A Companion to Cultural Geography

Blackwell Companions to Geography

Blackwell Companions to Geography is a blue-chip, comprehensive series covering each major subdiscipline of human geography in detail. Edited and contributed by the disciplines' leading authorities, each book provides the most up-to-date and authoritative syntheses available in its field. The overviews provided in each Companion will be an indispensable introduction to the field for students of all levels, while the cutting-edge, critical direction will engage students, teachers, and practitioners alike.

Published

1. *A Companion to the City*
Edited by Gary Bridge and Sophie Watson

2. *A Companion to Economic Geography*
Edited by Eric Sheppard and Trevor J. Barnes

3. *A Companion to Political Geography*
Edited by John Agnew, Katharyne Mitchell, and Gerard Toal
(Gearóid Ó Tuathail)

4. *A Companion to Cultural Geography*
Edited by James S. Duncan, Nuala C. Johnson, and Richard H. Schein

5. *A Companion to Tourism*
Edited by Alan A. Lew, C. Michael Hall, and Allan M. Williams

Forthcoming

6. *A Companion to Feminist Geography*
Edited by Joni Seager and Lise Nelson

7. *A Handbook to GIS*
Edited by John Wilson and Stewart Fotheringham

A Companion to Cultural Geography

Edited by

James S. Duncan
University of Cambridge

Nuala C. Johnson
Queen's University, Belfast
and
Richard H. Schein
University of Kentucky

Blackwell
Publishing

350 Main Street, Malden, MA 02148-5020, USA
108 Cowley Road, Oxford OX4 1JF, UK
550 Swanston Street, Carlton, Victoria 3053, Australia

The right of James S. Duncan, Nuala C. Johnson, and Richard H. Schein to be identified as the
Authors of the Editorial Material in this Work has been asserted in accordance with the UK
Copyright, Designs, and Patents Act 1988.

First published 2004 by Blackwell Publishing Ltd

Library of Congress Cataloging-in-Publication Data

A companion to cultural geography / edited by James S. Duncan, Nuala C.
Johnson, and Richard H. Schein.
    p. cm. – (Blackwell companions to geography)
  Includes bibliographical references and index.
    ISBN 0-631-23050-5 (alk. paper)
    1. Human geography. I. Duncan, James S. II. Johnson, Nuala Christina,
  1962– III. Schein, Richard H. IV. Series.

GF43.C65 2004
304.2 – dc21

                      2003008055

A catalogue record for this title is available from the British Library.

Set in 10 on 12pt Sabon
by SNP Best-set Typesetter Ltd., Hong Kong
Printed and bound in the United Kingdom
by TJ International Ltd, Padstow, Cornwall

For further information on
Blackwell Publishing, visit our website:
http://www.blackwellpublishing.com

Contents

Notes on Contributors

John Agnew is Professor of Geography at UCLA (University of California, Los Angeles) where he teaches political geography and the urban geography of Europe. He is the author, co-author, or co-editor of the following recent books: *Place and Politics in Modern Italy* (2002); *American Space/American Place: Geographies of the Contemporary United States* (2002); *Making Political Geography* (2002); and *Companion to Political Geography* (Blackwell, 2003). In 2000 he gave the Hettner Lectures at the University of Heidelberg on *Reinventing Geopolitics: Geographies of Modern Statehood*. He is co-editor, with David Newman, of the journal *Geopolitics*.

Clive Barnett works at the School of Geographical Sciences, University of Bristol. He has previously worked at the University of Salford and the University of Reading, and has held visiting positions at Ohio State University and the University of Natal, Durban. His current research includes work on media, communication, and democracy; media and citizenship in South Africa; cultural policy; and discourses of African postcolonialism. Clive does not think of himself as a cultural geographer.

Bruce Braun is the author of *The Intemperate Rainforest: Nature, Culture and Power on Canada's West Coast* and co-editor of *Remaking Reality: Nature at the Millennium* and *Social Nature: Theory, Practice, Politics*. He teaches at the University of Minnesota.

Dan Clayton teaches human geography at the University of St Andrews. He is the author of *Islands of Truth: The Imperial Fashioning of Vancouver Island* (2000), and is currently working on a book entitled *Colonialism's Geographies*.

Carl Dahlman is an Assistant Professor of Geography at the University of South Carolina and an Associate in the Walker Institute of International Studies. He teaches courses dealing with postconflict and humanitarian issues, as well as regional courses on Europe, the former Yugoslavia, and the Middle East. His current research focuses on the politics of identity and displacement among Kurds from Northern Iraq, and the international effort to reverse ethnic cleansing in Bosnia.

Stephen Daniels is Professor of Geography at the University of Nottingham. His publications include *Fields of Vision: Landscape Imagery and National Identity in England and the United States* (Polity, 1994) and *Humphry Repton: Landscape Gardening and the Geography of Georgian England* (1999).

Deborah Dixon is a Lecturer at the Institute of Geography and Earth Sciences, University of Wales-Aberystwyth. Her research addresses the spatialization of anti-essentialist forms of thought, with an emphasis on economic and cinematic geographies.

James S. Duncan teaches cultural geography at the University of Cambridge and is a Fellow of Emmanuel College. His publications include *The City as Text: The Politics of Landscape Interpretation in the Kandyan Kingdom* (1990) and *Landscapes of Privilege: The Politics of the Aesthetic in Suburban New York* (2003).

Nancy G. Duncan teaches cultural geography at the University of Cambridge and until 2001 was a Fellow of Fitzwilliam College. Her publications include *BodySpace: Destabilizing Geographies of Gender and Sexuality* (1996) and *Landscapes of Privilege: The Politics of the Aesthetic in Suburban New York* (2003).

Claire Dwyer is a Lecturer in Geography at University College London interested in transnationalism, ethnicity and gender. She is currently examining the transnational production and consumption of products within the British Asian food and fashion sectors and is the co-author of *Geographies of New Femininities* (1999).

Elizabeth A. Gagen teaches cultural Geography at the University of Manchester. Her research interests are in historical and cultural geographies of childhood, the history and philosophy of psychology and space, and performative geographies of gender, nation, and health. She has explored these interests in the context of early twentieth-century American playground reform and has published work on playgrounds, performativity, and play; national identity and children's bodies; and historical methodologies of childhood.

Nuala C. Johnson is a cultural-historical geographer at the School of Geography, Queen's University, Belfast. She has published a range of journal articles and book chapters on national identity, the heritage industry, monuments and memorials, and social memory. She is author of *Ireland, the Great War and the Geography of Remembrance* (2003).

John Paul Jones III is Professor and Head of the Department of Geography and Regional Development at the University of Arizona. His research interests are in human geography and geographic methodology.

Gerry Kearns teaches geography at the University of Cambridge and is a Fellow of Jesus College. His main research interests are the geographical dimensions of Irish national identities, the ideology and demography of nineteenth-century urban public health, and the history of the links between geography and imperialism.

Paul Kingsbury recently completed his doctorate in the Department of Geography, University of Kentucky. His dissertation, entitled "Transforming Corporate Tourism: Sandals Resorts International in Jamaica and the Politics of Enjoyment," uses Lacanian theory to critically analyze one of the most recent and important transformations in international tourism: the adoption and adaptation of alternative tourism policies and practices by conventional mass-tourism corporations.

James Kneale is a Lecturer in Geography at University College London. His interests in cultural and historical geography include popular fiction, reading practices, and spaces of drink. He is the co-editor (with Rob Kitchin) of *Lost In Space: Geographies of Science Fiction* (2002).

Audrey Kobayashi is a Professor of Geography and Women's Studies at Queen's University, Kingston, Ontario. Her interests include racism; gender; immigration; law, human rights, and geography; and Asian Canadians; and she has published widely in these areas. She also works as an activist in the areas of antiracism, disability rights, and employment equity.

Lily Kong is Professor of Geography at the National University of Singapore where she is also Dean of the Faculty of Arts and Social Sciences. She is a social-cultural geographer with broad interests, including geographies of religion, geographies of music, constructions of nation and identity, and constructions of nature and environment. Among her recent publications are *Constructions of 'Nation': The Politics of Landscapes in Singapore* (2003) and *Landscapes: Ways of Imagining the World* (2003).

David Lambert teaches cultural geography at the University of Cambridge and is a Fellow of Emmanuel College. He is author of several articles on White Caribbean culture and the cultural politics of anti-abolitionism.

Michael Landzelius is a Researcher in the Department of Geography at Lund University, Sweden. His international experience includes two years in the department of Geography at Cambridge University, UK, and one year in the Geography departments of Syracuse University and the University of California at Berkeley. He has published in journals such as *Environment and Planning D: Society and Space* and *The American Journal of Semiotics*, as well as in edited volumes. He presently researches the politics of space in case studies focusing on Swedish political hygienism in the 1930s and 1940s, and on scapes and flows of migratory paths in relation to cosmopolitanism and globalization.

Stephen Legg teaches cultural geography at the University of Cambridge and is a Fellow of Homerton College. His research interests include postcolonial theory and colonial urbanism.

David N. Livingstone is Professor of Geography at Queen's University, Belfast. He is the author of several books including *The Geographical Tradition* (Blackwell 1992) and *Putting Science in its Place: Geographies of Scientific Knowledge* (2003).

Cheryl McEwan is Lecturer in Human Geography at the University of Durham. Her interests span cultural, feminist, and postcolonial geographies. Her current research is concerned with gender and citizenship in post-apartheid South Africa and with broader issues of globalization, culture, and identities in transnational spaces. She is author of *Gender, Geography and Empire* (2000) and co-editor (with Alison Blunt) of *Postcolonial Geographies* (2002).

Don Mitchell is Professor and Chair of the Department of Geography, the Maxwell School, Syracuse University. In addition he is the director of the People's Geography Project based at Syracuse University. He is the author of *The Lie of the Land: Migrant Workers and the California Landscape* (1996); *Cultural Geography: A Critical Introduction* (Blackwell, 2000); and *The Right to the City: Social Justice and the Fight for Public Space* (2003).

Robert Shannan Peckham has held Research Fellowships at St Catharine's College, Cambridge and St. Peter's College, Oxford. He is the author of *National Histories, Natural States: Nationalism and the Politics of Place in Greece* (2001) and editor of *Rethinking Heritage: Cultures and Politics in Europe* (2003).

Richard Phillips teaches cultural geography at the European Studies Research Institute at the University of Salford. His publications include *Mapping Men and Empire: A Geography of Adventure* (1997) and *De-centring Sexualities: Politics and Representations Beyond the Metropolis* (2000).

Paul Robbins is Associate Professor of Geography at Ohio State University. His research on forests in Rajasthan, lawns in Ohio, and Elk in Montana, centers on the politics of landscape change and the cultural struggles inherent in the classification and measurement of the environment.

Sue Roberts is an Associate Professor of Geography and Member of the Committee on Social Theory at the University of Kentucky, USA. She is the co-editor (with Andrew Herod and Gearóid Ó Tuathail) of *An Unruly World? Geography, Globalization and Governance* (1998) and (with John Paul Jones III and Heidi Nast) *Thresholds in Feminist Geography* (1997).

James R. Ryan is Lecturer in Human Geography at Queen's University, Belfast. He is the author of *Picturing Empire: Photography and the Visualization of the British Empire* (1997) and editor (with Joan M. Schwartz) of *Picturing Place: Photography and the Geographical Imagination* (2003).

Richard H. Schein is an Associate Professor of Geography and Member of the Committee on Social Theory at the University of Kentucky. He thinks a lot about cultural landscapes.

Heidi Scott teaches cultural geography at the University of Cambridge and is a Fellow of Newnham College. Her main interests are in colonial and postcolonial theory, and colonial Latin America.

Joanne Sharp is Senior Lecturer in Geography at the University of Glasgow. Her research interests are critical geopolitics, gender and development, and public art. Her publications include *Condensing the Cold War: Reader's Digest and American Identity* (2000), *A Feminist Glossary of Human Geography* (1999) and *Space/Gender/Knowledge: Feminist Readings* (1997), both with Linda McDowell.

Jonathan M. Smith is a cultural-historical geographer primarily interested in the history of geographical ideas and geographical thought. He has published articles on various subjects, co-edited six books, and is co-editor of the journal *Philosophy and Geography*.

Nigel Thrift is a Professor in the School of Geography at the University of Oxford. His main interests are currently centered on nonrepresentational theory, the history of time, management knowledges, and the intersection between biology and information and communication technologies. Recent publications include *Cities* (with Ash Amin, Polity, 2002), *The Cultural Geography Handbook* (co-edited with Kay Anderson, Mona Domosh, and Steve Pile, 2003), and *Patterned Ground* (co-edited with Stephan Harrison and Steve Pile, 2003).

Karen E. Till is an Assistant Professor in the Department of Geography at the University of Minnesota and co-director of the Humanities Institute Space and Place Research Group. Karen is co-editor of the volume *Textures of Place: Geographies of Imagination, Experience, and Paradox* (2001) and has published numerous book chapters and articles about her research on social memory, identity politics, and urban landscapes in the US and Germany. She is currently completing a book based upon 10 years of research in postunification Berlin, tentatively entitled *The New Berlin: Memory, Politics, Place*.

Figures

Table

Chapter 1

Introduction

James S. Duncan, Nuala C. Johnson, and
Richard H. Schein

In the past two decades cultural geography has undergone significant theoretical, substantive, and methodological shifts. While cultural geography has a long and important place in the intellectual and institutional history of the discipline, the recent "spatial and cultural turns" in the humanities and social sciences have repositioned the field as one of considerable import to contemporary debates in Anglo-American human geography. During the first half of the twentieth century the concern of Carl Sauer and his students in the "Berkeley School" with human/environment relationships, material culture, and landscape interpretation marked out some of the terrain to which cultural geographers would continue to devote attention (Leighly 1963; Wagner & Mikesell 1962). The deployment of theoretical insights from cultural anthropology and landscape history during this period emphasized the interdisciplinary nature of cultural geography, a trend that continues today.

The importation into geography of positivist theory, behavioral psychology and highly abstract quantitative methods in the 1960s provoked cultural geographers to challenge the prevailing emphasis on spatial model building. Cultural geographers' emphasis on the symbolic dimension of human activities, the relevance of historical understanding of societal processes, and a commitment to an interpretative epistemology all challenged the scientific reductionism and economism of a positivist human geography. It was through cultural and historical geography that many of these issues were addressed and presented to a wider audience (Tuan 1974; Lowenthal 1961; Meinig 1979; Zelinsky 1973). During the 1980s there arose what some have termed a "new cultural geography" which questioned the predominant Berkeley School's use of the term culture as a reified "superorganic" explanatory variable (Duncan 1980) and offered in its place a more sociological and political approach which attempted to understand the "inner workings of culture" which had been consigned to a "black box" by earlier generations. British social geographers (Jackson 1980) who had previously dismissed cultural geography as irrelevant to contemporary urban social and political issues, began to turn to cultural history (Williams 1973) and the then rising field of cultural studies (Hall 1980) for inspiration in the development of this "new cultural geography." The study of "race" and ethnicity in historic and contemporary contexts for instance shifted from an emphasis on spatial mapping to an exploration of cultural representations of "race," which merged conventional concerns in social geography with more explicitly cultural interpretations (Anderson 1988; Jackson 1987; Ley 1974).

Similarly the emergence in the 1970s and 1980s of a radical human geography both invigorated cultural geographers' concern with a materialist basis for landscape interpretation (Cosgrove 1983; Daniels 1989) while simultaneously providing a focus for a broader critique of the limitations of economistic Marxist interpretations of human societies (Duncan & Ley 1982). Within cultural geography there also emerged a reassertion of the centrality of place to human geographical concerns (Agnew 1987; Entrikin 1991; Relph 1976). Feminist geographers too have had a marked impact on contemporary cultural geography by highlighting the prevalence of the detached male gaze in the study of landscape and other cultural phenomena (Rose 1993; Nash 1996). The promotion of a geography which would value the subjective, subaltern voices and cultural specificity, and which would employ a range of source material not normally used by geographers, would open up the discipline to methods and debates prevalent in philosophy, literary theory, cultural studies, and anthropology (Ley & Samuels 1978; Duncan & Duncan 1988; Gregory 1994; Doel 1995).

While cultural geography has always been an open, dynamic field, over the past decade there have been particularly rapid changes in what is now commonly referred to as the "cultural turn." These changes have regularly been animated by cultural geographers and have had wide-ranging effects in political, economic, and social geography. Issues of discourse, power, justice, the body, difference, hybridity, transnationalism, actor networks, resistance, transgression, performance, and representation have been particularly important in contemporary approaches within cultural geography and beyond. Feminist, Marxist, critical, psychoanalytical, postcolonial, and postmodern theorists have led the subfield in radically interrogating and transforming geographical conceptions of space, place, and landscape (Rose 1993; McDowell 1999; Mitchell 2000; Nast & Pile 1998; Jacobs 1996; Ryan 1997; Driver 2001; Thrift 1996; Gregory 2002). Since the 1970s, interdisciplinary inspiration has come from a wide range of thinkers such as Foucault, Barthes, Giddens, de Certeau, Benjamin, Deleuze and Guattari, Lefebvre, Bakhtin, Said, Butler, Harraway, Bourdieu, Habermas, Latour, and Lacan. Programmatic statements of the new directions that cultural geography has moved in are increasingly being matched by detailed empirical investigations.

Cultural geographers' traditional concern with human/environment relationships has continued, and over the past decade renewed debates about how nature is constituted and understood across different human societies have been particularly vigorous. Ranging from considerations of situated knowledges, environmental ethics, popular understandings of environmental issues to the unsettling of the nature/culture divide, cultural geography has been central in efforts to reconceptualize nature and critically examine environmental policy (Whatmore 2002; Fitzsimmons 1989; Castree & Braun 2001; Wolch & Emel 1998). In particular this is contributing to reestablishing stronger theoretical links between human and physical geography and has prompted a critical analysis of the basis of science. Cultural geographers' examination of the ways in which "scientific knowledge" has been deployed to support a range of colonial, imperial, and other economic and political projects has served to advance the notion that sociologies and histories of science may be inadequate without a cultural geography of scientific investigation.

Cultural geography therefore has been an important area of the discipline because of the centrality of its debates to the broader directions that geography is taking. Outside of disciplinary boundaries cultural geography has become increasingly visible to anthropologists, historians of science, cultural historians, archaeologists, and sociologists. Cross-disciplinary research and collaborative publication is a testament to this trend (e.g. Jackson et al. 2000). Cultural geography, however, is not only important in the arena of intellectual debate, but cultural geographers have also been having a small but increasing impact on policy-making communities (e.g. environmental planners, heritage managers, museum curators). The "field" is not simply a setting for research, but a network of political, management, and research worlds mutually incorporating diverse types of knowledge.

Structure

This volume begins with an introduction of key shifts in direction of cultural geography in the twentieth century. Secondly, the principal approaches that currently animate work in cultural geography are analyzed. Thirdly, the theoretical perspectives of the previous section are elaborated in a series of essays that focus on some of the major thematic areas to which cultural geographers have contributed. Collectively these chapters illuminate how the critical interventions of cultural geography have informed these specific realms of inquiry. Although the editors cannot (and would not want to) offer a single definition of cultural geography, they attempt to highlight the central ways in which ideas of culture have been debated, deployed, materialized, and contested across a range of spatial and historical contexts. In so doing the guiding principle of this book is the contingent, diverse, and contradictory manner in which human societies approach the hermeneutic project of making sense of their existential and material spaces for living. The editors recognize that cultural geography cannot be divorced from other branches of geography, and the dialogue that cultural geographers have engaged in with political, economic, historical, and social geographers will be woven throughout the volume.

The collection begins with an exploration of tradition in cultural geography (chapter 2). Richard Schein approaches the question of "tradition" itself, and explores a tentative genealogy of cultural geography that focuses upon the tensions inherent in positing a "traditional" versus a "new" cultural geography, especially as the latter engages with human geography's cultural turn. Given the strong feelings, both pro and con, which have been generated by the cultural turn within geography and more broadly within the social sciences, we thought that it might be productive to offer two views of its impact in geography, one by a cultural geographer sympathetic to the turn and the second by a non-cultural geographer who is considerably more skeptical. Heidi Scott (chapter 3) offers an overview of the impact of the cultural turn within contemporary geography over the past decade, while highlighting points of convergence with other fields. She offers an assessment of the strengths and weaknesses of the multiple practices of cultural geography while providing a sense of the power struggles both within the subfield over the nature of cultural explanation and between subfields over whether cultural explanation has tended to overshadow and detract from other areas of geography. Clive Barnett's essay (chapter 4) reflects a continuing uneasiness with the turn toward cultural explanation on the part of geographers in the various subfields that have only recently begun to take culture seriously. He expresses a more general concern that the consideration of culture could too easily become a central focus of geography as a whole.

Don Mitchell (chapter 5) argues that culture needs to be reintegrated into the social totality of capitalism as a moment of power. A historical-materialist cultural geography must understand that culture is a field of accumulations, not reducible to superstructural epiphenomena, but neither should an attention upon culture constitute a retreat into the immaterial as an explanatory realm. Joanne Sharp (chapter 6) traces the convergence between certain lines of feminist inquiry and cultural geography. She singles out as particularly fruitful the themes of identity politics, embodiment, and the debate over landscape and the masculine gaze. John Paul Jones and Deborah Dixon review key features of poststructuralism (chapter 7), especially as articulated through key ideas in cultural geography, such as representation and space, and including an attention to questions of methodology. They move from a synopsis of structuralism as a starting point, through basic theoretical tenets of poststructuralism, to discuss future articulations of poststructuralism with cultural geography. Paul Kingsbury addresses a general fear or distrust of psychoanalytic theory by geographers in general (chapter 8), before explicating how different psychoanalytic approaches have been reinterpreted and used by cultural geographers. He addresses Freudian approaches, object-relations theory, and Lacanian approaches in his treatment. Nigel Thrift (chapter 9) argues that nonrepresentational theory provides the basis for a different type of cultural geography than is offered by most cultural geographers. The core of his argument is that geographers should turn increasingly to the study of such embodied practices as dance, music, and crying as ways of engaging with the world.

David Livingstone's paper (chapter 10) highlights the significance of space in understanding the production and consumption of scientific knowledges. From the sites of production and the circulation of scientific theory and practice to the geographies of reception, Livingstone draws our attention to the new avenues of research stimulated by spatializing our understanding of the cultures of science. Bruce Braun tracks the relation between nature and culture in post-Second World War human geography (chapter 11). He specifically addresses four moments of the nature/culture problematic – cultural ecology, political ecology, cultural studies of the environment, and "beyond nature/culture" – through the work of Deleuze, Guattari, and Latour, finally calling into question the ontological distinction in the ordering categories themselves. Paul Robbins tackles practical and daily considerations of the nature/culture problematic through the lens of cultural ecology as the human production of and adaptation to the environment (chapter 12). He focuses particularly on critical contemporary problems of economic development, global poverty, and environmental change. In his review of environmental history, Gerry Kearns (chapter 13) explores the continuing importance of an ecological tradition both within geography and macrohistorical studies. He then examines the treatment of environmental history by Marxist geographers and new cultural geographers. Jonathan Smith (chapter 14) focuses on various approaches deployed to answer the question of whether it is ethical to shape the environment. Drawing on moral philosophy and adopting an historical perspective, Smith identifies key strands of thought that have characterized our moral position in relation to the environment from premodern to postmodern concerns.

Drawing from a range of contemporary political and social theory, John Agnew (chapter 15) charts the varied approaches that have developed to both understanding and, at times, dismissing nationalism. He surveys the strengths and limitations of territorial, diasporic, ethnic, religious, gendered, and landscape-based interpretations of the idea and practices of nationalism. Audrey Kobayashi approaches the concept of "race" as both a way of life deeply embedded in the European colonial past and lived out in the present as a taken-for-granted reality and as an analytical concept (chapter 16). The chapter begins with a review of the concept of "race" as it is understood in contemporary antiracist geography, then moves to a brief analysis of how the production of antiracist geography has developed in three contemporary Western and Northern contexts. Nancy Duncan and Stephen Legg (chapter 17) review the reasons why class has remained relatively neglected by cultural geographers, in spite of the tremendous interest shown in subjectivity and identity formation. They argue that while there are some good reasons why older notions of class in geography have been seen as unhelpful in understanding questions of identity, there is also no inherent reason why this should be so. In fact, they suggest, certain reworked Marxian and other dynamic and relational notions of class could contribute greatly to cultural analysis. Richard Phillips (chapter 18) considers the relationships between sexualities and space. Focusing both on heterosexual and homosexual dimensions of identity formation and drawing from a range of contemporary and historical contexts, Phillips examines the critical role of space in the construction and reconstruction of sexualized identities. Michael Landzelius (chapter 19) undertakes a sweeping survey of the way in which geographers have understood the body, from the behaviorists and phenomenologists of the 1970s to the psychoanalytic approaches of the late 1990s, and from the body–space nexus through impairment, illness, and the body.

James Kneale and Claire Dwyer (chapter 20) consider the varied meanings attending the concept of consumption. Drawing from a range of cultural theory, they explore the possibilities for developing a more nuanced understanding of the social nature of consumption and its materiality in contemporary society. Nuala Johnson (chapter 21) focuses attention on the manner in which ideas of public memory have been integrated into a geographical literature on identity formation and representation. She highlights the significance of space in particular in the articulation and conjugation of social memory.

Susan Roberts briefly reviews the manner in which "culture" and "economy" generally have been treated as things and as separate spheres (chapter 22), and explores the relations between economic and cultural geography that are central to geography's cultural turn. By way of example, she examines US maritime ports as places evincing a particularly interesting set of relations infused with economic, cultural, and (geo)political concerns. Karen Till (chapter 23) explores the complex ways that the interpretation of political landscapes is conceptualized through examining symbolic approaches to landscapes of the state; the material social relations revealed and hidden in landscapes of work, and the opportunities for developing an approach to understanding political landscapes which is embedded in everyday practice. Lily Kong (chapter 24) surveys the contributions of cultural geography to the study of religion. She draws attention to the significance of place in the understanding of religious belief systems and practices and she proposes a set of research questions for developing a "new" geography of religion. In chapter 25, James Duncan and David Lambert examine the complex and ambiguous notion of home. They do so by first reviewing notions of home as dwelling and its links to identity. They then go on to survey the idea of home place, with particular reference to the experiences of home in the British Empire. Elizabeth Gagen (chapter 26) explores the cultural geography of childhood by focusing upon the changing conceptions of childhood and the spaces, both adult and child-centered, in which such definitions are negotiated. She also addresses some of the particular methodological and ethical issues attendant in researching children. In chapter 27, Shannan Peckham examines the social and geographical context of cinema. He argues that a proper analysis of film must take into consideration its multiple geographies; not only those of its production, but those of its reception as well. The interconnections between landscape art and cultural geography since the 1980s is the subject of Steven Daniels' chapter 28. He considers both art and landscape to be "keywords" in the sense that the late Raymond Williams used the term. As such the chapter traces the interrelations between these terms as they are worked through a range of different representational practices.

Dan Clayton (chapter 29) situates the geographical study of colonialism both within the postcolonial turn and in relation to the recent historiographic interest in tracing the interlinkages between the practices of colonialism and the ideological and material support provided to it by contemporaneous geography. In chapter 30, James Ryan charts the relationship between postcolonialism and cultural geography. He investigates the dominant themes that have characterized research into geographical knowledge and colonial power, colonial and postcolonial identities, and the spaces of colonial encounter and resistance. Carl Dahlman explores the diaspora concept, including its relations to terms such as transnationalism, multiculturalism, and hybridity, before employing a critical (geo)political perspective to diaspora through the case of Kurdish emigration to Europe and North America (chapter 31). In chapter 32, Cheryl McEwan examines the major debates centered on cultural globalization and transnationalism. She interrogates the connections between cultural mobility and identities, citizenship and transnational spaces; and she highlights the possibilities for geographical scholarship harnessing the progressive and transgressive potential of transnationalism.

REFERENCES

Agnew, J. A. 1987: *Place and Politics*. London: Allen and Unwin.
Anderson, K. J. 1988: Cultural hegemony and the race-definition process in Chinatown, Vancouver: 1880–1980. *Environment and Planning D. Society and Space* 6, 127–49.
Castree, N. and Braun, B., eds. 2001: *Social Nature*. Oxford: Blackwell.

Cosgrove, D. 1983: Towards a radical cultural geography: problems of theory. *Antipode* 15(1), 1–11.

Daniels, S. 1989: Marxism, culture and the duplicity of landscape. In R. Peet and N. Thrift, eds., *New Models in Geography*, vol. 2. London: Unwin Hyman, 196–220.

Doel, M. 1995: Bodies without organs: schizoanalysis and deconstruction. In S. Pile and N. Thrift, eds., *Mapping the Subject*. London: Routledge, 226–40.

Driver, F. 2001: *Geography Militant: Cultures of Exploration and Empire*. Oxford: Blackwell.

Duncan, J. S. 1980: The superorganic in American cultural geography. *Annals of the Association of American Geographers* 70, 181–98.

Duncan, J. S. and Duncan, N. G. 1988: (Re)reading the landscape. *Environment and Planning D. Society and Space* 6, 117–26.

Duncan, J. S. and Ley, D. 1982: Structural Marxism and human geography. *Annals, Association of American Geographers* 72, 30–59.

Entrikin, J. N. 1991: *The Betweenness of Place*. Baltimore: Johns Hopkins University Press.

Fitzsimmons, M. 1989: The matter of nature. *Antipode* 21, 106–20.

Gregory, D. 1994: *Geographical Imaginations*. Oxford: Blackwell.

Gregory, D. 2002: *The Colonial Present*. Oxford: Blackwell.

Hall, S. 1980: Cultural studies and the Centre: some problematics and problems. In S. Hall et al., eds., *Culture, Media, Language*. London: Hutchinson/Centre for Contemporary Cultural Studies, 15–47.

Jackson, P. 1980: A plea for cultural geography. *Area* 12, 110–13.

Jackson, P., ed. 1987: *Race and Racism*. London: Allen and Unwin.

Jackson, P., Lowe, M., Miller, D., and Mort, F., eds. 2000: *Commercial Cultures*. Oxford: Berg.

Jacobs, J. 1996: *Edge of Empire: Postcolonialism and the City*. London and New York: Routledge.

Leighly, J., ed. 1963: *Land and Life: A Selection from the Writing of Carl Ortwin Sauer*. Berkeley, CA: University of California Press.

Ley, D. 1974: *The Black Inner City as Frontier Outpost*. Monograph no. 7. Washington, DC: Association of American Geographers.

Ley, D. and Samuels, M., eds. 1978: *Humanistic Geography: Prospects and Problems*. Chicago: Maaroufa Press.

Lowenthal, D. 1961: Geography, experience and imagination: toward a geographical epistemology. *Annals of the Association of American Geographers* 51, 241–60.

McDowell, L. 1999: *Gender, Identity and Place: Understanding Feminist Geographies*. Cambridge: Polity.

Meinig, D. W., ed. 1979: *The Interpretation of Ordinary Landscapes*. New York: Oxford University Press.

Mitchell, D. 2000: *Cultural Geography*. Oxford: Blackwell.

Nash, C. 1996: Reclaiming vision: looking at landscape and the body. *Gender, Place and Culture* 3(2), 149–69.

Nast, H. and Pile, S., eds. 1998: *Places through the Body*. London: Routledge.

Relph, E. 1976: *Place and Placelessness*. London: Pion.

Rose, G. 1993: *Feminism and Geography: The Limits of Geographical Knowledge*. Cambridge: Polity Press.

Ryan, J. 1997: *Picturing Empire: Photography and the Visualisation of the British Empire* London and Chicago: Reaktion Books.

Thrift, N. 1996: *Spatial Formations*. London: Sage.

Tuan, Y.-F. 1974: *Topophilia: A Study of Environmental Perception, Attitudes, and Values*. Englewood Cliffs, NJ: Prentice-Hall.

Wagner, P. and Mikesell, M., eds. 1962: *Readings in Cultural Geography*. Chicago: University of Chicago Press.

Whatmore, S. 2002: *Hybrid Geographies: Natures, Cultures, Spaces*. London: Sage.

Williams, R. 1973: *The Country and the City*. London: Chatto and Windus.

Wolch, J. and Emel, J., eds. 1998: *Animal Geographies*. London: Verso.

Zelinsky, W. 1973: *The Cultural Geography of the United States*. Englewood Cliffs, NJ: Prentice-Hall.

Part I Introducing Cultural Geographies

Chapter 2

Cultural Traditions

Richard H. Schein

Scholarly traditions often are presented in one of two ways. Either the tradition is held up as an honorable thing, and is presented as a teleological intellectual genealogy that naturally and inexorably leads to one's own conceptual or substantive or theoretical position within the academy. Or, the tradition is presented as a sort of intellectual 'other' – the defining foil for a more progressive or enlightened or sophisticated or somehow *better* way of approaching the subject at hand. Traditions are, of course, invented, as we learned a generation ago from Eric Hobsbawm and Terrence Ranger (1983). And although they were interested in cultural practices that seemed to serve a burgeoning (western) nationalism during the apogee of the modern nation-state, their observations are nonetheless instructive for this brief explication and exploration of traditions (and continuities) in cultural geography. More specifically, they taught us that traditions always serve a purpose – they serve a function, whether consciously intended or not – and often the interrogation of that function is as rewarding an enterprise as the examination of the 'tradition' *per se*. This position itself might be associated with the so-called 'new cultural geography' (which is really not so new anymore; the opening salvos in the once-called civil war in cultural geography having been fired some 20-plus years ago), for it presumes to take an ironic stance toward the question of 'traditional cultural geography' and its purpose is less to present an unquestionable, even unquestioned, historiography of an academic subdiscipline, than it is to raise certain positions, histories, genealogies, and debates that might serve to better place the pursuit of cultural geography *today*. Put another way, while this chapter might purport to offer a disciplinary road map of sorts, showing how we got here from then, the lessons of critical cartography tell us that all road maps are normative, and that to make claims about the past is as much about making claims on the future as it is in attempting to uncover some inalienable truth about the practice of, in this case, cultural geography.

At this point we also might take a cue from the resurgence of geographical interests in historiography, and particularly from one of the canonical works of that burgeoning literature, David Livingstone's *The Geographical Tradition* (1992). One of Livingstone's main points is that intellectual ideas and academic progress do not occur on the head of a pin. To understand the development of a tradition – or perhaps more accurately traditions – is to interrogate not only the ideas at the core of an intellectual enterprise *as* ideas, but also to realize the institutional contexts (in our case, usually academic or university ones) which nurture (or don't) particular kinds of scholarship, as well as the general societal contexts of those ideas and their framing institutions. Finally, one of the lessons of the past 20 years of geographical scholarship is a newfound appreciation for the way in which the particular subjectivity of the author makes a difference, and part of that subjectivity is bound in place. That is to say, it is important to realize my own location as author in writing this particular chapter in a cultural geography companion, as a middle-aged, white, male, US-trained scholar, at once an individual yet also influenced by the times and places I have studied (and have studied in), and so my chapter is likely to be different from the chapter immediately following this, which is written by a scholar much younger than I, who learned her cultural geography in a different time, and in a different place – in Britain to be precise; and those facts will, to a degree, differentiate our approaches to 'cultural geography.' Yet, in the end, we share a similar substantive interest in a number of topics that somehow cohere around the concepts of culture and geography, which are embodied in how, as scholars and citizens-of-the-world, we know and interrogate the world around us. We belong to a discursive or textual community; we identify with an academic discipline.

And so, after all of the caveats that mark these opening paragraphs, we are still left begging the historiographical questions: what cultural traditions and why do they matter? Without immediately taking a position on just what, exactly, cultural geography *is* (that is the purpose of this entire volume, after all), we can begin by acknowledging that there *has been* for the better part of a century, something recognized as cultural geography, especially in an American (here to mean US) context (thus it has a genealogy), which has served, more recently, as the intellectual foil (the conceptual other) that, in concert with a general disciplinary engagement with postempiricist and postpositivist epistemologies and ontologies, has helped to foster renewed (international) interests in something else called cultural geography. And while two (hypothetical) geographical scholars, each practicing their own cultural geography – one traditional, one new – and separated by the distance of 80 years and an ocean or two, might not necessarily recognize in each other's work an intellectual kinship apparent to us today, it is in making that kinship apparent, especially through institutional or disciplinary frameworks, that this chapter is interested. With full realization of the normative, teleological, and place-bound problematics of claiming a genealogy, I present here a few signposts toward understanding traditions and the place of traditions in cultural geography, primarily in an attempt to move from traditions to continuities to connections with the broadened interest in something called cultural geography in the Anglophone world.

Traditional cultural geography, as it is now known, was not called *traditional* cultural geography until 'it' became the focus or subject of scholarly critique over 20 years ago. It is through the nexus of critique, in this case positing a 'traditional' versus a 'new' cultural geography, that core disciplinary ideas are identified and refined, honed and retooled to meet the needs of contemporary scholars. And while critique is often seen as attack, resulting in an abandonment of the old, it also is important to remember that there had to be something intellectually valuable in the old to merit the attack in the first place, a set of concepts or substantive foci that are worth 'fighting over.' It is always dangerous, of course, to assume that a tradition of any kind is monolithic – that all practitioners who might be identified with a discipline think and act alike and are cast from the same mold. Yet key thinkers can always be identified, canonical works cited (and citations counted), and ideas can thus be traced to ascertain their dissemination and influence. In US cultural geography, the undisputed progenitor of cultural geography was Carl O. Sauer, often identified as the 'leader' of the Berkeley School of Cultural Geography (although like most such labels, this one was not self-ascribed, but assigned as a sort-of disciplinary shorthand for Sauer and his students and his devotees). Sauerian or Berkeley School Geography has served as a narrative for both approaches to 'tradition' which opened this essay: as a foil and as a genealogy to be revered. The mediation of those two approaches has been called a 'civil war' in cultural geography (Duncan 1994), and that civil war at the very least served as a forum for a set of debates that helped to clarify the various paths toward today's cultural geographies. With the privilege of hindsight, I take the position here that such debates – as long as they do not devolve into *ad hominem* attacks or overly vitriolic exchanges or hagiographic battles over patriarchy – are a good thing, for they mark an intellectual invigoration that 'keeps us honest' as scholars, making us always careful to elucidate and explicate our conceptual and theoretical positions, always accountable to the implications and ramifications of our scholarly practice. This, of course, is also a hallmark of a critical human geography more generally understood, wherein scholarship is seen never to be 'value free' and always carries with it (or should) what Gregory (1994) calls the anticipatory utopian moment. But to get to that point is to skip the beginning, and for many cultural geographers, the beginning is Sauer.

Carl Sauer was a prodigious scholar, and was perhaps an iconoclast who defies categorization. His academic career spanned over six decades, and one can hardly expect to pin down a thinking, active intellect over such a long period. But it is important, too, to remember that what we are after is key *ideas* rather than the essence of a particular man's scholarship, and while Sauer wrote many essays and books, a very few of them have come to stand above the others as disciplinary hallmarks, perhaps none more than 'The Morphology of Landscape,' published in 1925, when Sauer was relatively new to the Berkeley Geography department, having recently arrived from his Midwestern origins. 'Morphology of Landscape' is a highly sophisticated piece of theoretical rumination that still bears reading today. Its argument is multifaceted, but its most famous maxim posits the cultural landscape as the result of culture's action upon the medium of nature, and it is from that point that much of the recent critique evolved. It is the theoretical ramifications of 'Morphology' in a postpositivist intellectual milieu that have served as foil or conceptual other for the new cultural geography, particularly through a renewed interest in the concept of cultural landscapes from the 1980s. The place of a Sauerian or Berkeley School conception of landscape and culture *vis-à-vis* the new cultural geography is well documented elsewhere and so demands only a brief précis here (see, for example: Mitchell this volume; Cosgrove 1984, 2000a; Jackson 1989; McDowell 1994; Duncan 1990; Kobayashi 1989; Hugill & Foote 1994).

'Morphology of Landscape' (1925) was written in part as a result of Sauer's dissatisfaction with the then-dominant perspective of environmental determinism, especially as found in the work of Ellen Churchill Semple and Harlan Barrows. Sauer turned to Continental philosophy for philosophical guidance, his colleagues in Anthropology at Berkeley for theories of culture, and wrote 'Morphology' as part of "an effort to 'emancipate' himself from determinist thinking" (Williams 1983: 5). Sauer later claimed that methodological statements like 'Morphology' were part of an ongoing and shifting methodological position to which he rarely referred once they were written. Instead, he wrote, "they are best considered as successive orientations and have had utility as such; they belong to the history of geography, and if they are any good they represent change and growth" (as quoted in Williams 1983: 2).

While Sauer's position on theoretical and methodological change and growth is laudable, it is a highly personal statement and raises the question of how a wider readership responds to the writings of influential scholars. For example, 'Morphology' stood for several generations as a widely cited programmatic statement, and its influence still persists in some arenas of cultural geography today (look for it especially in introductory textbooks prepared for the US market). Additionally, Sauer's actual approach to the cultural landscape, as well as the work of his intellectual and scholarly 'offspring,' has been the subject of critique for a number of reasons. Cosgrove (1983: 2), for example, has suggested that "in the face of a strong determinism in geography" Sauer (along with Vidal) "laid emphasis on human culture as itself a deterministic force in transforming nature," and this emphasis was taken up by cultural geographers in general, especially those interrogating cultural landscapes. It is interesting in light of today's concern with the role of landscape as part and parcel of social (or socio-spatial) process, that Sauer's conception of the cultural landscape initially depended upon "apprehending the relationship between nature and culture dialectically, giving to neither an absolute dominance within a linear, determinist form of explanation" (Cosgrove 1983: 3). Nevertheless, Cosgrove continues,

Sauer's early insistence upon regarding human geography as a positive science (1925) and the methodological position he then espoused has been more readily followed than his concern with process, other than in studies of diffusion. The dialectic was not mediated through the historical specificity of human production, so that it dissolved into either the idealist reification of culture as an agent of change, or a semi-determinism dignified by the name "possibilism." (Cosgrove 1983: 3)

This, according to Cosgrove, "has left cultural geography theoretically impoverished, many of its studies existing in a theoretical vacuum, preserving a sense of cultural significance in understanding the landscape, but failing to extend this into a developing theoretical discourse" (Cosgrove 1983: 3).

A reified concept of culture in the practice of landscape interpretation may be traced to Sauer's (1925 [1963]: 343) 'Morphology,' where he wrote that "culture is the agent, the natural area is the medium, the cultural landscape is the result." Duncan (1980) has shown that this concept of culture has had wide import in the arena of landscape interpretation, and he has written on the implications of such a "superorganic" concept of culture. Duncan (1980: 181) claims that "the superorganic mode of explanation in cultural geography reifies the notion of culture, assigning it ontological status and causative power." A superorganic conception of culture posits "culture" as somehow external to individual human beings; culture becomes "an entity . . . not reducible to actions by the individuals who are associated with it, mysteriously responding to laws of its own" (Duncan 1980: 182). Duncan challenges many of the assumptions, or the intellectual baggage, implicit in employing a reified, superorganic concept of culture, including: the tendency to see humans as "relatively passive and impotent" (190); the idea that there exists an individual somehow apart from culture (189); the "assumption of homogeneity within a culture" (193); the tendency to create ideal types, and to "reduce the character of millions of people to a few traits" (193); the assumption of Pavlovian conditioning where "culture" is based upon unconscious and conditioned habit, rather than conscious intellectual activity (194); and failure to acknowledge other types of explanation beyond "culture as a determining force . . . hence many important questions are precluded" (191). Ultimately,

the most serious consequence of attributing causal power to culture is the fact that it obscures many important issues as to the origins, transmittal, and differentiation within a population of various "cultural characteristics." There is a surprising lack of many kinds of explanatory variables that are employed in other subfields of geography and in other social sciences; for example there is little or no discussion of social stratification, the political interests of particular groups, and the conflicts which arise from their opposing interests. Similarly, there is little discussion of government and other institutional policies, or the effects of business organizations and financial institutions on the landscape. Many of these things are seen as "given," or as cultural characteristics of a people that are not analyzed in any detail or used in explanation. Culture, which presumably includes the factors mentioned above, is seen to produce such effects on landscape. (191)

Mitchell (1995) has continued this critique of "culture" in cultural geography, most recently suggesting that even more recent, seemingly more-refined notions of culture as employed in cultural geography still reify the concept, granting it ontological and explanatory status. He suggests instead that there is no such thing as culture, only the *idea* of culture, to which several responses have been registered (Jackson 1996, Cosgrove 1996, Duncan & Duncan 1996, Mitchell 1996), including the challenge that even *ideas* themselves are "real" and have material and ideological consequences.

Sustained critique of the so-called "Sauerian" or "Berkeley" school of cultural geography, including its dominance of the landscape tradition in cultural geography, prompted Cosgrove and Jackson (1987) to suggest that there was on the horizon a "new" cultural geography, which was:

contemporary as well as historical (but always contextual and theoretically informed); social as well as spatial (but not confined exclusively to narrowly-defined landscape issues); urban as well as rural; and interested in the contingent nature of culture, in dominant ideologies and in forms of resistance to them. It would, moreover, assert the centrality of culture in human affairs.

From these points it can be argued that Sauerian cultural geography – no matter the 'accuracy' of its depiction – became little more than an opportunity for renewed engagement with questions of landscape interpretation, at first, and eventually for cultural geography more broadly; an engagement situated within then-current debates in geography more broadly aimed at moving away from positivist and empiricist human geographies. Thus Cosgrove's *Social Formation and Symbolic Landscape* (1984) represents geography's first sustained engagement with Marxism (see Mitchell this volume), while Duncan's doctoral dissertation from which the 'Superorganic' essay (1980) was drawn was a critique born of humanistic geography. It can be argued that this marks a turning-point in cultural geography's explicit (re)engagement with the discipline of Geography (Sauer himself generally withdrew from disciplinary engagement as Geography in the US, at least, underwent its 'quantitative revolution'); a move that perhaps brought cultural geography from the margins (in the US) or virtual non-existence (elsewhere) more solidly into the main streams of human geography, and took to that cultural geography subsequent concerns for literary theory, an anthropology struggling with a crisis of representation, questions of structure and agency and structuration, feminism, postcolonialism, critical race theory, and so on. But that brings us to this volume, and misses the point that some took exception to the critique, or at least to the manner in which it 'reinvented' cultural geography, and this was not necessarily deemed a good thing.

In a defense of a Sauerian tradition published in the *Annals of the Association of American Geographers*, Price and Lewis (1993: 1) took exception to what they saw as the "new cultural geographers" and "their critique of their academic forebears that has moved increasingly off-the-mark." While conceding the advancement of cultural research in several important ways, Price and Lewis's defense of the Sauerian tradition hinged primarily upon conflicting interpretations of just what that tradition is or was, and what they saw as the "faulty undergirding of the 'misrepresentation' of cultural geography by its critics." The essay and its rejoinders (Cosgrove 1993, Duncan 1993, Jackson 1993) are an important part of disciplinary dialogue, and provide insight into the nuances of 'paradigm clashes' as they are manifest in scholarly journals, as well as the manner in which 'traditions' are contested. Yet, one is left at the end of the clash with a vague sense that what was at stake was not so much the pursuit of a cultural geography as an institutionalized claim to a hagiographic tradition. Good points were made on both sides, of course – it is a rare debate that is entirely one sided, and the nuance of conflicting positions is always instructive for shattering a tendency to caricature another's scholarly practice. In the end one is tempted to agree with Price and Lewis's (1993: 2) claim that "in practice, old and new variants of cultural geography share precious little beyond their common name."

Yet, for some reason – filial loyalty? institutional attachment? a desire for continuity or lineage? a sense of genuine intellectual affinity? – there was (and perhaps still is), in the US at least, a *bona fide* attempt at *rapprochement* between the old and the new. Perhaps the hallmark of that *rapprochement* is the volume *Re-reading Cultural Geography* (Foote et al. 1994), in which a number of essays culled from the annals of traditional cultural geography were reprinted, alongside new essays and commentary by new cultural geographers. The book's foreword was written by Philip Wagner, who with Marvin Mikesell had published some 30 years earlier one of the more important programmatic statements in the traditional cultural geography's canon, *Readings in Cultural Geography* (Wagner & Mikesell 1962), a volume that had itself been a touchstone in the new cultural geography's critique. Wagner recanted, in part, that earlier volume's conception of culture, and wrote of the *Re-reading* collection (1994: 4):

What I invite you, the reader, to appreciate, then, is the diversity of original contributions, the mutability of messages, and yet the community of commitment that allows us to recognize our modest subdiscipline as a persistent, permissive, and open quest for a shared understanding, acknowledging multiple precedents and allowing for numerous metamorphoses within the diffusional universe that constitutes our common territory.

Wagner (p. 8) observed that "Cultural geography continues to flourish. Its locus of interest has changed, but not its logic of inquiry." And he hoped (p. 7) that:

Cultural geography can help to analyze and attack the human problems in our own societies that attach to race and poverty, age and gender, ethnicity and alienation. Spatial imagination, historical awareness, cultural sensitivity, and ecological insight, as well as that observational gift upon which field work depends, can all play a part in rendering service, and committed engagement will enrich our vision as well.

Similar bridge-building took place in Britain, most notably in Stephen Daniels' essay on the duplicity of landscape, in which he tried to theoretically accommodate the then-perceived divide between Marxian and humanistic inspired cultural geographies. Daniels (1989: 197) was particularly interested in furthering cultural geography's then-new engagement with Raymond Williams and John Berger (both Marxist cultural critics who also are central to the development of British cultural studies) in order to "open up the broad domain of geographical experience and imagination" which are central to their work. According to Daniels (p. 197), "this will involve making more of a rapprochement with Sauerian traditional cultural geography – in emphasizing observation, in emphasizing the importance of education, in reinstating the biophysical world, and in reinstating the idea of landscape, not despite of its difficulty as a comprehensive or reliable concept, but because of it." It would seem that Daniels, at least, and others most certainly, could see continuity in the gulf between the traditional and the new cultural geographies that involved more than a nostalgic desire for intellectual or patrimonial lineage.

Meanwhile, James Duncan's commentary, 'After the Civil War,' in the Foote volume, suggested, perhaps somewhat sympathetically to Wagner's point, that cultural geography be conceived of as an epistemological heterotopia rather than a "single contested space of power/knowledge." Duncan argued that "contemporary cultural geography . . . is no longer as much an intellectual site in the sense of sharing a common intellectual project as it is an institutional site, containing significant epistemological differences" (Duncan 1994: 402). Duncan reached this conclusion after noting that the younger generation of cultural geographers, "although still predominantly North American, has been joined over the past few years by British social geographers who have, under the influence of British cultural studies, taken the 'cultural turn' that is increasingly common in the social sciences," and so Duncan claimed a certain ennui regarding the civil war, as "the intellectual patrimony of the new cultural geographies has become so diffuse that many younger geographers see rebelling against a particular patriarch as increasingly obsessive and irrelevant."

And what exactly was the cultural turn, especially as it was manifest in cultural geography, new or old? That turn is the subject of at least two essays in this volume (those by Scott and Barnett), and has been recounted *vis-à-vis* cultural geography elsewhere in some detail (see, for example, Mitchell 2000). The cultural turn in geography drew upon a burgeoning interdisciplinary attention to 'culture' that was informed diversely by such intellectual forebears as E. P. Thompson, Raymond Williams, Louis Althusser, Richard Hoggart, Stuart Hall, Ashis Nandy, Donna Haraway, Gayatri Spivak, Homi Bhabha, Sara Suleri, Cornel West, bell hooks, Antonio Gramsci, Edward Said; and upon concepts such as semiotics, representation, discourse analysis, hegemony, subaltern studies, diaspora, queer studies, postcoloniality. Clearly, cultural studies, or the cultural turn, is a broad interdisciplinary field. Of particular relevance to cultural geography, however, is a set of characteristics summarizing what cultural studies aims to do (Sardar & Van Loon 1999: 9):

1   Cultural studies aims to examine its subject-matter in terms of *cultural practices* and their *relation to power*. Its constant goal is to expose power relationships and examine how these relationships influence and shape cultural practices.
2   Cultural studies is not simply the study of culture as though it were a discrete entity divorced from its social or political context. Its objective is to understand culture in all its complex forms and to analyze the *social and political context* within which it manifests itself.
3   Culture in cultural studies always performs two functions: it is both the *object* of study and the *location* of political criticism and action. Cultural studies aims to be both an intellectual and a pragmatic enterprise.
4   Cultural studies attempts to *expose and reconcile the division of knowledge*, to overcome the split between tacit (that is, intuitive knowledge based on local cultures) and objective (so-called universal) forms of knowledge. It assumes a common identity and common interest between the knower and the known, between the observer and what is being observed.
5   Cultural studies is committed to a *moral evaluation* of modern society and a *radical line* of political action. The tradition of cultural studies is not one of value-free scholarship but one committed to social reconstruction by critical political involvement. Thus cultural studies aims to *understand and change* the structures of dominance everywhere but in industrialist capitalist societies in particular.

These tenets are not unassailable. They are one attempt to characterize a broad and at times disparate interdisciplinary movement that also plays out differentially in different geographical contexts. It should not be a surprise that the genesis, adoption, and adaptations of cultural studies in Britain, notably through the Centre for Contemporary Cultural Studies, would appear differently than its counterparts in, say, Canada, New Zealand, Australia, the United States, or in India, Mexico, Malaysia, or Nigeria. And of course, as with any intellectual or scholarly 'movement,' cultural studies was and is open to critique itself, including, for example, charges that its earliest emphasis on class ignored equally important aspects of gender or race or sexuality in the constitution of everyday social life and power. So, too, the engagement by geographers with cultural studies has been variegated, depending upon the idea, places, and people involved.

And in geography, and for cultural, or increasingly culturally minded, geographers in several national and institutional contexts, the cultural turn in the human sciences provided at least two opportunities, perhaps even necessities. First, it provided an opportunity for geographers interested in 'culture' to take what was on their minds, or in their notebooks, as the basic stuff of a traditional cultural geography, and, through that material, engage with broader, interdisciplinary debates: a revalorization of culturally directed geographies, with a greater emphasis on questions of power, theory, and normativity. Second, the cultural turn's explicit attention to social theory fit nicely with burgeoning developments in geography more broadly, and perhaps brought cultural geographers more directly into swelling mainstream disciplinary currents; and perhaps also engaged heretofore economic or political or social geographers in cultural analysis and interpretation for the first time. In a sense, the new cultural geography took traditional cultural-geographic concerns as a point of departure, retheorized key concepts and ideas through cultural studies, and reengaged with the discipline at large through the concomitant attention to postpositivist and postempiricist theoretical frameworks, a commitment, in many cases, to a critical human geography, and ultimately to what Soja (1989) has called the reassertion of space in critical social theory – for let us not forget that what geographers had to offer the cultural turn and social theory was a practical history of attention to space, place, region, landscape, and society–nature dichotomies as key concepts of their twentieth-century discipline.

Cultural geography certainly is not alone in this potential elision, whereby a tradition is erected only to become the foil for perhaps entirely altogether different scholarly aims and directions. Fieldwork, once the bastion not only of empiricist epistemologies but an enterprise that carried within its practice the social reproduction of a male-dominated masculinist geographical practice, has been 'taken' on and redefined (reinvented?) as a broader, more catholic, and more reflexive set of practices (see, for example, Nast 1994). Fieldwork was central to a Sauerian tradition (see Price & Lewis 1993; or several of Sauer's own methodological statements, e.g. Sauer 1941, 1956). Yet recently a special issue of the *Geographical Review* titled 'Doing Fieldwork' (DeLyser & Starrs 2001) makes it clear that even in this arguably traditional journal (which published much in the Berkeley School tradition over the years) the core ideas of an intellectual enterprise can radically change, even while acknowledging a continuity of genealogy.

And so we are left with a genealogical problematic: whither tradition or wither tradition? Toward the second point, it is clear that today one can 'do' cultural geography without recourse to a 'traditional cultural geography' (see, for example, Shurmer-Smith & Hannam 1994). That position is probably more prevalent in Britain, where at times it might seem that all of human geography has become cultural geography. The next chapter, by Heidi Scott, more directly engages the cultural turn in geography from a decidedly British perspective (the bibliography is almost exclusively compiled from British-based academic publications, for example); and aside from an early reference to 'traditional cultural geography' which relegates the 'critique' to an American national context, the chapter generally gives credence to the development of a 'new' cultural geography almost exclusively out of a British cultural studies literature. There also are precedents that fall out of the predominant Sauerian teleology: where is the work of someone such as

Estyn Evans, for instance, in our rising new cultural geography? Yet one can argue that there is always internalized in that literature a critical space in which the Sauerian lives on, as a catalytic ghost that had to be exorcised for a clean break with an American tradition, if only, in the end, to avoid a name confusion. Or perhaps that is only the conservative curmudgeon in me writing, as every generation must come to terms with the fact that it might not be necessary for the next to read everything that was formative in one's own intellectual development.

Yet, that Sauerian ghost refuses to give up in some quarters. Clearly for some (Price & Lewis 1993, Robbins this volume) it is a sense of carrying on in key substantive research directions. In others, I suspect, its ghostly presence is a feature of institutional training. We read Sauer. We read the critique. We realized the path by which we got to the present state of affairs in cultural geography, and that the telling of the story is a central narrative in the ongoing redefinition of a tradition. Sometimes we need to do this for pedagogical reasons, in order to make clear in our graduate seminars the seemingly esoteric references that pervade the literature from the civil-war period. At other times we feel the need to clarify for colleagues who already carry with them an understanding of cultural geography exactly where we stand. In short, the critique is now perhaps tradition; and it carries 'traditional cultural geography' along with it. There are still others, perhaps, who take a middle ground, of sorts, me included. For example, in my own attempts to grapple with the idea(l)s of cultural landscapes (e.g. Schein 1993, 1997, 2003) I find that there is much that I learned from reading Sauer and the Berkeley School that I want to retain in my poststructuralist take on cultural landscapes as discourse materialized (Cosgrove 2000b), most notably an attention to detailed empirics (if not empiricism) for working through the theoretical implications of the landscape in reconstituting social life as well as a concern for the *long durée*, for the historical geographies of place that are central to the structuring qualities of those very places and landscapes. While I learned much from reading Foucault, I learned these things also from particular teachers, themselves devotees of Sauer, who believed in looking and thinking and, perhaps, in Sauer's (1956 [1963]: 393) 'morphologic eye': "a spontaneous attention to form and pattern . . . some of us have this sense of significant form, some develop it (and in them I take it to have been latent), and some never get it. There are those who are quickly alerted when something new enters the field of observation or fades out from it." One can take exception with the latent biological essentialism of Sauer's morphologic eye, but a charitable 'read' in a positive moment of genealogical reconstruction might make connections to more recent concerns with vision, ocular-centrism, and the lesson that these are learned and social epistemologies (see Cosgrove 1985; Rose 1992, 1993; Nash 1996). Learning from looking was central to the Sauerian tradition (Lewis 1983) and has not entirely faded from a retheorized contemporary cultural geography (Rose 2001). In short, there are elements of a 'traditional cultural geography' that bear retelling, revisiting, reformulating, and if the continuity is seen as forced or teleological, so be it. There is a certain ethical obligation to acknowledge intellectual forebears if, indeed, it is through their work that one's present position was achieved. And finally, there even has been in recent years a discovery of Sauer in other quarters that must be accounted for in geographical literatures. A prime example is the adoption of Sauer by William Cronon, especially in his groundbreaking *Changes in the Land* (1983), now a foundational text in American literatures on historical ecological change in an imperialist context.

In the end, there is a temptation to take a functionalist position on the matter of traditional cultural geography, especially at the institutional level. The *invocation* of the tradition is the point in the first place. Traditional cultural geography serves as part of a central narrative about how we practice our contemporary cultural geography, which is institutionalized to greater or lesser extent depending upon national disciplinary contexts and individual predilections.

There is a temptation also to recognize at the intellectual and scholarly level of ideas, that there is (through a positive historiographical interpretation) a grand continuity through some concepts and subjects basic to cultural geography of any definition. We can see in the Sauerian tradition attention to: the society/nature nexus, cultural landscapes, patterns and processes of imperialism and colonial domination, ecological change, historical as well as geographical process, detailed empirical work, and even the moral and ethical implications of our geographical practice, all topics that are very much a part of this volume. And these ideas resonate not just in a cultural-studies-derived (British) cultural geography, but across the Anglophone literatures in cultural geography. They can be found between the pages of (relatively) new journals such as *Cultural Geographies, Gender, Place, and Culture*, and *Journal of Social and Cultural Geography*, as well as in key books (such as Anderson 1995; Anderson & Gale 1992; Jacobs 1996; Fincher & Jacobs 1998; Wood 1998; Mitchell 1996, 2003; Henderson 1999; Hoelscher 1998; to mention only a few) by authors from a range of national disciplinary contexts beyond Britain. Traditions in the end are what you make of them. The tensions between critique and continuity, between old and new, between differing institutional sites of interrogation, between differing epistemologies, will always sit in uneasy opposition in any account of a tradition. In the end it is likely that no one will be entirely happy with any genealogical exercise, but it is the process of undertaking the interrogation that matters, after all, and not the quest for an ossified or reified set of essential characteristics by which we might model our scholarship, for then our traditions surely would wither as the world passed us by.

REFERENCES

Anderson, K. 1995: *Vancouver's Chinatown*. Toronto: McGill-Queen's University Press.

Anderson, K. and Gale, F. 1992: *Inventing Places*. London: Belhaven.

Cosgrove, D. E. 1983: Towards a radical cultural geography: problems of theory. *Antipode* 15, 1–11.

Cosgrove, D. 1984: *Social Formation and Symbolic Landscape*. London: Croom Helm.

Cosgrove, D. 1985: Prospect, perspective and the evolution of the landscape idea. *Transactions of the Institute of British Geographers* NS 10, 45–62.

Cosgrove, D. 1993: On "The reinvention of cultural geography" by Price and Lewis, commentary. *Annals of the Association of American Geographers* 83(3), 15–517.

Cosgrove. D. 1996: Ideas and culture: a response to Don Mitchell. *Transactions of the Institute of British Geographers* NS 21, 574–5.

Cosgrove, D. E. 2000a: Cultural geography. In R. J. Johnston et al., eds., *The Dictionary of Human Geography*, 4th ed. Oxford: Blackwell, 134–8.

Cosgrove, D. E. 2000b: Cultural landscape. In R. J. Johnston et al., eds., *The Dictionary of Human Geography*. Oxford: Blackwell, 138–41.

Cosgrove, D. E. and Jackson, P. 1987: New directions in cultural geography. *Area* 19, 95–101.

Cronon, W. 1983: *Changes in the Land*. New York: Hill and Wang.

Daniels, S. 1989: Marxism, culture, and the duplicity of landscape. In R. Peet and N. Thrift, eds., *New Models in Geography*, vol. II. London: Unwin Hyman, 196–220.

DeLyser, D. and Starrs, P. F. 2001: Doing fieldwork: editors' introduction. *Geographical Review* 91, iv–viii.

Duncan, J. S. 1980: The superorganic in American cultural geography. *Annals of the Association of American Geographers* 70(2), 181–98.

Duncan, J. S. 1990: *The City as Text: The Politics of Landscape Interpretation in the Kandyan Kingdom*. Cambridge: Cambridge University Press.

Duncan, J. S. 1993: On "the reinvention of cultural geography" by Price and Lewis, commentary. *Annals of the Association of American Geographers* 83(3), 517–19.

Duncan, J. S. 1994: After the civil war: reconstructing cultural geography as heterotopia. In K. E. Foote et al., eds., *Re-reading Cultural Geography*. Austin: University of Texas Press, 401–8.

Duncan, J. S. and Duncan, N. 1996: Reconceptualizing the idea of culture in geography: a reply to Don Mitchell. *Transactions of the Institute of British Geographers* NS 21, 576–9.

Fincher, R. and Jacobs, J. M., eds. 1998: *Cities of Difference*. New York: Guilford.

Foote, K. E., Hugill, P. E., Mathewson, K., and Smith, J. 1994: *Re-reading Cultural Geography*. Austin: University of Texas Press.

Gregory, D. 1994: *Geographical Imaginations*. Oxford: Blackwell.

Henderson, G. L. 1999: *California and the Fictions of Capital*. Oxford: Oxford University Press.

Hobsbawm, E. and Ranger T., eds. 1983: *The Invention of Tradition*. Cambridge: Cambridge University Press.

Hoelscher, S. D. 1998: *Heritage on Stage*. Madison: University of Wisconsin Press.

Hugill, P. J. and Foote, K. E. 1994: Re-reading cultural geography. In K. E. Foote et al., eds., *Re-reading Cultural Geography*. Austin: University of Texas Press, 9–23.

Jackson, P. 1989: *Maps of Meaning*. London: Unwin Hyman.

Jackson, P. 1993: On 'The reinvention of cultural geography' by Price and Lewis, Berkeley and beyond: broadening the horizons of cultural geography. *Annals, Association of American Geographers* 83(3), 519–20.

Jackson, P. 1996: The idea of culture: a response to Don Mitchell. *Transactions, Institute of British Geographers* NS 21, 572–3.

Jacobs, J. 1996: *Edge of Empire*. London: Routledge.

Kobayashi, A. *1989: A Critique of Dialectical Landscapes*. In A. Kobayashi and S. McKenzie, eds., *Remaking Human Geography*. London: Unwin Hyman, 164–83.

Lewis, P. 1983: Learning from looking: geographic and other writing about the American cultural landscape. *American Quarterly* 35(3), 242–61.

Livingstone, D. 1992: *The Geographical Tradition*. Oxford: Blackwell.

McDowell, L. 1994: The transformation of cultural geography. In D. Gregory, R. Martin, and G. Smith, eds., *Human Geography: Society, Space, and Social Science*. Minneapolis: University of Minnesota Press, 146–73.

Mitchell, D. 1995: There's no such thing as culture: towards a reconceptualization of the idea of culture in cultural geography. *Transactions of the Institute of British Geographers* NS 20, 102–16.

Mitchell, D. 1996: Explanation in cultural geography: a reply to Cosgrove, Jackson, and the Duncans. *Transactions of the Institute of British Geographers* NS 21, 580–2.

Mitchell, D. 1996: *The Lie of the Land*. Minneapolis: University of Minnesota Press.

Mitchell, D. 2000: *Cultural Geography: A Critical Introduction*. Oxford: Blackwell.

Mitchell, D. 2003: *The Right to the City*. New York: Guilford.

Nash, C. 1996: Reclaiming vision: looking at landscape and the body. *Gender, Place, and Culture* 3, 149–69.

Nast, H. J. 1994: Opening remarks on "women in the field." *Professional Geographer* 46(1), 54–66.

Price, M. and Lewis, M. 1993: The reinvention of cultural geography. *Annals of the Association of American Geographers* 83(1), 1–17.

Rose, G. 1992: Geography as a science of observation: the landscape, the gaze, and masculinity. In F. Driver and G. Rose, eds., *Nature and Science: Essays in the History of Geographical Knowledge*. London Group of Historical Geographers, Historical Geography Research Series no. 28.

Rose, G. 1993: *Feminism and Geography*. Minneapolis: University of Minnesota Press.

Rose, G. 2001: *Visual Methodologies*. London: Sage.

Sarder, Z. and Van Loon, B. 1999: *Introducing Cultural Studies*. Cambridge: Icon Books.

Sauer, C. O. 1925: The morphology of landscape. Berkeley: University of California Publications in Geography, 2(2), 19–54. Repr. in J. Leighly, ed., *Land and Life*. Berkeley: University of California Press, 1963, pp. 315–50.

Sauer, C. O. 1941: Foreword to historical geography. *Annals of the Association of American Geographers* 31, 1–24. Repr. in J. Leighly, ed., *Land and Life*. Berkeley: University of California Press, 1963, pp. 351–79.

Sauer, C. O. 1956: The education of a geographer. *Annals of the Association of American Geographers* 46, 287–99. Repr. in J. Leighly, ed., *Land and Life*. Berkeley: University of California Press, 1963, pp. 389–404.

Schein, R. H. 1993: Representing urban America: nineteenth century views of landscape, space, and power. *Environment and Planning D: Society and Space* 11, 7–21.

Schein, R. H. 1997: The place of landscape: a conceptual framework for interpreting an American scene. *Annals of the Association of American Geographers* 87(4), 660–80.

Schein, R. H. 2003: Normative dimensions of landscape. In C. Wilson and P. Groth, eds., *Everday America: Cultural Landscape Studies After J. B. Jackson*. Berkeley: University of California Press, 199–218.

Shurmer-Smith, P. and Hannam, K. 1994: *Worlds of Desire, Realms of Power: A Cultural Geography*. London: Edward Arnold.

Soja, E. 1989: *Postmodern Geographies: The Reassertion of Space in Critical Social Theory*. New York: Verso.

Wagner, P. L. and Mikesell, M. W., eds. 1962: *Readings in Cultural Geography*. Chicago: University of Chicago Press.

Wagner, P. L. 1994: Foreword: culture and geography: thirty years of advance. In K. E. Foote et al., eds., *Re-reading Cultural Geography*. Austin: University of Texas Press, 3–8.

Williams, M. 1983: "The apple of my eye": Carl Sauer and historical geography. *Journal of Historical Geography* 9(1), 1–28.

Wood, J. S. 1998: *The New England Village*. Baltimore: Johns Hopkins University Press.

Chapter 3

Cultural Turns

Heidi Scott

Recent decades have witnessed the meteoric rise of 'culture' and its study to a position of prominence across the social sciences and humanities. While this 'cultural turn' has been hotly contested and struggled over – no less so in geography than in other disciplines – it has nevertheless emerged as a reflection of, and timely response to, deep-rooted transformations that have taken place since the Second World War in the world's social and political landscapes. These changes have placed culture in the spotlight and made it a central focus of struggles over identity, belonging, and justice in the contemporary world.

The cultural geography that is associated with the recent transdisciplinary turn towards culture received its initial impetus from British geographers, who drew much of their initial inspiration from the work of Raymond Williams and the Birmingham Centre for Cultural Studies. In stark contrast to the old *Kulturkritik*, those working within cultural studies sought to reclaim culture for the population at large by embracing the view "from below" (During 1999: 25), and insisting upon the recognition of cultural diversity and processes of cultural change.

In the early 1980s, calls for a 'new' cultural geography were made by Jackson, who urged his colleagues to attend to the "inner workings of culture" (Jackson 1980: 112), and by Cosgrove, who proposed a radical cultural geography that would seek to understand symbolic production and "its role in the ordering of space" (Cosgrove 1983). In contrast to the traditional American cultural geography which it sought to critique,[1] the emergent field was closely linked to British social geography and sociology and deeply concerned with issues of space, power relations, and the diverse cultural practices of everyday life. Like cultural studies, the new cultural geography embraced and was profoundly shaped by feminist scholarship, as well as by poststructuralist, postmodern, and postcolonial theory. Since its early beginnings, it has been taken up and developed in diverse ways by geographers outside the UK, though almost exclusively within the English-speaking world. During the last 10 years, cultural geography has flourished to such an extent that it has become futile to try to conceptualize it as a unitary field with a coherent agenda or well-defined boundaries.

In what follows, I do not intend to dwell further on a discussion of cultural geography's genealogies, as this has been well-rehearsed elsewhere (see Jackson 1989; Mitchell 2000). Instead, I provide a brief sketch of the directions that geography's cultural turn has taken over the past decade or so, and then engage in a lengthier discussion of current developments, although for reasons of space and the sheer volume of the literature, I cannot hope to provide a comprehensive survey. More modestly, I aim to highlight some of cultural geography's most dominant contemporary trends and draw attention to significant parallels and points of connection with related fields of research.

Following the fall of the Berlin Wall and the rapid emergence of struggles over a "new world order," Cosgrove declared that a "spectacular agenda" had presented itself for cultural geography (Cosgrove 1992: 272). Initially, that agenda was overwhelmingly located in urban metropolitan areas of the industrialized West, as these came to be identified as key sites for the manifestation of social and political struggles that were being founded upon and expressed in terms of cultural difference. While research on lifestyle issues and the social construction of 'race' and gender featured prominently in work on the city, the material landscape was often of limited concern (Cosgrove 1992; Duncan 1993, 1994). The early preoccupation with first-world urban contexts may partly be understood as an endeavor on the part of new cultural geography to distance itself, like cultural studies, from an imperial past in which the term 'culture' – where it did not stand for the rarefied intellectual products of a privileged élite – was applied to the ways of life of 'primitive' non-Western peoples. At the same time, it constituted an understandable reaction to the traditional cultural geography's insistent and uncritical focus on rural and non-Western landscapes.

Despite the constant and continued prominence of the urban, research in cultural geography has embraced subject-matter of remarkable and ever-growing diversity. While the exploration of the relationships between nature and culture has proven to be an area of particular concern since the early 1990s, (post)colonial geographies, gender, sexuality and the body, national identities, travel writing, tourism and leisure, rural geographies, cultures of consumption, and globalization are just a few of the areas that have come under scrutiny. More recently, increasing attention has also been paid to cyberspace and internet technologies, to religion and to previously neglected social groups such as children and the disabled. At the same time, the predominantly visual focus of much work has been challenged by a growing interest in corporeal and sensual geographies that take account of touch, taste and hearing as well as of sight.[2]

Although sidelined by some early studies more concerned with issues of space and social construction, the last decade or so has witnessed the production of much significant research on landscapes and, as Matless illustrates in a review of work done by cultural geographers in 1995, a diverse range of topics has been examined through the prism of landscape (Matless 1996). If particular emphasis was initially placed on exploring the symbolism and textuality of landscapes (see e.g. Cosgrove & Daniels 1988; Duncan 1990; Barnes & Duncan 1992), later work reveals a gradual shift to the concept of landscape as a socionatural *process* and to thinking about how it *works* (Mitchell 1996; Matless 1998) – an approach which is equally apparent in archaeological and anthropological research (Bender 1993; Hirsch & O'Hanlon 1995).[3]

While reflecting its dynamism, the very proliferation of work in the new cultural geography has elicited cries of concern, not only from other areas of geography, but also from those who consider themselves practitioners within the field. From the early 1990s onwards, fears were repeatedly voiced over what some regarded as the indiscriminate overshadowing and 'colonization' of economic, political, and social concerns by the cultural, and the consequent overstretching of the term 'culture,' almost to the point of meaninglessness (see e.g. Thrift 1991; Gregson 1993; Barnett 1998). Bound up with this were worries that the cultural turn had caused geographers to lose their way in labyrinths of textuality and self-referentiality in which, predominantly concerned with linguistic games and the decoding of meanings, they had distanced themselves both from the material world and the political struggles that shape and take place within it. Although reprimanded on the one hand for abandoning substantive research in favor of ungrounded theoretical discussions, on the other, Thrift suggests, cultural geographers have also been accused of "hard-hearted empiricism" that reduces the world to a "lucky dip, a source of innumerable case studies waiting to be plucked, suitably agonized over . . . and published" (Thrift 2000: 1). While such charges are worth heeding, they are nonetheless guilty, I would argue, of frequent exaggeration and simplification. Geography's cultural turn most certainly involved a decisive turn towards text and representation, yet a concern for the material was by no means ever abandoned.[4] On the contrary, as Jackson indicates, interest in material culture is currently undergoing a renaissance (Jackson 2000).[5]

Despite the prominence of doubts and criticisms, cultural geographers continue to turn their attention to new areas of study with undiminished enthusiasm. However, the value of current work lies less in the subject-matter of new additions to a potentially infinite 'shopping-list' of topics that may be acquired for the field's consumption, but rather, I would suggest, in the ways in which cultural geography is being carried out and in the nature of its relationship with other areas of scholarship.

Cultural Geographies in Practice

If, as some have argued in recent years, the 'culture' concept has been used in a somewhat indiscriminate and careless manner, there is current evidence of a growing concern for paying close attention to the ways in which it is employed. Mitchell has been especially outspoken in criticizing cultural geographers for their willingness to concede to culture an amorphous multiplicity of meanings and, moreover, for what he regards as their repetition of traditional cultural geography's central error: that is, the reification of 'culture' as a "superorganic thing" or "realm," a perspective which has encouraged the "proliferation of examples that presumably *constitute* culture . . ." Instead, he argues, it is necessary to conceptualize culture as an *idea* and to concentrate on showing how it *works* in society (Mitchell 2000: 73–5). Mitchell's criticisms seem somewhat unfair given that, for many years, cultural geographers have in fact recognized culture as a process rather than as a 'thing' which may be possessed (see e.g. Anderson & Gale 1992 and 1999), although it is true that many studies pay scant attention to explaining how those processes work.

Nevertheless, it appears that Mitchell's suggestions have struck a chord within cultural geography. Shurmer-Smith provides enthusiastic support for Mitchell's understandings of culture in a new undergraduate textbook (Shurmer-Smith 2002), while Barnett, drawing on recent work in cultural studies that engages with Foucauldian notions of governmentality, proposes that culture

be understood as an historically variable range of practices that apply or deploy power to particular effects, and not as a realm that reflects, refracts or represents other modes of power. (Barnett 2001: 11)

In a range of disciplines beyond cultural geography, the turn of the century has been marked by comparable calls for revising the concept and usage of the term 'culture.' In cultural studies and literary criticism respectively, Mulhern and Eagleton warn against the collapsing of distinctions between culture and politics, a point which is also taken up by Barnett (Mulhern 2000; Eagleton 2000; Barnett 2001).[6] In anthropology, meanwhile, Ortner insists that "there is no longer anything we would call 'culture' or even 'cultures,' but that we want cultural interpretation to do different kinds of work" (Ortner 1999: 9).

If culture is done rather than possessed, growing emphasis is consequently being placed at present on the *doing* of cultural geography. This is perhaps most strikingly reflected in the title and style of Shurmer-Smith's *Doing Cultural Geography* (2002), which guides students through the application of theoretical perspectives and a range of methods in the practice of cultural geography. More widely, discussions about methods have gained prominence, and moves may be afoot for researchers to embrace broader, more engaged methods that go beyond textual analysis and traditional ethnographies. While Thrift would have cultural geographers learn from methods as diverse as street theatre, music and dance therapy and performative writing (Thrift 2000b: 3), Lilley suggests that mapping should not merely be treated as a practice to be deconstructed but recuperated as a creative strategy which offers "a way of connecting with landscape, and those who shape it" (Lilley 2000: 370).

Whether engaged research methods such as mapping will be widely adopted remains to be seen, but what their discussion does reflect is a more general, *theoretical* interest in issues of practice and performativity, and a related shift away from representation. Arguing that texts and representations can provide no more than a narrow and impoverished account of the world, Thrift proposes that we seek to valorize and apprehend the embodied, sensuous practices and noncontemplative knowledges that constitute the fabric of everyday life, a strategy which he terms "nonrepresentational theory."[7] While acknowledging the real and often tragic effects of power in the world, this approach seeks to escape from "the guilt-ridden, doom-laden and life-denying tone of much Western philosophical thought" (Thrift 1999: 302) and to celebrate the ways in which everyday creativity, imagination and play undermine and elude the workings of power (Thrift 2000a). The currency of these ideas is apparent, for example, in recent work on the embodied practices of caravanning and camping (Crouch 2001).

Notwithstanding current interest in nonrepresentational theory, it seems clear that the study of texts and other forms of representation will continue to play a

prominent, albeit less dominant, role in cultural geography. Recent work reveals a
sustained interest in travel writing and literature (Phillips 2001; Sharp 2002), as
well as in historical research, where medieval and early colonial geographies may
prove to be a new area of growth (Jones 2000; Wiley 2000; Harvey 2002). While
textual analysis will necessarily continue to be central to such historical work, it is
also apparent that texts are being engaged with in ways that bring the performative and material to the fore. The unearthing of meanings embedded within texts is
increasingly being sidelined by concerns for recuperating the spatial practices and
bodily performances that may be detected within them and which, until recently,
have largely been overlooked or dismissed. Such an approach is strongly evident,
for example, in recent work on imperial cities. While the study of texts and other
representations forms the basis of this work, it is argued that

> to understand the variety of ways in which cultures of imperialism were represented and
> negotiated in the European city, it is necessary to move beyond maps and texts to consider
> the relationship between different kinds of spaces – architectural, spectacular, performative
> and lived. (Driver & Gilbert 1999: 7–8)

Jacobs expresses related concerns with regard to the role of the city in the formation of colonial and postcolonial Australia. Seeking to move beyond mere spatial
metaphors by attending to "the 'real' geographies of colonialism and postcolonialism," her work explores the complex "spatial struggles" through which imperial
contests over identity and power have been articulated (Jacobs 1996: 1–5; see also
Taylor 2000).

At the same time, cultural geographers are increasingly attentive to tracing the
processes by which representations are *produced*, thereby reconnecting with the
material contexts and practices that shape them. The exploration of *acts* of mapping
thus provides the central theme of a recent collection of essays (Cosgrove 1999); in
a similar vein, Driver turns his attention to geographical fieldwork practices in the
high era of European exploration and imperialism (Driver 2001) and Brace examines the role of publishing and publishers in the formation of English rural identities in the mid-twentieth century (Brace 2001).

Returning to the theme of colonialism, a recent essay by Dubow moves away
from commonplace discussions of a disengaged "power-charged colonial gaze" to
exploring the ways in which colonial vision is created through dialogues between
sight, embodied desire and the experience of space (Dubow 2000). In the light of
Nash's recent warnings against the dismissal of representation and texts that some
proponents of nonrepresentational strategies appear to advocate, this work responds
to her call for the exploration of "the intersections between representations, discourses, material things, spaces and practices – the intertwined and interacting material and social world" (Nash 2000: 661).[8]

Just as much recent work in cultural geography seeks to reject 'either/or'
approaches in favor of more complex and textured accounts, so it also displays a
marked concern for overcoming – or at least challenging – some of the binary oppositions that have long been fundamental to Western thinking. Perhaps most prominent amongst these is the nature–culture dualism, which has attracted particular
attention in recent years from a range of disciplines within the social sciences and

humanities. If moves have been made for over a decade to recognize 'nature' as a cultural construct, the emphasis is now shifting towards drawing out the many ways in which the nonhuman, both animate and inanimate, is inextricably connected with and partly constitutive of human societies.

Drawing on actor-network theory,[9] geographers are challenging anthropocentric conceptions of the world by re-cognizing the human subject as just one form of agent whose actions are relationally shaped within hybrid networks of diverse agents – "human and nonhuman, technological and textual, organic and (geo)physical, which hold each other in position" (Whatmore 1999: 28; see also Whatmore 2000). The recent and related development of animal geographies is concerned not only with the ways in which human societies use and define animals and 'place' them both materially and imaginatively, but equally with examining – despite recurring fears about anthropomorphism – questions of animal agency and resistance to human orders (Philo & Wilbert 2000; Wilbert 2000).

The workings of power relations are currently being rethought in diverse contexts, in ways which reject any clear-cut oppositions between domination and resistance. This move is reflected in a recent publication which, while focusing on the domination/resistance couplet, seeks to undermine the binary model and draw out "the messy and inherently spatialised entanglements of domination/resistance, as always energised and traversed by the machinations and effects of power" (Sharp et al. 2000: 2). Geographical work on colonialism and imperialism is producing particularly nuanced accounts of power relations and identity which display sensitivity towards their enmeshed nature and the spatial processes and practices that constitute and shape them.[10]

Focusing on Victorian women travelers in nineteenth-century West Africa, McEwan draws attention to the inadequacy of adopting a feminist approach that recuperates and celebrates their agency without attending to issues of class, ethnicity and sexuality which cross-cut their relations with the colonized as well as with fellow Europeans. Thus, the ability of these women to exercise power over colonial subjects is undermined (as in the case of their male counterparts) both by acts of native resistance and by a frequently profound dependence on indigenous knowledges. At the same time, the textual *visibility* of this dependence reveals that, as women, they were unable (and also unwilling) to make claims for themselves as producers of geographical knowledge, and were largely denied membership of the Royal Geographical Society (McEwan 2000).

Such attentiveness to the internal differences and fractures that inflected the identity and (self)perceptions of European colonizers, and to how these were partly shaped in and by the periphery, is equally evident, for example, in work on white identities in colonial Barbados (Lambert 2001), in nineteenth-century South Africa and Britain (Lester 2001) and on European constructions of the tropics, to which a special issue of the *Singapore Journal of Tropical Geography* was recently dedicated. Introducing the papers, Driver and Yeoh draw attention to the ways in which they question the assumed "homogeneity and coherence in European systems of knowledge" and show how these views "may have been shaped by interactions with indigenous people and places" (Driver & Yeoh 2000: 3).[11]

Meanwhile, recent work by Martins and Abreu on imperial Rio de Janeiro undermines "conventional narratives of modernisation," which portray the rise of modernity on a global scale as the exclusive product of a dynamic and expanding Europe, by showing how early nineteenth-century processes of urban transformation "were shaped by a distinct local geography of globalisation" (Martins & Abreu 2001: 533).[12] While concerned with tracing global networks and flows of economic, cultural, and human capital as a consequence of European expansionism, much new work on imperialism and colonialism is therefore equally dedicated to the project of "provincializing Europe"[13] by emphatically drawing attention to the modulating effects of diverse local contexts, agencies and knowledge in the colonial 'peripheries.' Understandably, such approaches that seek to "blur the boundaries between centre and margin" (Anderson & Jacobs 1997: 21), have attained particular prominence in recent geographical (and anthropological) work that deals with issues of landscape, power and identity in (post)colonial Australia and New Zealand (see e.g. Morphy 1993; Jacobs 1996; Pawson 1999).

Transgressing Boundaries?

While cultural geographers and other scholars have become increasingly anxious to trace the ever-shifting networks that linked and mutually shaped local landscapes and global processes in the context of past centuries, this has become a goal of particular urgency where work of a contemporary nature is concerned. The dramatic effects of global capital, new technologies and the growing mobility of populations have made it imperative to rethink territorially bounded concepts of culture or culture groups in cultural geography, anthropology and cultural studies alike.[14]

Whereas initial reactions to globalization in the late twentieth century involved predictions of the future irrelevance of place and territoriality, these have given way to more measured accounts that acknowledge their continued significance. Focusing on local resistances to tourism in Goa, Routledge insists on the need to "remain attentive to place-specific discourses and practices of resistance" (Routledge 2001: 238), while Holloway and Valentine, who explore the use of the internet by British children, suggest that, rather than being placeless, "cyberspace is shaped through place-routed cultures" (Holloway & Valentine 2001: 153). At the same time, growing emphasis is placed on the difficulty of comprehending the production of local landscapes, identities, and practices without attending to the multiscalar networks of places and processes through which they are constituted. Such an approach is evident, for instance, in recent work on geographies of culinary authenticity in Britain, and on religion and suburban landscapes in south London. While the former study underlines the ubiquity of "mixed up, messed up, boundary defying culinary histories and practices" that defy countless national and cultural boundaries (Cook, Crang, & Thorpe 2000: 132), the latter illustrates how the London Mosque's suburban location is inextricably "tied to cultural, political and economic forces on a global scale" (Naylor & Ryan 2002: 50).[15]

Work on landscape in particular has long displayed a tendency to focus narrowly on the local. This, however, is clearly beginning to change, as reflected in a collection of essays on landscapes of defense edited by Gold and Revill. It is insufficient, they suggest, to study landscapes in isolation because of the interconnections that inevitably link them to other landscapes in relation to which they were formed (Gold & Revill 2000: 15). Their approach is applauded by Mitchell, who, making reference to his own work on California's contemporary landscapes, argues that those landscapes "do not just reflect but also incorporate and reify social processes working at a range of scales" and consequently "cannot be understood in isolation from other landscapes, other regions and other places" (Mitchell 2002: 383).

The transgression of traditional boundaries is evident not only in cultural geographers' current interests in tracing global processes that work across rather than within borders, but equally in terms of the growing connections that are being forged between cultural geography and other disciplines. Although fruitful exchanges and borrowings have long taken place, it now seems possible to detect the forging of stronger, more deliberate alliances that seek – actively and often with political intent – to weave connections across boundaries that have long maintained the existence of discrete disciplinary realms. While Featherstone and Lash suggest that the complex global processes of the contemporary world cannot be studied or comprehended through separate disciplines (1999: 2), Shurmer-Smith similarly questions the usefulness of maintaining the notion of 'cultural geography' as a distinct subdiscipline (2000: 524).

Although the imminent dismissal of labels such as 'cultural geography' seems highly unlikely, these concerns are nevertheless being actively engaged with in new publications that aspire to greater disciplinary hybridity by interweaving (rather than simply juxtaposing) methods and ideas from distinct areas of research. This approach is adopted in contributions to *Cultural Turns/Geographical Turns*, which aims to "break the boundaries of geography" by forging connections with work in diverse disciplines (Cook et al. 2000: xi), and is equally apparent in a major new volume on the archaeology and anthropology of landscape (Ucko & Layton 1999).

Current work on landscape in archaeology and cultural geography is particularly striking in its complementarity and common interests: while landscape archaeologists have displayed growing interest in landscape perceptions and the multiple meanings and power relations that shape and are shaped by material form (see e.g. Ucko & Layton 1999; Bradley 2000), cultural geography appears to be meeting them halfway in its present emphasis on the materiality of landscapes. At the same time, the prominence of actor-network theory in cultural geography is mirrored by new archaeological concerns for rethinking traditional divisions between human bodies and material things, and for constructing "a framework that acknowledges objects as a creative part of social life" (Gosden 2001: 164).

Despite cultural geography's growing involvement in such disciplinary transgressions and intertwinings, it may still be pertinent to question the extent to which it has really succeeded in overcoming other, no less traditional boundaries. In the early to mid-1990s, both Cosgrove and Duncan remarked on the tendency of work in new cultural geography to concentrate narrowly on the Western (and predominantly Anglo-American) world (Cosgrove 1992; Duncan 1994). More recently, Smith has suggested that, despite much talk of globalization, the field continues to be plagued by what he terms a "faux cosmopolitanism" (Smith 2001: 27–8).[16]

It cannot be doubted that much recent work, such as Bonnett's wide-ranging study of whiteness (Bonnett 2000), does indeed endeavor to look beyond the boundaries of the West, or that efforts are increasingly being made to include and review the work of scholars from beyond the Anglo-American realm in cultural and other human geography journals.[17] The recently-launched journal *Social and Cultural*

Geography, meanwhile, is notable for its inclusion of abstracts in French and Spanish. Nevertheless, many cultural geographers continue to show a striking disregard for literature written in languages and traditions other than English (unless it has been translated). Grossberg's recent criticisms, aimed at cultural studies, are equally applicable to cultural geography:

As a field, cultural studies remains too centered in Anglophone perspectives, traditions and disciplinary histories. These problems are exacerbated by the apparent reluctance of many English-speaking cultural studies scholars to grapple with empirical social and cultural contexts with which they are largely unfamiliar. (Grossberg 2002: 1)

Such lack of attention to non-English literatures and contexts is of no small consequence, given cultural geography's frequently proclaimed interest in decentering the West and its histories and geographies. Challenging the quietly accepted dominance of English should surely be central to the pursuit of this interest; otherwise, cultural geographers will continue to find themselves ironically bound by and reinforcing the very boundaries they wish to transgress. The persistence of linguistically determined barriers means that, even in a European context, geographers working within the Anglo-American tradition have largely maintained their distance from their non-Anglophone neighbors.[18]

While it is not my intention to suggest that all cultural geographers should necessarily become linguists, it is clear that cultivating greater attentiveness to other languages will further enrich an already diverse and dynamic field of research. The prominence that this issue has recently attained in human geography, as well as in related disciplines, suggests that such a move may soon be underway.

ACKNOWLEDGMENTS

I would like to thank Jim Duncan for his helpful editorial comments on an earlier draft of this chapter.

NOTES

1. See chapter 2, this volume, for a discussion of traditional cultural geography.
2. For reasons of space, I am unable to provide comprehensive references to this work. However, annual reviews of work done in cultural geography may be found in the journal *Progress in Human Geography*.
3. Although a geographically inspired lexicon of spatial and cartographic metaphors has been widely adopted across the humanities and social sciences, some of cultural geography's most fruitful and substantive exchanges appear to have been made with archaeology and anthropology.
4. As Matless observed in 1995, "most cultural work proceeds by putting into question any easy distinctions of materiality and representation" (1995: 396). Anderson and Gale (1999: 15) make a similar point: intensified interest in the politics of difference throughout the 1990s, they argue, has in fact "helped underline the inherent materiality of cultural life."

5. A possible consequence of this may be the forging of positive and productive links with the work of traditional cultural geographers who, in turn, seem increasingly receptive to approaches derived from new cultural geography.

6. This approach contrasts with Mitchell's rather strident assertion that "culture is politics by another name" (2000: 294).

7. This approach also involves a revision of traditional understandings of 'theory.' For Thrift, theory "becomes *a practical means of going on rather than something concerned with enabling us to see, contemplatively, the supposedly true nature of what something is*" (1999: 304); original emphasis.

8. The adoption of such a multifaceted approach appears to be reflected, for example, in recent work on postcolonialism and ecology in New Zealand (Dominy 2002), where textual analysis is combined with, rather than sidelined by, ethnographic fieldwork methods.

9. Initially developed by social theorists such as Callon, Latour, Law, and Serres, actor-network theory seeks to overcome the binaries and Euclidean certainties of Western thought. See e.g. Murdoch 1998 for a detailed discussion, and Whatmore 1999.

10. For a wide-ranging review of recent work on colonialism and imperialism, see Nash 2002.

11. Current work on European notions of the 'tropics' again reflects the enormous interest in issues of nature/culture, and their intersection with the study of colonialism and imperialism. Little explored until very recently, this may prove to be a significant area of future research for cultural geographers, cultural historians and literary critics alike. An interdisciplinary conference on tropicality was held in Greenwich (London), July 2002.

12. Recent work in history is similarly concerned with showing that 'globalization' is by no means a homogeneous and homogenizing product of the contemporary West, but rather a phenomenon that has emerged in diverse forms, places, and times. See e.g. Hopkins 2002.

13. I borrow this expression from Chakrabarty, cited in Rafael 1993: ix.

14. Anthropologists, for example, have recognized the inadequacy of traditional, Geertzian notions of 'culture' as bound to specific geographical locations and particular groups, and called for the need to "reconfigure the anthropological project in relation to the study of very complex social formations – nations, transnational networks, discontinuous discourses, global 'flows,' increasingly hybridized identities, and so forth" (Ortner 1999. 7).

15. Having said this, Peach (2002) argues that a *narrowing of scale* is currently apparent in cultural geography. I would strongly question the general applicability of this observation, but suggest that it may be so in the case of some work based on nonrepresentational and performative approaches, which tend to focus on microgeographies.

16. Arguably, such 'faux cosmopolitanism' applies above all to those who are at the 'center' of the new cultural geography (if such a thing exists). Scholars who work in areas such as environmental geography are showing interest in the ideas and approaches of cultural geographers, but without surrendering their interest in non-Western contexts. See e.g. Batterbury 2001.

17. Issues of language, and the need for Anglo-American geography to forge stronger links with geographers beyond that sphere, are discussed in a series of papers in vols. 18 and 20 of *Environment and Planning D: Society and Space*. Volume 18 also includes a review of Spanish and Portuguese literature.

18. Recent work in *Geographische Zeitschrift*, for example, shows that ideas central to Anglo-American cultural geography are being explored by geographers in other traditions, yet so far there is little evidence of reciprocity. Volume 88, for example, contains a series of papers on Orientalism. See especially Meyer 2000.

REFERENCES

Anderson, K. and Gale, F., eds. 1992: *Inventing Places: Studies in Cultural Geography*. Melbourne: Longman Cheshire.

Anderson, K. and Gale, F., eds. 1999: *Cultural Geographies*. Australia: Longman.

Anderson, K. and Jacobs, J. 1997: From urban Aborigines to Aboriginality and the city: one path through the history of Australian cultural geography. *Australian Geographical Studies* 35, 12–22.

Barnes, T. J. and Duncan, J. S., eds. 1992: *Writing Worlds: Discourse, Text and Metaphor in the Representation of Landscape*. London/New York: Routledge.

Barnett, C. 1998: Cultural twists and turns. *Environment and Planning D: Society and Space* 16, 631–4.

Barnett, C. 2001: Culture, geography, and the arts of government. *Environment and Planning D: Society and Space* 19, 7–24.

Batterbury, S. 2001: Landscapes of diversity: a local political ecology of livelihood diversification in south-western Niger. *Ecumene* 8, 437–57.

Bender, B., ed. 1993: *Landscape: Politics and Perspectives*. Providence, RI/Oxford: Berg Publishers.

Bonnett, A. 2000: *White Identities: Historical and International Perspectives*. Harlow: Prentice-Hall.

Brace, C. 2001: Publishing and publishers: towards an historical geography of countryside writing, c.1930–1950. *Area* 33, 287–96.

Bradley, R. 2000: *An Archaeology of Natural Places*. London/New York: Routledge.

Cook, I., Crang, P., and Thorpe, M. 2000: Regions to be cheerful: culinary authenticities and its geographies. In I. Cook et al., eds., *Cultural Turns/Geographical Turns: Perspectives on Cultural Geography*. Harlow: Prentice-Hall, 109–39.

Cook, I., Crouch, D., Naylor, S., and Ryan, J. R., eds. 2000: *Cultural Turns/Geographical Turns: Perspectives on Cultural Geography*. Harlow: Prentice-Hall.

Cosgrove, D. 1983: Towards a radical cultural geography: problems of theory. *Antipode* 15, 1–11.

Cosgrove, D. 1992: Orders and a new world: cultural geography 1990–91. *Progress in Human Geography* 16, 272–80.

Cosgrove, D., ed. 1999: *Mappings*. London: Reaktion Books.

Cosgrove, D. and Daniels, S., eds. 1988: *The Iconography of Landscape*. Cambridge: Cambridge University Press.

Crouch, D. 2001: Spatialities and the feeling of doing. *Social and Cultural Geography* 2, 61–75.

Dominy, M. D. 2002: Hearing grass, thinking grass: postcolonialism and ecology in Aotearoa – New Zealand. *Cultural Geographies* 9, 15–34.

Driver, F. 2001: *Geography Militant: Cultures of Exploration and Empire*. Oxford: Blackwell.

Driver, F. and Gilbert, D., eds. 2000: *Imperial Cities: Landscape, Display and Identity*. Manchester/New York: Manchester University Press.

Driver, F. and Gilbert, D. 1999: Imperial cities: overlapping territories, intertwined histories. In Driver and Gilbert, eds., *Imperial Cities: Landscape, Display and Identity*. Manchester/New York: Manchester University Press, 1–17.

Driver, F. and Yeoh, B. S. A. 2000: Constructing the tropics: introduction. *Singapore Journal of Tropical Geography* 21, 1–5.

Dubow, J. 2000: 'From a view *on* the world to a point of view *in* it': rethinking sight, space and the colonial subject. *Interventions* 2, 87–102.

Duncan, J. S. 1990: *The City as Text: the Politics of Landscape Interpretation in the Kandyan Kingdom*. Cambridge: Cambridge University Press.

Duncan, J. S. 1993: Landscapes of the self/landscapes of the other(s): cultural geography 1991–92. *Progress in Human Geography* 17, 367–77.

Duncan, J. S. 1994: After the civil war: reconstructing cultural geography as heterotopia. In K. Foote et al., eds., *Re-reading Cultural Geography*. Austin: University of Texas Press, 401–8.

During, S., ed. 1999: *The Cultural Studies Reader*. London/New York: Routledge.

Eagleton, T. 2000: *The Idea of Culture*. Oxford: Blackwell.

Featherstone, M. and Lash, S., eds. 1999: *Spaces of Culture: City, Nation, World*. London: Sage Publications.

Foote, K., Hugill, P., Mathewson, K., and Smith, J., eds. 1994: *Re-reading Cultural Geography*. Austin: University of Texas Press.

Gold, J. R. and Revill, G., eds. 2000: *Landscapes of Defence*. Harlow: Prentice-Hall.

Gosden, C. 2001: Making sense: archaeology and aesthetics. *World Archaeology* 33, 163–7.

Gregson, N. 1993: 'The initiative': delimiting or deconstructing social geography? *Progress in Human Geography* 17, 525–30.

Grossberg, L. 2002: 'A special editorial for 16(1).' *Cultural Studies* 16, 1–2.

Harvey, D. C. 2002: Constructed landscapes and social memory: tales of St. Samson in early medieval Cornwall. *Environment and Planning D: Society and Space* 20, 231–48.

Hirsch, E. and O'Hanlon, M., eds. 1995: *The Anthropology of Landscape: Perspectives on Place and Space*. Oxford: Clarendon Press.

Holloway, S. L. and Valentine, G. 2001: Placing cyberspace: processes of Americanization in British children's use of the Internet. *Area* 33, 153–60.

Hopkins, A. G., ed. 2002: *Globalization in World History*. London: Pimlico.

Jackson, P. 1989: *Maps of Meaning: An Introduction to Cultural Geography*. London: Unwin Hyman.

Jackson, P. 2000: Rematerializing social and cultural geography. *Social and Cultural Geography* 1, 9–14.

Jacobs, J. 1996: *Edge of Empire: Postcolonialism and the City*. London/New York: Routledge.

Jones, R. 2000: Changing ideologies of Medieval state formation: the growing exploitation of land in Gwynedd c.1100–c.1400. *Journal of Historical Geography* 26, 505–16.

Lambert, D. 2001: Liminal figures: poor whites, freedmen, and racial reinscription in colonial Barbados. *Environment and Planning D: Society and Space* 19, 335–50.

Lester, A. 2001: *Imperial Networks: Creating Identities in Nineteenth-century South Africa and Britain*. London/New York: Routledge.

Lilley, K. D. 2000: Landscape mapping and symbolic form: drawing as a creative medium in cultural geography. In I. Cook et al., eds., *Cultural Turns/Geographical Turns: Perspectives on Cultural Geography*. Harlow: Prentice-Hall, 370–86.

Martins, L. L. and Abreu, M. A. 2001: Paradoxes of modernity: imperial Rio de Janeiro, 1808–1821. *Geoforum* 32, 533–50.

Massey, D., Allen, J., and Sarre, P., eds. 1999: *Human Geography Today*. Cambridge: Polity Press.

Matless, D. 1995: Culture run riot? Work in social and cultural geography, 1994. *Progress in Human Geography* 19, 395–403.

Matless, D. 1996: New material? Work in cultural and social geography, 1995. *Progress in Human Geography* 20, 379–91.

Matless, D. 1998: *Landscape and Englishness*. London: Reaktion Books.

McEwan, C. 2000: *Gender, Geography and Empire: Victorian Women Travellers in West Africa*. Aldershot: Ashgate Publishing.

Meyer, F. 2000: Methodologische Überlegungen zu einer kulturvergleichenden Geographie oder: Auf der Suche nach dem Orient. *Geographische Zeitschrift* 88, 148–64.

Mitchell, D. 1996: *The Lie of the Land: Migrant Workers and the California Landscape.* Minneapolis: University of Minnesota Press.

Mitchell, D. 2000: *Cultural Geography: A Critical Introduction.* Oxford: Blackwell.

Mitchell, D. 2002: Cultural landscapes: the dialectical landscape – recent landscape research in human geography. *Progress in Human Geography* 26, 381–9.

Mitchell, W. J. T., ed. 1994: *Landscape and Power.* Chicago: University of Chicago Press.

Morphy, H. 1993: Colonialism, history and the construction of place: the politics of landscape in northern Australia. In B. Bender, ed., *Landscape: Politics and Perspectives.* Providence, RI/Oxford: Berg Publishers, 205–43.

Mulhern, F. 2000: *Culture/Metaculture.* London/New York: Routledge.

Murdoch, J. 1998: The spaces of actor-network theory. *Geoforum* 29, 357–74.

Nash, C. 2000: Performativity in practice: some recent work in cultural geography. *Progress in Human Geography* 24, 653–64.

Nash, C. 2002: Cultural geography: postcolonial cultural geographies. *Progress in Human Geography* 26, 219–30.

Naylor, S. and Ryan, J. R. 2002: The mosque in the suburbs: negotiating religion and ethnicity in South London. *Social and Cultural Geography* 3, 39–59.

Ortner, S. B., ed. 1999: *The Fate of "Culture": Geertz and Beyond.* Berkeley: University of California Press.

Pawson, E. 1999: Postcolonial New Zealand? In K. Anderson and F. Gale, eds., *Cultural Geographies.* Australia: Addison-Wesley Longman, 25–50.

Peach, C. 2002: Social geography: new religions and ethnoburbs – contrasts with cultural geography. *Progress in Human Geography* 26, 252–60.

Phillips, R. 2001: Decolonizing geographies of travel: reading James/Jan Morris. *Social and Cultural Geography* 2, 1–24.

Philo, C. and Wilbert, C., eds. 2000: *Animal Spaces, Beastly Places: New Geographies of Animal–Human Relations.* London/New York: Routledge.

Routledge, P. 2001: 'Selling the rain,' resisting the scale: resistant identities and the conflict over tourism in Goa. *Social and Cultural Geography* 2, 223–40.

Sharp, J. P. 2002: Writing travel/travelling writing: Roland Barthes detours the Orient. *Environment and Planning D: Society and Space* 20, 155–66.

Sharp, J. P., Routledge, P., Philo, C., and Paddison, R., eds. 2000: *Entanglements of Power: Geographies of Domination/Resistance.* London/New York: Routledge.

Shurmer-Smith, P. 2000: Cultural turns/geographical turns: perspectives on cultural geography. *Transactions of the Institute of British Geographers* 25, 524–6.

Shurmer-Smith, P., ed. 2002: *Doing Cultural Geography.* London: Sage Publications.

Smith, N. 2001: Socializing culture, radicalizing the social. *Social and Cultural Geography* 1, 25–8.

Taylor, A. 2000: 'The sun always shines in Perth': a post-colonial geography of identity, memory and place. *Australian Geographical Studies* 38, 27–35.

Thrift, N. 1991: Over-wordy worlds? Thoughts and worries. In C. Philo (comp.), *New Words, New Worlds: Reconceptualising Social and Cultural Geography.* St. David's University College, Lampeter: Social and Cultural Study Group, 144–8.

Thrift, N. 1999: Steps to an ecology of place. In D. Massey et al., eds., *Human Geography Today.* Cambridge: Polity Press, 295–322.

Thrift, N. 2000a: Entanglements of power: shadows? In J. P. Sharp et al., eds., *Entanglements of Power: Geographies Of Domination/Resistance.* London/New York: Routledge, 269–78.

Thrift, N. 2000b: Introduction: dead or alive? In I. Cook et al., eds., *Cultural Turns/ Geographical Turns: Perspectives on Cultural Geography.* Harlow: Prentice-Hall, 1–6.

Ucko, P. J. and Layton, R., eds. 1999: *The Archaeology and Anthropology of Landscape*. London/New York: Routledge.

Whatmore, S. 1999: Hybrid geographies: rethinking the 'human' in human geography. In D. Massey et al., eds., *Human Geography Today*. Cambridge: Polity Press, 22–39.

Whatmore, S. 2000: Heterogeneous geographies: reimagining the spaces of N/nature. In I. Cook et al., eds., *Cultural Turns/Geographical Turns: Perspectives on Cultural Geography*. Harlow: Prentice-Hall, 265–72.

Wilbert, C. 2000: Anti-this – against-that: resistance along a human–non-human axis. In J. P. Sharp et al., eds., *Entanglements of Power: Geographies of Domination/Resistance*. London/New York: Routledge, 238–55.

Wiley, J. 2000: New and old worlds: *The Tempest* and early colonial discourse. *Social and Cultural Geography* 1, 45–63.

Chapter 4

A Critique of the Cultural Turn

Clive Barnett

I. Turn: *'Move around so as to keep at the same distance from a center'*

There have been quite a few 'turns' in geography recently. There has been a 'moral turn,' an 'institutional turn,' and, a little while ago now, maybe even an 'empiricist turn' (this latter label was not meant as a compliment, unlike most other turns). But it is the 'cultural turn' that has attracted the most attention, and the one that has generated the most passionate debate. And it is not only geography that has been turning to culture. So have sociologists and historians (Bonnell & Hunt 1996), the-orists of the state (Steinmetz 1999), international relations theorists (Ninkovich & Bu 2000), to name but a few. There is even a set of arguments that the world itself has turned cultural in ways it apparently never used to be (Jameson 1998). Lots of these other fields also seem to have been turning geographical (see Cook et al. 2000), so that suddenly, everybody seems to be talking about culture *and* geography *at the same time*, even though the depth and extent of this geographical turn has been questioned by some (Agnew 1994; Martin 1999).

In this chapter, I want to worry away at the significance not so much of the cul-tural turn, as if there were such a thing, but rather at the rhetoric of 'the cultural turn.' In so doing, I want to air a pet hypothesis I have about the ways in which geography engages with theoretical ideas. This is the idea that size matters. Some people think the cultural turn is a turn for the worse (Martin 2001; Hamnett 2001), while some people think that it is a turn for the better (Philo 2000; Thrift 2000). Either way, there is a tendency to evaluate the pros and cons of shifts in intellec-tual fashion in terms of their overriding significance for the *whole* discipline. As either salvation or catastrophe, the idea of a cultural turn is only intelligible within a context in which commentators (like me) can imagine themselves to be part not so much of an imagined community, but of an actual, knowable community. Geog-raphy, after all, is a small discipline. I suspect the imagined coherence of a cultural turn depends in no small part on the sites and routines of academic gossip (Passmore 1998). The passions raised by the cultural turn in everyday academic set-tings (conferences, tearooms, pubs, lecture theaters) only makes sense if it is possible to imagine that a whole discipline either could, should, or should not, completely swerve from one path onto a wholly new one.

The rhetoric of a turn or turns tends to present academic disciplines as totalities. But more than this, the sense of a turn, with its strong undertones of progress, is perhaps an indication that geography is a discipline too small to be comfortable with its own intellectual pluralism. I realize this is a wholly counterintuitive proposition. I do not mean that geography does not allow the co-existence of all sorts of different ideas and methodologies. But geographers are not very relaxed about the degree of pluralism that does exist. This is evidenced by their chronic tendency to define the particular work they do in relation to what is going on elsewhere inside the discipline, even when the relevance of the connection is very tenuous indeed. A large part of the heat generated by the cultural turn depends on this inward looking orientation. As rhetoric, it is a turn around an axis very firmly anchored in geography.

II. Turn: *'Change from one side to another, invert, reverse'*

Everybody in geography seems to be talking about culture these days, but it is rather difficult to find anybody actually conceptualizing culture or the cultural as such. In fact, and here comes another pet hypothesis, I think the cultural turn in geography has worked in no small part through the determined *non*definition of culture. So, while human geographers have gone to great lengths to legitimize culture as a field of study by arguing that the predominant approaches to economic, political, and social phenomena have underestimated the cultural dimensions of this or that activity, it is never quite clear just what the neglected cultural dimension actually refers to. Most of the time, the sense of the cultural and culture derives from an oppositional staging of highly generalized, ontological categories which set the cultural off against the economic, the social, the material, and so on. The peculiar status of culture and the cultural as nonconcepts is registered by the fact that they are often held in suspension by quotation marks ('culture,' 'the cultural'). Citing 'culture' and 'the cultural' signals a deferral of conceptualization, either to a future moment, or to another academic field.

A recurring feature of discussions of the significance of the cultural turn in geography is the resort to diacritical narratives of distinction. In large part, the importance of the cultural turn emerges from declarations of what it is *not*. This helps to explain why substantive conceptualizations of culture and the cultural are fairly sparse in human geography. There are (at least) three axes of judgment and taste around which the importance of the cultural turn has been established.

1. Firstly, the cultural turn is about taking one's distance from a certain sort of Marxism. Of course, culture has long been a privileged locus for announcing the inadequacies of Marxist forms of social explanation. After all, one of the standard accusations levelled at Marxism is that it is *vulgar*. The 'Vulgar Marxism' tag tells us a lot more about the accuser (who is by definition staking a claim to be cultivated, sophisticated, able to appreciate complexity) than it does about the weaknesses of the tradition so impugned. The implication is that, by even suggesting that there may be some relationship between the higher things in life (opera, good wine,

pop music) and base considerations like work, causal explanation itself is guilty of bad taste. In turn, the appreciation of ambivalence and complexity come to be the benchmarks of social science endeavor.

The cultural turn has been heavily dependent upon a derivative postmodernist critique of 'totalizing' and 'essentialist' epistemologies of which Marxism is the primary suspect. Allied to this simplistic dismissal is the easy equation of Marxism with political economy, an effect of the particular empirical and theoretical emphases of geography's Marxism since the 1970s. In both its presences and its absences, Marxism in geography is distinguished from the Marxisms that have most influenced the development of cultural studies. But even the self-declared Marxist versions of cultural geography (e.g. Mitchell 2000) largely ignore the existence of a diverse tradition of Marxist *cultural* theory. Consequently, it has become common-sense for Marxism to be presented as unremittingly productionist, economistic, reductionist, deterministic, and class-based. This characterization underwrites an implicit understanding of the cultural as referring to an overlapping set of concerns with consumption, with forms of social relations other than class (which are also frequently conflated with being overwhelmingly about identity), with a focus upon agency rather than structure, and with an appreciation of contingency in social life. More generally, the hegemony of Marxist political economy over radical geography allows the cultural turn to be presented as a key moment in the flowering of theoretical diversity in the discipline. Contrary to this image, however, I think it is quite plausible to suggest that the theoretical reference points of the cultural turn have actually remained quite restricted, not least because of the sense of comfort provided by the 'not-Marxist anymore' narrative of progress. It certainly seems true that once cut adrift from Marxism, a poststructuralized critical human geography still tied to a rhetoric of radicalism only drifts further and further away from a normatively reflective tradition of liberal social science and political theory (Katznelson 1995). Insofar as its trajectory remains resolutely centripetal, the settling in of the cultural turn as an orthodoxy of its own might actively close off as many avenues of intellectual curiosity as it opens up.

2. But enough of this unseemly whining about Marxism. It is time to move on. If the cultural turn is about not being Marxist, or at least about not being caught dead being vulgar about one's residual Marxism, then it is just as much about proudly declaiming any tendencies towards positivism. This is the key methodological axis around which the cultural turn has been defined: it is about *not* being 'quantitative.' In this respect, the rhetoric of the cultural turn builds on and confirms a set of assumptions inherited from a previous generation of apostates (geography's theoretical involutions always seem to be distinguished by the vigour of renunciation). 'Cultural' has become synonymous with the use of certain methods of analysis, the thickly descriptive and thinly ethnographic. This is the sense in which whole swathes of work have come to be understood as being cultural, not least by those who do not use these qualitative methodologies. In geography, methodologies tend to be ascribed an enormous amount of political, and even moral efficacy (cf. Hammersley 1995). Yet the methodological self-righteousness that has become characteristic of critical human geography betrays a rather shaky pattern of political evaluation. The 'positivist' Vienna Circle was made up of liberals and radicals, after all.

Heidegger, on the other hand, one current favorite in geography, *was* a Nazi, and worse, he never even said sorry (Lang 1996). He is probably best read today as a salutary reminder of the moral hazards that attach themselves to an overly aestheticized disdain for the familiar, the countable, and the technological.

It is only by clinging to a somewhat discredited avant-garde conception of culture as an essentially aesthetic realm of self-realization that the value of numbers in progressing human welfare can be denied. In this respect, I wonder whether a progressive program for the analysis of culture can actually do without numbers. There are two senses in which this might be the case. Firstly, even the most resolutely qualitative of analyses tend to fall back on statements of quantity and numerical forms of reasoning to establish the general significance of the very detailed research findings they report (see Murdock 1997). Secondly, understanding the politics of culture in contemporary society with an eye to making a difference might depend on the use of numbers. The ability to intervene in public culture in pursuit of a progressive agenda of democratization depends in no small part on having the capacity to measure, compare, and assess cultural practices, tastes, and values (e.g. Barnett 2000; Ruddock 1998). Culture, in short, is too important to be defined against the instrumental, measurement, or numbers (Bennett et al. 1999; Lewis 1997). In this respect, perhaps the news is not all bad, insofar as there is an emerging interest in critical human geography in reassessing the importance of numbers not just as tools of domination, but as key resources in struggles for the extension of citizenship (e.g. Hannah 2001; see also Brown 1995). Perhaps we need a quantitative turn in cultural geography?

3. Finally, if the cultural turn constantly defines itself conceptually against Marxism and methodologically against quantification, then it also defines itself epistemologically as *not* being naively realist about knowledge claims. We are all social constructionists now, of one sort or another. This might have as much to do with taste as anything else, insofar as the cultural forms favored for analysis in canonical cultural theory tend to display a characteristically modernist aesthetic of difficulty. It is from this doubled canon of Works and Theory that one can trace the corollary of the overinflation of the political significance of different methodologies, which is the tendency to define cultural politics in narrowly formalistic terms by reference to a vocabulary of transgressing and disrupting established norms and conventions.

The operative understanding of 'social construction' that underwrites a whole genre of cultural analysis in human geography runs together a conceptual argument about the construction of identities with a methodological hodgepodge of 'textual' and 'discourse' analysis. Underwriting all of this is a generic recognition model of identity formation, in which individual and group identities are constituted by exclusion of the cultural other (see Oliver 2001). As a theoretical truth, the notion that identities are differentially constructed in relation to images of others, sanctions a methodology of reading texts, images, discourses (let's not be too fussy about the conceptual distinctions between these terms) on the grounds that these are the material out of which identities are made. This proves to be a very malleable assemblage of concepts and methods, which can be applied to the analysis of interview transcripts, geopolitical discourse, urban policy documents, colonial cartography, and much else besides. Social life thus gets reduced to a never-ending dance of Selves and Others, in which the focus of methodological analysis (representations of identity) is folded up with the main explanatory framework (identity formation has a self-confirming dynamic of desire, power, or intention).

Narratives of the cultural turn often bundle together all three of these diacritical gestures, the conceptual (not vulgarly Marxist), the methodological (not knowingly quantitative), and the epistemological (not naively realist) (e.g. Barnes 2001). The defining *not*-ness of the cultural turn is a symptom of a tendency to cling to geography ever more tightly as the whirly-gig of successive theoretical turns revolves more and more quickly. Each and every new idea or name stumbled across must be made to appear dramatically important to everyone, rendering all previous approaches old fashioned. The significance of the cultural turn is thus established by taking one's distance from both an 'uncritical' mainstream-mainstream (quantitative social science) and a 'not-critical-enough' critical-mainstream (Marxist social science), so that the cultural turn emerges as the route to attaining the genuinely critical 'critical' position. And it is from these sorts of stories of distinction, rather from any explicit work of conceptual elaboration as such, that the dominant senses of culture and the cultural emerge.

III. Turn: *'Give new direction to, take new direction, adapt, have recourse'*

My main point in all this is that geographers have not engaged in much detailed analysis of the concept that appears to be animating so much debate at the moment. Neither the proponents nor the detractors of the cultural turn move much beyond a rag-tag set of understandings of culture. So, culture is vaguely understood to be a generic feature of all social activity, referring in particular to the processes that make the world meaningful. A taken-for-granted symbolic understanding of culture is easily connected to the idea that culture is inherently differential. Meanings are contextual, specific, and contingent. And this is where geography comes in: because of culture, *things happen differently in different places*. Both the cultural and the geographical get defined as residual to general and abstract processes, and a culturally inflected geography emerges that provides contextual supplements to theoretical speculation that is carried on elsewhere.

This might seem an unlikely claim – that the cultural turn has been insufficiently theoretical – since the cultural turn has come to epitomize theoretical excess. But my argument is that while geographers have become very pluralistic in the use of culture and the cultural, this undefined usage is indicative of certain sort of theoretical discourse that might have negative as well as positive implications. In general, geographers have been content to construct 'theory' in terms of a set of propositions whose truth-status is already established by virtue of coming from somewhere else. The cultural turn has been legitimized by a two-way movement, referring to what is already going on in other fields while also insisting on the opportunity for geography to gain from broader engagements. This is also probably another side effect of being a small discipline.

The appeal to extradisciplinary sources of authority is just one means of resolving a fundamental paradox raised by postfoundationalist epistemologies of knowledge. Presuming to have undercut the grounds of truth-claims based on, for example, quantitative methodologies, dialectics, or critical realism, the newly en-cultured geographer is still left with the problem of what sorts of authority their own critical statements can carry. If one way round this uncomfortable conundrum is the appeal to other disciplines, then another closely related tactic is the recourse to the authority of the proper name of a *Theorist*. The cultural turn is thus associ-ated with a distinctive style of conceptual exposition whose most characteristic rhetorical device is "As X said," or "As X shows," followed by a more or less lengthy, more or less intelligible, citation. Deriving the truth-value of a statement from the simple fact that it was *said* only works as a persuasive argumentative strat-egy by implicitly calling on and reinstalling an aura of seriousness around select names. The names may alter (it could be Foucault or Lefebvre, Baudrillard or Haraway, Latour or Deleuze, Butler or Beck), but the textual apparatus of exposi-tion and persuasion remains remarkably constant. It gives rise to a cut-and-paste style of writing, in which a whole subgenre of theoretical writing takes the form of extended quotations from a limited assortment of writers, interspersed with gener-ally approving commentary, and uninterrupted by an excessive concern with criti-cal analysis or clarification. The almost total lack of irony characteristic of this genre encourages a suffocating degree of deference that closes down more avenues of serious thought than it opens. Even more seriously perhaps, it works to alienate a large part of any likely audience of students or fellow scholars (and in this, it again betrays an implicit avant-gardism, insofar as this alienation effect easily comes to be celebrated as an objective in and of itself). The reduction of theory to a set of slogans, bolstered by the author-effects of famous theorists' names, makes in par-ticular for really bad pedagogy. There is now an orthodox narrative of critical human geography, supported by textbooks, journals, and student dictionaries, in which the main characters are 'Positivism,' 'Structuralism,' and 'Poststructuralism.' This narrativization of the cultural turn has helped put in place a set of images of other research traditions that is at best a series of caricatures, and at worst involves teaching a series of half-truths and errors. This is perhaps the price of success. When 'critical' intellectual ideas become the basis of taught programs of instruction, being taught to a generation of students (including me) who do not share the contexts of personal struggle and engagement from which they earned their initial value, then the professionalization of 'being critical' becomes dependent upon inducting stu-dents into certain sorts of dispositions and attitudes by reference to heavily moral-ized constructions of 'mainstream' positions (Billig 2000).

In suggesting that the cultural turn has been insufficiently theoretical, I am not denying it has been the occasion for lots of theory-talk. But this is talk of a partic-ular sort. 'Theory' has become a kind of space-sharing performance art, in which what is registered is a set of common reference points. This theory-talk is an effort at constructing an audience in often unfamiliar, even hostile contexts. I have stolen this idea from someone else (probably more than one person, actually), so let me quote a favorite theorist of my own, Meaghan Morris, who has a good take on the nature of cultural theory in the contemporary English-speaking academy: "Cultural theory is a medium of diplomacy. This is why the term simultaneously refers, in media as well as academic usage, to a small but internationally recognized canon of names; to a subphilosophical jargon; and to a populist performance mode that aesthetically signposts its mixing of expository and narrative (or 'academic' and 'personal') rhetorics. All three practices are ways of creating a partial and often temporary commonality between people with little in common" (Morris 1998: 6). I think this description has a lot to commend it, and it certainly chimes with my own experiences, as both awed spectator and sometime bumbling performer. And in case you think I am being overly cynical about the whole enterprise, I do think there are all sorts of ways in which theory in this sense registers some welcome changes in the way academics do their thing (see Barnett 1998).

If theory functions in this way as a *lingua franca,* then it might be a very good thing indeed, providing a way of talking across divisions that might once have seemed unbridgeable. And this is not only about getting along with people from other disciplines. Kathryne Mitchell (1999) has argued that the vocabulary of culture has facilitated all sorts of *intra*disciplinary dialogues within geography, using work on immigration as her example. This is an argument that would see the vagueness of culture and the cultural as a huge advantage, insofar as it enables people from different perspectives to converge on a set of topics that have a high degree of overlap even if they lack strict conceptual coherence. Another field where culture has been doing this sort of work is in economic geography (see *Antipode* 2001). The culture and economy connection might take various forms, including a focus on cultures of work, cultures of the firm, culture as a synonym for consumption and identity, culture as subject to distinctive practices of commodification, or cultural as a reference to various qualitative methodological approaches (Ray & Sayer 1999). But one of the characteristic features of debates about culture and economy is a persistent tendency to present culture and economy as opposed principles in need of resolution. In most cases, the economic comes to stand for the abstract and the universal, and the cultural for the concrete and the particular. And geography invariably gets to be the site where these two sets of values are combined in context. So, *things happen differently in different places.*

In the final analysis, however, in all of these usages, even if culture remains only vaguely defined, it is never an entirely empty concept into which one can pour any sense at all. Culture can only serve its diplomatic function because it does indeed invoke a set of shared, overlapping understandings that do retain a degree of family resemblance. In particular, if we can all get along now by talking about culture, it is because there is something about culture that feeds on a particular understanding of what the geographical is all about. Culture and geography get connected as one side of an evaluative dualism that opposes specificity and difference to abstraction and universality. Here is another quote, one of my favorites, that makes the point very nicely: "You can't go wrong when you call something cultural, for it is the one term that, without necessarily specifying anything, carries the full weight of all possible forms of specificity" (Gallagher 1995: 309). I think this captures the essence of how geographers have used culture and the cultural, namely as a short-hand for specificity and difference: as what empirically escapes structural determination, and what conceptually disrupts abstraction and universalization. So it is that so much work that sits under the broad cultural banner combines very specific empirical case-studies with highly abstract explanatory categories (the West, Power, Desire), never quite stopping in between to flesh out the relays between the two.

IV. Turn: 'Remake (garment) with former inner side out'

So far, I have suggested that culture has not really been defined in geography, and that this might be what allows it to do the sort of work that it does as a nonconcept. But I want to conclude by suggesting that the real problem with the cultural turn might not be the nondefinition of culture. It might instead be the way in which this nondefinition almost completely elides the conceptualization of power and politics. Power and politics have become ubiquitous in culturally inflected research. It might be supposed that this is derived from Foucault, certainly subject to a standard reception that elevates a specific figure of power (the Panopticon) into a general theory (Barnett 1999). However, at a more mundane level, cultural analysis in geography has been heavily dependent upon an implicitly semiotic conception of power. Without necessarily being the subject of explicit conceptual discussion, the dominant strands of cultural theory upon which geographers have drawn have been shaped by a particular combination of post-Saussurean semiotics and Gramscian Marxism. What Saussure in particular bequeaths to cultural theory is a set of conceptual oppositions that have become the political unconscious of mainstream cultural studies: oppositions between arbitrariness and motivation, freedom and constraint, individuality and the social, the concrete and the abstract, the ideal and the material, use and system. If you splice these onto a reformulated notion of hegemony, liberally sprinkled perhaps with some psychoanalytic *linguisterie*, then one can quickly arrive at a notion of cultural power operating primarily through the semiotic process of coding and recoding signifiers (see Osborne 2000). Cultural politics comes to be defined in terms of the politics of meaning (cf. Grossberg 1998). And if meaning is an 'arbitrary' effect of articulating signs, then so one can understand not just cultural politics but *all* politics as a process through which interests and subjectivities are constructed through the (dis)articulation and (re)signification of identities. In this model, power is understood in a two-dimensional fashion to operate through *closure* (of the properly open play of signifiers), or *naturalization* (of the properly arbitrary nature of meanings), or *exclusion* (a necessary moment for the suturing of identity). The evaluative force of each of these categories turns on a zero-sum logic of *power* and *resistance*. And it follows that cultural politics, either in the classroom, the street, or sitting in front of the television in your living room, is understood on the analogy of critical reading, as the work of actively reinscribing chains of signifiers in order to produce new political subjectivities. It is worth noting that cultural politics in this sort of semiotic model of resistance still rests on a quite conventional, and distinctly un-Foucault-like conception of power, understood as the quantitative capacity of an individual or collective subject to realize their will (see Hindess 1996). In this case, politics is understood to turn on the differential capacity of social groups to make meanings stick, but the name of the game is still a battle between different actors to realize their own clearly defined interests.

This image of cultural politics is also, and despite first appearances, actually quite totalizing in its conceptual ambition. At its strongest, the idea of cultural politics in contemporary academic theory refers not just to the idea that there is a politics of culture, but to the much stronger claim that in a certain sense, culture is the privileged medium of *all* political conflict. It rests on the idea that 'material' power relations of class, gender, race, and so on are symbolized and contested in cultural practices. Perhaps the strongest version of this claim is to be found in the idea of a *circuit of culture* (Du Gay et al. 1996). According to this understanding, cultural practices can be understood in terms of a series of moments (production, regulation, consumption, representation, identity), each of which is inextricably linked to the others while retaining a degree of relative autonomy from them. At one level, this is a useful heuristic for a nonreductionist methodology, enabling one of these moments to be selected as an entry point for detailed research while keeping in mind the importance of the other practices. There is a stronger claim at work, however, insofar as what ties together each of these moments is the practice of meaning-making that runs through each of them. Meaning is both methodologically and conceptually privileged as being of the essence of cultural practice in this model. In the last instance, this idea that power relations are reproduced and resisted at the level of culture depends on a totalizing expressive conception of the relationships between meaning and the social formation, without which it would not be possible to suppose that the mundane practices of everyday life were saturated in political significance (Garnham 1997). One unfortunate result of this political saturation of culture is that the *ordinariness* of everyday life gets extremely short shrift.

This set of understandings of the relationships between culture and power underwrites an entire paradigm of engaged pedagogy. If power is understood to be reproduced through contingent acts of reproducing stable relations of meaning which naturalize the contingencies of power relations, then it is a short step to present the practice of revealing the constructedness of meanings (and by analogy of identities, interests, and subjectivities) as being an inherently political act. In the critical pedagogy paradigm (Heyman 2001), the classroom itself is reconfigured as a site where students are empowered to read critically. Any act of reading against the grain of received meanings (sometimes erroneously referred to as 'deconstruction') can thus be presented as either a political act in itself or as an essential preparation for it. This is a highly rationalistic, implicitly gendered conception of cultural politics, in which political resistance is presented as a matter of sloughing off the ideological blinkers of entertainment and distraction in favor of a hermeneutics of denaturalization and demystification. And furthermore, by reducing political intervention in cultural practices to the teaching and learning of appropriately critical acts of reading, a whole set of mundane power relations which shape classroom dynamics are finessed. Far from breaking with traditional methods of cultural pedagogy, critical pedagogy elevates their methods of distinction and disposition to a privileged status as political acts of resistance, while at the same time dodging all the difficult questions they raise about authority and responsibility (see Buckingham 1996, 1998).

Critical pedagogy rests on a third strategy for dealing with the cultural turn's self-induced crisis of epistemological authority. If one way of bolstering truth-claims is the appeal to extradisciplinary expertise, and another the "As X said" cut-and-paste approach, then a third is to align one's own academic analysis with the essential political goodness and moral rightness of the idealized struggles of ordinary people by deploying a rhetoric of 'resistance' (Brown 1996). This strategy depends upon an unproblematized politics of voice, in which analytical issues of plausible interpretation and explanation are brushed over by presenting surrogate critical readings of everyday practices that are couched in an all engulfing vocabulary of struggle, conflict, and transgression. In the face of scholar-activist representations of heroic everyday resistance, any purely academic questioning on methodological or conceptual grounds appears as a shocking act of moral and political betrayal.

I suspect that en-cultured geographers have been too content with displaying both the easy attitudes of critical disdain for other traditions and overt sympathy for various progressive causes, rather than working out just what culture is and how it does (and does not) connect up to power. The vogueishly vague, expansive nonde-finition of culture in geography has tended to elevate the moment of coding or meaning-making and identity over other aspects of cultural practice, such as the organizational, the institutional, the role of the state, or the central role of inter-mediaries (like us) in shaping cultural practices (Garnham 1995). Critical pedagogy does recognize this positioning of academics, but unfortunately reduces this to simply teaching the right attitudes to amazingly receptive students. But there is more to culture than meaning, and there are other cultural effects one could trace as well as those of signification and identity formation (Barnett 2001). We therefore require concepts and methods of analysis that are neither narrowly interpretative in their focus nor exclusively cultural in their frame of reference.

REFERENCES

Agnew, J. 1994: The hidden geographies of social science and the myth of the 'geographical turn.' *Environment and Planning D: Society and Space* 13, 379–80.

Antipode 33(2), 2001.

Barnes, T. 2001: Retheorizing economic geography: from the quantitative revolution to the "cultural turn." *Annals of the Association of American Geographers* 91, 546–65.

Barnett, C. 1998: The cultural turn: fashion or progress in human geography? *Antipode* 30, 379–94.

Barnett, C. 1999: Culture, government, and spatiality. *International Journal of Cultural Studies* 2, 369–97.

Barnett, C. 2000: Governing cultural diversity in South African media policy. *Continuum* 14, 51–66.

Barnett, C. 2001: Culture, policy and subsidiarity in the European Union. *Political Geography* 20, 405–26.

Bennett, T. et al., eds. 1999: *Accounting for Tastes*. Cambridge: Cambridge University Press.

Billig, M. 2000: Towards a critique of the critical. *Discourse and Society* 11, 291–2.

Bonnell, V. E. and Hunt, L., eds. 1999: *Beyond the Cultural Turn: New Directions in the Study of Society and Culture*. Berkeley: University of California Press.

Brown, M. 1995: The ironies of distance: an ongoing critique of the geography of AIDS. *Environment and Planning D: Society and Space* 13, 159–83.

Brown, M. F. 1996: On resisting resistance. *American Anthropologist* 98, 729–49.

Buckingham, D. 1998: Introduction: fantasies of empowerment? Radical pedagogy and popular culture. In D. Buckingham, ed., *Teaching Popular Culture: Beyond Radical Pedagogy*. London: UCL Press, 1–17.

Buckingham, D. 1996: Critical pedagogy and media education: a theory in search of a prac-tice. *Journal of Curriculum Studies* 28, 627–50.

Cook, I. et al., eds. 2000: *Cultural Turns/Geographical Turns: Perspectives on Cultural Geog-raphy*. London: Prentice-Hall.

Du Gay, P. et al., eds. 1996: *Doing Cultural Studies: The Story of the Sony Walkman*. London: Sage.

Gallagher, C. 1995: Raymond Williams and cultural studies. In C. Prendergast, ed., *Cultural Materialism: On Raymond Williams*. Minneapolis: University of Minnesota Press, 307–19.

Garnham, N. 1995: The media and narratives of the intellectual. *Media, Culture and Society* 17, 359–84.

Garnham, N. 1997: Political economy and the practice of cultural studies. In M. Ferguson and P. Golding, eds., *Cultural Studies in Question*. London, Sage, 56–73.

Grossberg, L. 1998: The victory of culture, part 1 (against the logic of mediation). *Angelaki* 3(3), 3–30.

Hammersley, M. 1995: *The Politics of Social Research*. London: Sage.

Hamnett, C. 2001: The emperor's new theoretical clothes, or geography without origami. In G. Philo and D. Miller, eds., *Market Killing*. London: Pearson.

Hannah, M. 2000: Sampling and the politics of representation in the US Census 2000. *Environment and Planning D: Society and Space* 19, 515–34.

Heyman, R. 2001: Pedagogy and the 'cultural turn' in geography. *Environment and Planning D: Society and Space* 19, 1–6.

Hindess, B. 1996: *Discourses of Power*. London: Routledge.

Katznelson, I. 1995: Social justice, liberalism, and the city. In A. Merrifield and E. Swyngedouw, eds., *The Urbanization of Injustice*. London, Lawrence and Wishart, 45–64.

Jameson, F. 1998: *The Cultural Turn*. London: Verso.

Lang, B. 1996: *Heidegger's Silence*. Ithaca: Cornell University Press.

Lewis, J. 1997: What counts in cultural studies? *Media, Culture and Society* 19, 83–97.

Martin, R. 1999: The new 'geographical turn' in economics: some critical reflections. *Cambridge Journal of Economics* 23, 65–91.

Martin, R. 2001: Geography and public policy: the case of the missing manifesto. *Progress in Human Geography* 25, 121–37.

Mitchell, D. 2000: *Cultural Geography*. Oxford: Blackwell.

Mitchell, K. 1999: What's culture got to do with it? *Urban Geography* 20, 667–77.

Morris, M. 1998: *Too Late Too Soon: History in Popular Culture*. Bloomington: Indiana University Press.

Murdock, G. 1997: Thin descriptions: questions of method in cultural analysis. In J. McGuigan, ed., *Cultural Methodologies*. London, Sage, 178–92.

Ninkovich, F. A. and Bu, L., eds. 2000: *The Cultural Turn: Essays in the History of US Foreign Policy*. Chicago: University of Chicago Press.

Oliver, K. 2001: *Witnessing: Beyond Recognition*. Minneapolis: University of Minnesota Press.

Osborne, P. 2000: *Philosophy in Cultural Theory*. London: Routledge.

Passmore, A. 1998: GeoGossip. *Environment and Planning A* 30, 8.

Philo, C. 2000: More words, more worlds: reflections on the 'cultural turn' and human geography. In I. Cook et al., eds., *Cultural Turns/Geographical Turns: Perspectives on Cultural Geography*. London: Prentice-Hall, 26–53.

Ray, L. and Sayer, A., eds. 1999: *Culture and Economy after the Cultural Turn*. London: Sage.

Ruddock, A. 1998: Doing it by numbers. *Critical Arts* 12(1–2), 115–37.

Steinmetz, G. 1999: *State/Culture: State Formation after the Cultural Turn*. Ithaca: Cornell University Press.

Thrift, N. 2000: Introduction: dead or alive? In I. Cook et al., eds., *Cultural Turns/Geographical Turns: Perspectives on Cultural Geography*. London: Prentice-Hall, 1–6.

Part II   Theoretical Intersections

Chapter 5

Historical Materialism and Marxism

Don Mitchell

> Historical Materialism offers to study social process in its totality; that is, it offers to do this when it appears, not as another "sectoral" history – as economic, political, intellectual history, as history of labour, or as "social history" defined as yet another sector – but as a total history of society, in which all other histories are convened.
>
> E. P. Thompson (1978: 70)

The first sustained attempt to develop historical materialism within cultural geography was by Denis Cosgrove.[1] Cosgrove (1983: 1) argued that "[b]oth Marxism and cultural geography commence at the same ontological point." Both "insist on characterizing the relationship between humans and nature as historical." But historical materialism differs from cultural geography by also insisting that humans "make their own history and themselves." Cosgrove argued that culture was best understood as "the production and reproduction of material life [as] necessarily a collective art, mediated in consciousness and sustained through modes of communication," and that cultural geographers needed to come to terms with the key debates that animated historical-materialist and Marxist theories of determination.

Historical Materialism . . .

The general philosophical position of materialism begins from the fundamental assertion that "matter" is the "primary substance of all living and non-living things" (Williams 1983: 197). The English word for "matter" derived from Latin and old French words designating building material: the physical substance of any *thing*. By extension, "matter" has come to designate the substance (obviously physical or not) of things, relationships, and events (1983: 198). Tracing philosophical materialism[2] to the fifth century BCE, Williams (1983: 198) suggests it really flourished in England (with Hobbes) in the seventeenth century and on the Continent soon thereafter as logical extensions were made from materialist philosophies of nature (e.g. nature as the result of "bodies in motion") to philosophies of society. Such philosophical materialism stands in opposition to idealism (and spiritualism) by denying that objects and relations derive their substance from ideas.

"*Historical* materialism" is a more modern variant, and typically signifies a particular set of concepts and affinities within Marxism: it indicates a body of *theory* (as well as a philosophical position). Trained in Hegelian philosophy, Karl Marx sought to transform the dialectics he learned into a theory and philosophy adequate to the political – revolutionary – social struggles he was engaged in. To do so, Marx rejected Hegel's idealism to develop instead a "materialist conception of history," which Engels later termed "historical materialism." Historical materialism is differentiated from broader materialism by its insistence, as Cosgrove (1983) noted, on humans' self-*production* of reality, of the worlds humans inhabit. For Marx, "self production," including the self-production of consciousness, was always deeply and inescapably *social* (rather than individual). And all social practice was itself historically and socially conditioned, determined by the dead weight of preceding practice and the institutions to which that practice gave rise. As Eagleton (1999: 5–6) put it, "Marx was aware that just for us to have an idea, a good deal else must already have taken place. What must already have happened in order for us to reflect? We must already be practically bound up with the worlds we are pondering and so already inserted into a whole set of social relations, material conditions, social institutions."

As a system of thought and analysis, then, historical materialism begins from certain premises:

The first premise of all human history is, of course, the existence of living human individuals. Thus the first fact to be established is the physical organisation of these individuals and their consequent relation to the rest of nature. . . . Men can be distinguished from animals by consciousness, by religion or anything else you like. They themselves begin to distinguish themselves from animals as soon as they begin to produce their means of subsistence, a step which is conditioned by their physical organisation. By producing their means of subsistence men are indirectly producing their actual material life. (Marx & Engels 1970: 42)

Given such arguments, Cosgrove made several related points critical to cultural geography. First, Marxism's "materialist conception of history" starts from a specific epistemological basis, namely that "the writing of history must set out from the natural bases of human life – the physical nature of human beings, and the natural conditions (geological, vegetational, climatic) in which they find themselves." Second, through the modification of these conditions – through the production of our very means of subsistence – humans produce themselves as human (and produce a new nature). Third, the production of the means of subsistence is social, it is conducted in a specific (historically determined) "mode." Fourth, and quoting Marx and Engels (1972), "this mode of production must not be considered simply as the reproduction of the physical existence of individuals. Rather it is a definite form of expressing their life, a definite 'mode of life' on their part." And fifth, the historical development of this "mode of life" in turn determines the form that social relations take.

. . . and Cultural Geography

These points suggested to Cosgrove (1983) that cultural geography could greatly benefit from a sustained encounter with Marxian historical materialism. Cosgrove

(1983: 3) noted that cultural geography already had many affinities with historical materialism, but up until then it had not developed what he called "the class dimension." Cultural geography, Cosgrove averred, needed a new *political* orientation. In particular, cultural geography possessed an inadequately differentiated and sociological notion of culture, and was thus ill-equipped to deal with questions of difference and power. As importantly, when questions of specific human agency entered cultural geography (e.g. Duncan 1980; Ley & Samuels 1978), they largely neglected "historical examinations of relations of production" and thus tended "towards phenomenological idealism" and radical individualism (Cosgrove 1983: 4).

In Cosgrove's view, then, there was a logical basis, and a real need, for a *rapprochement* between historical materialism and cultural geography, one that derived both from the political-intellectual agenda of Marxism (understanding society-nature as a totality and historically determined) and from the interest in ways of life that had animated early cultural geography. But for this *rapprochement* to be effected, a number of theoretical difficulties had to be addressed. Chief among these was the primary one that has bedeviled Marxism (and for that matter cultural geography) throughout its history: how to theorize the relations of determination that comprise the society–nature totality, and within it how best to theorize culture. This dual theorization of determination and culture needed to be a key task for materialist cultural geography.

Determination . . .

The classic statement of materialist determination comes in Marx's (1970: 20) Preface to his *Contribution to the Critique of Political Economy*:

In the social production of their existence, men inevitably enter into definite relations, which are independent of their will, namely relations of production appropriate to a given stage in the development of their material forces of production. The totality of these relations of production constitutes the economic structure of society, the real foundation, on which arises the legal and political superstructure and to which correspond definite forms of social consciousness. The mode of production of material life conditions the general process of social, political and intellectual life. It is not the consciousness of men that determines their existence, but their social existence that determines their consciousness.

Social existence – and the "conditions of possibility" that emerge through the production of the means of subsistence (no matter how simple or elaborate) – provides a foundation for social, political, and intellectual life. The direction of determination seems one-way: from economic foundation to social, political, and intellectual life. But as Cosgrove (1983: 5; see also 1984: 55) argued, "Marx's terms here are contingent. . . . They do not demand a deterministic interpretation." The question then is a practical one: just how *should* they be understood?

Reacting in part to the rise of an Althusserian notion of "overdetermination," Raymond Williams (1977: 87) argues that in Marx's work (and in historical materialism more generally) "determination" must be understood as both a "setting of limits" and an "exertion of pressures": "to determine or be determined to do something is an act of will and purpose. In a whole social process, the positive

determinations, which may be experienced individually, but are always social acts
... have very complex relations with the negative determinations that are experienced as limits." Moreover, according to Williams (1977: 87–8), the ultimate prove-
nance of both the positive exertion of pressure and the negative definition of limits
is human self-activity, human social practices:

> Determination ... is in the whole social process and nowhere else: not in an abstracted "mode
> of production," nor in an abstracted "psychology." Any abstraction of determination, based
> on the isolation of autonomous categories, which are seen as controlling or which can be
> used for prediction, is then a mystification of the specific, always related determinants which
> are the real social process – an active and conscious as well as, by default, a passive and
> objectified historical experience.

This is not how determination has always been understood within Marxism, especially within those parts of Marxism that concern themselves with "culture." Rather,
"in the transition from Marx to Marxism, and in the development of mainstream
Marxism itself, the proposition of a determining base and the determined superstructure has been commonly held to be the key to Marxist cultural analysis"
(Williams 1977: 76).

In Marx (if not in Marxism), the *relationship* between base and superstructure
was understood in a particular way:

> Upon the different forms of property, upon the social conditions of existence, as foundation,
> there is built a superstructure of diversified and characteristic sentiments, illusions, habits of
> thought, and outlooks on life in general. The class as a whole creates and shapes them out
> of its material foundation, and out of the corresponding social relationships. The individual,
> in whom they arise through tradition and education, may fancy them to be the true deter-
> minants, the real origin, of his activities. (Marx 1926: 55)

Note here that Marx argues that people, working in and with a set of "*social
conditions of existence*" (especially in relations of property, in this case), and
functioning within specific classes, *create* and *shape* the superstructure. The
superstructure is not "determined" in some mechanistic and autonomous way by
the "base." It is rather produced by people within a set of determinant and enabling
conditions defined by the totality of already-existing social relations.

Further, as Williams (1977: 76–7) points out, the use of "superstructure" here
(and elsewhere) indicates a rather complex concept that incorporates legal and political forms standing in relationship to relations of production; class-inflected forms
of consciousness; and a "process, in which over a whole range of activities, men
become conscious of a fundamental economic conflict and fight it out." These three
meanings of superstructure "direct our attention ... to (a) institutions; (b) forms of
consciousness; (c) political and cultural practices" (Williams 1977: 77), each of
which are *produced* by people living in and reproducing historically determinant
social conditions. A historical-materialist approach to social life, then, is one that
looks at social production and relates it to its historical and geographical development, and to the constant reproduction and transformation of the conditions of
existence, of "modes of life."

. . . and Culture

But what then of "culture"? "Culture" was not a key word in Marx's own work, but cultural theory has been an important and vital part of Marxism. Beginning with Gramsci's work in Italy in the 1920s, Lukács's theoretical and literary work in the same period, the Frankfurt School of Weimar Germany, and really accelerating (in different ways) in the "western Marxism" of post-Second World War France and Britain, theorizing culture became a focus of intense debate. "Culture," of course, is a remarkably multivalent concept, signifying everything from modes of thought and specific artistic productions to whole (infinitely complex) "modes of life."[3] It is impossible here to do justice to the range of meanings associated with the concept of culture; instead I will make a narrower argument about how culture has been figured in Marxism.

If we take as a starting point that culture is a concept that designates a "way of life" (and that, as Eagleton [2000: 1–2] says, "brings together both base and superstructure in a single notion"), and if we follow Williams (1958) in knowing that culture is ordinary (that it saturates every corner of life), then a Marxist approach to culture has two primary goals: (1) understanding how culture is produced – where it comes from; and (2) determining how it can be transformed through workers' own self-activity – how it can be made progressive and liberating rather than repressive and exploitative. These two goals have often been in tension in Marxism.

They were, however, brilliantly negotiated in the life and work of Antonio Gramsci. On the one hand, Gramsci's (1971) celebrated writings on hegemony (that sought to understand how power worked "culturally") turned attention to the analysis of the *institutions* through which power and domination were effected. On the other hand, such an institutional analysis indicated that institutional spaces could be created that promoted alternative modes of knowing, consciousness, and social struggle. Countercultural institutions were necessary to the development of counterhegemonies. Countercultural institutions (schools, newspapers, etc.) were vital components of the class struggle (Gramsci 1985: 20–46).

Despite his emphasis on class struggle, however, Gramsci's own definition of culture was decidedly conservative, almost Arnoldian in cast[4]. "I have a Socratic idea of culture; I believe it means thinking well, whatever one thinks, and therefore acting well, whatever one does" (1985: 25). But he differs from Matthew Arnold when he acknowledges that socialist "thinking well" will have to be organized: "Let us organize culture the same way that we seek to organize practical activity" (1985: 225). Culture, then, was an end in itself, *and* both a result and a means of organization. Proletarian cultural organization was particularly important because "the proletariat is a practical construct: in reality, there are individual proletarians, more or less educated, more or less equipped by the class struggle to understand the most refined socialist concepts" (1985: 32).

The development of countercultural institutions was critical because, in Gramsci's view, new modes of production are always "presupposed" by transformations of consciousness and social institutions; and yet these cultural transformations themselves can only become dominant – hegemonic – when the mode of production is revolutionized. In Gramsci's work, "culture" is both produced *for* workers and *by* workers. Workers' consciousness generally, and its class consciousness in particular, are the results of these two aspects of cultural production, which is exactly Williams' (1958) point when he insists that "culture is ordinary."

But if culture – and consciousness – is ordinary, then understanding its production required an even fuller understanding of its contours under capitalism. For Gramsci such an understanding could only come with the development of a robust communist party and a suite of cultural institutions associated with it. The Hungarian Marxist György Lukács, by contrast, turned to philosophy to understand the nature of the pressures and limits that determined culture. Reinserting Hegel in the center of Marx's analysis led Lukács to a more pessimistic set of conclusions about "hegemony" and its relationship to consciousness.

Writing in the immediate aftermath of the First World War, and in the midst of the rapid economic restructuring that Gramsci called "Fordism," Lukács sought to uncover the relationship between the fetishization of both commodities – which he called their "reification" (which itself can be roughly described as their "thingification": Lukács 1968: 86–7) – and working peoples' consciousness. His goal was to show how processes of reification in the social world (especially the world of work) produced a similar reification of consciousness.

Since, as Marx (1987 ed.: 45) noted, a "commodity is in the first place, a thing outside us" that fulfills needs, and since the exchange of commodities establishes a social world in which relations between people appear as if they are relations between things, the production of commodities is *necessarily* alienating. Under capitalism, this alienation is deep because labor-power itself is commodified. As divisions of labor are extended and deepened, labor-power's *formal equality* – that is, its abstraction in the marketplace to some quantity of socially necessary labor-time (1987 ed.: 47–8) – ensures that the "finished article ceases to be the object of the work process" (Lukács 1968: 88). It becomes possible "to separate forcibly the production of use-values in time and space" (Lukács 1968: 89) so as to better control and rationalize their production. This is important because:

[T]his fragmentation of the object of production necessarily entails the fragmentation of its subject. In consequence of the rationalisation of the work-process the human qualities and idiosyncrasies of the worker appear increasingly as *mere sources of error*. . . . Neither objectively nor in his relation to his work does man appear as the authentic master of the process; on the contrary, he is a mechanical part incorporated into a mechanical system. (1968: 89; see also Marx 1987 ed.: 306)

In such a system, the bourgeoisie as much as the proletariat is subject to alienation:

The atomisation of the individual is . . . only the reflex in consciousness of the fact that the "natural laws" of capitalist production have been extended to cover every manifestation of life in society; that – for the first time in history – the whole of society is subjected, or tends to be subjected, to a unified economic process, and that the fate of every member of society is determined by unified laws. (Lukács 1968: 91–2)

The only recourse is to fight against this: to defeat alienation and the reification of consciousness, "revolution is a categorical imperative" (Berman 1989: 142) – as is a communist party or other revolutionary organizations that seek to instill an oppositional culture. For, as Berman (1989: 142–243) argues, "Without culture and consciousness," without the "development of a vibrant, dynamic, self-critical, and self-renewing radical culture," working people "will not be able to grow in awareness and autonomy, to develop their critical will and their sense of power. If they do not grow and develop this way, the reification-machine will go on running" – as indeed it did in the subsequent evolution of the Soviet Union and its client states (see Buck-Morss 2000).

Lukács, like Marx, argued that the "natural laws" of capitalist production extended into every "manifestation of life in society." The expansion of capital – accumulation for accumulation's sake – is the imperative. But capital's own expansion inevitably runs up against its own limits as a system: there is demand for only so many cars, so many bananas, or so many light bulbs. The expansion of capital therefore necessitates a constant search for new markets (new buyers of cars, bananas, and light bulbs); the development of new needs and wants (the desire for a more luxurious car, a yellower banana, or a brighter light bulb); or the colonization by the commodity of new parts of social life (the commodification of back-seat sex; the commercialization of the *meaning* of the banana; or the turning into property of the very *idea* that a light bulb going on over a head is meant to represent). "Culture," as a way of life, as social meanings, and as artistic production, is inextricably bound up with commodity production.

All three strategies for the expansion of commodity production are important, but it was the third that drew the specific attention of theorists associated with the "Frankfurt School" (see Jay 1973). In the wake of the Second World War and reflecting on the rise of American mass entertainment, its two leading theorists, Adorno and Horkheimer, both cognizant of their debts to Lukács, focused squarely on what they came to call "the culture industry." They were concerned to theorize the changing role of art in social life. "Movies and radio no longer pretend to be art," they wrote. "The truth that they are just business is made into an ideology to justify the rubbish they deliberately produce" (Adorno & Horkheimer 1993: 31). This "rubbish" is differentiated not by subject, but through market segmentation. "Marked differentiations such as those of A and B films, or of stories in different price ranges, depend . . . on classifying, organizing, and labeling consumers. Something is provided so that none may escape" (1993: 32). "Culture" is here something that it produced as a commodity so it may be consumed as a commodity. Its value is realized in exchange. Use-value is merely a vehicle towards the consummation of that exchange.

But cultural commodities like films or radio shows are more insidious than other types of commodities because when they are used, they inevitably seep into and help to shape consciousness: "The whole world is made to pass through the filter of the culture industry" (Adorno & Horkeimer 1993: 33). Or as the French situationist Guy Debord (1994: 29) later put it: "commodities are now *all* there is to see; the world we see is the world of the commodity." If the culture industry has developed out of the imperative of capitalist expansion – out of the imperative to find additional corners of social life to commodify – it is nonetheless important that it plays a crucial *ideological* role in contemporary society:

What is decisive today is . . . the necessity inherent in the system not to leave the customer alone, not for a moment to allow him any suspicion that resistance is possible. The principle dictates that he should be shown all his needs as capable of fulfillment, but that those needs should be so predetermined that he feels himself to be the eternal consumer, the object of the culture industry. Not only does it make him believe that the deception it practices is satisfaction, but it goes further and implies that, whatever the state of affairs, he must put up with what is offered. . . . Pleasure promotes the resignation which it ought to help forget. (Adorno & Horkheimer 1993: 40)

The culture industry's industrial and ideological roles are mutually supportive, equally important, and ingeniously unified. The reification of consciousness is – not even subtly – advanced.

Questions of ideology also animated the French communist theorist Louis Alhusser. Althusser's legacy, both politically and intellectually, is complex. For Cleaver (2000: 50), Althusser's theoretical efforts to create a "structuralist" Marxism in the 1960s and 1970s constituted a (failed) attempt to develop a Marxism palatable to the still Stalinist French Communist Party, and should pretty much be dismissed as such. Cleaver is right, but unfortunately, Althusser's theoretical arguments have nonetheless had an enormous impact on subsequent radical cultural theory. In his famous essay on what he called "Ideological State Apparatuses" (ISAs), Althusser (1971) asserted that ideology is the set of representations and images through which people live – or experience – their "conditions of existence." But these images and representations are always grounded in some set of institutions (such as church, school, or media) which served as functionaries of the state by assuring the "interpellation" – or "hailing" of "subjects" (see Hall 1996). ISAs always possessed a "relative autonomy" from the economic "base," even if that base was always determinant "in the last instance" (Althusser 1971). Althusser borrowed from Freud and Lacan the notion of "overdetermination" to explain this relative autonomy, arguing that any subject position, like any "moment" in a social formation, was always the product of not just a single determinant, but the pressures and forces of a large suite of determinations. Ideology, embodied in ISAs, hailed people into place, established them as subjects in their social worlds, and presented them with the images and representations through which they could make sense of both their subjectivity and their place in the world.

When "overdetermination" was connected to the notion of social formation, Althusser claimed that it reoriented materialism towards a "middle ground" between a generalized mode of production and the specificity of everyday life, presumably "hitch[ing] together the base and superstructure" that Althusser thought Marx had "formally detached" (Inglis 1993: 83), and allowing for "a close material and conceptual analysis of social relations within a given place at a given time" (Smith 2000: 752). The ultimate irony of Althusser and many of his closest followers in structural Marxism is that this is exactly what they *did not* do, and on their failure to move beyond the formal and the conceptual, the theoretical and the abstract, English Marxists like E. P. Thompson (1978) and Raymond Williams (1977) launched withering attacks.

In particular, Thompson showed that sitting at the heart of the Althusserian project was a deep *idealism*. In language that still has deep resonance today (since it names exactly the problem that remains in contemporary structuralism, including that which goes by the name "poststructuralism"), Thompson (1978: 148 original emphasis) found lurking "behind Althusser's grotesque notion of ideological 'interpolation' or 'hailing' . . . even more *chic* notions of men and women (*except*, of course, select intellectuals), not thinking or acting but being *thought* and being *performed*." Men and women were creatures of systems – of systems of *thought* – and thus merely bearers of social relations, not shapers of them, not resisters against them, not people *experiencing*, and therefore transforming social life.

There is, thus, a significant difference between Althusser's antihumanism and the deep cultural pessimism of Adorno and Horkheimer. For the former, people are hailed into preestablished ideological and social places, places constructed by the "structure." For the latter, the very *will* of people is recognized right from the beginning. What is decisive, they say, is the necessity of not leaving people alone, because as soon as they are left to their own devices, they will struggle against the shackles that contain them, they will seek to break out of them and create something new. People are not *hailed* into position as (for example) consumers, but must be *induced* into shaping themselves as consumers, into finding being a consumer the best way to live, the best way to organize experience. The reproduction and expansion of capital requires, against all countervailing forces, that social life be limited, and pressures exerted in such a way that people need and want to consume so as to live, and to live well and enjoyably.

Experience, for Thompson (1978), thus had to be placed at the center of Marxist analysis, and when this was done then the sort of base–superstructure argument that Althusser advanced can be seen to be little more than nonsense. In perhaps some of the most famous lines from his long critique of Althusser, Thompson (1978: 96) lays out this argument in reference to his own research on the historical role of law in shaping English capitalism:

I found that law did not keep politely to a "level" but was at *every* bloody level; it was imbricated within the mode of production and productive relations themselves (as property-rights, definitions of agrarian practice) and it was simultaneously present in the philosophy of Locke; it intruded briskly within alien categories, reappearing bewigged and gowned in the guise of ideology, it danced a cotillion with religion moralising over the theatre of Tyburn; it was an arm of politics and politics was one of its arms; it was an academic discipline, subjected to the rigour of its own autonomous logic; it contributed to the definition of the self-identity both of rulers and of ruled; above all, it afforded an arena for class struggle, within which alternative notions of the law were fought out.

Law was experienced; law was an experience; the experience of law shaped social life; social life struggled back against the law; social formations were shaped and transformed. To understand this required not a flight into idealist fantasies about structure and ISAs, but careful historical-materialist analysis: a careful analysis of the historical record.

For a Marxism without *historical* materialism was no Marxism at all, and it certainly wasn't *materialist*: that was exactly Thompson's charge against Althusser. It was also Williams' (1977: 92). The problem with structural Marxism, according to the latter, was not (as often charged) that it was "too materialist" (leaving too little room for consciousness, ideas, and the accidents of social life), but that "it was never materialist enough."

Marxist Geography . . .

Cosgrove's 1983 call for a historical-materialist cultural geography was written in the context of these debates. As he put it in his landmark *Social Formation and Symbolic Landscape*, the key relationship that geographers needed to explore was "between cultural production and material practice" (1984: 2):

A cultural concept like the landscape idea does not emerge unprompted from the minds of individuals or human groups. . . . [H]istorically and theoretically it is unsatisfactory to treat the landscape way of seeing in a vacuum, outside the context of a real historical world of productive human relations . . . (1984: 2)

Thompson- or Williams-style historical materialism thus had to be at the heart of radical cultural geography, as Cosgrove made so clear in the second chapter of *Social Formation*.

But there was another foundation for Cosgrove's call for a materialist and radical cultural geography: the development of Marxism in geography itself. Marxism entered geography not through cultural theory, nor even through economic theory, but rather through the activist engagements of scholars radicalized by the upheavals of the 1960s (Peet 1977, 1998). In this regard, the turn to Marxism came as part of a much wider radical transformation of geography that included developments in anarchism, feminism, ecology, and humanism as geographers sought to theoretically ground their own growing activism.

Dissatisfaction with the dominant positivist spatial science of the day (which he had done so much to codify) led David Harvey (1973) to turn first to liberal and then to Marxist theories of social justice, and in doing so to lay out (for the first time in geography, though there were precedents in urban sociology) an explicitly Marxist and explicitly geographic urban theory. Harvey's goal was to expose the systematic *roots* of urban injustice, not just map its effects (as liberal and positivist theory was limited to doing). For Harvey, however, a Marxist reconfiguration of geography demanded geographic reconfiguration of Marxism. The space and spatiality which is implicit in Marx's work had to become explicit. The result was *Limits to Capital* (Harvey 1982). *Limits* focused on processes of capital circulation, its ossification in the built environment, and the contradictions to which these two processes gave rise. Together with Massey's (1984) *Spatial Division of Labor* and Smith's (1984) *Uneven Development*, *Limits* set the stage for the development of a rigorous Marxist economic geography that examined capitalist development and restructuring, uneven development, and labor market dynamics.

Much of the work inspired by these three books was, understandably, focused on the spatial dynamics of the capitalist economy. It was, in these terms, "economistic," and as such some critics found in the Marxist geography of the 1980s a too narrow, even two-dimensional analysis of social life, one that seemed little interested in the complexity of society and its cultures in place. While some of this critique came from within the broadly Marxist camp, some also came from outside it, as with, for example, Duncan and Ley's (1982) accusation that Marxist geography was "structuralist" and thus theoretically annihilated the real living people who actually produced social life.[5] Marxist geography was seen to be too closely cleaved to political economy.[6]

Even so, as Cosgrove's *Social Formation* made clear, there was exceptional scope within geographical Marxism for developing workable, spatial theories of culture and landscape. This scope was to some extent given shape in Peter Jackson's (1989) important text, *Maps of Meaning*, which sought to construct a cultural-materialist cultural geography sufficient to what seemed to be "new times" (cf. Hall & Jacques 1989). These "new times" quickly came to be called "postmodern," and Jackson's book was launched into geography concurrent with two others that sought to define the *Zeitgeist*, Harvey's (1989) *The Condition of Postmodernity* and Soja's (1989) *Postmodern Geographies*. In retrospect, these three books, focused on understanding the relationship between culture, social life, and economy, announced the coming of what has been called the cultural turn in geography, and with it a significant reinvigoration of cultural geography, much, but not all, of it grounded in historical materialism.

. . . and Cultural Marxism in Geography

Two related impulses shaped Jackson's *Maps of Meaning*. The first was to closely tie social and cultural geography to the project of British cultural studies. The second was to use "cultural materialism" as the twine that bound these two fields. Jackson's (1989: ch. 8) "agenda for cultural geography" thus focused on the (complex) material bases for, and explanation of, ideology, race, language, gender, popular culture, and class (as lived experience). Jackson (1989: 182) faulted Marxist geography for developing "a thoroughly de-cultured view of society where social relations are rigidly structured by an inflexible political economy." His goal was thus to interweave the economic Marxism of geography with some brands of cultural studies to produce a "materialist cultural geography" (1989: 43) that focused on the ways that people made culture as much as it focused on the structural constraints within which that making was advanced or limited.

The publications of Harvey's *Condition*, therefore, must have both heartened and disappointed Jackson. On the one hand, Harvey clearly took culture seriously, seeking to ground it in material social practices. On the other hand, Harvey more or less resuscitated something like a base–superstructure model of society,[7] arguing that the "surface froth" of cultural change derived from more "fundamental" transformations in the political economy, in this case the shift from fordist to postfordist regimes of accumulation. The ferment that so much postmodernist culture seemed to celebrate was, in Harvey's telling, inextricably linked to changing modes of exploitation; therefore any celebration was premature, at the very least.

In partial contrast, Soja (1989: 5) considered postmodernism – as a sociospatial *ontology* – to be "a possibly epochal transition in both critical thought and material life." *Postmodern Geographies* develops largely as a critique of social theory, but it does so through constant reference to political-economic change at the urban and regional scales, especially as they are worked out in Los Angeles. What is most striking in Soja's account of new spatial ontologies – particularly given his later work (cf. 1996, 2000) – is its relative inattention to the ways in which these ontologies, linked in his telling to economic restructuring, are *hegemonic* rather than already-complete totalizations of social life. This is all the more surprising because beginning in the mid-1980s, the Gramscian concept of hegemony had become central to much geographical discourse. For Jackson (1989: 53ff.), "hegemony" allowed for an examination of how power worked through both persuasion and coercion and thus why culture was so critical and always more than something that could be reduced to an effect of the economic base. After all, as Marx (1987 ed.: 537) argued, "the maintenance of the working-class is, and must ever be, a necessary precondition to the reproduction of capital."

"Reproduction" is a critical term. Socialist feminists in the 1970s and 1980s argued that much stronger attention needed to be paid within Marxism to the processes of *re*production, and the ways that they structured and were structured by gender, sexuality, and race. Such work took the quotation from Marx above seriously and made it clear that a focus on production, and on the workplace, was insufficient. The home, the family, the neighborhood, the school, and the store, were all key sites for negotiation and struggle over capitalism and its social formations. Moreover, any adequate theory of capitalist crisis demanded a much closer attention to crises of reproduction than was common in geographical Marxism (cf. Katz 1991a, 1991b, 2001). "Reproduction" needed to be understood as the site of "culture," as the place where the social totality was felt and lived.

Struggle and the exercise of power within the domain of "culture," then, is a precondition to the reproduction of capitalism. For Jackson (1989: 80), the key to a truly materialist study of culture in geography was to "view culture as the medium or idiom through which meanings are expressed. If one accepts . . . arguments for the plurality of cultures, then 'culture' is the domain in which these meanings are contested." Cultural geography is thus assigned the task of examining the content of these struggles, while at the same time exploring the varying spatialities to which they give rise. A cultural-materialist approach to culture focuses both on cultural politics and the politics of culture: "the cultural is the political" (Jackson 1989: 4).

In an article published in 1995, I accepted that the cultural is always political, but took issue with theories that constructed culture as a specific "realm," "domain," or "signifying system." To me, such theories both re-reified culture, and rehabilitated something like a base–superstructure model, only this time with causality running in the opposite direction. I argued (though not exactly in these terms) that "culture" needed to be reintegrated into the social totality of capitalism as a moment of *power*. Culture was an effect of struggles over power that was expressed as a reification of meaning, certain ways of life, or patterns of social relations: it is a materially based idea (or ideology) about social difference. "Culture" may be different from economic relations, but it could not be severed from them. Within capitalism, "culture" is always linked, directly or indirectly, to strategies and politics of accumulation. A fully materialist study of culture would focus on these strategies and politics (Mitchell 1995).

My article was published in the midst of a torrent of theoretical exploration, debate, and empirical work in geography on questions of culture. Later labeled the "cultural turn," cultural analysis took the geographical academy by storm in the 1990s. In a way that it had not been before, "culture" became both an object of analysis and a means for explanation. And it was, for many geographers, a turn *away* from materialism and towards what Philo (1991, 2000) identified as the "immaterial": the world of ideas and meanings, discourses and texts, signifying systems and "values" in their most ethereal, most ungrounded sense.

But there remains a vital need to connect values to value, to see how, as Marx would have it, values are always conditioned, always the product of limits and pressures. In a world where even ideas are now property, hedged in by capitalist laws and traded as if they were so many tons of grain, the need for a fully materialist cultural geography is now greater than ever (cf. Barnett 1998), and thus the retreat into the immaterial, and the focus on "culture" as an explanatory realm, that has so marked the cultural turn, comes at an unacceptable cost. Just because geographers have become infatuated with "meaning" and "discourses," processes and crises of accumulation have not come to a halt – nor has the reification machine stopped running. A cultural geography that is really meaningful will have to return to the fact that in the world we live in, the imperative of accumulation sits at the heart of what Williams called "determination of [a] whole kind" which exists "in the whole social process and nowhere else: not in an abstracted 'mode of production,' nor in an abstracted 'psychology' " – which is to say that to ignore the mode of production in our analyses of social and cultural life is every bit as much an error as to reduce all life to that mode of production. And at the same time, historical materialist cultural geography must understand that "culture" itself is a field of accumulation, a locus of and for commodity production. Capitalism is imperialist in its needs and ambitions, seeking to colonize every last corner of our lives. The new (too often idealist, too often immaterial) cultural geography ignores this fact at its – and our – peril.

NOTES

1. Blaut (1980) had earlier suggested that Sauerian cultural geography shared much in common with historical materialism, but he did not develop the point.
2. "The opinion that nothing exists except matter and its movement and modifications; also . . . the opinion that the phenomena of consciousness are wholly due to the operations of materials agencies." *OED: Materialism.*
3. For a cogent discussion see Eagleton 2000.
4. For Matthew Arnold (1993: 79), culture was "the *best* knowledge and thought of the time."
5. Duncan and Ley's (1982) argument was built on a tissue of misapprehensions and perhaps willing distortions of the nature of Marxist geography, which with only a few exceptions was quite anti-Althusserian, but it nonetheless had a great resonance with many not predisposed to Marxism in the first place.
6. Such accusations missed much of what was being written in Marxist geography (including Harvey's [1979] brilliant historical-materialist iconographic reading of the Basilique du Sacré Coeur and the growing focus on society–nature interactions).
7. It should be noted that Harvey's take on the base–superstructure problem is decidedly different from Althusser's. Harvey refuses to trade in the sort of idealist abstractions that were Althusser's bread and butter, seeking instead to show both theoretically and historically the nature of economic determination (in the sense of pressure and limits) of cultural forms.

REFERENCES

Adorno, T. and Horkheimer, M. 1993: The culture industry: enlightenment as mass deception. In S. During, ed., *The Cultural Studies Reader*. London and New York: Routledge, 29–43.

Althusser, L. 1971: Ideology and ideological state apparatuses. In *Lenin and Philosophy and Other Essays*. New York: Monthly Review.

Arnold, M. 1993: *Culture and Anarchy and Other Writings*, ed. S. Collini. Cambridge: Cambridge University Press.

Barnett, 1998: The cultural turn: fashion or progress in human geography. *Antipod* 30, 379–94.

Berman, M. 1989: Georg Lukács's cosmic chutzpah. In J. Marcus and Z. Tar, eds., *Georg Lukács: Theory, Culture and Politics*. New Brunswick: Transaction Publishers, 137–52.

Blaut, J. 1980: A radical critique of cultural geography. *Antipode* 12(2), 25–9.

Buck-Morss, S. 2000: *Dreamworld and Catastrophe: The Passing of Mass Utopia in East and West*. Cambridge, MA: MIT Press.

Cleaver, H. 2000: *Reading Capital Politically*. Edinburgh: AK Press.

Cosgrove, D. 1983: Towards a radical cultural geography. *Antipode* 15, 1–11.

Cosgrove, D. 1984: *Social Formation and Symbolic Landscape*. London: Croom Helm, 2nd ed., Madison: University of Wisconsin Press, 1998.

Debord, G. 1994: *The Society of the Spectacle*, tr. D. Nicholson-Smith. New York: Zone Books.

Duncan, J. 1980: The superorganic in American cultural geography. *Annals of the Association of American Geographers* 70, 181–98.

Duncan, J. and Ley, D. 1982: Structural Marxism and human geography: a critical assessment. *Annals of the Association of American Geographers* 72, 30–59.

Eagleton, T. 1999: *Marx*. London: Routledge.

Eagleton, T. 2000: *The Idea of Culture*. Oxford: Blackwell.

Gramsci, A. 1971: *Selections from the Prison Notebooks* ed. and tr. Q. Hoare and G. Nowell-Smith. London: Lawrence & Wishart.

Gramsci, A. 1985: *Antonio Gramsci: Selections from the Cultural Writings*, eds. D. Forgacs and G. Nowell-Smith. Cambridge: Harvard University Press.

Hall, S. 1996: Introduction: who needs "identity." In S. Hall and P. de Gay, eds., *Questions of Cultural Identity*. London and Thousand Oaks, CA: Sage, 1–17.

Hall, S. and Jacques, M., eds. 1989: *New Times: The Changing Face of Politics in the 1990s*. London: Lawrence & Wishart.

Harvey, D. 1973: *Social Justice and the City*. Baltimore: Johns Hopkins University Press (republished 1988 by Blackwell, Oxford).

Harvey, D. 1979: Monument and myth. *Annals of the Association of American Geographers* 69, 362–81.

Harvey, D. 1982: *The Limits to Capital*. Chicago: University of Chicago Press (republished 1999 by Verso, London).

Harvey, D. 1989: *The Condition of Postmodernity*. Oxford: Blackwell.

Inglis, F. 1993: *Cultural Studies*. Oxford: Blackwell.

Jackson, J. 1989: *Maps of Meaning: An Introduction to Cultural Geography*. London: Unwin Hyman.

Jay, M. 1973: *The Dialectical Imagination: A History of the Frankfurt School and the Institute of Social Research, 1923–1950*. Boston: Little, Brown.

Katz, C. 1991a: An agricultural project comes to town: consequences of an encounter in Sudan. *Social Text* 28, 31–8.

Katz, C. 1991b: Sow what you know: the struggle for social reproduction in rural Sudan. *Annals of the Association of American Geographers* 81, 488–514.

Katz, C. 2001: Hiding the target: social reproduction in the privatized urban environment. In C. Minca, ed., *Postmodern Geography: Theory and Praxis*. Oxford: Blackwell, 94–110.

Ley, D. and Samuels, M. 1978: *Humanistic Geography: Prospect and Problems*. London: Croom Helm.

Lukács, G. 1968: *History and Class Consciousness: Studies in Marxist Dialectics*, tr. R. Livingstone. Cambridge, MA: MIT Press.

Marx, K. 1926: *The Eighteenth Brumaire of Louis Bonaparte*. London: G. Allen and Unwin.

Marx, K. 1970: *A Contribution to the Critique of Political Economy*, tr. S. Ryazanskaya. Moscow: Progress Publishers.

Marx, K. 1987: *Capital*, vol. 1. New York: International Publishers.

Marx, K. and Engels. F. 1970: *The German Ideology*, ed. and with an intro. by C. J. Arthur. New York: International Publishers.

Marx, K. and Engels, F. 1972: *Feuerbach: Opposition of the Materialistic and Ideological Outlook*. Moscow: Progress Publishers.

Massey, D. 1984: *Spatial Divisions of Labour: Social Structure and the Geography of Production*. London: Methuen.

Mitchell, D. 1995: There's no such thing as culture: towards a reconceptualization of the idea of culture in geography. *Transactions of the Institute of British Geographers* 20, 102–16.

Peet, R., ed. 1977: *Radical Geography: Alternative Viewpoints on Contemporary Social Issues*. Chicago: Maaroufa.

Peet, R. 1998: *Modern Geographical Thought*. Oxford: Blackwell.

Philo, C. 1991: Introduction, acknowledgements and brief thoughts on older words and older worlds. In C. Philo (comp.), *New Words, New Worlds: Reconceptualizing Social and Cultural Geography*. Lampeter: Social and Cultural Geography Specialty Group.

Philo, C. 2000: More words, more worlds: reflections on the "cultural turn" and human geography. In I. Cook, D. Crouch, S. Naylor, and J. Ryan, eds., *Cultural Turns/Geographical Turns*. Harlow: Pearson Education, 26–53.

Smith, N. 1984: *Uneven Development: Nature, Capital, and the Production of Space*. Oxford: Blackwell; 2nd ed. 1990.

Smith, N. 2000: Social formation. In R. Johnston, D. Gregory, G. Pratt, and M. Watts, eds., *The Dictionary of Human Geography*, 4th ed., 752–3.

Soja, E. 1989: *Postmodern Geographies: The Reassertion of Space in Critical Social Theory*. Oxford: Blackwell.

Soja, E. 1996: *ThirdSpace*. Oxford: Blackwell Publishers.

Soja, E. 2000: *Postmetropolis: Critical Studies of Cities and Regions*. Oxford: Blackwell.

Thompson, E. P. 1978: The poverty of theory: an orrery of errors. In *The Poverty of Theory and Other Essays*. New York: Monthly Review Press, 1–210.

Williams, R. 1958: *Culture and Society*. London: Chatto and Windus.

Williams, R. 1977: *Marxism and Literature*. Oxford: Oxford University Press.

Williams, R. 1983: *Keywords*. London: Fontana Press.

Chapter 6

Feminisms

Joanne Sharp

Introduction

Until relatively recently, feminist and cultural geographies did not have much in the way of common interests. The descriptive accounts of cultural landscapes and regions of Carl Sauer (1963) and his intellectual legacy offered little to feminists who wished to explain the effects of patriarchy on the spaces through which women's roles were constrained and enabled, and the spatialities through which gender identities and relations were maintained and expressed. This changed with the "cultural turn," where "new" cultural geographies turned to the less material, observable facets of cultural production, in the geographies of landscape but also through a plethora of everyday practices and activities. Hence both feminist and cultural geographers study the power relations woven through the practices of everyday life to understand the production of identities, inclusions, exclusions, and cultures of domination and resistance. This chapter will examine where cultural and feminist geographies converge and where they diverge. The chapter will conclude with a discussion of possible areas of research in the future.

Feminist Geography and New Cultural Geography

The famous feminist call of "the personal is political" was important in academic analyses because it turned attention away from study of formal institutions of power and politics, to understanding the importance of beliefs and meaning systems and the common-sense values of culture in the construction of gender roles and identities. Rather than only examine the formal spaces of work, for instance, feminists turned to understand the processes which constructed separate spheres of work and home, and why these became gendered (McDowell 1983). Similarly, feminists have examined the construction of spheres of politics and nonpolitical spheres, this social division itself an operation of power (Enloe 1989; see also McDowell & Sharp 1997). And so, feminists have increasingly pointed to the importance of the everyday to the geographies of gender relations.

New cultural geography similarly moved on from its previous concentration on the formal processes and material expressions of culture – the culture region and culture area of Sauer (1963), the material expressions on the cultural landscape of Kniffen (1962) – to look at the processes through which cultural systems are produced and reproduced. Drawing on the work of cultural theorists, perhaps most significantly Said (1979), new cultural geographers have prioritized a politics of representation, and attempts to open up a space for those whose meanings are represented (and marginalized) by hegemonic assemblages, discourses, and practices. Feminist concerns are integral to new cultural geography which understands gender relations (and other facets of cultural identity) to be involved in the constant (re)production of culture, but also the signification of gender norms in cultural systems. There are three areas where feminist geographers have particularly important contributions to make to cultural geography: identity politics, landscape and the body. I will now examine each in turn.

Identity Politics

Feminist geography has understood the construction of gendered identities through a number of different conceptual frameworks. The "three waves" of feminism have each understood the construction of masculine and feminine in differing ways. The "first wave" of feminists believed that men and women were essentially the same. Thus, in a society which privileged men due to historical domination of men over women, all that is required for equality is that women be given the same opportunities as men: equal opportunities in the job market, in voting, and so on.

"Second wave" feminists saw gender as a much more pervasive element in the construction of social roles and opportunities, and so were more concerned with emancipation of women than with attaining equality with men. This meant that rather than try to deny differences between men and women, these feminists drew out the differences. Men and women *are* fundamentally different as far as second wave feminists are concerned. Whether as a result of nature (biological difference) or nurture (socialization), men and women have different understandings of the world, different ways of knowing it, and a different set of abilities, talents, characteristics and so on. Furthermore, because culture and society have been dominated by men for so long, they have taken on masculinist traits, most often explained as confident cultures of competitiveness and individualism, based around aggression, rationality, or objectivity (or some combination). Therefore, providing women with the same opportunities (access to the labor market or education, for example) will not result in equality because women will be struggling to compete with men within a culture which recognizes and rewards masculinist traits, rather than feminist traits (of compassion, support, and emotion). Those women who have been successful – female political leaders such as Margaret Thatcher are most often produced as an example here (see Enloe 1989) – have only achieved what they have, say second wave feminists, because of their expulsion of their female traits and adoption of a hypermasculine cultural identity.

Due to this focus on the essential differences between men and women, most usually seen to be the result of the biological "facts" of sexual difference, cultural expectations of what women "should" look and act like have come under particular criticism from second wave feminists.[1] 'No More Miss America' demonstrations and global women's protests against Miss World competitions represented this rejection of dominant norms, and at such rallies, there were 'Freedom Trash Cans' "into which were thrown bras, along with girdles, curlers, false eyelashes, wigs, copies of the *Ladies' Home Journal, Cosmopolitan, Family Circle* etc." (Bordo 1993: 19, quoted in McDowell 1999: 244–5). Feminists were particularly critical of "the beauty myth" (Wolf 1991) which primarily reduced women to an aesthetic object of the male gaze rather than as active agents themselves. Feminist geographers have highlighted the spatially restraining effects of the beauty myth, whether the simple difficulties of walking quickly and assertively in narrow skirts and high-heeled shoes, or the reproduction of an image of women as frail and thus constrained from their independent use of social space (McDowell 1983; Valentine 1993). The feminist claim that 'the personal is political' has meant that campaigns around issues such as pregnancy, abortion, and maternity leave became an important part of feminist "body politics" (McDowell 1999).

There are other expressions of this difference between masculinist and feminist cultures. Ecofeminists for instance believe that because masculinist culture has dominated in Western society, the environment has been aggressively stripped of resources, mined for minerals and rendered an economic good. They believe that women have more in common with nature due to the common oppression under patriarchal power relations and so a female-dominated culture would be more likely to facilitate sustainable management of nature and a more equitable distribution of resources (e.g. Shiva 1989). The rise of capitalist modes of production, modern scientific practice and Enlightenment thought together changed conceptions of Nature as being a (divine) order to being disordered and in need of the controlling influence of man's intervention (Merchant 1980). By this time, "man" was no longer seen as part of Nature, as Haraway has argued in her genealogy of primatology, "it is the white man who has excluded himself from 'nature' by both history and a Greek-Judeo Christian myth system" (Haraway 1989: 159). Similar arguments are made for the inevitability of war and conflict in masculine-dominated societies (Enloe 1989, 1993; Seager 1993).

The second wave of feminism was incredibly powerful politically in that it drew up clear lines of opposition between men and women. In addition, it challenged the apparent universality of Western knowledge, claiming it to be an extension of masculinist ways of knowing and therefore partial. This opened the way for later, more fundamental epistemological challenges to dominant thought such as Haraway's (1988) insistence on the situatedness of knowledge claims, or relativist positions of postmodernist theorists such as Lyotard (1984).

However, more recently, a number of different groups of women have drawn attention to their alienation from the nature of "woman" used in many second wave claims in their name. Robin Morgan's "global sisterhood" was one such attempt to look at the commonality which was the "result of a *common condition* which, despite variations in degree, is experienced by all human beings who are born female" (Morgan 1984: 4). A number of Third World feminists have challenged Morgan's image of a global sisterhood arguing that it ignores all of the differences, inconsistencies, and histories which make up the notion of womanhood in different places. For Mohanty (1997: 83) this automatic alliance erases the agency of

women in particular historical struggles, and requires that "the categories of race
and class have to become invisible for gender to become visible." For Third World
feminists like Mohanty, the global sisterhood image silences the histories of colonialism, imperialism and racism from which Western feminists still benefit. Post-
communist feminists have similarly critiqued Western feminism for its liberal,
middle-class assumptions (Funk & Mueller 1993). Other groups of women have
also started to be more vocal in their insistence that their experiences and identities
be included into understandings of what it is to be female in different societies:
lesbian and bisexual women have challenged the "compulsory heterosexuality" of
much feminist politics, working class women have challenged the predominant idea
in liberal notions of feminism that it is liberating to leave the house to find work
(for them, this simply becomes yet another burden on their time), and disabled
women critique the embodied assumptions underlying much feminist thought and
politics (see Rich 1986; Nast 1999; Chouinard & Grant 1995).

Thus, in response to these critiques of earlier incarnations, "Third wave" feminism takes a more complex view of gender relations. Here gender is a central axis
of power and identity, but one which cannot be understood in isolation of other
elements of identity such as race, class, nationality and sexuality. Third-wave feminists have acknowledged the greater complexity of gender relations, not simply
operating around a male–female binary, but cross-cut by issues of race, class, and
sexuality. Such feminists have moved from the essentialist arguments of previous
feminisms: gender identity is not defined as stable and bounded but instead as fluid.
Rather than regard gender identities as having fixed boundaries – as male or female
– this approach regards them as constantly in flux. In other words, a rejection of
boundaries is, for some, epistemologically a feminist move. French and Italian feminists in particular have been resistant to attempts to delimit and name the feminine, arguing that femininity is constructed as "that which disrupts the security of
the boundaries separating spaces and must therefore be controlled by a masculine
force" (Deutsche 1996: 301). Feminists such as Cixous (see Shurmer-Smith 1994)
and Irigaray (1985) regard the establishment of boundaries as a fundamentally
masculinist move, a will to power through the defining and delimiting of an essence
into something known. Instead, Cixous and Irigaray see feminism as always being
in excess, always escaping categorization and limitation, always more than can
be known and thus always subversive of accepted ways of knowing. Elements
of recent developments in cultural geography have also embraced this fluidity of
categories.

Cultural geographers influenced by poststructuralism have also challenged coherent and bounded notions of the subject. Most influential is the work of Michel
Foucault (see especially Foucault 1977; 1978). For Foucault, "subjectivity is an
epiphenomenon of discourse: there is no ontological self, but rather a sense of selfhood is an effect of discourse, and a location within networks of power/knowledge"
(Sharp 1999: 267). There is no subject prior to knowledge, power, and discourse.
In his earlier work on the subject (Foucault 1977), he focuses on attempts to
"produce" docile subjects through the construction of particular spaces through
practices of disciplining and surveillance (for example, schools, hospitals, and
prisons). In the later *History of Sexuality* volumes, Foucault (1978) looks at the
"technologies of the self" through which individuals are taught to assume – but

more importantly they choose to assume – certain subjectivities (his example is of sexed selves).

Feminist theorist Judith Butler (1990) has been key in understanding gender identities from this more fluid perspective. She considers the ways in which gendered identities are reproduced through the repetition of mundane activities rather than there being any essentialist biological definition of gender, or any stable identity established through social construction. It is the deed and not the doer that is of significance. The notion of a coherent and independent identity – or "the subject" – is the effect of constant performance. On the whole, she argues, repetition works to reinforce the norm of heterosexuality. It is only through the constant repetition of heterosexualized actions that the illusion of a heterosexual norm can emerge. Everyday practices such as looking at advertising images, following soap opera storylines, placing pictures of families on office desks, unselfconsciously reproduce heterosexuality as the norm (see also Valentine 1993). Butler (1990) argues that queer politics resists these practices through a reversal. From a mass of possible sexual performances emerges a conceptual map on which clear and distinct lines can be drawn dividing "straight" from "gay," "normal" from "deviant." However, Butler's is not such a monolithic theory. There is always the possibility of resistance and transgression in this model which is so dependent on correct repetition. Alternative practices – whether consciously or unconsciously performed – can destabilize and ultimately undermine these fragile assemblages. Feminist geographers have embraced Butler's ideas, particularly the importance she gives to the historical and geographical specificity of each performance. As a result, there have been studies of the geographies of sexual performance, with feminist geographers considering the role of both private spaces in the construction of gay identities (e.g. Rothenberg 1995; Johnston & Valentine 1995), performances of gender in spaces of work (e.g. McDowell 1997), the importance of challenges to the heterosexism of public space (e.g. Knopp 1995), and the significance of transgressions known only to the individual(s) involved in the act (e.g. Bell & Valentine 1995). Some feminists have argued that space itself should be seen as performatively enacted (Rose 1993), or have suggested that it is important to resist images of space and place that are fixed and quotidian – in a binary gender system, feminine – in comparison to the transformative masculinism of time (see Massey 1993).

Performance and fluidity have also recently been embraced in cultural geography. The figure of the hybrid or mobile subject has become central to much cultural theory and cultural geography, from Clifford's (1992) "traveling culture" to celebrations of the nomad as the rootless subject that is freely able to traverse global space and resist dominant codings (Doel 1995; Routledge & Simons 1995). For the latter cultural geographers, influenced by Deleuze and Guattari (1983; 1987), the state apparatus is part of a cultural drive towards immobility and fixity. Nomadism is a fluid positionality which blurs boundaries and subverts stable definitions, whether this mobility is actual movement across space, or a metaphorical state of being. The figure of the nomad resists settled patterns of thought and as such has been held up as the decentered or fragmented subject of postmodernism and poststructuralism, or the figure of resistance in critical theory (see Routledge & Simons 1995). Deleuze and Guattari (1987) hold up the nomad as the figure resisting that paranoiac desire emanating from the territorializing and repressive effect of institutions (such as the state, family and school). They hold up schizophrenic desire as the nomadic subversion of these fixed and bounded identities.[2] This desire deterritorializes: transcending borders and resisting any attempts to contain or discipline. These desires also have spatial expressions: territorialization produces "striated spaces" of control and limitation, while deterritorialization produces "smooth spaces" of movement.

This understanding of the mobile subject has been critiqued by Kaplan (1987) who argues that such mobility is only available to privileged white males (see also Braidotti 1994; Massey 2000). Certain women (and minorities) do not have access to the technologies of mobility, and are often very much situated in place. Various images of a shrinking and fluid globe are, argues Massey (2000), a geographical imagination situation in the West, particularly in the imaginations of white men, rather than being a newly emerging and resistant global sense of place. For those who have the economic and cultural capital, the world is indeed becoming a smaller place linked by jet travel and the electronic communities of the internet. For others however, the globe is as much a "striated space" as it ever was, marked as it is by spaces of danger, barriers of nation-state borders, the cost of travel and the perpetuation of colonial discourses of race. Although recognizing the extralocal nature of definitions of place, Massey (1993) argues that global space is nevertheless subject to the laws of a set of "power geometries" based in wealth, patriarchy, and Western-centrism. Global space is thus constructed to ensure that mobility is not available to all, that certain groups are still subject to the constraints of place, to be exploited by the power of capital which is mobile across the globe. This issue is of particular importance to feminists in that global poverty is increasingly a gendered condition with women now estimated to comprise the majority of the world's poor.

Furthermore feminists have been anxious about embracing fluid notions of subjectivity and identity for fear that they will lose the ability to define boundaries of identity and as a result lose the power of fighting for the cause of female emancipation. As Linda Alcoff suggests, Foucault ignores the fact that, sometimes, "thinking of ourselves as subjects can have, and has had, positive effects contributing to our ability effectively to resist structures of domination" (Alcoff 1990: 73). Although postmodernist versions of relativism are in some ways allied with feminism in their challenge to any universalist claims by Western knowledge, and for fragmenting the unified (masculinist) subject, they also challenge the efficacy of feminist politics. Some feminists have suggested that, despite the radical propositions of relativism, it is in actuality a politically conservative position. As Fox-Genovese (1986: 121) has remarked,

Surely it is no coincidence that the western white male elite proclaimed the death of the subject at precisely the moment at which it might have had to share that status with women and peoples of other races and classes who were beginning to challenge its supremacy. (See also Mascia-Lees et al. 1989)

A number of feminists have taken up Gayatri Spivak's suggestion of a "strategic essentialism" from which women can fight patriarchal oppression (Mohanty 1988; Fuss 1989). In this sense, in addition to being a cultural identity, strategic essentialism is a political concept. Mohanty (1988) argues that coalitions are formed not because they are necessarily enjoyable but because they are required for survival. This offers the possibility of retaining the idea of a "feminist politics" and the desire to make things better without the necessity of a belief in biological essentialism or universalism. For others, feminist knowledge is much more ambivalent (Rose 1991) – both accepting the necessity of the identity of woman despite the limitations that this sets, and acknowledging that the experiences of women will always be in excess of this one identifier.

Feminists have striven to facilitate the entry of women's voices into the exclusively masculinist institutions of academia, but notions of inclusion are also methodologically important for feminist geographers. Feminist methodology has always stressed the importance of listening to the voices of others so that research is a collaborative process rather than the product of an expert "analysis" or "reading" of the world (see Moss 2002). The inclusion of the voices of those who have experience of different situations and those who have different and marginalized viewpoints is central to much feminist methodology (see Moss 2002). Cultural geography has followed and developed this trend with many turning attention from the production of official or dominant cultures to those subcultures of marginal groups (see Duncan 1993). While embracing this widening challenge to academic authority, feminist geographers have been wary of what can appear to be a constant search for a new marginal group to study, something which might be considered to be "fetishizing" the "other." There is also a danger that by regarding all marginal groups as equally valid and important – merely by dint of their marginality – complex power relations might be missed. Some feminist geographers have written of their fear that they could become voyeuristic regarding various groups they might be involved in researching: by being enticed by the exoticism of the other, or choosing a difference to study for its difference rather than any particular commitment to the group in question (see England 1994; Katz 1994). For example, Cindy Katz uses a comparative approach, not only to foreground her relationship to those involved in the research, but also to allow the research to reflect upon larger-scale processes:

By displacing the field and addressing the issue in rural Sudan and East Harlem, New York – settings that on the surface appear to have little in common – I am able to tell a story not of marginalization alone where "those poor people" might be the key narrative theme, but of the systemic predations of global economic restructuring. (Katz 1994: 68)

Here feminist geographers can achieve an understanding of the specifics of particular situations, can find space for the voices and concerns of the people participating in the research, without simply regarding them as "different." The comparative dimension facilitates an understanding of regional and global connections, placing the researcher and researched in the same cultural landscape, and teasing out relationships of power and knowledge that link the two.

Landscape

Cultural geography has, of course, long been interested in the role of landscape in the reproduction of cultural geographies. New cultural geographers look to the landscape as a "signifying system" (Duncan 1990) through which meanings are made and remade. Some feminist geographers have looked to the landscape to provide information on how gendered identities are constructed. The imagery of nation is particularly important in the landscape and reinforces the gendered expectations of national citizens: that men are the active agents of national liberation as soldiers and statesmen, while women are metaphorical images of the nation to be protected by their menfolk (see McClintock 1993; Sharp 1996). Warner (1985) has shown the constant use of such images in the reproduction of national landscapes, while Johnson (1995) has studied the role of public statuary in Dublin for the reproduction of masculinist images of the nation and prescriptive models of "good" womanhood. Other work on dominant and resistant landscape imagery shows how performance around the landscape, in telling stories and singing songs, can both reinforce and challenge inherited gender identities (Dowler 1998).

However some feminist geographers have been wary of adopting the landscape approach altogether. Geography is, by tradition, a highly visual discipline concerned with such issues as cartographic representation, the problems of the description of landscapes and regions. Drawing on the pioneering work of John Berger (1972), cultural geographers such as Cosgrove and Daniels (1988) have argued that landscape should be regarded as a "way of seeing," which emerges from historically and geographically specific "visual ideologies." Rose (1993) has critiqued them, however, for omitting a discussion of the gendered and sexed taint to the landscape gaze, and, drawing on Mulvey's (1989) characterization of "the gaze" as an element of the "uneasy pleasures of power," she suggests that this form of cultural geography is therefore complicit in the reproduction of the gendering of the gaze (Rose 1993: 86).

Rose (1993) goes further to argue that gazing on the landscape inevitably casts it as feminine giving the viewer pleasure in his (sic) seeing, knowing, and unveiling of its secrets. Rose (1993) warns of the objectifying and voyeuristic position adopted by the expert cultural geographer decoding the landscape (see also Gregory 1996 for a discussion of the elitism of the gaze on the landscape). For instance, Shurmer-Smith and Hannam (1994: 95) suggest that the "thrill that Harvey gets at playing the voyeur is all too obvious in his recent books, whilst Soja's penchant for monumentalism has not gone unnoticed." In the social context of patriarchy, the concept of the gaze represents the split between the active male surveyor and the passive female who is being surveyed. Cultural and feminist theorists argue that dominant constructions of femininity are established through the gaze (Berger 1972; Mulvey 1989), thus making it a contradictory position for female geographers to adopt. Some feminists have presented the figure of the *flâneur* – who walks through the modern metropolis unseen but seeing everything – as the voyeur of the landscape, arguing it to be an inherently masculinist position as women must always be the object of the gaze. However, Wilson (1992) seeks to challenge this representation arguing that it depends upon too simplistic an image of gender. While the city does represent a space of masculinist order and control, it also encapsulates movement, disruption and decentering – traditionally feminine characteristics – certainly offering all sorts of challenges and opportunities to women, rather than rendering them little more than disempowered objects of the male gaze.

Furthermore, Nash (1996) challenges Rose's account of the cultural geographers' gaze because she see Rose's argument as equating visual representations directly with "generalized notions of masculinism, imperialism and oppression" (Nash 1996: 151). Through her reading of women's depictions of male bodies as land-scapes, Nash (1996) suggests that there is nothing inherently oppressive in either the landscape or the gaze, and offers the possibility of female heterosexual pleasure as well as homoerotic gazes (see also the discussion in Mitchell 2000: 223–9). Similarly, photographer Ingrid Pollard uses representations of the English landscape to challenge the viewer's gaze for its inherent assumptions about nation, gender, and race (Pollard 1993).

Embodiment

Since the establishment of second-wave ideas, feminists have been concerned both with the material body and the body as represented in medical, philosophical, and cultural texts (Pringle 1999: 17–20). This interest has become more intense with many geographers' fear of the overly abstract nature of much geography in the wake of the cultural turn which emphasized texts and representations. Philo expresses his concern,

about this dematerializing of human geography: this preoccupation with immaterial cultural processes, with the constitution of intersubjective meaning systems, with the play of identity politics through the less-than-tangible, often-fleeting spaces of texts, signs, symbols, psyches, desires, fears and imaginings. I am concerned that, in the rush to elevate such spaces in our human geographical studies, we have ended up being less attentive to the more 'thingy,' bump-into-able, stubbornly there-in-the-world kinds of matter (the material) with which earlier geographers tended to be more familiar. (Philo 2000: 33)

Thus many feminist geographers have turned to the body as a method of re-establishing the material. This is not a naive antitheoretical turn but an attempt to unite the discursive elements of cultural production with the emotions, pains, joys, passions, and requirements of various bodies. Foucault's work on the effects of power, surveillance and discipline has again been influential here. His research demonstrated the ways in which different bodies emerged from different discursive power/knowledge regimes. Although Foucault did not focus on gender as a signif-icant element in the construction of bodies, his work has been an important point of departure for a number of feminist theorists (see Butler 1993; Nast and Pile 1998). This position argues for the need to think of bodies as sites of performance in their own right rather than simply simple surfaces for discursive inscription. Bodies are the "sites and expressions of power relations" (McDowell 1995: 79). Discourses do not simply write themselves directly onto the surface of bodies as if these bodies offered blank surfaces of equal topography. Furthermore, the spaces through which bodies move, and in which they are made and remade through various practices, are integral to the form the bodies take, making this a significant interest of cultural geographers. For example, McDowell (1997) looks at the ways in which discourses of appropriate work behavior materialize in the space of mer-chant banks through various embodied performances, while Longhurst (1995, 1996) has examined the specific geographies of pregnant bodies.

Methodologically, this is important as a focus on bodies can ground under-standings of cultures in everyday practices, and, perhaps even more importantly, ground the researcher in the cultural processes which are being examined. Despite its associations with the masculinist exploits of empire (see the exchange between Stoddart [1991] and Domosh [1991]), feminist geographers have a commitment to fieldwork for the possibility it offers for the inclusion of other voices into various parts of the research process, and for the genuine collaboration which this type of work can facilitate (see the *Professional Geographer* special issue, 1994). This means that, on the whole, feminist geography has largely resisted the discursive dominance of cultural geography, and instead examined the material effects of different discursive regimes. Commentators have noticed a shift to "research 'on the ground'" in recent geographical conferences, and on struggles with what could be done to make things better, with prominent sessions on activist politics (see Dowler & Sharp 2001).

Conclusions

There are many common points of interest between feminist and cultural geographies but also places where many feminists are wary of the direction cultural geography might take them. More recent developments into nonrepresentational theory and actor-network theory have, for example, offered feminists an important critique of the sometimes over-determining discursive analyses that have come to dominate cultural geography (see Bingham & Thrift 2000). However, these approaches, while interesting in examining the effects of micropractices of everyday life, are perhaps too descriptive for the overtly political aims of much feminist geography which seeks not only to describe how it is that women and men are guided towards particular identities, roles, and practices, but also how to intervene to change them.

NOTES

1. This work has predominantly examined Western cultural expectations.
2. The romanticization of homelessness and psychological disorders in the ideas of nomadism has faced critique, however, by those who argue that the metaphorical use of these terms denies the pain of their physical reality (see Parr & Philo 1995).

REFERENCES

Alcoff, L. 1990: Feminist politics and Foucault: the limits to a collaboration. In A. Dalley and C. Scott, eds., *Crises in Continental Philosophy*. Albany: SUNY Press.
Bell, D. and Valentine, G. 1995: The sexed self: strategies of performance, sites of resistance. In S. Pile and N. Thrift, eds., *Mapping the Subject*. London: Routledge, 143–57.
Berger, J. 1972: *Ways of Seeing*. Harmondsworth: BBC/Penguin.
Bingham, N. and Thrift, N. 2000: Some new instructions for travellers: the geography of Bruno Latour and Michel Serres. In M. Crang and N. Thrift, eds., *Thinking Space*. London: Routledge, 281–301.
Bordo, S. 1993: *Unbearable Weight*. Berkeley: University of California Press.
Braidotti, R. 1994: *Nomadic Subjects*. New York: Columbia University Press.
Butler, J. 1990: *Gender Trouble: Feminism and the Subversion of Identity*. London: Routledge.

Butler, J. 1993: *Bodies that Matter*. London: Routledge.

Chouinard, V. and Grant, A. 1995: On not being anywhere near 'the project': revolutionary ways of putting ourselves in the picture. *Antipode* 27, 137–66.

Clifford, J. 1992. Traveling culture. In L. Grossberg et al., eds., *Cultural Studies*. New York: Routledge.

Cosgrove, D. and Daniels, S. 1988: *The Iconography of Landscape*. Cambridge: Cambridge University Press.

Deleuze, G. and Guattari, F. 1983: *Anti-Oedipus*. Minneapolis: University of Minnesota Press.

Deleuze, G. and Guattari, F. 1987: *A Thousand Plateaus*. Minneapolis: University of Minnesota Press.

Deutsche, R. 1996: *Evictions*. Cambridge, MA: MIT Press.

Doel, M. 1995: Bodies without organs: schizoanalysis and deconstruction. In S. Pile and N. Thrift, eds., *Mapping the Subject*. London: Routledge, 226–40.

Domosh, M. 1991: Towards a feminist historiography of geography. *Transactions, Institute of British Geographers* 16, 95–104.

Dowler, L. 1998: 'And they think I'm just a nice old lady': women and war in Belfast, Northern Ireland. *Gender, Place and Culture* 5, 159–76.

Dowler, L. and Sharp, J. 2001: A feminist geopolitics? *Space and Polity* 5, 165–76.

Duncan, J. 1990: *The City as Text*. Cambridge: Cambridge University Press.

Duncan, J. 1993: Landscapes of the self/landscapes of the other(s): cultural geography 1991–2. *Progress in Human Geography* 17, 367–77.

England, K. 1994: Getting personal: reflexivity, positionality and feminist research. *The Professional Geographer* 46, 80–9.

Enloe, C. 1989: *Bananas, Beaches and Bases: Making Feminist Sense of International Relations*. Berkeley: University of California Press.

Enloe, C. 1993: *The Morning After: Sexual Politics at the End of the Cold War*. Berkeley: University of California Press.

Foucault, M. 1977: *Discipline and Punish: The Birth of the Prison*. London: Allen Lane.

Foucault, M. 1978: *The History of Sexuality, Volume I: An Introduction*. London: Allen Lane.

Fox-Genovese, E. 1986: The claims of a common culture: gender, race, class and the canon. *Salmagundi* 72, 119–32.

Funk, N. and Mueller, M., eds. 1993: *Gender Politics and Post-Communism: Reflections From Eastern Europe and the Former Soviet Union*. New York: Routledge.

Fuss, D. 1989: *Essentially Speaking: Feminism, Nature and Difference*. London: Routledge.

Gregory, D. 1996: *Geographical Imaginations*. Oxford: Blackwell.

Haraway, D. 1988: Situated knowledges: the science question in feminism and the privilege of partial perspective. *Feminist Studies* 14, 575–99.

Haraway, D. 1989: *Primate Visions: Gender, Race and Nature in the World of Modern Science*. New York: Routledge.

Irigaray, L. 1985: *Speculum of the Other Woman*. Ithaca: Cornell University Press.

Johnson, N. 1995: Cast in stone: monuments, geography, and nationalism. *Environment and planning D: Society and Space* 13, 51–65.

Johnston, L. and Valentine, G. 1995: Wherever I lay my girlfriend, that's my home: the performance and surveillance of lesbian identities in domestic environments. In D. Bell and G. Valentine, eds., *Mapping Desire: Geographies of Sexualities*. London: Routledge, 99–113.

Kaplan, C. 1987: Deterritorializations: the rewriting of home and exile in western feminist discourse. *Cultural Critique* 6, 187–98.

Katz, C. 1994: Playing the field: questions of fieldwork in geography. *Professional Geographer* 46, 67–72.

Kniffen, F. 1962 [1936]: Louisiana house types. In P. Wagner and M. Mikesell, eds., *Readings in Cultural Geography*. Chicago: University of Chicago Press.

Knopp, L. 1995: Sexuality and urban space: a framework for analysis. In D. Bell and G. Valentine, eds., *Mapping Desire: Geographies of Sexualities*. London: Routledge, 149–61.

Longhurst, R. 1995: The body and geography. *Gender, Place and Culture* 2, 97–105.

Longhurst, R. 1996: Refocusing groups: pregnant women's geographical experiences of Hamilton, New Zealand/Aotearoa. *Area* 28, 143–9.

Lyotard, J.-F. 1984: *The Postmodern Condition*. Minneapolis: University of Minnesota Press.

Mascia-Less, F., Sharp, P., and Cohen, C. 1989: The postmodern turn in anthropology: cautions from a feminist perspective. *Signs* 15, 7–33.

Massey, D. 1993: Politics and space/time. In M. Keith and S. Pile, eds., *Place and the Politics of Identity*. London: Routledge, 141–61.

Massey, D. 2000: *Imagining Globalisation*. Lecture at the University of Strathclyde, Feb. 23.

McClintock, A. 1993: Family feuds: Gender, nationalism and the family. *Feminist Review* 44, 61–80.

McDowell, L. 1983: Towards an understanding of the gender division of urban space. *Environment and planning D: Society and Space* 1, 59–72.

McDowell, L. 1995: Body work: heterosexual gender performances in city workplaces. In D. Bell and G. Valentine, eds., *Mapping Desire: Geographies of Sexualities*. London: Routledge.

McDowell, L. 1997: *Capital Culture: Gender at Work in the City*. Oxford: Blackwell.

McDowell, L. 1999: Second wave feminism. In L. McDowell and J. Sharp, eds., *A Feminist Glossary of Human Geography*. London: Arnold, 244–5.

McDowell, L. and Sharp, J., eds. 1997: *Space/Gender/Knowledge: Feminist Readings*. London: Arnold.

McDowell, L. and Sharp, J., eds., 1999: *A Feminist Glossary of Human Geography*. London: Arnold.

Merchant, C. 1980: *The Death of Nature: Women, Ecology, and the Scientific Revolution*. New York: Harper & Row.

Mitchell, D. 2000: *Cultural Geography*. Oxford: Blackwell.

Mohanty, C. T. 1988: Under Western eyes: feminist scholarship and colonial discourses. *Feminist Review* 30, 61–88.

Mohanty, C. T. 1997: Feminist encounters: locating the politics of experience. In L. McDowell and J. Sharp, eds., *Space, Gender, Knowledge: Feminist Readings*. London: Arnold, 82–97.

Mohanty, C., Russo, A., and Torres, L., eds. 1991: *Third World Women and the Politics of Feminism*. Bloomington: Indiana University Press.

Morgan, R. 1984: *Sisterhood is Global: The International Women's Movement Anthology*. New York: Anchor Press/Doubleday.

Moss, P. 2002: *Feminist Geography in Practice*. Oxford: Blackwell.

Mulvey, L. 1989: *Visual Pleasure and Other Pleasures*. London: Macmillan.

Nash, C. 1996: Reclaiming vision: looking at landscape and the body. *Gender, Place and Culture* 3, 149–69.

Nast, H. 1999: Compulsory heterosexuality. In L. McDowell and J. Sharp, eds., *A Feminist Glossary of Human Geography*. London: Arnold.

Nast, H. and Pile, S., eds. 1998: *Places Through the Body*. London: Routledge.

Parr, H. and Philo, C. 1995: Mapping 'mad' identities. In S. Pile and N. Thrift, eds., *Mapping the Subject*. London: Routledge, 119–25.

Philo, C. 2000: More words, more worlds: reflections on the 'cultural turn' and social geography. In I. Cook et al., eds., *Cultural Turns/Geographical Turns*. London: Longman Higher Education, 26–53.

Pollard, I. 1993: Another view. *Feminist Review* 45, 46–50.

Pringle, R. 1999: Body. In L. McDowell and J. Sharp, eds., *A Feminist Glossary of Human Geography*. London: Arnold, 17–20.

Professional Geographer. 1994: Women and the field. Special issue 46(1).

Rich, A. 1986: *Blood, Bread and Poetry: Selected Prose 1979–1985*. New York: Norton.

Rose, G. 1991: On being ambivalent: women and feminisms in geography. In C. Philo (comp.), *New Words, New Worlds*. Aberystwyth: Cambrian Printers.

Rose, G. 1993: *Feminism and Geography*. Oxford: Blackwell.

Rothenberg, T. 1995: 'And she told two friends': lesbians creating urban social space. In D. Bell and G. Valentine, eds., *Mapping Desire: Geographies of Sexualities*. London: Routledge, 165–81.

Routledge, P. and Simons, J. 1995: Embodying spirits of resistance. *Environment and Planning D: Society and Space* 13, 471–98.

Said, E. 1979: *Orientalism*. New York: Vintage.

Sauer, C. 1963 [1925]: The morphology of landscape. In J. Leighly, ed., *Land and Life: A Selection from the Writing of Carl Ortwin Sauer*. Berkeley: University of California Press.

Seager, J. 1993: *Earth Follies*. London: Routledge.

Sharp, J. 1996: Gendering nationhood: a feminist engagement with national identity. In N. Duncan, ed., *BodySpace: Destabilizing Geographies of Gender and Sexuality*. London: Routledge, 97–108.

Sharp, J. 1999: Subject/subjectivity. In L. McDowell and J. Sharp, eds., *A Feminist Glossary of Human Geography*. London: Arnold, 267–9.

Shiva, V. 1989: *Staying Alive: Women, Ecology and Development*. London: Zed Books.

Shurmer-Smith, P. 1994: Cixous' spaces: sensuous spaces in women's writing. *Ecumene* 1, 349–62.

Shurmer-Smith, P. and Hannam, K. 1994: *Worlds of Desire, Realms of Power: A Cultural Geography*. London: Edward Arnold.

Stoddart, D. 1991: Do we need a feminist historiography of geography – and if we do, what should it be like? *Transactions, Institute of British Geographers* 16, 484–7.

Valentine, G. 1993: (Hetero)sexing space: lesbian perceptions and experiences of everyday spaces. *Environment and planning D: Society and Space* 11, 395–413.

Warner, M. 1985: *Monuments and Maidens: The Allegory of the Female Form*. London: Picador.

Wilson, E. 1992: The invisible flâneur. *New Left Review* 191, 90–110.

Wolf, N. 1991: *The Beauty Myth: How Images of Beauty are Used Against Women*. New York: Doubleday.

Chapter 7

Poststructuralism

Deborah P. Dixon and John Paul Jones III

Our purpose in this chapter is to review key features of poststructuralism and to describe some of the ways this theory is employed within cultural geography. Following some introductory remarks that situate poststructuralism, we provide a synopsis of structuralism, the foundational theoretical framework against which early poststructuralist thought was directed and received its name. From this backdrop we then move to a discussion of some of the more important theoretical tenets of poststructuralism, introduced by way of two influential theorists, Jacques Derrida and Michel Foucault. We then offer a poststructuralist theorization of representation and space, two important categories in cultural geography. The penultimate section offers some thoughts on the poststructuralist methodology of deconstruction. We conclude with a discussion of future articulations between poststructuralist theory and cultural geography.

Poststructuralist thought emerged in geography in the late 1980s and early 1990s. Challenging forms of thought that relied upon traditional theories of objectivity and subjectivity, center and margin, materialism and idealism, truth and fiction, regularity and difference, and certainty and indeterminacy, poststructuralism brought to the entire field of geography a critique that unsettled the ontological and epistemological moorings of extant theoretical frameworks (see, for example, Dixon & Jones 1996, 1998; Doel 1999; Gregory 1994; Keith & Pile 1993; Nast & Pile 1998; Olsson 1992; Pile 1996; Pile & Thrift 1995). What were these existing frameworks, and why did the poststructuralist alternative find currency among cultural geographers? The answers to these questions are related, for at the time of poststructuralism's arrival in the discipline, most geographers worked with one of three metatheories, or 'paradigms' – spatial science, critical realism, and humanism (Johnston & Claval 1984)[1] – and cultural geographers had an uneasy relationship with each of them. First, consider that many so-called traditional cultural geographers were, like many of their spatial scientist counterparts, naive empiricists (Jackson 1994), comfortable in focusing on mapped phenomena with little in-depth analysis of the deeper structures that might underlie these objects (compare, for example, Duncan's 1980 critique of cultural geographers' theory of culture to Peet's

1977 critique of theory within spatial science). Yet most cultural geographers at the time explicitly rejected spatial science: they were skeptical of its adherence to objective modes of social investigation and to its often mechanistic search for order (Ley 1980). Critical realism (Sayer 1984, 2000), by contrast, offered a deeper route to understanding through a structured yet flexible ontology of direct forces and indirect mediations. One might think that critical realism would have proven attractive to many theoretically-minded cultural geographers, but in practice this paradigm was largely silent on issues of interpretation and representation, which had long been central analytic concepts for cultural geographers (Lewis 1979; Meinig 1979). Critical realists also tended to privilege economic over cultural explanations; these were seen as reductionist by some cultural geographers (e.g. Duncan & Ley 1992, 1993). If the 1970s came close to offering a coherent theoretical framework for cultural geography, it was humanism (Buttimer 1976; Relph 1976; Tuan 1976, 1977), and indeed many traditional cultural geographers could be so labeled. But a humanistic geography that focused on the recovery of the experiences and meanings of individuals, when theorized as relatively unmarked by wider social forces, was viewed as overly volunteerist (e.g. Gregory 1981). It is within this uneasy conceptual context that a number of cultural geographers turned to poststructuralism.[2]

It is important to emphasize at the outset that poststructuralism did not offer a clear counterontology to spatial science, critical realism, or humanism. Rather, poststructuralism appeared to undermine each of these frameworks by claiming that any ontology is 'always already' an outcome of epistemology, of our socially constructed ways of knowing. In so throwing ontology into doubt, poststructuralism asks us to reflect not only how we know, but also how elements of ontology – such as space, place, nature, culture, individual, and society – become framed in thought in the first instance. In posing such questions, poststructuralism finds a productive moment in examining how social relations of power fix social practices, objects, events, and meanings as self-evident, given, natural, and enduring. In regard to geography, this requires an analysis of why some objects rather than others are taken to be central to geographic inquiry, as well as an analysis of how those objects are understood to exist and relate to one another.

Such theoretical concerns proved attractive for many cultural geographers. In particular, they focused attention on the 'crisis of representation' that had otherwise escaped critical analysis in geography, thereby introducing such questions as: How has the 'real' world been constructed as a given ontological fact, and who has the power to produce these truths? How can we think about meaning as both indeterminate and contextual? How should we theorize the relationships between meanings, practices, and the material world? And, what is the position of the cultural geographer in this process: as the expert 'decoder' of cultural forms and practices, or as a situated 'interpreter' who can only re-present these forms and practices once again?

Before we begin to address these questions, it seems worthwhile to emphasize that though its intellectual roots are in continental philosophy and literary theory, poststructuralism knows no boundaries when it comes to objects of analysis. So, though its impact has been strongly felt in cultural geography, where it has not only invigorated research questions but has also led to the identification of new objects of analysis – including many reviewed in this volume – its critical stance toward simplistic forms of truth, representation, and politics have become points of engagement between it and other geographic subfields, including economic geography (Barnes 1996; Gibson-Graham 1996); geopolitics and the state (Hanna 1996; Ó Tuathail 1996); rural geography (Cloke & Little 1997; Dixon & Hapke 2003; Lawrence 1995); cartography (Harley 1989); social geographies of gender (McDowell & Sharp 1997; Rose 1993), 'race' (Kobayashi 1994; Mahtani 2002; Nast 2000; Pred 2000), and bodies (Nast & Pile 1998; Pile & Thrift 1995); tourism geography (Del Casino & Hanna 2000; Hanna & Del Casino 2003); virtual geographies (Crang et al. 1999; Hillis 1999; Kitchen & Dodge 2001); postcolonial geographies (Jacobs 1996; Gregory 1994; Howitt & Suchet 2003; Sparke 1998); and nature–society studies (Braun & Castree 1998; Castree & Braun 2001; Demeritt 2002; Willems-Braun 1997). Moreover, poststructuralism can be credited with destabilizing the very demarcations that permit the identification of 'subfields' – in short, the boundaries between the cultural, social, economic, political, and environmental spheres are far less distinct under poststructuralism than they once were (Dixon & Jones 1996, 1998). It is through this process of destabilization that poststructuralism within cultural geography has wide-ranging implications for geography at large.

Before the Post: What was Structuralism?

The literature associated with structuralism is both complex and wide-ranging, but in all its forms it holds that phenomena, including all manner of practices, objects, events, and meanings (let us call these POEMs for short), are taken to exist not as discrete entities, but as parts relationally *embedded within*, and *constituted by*, underlying wholes, or structures. It is not unusual to see structuralism rendered as an inflexible and static framework, so let us clear up a few misunderstandings. A structure should not be conceived of as an external architecture upon which POEMs are hung, for such a view implies that a structure exists independently of the parts it embeds; instead, structures are constituted solely from the relations among their constitutive elements, or parts. And, since they do not exist independently of POEMs, structures are dynamic and spatially differentiated fields of relations. Finally, structures do not have material form nor do they have the ability to act; they are not visible in the empirical realm, but inasmuch as they systematize the relations and therefore the causal efficacy of POEMs, they are presumed to operate.

The most important structuralist thinker for the development of poststructuralism was the Swiss linguist Ferdinand de Saussure (1857–1913). His goal was to understand the abstract structures behind all forms of social communication, from painting and religious rituals to chess games and the rules of courtship. As a linguist, Saussure applied his theory of semiotics – that is, the science of signs – to the study of language. In doing so, he rejected the traditional, historical approach to the study of language, a philological endeavor focusing on detailed descriptions of the historical evolution of particular languages and language families. He also rejected the positivist line of research dominant in his day, which sought to understand language through analysis of sounds and their impact on the nervous system. For Saussure, elements of language gain their currency according to the structure within which they are embedded (Saussure 1974). A particular language, therefore, must be studied as a systematized collection of sounds and inscriptions, each of which, as in structuralism more generally, can only be assigned a value, or meaning, when thought of in relation to the remainder of the elements. But how does language work to transmit meanings from one person to another? In analyzing the relations among these elements, Saussure struck an analytic distinction between the 'signified,' which is the mental construct, or idea, of a particular phenomenon, and the 'signifier,' which takes the form of a distinguishable 'mark,' such as a sound, inscription, or special body movement. Within a language, signifieds are associated with particular signifiers to form a 'sign'; in consequence, when people communicate they use particular signs to convey and understand meaning. And, because signifiers are considered to exist within the realm of the symbolic, that is, as abstract representations that refer to real-world phenomena, the systems of communication within which they are embedded can be thought of as relatively autonomous from any real-world referent. Given that there is no necessary relationship between the signifier and the signified, the actual choice of signifier is arbitrary. This is why, of course, various languages can have different words (signifiers) for the same object (the signified). Indeed, the signifier only has value when it can be differentiated from other signifiers and used to convey a particular signified again and again. All languages, then, depend upon the fact that we learn to recognize this difference between signifiers.

Now the very fact that communication can occur through signifiers that are fundamentally arbitrary, implied for Saussure that a system, or set of rules, must exist by which people can indeed be taught to differentiate between signifiers, and to which all must subscribe if communication is to proceed unhindered. Just as chess and courtship (both systems of signs) are built around certain rules of the game (the moves of the knight, the lingering glance), so too are all languages founded upon abstract regulations that shape the ways in which they are played, or manifested in practice. Within this conception, the underlying structure that allows communication to take place is called the *langue*, while the actual practices by which communication takes place Saussure called the *parole*. To sum up, for Saussure the elements of language constitute interrelated signs, whose mark or signifier is embedded in a structure of langue, which itself may be transformed through the practice of parole.

That Saussure's model could be applied to any number of sign systems in any language and across myriad communication systems accounts in part for its popularity well into the 1960s in a variety of disciplines, including literary theory and philosophy. Freud's psychoanalysis, in particular his analyses of dreams, was also rooted in structuralism. So too was anthropologist Lévi-Strauss's search for the organizing principles of culture. And, in some versions of Marxism, structuralism underwrote attempts to explain many aspects of social life as determined by the underlying mode of production.[3]

Post-ing Structuralism

Though elements of poststructuralism can be found in the work of philosophers such Friedrich Nietzsche and Martin Heidegger, its formal recognition as a body of theory can be traced to a host of more contemporary social, cultural, and literary theorists. Here we discuss the work of two of the most important theorists, Jacques Derrida (b. 1930) and Michel Foucault (1926–1984).

It was Derrida who, at a 1966 conference on structuralism in the city of Baltimore, introduced poststructuralist thought to an international audience through the presentation of a paper titled 'Structure, Sign, and Play in the Discourse of the Human Sciences.' The major goal of the conference was to stimulate innovation in structuralist thought across a wide variety of disciplines. Yet Derrida's paper (published in 1970 and reissued in 1972) critiqued the very notion of structure by analyzing the process of 'centering' upon which diverse forms of structuralist thought were constructed. Tracing back particularly significant manifestations of this centering process in Western thought, Derrida suggested that what seemed to be secure ontological categories, such as presence, essence, existence, cause, origin, substance, subject, truth, God, and 'man,' were merely epistemological constructs handed down through generations of philosophers and scientists.

Specifically, Derrida noted that in fixing a structure's parts, the whole must simultaneously exclude all of those other elements that do not have some form of relation with its center. In the process, an inside and an outside of the structure are posited. This center around which a structure is assembled holds a paradoxical position, in that while it is related to all of those elements within the structure, it is also held to be fixed and inviolable. As Derrida argues:

> it has always been thought that the center, which is by definition unique, constituted that very thing within a structure which governs the structure, while escaping structurality. This is why classical thought concerning structure could say that the center is, paradoxically, *within* the structure and *outside* it. The center is at the center of the totality, and yet, since the center does not belong to the totality (it is not part of the totality), the totality *has its center elsewhere*. The center is not the center. The concept of centered structure . . . is contradictorily coherent. And as always, coherence in contradiction expresses the force of a desire. (1972: 248; emphasis in original)

As Derrida went on to note, this centering process is the product of a binary – an either/or – epistemology. Such a way of thinking about the world stabilizes not only the meaning of one term, such as Truth, but through the assignation of a periphery, defines an 'other' that falls outside of its purview, fiction. In a similar vein, binary thought produces sharp contrasts between essence and contingence, cause/ effect and serendipity, substance and chimera, subject and object, God and idol, and 'man' and nature.

Poststructuralists register three complaints with this mode of thought. First, and following on from the work of Derrida, poststructuralists maintain that in all of these binary systems, what appears to be the 'foundation' for a system of thought is but a hypothetical construct, one that reveals more about the society that produced it than the supposed character of the real world. In this case, poststructuralists turn their attention to the production of centers, margins, and the boundaries that demarcate them. In recognizing centers and margins as products of an either/or mode of thinking rather than the natural state of affairs, poststructuralists are drawn to several key questions. One the one hand, they ask who has the social power to draw the boundary between a center and margin; on the other hand, they question

to what end is any such system of differentiation directed. In recognizing categorizations as the product of social relations of power, attention turns to which social
groups have the discursive resources to construct categories; that is, who has the
ability to name the world? Thus, a major component of poststructuralist research
involves inquiries into the categories that frame 'reality' according to either/or
binaries.

Second, binaries presume a 'totalizing' epistemology, so termed because either/or
thought can only posit a world in which everything either 'is' or 'is not.' Epistemologically speaking, the effect of binary thought is to constrain what can be conceived about the world. Now, in some instances binary thought can be productive,
as in, for example, the formulation of computer languages that operate on an underlying system of ones and zeroes. But in other instances, binaries so stricture what
knowledge is possible, that they unduly limit what can be conceived in the world.
In this way, the binary epistemology ultimately infuses ontological concepts (e.g.,
the individual vs. society, local vs. global, chaos vs. order). Consider, for example,
our understanding of phenomena as either natural or cultural. Such binary thinking will ultimately organize virtually all questions researchers might want to ask
about social or physical systems. These questions, however, can ultimately be
exposed as circular in character, for, though researchers may think they are posing
questions about 'real' categories, they are by default investigating the products of
their own binary epistemology.

A third complaint about binary modes of thinking is that they are not, in fact,
as fully relational as structuralism claims them to be. For example, while Saussure's
model assumes that language is comprised of an arbitrary system of signifiers whose
elements become meaningful through their relation to each other (the word 'cat'
does not sound like 'dog' and thus permits us to understand the difference), for him
the concept of a feline four-legged mammal (the signified) faithfully re-presented the
real-world animal, or referent, independent of the existence of its canine variant.
Using Derrida's critique of Saussure, however, we could argue that the mental construct of a feline is not grounded in the one-to-one relationship between it and the
referent, but is definable only in relation to all other concepts that give feline its distinction by referring to what feline is *not*. Thus, feline is *negatively* defined in relation to a host of other concepts such as canine, leonine, equine, lupine, and bovine.
As such, signifieds are not only relational, but also arbitrary, at least in the sense
that biologists have defined classification systems that permit differentiation among
these animals. In this manner, poststructuralism throws doubt onto all certainties
regarding researchers' ability to 'correctly' represent reality, for our concepts do not
simply re-present that reality, in the sense of mirroring their referent, but represent
reality within a fully relational system of understanding that permits the referent to
be cognized as it is. It was at this point in the development of poststructuralism –
the point when theorists saw that centers have no natural locus – that:

language invaded the universal problematic; that in which, in the absence of a center or origin,
everything became discourse . . . that is to say, when everything became a system where the
central signified, the original or transcendental signified, is never absolutely present outside
a system of differences. The absence of the transcendental signified extends the domain and
the play of signification *ad infinitum*. (Derrida 1972: 249)[4]

A second influential theorist of poststructuralism was the French philosopher-historian Michel Foucault.[5] Whereas Derrida focused on the dualistic presumptions of Western Philosophy, Foucault undertook to problematize the production of modernist forms of knowledge, noting how 'Western' scientific ideas and practices since the eighteenth century produced a series of non-normal 'others,' such as the insane and the sexually perverted. In doing so, he drew attention to how this modernist undertaking has been underwritten by a particular conception of 'Man' as a unique being, capable of describing, explaining, and mastering the operation of body and mind, as well as society and nature. Hence, within these scientific analyses, Man is not only the object and the subject of his own understanding, he is also understood to orchestrate the social and physical realms within which he lives.

In placing Man within these contexts, Foucault argues, modernist forms of knowledge necessarily establish a series of insurmountable paradoxes. First, Man himself appears as an object to be studied empirically alongside other objects, but is also posited as the transcendental source from which the possibility of all knowledge can flow. Second, in determining the domain of 'conscious thought,' Man has also framed the 'unconscious.' And yet, in presenting 'himself' as the source of intelligibility, Man must attempt to explain this latter realm; that is, to think the unthinkable. And third, Man conceives of himself as the product of history, and yet posits himself as the source of that very history. As Foucault concluded in *The Order of Things* (1973a), modernist sciences of Man simply cannot produce a comprehensive account of their subject/object, and so must disintegrate under the weight of their own contradictions.

Foucault's own historical analyses can be considered a commentary on this same condition, but also a means of stepping outside of the traditional terms of debate in order to produce knowledge that is nonmodernist in technique as well as intent. Among the most important of his concepts is that of "discursive practice." Put briefly, a discursive practice is a regularity that emerges in the very act of articulation. As such, it should not be thought of as an idealized theory of something, nor as a set of meanings that are somehow 'imprinted' onto real-world phenomena. These rely on an idealist understanding of the mind as the source of knowledge, and presume an unwarranted distinction between mind and body, self and social. For Foucault, each articulation establishes the conditions of possibility for thought and action; that is, it posits what is appropriate and reasonable to be thought and practiced. As such, an articulation is more than mere communication – it is an active intervention in the social and physical realms. From this position, Foucault derived two analytic projects.

First, Foucault noted that each articulation is produced and understood within a given context, such that it is afforded meaning. The kinds of articulations Foucault was interested in were those that had gained sufficient authority such that they were deemed to be valid even when they were taken out of context. That is, they had gained the status of truth. Hidden in previous analyses of communication, argued Foucault, were the means by which these particular articulations gained distinction. Within a discourse, he maintained, a disciplining process takes place within and between strategies of power, which are all those techniques by which a statement is accepted as valid and appropriate, and by which that statement could not but be articulated in the way it was. In regard to social research, for example, these techniques would include empirical confirmation, dialectical argument, and phenomenological bracketing. Each of these allows for the privileging of some articulations over and above others as valid claims concerning the nature of 'reality.' For Foucault, power is considered within this context to operate through discourse, and to be complicit with the production of specific forms of knowledge that not only claim to provide insight into how the world works, but which are also deployed in the active management of that world. Key to this process is the emergence of a specialized cadre of experts, such as scientists and educators, who draw on these bodies of knowledge to further enhance their own status by ensuring the diffusion of particular ideas and concepts through society. Importantly, this legitimacy ensues not from their 'personal' character, but from the positions they hold within an institutional framework, as well as within a given set of social relations. A discourse, then, is not something that is simply produced and received by people; rather, it is tied into a discursive site, such as a school, church, office, scientific laboratory, and so on, where knowledge is actively produced and disseminated.

A relevant example of this mode of analysis is Foucault's commentaries on space. According to Foucault (1984), eighteenth-century France saw a shift in how, and by whom, space was conceived and discussed. Previously, space had been the domain of the architects, who envisioned the governed city as a metaphor for the governed territory. The primary spatial trope was one of penetration, whereby all of the city, and by projection, all of the state, was laid open to the regulatory surveillance and practices of the police. As the century progressed, new cadres of experts, including engineers and builders, emerged as the authoritative sources of knowledge on transport linkages and planning. The associated discourses addressed space in terms of speed, mobility, and networks, and entailed a revisioning of the links between the exercise of political power and the space of both the city and the territory.

Second, and following Saussure's focus on semiotics as a science of signs, Foucault interpreted the term 'discourse' far beyond speech to include the inscription of social relations (and thereby the exercise of power) on and through the body itself. The complex interplay of social relations of power both enables and constrains the body in certain ways: that is, the capacity of the body to be shaped and to act. Foucault refers to the emergence of what he termed "technologies of the self" – disciplinary actions that have become taken for granted. These range from new standards of punctuality to the self-regulation of dress and hygiene. In making this argument, Foucault's aim is not to reiterate the imposition of coercive power over individuals, but to show the tendency for modern-day power to be depersonalized, diffused, relational, and anonymous. Power is not held by one particular group, but rather is exercised through a series of everyday activities. For some critics, such as Terry Eagleton (1990), this position denotes a hopeless pessimism, in that power is understood to 'discipline' and 'normalize' more and more dimensions of everyday life. For Foucault, however, the means of resisting relations of power lie in the disruption of this daily performance. It is at the local level, even unto the site of the body itself, that resistance takes place.

The case studies Foucault chose to pursue, consisting of penal, education, and medical systems, focus accordingly on the ways in which the 'self' is constructed through discursive practices. The ensuing histories are also, however, illustrative of

Foucault's attempt to produce a body of work that does not operate according to modernist modes of interpretation. In *The Archaeology of Knowledge* (1974), he writes:

My aim was to analyse . . . history in the discontinuity that no teleology would reduce in advance; to map it in a dispersion that no pre-established horizon would embrace; to allow it to be deployed in an anonymity on which no transcendental constitution would impose the form of the subject; to open it up to a temporality that would not promise the return of any dawn. (p. 203)

For Foucault, there is no necessary trajectory to history, nor is there a definitive causal mechanism, such as human agency, that lies at the heart of social change. In representing history, then, each mode of analysis – or "genealogy" – must be considered as conceived and articulated around present-day issues and concerns, such that succeeding analyses of the same topic must necessarily rewrite the past from the perspective of the present. Nevertheless, his own project was to bring to light how particular clusters of discourse/power worked to produce, fill, and maintain the categories by which we claim to know the world, such as culture, nature, history, geography, individual, society, modern, primitive, objective, subjective, and so on. All of these terms have an "archaeology" to them, by which Foucault means a series of contexts within which they have been endowed with meaning and significance.

In sum, for Foucault, social researchers cannot, and should not, pursue truth, at least when interpreted as a category with the status of a universal, timeless quality (that is, Truth with a big 'T'). This is because each society has its own regime of truth, the specifics of which are fashioned by: the types of discourses deployed (these can be legal, moral, rational, and teleological, among others); the techniques and procedures used to distinguish between true and false statements; and the status of those who are charged with saying what counts as true (1980: 131). It is at this point that we can see an affinity between Foucault's account of discursive practices and Derrida's concern to destabilize those centers – such as origin, subject, essence, and Truth – by which explanatory modes of analysis operate. The project of both theorists is to work against accepted ways of thinking, researching, and writing about the world and in so doing open up the question of what it is to 'know.' In the next section we illustrate this rethinking by reference to two important categories within cultural geography – representation and space.

Representation, Space, and their Intersections

Representation stands as a key concept in poststructuralist thought. It can be theoretically distinguished from *re-presentation* by reserving the latter's meaning as implying the impossible, namely, capturing and reflecting – as in confining and mirroring – a real-world referent in thought, language, and visual media. Representation, by contrast, refers to the social mediation of the real world through ever-present processes of signification (Aitken & Zonn 1994; Barnes & Duncan 1991; Cresswell & Dixon 2002; Del Casino & Hanna 2003; Duncan 1990; Duncan & Sharp 1993; Hanna 1996; Harley 1989; Harvey 2003; Jones & Natter 1999; Natter & Jones 1993). By illustration, we can return to the relationships among signifiers, signifieds, and real-world referents. As should be clear, within poststructuralism such relations are not taken for granted; rather, they become foci of analysis in their own right. This is because signifieds are not presumed to stand alone, but are considered to be defined in relation to each other through the socially constructed discourses that give them their definition and character. As a result of the embeddedness of signifieds in discourse, no signifier can be presumed to stand in a one-to-one relationship with a real-world referent. In light of this reconceptualization, poststructuralists refer to representational processes instead of re-presentation, and they direct their investigations toward an understanding of the mediating role of discourses in representational processes.[6]

Let us consider now some of the implications of this theoretical position. First, poststructuralists take note of and critique forms of thought that distinguish between the "real" world and its "mere" re-presentation in communication, whether conceived in terms of language, sensory perceptions, or electronic media. This critique is a source of continuing conceptual confusion between poststructuralists and other theorists, since much traditional social thought is predicated on the very distinction between the real world of POEMs and their re-presentation in thought and language. Conflated with real/representation are other binary formulations such as materiality/ideology and concrete/abstract (see, for example, Mitchell's 1995, 2000, and 2002 critiques of an 'immaterial' cultural geography). For nonpoststructuralists, this distinction and the impulse to resolve it implies a faith in the possibility of unmediated re-presentation, wherein researchers might actually "get it right." For poststructuralists, by contrast, there is no Truth lurking behind real-world objects. This is not to reject the existence of the world *per se* (cf. Peet 1998), but rather to maintain that the world can never be known in a manner that is not somehow socially mediated. What is more, any claim to know one can emerge as complicit with authoritarian forms of power in which a particular group names and frames "reality" for all (Deutsche 1991). And, it is this non-innocent character of constructs that points to the importance of all the other constructs and to the entire social context within which their interdependencies become fixed and stabilized.

Second, in taking into account these interdependencies, poststructuralists take note of both "context" and "intertext." The former refers to the temporary stabilization of meanings drawn together in the articulation of a discourse that communicates those meanings in a sensible form by establishing differences among them. Context, then, fixes the relational field of meaning, but it does so only by drawing upon previous contexts that are themselves embedded in still other contexts.[7] This intercontextual character of the relations among constructs is intertext, a term specifying how one context is related to others, but also how they might be transformed. In this sense, intertext is the relational field – of flows and concatenations – for the production of new contexts. To give an example, in reading a book, context might be temporarily established by an author who draws upon meanings established within a genre. The act of reading, however, involves the production of a new field of meaning by the reader, within which those meanings are destabilized and restabilized yet again. In this view, and in virtue of the intertextual character of all communication, meanings cannot be permanently fixed according to: the intent behind their production; their content, genre, or mode of dissemination; or the perspectives of the reader (Natter & Jones 1993). Thus, the meanings that adhere to signifieds cannot be presumed as fixed or fully present, but are always in process, awaiting their deployment in new contexts.[8]

While the above points to the open and unfinished character of representation, it also suggests a problem for reflexive social analysts – that is, those willing to judge their own work within the purview of representation. Put somewhat differently, if representation within poststructuralism denies the disclosure of Truth, and if the subject is no longer speaking with the security and advantage of Identity, then how are we to trust our and others' analyses? Feminists have grappled with these issues at some length (Butler & Scott 1992; Harding 1987; in geography, see Nast 1994). One widely accepted response is to reflect on one's social positionality ('white, heterosexual, male') *vis-à-vis* researched participants and texts, recognizing that the outcome of those inquiries are influenced by the different standpoints (Collins 1990; Hartsock 1985) that infuse the research process. But others (e.g. Scott 1993) have argued, following poststructuralism, that the register of social experience that gives these standpoints their presumed stability (however temporary) is no guarantee of identity. Moreover, in the wake of the 'death' (or dissemination) of the author, the postmodernist claim to recover marginalized voices through a sensitivity to multiple knowledges becomes suspect (see again note 2). The 'differences' that postmodernist inquiry seeks to activate will not be fully relational if inquiry is driven by an underlying faith in the researcher's ability to demarcate center from margin, or, for that matter, to 'fix' the relationship between the real and the represented.

In considering these claims, some critics have responded with the argument that what is lost in the poststructuralist 'crisis of representation' is any possibility of strong evaluation; in particular, poststructuralism is charged with relativism and nihilism (Wolin 1992). But while it is certainly the case that this approach eschews the notion of an external vantage-point from which judgments concerning accuracy and ethicality can be made, this need not lead directly to either relativism or nihilism (Dixon & Jones 1997; Jones 1994). This is because, first, the destabilization of centers – Derrida's "cracking of nutshells" (Caputo 1998) – is very much a political project in the way it points to the constructedness and, hence, the contingency, of all kinds of authoritative claims. To choose to undertake poststructuralist analysis is therefore already a form of evaluation *and* intervention. Second, we can acknowledge that poststructuralism holds that all evaluative-ethical projects, including those undertaken in the name of liberty, community, and democracy, can only be 'evaluated' within the particular spatial-historical contexts of their articulation (Jones & Moss 1995). But even though they exist as discursive, ideal forms without guarantees – how could they be otherwise? – this does not imply the end of politics or of evaluation. Quite the opposite, in fact:

the idea of radical and plural democracy implies that we accept the possibility of contestation, that we accept that conflict is part of the vitality of a modern pluralistic democracy which, of course, means that it will always depend on the capacity of the radical democratic forces to maintain their hegemony. (Mouffe 1993: 92)

In short, whereas in structuralist forms of inquiry the researcher takes on the certainties invested in the roles of arbiter, analyst, and decoder, in poststructuralism the researcher interprets, activates, and transmutes meanings and their contexts. Indeed, rather than work within the domain of the Same, researchers can explicitly proliferate difference by acting out the multiplicities of a mobile researcher (Rose 1993). Another appropriate methodological strategy might be found in what Cindi Katz (1996) calls "minor theory" – that attempt to work the disruptions of a discourse, seeking weak signs so as to subvert from within, and pushing displacements to the limit.

With these comments on representation in mind, let us now turn to the spatialities of representation by introducing a twofold agenda for geographic research: one, to investigate the spatial character of discourses through an investigation of the geographic meanings embedded in particular representations and discursive sites, and two, to understand the representational character of space itself (Jones & Natter 1999). Regarding the former, we can assert not only that representations signify spatially, say by invoking particular places and stamping them with particular meanings, but also that any signification or discourse is 'always already' spatial. How can this strong view of spatiality within representation be maintained?

An answer is to be found in the dialectic of space and social power elaborated by writers such as Lefebvre (1991) and those geographers who have been influenced by his work (Gregory 1994; Harvey 1989, 1990; Soja 1989, 1996; Massey 1994). Whether conceived as a sublation of dialectical moments or as an overdetermined condition, Lefebvre's concept of social space points to the indivisibility of space and social power – from the ways that social relations are constituted in and unfold through spatial distributions, built environments, and spatial significations, to the ways that space itself is socially produced through relations of social power (Lefebvre 1991). In this view, it is untenable to conceive of social relations of class, gender, race, or nation as falling outside of the purview of the spatiality through which they are practiced and reproduced in everyday life. Even the discourses of progress, morality, and reason (to name just a few) emanating from these relations are spatial – marking sociospatial constructs such as public/private, global/local, and chaotic/orderly. These discourses also carry with them spatial concatenations, attenuations, and disjunctures; that is, they mark the 'other spaces' of stagnation, immorality, and insanity. The analysis of representation is therefore a thoroughly spatial task that falls on all sides of an analytic that specifies communication in terms of production, content (including genre, see White 1987), and reception, and all of these, in turn, are interconnected through myriad spatial contexts that ultimately unhinge this analytic's limits (Natter & Jones 1993; also Doel 1999).

The second moment in this agenda is to consider the representational character of space itself. It is worthwhile first to point to spatial epistemology – our ways of knowing space. Under the aegis of Western reason, this epistemology has been suffused with ocularcentrism, Cartesian perspectivalism, and lineation (Dixon & Jones 1998; also Cosgrove 2003; Driver 1995). Whereas ocularcentrism privileges vision over other forms of knowing and is one basis for social power through surveillance, perspectivalism coordinates vision by situating the viewer from a vantage-point above (Schein 1993); lineation, meanwhile, is the basis for gridding social space – the Cartesian counterpart to categorization more generally. Any number of histories can be written about the imposition of reason's grid epistemology, from the configuration of social space in the projects of colonialism and nation-building

(Anderson 1991; Driver 2000; Gregory 1994; Hannah 2000; Mitchell 1991, 2002; Sidaway 2000), to the carving of towns out of nature and bringing them together through systems of transport (Foucault 1984: 239–56; Scott 1999), to the policing and self-disciplining of bodies in the gendered microspaces of everyday life (Butler & Parr 1999; Crang 1994; de Certeau 1984; Driver 1985; Gregson & Rose 2000; Lewis & Pile 1996; McDowell 1995). Even our concept of scale – cascading as it does through the above examples – can be thought of as an outcome of the grid epistemology (Jones 1998; Strohmayer 2003).

Alternative spatial epistemologies, however, are also lodged in space. Working from a poststructuralist feminist perspective, Gillian Rose (1993) describes a mobile, nonmasculinist, nonspectral, and nontransparent "paradoxical" space, one that is fused (as both/and rather than either/or) with multiple oppositional moments, including Same/Other, oppression/resistance, exclusion/inclusion, and center/margin. This space, partly imagined and partly within grasp, bears affinities to the hybrid 'thirdspace' of Homi Bhabha (1994), which has been elaborated through Lefebvre in the work of Ed Soja (1996). His thirdspace is:

the space where all places are capable of being seen from every angle [see note 5], each standing clear; but also a secret and conjectured object, filled with illusions and allusions, a space that is common to all of us yet never able to be completely seen and understood, an 'unimaginable universe.' (Soja 1996: 56)

Like Rose, Soja offers a space of "all-inclusive simultaneity" that "opens up endless worlds to explore and, at the same time, presents daunting challenges" (1996: 57).

From this theorization of the ways in which spaces are already invested with epistemology, we can proceed to rethink one of cultural geography's traditional objects of inquiry, the landscape. Whereas previous theorizations understood landscapes to be the imprint of a culture (Sauer 1963, originally 1925) or the effect of a social process such as capitalism (Cosgrove 1983; Knox 1984), poststructuralism has pointed to their status as a complex assemblage of significations and discourses that are intertextually bound with a host of other landscapes and discourses (e.g. Schein 1997). The landscape-as-text metaphor thus sees place as intersecting with an infinite number of other texts and contexts, such that we cannot demarcate where one starts and another begins. What is more, these multiple sites of discursive propagation open a circuit that is beyond landscapes, seeping into other representational media such as film, television, cyberspace, the body, political discourse and other forms of speech, and written texts of all kinds, including maps.[9]

Deconstruction as Poststructuralist Methodology

In this section we introduce – theoretically but with an eye towards 'doing' – the poststructuralist methodology of deconstruction. The term has entered the lexicon of many areas of the academy, from geography and comparative literature to architecture and anthropology. It has also received wide purchase in popular culture (witness, for example, "deconstructive fashion"). Though in popular usage "deconstruction" usually refers to any attempt at critiquing an established order of one form or another (as in the bumper sticker entreating us to "subvert the dominant paradigm"), in this section we provide a narrower, analytic understanding of this research method, one that maintains a close association with the theoretical tenets laid out above. We do this not to put tight constraints around deconstruction as a research strategy, for even Derrida, the archetypal deconstructor, resists defining it, arguing that to do so is not only contrary to deconstruction itself but also might limit and tame the methodology's political potential. We do, however, want to give sufficient guidelines so that readers can see how deconstruction might be "applied" in geographic research.

For something to be de-constructed, it clearly must have been constructed in the first instance, and it is in this sense that we can identify an entry point to this form of analysis. Deconstruction begins by focusing attention on centers, defined in an earlier section of this chapter as the organizing principles of structures. Centers carry with them a number of qualities consistent with the structuralist enterprise, including an either/or epistemology, an apparently noncontingent, natural, and enduring nature, and a seemingly independent, self-positing and self-defining, presence. To deconstruct one must therefore first recognize the existence of a center, and with it, both a marginalized periphery (the "other") and a boundary that produces and maintains – as opposed to merely "indicates" – the difference.

Now, as described above, the binaries comprising centers and peripheries do not simply re-present the world, but are instead socially defined representations of it. This means that the process of constituting a center and a periphery will never be a neutral one. Indeed, at stake in the naming of centers and the drawing of boundaries is social capital of many forms, since these representations influence the thoughts and actions of people. For example, inasmuch as centers and peripheries are dependent upon a binary epistemology, we might first note that those who stand to gain from this epistemology are often the same persons who can, in political discourse, mark the difference between the feasible and the impossible, or the realistic and the fantastic (to mention just two common either/or categorizations). And these will usually be the same persons who find utility in defining centers as stable, natural, and enduring, and who stand to gain from their seemingly self-evident qualities.

In this view, it is reasonable to expect that poststructuralists might look to forms of ideology, political persuasion, or coercion as sites of centering and marginalization. One might look, for example, in the languages and assumptions of formal institutions such as the state, in the discourses and practices of economic enterprises, and in the cultivated trappings of influential social groups, such as men, whites, religious leaders, scientists, and so on. It is through the rules, regulations, practices, and discourses of such institutions and groups of persons that centers and margins are reproduced and policed, and become available for the further exercise of social power.

To help illustrate the process of centering and the deconstructive response to it, let us consider as an example the structure of racism, which in some forms posits a "white" center and a racialized "other" comprised of those grouped as blacks, Indians, Hispanics, and so on, as well as those who do not easily fit into any of these categories. Now, one powerful yet pre-deconstructive form of critique of this system involves an assessment of the unequal distribution of the social surplus by, for example, demonstrating that racialized persons have lower income, poorer housing, inadequate healthcare, and inferior education (see Bonnett 1997). By contrast, a classically deconstructive approach is to focus on the relational character of race and on the centering processes that enable the designations of "white" and "other." This form of analysis would critique "white" as a self-sufficient category, one beyond social construction. The goal of inquiry of this approach would be to make the category visible to analysis by pointing to the ways in which "whiteness" is itself dependent upon marginalized races, such that it becomes the foundational race – ahistorical and invariant – against which all other races are compared and contrasted (Dwyer & Jones 2002). The aim of identifying a center such as whiteness would be to disclose and undermine the grounds by which it, and therefore white privilege, is asserted and maintained. One might, for example, examine everyday political language, which is replete with claims both about the benefits of majoritarianism, a discourse that works to maintain "white" as a center, and about the need for racialized groups to "bootstrap" themselves rather than rely upon "mainstream" society. It is in these ways, and countless others (in, for example, the popular media), that an "us/them" system of race is maintained and reproduced, serving ultimately to protect whiteness and white privilege.

This example points us to a second step in deconstruction, wherein having identified a center, one conducts research on the processes that both maintain it and permit its subversion. These inquiries are directed toward the discourses through which centers are constructed from margins (Derrida's "constitutive outside," 1988) and buttressed through discursive sites from which those centers are propagated. Thus in deconstructing whiteness a poststructuralist might investigate, first, when and how "white" emerged as the organizing principle of the structure of race. Such research involves analysis of the emergence of the concept in particular times and places, thereby pointing not only to its arbitrary sociohistorical character, but also to the context within which it became defined and asserted. A second and related task involves tracing the interrelations and limits of a center by examining the discourse associated with it. Here one seeks to determine which discourses have been associated with whiteness, and how they work to reproduce it. For example, one might examine how discourses of orderliness, sanitation, purity, and beatification link whiteness with a host of positive connotations. Or one might trace the conflation of whiteness with other central constructs such as masculinity or sexuality. In these cases, one might ask: what are the discourses that link these constructs? For example, how does a subject position such as white-heterosexual-male become the organizing principle against which all "other" subject positions are defined as "other"?

These sorts of analyses can be grounded through an assessment of particular discursive sites, the "locations" from which discourses emanate. They include, first, sites of linguistic and visual representation, such as speech-acts, written communication, paintings, photographs, and electronic media. Even bodies are categorized as linguistic and visual sites, since how one speaks and looks conveys meanings that tap into larger discourses (about, for example, race or masculinity). Second, institutional positions are discursive sites, ones that are independent of the particular individual occupying the site. Such positions include, for example, those held by politicians and judges, religious and secular leaders, and business persons and public intellectuals. In such sites are vested particular forms of power that circulate through the enunciations and practices of the individuals occupying the positions. Third, and of particular significance to cultural geographers, are built environments, which, like institutional positions, are vested with power by virtue of the meanings people associate with particular places. These include not only sites obviously invested with sociopolitical meaning, such as churches, courthouses, and monuments and memorials, but also those more everyday sites that likewise reproduce meanings in society, such as stadiums, shopping centers, highways, gated communities and more.

A research project that seeks to deconstruct whiteness, then, would make use of the following questions: What are the discursive locations from which whiteness is centralized and propagated? Which linguistic and visual representations support skin color – as opposed to eye color (Morrison 1993) – as the defining principle of the structure of race? How do racialized bodies convey meanings in political discourse, textbooks, and popular culture? How and with what effect do institutions such as the census bureau propound "race" as a category through the practice of naming the racialized origins of persons, and how, even, do such categories as "multiracial" work within, rather than confront, the centrality of whiteness? And, finally, how is the structure of race reproduced through daily practices within and through built environments? How are certain places normalized as the home of particular racialized groups, from gated communities to "ghettos" (Natter & Jones 1997)?[10]

As this example shows, deconstructive analysis is far from stripped of political potential. This is because centers, though they circulate within diverse and oftentimes conflated sets of discourses operating throughout society, typically serve to maintain the dominant social powers and institutions with that society. Yet, in assessing the politics of deconstruction, one must recognize that it not only animates, but also qualifies, the study of the transgressive potential located in peripheries (also see Sharp et al. 2000, esp. ch. 1). On the one hand, deconstruction provides the basis for examining the transgressions and transgressive potential of peripheries. In making visible centers and contesting their effrontery, deconstruction taps the always-existing power within marginality, a power to disclose the constitutive trace of the periphery within the center. In this view, discourse and discursive sites can be conceptualized just as much as sites of contestation as of domination. On the other hand, it must also be emphasized that the goal of deconstruction is not to reverse a binary mode of thinking by asserting the centrality of peripheries, for this would merely reinscribe a structuralist mode of thinking about the world. Nor is the goal simply to undermine the certainties of those social powers and institutions. Rather, by prying apart the stability of centers, deconstruction serves to open up new ways of naming and relating meanings, ones that are deliberated upon rather than taken for granted. In this view, deliberation does not mean the abolition of categories and centers, for this would be an impossible project, but rather implies that attention be directed both toward the sociohistorical context within which any category is deployed and the ramifications of its deployment.

Future Articulations between Poststructuralism and Cultural Geography

As we have shown, poststructuralism unsettles routine modes of social inquiry relying on handed-down concepts that purport to contain either essential truths (e.g., progress, reason) or worldly objects and events (e.g., nature, resistance). These concepts and the centering effects they produce are taken as significant objects of inquiry in and of themselves; accordingly, deconstructive analysis asks how, and with what effect, such concepts operate, and to whose benefit.

Significantly, poststructuralism has been helpful in rethinking the subfield of cultural geography, both in terms of its constitutive elements and its development over time. Consider the nodding acquiescence we give to the repetitive invocation of scores of normalized cultural categories, and their denotative and connotative associations, such as: community, nature, public, identity, scale, territory, experience, attachment, rhetoric, individual, landscape, animals, periphery, development, place, history, justice, family, agency, locality, authenticity, values, region, environment, borders, citizen, habituation, the everyday, gender, race, transgression, memory, nation, spectacle – even "culture" and "post" do not escape normalization. Poststructuralism unhinges these concepts from their securities, tossing them into a differential 'space' of relational meanings buttressed by wide socio-spatial-historical contexts and everyday social articulations; peering into that space we can examine their stabilizations and destabilizations, their inexact certitude and their exacting uncertainties. Under poststructuralism, all our POEMs are porous, more likely to hemorrhage than to contain and capture. Space too is "affected" (in both senses of the term): it is pulsing, vibrating, crumpled and folded, rather than stable, transparent, flat, and dimensional (Doel 2000). To undertake such analyses, cultural geographers have had to adopt a new set of analytic metaphors necessary to the task, including: mobility (as opposed to rootedness); networks of connection and disconnection (as opposed to centers and margins); and fluidities and flows (as opposed to cause→effect).

Importantly, this reworking of phenomena has entailed an appreciation of the constructed, partial, and always contextualized figure of the researched and the researcher. We are differentially and continually entangled in a host of social relations that constitute what it means to be a subject. Our own embeddedness in discourse, within which we perform in a process of self-construction by means of reiteration (Butler 1990), extends much further than was previously thought; as Hinchcliffe (2003) points out, many of the terms traditionally used within cultural geography, such as landscape, place, and inhabitation, rest upon a binary that arbitrarily demarcates between human and nonhuman, such that our analyses of culture, as traditionally conceived, is thoroughly anthropocentric and nonrelational. The haunting 'traces' of this particular mode of centering – the bestial and the techno-logic – have since been brought to light (Haraway 1991; Philo & Wilbert 2000; Whatmore 2001; Wolch 1996; Wolch & Emel 1998).

Poststructuralism has also had an impact upon how we think about the history of, and the histories within, cultural geography. Poststructuralism rejects the notion that there is an ordered trajectory to the emergence and development of the subfield based around the unlocking of concepts such as landscape and place. It also shows that historical writing is not a recovery of a place and period but a form of writing from the perspective of the present. Following Foucault's theory of history, these imply that we recognize our present situatedness in our attempts to write the past; that we pay attention not to the essential agent behind actions and more to the effects and affects that subjects generate through discursive practices; and that we reject any notion of continuity or order in historical analysis.

This reassessment of cultural geography – for example, in how we construct places in our writings – puts poststructuralism in an antithetical position *vis-à-vis* those theoretical approaches that lay claim to an objective analysis of an ordered world and orderly subjects, namely spatial science, humanism, and critical realism. And though this 'difference of opinion' appears to confirm their distinct approaches, each peering through their own particular lens, this would be, under poststructuralism, a misleading understanding. Certainly each draws differently, through affirmation and repudiation, upon a complex and dynamic field of meanings concerning the character of social life and its investigation. Yet, as we have argued elsewhere (Dixon & Jones 1996), none of these paradigms can escape this fully relational field of knowledge, within the discipline and beyond. Accordingly, poststructuralism would suggest that the peripheries of our epistemological concepts are lodged into their respective centers and hence – importantly – into each paradigm's "others." We should not be too surprised, then, to discover shared assumptions and practices, even in repudiation. This is why we can, for example, track concepts such as scale and relationality across poststructuralism (via the notion of context), through Marxism (via internal and external relations), and on to humanism (via the notion of intersubjectivity) and spatial science (via the identification of autocorrelation). We can equally track ontological concepts, such as 'community' (Joseph 2002), across different paradigms. And, we can follow the twists and turns of a material–discourse binary within all manner of research, regardless of theoretical allegiances. In sum, the bodies of work that comprise cultural geography are very much embedded in a web of differential and relational understandings. If nothing else, this should put an end to the hubris that underwrites the affirmation of one particular framework over another. And yet curiously, it was through poststructuralism, which we should add *already carries structuralism within it*, that this understanding became clear.

NOTES

1. Paradigms have traditionally been held to denote "the working assumptions, procedures, and findings routinely accepted by a group of scholars, which together define a stable pattern of scientific activity" (Gregory 2000: 571). The term 'paradigm' gained currency with the publication of Kuhn's 1962 book, *The Structure of Scientific Revolutions*. It was adopted by spatial scientists to describe their quantitative and theoretical 'revolution' (Berry & Marble 1968). This maneuver has not been without controversy in the field of geography (e.g., Mair 1986; Johnston 1991; see Gregory 2000 for an excellent short review and critique). Notwithstanding these criticisms, we employ the term here with the following understanding: (i) they are metatheoretical clusters of thought defined by the historically congealed incorporation and repudiation of the elements of binary relations that exist at the ontological and epistemological levels (e.g., objectivity–subjectivity, order–chaos, materialist–idealist, determinacy–uncertainty, discrete–relational; rational–emotional); (ii) they are, as Gregory's definition indicates, widely accepted in practice, guiding research programs by suggesting appropriate objects of analysis and their theorization, and informing the research strategies brought to bear on those objects; and (iii) in spite of their congealed and commonly agreed-upon character, they are not static, undifferentiated, mutually exclusive, or hegemonic: the

objects they define, the concepts they help to generate, and the procedures they inform are always open and in negotiation – this is the result of the multiply situated agencies that individuals bring to the research process (see Dixon & Jones 1996).

2. Many cultural geographers also turned to postmodernism, a diffuse set of ideas and practices that have been associated in diverse ways with poststructuralism. In brief, postmodernism can be conceived of as a significant object of study as well as an epistemological stance with respect to modernist forms of knowledge and practice. As an object of study, postmodernism has been understood as an emergent social condition; that is, the economic changes wrought under late capitalism have, it is argued, led to a transformation in the way in which we experience the world (see Harvey 1989; Jameson 1991). These include changes in the way we experience space and place (Ley 1989; Soja 1989), the built environment (Ellin 1996; Sorkin 1992; Zukin 1991) and urban culture (Chambers 1986, 1988). As an epistemological stance, postmodernism has much in common with poststructuralism, in that there is a suspicion of modernist 'grand theory' that purports to comprehensively explain the social and physical realms (Lyotard 1985). In contrast, postmodernism assumes a plurality of knowledges, and offers an attention to difference and diversity, such that previously marginalized understandings can be brought to light. For some, geography is uniquely placed to make these arguments, in that a traditional hallmark of the discipline has been sensitivity to differentiation (Gregory 1989a, 1989b; Philo 1991; Soja 1987; Strohmayer & Hannah 1992). An entry into these debates can be found in Benko 1997. An overview of the interfiliations between postmodernism and poststructuralism can be found in Best and Kellner's (1991) *Postmodern Theory*.

3. For students interested in reading further, Selden 1989 and Sarup 1993 provide good introductions to structuralism (and poststructuralism) in literary theory, while Lechte 1994 offers useful, reference-like synopses of the work of a wide range of associated theorists. Students can follow up on many of the thinkers found in Selden and Lechte by reading the selections of original writings in Lemert's authoritative collection (1999). Likewise, Leach 1997 offers well-chosen excerpts with an eye to architecture and space. In cultural geography, structuralism largely came through the door of semiotics – the study of signs – by way of the work of A. J. Greimas, Charles Peirce, and the early writings of Roland Barthes and Jean Baudrillard (see note 6, below). Structuralist semiotics influenced the work of some of the essayists in Cosgrove and Daniels (1988), while Barnes and Duncan's 1991 collection marks an effort to shift to poststructuralism. Other important texts to compare are Cosgrove 1984, Duncan 1990, and Gottdiener 1994 on landscapes, and Jackson 1994 and Cresswell 1996 on cultural politics. Barnes and Duncan 1991 (ch. 1), Duncan and Duncan 1988, Natter and Jones 1993, and Olsson 1996 explicitly take up the relationship between literary theory and geography.

4. Derrida's many translated writings include *Of Grammatology* (1976), *Writing and Difference* (1978), *Limited Inc* (1988), the collection *A Derrida Reader* (1991), and *Specters of Marx* (1994). A good introduction to Derrida's thought can be found in Caputo's (ed.) *Deconstruction in a Nutshell* (1998). An excellent advanced analysis is found in *The Tain of the Mirror* (Gasché 1988). Marcus Doel has written more on Derrida than any other geographer; see his *Poststructuralist Geographies* (1999).

5. Foucault's translated works on the writing of history include *The Order of Things: An Archaeology of the Human Sciences* (1973a) and *The Archaeology of Knowledge* (1974). His genealogical analyses include *Madness and Civilization: A History of Insanity in the Age of Reason* (1973b), *The Birth of the Clinic: An Archeology of Medical Perception* (1975), *Discipline and Punish: The Birth of the Prison* (1977), and the *History of Sexuality*, vols. 1 (1979), 2 (1985) and 3 (1986). Dreyfus and Rabinow 1982 offers a serious book-length treatment. Interviews and shorter essays can be found in

Power/Knowledge (1980), *The Foucault Reader* (1984), and *Politics, Philosophy, Culture* (1988), and in Foucault (1997). Within geography, the importance of Foucault's ideas is discussed in works by Felix Driver (1985, 1997), Matt Hannah (1993), David Matless (1991), and Chris Philo (1992).

6. Though we do not address their work in-depth in this chapter, both Roland Barthes and Jean Baudrillard have had a tremendous impact on the analysis of representations. For example, while Barthes's earlier work (1953, 1957, 1964, 1967) had much in common with the semiotic analyses of Saussure, he went on to critique the retention of a structuralist emphasis on surface (re-presentation) and depth (reality). Barthes's initial impulse was to target the "bourgeois norm" via an interrogation of the social production of the "falsely obvious," an impulse best encapsulated in his *Mythologies* (1957). In understanding how such norms have reached the unquestioned status of myth, Barthes expanded upon Saussure's categorization of language into signifiers (words/ practices), signifieds (intent/meaning), and signs (the combination of the two in a particular system of communication), via the addition of what he termed a primary signifier and a secondary signifier. The former relates to the initial association of an inscription with a mental image. The second relates to the way in which this initial signifier can then become the signified in a second process. The word 'cat,' for example, is the signifier for the mental image of a feline. This signifier can then be used as a descriptor for a human being, such that the word cat is now the signified. The primary signifier can be termed the level of denotation, the secondary the level of connotation. Myth ensues from the fixing of the secondary connotations of terms, such that the resulting associations can be considered the dominant, or hegemonic, mode of thinking. Myth does not 'hide' meaning, as in some understandings of ideology, but rather celebrates the 'givenness' of a particular construction of reality. In his later work, however, Barthes (1973, 1978, 1985) retreated from this structuralist stance toward meaning, arguing that signifiers do not reference underlying signifieds, but rather other signifiers, such that meaning is always in process – a temporary stop in a continuing flow of interpretations of interpretations – and as such cannot be held up as the originary moment for any explanation. Meanings, therefore, cannot be demarcated according to the intent behind their production, their mode of dissemination, or the perspectives of the reader, precisely because each of these three contexts cannot be considered autonomous from other contexts, or indeed from each other. In sum, for Barthes, meanings are *polysemic* in character.

Baudrillard's early work (1968, 1970, 1972) is similarly embedded in semiotics. It addresses the ways in which objects within a capitalist society are afforded meaning and value. Baudrillard adds sign value, which is the differentiation of objects from one another, and symbolic exchange (the gift), to the Marxist concepts of use value (utility) and exchange value (commodification). In his *Symbolic Exchange and Death* (1976), however, Baudrillard explicitly takes on the issue of representation, arguing that we can no longer talk of the mere copying of an 'original.' This is because there is no longer an analytic distinction to be made between representation and reality. In his later works, Baudrillard (1981, 1986, 1990) expands on the idea that representational processes have undergone a profound transformation: whereas in the Renaissance one could talk of counterfeit, and in the Industrial era of production, in the current 'hyperreal' era we deal primarily with simulation, in the form of virtual reality, global media, and fashion. The focus of attention lies not on the process by which reality is mediated, but rather on the mechanisms by which a continuous flow of simulacra are generated. And, in the face of such a totalizing system, whereby simulacra re-represent simulacra, we should eschew 'banal' theories that seek to judge and rationalize in favor of 'fatal' theories that entail fascination, ironic amusement, and even ecstasy before the image itself.

7. Derrida has perhaps the broadest understanding of context: "the entire real history of the world" (1988: 136). This is why his aphoristic phrasing, "there's nothing outside the text" (*il n'y a pas de hors-texte*) is not, as is sometimes alleged, idealist, for in Derrida's work, all texts are in context. Deconstruction, the poststructuralist methodology we describe below, animates from this understanding. Derrida describes it as the effort "to take this limitless context into account, to pay the sharpest attention possible to context, and thus to an incessant movement of recontextualization" (1988: 136). This view of the macrocosm embedded within the microcosm has parallels to Jorge Luis Borges's story, 'The Aleph,' described as a "sphere whose center is everywhere and whose circumference is nowhere . . . one of the points in space that contains all other points" – in other words, a structure without a center (1979: 23, 26; see Soja 1996).

8. Such a position entails what Barthes (1978) referred to as the "death of the author." Meaning cannot originate from the author because this 'person' is a socially and historically constituted subject, and hence does not exist prior to or outside of language. For Barthes, this is a liberating stance, in that each reader can add to, alter, or simply edit a text through the act of reading, and, further, can move through a text in an aleatory, nonlinear fashion, thereby 'writing' the text anew. Importantly, the reader does not then become the 'authority,' but rather each subject is understood to contribute to the stabilization and destabilization of a field of meanings (see discussion of context and intertext, above). Analyses of the flow of meanings though texts can be found throughout media studies of film (De Lauretis 1984; Mulvey 1989), television (Allen 1992), and literature (Fish 1982; Jauss 1982).

9. Marcus Doel (1999, 2000, 2003) goes even further, providing a new theory of space drawn from Gilles Deleuze and Félix Guattari (1972, 1987). They were known for proliferating a large number of spatiophilosophical in(ter)ventions, including such distinctions as: striated vs. smooth space; mapping vs. tracing; trees vs. rhizomes; points vs. flows; and the dynamic spatial processes of territorialization, deterritorialization, and reterritorialization (see Doel 2000). Deleuze and Guattari are resolutely materialist *and* poststructuralist – for them the world exists in the spacing of difference – and they reject that their concepts are in any way metaphors (1987). Doel puts it this way: "*As fanatical materialists, we are struck by everything* – nothing will be set aside from the play of force; nothing will be spirited away onto a higher plane or exorcised into a netherworld. It is true that we take up signs, words, images, quantities, figures, maps, photographs, money, hypertext, gardening advice, lipstick traces, the exquisite corpse, and so on and so forth – but we take them up as force: as strikes and counter-strikes; as blows and counter-blows" (2003, in press, emphasis in the original). This effort to wrest materialism from the materialists (e.g. Peet 1998) is the latest poststructuralist reversal, one that overturns the valences of the real vs. representation opposition within geography.

10. Students looking for methodological assistance should consult Hall 1997 (ch. 1) and Rose 2001. Both give clear accounts of the differences between structuralist semiotics and poststructuralist discourse analysis. Another useful work, particularly for a Derridian reading of texts, is provided by Denzin 1994.

REFERENCES

Aitken, S. and Zonn, L. 1994: Representing the place pastiche. In S. Aitken and L. Zonn, eds., *Place, Power, Situation and Spectacle: A Geography of Film*. Lanham, MD: Rowman and Littlefield, 3–25.

Allen, R. C., ed. 1992: *Channels of Discourse: Television and Contemporary Criticism*. Chapel Hill, NC: University of North Carolina Press.

Anderson, B. 1991: *Imagined Communities: Reflections on the Origin and Spread of Nationalism*. London: Verso.

Barnes, T. 1996: *Logics of Dislocation: Models, Methods and Meanings of Economic Geography*. New York: Guilford.

Barnes, T. and Duncan, J., eds. 1991: *Writing Worlds: Discourse, Text, and Metaphors in the Representation of Landscape*. London: Routledge.

Barthes, R. 1953: *Writing Degree Zero*, tr. A. Lavers. New York: Hill and Wang.

Barthes, R. 1957: *Mythologies*, tr. A. Lavers. St. Albans: Paladin.

Barthes, R. 1964: *Elements of Semiology*, tr. A. Lavers. New York: Hill and Wang.

Barthes, R. 1967: *The Fashion System*, tr. M. Ward. New York: Hill and Wang.

Barthes, R. 1973: *The Pleasure of the Text*, tr. R. Miller. New York: Hill and Wang.

Barthes, R. 1978: *Image-Music-Text*, tr. S. Heath. New York: Noonday Press.

Barthes, R. 1985: *The Responsibility of Forms: Critical Essays on Music, Art and Representation*, tr. R. Howard. New York: Hill and Wang.

Bhabha, H. 1994: *The Location of Culture*. London: Routledge.

Baudrillard, J. 1968: *Le Système des Objects*. Paris: Denoël.

Baudrillard, J. 1970: *La Société de la Consommation*. Paris: Gallimard.

Baudrillard, J. 1972: *For a Critique of the Political Economy of the Sign*, tr. C. Levin. St. Louis: Telos Press.

Baudrillard, J. 1976: *Symbolic Exchange and Death*, tr. I. Grant. London: Sage.

Baudrillard, J. 1981: *The Evil Demon of Images and the Precession of Simulacra*, tr. P. Patton and P. Foss. Sydney: Power Institute.

Baudrillard, J. 1986: *America*, tr. C. Turner. New York: Routledge.

Baudrillard, J. 1990: *The Transparence of Evil: Essays on Extreme Phenomena*, tr. J. J. St. John. London: Routledge.

Benko, G. 1997: Introduction: modernity, postmodernity and the social sciences. In G. Benko and U. Strohmayer, eds., *Space and Social Theory: Interpreting Modernity and Postmodernity*. Oxford: Blackwell, 1–44.

Berry, B. and Marble, D. F., eds. 1968: *Spatial Analysis: A Reader in Statistical Geography*. Englewood Cliffs, NJ: Prentice-Hall.

Best, S. and Kellner, D. 1991: *Postmodern Theory*. New York: Guilford.

Bonnett, A. 1997: Geography, 'race,' and whiteness: invisible traditions and current challenges. *Area* 29, 193–9.

Borges, J. L. 1979: *The Aleph and other Stories, 1933–1969*. New York: Dutton.

Braun, B. and Castree, N., eds. 1998: *Remaking Reality: Nature at the Millennium*. London: Routledge.

Butler, J. 1990: *Gender Trouble: Feminism and the Subversion of Identity*. London: Routledge.

Butler, J. and Scott, J., eds. 1992: *Feminists Theorize the Political*. London: Routledge.

Butler, R. and Parr, H., eds. 1999: *Mind and Body Spaces: Geographies of Illness, Impairment and Disability*. London: Routledge.

Buttimer, A. 1976: Grasping the dynamism of the lifeworld. *Annals of the Association of American Geographers* 66, 277–92.

Caputo, J., ed. 1998: *Deconstruction in a Nutshell: A Conversation With Jacques Derrida*. Fordham: Fordham University Press.

Castree, N. and Braun, B., eds. 2001: *Social Nature: Theory, Practice and Politics*. Oxford: Blackwell.

Chambers, I. 1986: *Popular Culture: The Metropolitan Experience*. London: Routledge.

Chambers, I. 1988: Contamination, coincidence and collusion: pop music, urban culture and the Avant Garde. In C. Nelson and L. Grossberg, eds., *Marxism and the Interpretation of Culture*. Urbana, IL: University of Illinois Press, 607–11.

Cloke, P. and Little, J., eds. 1997: *Contested Countryside Cultures: Otherness, Marginalisation, and Rurality*. London: Routledge.

Collins, P. H. 1990: *Black Feminist Thought: Knowledge, Consciousness, and the Politics of Empowerment*. London: Routledge.

Cosgrove, D. 1983: Towards a radical cultural geography: problems of theory. *Antipode* 15, 1–11.

Cosgrove, D. 1984: *Social Formations and Symbolic Landscapes*. London: Croom Helm.

Cosgrove, D. 2003: Landscape and the European sense of sight. In K. Anderson, M. Domosh, S. Pile, and N. Thrift, eds., *Handbook of Cultural Geography*. Thousand Oaks, CA: Sage, 249–68.

Cosgrove, D. and Daniels, S., eds. 1988: *The Iconography of Landscape: Essays on the Symbolic Representation, Design and Use of Past Environments*. Cambridge: Cambridge University Press.

Crang, M., Crang, P., and May, J., eds. 1999: *Virtual Geographies: Bodies, Space and Relations*. London: Routledge.

Crang, P. 1994: It's showtime: on the workplace geographies of display in a restaurant in south east England. *Environment and Planning D: Society and Space* 12, 675–704.

Cresswell, T. 1996: *In Place/Out of Place: Geography, Ideology, and Transgression*. Minneapolis: University of Minnesota Press.

Cresswell, T. and Dixon, D. P., eds. 2002: *Engaging Film: Geographies of Mobility and Identity*. Lanham, MD: Rowman and Littlefield.

De Certeau, M. 1984: *The Practice of Everyday Life*. Berkeley: University of California Press.

De Lauretis, T. 1984: *Alice Doesn't: Feminism, Semiotics, Cinema*. Bloomington: Indiana University Press.

Del Casino Jr., V. J. and Hanna, S. P. 2000: Representations and identities in tourism map spaces. *Progress in Human Geography* 24, 23–46.

Del Casino Jr., V. J., and Hanna, S. P. 2003: Mapping identities, reading maps: the politics of representation in Bangkok's sex tourism industry. In Hanna and Del Casino Jr., eds., *Mapping Tourism*. Minneapolis: University of Minnesota Press, 161–85.

Deleuze, G. and Guattari, F. 1972: *Anti-Oedipus: Capitalism and Schizophrenia*, tr. R. Hurley, M. Seem, and H. R. Lane. New York: Viking.

Deleuze, G. and Guattari, F. 1987: *A Thousand Plateaus: Capitalism and Schizophrenia*, tr. B. Massumi. Minneapolis: University of Minnesota Press.

Demeritt, D. 2002: What is the 'social construction of nature'? A typology and sympathetic critique. *Progress in Human Geography* 6, 767–90.

Denzin, N. 1994: Postmodernism and deconstructionism. In D. R. Dickens and A. Fontana, eds., *Postmodernism and Social Inquiry*. London: University College London Press, 182–202.

Derrida, J. 1970 [reissued 1972]: Structure, sign and play in the discourses of the human sciences. In R. Macksey and E. Donato, eds., *The Structuralist Controversy*. Baltimore: Johns Hopkins University Press, 247–65.

Derrida, J. 1976: *Of Grammatology*, tr. C. Spivak. Baltimore: Johns Hopkins University Press.

Derrida, J. 1978: *Writing and Difference*, tr. A. Bass. Chicago: University of Chicago Press.

Derrida, J. 1988: *Limited, Inc*, tr. S. Weber. Evanston, IL: Northwestern University Press.

Derrida, J. 1991: *Between the Blinds: A Derrida Reader*, ed. P. Kamuf. New York: Columbia University Press.

Derrida, J. 1994: *Specters of Marx: The State of the Debt, the Work of Mourning, and the New International*, tr. P. Kamuf. London: Routledge.

Deutsche, R. 1991: Boys town. *Environment and Planning D: Society and Space* 9, 5–30.

Dixon, D. P. and Hapke, H. 2003: Cultivating discourse: the social construction of agricultural legislation. *Annals of the Association of American Geographers* 93, in press.

Dixon, D. P. and Jones III, J. P. 1996: For a *supercalifragilisticexpialidocious* scientific geography. *Annals of the Association of American Geographers* 86, 767–79.

Dixon, D. P. and Jones III, J. P. 1997: On the 'con's in deconstruction. *The California Geographer* 37, 32–5.

Dixon, D. P. and Jones III, J. P. 1998: My dinner with Derrida, *or* spatial analysis and poststructuralism do lunch. *Environment and Planning A* 30, 247–60.

Doel, M. 1999: *Poststructuralist Geographies*. Edinburgh: University of Edinburgh Press.

Doel, M. 2000: Un-glunking geography: spatial science after Dr. Suess and Gilles Deleuze. In M. Crang and N. Thrift, eds., *Thinking Space*. London: Routledge, 117–35.

Doel, M. 2003: Poststructuralist geographies: the essential selection. In P. Cloke, P. Crang, and M. Goodwin, eds., *Envisioning Human Geographies*. London: Arnold, in press.

Dreyfus, H. L. and Rabinow, P., eds. 1982: *Michel Foucault: Beyond Structuralism and Hermeneutics*. Chicago: University of Chicago Press.

Driver, F. 1985: Power, space and the body: a critical assessment of Foucault's *Discipline and Punish*. *Environment and Planning D: Society and Space* 3, 425–46.

Driver, F. 1995: Visualising geography: a journey to the heart of the discipline. *Progress in Human Geography* 19, 123–34.

Driver, F. 1997: Bodies in space: Foucault's account of disciplinary power. In T. Barnes and D. Gregory, eds., *Reading Human Geography: The Poetics and Politics of Inquiry*. London: Arnold, 279–89.

Driver, F. 2000: *Geography Militant: Cultures of Exploration and Empire*. Oxford: Blackwell.

Duncan, J. 1980: The superorganic in American cultural geography. *Annals of the Association of American Geographers* 70, 181–98.

Duncan, J. 1990: *The City as Text: The Politics of Landscape Interpretation in the Kandyan Kingdom*. Cambridge: Cambridge University Press.

Duncan, J. and Duncan, N. 1988: (Re)reading the landscape. *Environment and Planning D: Society and Space* 6, 117–26.

Duncan, J. and Ley, D. 1992: Structural marxism and human geography: a critical assessment. *Annals of the Association of American Geographers* 72, 30–59.

Duncan, J. and Ley, D. 1993: *Place/Culture/Representation*. New York: Routledge.

Duncan, N., ed. 1996: *Bodyspace: Destabilizing Geographies of Gender and Sexuality*. London: Routledge.

Duncan, N. and Sharp, J. 1993: Confronting representation(s). *Environment and Planning D: Society and Space* 11, 473–86.

Dwyer, O. and Jones III, J. P. 2002: White socio-spatial epistemology. *Social and Cultural Geography* 1, 209–22.

Eagleton, T. 1990: *The Ideology of the Aesthetic*. Oxford: Blackwell.

Ellin, N. 1996: *Postmodern Urbanism*. Princeton: Princeton Architectural Press.

Fish, S. 1982: *Is There a Text in this Class?* Cambridge MA: Harvard University Press.

Foucault, M. 1973a: *The Order of Things: An Archaeology of the Human Sciences*, tr. R. Howard. New York: Vintage Press.

Foucault, M. 1973b: *Madness and Civilization: A History of Insanity in the Age of Reason*, tr. R. Howard. New York: Vintage Press.

Foucault, M. 1974: *The Archaeology of Knowledge*, tr. A. Sheridan. London: Tavistock.

Foucault, M. 1975: *The Birth of the Clinic: An Archaeology of Medical Perception*, tr. A. Sheridan. New York: Vintage Books.

Foucault, M. 1977: *Discipline and Punish: The Birth of the Prison*, tr. A. Sheridan. London: Allen Lane.

Foucault, M. 1979: *The History of Sexuality, Volume 1: An Introduction*, tr. R. Hurley. London: Allen Lane.

Foucault, M. 1980: *Power/Knowledge: Selected Interviews and other Writings 1972–1977*, ed. C. Gordon. New York: Random House.

Foucault, M. 1984: *The Foucault Reader*, ed. P. Rabinow. New York: Pantheon.

Foucault, M. 1985: *The History of Sexuality, Volume 2: The Use of Pleasure*, tr. R. Hurley. New York: Pantheon.

Foucault, M. 1986: *The History of Sexuality, Volume 3: The Care of the Self*, tr. R. Hurley. New York: Pantheon.

Foucault, M. 1988: *Politics, Philosophy, Culture: Interviews and Other Writings, 1977–1984*, ed. L. D. Kritzman. London: Routledge.

Gasché, R. 1988: *The Tain of the Mirror: Derrida and the Philosophy of Reflection*. Harvard: Harvard University Press.

Gibson-Graham, J.-K. 1996: *The End of Capitalism (As We Knew It): A Feminist Critique of Political Economy*. Oxford: Blackwell.

Gibson-Graham, J.-K. 2000: Poststructuralist interventions. In E. Sheppard and T. Barnes, eds., *A Companion to Economic Geography*. Oxford: Blackwell, 95–110.

Gottdiener, M. 1994: *Postmodern Semiotics*. Oxford: Blackwell.

Gregory, D. 1981: Human agency and human geography. *Transactions of the Institute of British Geographers* NS 6, 1–18.

Gregory, D. 1989a. Areal differentiation and post-modern human geography. In D. Gregory and R. Walford, eds., *Horizons in Human Geography*. Lanham, MD: Rowman and Littlefield, 67–96.

Gregory, D. 1989b: The crisis of modernity? Human geography and critical social theory. In R. Peet R. and N. Thrift, eds., *New Models in Geography*, vol. II. London: Unwin Hyman, 348–85.

Gregory, D. 1994: *Geographical Imaginations*. Oxford: Blackwell.

Gregory, D. 2000: Paradigm. In R. J. Johnston, D. Gregory, G. Pratt, and M. Watts, eds., *The Dictionary of Human Geography*, 4th ed. Oxford: Blackwell, 571–2.

Gregson, N. and Rose, G. 2000: Taking Butler elsewhere: performativities, spatialities and subjectivities. *Environment and Planning D: Society and Space* 18, 433–552.

Hall, S., ed. 1997: *Representation: Cultural Representations and Signifying Practices*. Thousand Oaks, CA: Sage.

Hanna, S. P. 1996: Is it Roslyn or is it Cicely? Representation and the ambiguity of place. *Urban Geography* 17, 633–48.

Hanna, S. P. and Del Casino Jr., V. J. 2003: Tourism spaces, mapped representations, and the practices of identity. In S. P. Hanna and V. J. Del Casino Jr., eds., *Mapping Tourism*. Minneapolis: University of Minnesota Press, pp. ix–xxvii.

Hannah, M. 1993: Foucault on theorizing specificity. *Environment and Planning D: Society and Space* 11, 349–63.

Hannah, M. 2000: *Governmentality and the Mastery of Knowledge in Nineteenth-Century America*. Cambridge: Cambridge University Press.

Haraway, D. 1991: *Simians, Cyborgs, and Women: The Reinvention of Nature*. London: Routledge.

Harding, S., ed. 1987: *Feminism and Methodology*. Bloomington: Indiana University Press.

Harley, J. B. 1989: Deconstructing the map. *Cartographica* 26, 1–20.

Hartsock, N. 1985: *Money, Sex and Power: Toward a Feminist Historical Materialism*. Evanston, IL: Northwestern University Press.

Harvey, D. 1989: *The Condition of Postmodernity: An Enquiry into the Origins of Cultural Change*. Oxford: Blackwell.

Harvey, D. 1990: Between space and time: reflections on the geographical imagination. *Annals of the Association of American Geographers* 80, 418–34.

Harvey, F. 2003: Knowledge and geography's technology: politics, ontologies, representations in the changing ways we know. In K. Anderson, M. Domosh, S. Pile, and N. Thrift, eds., *Handbook of Cultural Geography*. Thousand Oaks, CA: Sage, 532–43.

Hillis, K. 1999: *Digital Sensations: Identity, Embodiment and Space in Virtual Reality*. Minneapolis: University of Minnesota Press.

Hinchcliffe, S. 2003: Inhabiting – landscapes and natures. In K. Anderson, M. Domosh, S. Pile, and N. Thrift, eds., *Handbook of Cultural Geography*. Thousand Oaks, CA: Sage, 207–25.

Howitt, R. and Suchet, S. 2003: Ontological pluralism in contested cultural landscapes. In K. Anderson, M. Domosh, S. Pile, and N. Thrift, eds., *Handbook of Cultural Geography*. Thousand Oaks, CA: Sage, 557–69.

Jackson, P. 1994: *Maps of Meaning: An Introduction to Cultural Geography*. London: Routledge.

Jacobs, J. 1996: *Edge of Empire: Postcolonialism and the City*. London: Routledge.

Jameson, F. 1991: *Postmodernism, or, the Cultural Logic of Late Capitalism*. Durham, NC: Duke University Press.

Jauss, H. R. 1982: *Toward an Aesthetic of Reception*, tr. T. Bahti. Minneapolis: University of Minnesota Press.

Johnston, R. J. 1991: *Geography and Geographers: Anglo-American Geography since 1945*, 5th ed. London: Arnold.

Johnston, R. J. and Claval, P., eds. 1984: *Geography since the Second World War*. Lanham, MD: Rowman and Littlefield.

Jones, K. T. 1998: Scale as epistemology. *Political Geography* 17, 25–8.

Jones III, J. P. 1994: Review of *The Terms of Cultural Criticism: The Frankfurt School, Existentialism, Poststructuralism*, by R. Wolin. *Environment and Planning, D: Society and Space* 12, 127–8.

Jones III, J. P. and Moss, P. 1995: Democracy, identity, space. *Environment and Planning D: Society and Space* 13, 253–7.

Jones III, J. P. and Natter, W. 1999: Space 'and' representation. In A. Buttimer, S. D. Brunn, and U. Wardenga, eds., *Text and Regional Image: Social Construction of Regional Knowledges*. Leipzig: Selbstverlag Institut für Länderkunde, 239–47.

Joseph, M. 2002: *Against the Romance of Community*. Minneapolis: University of Minnesota Press.

Katz, C. 1996: Toward minor theory. *Environment and Planning D: Society and Space* 14, 487–99.

Keith, M. and Pile, S., eds. 1993: *Place and the Politics of Identity*. London: Routledge.

Kitchen, R. and Dodge, M. 2001: *Mapping Cyberspace*. London: Routledge.

Knox, P. 1984: Symbolisms, styles, and settings: the built environment and the imperatives of urbanized capitalism. *Architecture and Behavior* 2, 107–22.

Kobayashi, A. 1994: Coloring the field: gender, "race" and the politics of fieldwork. *The Professional Geographer* 46, 73–80.

Kuhn, T. 1962: *The Structure of Scientific Revolutions*. Chicago: University of Chicago Press.

Lawrence, M. 1995. Rural homelessness: a geography without a geography. *Journal of Rural Studies* 11, 304–16.

Leach, N., ed. 1997: *Rethinking Architecture: A Reader in Cultural Theory*. London: Routledge.

Lechte, J. 1994: *Fifty Key Contemporary Thinkers: From Structuralism to Postmodernity*. London: Routledge.

Lefebvre, H. 1991: *The Production of Space*, tr. D. Nicholson-Smith. Oxford: Blackwell.

Lemert, C., ed. 1999: *Social Theory: The Multicultural and Classic Readings*. Boulder, CO: Westview.

Lewis, C. and Pile, S. 1996: Woman, body, space: Rio carnival and the politics of performance. *Gender, Space and Culture* 3, 23–41.

Lewis, P. 1979: Axioms for reading the landscape: some guides to the American scene. In D. Meinig, ed., *The Interpretation of Ordinary Landscapes: Geographical Essays*. New York: University Press, 11–32.

Ley, D. 1980: *Geography without Man: A Humanistic Critique*. Oxford: Oxford University Press.

Ley, D. 1989: Modernism, postmodernism and the struggle for place. In J. Agnew and J. Duncan, eds., *The Power of Place: Bringing Together the Geographical and Sociological Imaginations*. London: Unwin Hyman, 44–65.

Lyotard, J.-F. 1985: *The Postmodern Condition: A Report on Knowledge*, tr. B. Massumi. Minneapolis: University of Minnesota Press.

Mahtani, M. 2002: Tricking the border guards: performing race. *Environment and Planning D: Society and Space* 20, 425–40.

Mair, A. 1986: Thomas Kuhn and understanding geography. *Progress in Human Geography* 10, 345–70.

Massey, D. 1994: *Space, Place and Gender*. Minneapolis: University of Minnesota Press.

Matless, D. 1991: An occasion for geography: landscape, representation and Foucault's corpus. *Environment and Planning D: Society and Space* 10, 41–56.

McDowell, L. 1995: Body work: heterosexual gender performances in city workplaces. In D. Bell and G. Valentine, eds., *Mapping Desire: Geographies of Sexualities*. London: Routledge, 75–95.

McDowell, L. and Sharp, J., eds. 1997: *Space, Gender, Knowledge: Feminist Readings*. London: Arnold.

Meinig, D. 1979: The beholding eye: ten versions of the same scene. In D. Meinig, ed., *The Interpretation of Ordinary Landscapes: Geographical Essays*. New York: Oxford University Press, 32–48.

Mitchell, D. 1995: There's no such thing as culture: towards a reconceptualization of the idea of culture in geography. *Transactions of the Institute of British Geographers* 20, 102–16.

Mitchell, D. 2000: *Cultural Geography: A Critical Introduction*. Oxford: Blackwell.

Mitchell, D. 2002: Cultural landscapes: the dialectical landscape – recent landscape research in human geography. *Progress In Human Geography* 26, 382–9.

Mitchell, T. 1991: *Colonising Egypt*. Berkeley: University of California Press.

Mitchell, T. 2002: *Rule of Experts: Egypt, Techno-Politics, Modernity*. Berkeley: University of California Press.

Mouffe, C. 1993: An interview with Chantal Mouffe (conducted by M. Bosman and L. Barre). *disClosure* 3, 87–104.

Morrison, T. 1993: *Playing in the Dark: Whiteness and the Literary Imagination*. New York: Vintage Books.

Mulvey, L. 1989: *Visual and Other Pleasures (Theories of Representation and Difference)*. Bloomington: Indiana University Press.

Nast, H. 2000: Mapping the "unconscious": racism and the oedipal family. *Annals of the Association of American Geographers* 90, 215–55.

Nast, H., ed. 1994: Women in the field: critical feminist methodologies and theoretical perspectives. (Special section.) *Professional Geographer* 46, 54–102.

Nast, H. and Pile, S., eds. 1998: *Places Through the Body*. London: Routledge.

Natter, W. and Jones III, J. P. 1993: Signposts toward a poststructuralist geography. In J. P. Jones III, W. Natter, and T. Schatzki, eds., *Postmodern Contentions: Epochs, Politics, Space*. New York: Guilford, 165–204.

Natter, W. 1997: Identity, space, and other uncertainties. In G. Benko and U. Strohmayer, eds., *Space and Social Theory: Geographic Interpretations of Postmodernity*. Oxford: Blackwell, 141–61.

Olsson, G. 1992. *Lines of Power: Limits of Language*. Minneapolis: University of Minnesota Press.

Ó Tuathail, G. 1996: *Critical Geopolitics: The Politics of Writing Global Space*. Minneapolis: University of Minnesota Press.

Peet, R. 1977: The development of radical geography in the United States. In R. Peet, ed., *Radical Geography*. Chicago: Maaroufa, 6–30.

Peet, R. 1998: *Modern Geographic Thought*. Oxford: Blackwell.

Philo, C. 1991: The differences of postmodern human geography. In P. Cloke, C. Philo, and D. Sadler, eds., *Approaching Human Geography: An Introduction to Contemporary Theoretical Debates*. New York: Guilford Press.

Philo, C. 1992: Foucault's geography. *Environment and Planning D: Society and Space* 10, 137–61.

Philo, C. and Wilbert, C., eds. 2000: *Animal Spaces, Beastly Places: New geographies of Human-Animal relations*. London: Routledge.

Pile, S. 1996: *The Body and the City: Psychoanalysis, Space and Subjectivity*. London: Routledge.

Pile, S. and Thrift, N., eds. 1995: *Mapping the Subject: Geographies of Cultural Transformation*. London: Routledge.

Pred, A. 2000: *Even in Sweden: Racisms, Racialized Spaces, and the Popular Geographical Imagination*. Berkeley: University of California Press.

Relph, E. 1976: *Place and Placelessness*. London: Pion.

Rose, G. 1993: *Feminism and Geography*. Cambridge: Polity.

Rose, G. 2001: *Visual Methodologies*. Thousand Oaks, CA: Sage.

Sarup, M. 1993: *Introductory Guide to Post-Structuralism and Postmodernism*. Athens, GA: University of Georgia Press.

Sauer, C. O. 1963 [originally 1925]: The morphology of landscape. In J. Leighly, ed., *Land and Life: A Selection of the Writings of Carl Ortwin Sauer*. Berkeley: University of California Press, 315–50.

Saussure, F. de. 1974: *Course in General Linguistics*. London: Fontana.

Sayer, A. 1984: *Method in Social Science: A Realist Approach*. London: Hutchinson.

Sayer, A. 2000: *Realism and Social Science*. Thousand Oaks, CA: Sage.

Schein, R. 1993: Representing urban America: nineteenth century views of landscape, space, power. *Environment and Planning D: Society and Space* 11, 7–21.

Schein, R. 1997: The place of landscape: a conceptual framework for interpreting an American scene. *Annals of the Association of American Geographers* 87(4), 660–80.

Scott, J. 1993: The evidence of experience. In H. Abelove, M. A. Barale, and D. M. Halperin, eds., *The Gay and Lesbian Studies Reader*. London: Routledge, 397–415.

Scott, J. C. 1999: *Seeing Like a State: How Certain Schemes to Improve the Human Condition Have Failed*. New Haven: Yale University Press.

Selden, R. 1989: *Practicing Theory and Reading Literature: An Introduction*. Lexington, KY: University of Kentucky Press.

Sharp, J., Routledge, P., Philo, C., and Paddison, R., eds. 2000: *Entanglements of Power: Geographies of Domination and Resistance*. London: Routledge.

Sidaway, J. 2000: Postcolonial geographies: an exploratory essay. *Progress in Human Geography* 24, 591–612.

Soja, E. 1987: The postmodernization of geography: a review. *Annals of the Association of American Geographers* 77, 289–94.

Soja, E. 1989: *Postmodern Geographies: The Reassertion of Space in Critical Social Theory*. London: Verso.

Soja, E. 1996: *Thirdspace: Journeys to Los Angeles and Other Real-and-Imagined Places*. Oxford: Blackwell.

Sorkin, M., ed. 1992: *Variations on a Theme Park: The New American City and the End of Public Space*. New York: Noonday.

Sparke, M. 1998: A map that roared and an original atlas: Canada, cartography, and the narration of nation. *Annals of the Association of American Geographers* 88, 464–95.

Strohmayer, U. 2003: The culture of epistemology. In K. Anderson, M. Domosh, S. Pile, and N. Thrift, eds., *Handbook of Cultural Geography*. Thousand Oaks, CA: Sage, 520–31.

Strohmayer, U. and Hannah, M. 1992: Domesticating postmodernism. *Antipode* 24, 29–55.

Tuan, Y.-F. 1976: Humanistic geography. *Annals of the Association of American Geographers* 66, 266–76.

Tuan, Y.-F. 1977: *Space and Place: The Perspective of Experience*. London: Arnold.

Whatmore, S. 2001: *Hybrid Geographies: Natures Cultures Spaces*. Thousand Oaks, CA: Sage.

White, H. 1987: *The Content of the Form: Narrative Discourse and Historical Representation*. Baltimore: Johns Hopkins University Press.

Willems-Braun, B. 1997: Buried Epistemologies: The politics of nature in (post)colonial British Columbia. *Annals of the Association of American Geographers* 87, 3–31.

Wolch, J. 1996: Zoöpolis. *Capitalism, Nature, Socialism* 7, 21–48.

Wolch, J. and Emel, J., eds. 1998: *Animal Geographies: Place, Politics and Identity in the Nature-Culture Borderlands*. London: Verso.

Wolin, R. 1992: *The Terms of Cultural Criticism: The Frankfurt School, Existentialism, Poststructuralism*. New York: Columbia University Press.

Zukin, S. 1991: *Landscapes of Power: From Detroit to Disney World*. Berkeley: University of California Press.

Chapter 8

Psychoanalytic Approaches

Paul Kingsbury

We are threatened with suffering from three directions: from our own body, which is doomed to decay and dissolution and which cannot even do without pain and anxiety as warning signals; from the external world, which may rage against us with overwhelming and merciless forces of destruction; and finally from our relations to other men. (Freud 1961: 26)

The best image to sum up the unconscious is Baltimore in the early morning. (Lacan 1972: 189)

Introduction

On the 27th of August 1909, the *George Washington* ocean liner entered New York City's harbor. Aboard, Sigmund Freud reportedly turned to fellow psychoanalyst Carl Jung and said, "don't they know we're bringing them the plague?" A fortnight later, Freud delivered five lectures at Clark University and sealed the international status of psychoanalysis. How, then, could Freud, having coined the word only 15 years previously, boldly compare psychoanalysis to a plague? Given that the vocabulary of contemporary popular culture has become suffused with phrases such as the "Ego," "fetish," and "unconscious," what is still so virulent about psychoanalysis that makes geographers like Steve Pile compare psychoanalytic theory to an "unpleasant experience, just like measles" (Pile 1996: 81)? And why should cultural geographers risk infection, prompting Gillian Rose to report in *The Dictionary of Human Geography* (2001) that "despite its dangers, psychoanalytic theory is being used by some geographers as a critical tool to reinterpret and reconfigure different kinds of geographies" (Rose 2000: 654)?

Unlike the disciplines of Art Criticism or English Literature, thorough engagements with psychoanalysis in Geography have emerged only recently. Pile has argued that most geographers have assumed that psychoanalysis is obsessed with the person(al) and unable to critique cultural-political struggles (1998: 204). And yet, innovative analyses of space and culture pervade many psychoanalytical writings. In the first epigraph, for example, Freud articulates human vulnerability through the ineluctable spatial relations between bodies, psyches, environments, and social relations. The psychoanalytic insistence on the persistence of space in, through, beyond, and between material and psychical ellipses of selves, others, and worlds leads Pile to declare that "[p]sychoanalysis is, after all, a spatial discipline" (1996: 77).

Psychoanalysis is composed of methods, *praxes*, and complex theories revised and contested between and within its various 'schools of thought.' This chapter examines the ways in which differing psychoanalytic approaches have been reinterpreted and used by cultural geographers. Now, French psychoanalyst Jacques Lacan reminds us that "[s]aying it all is literally impossible: words fail" (Lacan 1990: 3). This little chapter will inevitably fail to do justice to the theoretical breadth and intricacies of psychoanalysis and the approaches. Readers are therefore advised to scrutinize the references (and their references) cited ahead.[1] I now turn briefly to consider two premises that made Freud's psychoanalytical discoveries so infectious.

Two Fundamentals of Psychoanalysis[2]

It is often claimed that Freud dealt humanity's pride a third blow. Nicolaus Copernicus discovered that the earth was not the center of the universe. Charles Darwin claimed that humans were biologically more similar to evolved apes than God's creation. Freud ushered in a new mode of science and reflexivity by refusing to equate the mind (Ego) with consciousness by 'discovering' the existence of the dynamic unconscious that could speak.

The unconscious

As an adjective the Freudian unconscious refers to psychical processes that are not subject to consciousness at a given moment. As a noun, the unconscious refers to one of the three "psychical localities" outlined in Freud's first "topographical" theory of the mind composed of the conscious, preconscious, and the unconscious. In this model, the unconscious is not opposed to consciousness but is the radical division and irreducible difference between consciousness and itself. The unconscious is an unrealized discourse from an "Other Scene" beyond space, time, negation, and contradiction. Composed of traumatic prohibitions and cruel injunctions, the unconscious comprises repressed painful "ideational representatives" – signifiers and memories usually of a sexual nature. The unconscious is not (as is commonly supposed) a hidden repository of wild emotions or improper urges. The unconscious *pulsates from within* everyday consciousness and emerges when 'things go wrong.' It speaks capriciously and stubbornly through distortions or symptoms exemplified by dreams and slips of the tongue. Freud eventually developed a "structural" theory of the psyche composed of three interrelated "agencies": the negotiating Ego that adapts to and guides reality; the censorious Super-Ego constituted by parental prohibitions and demands; and the chaotic Id associated with illicit drives.

The drive

Freud argued that human pleasure and procreation do not coincide easily. In contrast to the biological and innate attributes of "instinct," Freud argued that a psychical montage of "drives" coordinated human sexuality. Distinct from natural functions and independent from a particular object of satisfaction, the drives are highly variable and determined by our cultural and historical backgrounds. Freud contended that sexuality was connected to the unconscious and emerged once the drive was isolated from natural functions. Freud asserted that perversity (fetishism, same sex desire, and masturbation) was the condition of sexuality *per se* and constituted infantile sexuality. According to Freud, babies lack a self-image of a unified body and a predetermined sexual object choice. Babies are "polymorphously perverse" – composed of multiple bodily erotogenic zones that exist prior to cultural naturalization. Freud radically announced that "all human beings are capable of making a homosexual object-choice and have in fact made one in their unconscious" (Freud 1975: 11).

Approaching Psychoanalytic Geography

When Freud elucidates psychoanalytic concepts he usually unravels their unique spatialities. In *Civilization and Its Discontents* (1961: 17), for example, Freud discusses the preservation of "memory-traces" using the analogy of the "history of the Eternal City": Rome (see also Pile 1996: 241–3). *Civilization and Its Discontents* is Freud's most sustained psychoanalytic critique of Western culture's cultivation of anxiety, guilt, and enmity. Freud discusses tensions between necessary repression, social harmony, and individual aggressivity. He counterposes the biblical injunction "Thou shalt love thy neighbor as thyself" with the Latin dictum "man is a wolf to man" (1961: 65–9), and concludes the essay with somber speculations on the menacing auspices of Hitler and Fascism.

Clearly, psychoanalysis is not a kind of *psyche*analysis – restricted to the analyses of interior minds on indoor couches (see Bondi 1999). The unconscious is *outside* (Lacan 1998: 131) *qua* the symbolic and material cultures of malls, magazines, and monuments. Transference – the displacement of affect from one idea or person to another – moves in mysterious ways across these pages, down optic cables, resonating in the lives and lines of movie stars and fans, politicians and voters, taxi drivers and passengers. Even fantasies reside in airplane safety instructions that depict passengers in postcrash scenarios "like a nice collective lagoon holiday . . . under the guidance of an experienced swimming instructor" (Žižek 1999: 91).

Psychoanalysis, then, lures cultural geographers because its categories are already thoroughly spatial providing theoretical orientation to examine complex cultural practices, identities, discourses, and landscapes. Freudian and psychoanalytic space is precariously and terminally liminal, swarming amidst the porosity of borders, spectrality of objects, and the uncanniness of the familiar. Moreover, psychoanalysis enables geographers to theorize space itself by showing how spaces of cultural difference teem with recurrent forces of pain, destruction, and aggressivity borne out of psychical conflicts and deficiencies.

Reproaching Psychoanalytic Geography

Do not get carried away though! Psychoanalysis, the "universalizing, decorporealized, and culturally decontextualized account of psychosexual development" (Blum

& Nast 1996: 571) has been justifiably submitted to numerous *cultural* critiques. For many scholars, psychoanalysis enforces patriarchal reinscriptions of the 'feminine,' normative, heterosexist structures of gender, repressive understandings of power and subjectivity, and disavows its geographical and historical biases for studying predominantly Western white bourgeois nuclear families. These charges are serious but extremely valuable in making psychoanalytic approaches in geography more vigilant and responsible. The 'bad press' that psychoanalysis occasionally gets, however, is usually symptomatic of valuable critical engagements rather than an inherent inability to explicate various cultural geographies.

Similarly, in *The Body and the City: Psychoanalysis, Space, and Subjectivity* (1996), Pile cautions that psychoanalytic concepts cannot "be easily transposed into, superimposed onto, or mapped alongside, geography – regardless of the kind of geography" (1996: 81). Pile bemoans that when geographers have found it expedient to acknowledge psychoanalysis they have usually misunderstood or simply ignored its theoretical premises. Pile notes that despite a mutual interest in perception, behavior, and the mind, the subdiscipline of behavioral geography did not engage with psychoanalysis. Premised on a "black box" model of the mind and a disbelief in the dynamic unconscious, Pile argues that behavioral geography was ultimately unable to specify exactly how the mind worked in its interaction with the phenomenal environment.

Pile observes that in the late 1970s and early 1980s, most critiques of behavioral geography came from 'humanistic' and 'radical' geographers. The former (influenced by phenomenology) examined cultural symbolic meanings, and the latter (influenced by Marxism) critiqued cultural power structures. Attempting to go beyond the "conscious, observable, known world" (1996: 73), both humanistic and radical geography addressed the question of human subjectivity and agency. Pile argues, however, that nonpsychoanalytic investment in the category of "experience," the binary of "structure and agency," and an assumption that cultural meanings were transparently communicable limited their critiques.

Pile's book is a fascinating and extremely useful introduction to psychoanalysis and geography that also offers strategies to critically understand subjectivity and spatialities of the body in urban contexts. Pile triangulates Henri Lefebvre's formula of "spatial practice, representation of space, and representational space," with Freud's "unconscious, preconscious, and conscious," and Lacan's "Real, Imaginary, and Symbolic" (1996: 155). Pile also addresses the political possibilities of various approaches to a "psychoanalysis of space" (1996: 181), and it is to these various psychoanalytic approaches within geography that I now turn.

Freudian Approaches

Dream spaces

Dreams – and cities – remain the guardians of the moderns' sleep: an elaborate play of remembering and forgetting; showing and disguising. (Pile 2000: 83–4)

In "Freud, Dreams and Imaginative Geographies," Pile sets up a "dialogue between Freud's ideas and the ways in which geography is imagined" (Pile 1998: 205). Dreams for Freud are the "royal road to the unconscious" and prove the mind is split between consciousness and restless creativity. According to Pile, Freud did not need to revise his theory of dreams presented in *The Interpretation of Dreams* (1965) because of "the way in which he thought *spatially* about the mind" (1998: 206).

Freud understands dreams as the "[disguised] fulfillment of a [suppressed or repressed] wish" and "the guardians of sleep" (Pile 1998: 209). Dreams guard sleep by staging *disguised* situations that dramatize wishes. The transcription process of "dream-work" involves "condensation, displacement, the means of representation and secondary revision" (1998: 209). Images – the "manifest content" of dreams are composed of symbols that condense a vast array of contradictory meanings – the dream's "latent thought." Pile contends that Freudian "dream space" is not a "container" but rather a connective medium of "associative paths" (1998: 211) composed of psychical "density and intensity produced by their location in the interweaving of thought, feelings, and meanings" (Pile 1998: 211). The process of "displacement" transfers or partially censors the intensity of psychical investments through relocation. Using spatial analogies and relationships, dreams displace psychical intensity by investing and overdetermining "seemingly meaningless images with apparently inexplicable feelings" (1998: 212). Pile (1998: 213) declares "there is a geography to dreams" where "locality is almost a paradigm for dreams" blending dreaming and waking life. Pile describes the personal and cultural geographies of desire, identity, meaning, and power in a dream documented by Freud as follows:

> the desire for sex which produced the dream of the policeman, the church and the landscape is located within a web of meanings which have 'anchoring points' not only in a fantasized topography of the male and female body and also in the imaginative spatiality of fucking (as a number of steps, whether peaceable or difficult), but also in the social construction of the male body as active (like a person) and the female body as passive (like a landscape) and also in the social relations of marriage, sexuality, religion, work, class, criminality and morality. (Pile 1998: 213)

Dream spaces are networks under constant erasure and revision that rework causality through "collocation, juxtaposition, fragmentation . . . recomposition, reversals . . . [and] spatial analogies" (Pile 1998: 215). Freud's "spatial thinking," specifically his theory of "dream-work" allows Pile to conceptualize imaginative geographies of interior and exterior worlds articulated in Edward Said's understanding of "Orientalism." The Orient is an imagined colonized place, produced discursively through stories and stereotypes as Europe's "collective day-dream" (Said quoted in Pile 1998: 222). Orientalism "allowed the West to dream of adventures, sexual encounters, fame and fortune – and of Empire" (1998: 222). Overinvested with meaning and echoing the process of dream-work, imaginative geographies dramatize differences of meanings by localizing and distancing the East from the West through displacement.

The Dreamcity

In "Sleepwalking in the Modern City: Walter Benjamin and Sigmund Freud in the World of Dreams," Pile (2000) contends that urban spaces are comparable to dreams (see also Robinson 1998). Pile examines Walter Benjamin's use of dream analysis in *One Way Street*, written in 1925. Benjamin aims to "induce a shock that would wake up the [alienated] moderns" (Pile 2000: 79) from a culture that fetishizes commodities. Benjamin fans revolutionary sparks in writing about the "dreamhouses of modernity" (2000: 79) – restless urban spaces exemplified by derelict Parisian arcades. Similarly, Pile's notion of a "Dreamcity" conceals fears and desires through its "dreamcity-work" or "unconscious logics" that produce "seemingly desireless, fearless, and absurd elements" (2000: 84). Pile contends that there is "no one dream that articulates the city, nor one aspect of the city that defines its dreaming" (2000: 84). That Pile acknowledges that someone's dream may be another person's nightmare leads us to examine the possible relationship between the political and psychoanalysis.

Racist Oedipalization

The mapping of incest onto blackness onto the end of civilization itself thus informed bodily and spatial forms of segregation that were culturally, politically, and economically upheld for unconscious and racist familiarized reasons in cities and rural areas across the country. (Nast 2000: 231)

The political and psychoanalytic scope of Heidi Nast's "Mapping the 'Unconscious': Racism and the Oedipal Family" (2000) is prefigured in the article's key words: "family," "racist-oedipal hysteria," "slavery," "unconscious," "urban renewal," and "white supremacy." Nast's paper examines eight "mappings" that include US plantation (post)slavery settings in the south and urban racial segregation in mid-twentieth-century Chicago. Examining cultural practices at various geographic scales, Nast theorizes how "embodied unconscious emotions and desires have impelled the construction of many racist landscapes" (2000: 217).

How can the unconscious be political or even racist? For Nast, an irreducible and incommensurable cultural split between a prelinguistic *imaginary* (infant–maternal relations, practice, ritual, and performance) and a linguistic *symbolic* (law of the father, language, and the spoken) that is *"unconsciously instrumental to modern forms of exploitation"* and "understood as a strategic political geographic device" (Nast 2000: 243). Nast uses "the word 'unconscious' to connote a kind of blinding of oneself to the ways in which the body and desire speaks itself" (2000: 242) through symbolic *and* imaginary spaces. "Oedipal relations" are created and managed to negotiate this traumatic split and also maintain racist "colonial-familial relations instrumental to plantation and industrial capitalism" (2000: 243). Nast's understanding of culture draws on Freud's theories of Oedipal myths that she argues work "precisely because *they are made* to carry out work – just as in any other culture, beliefs and practices repose through mythical tales and places" (2000: 243).

Freud thought culture could only exist once prohibitions deflected incestuous desires away from the family and toward the domain of the "law of the Father." Freud argues that Oedipal desire disappears when the son submits to the law of the Father and displaces maternal desire to female persons outside the maternal body and home. The idealized modern US Oedipal-cultural triad of Mother–Son–Father, Nast argues, is coded white, while the prohibitive incestuous threat – "the Repressed" – is typically "colored" black. The symbolically white mother, then, is unconsciously defined as a vulnerable object of incestuous desire from black "boys"

– carriers of unconscious desires. Accordingly, incest with the white mother was unconsciously racialized and black male exploitation in the US was libidinized. Nast argues that white fears could not be spoken because they were so psychically and culturally repressed in a "labyrinthine maze" of familial desire, political-economy and symbolic necessity. As a result, white fears could only be spoken through the idiom of violence in the reassertion of their supposedly racially superior symbolic fatherhood.

Nast demonstrates how unconscious space is an embodied, structured, libidinized, and violent *sociospatial effect* that emerged "as an embodied spatial effect unevenly across space and time in tandem with European colonialisms across the world" (2000: 215) in the racist and familialized strictures of industrial capitalism. Colonial conquests and violence were sexualized and spatially displaced or repressed by white Oedipal families into the cultural unconscious. During the post-Reconstruction period in the US, black men were lynched and castrated whenever a "mythological black man was seen as potentially touching, approaching, or raping a white woman" (Nast 1999: 217). To compound their subordination to white heteropaternal Oedipal 'law,' enslaved black men were infantilized. Through the denial of a last name and interpellations of "son" and "boy," black slaves were controlled yet feared members of a white cultural family.

Nast's argument is powerful and instructive. First, we read how the dynamic unconscious is materialized in cultural practices and meanings. Second, her psychoanalytic approach differs from Marxian analyses of "capitalist logics" in ideology by examining the "illogical rages and actions" to provide a potentially "greater explanatory force to 'race'" (2000: 217). Third, Nast's paper challenges the belief that simply modifying the causal relation between cultural landscapes and psyches can easily solve heterosexism and racism. Finally, Nast argues that potentially racist and colonial forces implicit in Freud's theorizations of Oedipal drama must be acknowledged to avoid further compliance with racism.

Uncanny landscapes and sexed cities
Robert Wilton's "The Constitution of Difference: Space and Psyche in Landscapes of Exclusion" examines how cultural relations may be "troubled by the proximity of difference" (1998: 176). Wilton uses Freud's notion of the "uncanny" that designates feelings and things that are unsettling but involve the reappearance of unusually familiar elements from unconscious concealment. Wilton chooses a psychoanalytic approach because "existing [urban] studies fail to adequately conceptualize the origins of people's behavior" (1998: 180). He provides a case study of a 25-bed AIDS hospice in a Los Angeles neighborhood where illness and death deeply disturbs local residents. The effects on the community are uncanny because the hospice symbolized vulnerability and mortality, "supposedly the very antithesis of the living body and yet something which people find disturbingly familiar" (1998: 181).

In "Sexing the City" (1998), Liz Bondi argues that feminist interpretations of urban landscapes relying on the nonpsychoanalytic distinction between gender and sex generally close off questions of sex, sexuality, and sexual practice (see also Nast 1998). Bondi contrasts this "sex-free" tendency, where heterosexuality appears as an integral part of considerations of gender identity, with gay and lesbian studies of the city that critique hegemonic forms of heterosexuality. Arguing that gender is "far more complex than implied by the categories 'women' and 'men'" (1998: 178),

Bondi's feminist approach utilizes a Freudian perspective of feminine and masculine identities that "are more like masks or fictions we create in order to sustain myths about our subjective integrity, which we need to operate within our rule-governed social milieus" (1998: 183). Bondi analyzes the cultural politics of gentrification and prostitution in neighborhoods of Edinburgh, Scotland.

Object-relations Theory

The main proponents of object-relations theory were Michael Balint, Donald W. Winnicott, and W. R. D. Fairbairn. The theory was established in England during the interwar years and became one of the most prominent post-Freudian psycho-analytic approaches. Object-relations theory includes a number of theoretical points of view, but generally deemphasizes the role of the drive by focusing on the embod-ied intersubjective formation of the psyche in relation to 'objects.' These objects of mediation include mothers, fathers, fantasies, toys, and parts of the body (typically breasts, fingers, and mouths) oscillating between the external environment of the "not me" and the child's internalized mental representations. Psychical boundaries are installed to separate good (sources of comfort) and bad (anxiety-provoking) objects to prevent the dissolution of the self. Objects, however, sometimes embody good and bad qualities, as is exemplified by the primary caretaker, usually codified as the mother who provides and withdraws love. Furthermore, introjection, the evaluation of the self or ego by living through and taking in objects, may be con-tinuous and excessive so that the child 'disappears' into a dependent relation with objects. Projection is the attribution of feelings, typically love and hate, to other objects, and can be excessively hostile and impair the child's capacity for empathy (Sibley 1995: 6).

Geographies of exclusion

The construction of community and the bounding of social groups are part of the same problem as the separation of self and other. Collective expressions of fears of others, for example, call on images which constitute bad objects for the self and thus contribute to the definition of the self. (Sibley 1995: 15)

In *Geographies of Exclusion: Society and Difference in the West* (1995), David Sibley endorses an object-relations approach to cultural analyses and notes that Melanie Klein views the "emerging sense of the border, of separateness and self, as a social and cultural process" (1995: 6). Sibley maps cultural geographies of the discrepant – composed of exclusion, rejection, purification, transgression, and distancing – "between the inner (pure) self and the outer (defiled) self" (1995: 7). According to Sibley, these geographies collapse public and private spheres, and amplify binaries between cultural 'selves' and 'others.' In this way, dominant cul-tural groups attempt to consolidate power by marginalizing the threats of 'others' exemplified by the elderly, disabled, women, criminals, blacks, gays, and children.

"Geographies of exclusion" mobilize cultural stereotypes of 'good selves' and 'bad others.' Sibley uses examples of photographs of gypsies labeled as "criminal types" and the European regulation of colonial and racial spaces through the moral use of the color black to codify disease and shame, and white to codify innocence and safety. Similarly, Sibley's chapter "Mapping the Pure and Defiled" demonstrates how modern media represents cultures of vulnerability and threat. Examples include television advertisements that portray the vulnerability of a child in the "defiled environment of New York City" (1995: 63) and the wild behavior of children requiring the civilizing effects of detergent, mothers, and the home. Sibley uses the same arguments in his Part II, "The Exclusion of Geographies," to analyze the exclusion of "academics as subjects" who were considered to possess dangerous knowledge. Focusing on the urban sociological studies of W. E. B. Dubois, Sibley shows how "processes of social segregation observable in the modern city, for example, are mirrored in the segregation of producers" (1995: xvi).

Transitional spaces and potential places

Characterizing children as *other* is a particularly thorny problem. (Aitken & Herman 1997: 63)

Stuart Aitken and Thomas Herman's "Gender, Power, and Crib Geography: Transitional Spaces and Potential Places" (1997) attempts to contribute to post-Enlightenment thought by offsetting the tendency to privilege "reason, logic, orderly development" over "frivolity, intuition, emotion, discursive practice, holistic acceptance and collective experience" (1997: 64). Aitken and Herman argue that Winnicott's (1971) concept of "transitional space" – the nonlinear, playful, intuitive, and experimental space that blurs distinctions between self and object and the space from which culture emerges – can illuminate understandings of children's identity formation without serving adults and patriarchy. They argue that Winnicott's ideas parallel Lefebvre's and diverge from the objective distancing and compartmentalizing tendencies of Freud, Lacan, and Jean Piaget, which "[fails] to place the emotional, feeling and playing child within an irreducible web of cultural meaning" (1997: 67). For Aitken and Herman, "what may be missing in geography and child development studies is attention to the ways that play, culture, racial identities and gender formations are conflated within transitional spaces" (1997: 75). "Crib Geography" poses the following questions:

How can we, as adults, imagine the place of children? It is possible to see ourselves in our children and we can relive some of our own childhood pains and joys through them, but can we fully appreciate the nuances that comprise a child's world? (1997: 64)

These questions are examined in various Western cultural contexts that include adult controlled spaces and designed built environments that belie a dogma of supervision, protection, and behavioral training of children (see also Aitken 2001). They note that the "seemingly neutral space" (1997: 80) of crib, bedroom spaces, and institutions of childcare centers, homeless shelters, residential psychiatric wards, are cultures underpinned by unquestioned adult authority and white, middle-class values. Aitken and Herman caution against using a psychoanalytic approach to reconceptualize play and culture. They assert that Freud's "instinct theory" [*sic*] means "psychoanalytical theory is inherently depoliticizing" (1997: 71), while "Winnicott may be complicit with a patriarchal idealization of child development" (1997: 82).[3] We may now consider how geographers use a Lacanian approach to negotiate another thorny issue – gender and psychoanalysis.

Lacanian Approaches

Lacan has emerged as one of the most influential and original psychoanalytic the-orists since Freud and is immensely popular in film, gender, and cultural studies. Lacan's work, however, is often debunked for its dense elliptical style or provoca-tive statements such as "the unconscious is structured like a language," and "there is no such thing as a sexual relationship." The clinical dimension and conceptual variations in Lacan's 50 years of work (most of which has not been translated into English), however, have been overlooked by most Anglo-American scholars.

Lacan's complex concepts, such as the "phallus," "mirror stage," "*objet petit a*," and "*jouissance*" revolutionized psychoanalytic debates over theory and practice. Lacan challenges other psychoanalytic approaches (most notably object-relations theory and Ego psychology) through his "return to the meaning of Freud" and recast-ing of concepts such as displacement and condensation into linguistic equivalents (metaphor and metonymy). Lacan's theory of the registers is arguably the most con-stant reference throughout his entire work. Lacan argues that psychic life is coordi-nated by dynamic interconnections between the "Imaginary" (image, illusion, deception, seduction, meaning, alienation, luring, and rivalry), the "Symbolic" (lan-guage, universality, absence, death, and lack), and the "Real" (trauma, indetermi-nate, unknowable, anxiety, impossibility). One reason for Lacan's popularity is how his theoretical insights prefigure the predominant psychodynamics of fantasy, nar-cissism, and the visual in modern Western culture (see Blum & Nast 2000: 183, 200).

Shopping with Lacan

The subfield "geographies of consumption" echoes Lacanian psychoanalysis with its interest in cultures of self-actualization, images, fetishism, spectacle, and plea-sure. In "Once-upon-a-Time in the Commodity World: An Unofficial Guide to Mall of America" (1999), Jon Goss argues that Mall of America's spaces of nature, col-lective myth, individual fantasy, and memory fulfill vital cultural and psychological functions. Goss critically aligns the Lacanian Real with the Mall's "specks of dirt," that betray its illusion of semiotic perfection and exploitative relations of produc-tion (1999: 72), and the Lacanian Symbolic to facilitate understandings of com modity fetishism that do not

misperceive objects as reifications of social relations, or that relations between things displace relations between people, although this is true, but rather that complex relations between people and things, or better, people-things, are constitutive parts of the symbolic order. (1999: 71)

Following the psychoanalytically inflected writings of Benjamin and Lefebvre, and Slavoj Žižek's Lacanian rendering of ideology (1997), Goss approaches com-modity fetishism by neither conceiving the consumer as dupe nor asking "what The Mall really is, to seek 'the real' beneath the 'plague of fantasies.'" Instead, Goss wants to "take pleasure [*jouissance*] [*sic*] in the play of reality and fantasy, while critically examining how we actually believe in this distinction" (1999: 49).

Lacan 'for' feminism

What if this real, this claim that there is a real space, itself depends on desire, is itself an imagined fantasy? . . . Whose desire, whose space would this be? Who would it constitute? Who would dwell in it, and how? (Rose 1996: 62, emphasis in original)

Three French feminists, Hélène Cixous, Julia Kristeva, and Luce Irigaray, appropriated psychoanalytic theoretical premises to expose the systematic repression of feminine and maternal experiences and the undue bias toward masculinity in Western thought. Lacan was openly hostile to feminism and ridiculed its political aspirations. Yet some feminists (including geographers) have found Lacan's theories useful to subvert binary conceptions of innate and fixed gender differences by emphasizing their precarious psychical-linguistic dimensions constituted by patriarchal culture.

In "As if the Mirrors had Bled: Masculine Dwelling, Masculinist Theory and Feminist Masquerade" (1996), Gillian Rose situates her writing in " 'a between' between us, an around, a space, in order to initiate a dialogue" (1996: 61) with Irigaray – a practicing analyst and former student of Lacan. Irigaray's notion of the "imaginary" that conflates the symbolic, bodily, and cultural, enables Rose to question the masculinist insistence by geographers "to distinguish between real and non-real space" (1996: 62). Rose (1995) also draws on Lacan's notions of "the gaze" and "symbolic castration" to theorize the fragility inherent to masculine cultural understandings of visualized spaces of self/knowledge and the politics of representation therein.

Jenny Robinson's article "Feminism and the Spaces of Transformation" (2000) draws on the work of Kristeva, who "encourages us to read psychoanalytic narratives within a sociohistorical frame, and to question their gendered assumptions" (2000: 297). Robinson illustrates Kristeva's insistence that the Symbolic (cultural relations and practices) can be "shattered" and that "the semiotic" and "abjection" can provide a conceptual basis to show "the persistent *failure* of borders, distinctions and separations" (2000: 296).

Bondi (1997) asserts, in "In Whose Words? On Gender Identities, Knowledge and Writing Practices," that despite Lacan's antifeminism, androcentricism, and chauvinism, he offers "a strategy of unsettling patriarchal practices from a position self-consciously within that heritage" (1997: 251) that "undercuts men's as well as women's claims to authoritative speaking positions" (1997: 253–4). In "Jacques Lacan's Two-dimensional Subjectivity" (2000), Blum and Nast have deftly argued that "Lacan's analysis of human subjectivity is flawed" (2000: 200) because it privileges the visual, suppresses the material-maternal body, relies on "normative heterosexuality," restricts the world to "a closed system of mirror and phallus" (2000: 201), and reduces infantile sexual alterity "through renouncing the mother's body" (2000: 185). Nonetheless, they conclude that Lacan still presents geographers with important theoretical orientations to renegotiate heteropatriarchy and spatial oppressions (see also Blum 1998; Blum & Nast 1996). Moreover, psychoanalysis still presents geographers with important opportunities to interrogate what is meant by "culture."

Conclusion: *More* Psychoanalytic Approaches?

Hopefully, the epigraph where Lacan compares the unconscious with Baltimore appears less peculiar now. Psychoanalysis does not so much blur boundaries between inner and outer as it explicates how supposed intimate inner spaces are inhabited by supposed alien outer and vice versa. The unconscious, for example, is thus externally materialized in everyday cultural contexts, "or to quote *The X Files* motto: 'The truth is out there'" (Žižek 1999: 89). Geographers choose psychoanalytic approaches because they show how the restrictive binaries (self versus other, material versus ideal, and subjective versus objective) that are operationalized in culture are always out of sync. Psychoanalysis enables powerful *critical explanations* at various geographic scales of seemingly irrational or normative cultures of sexism, racism, and economic exploitation configured in 'human, all too-human' geographies of fear, violence, and fantasy.

Nonetheless, more intensive psychoanalytic approaches are possible. To be sure, "[t]he size and complexity of the field make any engagement with psychoanalysis appear somewhat daunting" (Pile, quoted in Wilton 1998: 183), and sometimes "[i]t still feels like musing, all this talk of dreams" (Pile 2000: 85). The complexity of psychoanalysis and the potential radicalism of psychoanalytic approaches have for the most part been compromised. Many cultural geographers have relied heavily on secondary literatures that often assimilate versions of psychoanalysis conforming to understandings of culture *qua* the deconstructive effects of deferred (con)textual signification or constructive discursive practices, rather than the *psychospatial* vicissitudes of the unconscious, fantasy, and desire (see Callard 2003; Kingsbury 2003). Little wonder, then, that for most cultural geographers the writings of Jacques Derrida and Michel Foucault have appeared more palatable and easier to understand than the writings of Freud or Lacan.

NOTES

1. Readers are also advised to read the *Journal of Social & Cultural Geography*, vol. 4 (2003), a theme issue on 'Psychoanalytic Geographies' published just before this book went to press.
2. Cf. Lacan 1998.
3. Aitken and Herman repeat the standard mistake of failing to distinguish between Freud's words *Trieb* (drive) and *Instinkt* (instinct). Psychoanalysis can be 'inherently' politicizing (see Nast 2000; Kingsbury 2003; Žižek 1997, 1999).

REFERENCES

Aitken, S. 2001: *Geographies of Young People: The Morally Contested Spaces of Identity.* London and New York: Routledge.

Aitken, S. and Herman, T. 1997: Gender, power and crib geography: transitional spaces and potential places. *Gender, Place and Culture: A Journal of Feminist Geography* 4(1), 63–88.

Blum, V. 1998: Ladies and Gentleman: train rides and other Oedipal stories. In H. Nast and S. Pile, eds., *Places Through the Body*. New York: Routledge, 263–80.

Blum, V. and Nast, H. 1996: Where's the difference? The heterosexualization of alterity in Henri Lefebvre and Jacques Lacan. *Environment and Planning D: Society and Space* 14, 559–80.

Blum, V. and Nast, H. 2000: Jacques Lacan's two-dimensional subjectivity. In M. Crang and N. Thrift, eds., *Thinking Space*. New York: Routledge, 183–204.

Bondi, L. 1997: In whose words? On gender identities, knowledge and writing practices. *Transactions of the Institute of British Geographers* 22, 245–58.

Bondi, L. 1998: Sexing the city. In R. Fincher and J. Jacobs, eds., *Cities of Difference*. New York: Guildford, 177–99.

Bondi, L. 1999: Stages on journeys: some remarks about human geography and psychotherapeutic practice. *The Professional Geographer* 51, 11–24.

Callard, F. 2003: The taming of psychoanalysis in geography. *Social & Cultural Geography* 4, 295–312.

Freud, S. 1961: *Civilization and Its Discontents*. New York: W. W. Norton.

Freud, S. 1962: *Three Essays on the Theory of Sexuality*. New York: Basic Books.

Freud, S. 1963: *Character and Culture*. New York: Macmillan.

Freud, S. 1965: *The Interpretation of Dreams*. New York: Avon.

Goss, J. 1999: Once-upon-a-Time in the Commodity World: An Unofficial Guide to Mall of America. *Annals of the Association of American Geographers* 89, 45–75.

Johnston, R. J., Gregory, D., Pratt, G., and Watts, M. 2001: *The Dictionary of Human Geography*. Oxford: Blackwell.

Kingsbury, P. 2003: Psychoanalysis, a gay spatial science? *Social & Cultural Geography* 4, 347–67.

Lacan, J. 1972: Of structure as an inmixing of an Otherness prerequisite to any subject whatever. In R. Macksey and E. Donato, eds., *The Structuralist Controversy: The Languages of Criticism and the Sciences of Man*. Baltimore: Johns Hopkins Press, 186–200.

Lacan, J. 1977: *The Four Fundamental Concepts of Psychoanalysis: The Seminar of Jacques Lacan, Book XI*, tr. A. Sheridan. New York: W. W. Norton.

Lacan, J. 1990: *Television/A Challenge to the Psychoanalytic Establishment*. New York: W. W. Norton.

Nast, H. 1998: Unsexy geographies. *Gender, Place and Culture* 5, 191–206.

Nast, H. 2000: Mapping the "unconscious": racism and the oedipal family. *Annals of the Association of American Geographers* 90, 215–55.

Pile, S. 1996: *The Body and the City: Psychoanalysis, Space, and Subjectivity*. New York: Routledge.

Pile, S. 1998: Freud, dreams, and imaginative geographies. In A. Elliott, ed., *Freud 2000*. New York: Routledge, 204–34.

Pile S. 2000: Sleepwalking in the modern city: Walter Benjamin and Sigmund Freud in the world of dreams. In G. Bridge and S. Watson, eds., *A Companion to the City*. Oxford: Blackwell, 75–86.

Robinson, J. 1998: (Im)mobilizing space – dreaming of change. In H. Judin and I. Vadislavic, eds., *Blank ____: Architecture, Apartheid and After*. Rotterdam: Netherlands Architecture Institute, 163–71.

Robinson, J. 2000: Feminism and the spaces of transformation. *Transactions of the Institute of British Geographers* 25, 285–301.

Rose, G. 1995. Distance, surface, elsewhere: a feminist critique of the space of phallocentric self/knowledge. *Environment and Planning D: Society and Space* 13, 761–81.

Rose, G. 1996. As if the mirrors had bled: masculine dwelling, masculinist theory and feminine masquerade. In N. Duncan, ed., *BodySpaces*. New York: Routledge, 56–74.

Rose, G. 2000: Psychoanalytic theory and geography. In R. J. Johnston, D. Gregory, G. Pratt, and M. Watts, eds., *The Dictionary of Human Geography*, 4th ed. Malden, MA: Blackwell Publishing, 653–5.

Sibley, D. 1995: *Geographies of Exclusion: Society and Difference in the West*. New York: Routledge.

Wilton, R. D. 1998: The constitution of difference: space and psyche in landscapes of exclusion. *Geoforum* 29, 173–85.

Winnicott, D. W. 1971: *Playing and Reality*. London: Tavistock.

Žižek, S. 1997: *The Plague of Fantasies*. London: Verso.

Žižek, S. 1999: *The Žižek Reader*. Oxford: Blackwell.

Chapter 9

Performance and Performativity: A Geography of Unknown Lands

Nigel Thrift

This my hand will rather
The multitudinous seas incarnadine
Making the green one red.
Thomas De Quincy

Bow, stubborn knees and heart with strings of steel
Be soft as sinews of the new-born babe
Hamlet 3.3.70–1

Crying is a puzzler.
Charles Darwin 1838

Introduction: An Awkward Perspective

I take it as axiomatic that cultural geography has lost its way. A particular picture of the world has held it captive, a picture based on just a few brushstrokes: a stubbornly humanist metaphysics, the repeated application of methodologies that just confirm that world's existence, and a politics which still attempts to take the moral high ground. The result, at least, is clear. Cultural geography has become intellectual work as usual, cutting itself off from its radical origins.

But there is another way. In this chapter, I will sketch out some of the elements of what a revivified cultural geography might look like, one not based just on the academic grind of text and countertext but on an ethos of constant experimentation across many registers of experience in a world "saturated with phenomena," to use Helen Vendler's (1995) pregnant phrase. I will argue that this reformulation requires three main elements, each of which forms a key part of the chapter. One is to recognize the richness of the world. Another is to take an expressively formed embodiment into our thinking. And the last is to produce a different ethos of engagement with the world.

In each case, what is being attempted is to produce a new kind of political weave to the world, one which attempts to meet despoliation with an ethos of creation rather than just resistance. It is engaged, above all, with forcing new kinds of sur-facings, born out of the burn of raw energy released by making implicit and pow-erful connections (Taussig 1999; Thrift 2002). What is being aimed for, in other words, is a definition of the political which avoids a model of a hallowed ground of politics surrounded by a desert of quietism, in favor of "continuously" political activity woven into the fabric of life.

Such a change of horizon can be located as part of a broader project, which is to finally slough off the perpetually futile but seemingly ever-renewed legacy of thinking of history and geography through totalizing systems, with an utter dis-proportionality between the types of questions posed (most of them by the great systems of Christian theology) and the vaulting types of answers provided as thinkers felt compelled to " 'reoccupy' the 'position' of the medieval Christian schema of creation and eschatology – rather than leave it empty, as a rationality that was aware of its own limits might have done" (Wallace 1983: xx–xxi). In other words, as Hans Blumenberg (1983: 48–9) puts it in his magisterial *The Legitimacy of Modern Reason*, the attempt to "answer a medieval question with the means available to a postmedieval age" is a case of "the wrong tools for the wrong job" (Rabinow 2002: 14). But now we are finally facing up to the fact that we need new forms of more modest theoretical curiosity which are minded to overcome prob-lems in quite different ways. Not coincidentally, such a move requires a reworking of space – as we shall see.

But let me start with a prayer, Jorie Graham's (2000: 36), to be precise.

> What of   the quicksand.
> My desperate eye   looking too hard.
>
> Or the eye   of the world
> looking too hard
>
> for me. Or, if you prefer, *cause*,
>
> looking to take in
> what could be sufficient—
>
> Then the sun goes down   and the sentence
>
> goes out. Recklessly towards the end. Beyond
> the ridge. Wearing us as if lost in
>
> thought with no way
> out, no eye at all to slip through,
>
> none of the hurry or the between-
> hurry thinkings to liquefy,
>
> until it can be laid on a tongue
>
> oh quickness – like a drop. Swallow.
> Rouse says the dark.

The act of prayer. For 40 years or so, that act has been at the center of debate in the social sciences and humanities, ever since Louis Althusser revived Pascal's dictum "kneel down, move your lips in prayer and you will believe" as a means of berat-

ing humanism and moving beyond reading techniques based on the standard rhetorical and semiotic models. As Graham's reworking of fragments from Hölderlin
makes clear, we can now see that numinous historical moment returning in full force
as a series of belated recognitions – of the urgency of thinking materiality anew, of
the importance of technologies of carnality to what we call thinking, and of the
consequent need to instigate another way of proceeding. These three reformulations
will make up the main part of this chapter. Having touched on these reformulations, I will then at least begin the task of showing how they show up in the many
acts of performance and so provide a capacity to know the world from "an *awkward
perspective*" (Hölderlin, cited in Fenves 2001: 1; my emphasis) which cannot, or so
I believe, be easily kept in play in other ways. By way of a conclusion, I will then
touch on what all this might mean for how geography is once it no longer expects
to get its bearings.

The World is Rich

I want to start this process of re-cognition by revisiting the vexed question of *materiality*. For one of the most striking developments of the last few years has been the
series of struggles to make a new compact with this term, partly the result of the
renaissance of a certain kind of vitalism (see May & Thrift 2001), partly the result
of new technological developments which seem to presage a new kind of lightness
to being, and partly the result of a desire to inject a sense of wonder[1] and aston-
ishment back into a world which sometimes seems to have become tarnished by
spectacle.[2] This new sense of materiality challenges a whole series of traditional divisions – between organic and inorganic, science and art, and space and time, for
example – in its hunger to redefine how the world is/could/should be.[3] What are the
chief aspects of this new sense of materiality? I think there are three. The first is
what we might call, following Tiffany (2000), a lyric materiality. It is becoming
commonplace to identify the point at which materialism both breaks free and simultaneously stultifies with Marx's doctoral thesis on Democritus and Epicurus (e.g.
Bennett 2001; Tiffany 2000). In that thesis, Marx half-animates the world. He uses
Epicurean philosophy to show that the "sensuous appearance" of the world is built
into its very character and is not just a subjective impression but then, falling back
on Democritus, he only allows that sensuousness limited play, and so ends up with
a standard philosophical anthropology in which exaltation, enchantment, and
derangement are marked human (some might say all too human). "By the time Marx
gets done with it, the fighting spirit of matter has settled down into the bodies of
men" (Bennett 2001: 120). Marx therefore loses touch with the appreciation of
agency within nature that Epicurus's fundamental atomic property of swerve affirms.

But now there are attempts to reinstate exaltation, enchantment, and derangement back into materialism in a way already prefigured by writers like Walter Benjamin. How does this kind of "aesthetically disposed" materialism differ from the
old materialism? First, it extends the imagination into matter, rather than seeing the
two as separate and distinct, by exploring the poetic dimension. We cannot escape
the fact that our means of depicting the world is bound up with what we take the
world to be. It is not the case that this is just a simple depiction of the real by the
imagination, however. For material substance is:

A medium that is inescapably informed by the pictures that we compose of it. We are confronted with the idea that a material body, insofar as its substance can be defined, is composed of pictures, and that the conventional equation of materialism and realism depends on the viability of the pictures we use to represent an invisible material world. (Tiffany 2000: 9)

And the lyric nature of substance is, if anything, being underlined. Why? Because, at this point in history,

Science becomes rich in visualizing skills and art gains many entries into the object. Fiction is no longer free under the pretext that it would be subjective or impotent, and science is no longer merely "accurate," because to be so it would also need to be unmediated, unsituated and unhistorical. (Latour 1999: 428)

And this tendency can only expand as more and more of the practices of science, spurred on by powerful technical media, rely on imagining the invisible (Ede 2000).

A second aspect of the new materiality that is inherent in the lyric is what we might call a sense of wonder. Fisher (1998) argues that wonder disrupts ordinary narrative expectations by producing sudden experiences in an instant of time in which all details are present at once in a kind of spatial crowding. The everyday is shuffled and displaced by a rare or even singular and utterly compelling event. It is therefore something more than surprise, because "wonder does not depend on awakening and then surprising expectation, but on the complete absence of expectation" (p. 21). Again, wonder is something more than the by now overly familiar notion of shock; "shock is a rejuvenation within fatigued systems of representation and thought. That is why the classical and religious mind of Baudelaire gave us our greatest poet of the aesthetics of shock. With shock we face the all or nothing, the Russian roulette of a mind or a system at the end of its rope" (p. 5). Rather, wonder is a kind of local intelligibility, as Fisher (1998: 9), in a wonderful passage, makes clear.

Socrates insisted that to know what it is that we do not know is the humbling first step of true knowledge. We need to add that the impossibility of knowing any such thing is one of the things that strikes us when we look closely at the reasoning and science of the past, even in the moments of its greatest accomplishments . . . When we look at the history of successful explanation and ask how it could be that it remained undamaged by the unreliable tools, unavailable technology, hidden errors carried on through the entire project of thought, inadequate basic terminology, sectors of ignorance built in like blank spots on a map and sometimes taking up 90 per cent of the map itself, then we can see just how fruitful the idea of local intelligibility is as the necessary alternative to certain knowledge. Defective but still manageable rationality is what we actually have to use to make sense of the objects of our curiosity.

Wonder drives and sustains the defective rationality that gives us intelligibility under conditions where we will not even know that we have reached certain knowledge when and if we have.

A third aspect of the new materiality I will call involution, calling to mind the great and interlinked dream metaphors that De Quincy called "involutes" that reveal new connections, making the green one red. Nowadays, this aspect of materiality is often tagged as neobaroque, bringing to mind a tradition of conceiving of complexity that reaches back to Whitehead and finds its current keenest exponent in the works of Benjamin (1985) and Deleuze (1993). In this tradition, the world appears as a heap of highly significant fragments (somewhat akin to Leibnizian monads), rather than a seamless web which adds up to a superorganic whole. This is a constantly fluctuating world of the side-by-side existence of mutually exclusive realities, realities in turbulent motion forming short-lived patterns with each other – when patterns exist at all. The "emancipation of dissonance" (Kwa 2002) that results from such a vision emphasizes the creative aspect of the world in its attention to the swerve. In the neobaroque tradition, then, the world is contingent and complex, a space for opportunities and events. This is the opposite of the view that sees general laws in every single local instance and event for "when we cannot predict the future course of a complex system, it is not because we don't know enough. The world is uncertain. Uncertainty in the baroque case is ontological rather than epistemological" (Kwa 2002: 47).

This new sense of materiality takes the world into new territories. To begin with, it takes the poetics of metaphor seriously, where metaphor is not taken to be something cozy and familiar but what Husserl once called a "resistance to harmony" which is also simultaneously an act of restitution. It strains against both disciplined experience and the objective univocity of certain kinds of abstraction in that it contains more than it is selected for. As Blumenberg (1997: 84–5) so brilliantly puts it,

This is the model of what is claimed for hermeneutics, but in this case it runs in the opposite direction: interpretation does not enrich the text beyond what the author consciously puts into it; rather, the alien relationship flows unpredictably into the production of texts. Metaphor's imprecision, now scorned in the rigorous self-sharpening of theoretical language, corresponds in a different way to the maximal abstraction of such concepts as "Being," "History," "World," which have not ceased to impress us. However metaphor retains the wealth of its heritage, which abstraction must deny.

Then, the new sense of materiality takes investments of affective energy in objects seriously. So, for example, the investment of such energy in commodities is no longer peremptorily dismissed as fetishism. It does not only entail a kind of mindless amusement but all kinds of pleasurable affirmations. More importantly, objects become elements of ethologies which can go wild, making new paths and clusters, distributing themselves as key parts of various passions (Attfield 2000).

And, to finish up, the new sense of materiality necessarily involves itself in trying to trace out the political unconscious of the material world as a kind of performative agency in the shape of those physical automatisms, based on the mimetic dimension, which provide most of our grounding in the world. These "lyrics" – a host of historically contingent expressions, with their attendant traumas, joys, and conversions – are "songlines" which are now drawn on not just media like the body and the movement of air but also the screen and the mundane para-ethnographic apparatus of such incessant and insistent objects as networks of pipes, families of formulae and clearing systems (Marcus 2002; Riles 2002).

Thinking Embodiment

Again, what we can take from the example of Graham's prayer is the need to be careful not to assume that the message is the be-all and end-all of life. In a certain sense, the medium really is the message in that if the body conforms then the doctrine follows on, as Bourdieu, in Pascalian vein, so often demonstrated (e.g. Bourdieu 1999). Belief is about sedimenting the body.

But, more than that, her careful mixing of metaphors also shows the importance of questioning what is meant by the body. Thus, recent work has tended to radically undermine the idea that the body is a finished organic whole beginning or ending at the wall of skin. Rather, the body is seen as a set of interdependent associations or interactions or populations, stressing commonality over isolation, which are born out of the force, even vehemence (Fisher 2002), of expression as *embodiment*. And this really does mean commonality out of force. So, to begin with, embodiment is a set of spatially and temporally distributed series: body a-whereness rather than body awareness. It consists of the differential flow of a particular kind of constantly moving carnality which has its reasons and its modes of reasoning, but these are not necessarily cognitively framed. Modern dance has often tried to make this point by arranging moving bodies in such a way that "disconnected movements can take off and develop at the same time in the same body" (Gil 2002: 118–19), inducing the simultaneous superposition of multiple positions in time and space, proliferating articulations which demonstrate that movement can become its own motivation. Take the case of Merce Cunningham. He

decomposes gestures in the balancing act of the body-in-movement, so that the nexus of positions of bodily parts is no longer that of an organic body. One could even say that to each of the simultaneously held positions there corresponds a different body. (Organic, yes, but out of the multiplicity of organic virtual bodies that constitute one same body there emerges an impossible body, a sort of monstrous body: this is the virtual body.) This body prolongs gesture into virtuality since what follows from gesture can no longer be perceived by and in an empirical, actual body.

It follows that there is no single body, like the "proper" body of phenomenology, but rather multiple bodies. (Gil 2002: 123)

Then, embodiment does not just consist of the particular consistencies of flesh. It is radically extended by tools of various kinds which are an integral part of what we call humanity, rather than being something set to one side of individual human bodies as means through which these bodies attain various goals and meanings (Leroi-Gourhan 1983). Gradually, the human has come to consist of more and more "body parts" – and more and more wordly "counterparts" – each learning to affect the other. As Latour (1999: 147) puts it, "the pair human–nonhuman does not involve a tug-of-war between two opposite forces. On the contrary, the more activity there is from one, the more activity there is from the other." Because of this active intermediation, intersubjectivity must be seen as much as an outcome of capture by various kinds of tool (texts, devices, and body disciplines) as a driving force.

In turn, this leads us to a last point. The nonhuman counts. Not as a back-up or an interface or a possession but as a more or less extensive architecture of action whose concerns do not just impinge on "us" but make "us" what "we" are. Massumi (2002a: xxix–xxx) puts it well:

There are any number of non-human strata in the world, with their own "perceptual" mechanisms: means for picking up a charge of potential aflow in the world and capturing it in a stratum-forming self-production or reproduction. Many of these non-human formations are in fact integrated in the human body. A ray of light passing into the human eye strikes on the level of physics. Its impulse passes through many an interlocking level, from the physical to the chemical to the biological. On each level, it produces a dedicated effect that is captured as a content, and around which certain functions alimenting the self-regulating system will come to revolve. The cascading generation of alimentary effects and functional capture continues across the gaps between bodily strata. When it reaches the brain, the whole series repotentializes. Brain functioning serves as a hinge between the internal stratifications contained by the skin and the wider systems of capture into which the human organism as a whole is in turn integrated.

So, to summarize, embodiment may best be thought of as a set of circulating ethologies, architectures of unlike things which come together and are aligned as particular functionings (that is bodies of sensation that do not refer to the perception of an object or the affections of a subject) with particular capacities to produce effects and affects. These ethologies are moving "thought-ways," ways of doing/thinking world, what Deleuze calls "refrains," orderings that drive across and produce regions by constantly making and remaking alliances and relationships: the work of doing relation.

Engaging the World

In turn, this kind of depiction of a rich and sensuous materiality suggests a very different kind of ethos of engagement with the world, what I have called elsewhere "summoning life" (Thrift 2002). This is an attempt to carve out a different kind of ethos from that which currently takes up and deadens so much of our energies, one which adds to the world by framing the energetics of encounters in creative and caring ways which add to the potential for what may become, one which – in the teeth of all the evidence – is always moving towards possible celebration. It tries to produce more artful responses to the questions encounters continuously ask of us, expanding just a little the spaces of joy and generosity that so often show up but are mutilated by the assumptions of what the circumstances must be. This is not a romantic conception of a political ethic, I hasten to add, since it assumes that what is being striven for at most times is agonistic respect (what is often called deep pluralism) born out of an expanded sense of what constitutes sensibility and thoughtfulness. But it is a hopeful conception – or so I hope – which attempts to undo some of the damage inflicted by numerous orderings on our capacity for thoughtfulness and to amplify responsiveness.

Producing such an ethos therefore depends upon making assumptions about how the world will be disclosed.

One of those assumptions is that the world will *not* turn up as a secularized modernity. I have no truck with an account of the world as a realm of disenchantment (Thrift 1996; Bennett 2001). Instead, I see our current conjuncture as no less full of gods and spirits than the medieval period, though they may take on radical forms. I simply do not believe that capitalism or bureaucracy or science has the power to iron out the imagination, though they certainly condition and channel it.[4] I see these kinds of secular orderings (and since they are themselves shot through with manifestations of superstition, leaps of the imagination and affective energy, I might question the use of the description "secular") as attempts to produce efficacious organizations of public space which will crowd out precisely these kinds of manifestations. Of course, the repressed then returns, but powered up by these secular conditions orders enormous organizational resources into counterproductive conflicts, schisms, and wars.

Another assumption is that politics operates at all manner of levels, of which one of the most important, as Connolly (1999) has pointed out, is the "visceral" register of the amygdala, stomach, and numerous other body parts (not all of which, as we have seen, are in what has conventionally been regarded as the body) which generate intensities, images, and feelings. Connolly concentrates on this visceral register for a number of reasons – in part to show just what is lost if a Kantian and Habermasian notion of public discourse is asserted, in part to allow him to listen receptively to politics at points of inception other than those at which its practices are conventionally understood to kick in, and in part as a political ambition in itself; to be able to modify the "infrasensible" aspects of this register of feeling in order to allow new energies and surprising experiments to emerge.

One more assumption is that we need to inhabit and take responsibility for the world differently. That is we need to be more open to attentive openness and less concerned about control. But how to express this? One analogy that comes to mind is with the display quality of the sentient world. As Arendt (1978: 29) puts it, using – significantly for this context – a theatrical metaphor, "whatever can see wants to be seen, whatever can hear calls out to be heard, whatever can touch presents itself to be touched." In other words, "sentient creatures . . . possess an active response to being perceived – in the form of an impulse to distinguish themselves. Thus 'what is' is constantly contributing to and bringing forth the wild spectacular quality of the world" (Curtis 1999: 31). In a remarkable paper, Read (2000) has demonstrated how this performance imperative produces a recognition of alterity and a certain vulnerability which can in turn produce a kind of ethical stance.

What such an ethic of engagement is trying to work on above all might be summarized as affective capacity, a capacity which constitutes something more than the personal quality of emotion but which retains the emphasis on feeling (Brown & Stenner 2001). Affect is understood here in a classical Spinozan fashion as "the modifications of the body by which the power of action of the body is increased or diminished, aided or restrained, and at the same time the idea of these modifications" (Spinoza, *Ethics*, part III, def. 3). Of course, the Spinozan body means here something different from the individual organic body, something more like dispositions for movement or transition within a particular diagram of encounters which are both affecting and affected.[5] As Massumi (2002b: 15) so clearly puts it:

For Spinoza, the body was one with its transitions. Each transition is accompanied by a variation in its capacity: a change in which powers to affect and be affected are addressable by a next event and how readily addressable they are – or to what degree they are present as futurities. That degree is a bodily intensity, and its present futurity a tendency. The Spinozist problematic of affect offers a way of weaving together concepts of movement, tendency, and intensity in a way that takes us right back to the beginning: in what sense the body coincides with its own transitions and its transitioning with its potential.

And it is important to note that the variation in intensity is felt: it is the felt reality of the work of relation. Out of such an understanding of affect and body, Spinoza forged an ethics of expression which has now come back to haunt us. Massumi (2002a: xxii, author emphasis) puts that ethics into words so:

What expression is most emphatically not dependent upon in the first instance is any purportedly generally applicable moral rule of assigning responsibility for it or toward it. There is indeed an ethics of expression, which Deleuze and Guattari acknowledge and accept as a central problem. They insist on the term "ethics," as opposed to morality, because the problem in their eyes is not in any primary fashion that of personal responsibility. It is a basically pragmatic question of how one *performatively* contributes to the stretch of expression in the world – or conversely prolongs its capture. This is fundamentally a *creative* problem. Where expression stretches, potential determinately emerges into something new. Expression's tensing is by nature creative. Its passing brings into definite being. It is *ontogenetic*. To tend the stretch of expression, to foster and inflect it rather than trying to own it, is to enter the stream, contributing to its probings: this is co-creative, an aesthetic endeavour. It is also an ethical endeavour, since it is to ally oneself with change: for an ethics of emergence.

And So To Performance

I hope it now becomes clearer why I and others have become so interested in the topos of performance in recent years (Thrift 2000; Thrift & Dewsbury 2000). For performance asks the right questions in the right way, born out of an intense desire to work on the imagination in order to add something into the world, in a world in which constantly altering demands to perform have become commonplace (McKenzie 2001). I tend to see performance as the modern equivalent of prayer in its focus, intensity and ethical commitment whilst remaining different in its desire to use repetition to do something different each time. It is not, of course, a panacea but it starts to provide a body for the thoughts I have worked between on a screen. Performance has built up a knowledge about technologies of carnality, space and time which is aware of itself and its effects. It can do the grand and the epic but it is also aware that the "smallest" things – from the flicker of an eyebrow to the positioning of a chair, from the track of a tear to the staging of an entrance – matter.

Performance does many things – that is its point – but here I will concentrate on just its ability to perturb. We need to be careful here. Much performance simply cements established orders: it is not an orgy of guerilla tactics and incursionary resistances but a part of dominant cultural orders (McKenzie 2001; see also Genosko 2002). But enough of it is different to provide a base for thinking other.

Perhaps the best way of thinking about performance is as a cultural store of expressive longings, sometimes explicitly articulated, sometimes, like a lover's glance across a room, left unsaid. And these longings are not by any means always in the cognitive domain. Many of them are only expressed as prereflexive signs, little mo(ve)ments of affect pointing towards something without being able to say what it is.

In what follows, I will just – very briefly indeed – note how these performative moments can sometimes (and sometimes not, which often proves just as interesting) produce a certain kind of ascension by pointing to cases from musical performance, specifically opera and country music. (In doing so, I have tried to select for different aspects of the contemporary performative agenda which point up different ways of doing different, in the sure knowledge that all I am doing is scratching the surface.) These choices may not, at first sight, seem very promising. After all, in most incarnations, neither of them exactly conjure up the avant-garde. Then, both opera and country music work to well-worn performative scripts which pass "into performers' bodies, performers who are in a chimerical state between aliveness and deadness, singers [and musicians] who produce sound that has violent force" (Abbate 2001: 18, my addition). And both opera and country music are not only routinely recorded but that recording may indeed be the main motive force.[6] Given these glosses, how can we understand performance in genres like opera and country music without falling back on the usual stereotypes of performance as either a form of puppetry only brought to life by a master script or score or an illicit improvisation which functions as the equivalent of radical political action. What is playing the instrument–performer–audience? The answer, in large part, is to try to better understand performance networks' affective dimensions and especially their ability to "possess" both performers and audience. Abbate (2001: xv–xvi) gives some sense of the process in opera as it gives expression to powerful affective forces when she writes about the virtuoso performances that she still remembers as if they were yesterday:

They conveyed the impression that the work was being created at the moment, "before one's eyes," never seeming to invite comparison between what was being heard and some lurking double, some transcendent work to which they had to measure up. In other words, they never produced the sinking feeling that one was in the presence of *werktreue*, that "this is a good performance of that." Though they were performances of pieces that I knew well, the template had been forgotten. Suggesting that what one heard was simultaneously being invented and fading away, they produced a strange undertone, inviting held breath as if they could arrest all loss. At the same time they were distinctly, exaggeratedly material, directing attention to the physical reality of the musicians and the sounds they create, and one's place as a listener or performer within that sound. There were acoustic irregularities or odd visual angles, all sorts of surplus allied to unique circumstances. Revisited in memory, they have often directed what I write about music. They raise an interesting question: how mortal is performance, if it can resonate this powerfully this long?

That same question is raised in a different way by country music. Country is often seen as the anthems of a reactionary pathos and therefore dismissed by many intellectuals; but, as Shusterman (2000) has argued so effectively, part of the reason for this dismissal is precisely its recognition and use of affect in performance: "extreme emotion or sentimentality is a trademark of country music and a prime reason why intellectuals dismiss it as vulgar kitsch" (Shusterman 2000: 85). According to Shusterman country music demands the construction of sincerity which requires the deployment of emotional styles which can signal authenticity and which themselves, through continuous use, trigger the expectation of emotional response in the audience. Relying on this emotional style archive, a relatively limited musical repertoire, and a strong narrative push, country music is often able to use the common failures of life to construct a kind of affirmation.

However, what is particularly interesting about musical performance is when things get awkward so that the process of emergence is exposed in all its workings. Most performances are not perfect reproductions; there are dropped notes, missed cues, and fluffed entrances.

Error and breakdown are byproducts, exposing the dead-object problem, an aspect of the performance network that few wish to see. This is one reason why performances that go wrong – where someone forgets, or when the music making threatens to fumble or stop – do not simply create frustration or disapproval in the audience. The emotions are more complicated. There is a sense of fear, of anxiety or even panic. And not only from sympathetic identification with those on stage: the spectacle has shown its other face, as a moribund collective that has somehow gotten derailed from the commands that have supplied it with temporary, harmonious life. (Abbate 2001: 45)

I want to illustrate some of these thoughts more fully by considering one of the most neglected of embodied affective states, namely crying. Part of the reason for this neglect is that crying has proved a genuine conundrum, both because of its extreme obviousness and, simultaneously, its extreme opaqueness. Thus the cultural history of crying is at one and the same time a history of attempts to practice crying appropriately and to categorize and explain what crying is. From the early categorization of Saint Augustine to the latest thoughts of psychotherapists (e.g. Kottler 1996) to the almost constant struggles by scientists from Darwin (1998/1872) onwards to put any kind of functional meaning on crying, tears have proved a primary way of thinking a usually highly gendered expectation of how embodiment shows up.[7] And we can be quite sure, as a result of this history, that crying varies widely in its frequency, uses and effects in cultures now and through the historical record (Vincent-Buffault 1991; Hvidberg 1992; Lange 1996; Lutz 1999; McEntire 1990; Reddy 2001).

What interests me about crying in current Western cultures is both crying's generality – as Frey (1985: 21) puts it, "adult tears can appear in response to almost any imaginable situation" – and its often extreme awkwardness: though there are sad or joyful situations where crying is accepted as appropriate and even, in some senses, pleasurable (at funerals and goodbyes, as an element of reconciliation or solace, as a public declaration of sincerity, as an expression of wonder, as a release when watching certain kinds of performance like "tear-jerker" movies or listening to certain kinds of music – such as country music), quite often crying can prove highly inappropriate and difficult to deal with, both for those who are crying and those who are also involved (Cavell 1996). I would argue that crying is often therefore best understood as an act of theatre, a practical means of becoming awkward announcing a change of affective state, a means which, in particular, circumvents some of the expressive limitations of language; "crying emerges when culture forces people to embody a response that they cannot say" (Katz 1999: 198). There is a dramatics to the crying body: as Katz (1999: 179) again puts it, crying is "a panoply of distinctive, aesthetically guided ways of mobilizing the expressive body." In turn such crying is often highly experimental; it has no exact goal in mind but is rather simply a means of changing the situation in order to see what will turn up, which may well simply be another form of awareness/appreciation of that situation. An artful and sensual bridge to something else. The need to bridge can take many forms – between small and large social worlds, between absence and presence, between hubbub and silence – but what cannot be denied is a high aesthetic competency which allows events to be molded: "crying exhibits a poetic logic by which people bring to the surface and mark things that are routinely effaced in ordinary non-emotional conduct. They hit upon, transform, and present dimensions of the routinely invisible, natural three-dimensionality of their conduct" (Katz 1999: 213). In other words, they move into another register of embodiment which precisely underlines and indeed searches out the degree to which they are embodied: "the flow that intertwines person and world metamorphoses as it moves from the background to the foreground of experience" (Katz 1999: 220) Various parts of the body search out new counterparts, transforming the metaphoric structuring of experience. Breathing is a good example. The catch of breath in crying brings to the fore an action that is normally considered to be automatic (at least in the West) and can be used to artful material effect in numerous forms of event. As Irigaray (2002) makes clear, air too can be cultivated and shared, and crying does exactly this as it breathes out of tune.

Conclusions: Jangling Space and Time

What I want to conclude this chapter with – at last, some will say – is the kinds of geographies that turning in the direction I have pointed to will allow to come to the fore. I hope that by now the political goal is clear: to show up the work of relation in new ways which concentrate on boosting powers of emergence. It follows that the kind of approaches to timespace that will be preferred are those forms of radical empiricism and pragmatics that show up the ways in which circulations emerge and are maintained, of the kind to be found in the work of, for example, Whitehead, Deleuze, and Latour. Such approaches are unlikely to have much truck with "natural" boundaries and relationships, will refuse to deal in fixed warrants such as "nature" or "reason," and are wary of predetermined lines of knowing. They paint, instead, a picture "of a social order constantly threatened by immediate decomposition because no component is ever fully part of it" (Latour 2002: 124).[8]

The point, of course, is that we are only just beginning to explore these timespaces and their different potentials, so I cannot bring back from the front dispatches full of tales of great disaster and even greater triumphs. But, I should also add that it is in the nature of these kinds of approaches to shy away from precisely these kinds of narratives, and to concentrate on something altogether more modest. No single spatio-temporal logic can encompass all the ins and outs of the world. So I find much more *political* sustenance in the few recent "geopathic" (Chaudhuri 1995) attempts to dwell on performance by writing about music (e.g. Smith 2000), walking (e.g. Wylie 2003), and other preternaturally expressive practices. What all these attempts have in common is their tentative character as they try to track their own process of emergence as part of a more general lesson about drawing out.[9] And each of them draws on methodological knowledges that can provide sustenance for expressive points of view, most especially those knowledges: that do not forswear the lyric; that privilege movement; that realize that bodies speak in all kinds of different ways; that value indeterminacy and; that believe that there is a politics of the ordinary which can be and sometimes is extraordinary. These knowledges are necessarily eclectic, drawn from all aspects of the variable mappings provided by "performance," whose "phenomenology" is both conceptual and physical from the start (Chaudhuri 1997; Rehm 2002).

And what spaces do they discover? Spaces that have to come to life because they are in play and so can track and intervene in the play of space. As I have noted elsewhere (e.g. Thrift 2000), play is often considered to be a lightweight activity. But it is equally possible to argue that play is one of the most serious activities that it is possible to participate in, not least because its sense of space depends upon the inversion of the relation of position to movement. In play space "movement is no longer indexed to position. Rather, position emerges from movement, from a relation of movement to itself" (Massumi 2002b: 180).

Thinking space through movement is, of course, exactly what performance does but the insight can be generalized up (e.g. Amin & Thrift 2002). And, in turn, we can see this kind of thinking starting to have impacts upon how the spaces around us function, in various new forms of topological architecture, in experiments with the mobile technologies and new forms of mobile address that are beginning to surround us (Thrift 2002), in the continual performances made possible by the internet (from music to prayer), in certain new forms of radical economic activity, and so on. This is akin to Massumi's (2002b: 207) "translogic":

A translogic is different from a metalogic. It doesn't stand back and describe the way multiple logics and the operative levels they model hold together. It enters the relations and tweaks as many strands as it can to get a sense of what may come. It imaginatively enters the fabric of transition and pulls as many strands as it can to see what emerges. It is effective. Rather than metalogical, it is supermodulatory.

Use imagination. Unfold, experiment, modulate, become. Formation not form. Life as more life.[10]

In closing, I want to suggest that such a stance provides the most wonderful opportunities – if only we have the nerve to take them. It will not be easy. The discipline's body image of itself, so to speak, will require changing and that will be deeply threatening to more than a few, and most especially those who believe that they and only they have true knowledge of how the world is and ought to be. As I have argued, following Hölderlin's interpretation of Sophocles, what is needed instead is an awkward perspective, a "perspective that cannot get its bearings, achieve a stable stance and set itself on the right course" (Fenves 2001: 1), a perspective that does not just detach itself from the privileged vantage points sanctioned by the order of law but actively tends perspectives that are likely to go awry, not out of some adolescent need to simply favor the contrary but out of a deep-seated conviction that securing a point of view that never goes wrong cannot add to the world and detracts precisely from those lyric qualities that it is important to tend. "Awkwardness, to paraphrase Spinoza, is the index of itself" (Fenves 2001: 12).

The sentence goes out, it ends – but it does not finish.

NOTES

1. Complicating the idea that any intellectual history is straightforward, it is worth recalling that one of the first cogent discussions of wonder was by Descartes (see Fisher 1998).
2. Though it is worth remembering the enormous efforts, many of them involving sophisticated performative techniques full of "special effects," made by the medieval church.
3. To prefigure my argument, I think that this conjures up a wonderful picture of the world as a set of continually instantiated longings, prayers, and curses (I did not say the picture

was necessarily a beautiful one) which have built up effective repetitions that resonate in our lives and lead us on. But I mean to go farther than this in trying to show why this picture of continually circulating prayers and curses itself provides a platform for rethinking materialism.

4. For me, such attitudes betray the lack of a convincing historical imagination.
5. At times, Spinoza does indeed refer to individual human bodies, and this needs to be kept in mind in reading his work.
6. There is a lively debate over whether in such a media-saturated world a notion of liveness still makes sense (see Auslander 2000).
7. Though as Lutz and others make clear, not always as expected. For example, as he points out, it is becoming acceptable for male politicians to be seen to cry in the media, but this would cause problems for female politicians.
8. As Tarde, writing in 1898, (cited in Latour 2002: 124) puts it:

> It is always the same mistake that is put forward: to believe that in order to see the regular, orderly, logical pattern of social facts, you have to extract yourself from their details, basically irregular, and go upwards until you embrace vast landscapes panoramically: that the principal source of any social coordination resides in a very few general facts, from which it diverges by degree until it reaches the particulars, but in a weakened form; to believe in short that while man agitates himself, a law of evolution leads him. I believe exactly the opposite.

> It has taken us nigh on a hundred years for the ramifications of such a statement to be fully understood.

9. This was of course the original meaning of the verb, to educate (Roach 2002).
10. I have abused Simmel's famous usage here for my own ends.

REFERENCES

Abbate, C. 2001: *In Search of Opera*. Princeton: Princeton University Press.
Amin, A. and Thrift, N. J. 2002: *Cities: Re-imagining Urban Theory*. Cambridge: Polity Press.
Arendt, H. 1978: *The Life of the Mind*. New York: Harcourt Brace Jovanovich.
Attfield, J. 2000: *Wild Things: The Material Culture of Everyday Life*. Oxford: Berg.
Auslander, P. 2000: *Liveness*. New York: Routledge.
Benjamin, W. 1985: *The Origin of German Tragic Drama*. London: Verso.
Bennett, J. 2001: *The Enchantment of Modern Life*. Princeton: Princeton University Press.
Blumenberg, H. 1983: *The Legitimacy of the Modern Age*. Cambridge, MA: MIT Press.
Blumenberg, H. 1997: Prospect for a theory of nonconceptuality. In *Shipwreck with Spectator: Paradigm of a Metaphor for Existence*. Cambridge, MA: MIT Press, 81–102.
Bourdieu, P. 1999: *Pascalian Meditations*. Cambridge: Polity Press.
Brown, S. D. and Stenner, P. 2001: Being affected: Spinoza and the psychology of emotion. *International Journal of Group Tensions* 30, 81–105.
Cavell, S. 1996: *Contesting Tears: The Hollywood Melodrama of the Unknown Woman*. Chicago: University of Chicago Press.
Chaudhuri, U. 1995: *Staging Place: The Geography of Modern Drama*. Ann Arbor: University of Michigan Press.
Connolly, W. E. 1999: *Why I Am Not A Secularist*. Minneapolis: University of Minnesota Press.
Curtis, K. 1999: *Our Sense of the Real: Aesthetic Experience and Arendtian Politics*. Ithaca, NY: Cornell University Press.

Darwin, C. 1998 [1872]: *The Expression of Emotions in Man and Animals*. London: Harper Collins.

Deleuze, G. 1993: *The Fold: Leibniz and the Baroque*. Minneapolis: University of Minnesota Press.

Deleuze, G. 2001: *Pure Immanence: Essays on a Life*. New York: Zone Books.

Ede, S., ed. 2000: *Strange and Charmed: Science and the Contemporary Visual Arts*. London: Calouste Gulbenkian Foundation.

Fenves, P. 2001: *Arresting Language: From Leibniz to Benjamin*. Stanford: Stanford University Press.

Fisher, P. 1998: *Wonder, the Rainbow and the Aesthetics of Rare Experiences*. Cambridge, MA: Harvard University Press.

Fisher, P. 2002: *The Vehement Passions*. Princeton: Princeton University Press.

Frey, W. H. 1985: *Crying: The Mystery of Tears*. Minneapolis: Winston Press.

Game, A. and Metcalfe, A. 2002: *The Mystery of Everyday Life*. Sydney: Federation Press.

Genosko, G. 2002: *Felix Guattari: An Aberrant Introduction*. London: Continuum.

Gil, J. 2002: The dancer's body. In B. Massumi, ed., *A Shock to Thought: Expression after Deleuze and Guattari*. London: Routledge, 117–27.

Graham, J. 2000: Prayer. In *Swarm: Poems*. New York: Ecco Press.

Hvidberg, F. F. 1962: *Weeping and Laughter in the Old Testament*. Leiden: Brill.

Irigaray, L. 2002: *Between East and West: From Singularity to Community*. New York: Columbia University Press.

Katz, J. 1999: *How Emotions Work*. Chicago: University of Chicago Press.

Kottler, J. A. 1996: *The Language of Tears*. San Francisco: Jossey-Bass.

Kwa, C. 2002: Romantic and baroque conceptions of complex wholes in the sciences. In J. Law and A. Mol, eds., *Complexities: Social Studies of Knowledge Practices*. Durham, NC: Duke University Press, 23–52.

Lange, M. E. 1996: *Telling Tears in the English Renaissance*. New York: Brill.

Latour, B. 1999: *Pandora's Hope: Essays in the Reality of Science Studies*. Cambridge, MA: Harvard University Press.

Latour, B. 2002: Gabriel Tarde and the end of the social. In P. Joyce, ed., *The Social in Question: New Bearings in History and the Social Sciences*. London: Routledge, 117–32.

Leroi-Gourhan, A. 1993: *Gesture and Speech*. Cambridge, MA: MIT Press.

Lutz, T. 1999: *Crying: The Natural and Cultural History of Tears*. New York: Norton.

Marcus, G. 2002: Paper presented to SSRC workshop on Oikos and Anthropos, Prague.

Massumi, B. 2002a: Introduction: like a thought. In B. Massumi, ed., *A Shock to Thought: Expression After Deleuze and Guattari*. London: Routledge, xiii–xxxix.

Massumi, B. 2002b: *Parables for the Virtual: Movement, Affect, Sensation*. Durham, NC: Duke University Press.

May, J. and Thrift, N. J., eds. 2001: *Timespace: Geographies of Temporality*. London: Routledge.

McEntire, S. J. 1990: *The Doctrine of Compunction in Medieval England: Holy Tears*. Lewiston, NY: Edwin Mellen.

McKenzie, J. 2001: *Perform or Else*. New York: Routledge.

Rabinow, P. 2002: Midst anthropology's problems. Paper presented to SSRC Workshop on Oikos and Anthropos, Prague.

Read, A. 2000: Acknowledging the imperative of performance in the infancy of theatre. *Performance Research* 5, 61–9.

Reddy, W. M. 2001: *The Navigation of Feeling: A Framework for the History of Emotions*. Cambridge: Cambridge University Press.

Rehm, R. 2002: *The Play of Space: Spatial Transformation in Greek Tragedy*. Princeton: Princeton University Press.

Riles, A 2002: Paper presented to SSRC workshop on Oikos and Anthropos, Prague.

Roach, J. 2002: Foreword. In A. Mertz, ed., *The Body Can Speak: Essays on Creative Movement Education with Emphasis on Dance and Drama*. Carbondale: Southern Illinois University Press, xi–xii.

Shapiro, M. J. 1999: *Cinematic Political Thought: Narrating Race, Nation, and Gender*. New York: New York University Press.

Shusterman, R. 2000: *Performing Live: Aesthetic Alternatives for the Ends of Art*. Ithaca: Cornell University Press.

Smith, S. J. 2000: Performing the (sound)world. *Environment and Planning D: Society and Space* 18(5), 615–37.

Targoff, R 1997: The performance of prayer: sentiment and theatricality in modern England. *Representations* 60, 49–69.

Taussig, M. 1999: *Defacement: Public Secrecy and the Labor of the Negative*. Stanford: Stanford University Press.

Thrift, N. J. 1996: *Spatial Formations*. London: Sage.

Thrift, N. J. 2000: Afterwords. *Environment and Planning D: Society and Space* 18(2), 213–55.

Thrift, N. J. 2002: Summoning life. In P. Cloke, M. Goodwin, and P. Crang, eds., *Envisioning Geography*. London: Arnold.

Thrift, N. J. and Dewsbury, J. D. 2000: Dead geographies – and how to make them live. *Environment and Planning D: Society and Space* 18(4).

Tiffany, D. 2000: *Toy Medium: Materialism and Modern Lyric*. Berkeley: University of California Press.

Vendler, H. 1995: *Soul Says: On Recent Poetry*. Cambridge, MA: Harvard University Press.

Vincent-Buffault, A. 1991: *The History of Tears: Sensibility and Sentimentality in France*. London: Macmillan.

Vingerhoets, J. J. M. and Cornelius, R. R., eds. 2001: *Adult Crying: A Biopsychosocial Approach*. London: Brunner-Routledge.

Wallace, R. M. 1983: Translator's introduction. In H. Blumenberg, ed., *The Legitimacy of Modern Reason*. Cambridge, MA: MIT Press, i–xxxi.

Warhol, R. 1992: As you stand, so you feel and are: the crying body and the nineteenth century text. In F. Mascia-Lees and P. Sharpe, eds., *Tattoo, Torture, Mutilation and Adornment: The Denaturalization of the Body in Culture and Text*. Albany, NY: State University of New York Press.

Wylie, J. 2003: An essay on ascending Glastonbury Tor. *Geoforum* 33, 441–54.

Part III   Nature/Culture

Chapter 10

Cultures of Science

David N. Livingstone

In 1863 the New Zealand *Southern Monthly Magazine* expressed its enthusiasm for Darwin's theory of evolution. Darwinism, so the magazine's readers were told, had cast new light on the process of colonization by showing how a "weak and ill-furnished race" necessarily had "to give way before one which is strong and highly endowed" (quoted in Stenhouse 1999: 83). Darwinism, evidently, suited to perfection the needs of New Zealand imperialists. It enabled the Maori to be represented in the language of savagery and thus to provide scientific legitimacy for the land-hungry settlers who welcomed the prospect of Maori extinction. As John Stenhouse (1999: 81) has observed "New Zealanders embraced Darwinism for racist purposes." In the American South, things were different. Here Darwinian evolution was routinely resisted by proponents of racial ideology. For it could destabilize long-held views about the separate creation of the different human races and undermine the belief that they had been endowed with different levels of cultural and intellectual excellence by the Creator. In this environment, the Darwinian idea that all humans were descended from a common stock could be politically disturbing (Stephens 2000). For racial reasons, it seems, Darwin's theory enjoyed different fortunes in Wellington and Charleston. Thus we find the New Zealand materialist and physician Alfred Kingcome Newman using Darwinian language in 1882 to callously condone the extinction of the Maori by a 'superior race' in the struggle for existence between nations. By comparison, in the southern states of America, the anti-Darwinian John McCrady devised his own 'law of development' to sustain his belief that the South was a higher form of civilization superseding the rest of the United States and that each race was a distinct species limited to its own geographical province.

Of course we should not generalize too readily from these particular cases. In both New Zealand and the American South different evaluations of Darwin's theory were to be heard during the second half of the nineteenth century. But these two episodes do nevertheless expose something of how scientific theories are encountered differently in different cultures and can be used as resources to justify various – sometimes contradictory – causes. In the light of these circumstances, it is clear that the meaning of any scientific theory is not stable; rather it is mobile and changes from one place to another. In one location Darwinism could be read as underwriting long-standing racial politics; in another it was seen to imperil traditional race relations. In each situation the meaning of Darwinism, and its implications, were locally constructed.

Other examples could readily be enumerated. Nineteenth-century Russians, for example, resisted Darwin's competitive metaphor of a struggle for existence but embraced versions of the theory that played up cooperation between species – a stance that mirrored the Russian political economy which was devoid of a market-driven middle class (Todes 1989). Besides, the climatic extremes of the Siberian north just did not seem like the kind of environment Darwinians had in mind when they spoke of teeming life-forms, lush vegetation, and tight ecological niches. Both the political and physical geography of Russia conditioned how evolutionary theory was construed. In Canada, it was only when romantics began to depict the harsh northern reaches as the wellspring of the race and the source of vigor and vitality that the language of Darwinism began to blossom. Not surprisingly, when Canadian scientists did turn to the application of Darwinian theory they tended to focus on the geographical distribution and morphological adaptations of Arctic plants (Zeller 1999).

All of this confirms that, just like covered bridges or private wealth, scientific knowledge is not uniformly distributed across the face of the earth. Its complexion differs from place to place, and across the spectrum of scales. Because scientific knowledge is produced differently in different spaces, because it is confronted differently in different arenas, and because it migrates from one location to another, it makes sense to think of scientific enterprises as geographically constituted. This is beginning to be recognized both by geographers and sociologists who have, in recent years, begun to explore more systematically the role of space in the making and circulation of scientific knowledge (for example Ophir & Shapin 1991; Livingstone 1995, 2003; Demeritt 1996; Shapin 1998; Smith & Agar 1998; Withers 1999). The range of ways in which scientific culture may be geographically interrogated, of course, is vast. Here I want to tackle the issue on just three fronts. First I want to dwell at the regional scale in order to uncover something of the ways in which scientific endeavor has been shaped by regional culture. Second, the focus sharpens and attention falls on specific sites of scientific inquiry. Here the significance of spaces of knowledge – laboratories, libraries, stock farms, museums, tents, field stations – in cognitive enterprises can begin to be glimpsed. Finally, because people, ideas, and instruments move from place to place, scientific undertakings disclose distinctive geographies of reception and consumption. Just what bearing these have on the local construction and meaning of scientific theories warrants scrutiny.

Regional Cultures of Science

Something of the scientific significance of regional dynamics surfaces when we turn to the making of scientific Europe several centuries ago. It is important to recall at the outset, of course, that Europe has never been a self-contained or uncontested space, and that the scientific developments that took place here were fashioned in profound ways by extramural influences. Chinese alchemy, for example, exercised an immense influence on European medicine; Islamic geodetic methods of determining the 'sacred direction' of Mecca for daily prayer informed European astronomy and cartography (see Goodman & Russell 1991). At the same time a variety of Greek medical and scientific works, such as Archimedes' mathematics and Ptolemy's geography, were translated in Baghdad and from there spread west through Europe. In numerous ways, Europe owed much to cultural transmissions from 'the East' (Montgomery 2000).

Inside Europe too, regionalism was crucially important in the shaping of scientific knowledge. When Voltaire crossed the English Channel, he entered a different world. "A Frenchman arriving in London," he wrote in 1734, "finds things very different, in natural science as in everything else. He has left the world full, he finds it empty. In Paris they see the universe as composed of vortices of subtle matter, in London they see nothing of the kind. For us it is the pressure of the moon that causes the tides of the sea; for the English it is the sea that gravitates towards the moon . . . In Paris you see the earth shaped like a melon, in London it is flattened on two sides. . . . The very essence of things has totally changed." Voltaire's rhetorical gibe at the supposed universalism of European natural philosophy advertises something of the regional geography of scientific knowledge at the height of the Scientific Revolution. This had long been the case as a brief consideration of conditions in two European regions during the sixteenth century – the Italian and the Iberian peninsulas – will disclose.

Cultural circumstances in sixteenth-century Italy made it, at once, one of the most precarious yet productive regions in Europe for engagement in what would now be considered scientific pursuits. On the one hand, the Italian peninsula was already one of the most highly urbanized areas of the world with the flourishing of such centers as Palermo, Milan and Venice, a culture of book gathering, and a history of banking. The home of such venerable universities as Bologna and Padua, it stood at the center of the Renaissance revival of ancient learning. On the other hand, the impulse towards theological surveillance, manifest in the emergence of the Society of Jesus (1540), the Council of Trent (1543), and the Index of Prohibited Books (1543), made Italy a precarious enough environment for certain kinds of scientific endeavor.

For scientific inquiry to flourish in this environment, princely patronage was of critical importance, not least because technological innovations could bring financial rewards. Commercial potential, but, just as often, a lust for prestige and distinction, prompted dynastic families, like the Medici, to invest in natural philosophy as cultural capital. In such circumstances, it was much to the advantage of anyone with a taste for empirical inquiry to seek out ways of presenting to baroque rulers some scientific boon that would bring renown to them. Name a newly observed star after one of them and a hitherto precarious future could be guaranteed. In turn, good standing with the princely powers conferred on practitioners of scientific arts legitimacy in matters of natural knowledge. It worked both ways: rulers got glory, philosophers got credibility. In such a knowledge economy, neither observational nor computational skills were enough to deliver to a scientific practitioner the right to be heard. What counted was courtly status and esteem. And this casts an important light (though by no means the only light) on the infamous case of Galileo whose advocacy of heliocentrism led to his being condemned as a heretic in 1633.

That story really begins when Galileo secured the patronage of the Medici family when he shrewdly named the satellites of Jupiter 'the Medicean stars.' Soon he found himself at the court of the Grand Duke of Tuscany, a move that dramatically improved his status yet brought him closer to watchful pontifical eyes where any departures from Aristotelian orthodoxy were likely to attract attention. At the same time the shape of Galileo's developing science bore the stamp of seventeenth-century Italy's courtly culture (Biagioli 1992). Established conventions of debate at the court encouraged Galileo to develop a theatrical style of rhetoric and a combative tone that would have been regarded as inappropriate in, say, the gentlemanly culture of seventeenth-century England's Royal Society. There, by contrast, sensationalism in natural philosophy was regarded as vainglorious conceit. In Italy scientific bravado earned courtly esteem; but it cost Galileo the very papal legitimacy he sought and led to his eventual denunciation. Here the particularities of regional culture had much to do with the struggle between the new astronomy and ecclesiastical authority.

Along Europe's western margins, on the Iberian peninsula, regional culture conditioned empirical inquiries in a rather different way (Goodman 1988). Proximity to North Africa, for example, meant that the diffusion of Arabic astronomical and medical works made their influence felt. But the peninsula's maritime impulses were no less significant and fostered a tradition of scientific endeavor markedly different from that of the Italian court. Here navigational matters were to the fore even if there is little solid evidence for the existence of the nautical academy that Prince Henry 'the Navigator' was supposed to have established at Sagres. For imperial and commercial purposes, Iberian monarchs actively promoted what has been called the haven-finding arts by retaining the services of a range of remarkable Jewish practitioners of practical mathematics, astronomy and cartography – particularly the Cresques family. The Iberian scientific tradition thus bore the stamp of imperial utility. Advances in the study of terrestrial magnetism, medicinal botany and mercantile mathematics, for example, were all marked by what might be called the expeditionary 'far side.' On his voyage to India in the late 1530s, Joao da Castro engaged in investigations of terrestrial magnetism to challenge current orthodoxy on the issue of magnetic declination, the pharmaceutical value of tropical plants like the mango and camphor was investigated by the physician Garcia d'Orta, and computational methods of working between different weights and measures were developed by Gaspar Nicolas.

These two cases can be seen as emblematic of how, in one way or another, regional particularity may impose itself on scientific enterprises. Iberian science, fashioned on an imperial template was a rather different activity from the performances that entertained the Italian court and landed advocates of the new astronomy in deep theological water. In one situation, credibility was a function of courtly status; in another, it was proficiency in the practicalities of reading land and sea that delivered cognitive authority. This means that scientific endeavor in different regional arenas meant very different things – in what was investigated, who had the power to make knowledge, and why certain lines of inquiry were pursued. Of course this does not mean that there were no common threads knitting together scientific Europe, nor that regions were hermetically sealed off from one another. There is nothing fixed about regions; they are contingent, mobile, unstable. Yet they are sufficiently robust to confirm that it makes sense to append them as geographical adjectives to particular kinds of scientific endeavor and to speak coherently of, say, *French* physics in the eighteenth century, *English* geology in the Victorian period, or *German* medicine under the Nazis.

Local Sites of Science

Scientific endeavor carries the imprint of the regional culture in which it is practiced. But it is also conditioned by the specific sites in which inquiry is conducted. The range, of course, is enormous. Laboratories, hospitals, observatories, libraries, museums and field sites are all recognizable as spaces of scientific endeavor. But scientific knowledge has also been made on ships' decks, stock farms and exhibition stages, in tents, coffee shops, and cathedrals. The list could go on and on. Take the Victorian public house, for example, a place not usually associated with scientific endeavor. Here, during the early decades of the nineteenth century, artisan botanists would congregate on Sunday mornings to engage in discussion about plants, to share expertise, to exchange specimens, and to consult botanical texts (Secord 1994). In the cozy atmosphere of the village inn, florists, gardeners and herbalists – many of whom had an enviable command of Linnaean taxonomy – pushed forward the frontiers of botanical science and, from time to time, attracted the attention of gentlemen botanists like those at Kew Gardens who resorted to them for quality samples. The pub provided them with a distinct social space that enabled them to challenge traditional distinctions between philosophers and practitioners, between head work and hand work. It was a cultural location that contested the dominant scientific arenas of the time.

Sites of scientific pursuits influence practice in various ways. Often the site is constructed so as to foster or constrain communication; often it is regulated by formal and informal mechanisms of boundary policing to control access to the space and to mark an invisible line between 'insiders' and 'outsiders.' At the same time, it is in these sites that scientific practitioners acquire and reproduce the core values, customs and conceptions of their tradition of inquiry. In these, and numerous other ways, the microgeography of knowledge-production sites fashions scientific practice. So whether it is Robert Boyle carrying out experiments on the physical properties of air in the basement of his sister's London residence, Charles Darwin doing his barnacles at home in Down House, Bronislav Malinowski inquiring into social institutions in the Trobriand Islands, or Josef Mengele carrying out investigations into what was euphemistically called 'racial hygiene' at Auschwitz, the site-specific conditions of knowledge-making were hugely different, as were the ways in which the knowledge acquired migrated from its source out into the public sphere.

Something of the geographical dynamic at work in sites of scientific production can be glimpsed by considering a range of different *forms of spatiality* that are in play in a range of scientific engagements. The rudimentary taxonomy that I am advancing here, of course, is intended to be suggestive rather than comprehensive. Though at best a first approximation towards a more thoroughgoing spatial interrogation of science, the classification I am developing nonetheless serves to highlight dominant cognitive forces that are embedded in different sites of inquiry.

The laboratory is often taken as a space, *par excellence*, of scientific performance because here the aim is to manipulate the natural order through experimental interrogation in such a way that investigators can make sense of how the physical world operates. Laboratories, then, can be thought of as *sites of manipulation*. In such locations, geography matters in various ways. Take the early laboratories that developed in seventeenth-century England. Here we can profitably distinguish between two zones. First, there is the 'back space' where what was called the 'trying' of an experiment was carried out. Here various servants, mechanics, and laborants struggled to make the experiment work, to make nature behave in certain ways. Often things did not go according to plan, and the experiment would be tried over and over again. Only when the processes were thoroughly mastered – when nature was made to properly perform – did the experiment move out into the 'front' region of 'showing.' This was when the natural philosopher would demonstrate the fruits of his endeavors to peers in order to secure their warrant and to confirm his results. Only when this circuit was successfully completed could a claim achieve the status of knowledge. The justification of a scientific claim required that it move from the private space of delving into the public space of demonstrating. The production of laboratory knowledge was thus a fundamentally geographical activity. And it was geographical in another way too. Only when the showing had been approved by accredited observers did it pass as genuine knowledge. But not just anyone could be a witness. Only those with the right social standing and appropriate credentials counted. To be included in the knowledge-making community, then, one had to simultaneously occupy a spatial triad: physical space (the laboratory site itself), social space (be a member of the gentlemanly class), and epistemic space (be an accredited natural philosopher). No wonder that Steven Shapin (1988) observes that only 'geographically privileged persons' had the right to make scientific knowledge.

Spatial occupancy is crucial to the making of knowledge in other sites too, notably in *sites of expedition*. Here, raw experience of unmanipulated nature is typically portrayed as fundamental to the acquisition of real knowledge. Sneering at the speculations of the armchair philosopher, the heroic explorer typically despises stay-at-home theoreticians for their lack of field experience. Hence the Victorian glacial geologist James David Forbes repudiated the claims about glacial motion that the Cambridge mathematical physicist William Hopkins had put forward, precisely because Hopkins had never experienced what Forbes referred to as "protracted residence among the Icy Solitudes" (quoted in Hevly 1996: 70). To Forbes, experimentation on liquids and forces in the lab just could not deliver reliable scientific knowledge about glacial motion. Plainly for him *where* knowledge was acquired counted as a critical component in its reliability. Of course, the sites of expedition in which field work is carried out routinely present epistemological predicaments of various stripes. Replication cannot easily be effected in the field, the environment cannot be rigorously controlled, and – perhaps most significant of all – the very presence of field scientists constitutes what passes as 'the field' through the academic projects they pursue. The geographies of field sites thus shape both epistemologically and practically the knowledges that are produced there. Besides this, there are occasions when the objects under scrutiny in the field are actively constructed by the performances of field workers. In one celebrated case, anthropologists studying native Amazonians cast them as sociobiological entities and stood by watching while they were devastated through the use of a defective vaccine. Real people were translated in anthropological vision into Darwinian life forms and scrutinized for their adaptive responses to a dramatically new aggressive environment.

Sites of presentation differ from both the laboratory and the field in significant ways. In sites like museums, botanical gardens, and zoos, it is the arrangement and display of specimens and artifacts that predominates. As storehouses for collected articles, these seem unproblematic spaces of accumulation. But, historically, the amassing of objects of one kind or another constituted a radically new form of knowledge. It was the seventeenth-century natural philosopher Francis Bacon who gave legitimacy to this style of inquiry by insisting on the importance of collecting particular items in opposition to the syllogistic reasoning of his day (Daston & Park 1998). The opening up of sites of accumulation was thus a critical new epistemic move. But spatiality is engaged in these sites in another way too. In addition to acquisition, museums and botanical gardens are implicated in presentation – spatial arrangement of one sort or another. Early botanical gardens, for instance, sought to recover the glories of the garden of Eden by laying out plants according to what was thought to be divine patterns. Later, during the era of the voyages of reconnaissance, gardens were arranged into four quarters, one each for plants from Europe, Asia, Africa, and America. By what was called 'geographical planting' the symmetry of global botany could be re-presented (Prest 1991). Practices of this sort, of course, could have directly political implications. The Victorian anthropologist Henry Pitt-Rivers was convinced that the proper placing of the specimens in his ethnological museum itself constituted a political text. Disclosing the slow, gradual, progressive pattern of anthropological history, he believed, could counter radical inclinations. "Anything which tends to impress the mind with the slow growth and stability of human institutions," he wrote, " . . . must, I think, contribute to check revolutionary ideas" (quoted in Asma 2001: 260). The proper placing of exhibits was thus an inherently political exercise. Sites of presentation are essentially about spatial formations of knowledge.

Sites of manipulation, expedition and presentation are not static spaces. Frequently they are also nodes in systems of interchange through which ideas, objects, practitioners and instruments pass. This recalls to our attention the importance of mobility in scientific ventures and underscores the role played by *sites of circulation*. Consider botanical and zoological gardens. These are centers in the circuitry of scientific commodities. Kew Gardens, for example, became one of the great exchange houses of the British empire by harvesting the world's botanical bounty, redistributing specimens to satellite gardens, and serving the needs of British agronomy (Drayton 2000). Such practices were emblematic of the more general principle that metropolitan science depended for its life-blood on a global capillary network through which species, specimens, and samples all coursed.

At the same time, sites of circulation are often centers of calculation. When items of scientific interest are transported from their point of collection to an assemblage space, they can be compared with samples from the other side of the world, modified by instrumental devices of various kinds, reorganized into a host of new taxonomic associations, subjected to a suite of statistical manipulations, and so on. The sites where such transformations take place wield immense power for they have the capacity to break the world apart, put it together in new combinations, and reduce it to the scale of a map, chart, table, or catalog. Out of the miscellaneous materials they acquire – physical objects, photographic representations, mathematical symbols, sketch maps, satellite images – sites of circulation forge global panoramas. As Bruno Latour (1999: 39), fastening on the way in which plant specimens brought back from the Amazon forest to the laboratory circulate and recombine in new conceptual formulations, puts it "The plants find themselves detached, separated, preserved, classified, and tagged. They are then reassembled, reunited, redistributed according to entirely new principles that depend on the researcher, on the discipline of botany."

Geographies of Scientific Reception

So far our attention has been directed, by and large, to the production end of the scientific knowledge circuit. Where scientific knowledge originates and how different spatial settings shape scientific inquiry have been at the forefront of our concerns. The consumption sector of the knowledge economy now demands scrutiny. For scientific texts and theories are received in different ways in different geographical locations. What James Secord (2000) has judiciously referred to as 'geographies of reading' is relevant at this point, as is Edward Said's (1991) insistence that as theory travels from place to place it is transformed. In matters of intellectual transmission, migration is never mere replication. Just as scientific claims are always the product of time and place, so they are always appropriated in time and place.

Two cases of how scientific works were differently read in different settings will illustrate something of what attention to the geography of reading can deliver. Then a few reflections on how Darwin's theory was encountered in two Victorian cities will demonstrate something of how the meaning of a scientific theory and its wider implications are the products of local circumstances. Taken together these exhibit what I have in mind by the 'geographies of scientific reception'.

How Alexander von Humboldt's writings were received in a variety of national settings during the first half of the nineteenth century usefully introduces the theme (Rupke 1999). His major work, *Kosmos*, for example, for which he is now most remembered by geographers, enjoyed much less attention in his own day than his researches on Mexico, no doubt on account of the latter's geopolitical and commercial implications. Moreover, Humboldt's contribution to scientific endeavor was rather differently evaluated in different contexts. English reviewers of his Mexican writings, for instance, were far more critical than French and German reviewers. They were also far more inclined to judge the work by how it handled questions that British natural scientists routinely brought within the scope of natural theology. And while their continental counterparts tended to dwell on Humboldt's improved determinations of latitude and longitude, it was the work's strategic significance for global traffic – not least Humboldt's proposals for excavating a navigable canal route between the Pacific and the Atlantic – that most attracted British interest.

As the geography of Humboldt's reviews makes clear, textual meaning differs from place to place. It is not stable. Whatever Humboldt may have intended by his various pronouncements, his readers heard him say different things. If this realization prompts us to query the unitary simplicity of notions of 'the author' and 'authorial intention,' it renders no less problematic the idea of 'the audience.' Humboldt had many audiences, and the meaning of the Humboldt phenomenon was differently construed by each. All this implies that distinctive cultures of reading exist within regions and between them, within cities and between them, within neighborhoods and between them. We can thus appropriately speak of 'geographies of reading.' This is the phrase that the historian of science, James Secord, calls upon in his elucidation of how, in different spaces, the sensational Victorian evolutionary work by Robert Chambers, *Vestiges of the Natural History of Creation* (which was first published in 1844) was encountered (Secord 2000). A controversial pre-Darwinian portrayal of cosmic evolution, it caused a furor at the time in its presentation of a speculative developmental account of everything from the solar system to the human species. And its meaning was variously made in various locations. Amongst London's aristocratic readers, it was regarded as poisonous, and refutations from the pens of scientific critics were warmly embraced. To progressive Whigs, by contrast, it was boldly visionary and gloriously free of bigotry or prejudice. In Unitarian conversation, the book's emphasis on change from below was seen as a telling blow against a smug ecclesiastical establishment. Outside London, the book also fared differently. In Oxford it was read as supportive of new scientific insights. In Cambridge it was vilified by writers like the clergyman-geologist Adam Sedgwick, who thought it an example of the most degrading species of materialism. In Liverpool, where it stirred up more sustained print controversy than anywhere else in Britain, the way it was read mirrored the social microgeography of the city. It sold briskly among those pressing for urban reform, for example, because it could be taken as scientific justification for social improvement.

One further factor in this particular case highlights, I think, the significance of the cultural geography of textual encounter. Originally *Vestiges* was published anonymously. The reasons why need not detain us here. What is noticeable is that what might be called a geography of authorial suspects rapidly surfaced. As Secord (2000: 24) puts it: "Names that seemed likely in Liverpool or Edinburgh were barely canvassed in Cambridge or Oxford; those that were common in London's fashionable West End were barely known in the Saint Giles rookeries only a few blocks away." Speculation was intense. All sorts of candidates were put forward. Why? Because *aligning an author* was required for *fixing a reading*.

From even these cursory remarks, it is clear that textual encounter is not to be thought of as a passive 'consumption' of knowledge. To the contrary. Textual reception is an active hermeneutic engagement. For the meaning of a text is made and remade through the diverse ways in which it is read. And the ways in which meanings are created through how a text, not least a 'classic' text, is edited, introduced, staged, reprinted, and so on, further complicate the story. If we are to discern something of how texts are confronted, interpreted and mobilized for particular causes, I think we will need to attend in a more sustained way to the geographies of reading, that is, to the spaces in which textual encounter literally takes place.

In the light of these textual cartographics, it is clear that scientific theories display distinctive regional geographies of reception. Darwin's theory of evolution, for example, enjoyed different fortunes in different cities because he was heard to say different things and because different rhetorical strategies were deployed in these theaters of operation to meet the challenges he was taken to be provoking (Livingstone 1999). Let me briefly illustrate.

In late nineteenth-century Belfast and Edinburgh, radically different assessments of Darwin's evolutionary theory were to be heard. Generally speaking, angry opposition to the theory was to be heard from leading churchmen in Belfast while it was warmly embraced by their counterparts in Edinburgh. Why? Two public spectacles, each of which made headline news at the time, profoundly conditioned just how evolutionary theory in general, and Darwinism in particular, were read by the religious elites in the two cities. In the Belfast case, the coming of the British Association for the Advancement of Science to the city during the summer of 1874 was crucial. For on that occasion, the Darwinian materialist, John Tyndall – himself an Irishman – in his infamous 'Belfast Address' took the opportunity of attacking conventional religion's dabbling in scientific affairs and pushed forward his campaign to divert cultural authority away from the old clerical brigade and into the hands of the newly professionalized scientific fraternity. His challenge so traumatized religious leaders in the city that they hastily put together a set of winter lectures for the general public in which they systematically sought to defend the faith from scientific assault. In this environment it was extraordinarily difficult to read Darwin or his allies sympathetically. Tyndall just made conciliatory readings of evolution well nigh impossible. In Edinburgh, a few years later, the ecclesiastical trial of one of Scotland's leading scholars, William Robertson Smith, made headline news. Smith had become acquainted with German critical scholarship and had applied it to the Bible arguing that it embodied various mythological elements. He developed too anthropological theories of early sacrifice, ritual cannibalism, female infanticide, and polyandry which, while profoundly impressive to figures like Durkheim and Freud, did little to endear him to members of his own religious community. In this environment, and given Scotland's long-standing enthusiasm for solid empirical science, Darwin seemed tame and *The Origin of Species* was perceived to pose few threats of epic proportions. Evidently, the meaning of Darwin and Darwinism was constructed very differently on each side of the Irish Sea. How evolutionary theory was read in each space was shaped by contingent public events that challenged, to the core of their being, the cultural identity of elite groups in both cities.

Conclusion

Science has many geographies. Both the production and consumption of scientific knowledge are stamped by geographical factors. Here I have focused on the importance of regional culture in the emergence of European science, on the significance of very specific sites in the generation of scientific knowledge, and on how works of scientific scholarship are differently read and mobilized in different cultural settings. The episodic examples I have drawn upon are only intended to be suggestive of the range of subjects that come under the rubric of 'cultural geographies of science.' Numerous other issues merit scrutiny, of which the geographies of scientific finance, the role of buildings in the building of science, the impact of technological change on scientific culture and geographies of scientific popularization are only a few examples. The study of the geographies of scientific culture, I believe, has only just begun.

REFERENCES

Asma, S. T. 2001: *Stuffed Animals and Pickled Heads: The Culture and Evolution of Natural History Museums.* New York: Oxford University Press.

Biagioli, M. 1992: Scientific revolution, social bricolage, and etiquette. In R. Porter and M. Teich, eds., *The Scientific Revolution in National Context.* Cambridge: Cambridge University Press, 11–54.

Daston, L. and Park, K. 1998: *Wonders and the Order of Nature, 1150–1750.* New York: Zone Books.

Demeritt, D. 1996: Social theory and the reconstruction of science and geography. *Transactions of the Institute of British Geographers* 21, 484–503.

Drayton, R. 2000: *Nature's Government: Science, Imperial Britain, and the 'Improvement' of the World.* New Haven: Yale University Press.

Goodman, D. 1988: *Power and Penury: Government, Technology and Science in Philip II's Spain.* Cambridge: Cambridge University Press.

Goodman, D. and Russell, C. A., eds. 1991: *The Rise of Scientific Europe 1500–1800.* London: Hodder & Stoughton.

Hevly, B. 1996: The heroic science of glacier motion. *Osiris* 11: 66–86.

Latour, B. 1999: Circulating reference: sampling the soil in the Amazon forest. In *Pandora's Hope: Essays on the Reality of Science Studies.* Cambridge, MA: Harvard University Press, 24–79.

Livingstone, D. N. 1995: The spaces of knowledge: contributions towards a historical geography of science. *Society and Space* 13, 5–34.

Livingstone, D. N. 1999: Science, region, and religion: the reception of Darwinism in Princeton, Belfast, and Edinburgh. In R. L. Numbers and J. Stenhouse, eds., *Disseminating Darwinism: The Role of Place, Race, Religion, and Gender.* New York: Cambridge University Press, 7–38.

Livingstone, D. N. 2003: *Putting Science in its Place: Geographies of Scientific Knowledge.* Chicago: University of Chicago Press.

Montgomery, S. L. 2000: *Science in Translation: Movements of Knowledge Through Cultures and Time.* Chicago: University of Chicago Press.

Ophir A. and Shapin, S., eds. 1991: *The Place of Knowledge: The Spatial Setting and its Relations to the Production of Knowledge.* Special issue of *Science in Context,* 4.

Prest, J. 1991: *The Garden of Eden: The Botanic Garden and the Re-Creation of Paradise.* New Haven: Yale University Press.

Rupke, N. 1999: A Geography of enlightenment: the critical reception of Alexander von Humboldt's Mexico work. In D. N. Livingstone and C. W. J. Withers, eds., *Geography and Enlightenment.* Chicago: University of Chicago Press, 319–39.

Said, E. W. 1991: Travelling theory. In *The World, the Text and the Critic.* London: Vintage, 226–47.

Secord, A. 1994: Science in the pub: artisan botanists in early nineteenth-century Lancashire. *History of Science* 32: 269–315.

Secord, J. A. 2000: *Victorian Sensation: The Extraordinary Publication, Reception, and Secret Authorship of 'Vestiges of the Natural History of Creation.'* Chicago: University of Chicago Press.

Shapin, S. 1988: The house of experiment in seventeenth-century England. *Isis* 79, 373–404.

Shapin, S. 1998: Placing the view from nowhere: historical and sociological problems in the location of science. *Transactions of the Institute of British Geographers* 23, 1–8.

Smith, C. and Agar, J., eds. 1998: *Making Space for Science: Territorial Themes in the Shaping of Knowledge.* London: Macmillan.

Stenhouse, J. 1996: 'A disappearing race before we came here': Doctor Alfred Kingcome Newman, the dying Maori, and Victorian scientific racism. *New Zealand Journal of History* 30, 124–40.

Stenhouse, J. 1999: Darwinism in New Zealand, 1859–1900. In R. L. Numbers and J. Stenhouse, eds., *Disseminating Darwinism: The Role of Place, Race, Religion, and Gender.* New York: Cambridge University Press, 61–89.

Stephens, L. D. 2000: *Science, Race, and Religion in the American South: John Bachman and the Charleston Circle of Naturalists, 1815–1895.* Chapel Hill: University of North Carolina Press.

Todes, D. P. 1989: *Darwin Without Malthus: The Struggle for Existence in Russian Evolutionary Thought.* Oxford: Oxford University Press.

Withers, C. W. J. 1999: Towards a history of geography in the public sphere. *History of Science* 34: 45–78.

Zeller, S. 1999: Environment, culture, and the reception of Darwin in Canada, 1859–1909. In R. L. Numbers and J. Stenhouse, eds., *Disseminating Darwinism: The Role of Place, Race, Religion, and Gender.* New York: Cambridge University Press, 91–122.

Chapter 11

Nature and Culture: On the Career of a False Problem

Bruce Braun

This essay tracks the career of a problem that has long occupied cultural geography: the *relation* between culture and nature. To speak of a problem in terms of its career is to call attention to its historicity. However, I am less interested in providing a progressive disciplinary history concerning attempts to understand the 'relation' between nature and culture, than in exploring how this problem has come to be defined, taken up, and debated within a shifting configuration of ideas, institutions and practices. Thus, while this chapter explores the changing fortunes of the 'nature–culture' problem within cultural geography (and the currency of various theoretical and empirical approaches that cultural geographers have used to understand it), it also suggests a way of reading disciplinary knowledges, not as the progressive unfolding of truth, but as truth-claims that carry within them multiple and diffuse genealogies. Such an approach may enable us to see the *problem* of the relation between nature and culture as itself historical – perhaps even what Deleuze (1991) defined as a 'false' problem – and thus to imagine – much as Foucault (1970) imagined for the figure of 'man' – the moment when it passes from the stage of history.[1]

To simplify this task I will divide the career of the nature–culture problematic in post-1950s Anglo-American geography into four 'moments': cultural ecology, political ecology, cultural studies of the environment, and actor-network theory (or 'nonmodern' ontologies).[2] These are somewhat arbitrary distinctions: there are, after all, many points of continuity between them, and many scholars would imagine their work fitting well within several designations. Also, although I present these 'moments' in succession, it would be a mistake to assume that one follows the next like links in a chain. That is not how knowledges change. We will see, for instance, that work informed by actor-network theory in the late 1990s has a certain (uncanny) resemblance to the work of cultural ecologists from the 1960s, even as it rejects much of what traveled under the banner of political ecology or cultural studies of the environment in the intervening years. We will also see that each 'moment' is conjunctural – emerging at the intersections of many different intellectual and political projects. To take only one example, although cultural studies of the environment can be read in terms of its *departures* from political ecology, very few of its practitioners have taken political ecology as their reference point, looking instead to fields as diverse as literature, philosophy, and cultural studies, in order to develop novel approaches to the study of nature and society. The temporality of this 'problem,' then, is neither linear nor singular. The distinctions I draw are meant to function heuristically, with the objective of calling attention to varied ways that the relation between culture and nature has been understood in the discipline since the 1950s, and with the goal of identifying what is at stake in the differences.

This chapter is more than a summary, however. I deploy the notion of 'moments' deliberately. This allows me not only to posit a changing career for this problem, but to posit its future passing. I will develop this argument later, although its outline can be briefly sketched here. The first three moments, I will suggest, did far more than investigate a problem located 'in' the world; they worked, each in their own way, to constitute 'nature' and 'culture' as separate domains, and to imagine the relation between them *as* a problem. In this sense, each of these moments is *performative* – they bring into being the very problem they seek to resolve. The fourth moment, I argue, is different from the others, since it produces a crisis within the problem itself. Its difference is not that it lies outside history, culture and politics (and thus in a different relation to the real); rather, unlike the other moments, it does not seek to find an answer to the question – "what is the *relation* between nature and culture?" – but instead sets out to displace this question and its founding categories altogether.

Read from the perspective of this last moment, the first three moments can be seen to follow – and reinforce – the terms of what Bruno Latour (1993) has called the "modern Constitution," which, among its various clauses includes the *separation* of nature and culture into distinct ontological domains. Viewed in this way it also becomes possible to see that in respect to its concern over the relation between nature and culture, the discipline of geography is symptomatic of a 'modern' episteme in which certain problematics presented themselves as self-evident, and in urgent need of investigation. To say this in somewhat different terms, as the discipline most concerned with the 'nature–culture' problem, geography filled a slot provided for it by the very terms of the modern Constitution. Indeed, we might press this further to suggest that in this respect geography is, paradigmatically, the *most* modern of disciplines, for unlike other disciplines, like sociology and political science, which have sought to explain the dynamics of the 'cultural' side of this dualism (through the analysis of 'culture,' 'society,' 'politics,' 'economy'), or, like physics and ecology, which have sought to explain the 'natural' side of this dualism (through the analysis of 'force,' 'energy,' and 'matter'), geography has made *both sides* of this dualism its object of investigation, not by placing them within the same analytical field, *but by continuously worrying over their relation*! In this sense geography must be read not only as an effect or symptom of this Constitution, but also a key source for its continued institutional and imaginative hold.

As we will see, the fourth moment that I track in this essay – nonmodern ontologies – does much more than displace the problem of culture and nature by attacking the terms of the modern Constitution, it also produces a crisis within the very notion of *disciplinarity*, and raises serious questions for how we understand 'cultural' geography or, indeed, the discipline of geography itself.

Culture and Nature: Tracking the Career of a Problematic

How are 'culture' and 'nature' related? What governs this relation? These questions have concerned geographers since the inception of the discipline in the nineteenth century. My goal here will not be to develop an exhaustive account of the different ways that these questions have been answered, reaching back to the time of figures such as Humboldt, Marsh, and Ratzel, but instead to map a distribution of competing contemporary approaches. For the sake of brevity, my descriptions will be necessarily coarse; a more careful examination of each position would locate many nuances that are not addressed here, as well as ways in which the positions bleed into each other. All three approaches that I initially examine – cultural ecology, political ecology, cultural studies of the environment – have developed highly influential accounts of the relation between culture and nature (or 'society–environment relations'), and have provided analytical tools that have been of great importance to geographers and scholars working in related disciplines.

Dreams of unity: cultural ecology and the seductions of systems theory

Cultural ecology – sometimes called human ecology – represents one of the most fascinating efforts in the history of geography to systematically investigate the relation between nature and culture. It gained prominence in geography in the late 1960s and early 1970s, leaning heavily on the work of ecological anthropologists for its intellectual resources and methods. Although its influence has waned, it continues to cast a long shadow over the discipline, and still claims many adherents (see Turner 1989, Butzer 1989).

Stated in broad terms, cultural ecology sought to develop a *unified theory* of culture and nature, one which would dissolve the culture–nature dualism and replace it with a single totality. To achieve this it drew extensively on the science of *ecology*, the field of *cybernetics*, and *systems theory* more generally. At the very outset, this tells us something about the traffic in ideas between disciplines – how ideas developed in certain contexts come to be *translated* into other contexts and with what effects. At the time, ecology, systems theory and cybernetics were immensely popular resources not only for geographers, but for scholars across the social sciences, much as political economy, poststructuralism, and cultural studies would be in the 1980s and 1990s.[3] From these resources cultural ecology developed one of its central and most controversial claims: that human activities, much like the activities of other organisms, played *functional roles* within ecological systems, roles which contributed to the integrity and continuity of these systems. This central concept provided the basis for a research agenda that saw scholars fan out across the globe to investigate the ecological function of specific cultural practices (such as methods of cultivation, property ownership, or rituals), and to attempt to understand these practices in terms of *adaptation to* and *regulation of* specific environmental conditions. The resulting studies provided a wealth of fine-grained empirical studies that enumerated the cultural practices of various 'traditional' societies, gathered data on climate and ecology, evaluated cultural practices in terms of flows of energy and matter (measured in units such as calories), and mapped the complex feedback loops that connected cultural practices and local ecologies.

These efforts were fraught with both logical and logistical difficulties, but before turning to these I wish to suggest that the objectives of cultural ecology were more interesting than many of its critics have allowed. In important respects cultural ecology was a reaction to developments in anthropology (and elsewhere in the social sciences) which had resulted in 'culture' (or 'society') being understood to develop according to its own internal dynamics, entirely *autonomous* from its physical environments. As Marvin Harris (1974) complained, anthropology had increasingly accepted the position that culture begot culture, and thus had lost its ability to understand the *material conditions* within which cultural practices emerged and to which they adapted (in anthropology Harris's position came to be known as 'cultural materialism'). The culturalism of mid-century anthropology, of course, was quite understandable, having developed in reaction to the earlier influence of environmental determinism (or anthropogeography – the belief that the environment determined the traits of individuals and societies) and in response to possibilism (the belief that nature set certain parameters within which humans exercised choice or will). Geographers and anthropologists had rightly identified both as harboring dubious, even racist, conclusions. Indeed, it should be noted that many cultural ecologists were as wary of these positions as their so-called culturalist colleagues. Or, more precisely, while they accepted the *interrelationship* of culture and nature posited by environmental determinism and possibilism, they rejected what Clifford Geertz (1963) called their 'holism' (see also Vayda & Rappaport 1968). This was essentially an argument about scale and level of abstraction. As Geertz explained, these earlier approaches had understood both culture and ecology in such *broad* terms as to be virtually meaningless: 'Eskimos' and 'Aborigines,' understood in terms of 'polar regions' and 'deserts.' The conclusions drawn at this level of abstraction, he argued, could not possibly be substantiated. Yet, for ecological anthropologists, the *rejection* of environmental determinism and possibilism was seen as equally problematic, since it had led scholars to privilege historical or cultural influences as the sole determinants of cultural phenomena, thereby severing any connection with the environment (Vayda & Rappaport 1968) or material conditions (Harris 1974).[4]

As we will see later, these arguments anticipate many of the criticisms put forward by actor-network theorists, who some three decades later would argue that Western societies had lost their ability to recognize the ways that people and things were intimately connected. Bruno Latour (1993), for instance, has argued that our failure to locate people and things on the same ontological and analytical plane is the reason we 'shuttle' between two opposed positions – that people are all-powerful and can transform their culture in whatever way they pleased (culture begets culture), or that people are impotent and can do nothing, since culture is determined by nature (environmental determinism). In a sense cultural ecologists sought to resolve this contradiction by seeking a middle ground that avoided the excesses of environmental determinism, but that also rejected the idea of the autonomy of 'culture.' This would be accomplished, some of its practitioners thought, by developing more thorough, fine-grained understandings of the *specific relations* that existed between local communities and their surrounding environments.

This put great emphasis on fieldwork, as individuals and research teams enumerated, measured, and diagrammed the "complex, systemic interrelationships"

(Butzer 1989) that bound peoples and ecologies in particular places. These efforts were initially led by a number of ecological anthropologists, including prominent figures such as Julian Steward, Andrew Vayda, Roy Rappaport, Marvin Harris, and Clifford Geertz. Steward (1955) outlined some of cultural ecology's first methodological principles, including that the researcher must first isolate those aspects of cultural practice whose functional ties to the environment were most explicit, or where the interdependencies of cultural practices and organism–environment relationships were seen to be most crucial. Not insignificantly, Steward called these practices the 'cultural core,' in contrast to other cultural practices which he considered contingent or secondary. In turn, the cultural ecologist would isolate the ecological relations and processes that appeared most important for the human 'adaptations' that had been identified. Geertz (1963: 8) considered this a relatively straightforward task:

If one empirically determines the constellation of cultural features which are most unequivocally related to the processes of energy interchange between man and his surroundings in any given instance, one necessarily also determines which environmental features have primary relevance for those same processes.

Beginning with a cultural practice, researchers would carefully detail its ecological consequences – modifications of soils, vegetation and animal life, number of calories produced as food – and outline the various relations and feedback loops in the system, thereby revealing how existing practices had 'adapted' to environmental conditions. Significantly, neither Steward nor Geertz sought to collapse *all* cultural practices and *all* ecological processes into a single system. Geertz, in particular, argued that some practices were completely unrelated to environmental conditions, and rejected Steward's designation of 'core' and 'contingent.'

These limited qualifications would appear to go some way to rescuing cultural ecology from accusations that it merely packaged an updated environmental determinism. But others were far less cautious and sought to extend the emerging discipline further in the direction of finding 'adaptation' as the key to culture. Andrew Vayda and Roy Rappaport (1968), for instance, argued that Steward had a far too limited view of *which* cultural practices had ecological significance, and thus which practices could properly be seen as adaptive responses to environmental conditions. In particular, they chastised Steward for disregarding religious practices, especially rituals. Within anthropology at the time it was common to explain (or dismiss) these as functioning merely to mediate the fear and powerlessness of primitive peoples in the face of natural forces – a cultural response to the terror of sublime nature. Of those studies that sought to understand such 'secondary' practices in terms of ecological functions, Roy Rappaport's (1967) infamous study of the ritual of pig killing in New Guinea is perhaps most widely cited. In his study Rappaport argued that pig-killing rituals had important *ecological* functions. His conclusions are worth quoting at length:

The Tsembaga ritual cycle has been regarded as a complex *homeostatic* mechanism, operating to maintain the values of a number of variables within 'goal ranges' (ranges of values that permit the perpetuation of a system, as constituted, through indefinite periods of time). It has been argued that the regulatory functions of ritual among the Tsembaga and Maring help to maintain an undegraded environment, limits fighting to frequences that do not endanger the existence of the regional population, adjusts man-land ratios, facilitates trade, distributes local surpluses of pig in the form of pork throughout the regional population, and assures people of high-quality protein when they most need it. . . . The Tsembaga, designated a 'local population,' have been regarded as a population in the animal ecologist's sense: a unit composed of an aggregate or organisms having in common certain distinctive means whereby they maintain a set of trophic relations with other living and nonliving components of the biotic community [with?] which they exist together. (p. 224)

Similar conclusions about 'ritual' were reached by other researchers, from shoulder-blade divination among North American caribou hunters (Moore 1957), to sexual license during the ceremonial season among the Indians of the Central Desert of Baja California (Aschmann 1959). Such studies came perilously close to reproducing the environmental determinism of anthropogeography, and the possibilism of the French geographer Vidal de la Blache.

In geography, cultural ecology would gain importance in the 1970s, led by figures such as Bernard Nietschmann, Karl Butzer, William Denevan, Alfred Siemens, and Philip Porter. These studies would for the most part follow the theoretical and methodological innovations of ecological anthropology. Nietschmann's research on the Miskito Indians on the Caribbean coast of Central America is in many ways typical. Following the lead of Steward and others, Nietschmann (1973: x, 1) sought to determine "how a particular population had adapted to local ecosystems and modified them," beginning with the assumption that "many indigenous cultures which interact with these [Latin American] ecosystems have adapted their food resource strategies so that ecological integrity is protected." To be sure, this was not a unidirectional imprinting of nature on culture; rather, through recourse to systems theory, the environment and human populations were understood as "parts of an interacting system which, through its circular relationships and systems of negative and positive feedback, influences and modifies each one and changes them together" (p. 4). Similar to the ecological anthropologists, for Nietschmann 'ecosystem' became the master term, borrowed directly from Eugene Odum's 1959 classic, *Fundamentals of Ecology*.

These studies would later come under harsh criticism, but it is not hard to see why it should have been viewed with such promise, or why the work of cultural ecologists has received renewed, albeit critical, attention in recent years. The payoff, Geertz (1963: 8) argued, was that

the sharpness of the division between analysis from the side of 'man' and analyses from the side of 'nature' . . . disappears, for the two approaches are essentially alternative and interchangeable conceptualizations of the same systemic process.

Cultural ecologists, Geertz explained, could achieve an "exact specification" of the "relation between selected human activities, biological transactions, and physical processes" (p. 2), and could do so by "including them within a single analytical system, an ecosystem." In short, Geertz imagined that it was possible to understand cultures and their environments as *single* entities, anticipating in a somewhat uncanny manner similar calls made across the social and ecological sciences several decades later. Indeed, read from the perspective of the nonmodern ontologies that

I will discuss below, Geertz's critique of existing approaches to the 'culture and nature problematic' is worth quoting at length. Speaking of anthropogeography and possibilism, he wrote:

Both initially separate the works of man and the processes of nature into different spheres – 'culture' and 'environment' – and then attempt subsequently to see how as independent wholes these externally related spheres affect one another. With such a formulation, one can ask only the grossest of questions: "how far is culture influenced by environment?" "How far is the environment modified by the activities of men?" And can give only the grossest of answers: "To a degree, but not completely." (p. 2)

Andrew Vayda put it similarly:

Although there have been numerous pleas for treating cultural, environmental, and human biological variables as parts of one system, these pleas have been but little heeded by most social scientists. Even among the relatively few contemporary social scientists who are especially concerned with the relation between cultural and noncultural phenomena, the prevailing tendency has been to define the cultural variables and the other ones as belonging to separate systems and then to ask about the influence of the systems upon one another. (1967: xii–xiii)

Taking an 'ecological' approach, Geertz explained, would not separate the works of man from the processes of nature, but instead understand them as an *integrated whole*, since "material interdependencies" would "form a [single] community."

I will revisit these claims later. For my present purposes, what is of interest is less cultural ecology's call for a unified theory, than how this unity was conceived. As already noted, cultural ecology emerged during the heyday of ecosystem ecology, systems theory, and cybernetics. From ecology, cultural ecologists borrowed more than an increased awareness of biological processes and ecological relations, but also the notion of *interrelated wholes*, captured most fully in the notion of 'ecosystem.' From systems theory they took on board the notion of complex feedback loops, often appealing to the elegant diagrams of the ecologist Eugene Odum. And from cybernetics they found a new basis for an age-old belief in homeostatic systems and the balance of nature (see Demeritt 1994).

This potent combination may have promised to bridge the poles of nature and culture (Zimmerer 1996: 172), but it also provided the conceptual scaffolding for cultural ecology's most significant – and problematic – claim: that cultural practices had *functions* within larger ecological systems, and could be understood and analyzed in these terms (a claim that aligned cultural ecology with forms of Darwinism). Under the sway of systems theory, cultural practices were often taken to exist solely as *adaptive mechanisms* whose purpose was to retain *equilibrium* in the system as a whole. In his study of pig-killing rituals, for instance, Rappaport (1967: 4) made much of the 'self-regulating' nature of systemic relationships, drawing an analogy between cultural practices and thermostats. Each was seen to regulate the environment in a way that kept conditions relatively constant. Even Geertz, known later for his 'thick description' of cultural practices, drew inspiration from Odum in order to argue that the "maintenance of system equilibrium or homeostasis is the central organizing force" of specific cultures and cultural practices.

Although far from uniformly applied, this reliance on general systems theory and its associated notions of balance and self-regulation would eventually come under withering attack. Foremost among the charges leveled at cultural ecologists was that of functionalism – that theories of 'cultural adaptation' falsely imputed the *effects* of cultural practices as their *cause*. As Zimmerer (1996) notes, this problem was exacerbated by the tendency of such studies to be synchronic and ahistorical. Few researchers made any effort to develop historical accounts of how specific cultural practices emerged, or how they came to be extended across space and time. As complex as were cultural ecology's charts of energy flows, and as finely grained as were its descriptions of the ecological role of cultural practices, it was never quite able to adequately answer the 'why' question of cultural practices. Neither the *genesis* of cultural practices nor their *transformation* could be explained, except through vague appeals to 'adaptation.'

Equally as problematic, while writers like Geertz imagined that these studies finally transcended the culture–nature dualism, showing culture and nature to exist as a *single* unit, they in large part did so through a sleight-of-hand – by collapsing culture *into* nature. To be sure, human actors did things – they plowed, told stories, performed rituals – but nature largely predetermined what these actions would be. Nature and culture were brought together, critics asserted, but at the price of losing half of the actors!

During the 1980s, challenges to cultural ecology's central concepts – adaptation, trophic systems, feedback loops, homeostasis – intensified. To charges of functionalism would be added the charge of historicism, since the field's assumption of homeostasis – again borrowed from systems theory and ecosystem ecology – conspired to make its accounts remarkably teleological. All cultural practices were seen to lead to the same inevitable end (ecosystem integrity). To be sure, not all cultural ecologists fell into these traps. Its more astute adherents carefully distinguished between approaches which claimed to *explain* cultural practices, and those which merely noted the ecological *function* that cultural practices appeared to have, without imputing cause (Vayda & Rappaport 1968). As Vayda (1967: x) put it in a spirited defense of cultural ecology, the object of analysis was "a demonstration of how things work rather than an explanation of why they exist or how they have come to be." Yet the line between description and explanation was often blurred and the notion of adaptation frequently smuggled in the very assumptions that Vayda fought to excise. Other cultural ecologists noted that not all cultural practices led to homeostasis: some produced catastrophic change. But more often than not these were seen as a result of the introduction or diffusion of new or foreign practices that upset the fine-tuned balance that had been achieved between local communities and their environments. That cultural ecologists almost universally studied 'traditional' societies no doubt contributed further to this sense of socio-ecological balance, tapping into widespread understandings of modernity as rupture and premodern societies as inherently ecological.

Other critics focused on how cultural ecologists conceived of 'culture,' faulting practitioners for presenting culture as monolithic, static and bounded, and for erasing history and politics (see Duncan 1980; Cosgrove & Jackson 1987; Gupta

& Ferguson 1997). Indeed, for many critics, the language of ecology was partly to blame. In the texts of some cultural ecologists culture had itself come to be understood like an organism – and as an organism, a functional part of an eco-system – rather than as an outcome of political contestation, as cultural anthro-pologists and the 'new' cultural geographers claimed it to be, or as bound up with social and economic forces, as political economists increasingly argued it was. As a result, critics suggested, *relations of power* were ignored entirely, except in the broad historical frame of culture groups being 'displaced' by others (cf. Peet & Watts 1996).

Beginning in the late 1970s, competing approaches emerged in geography that contrasted with, and often directly contested, the functionalism and teleology of cul-tural ecology, and which sought to understand the decisions of individual actors – what Blaikie and Brookfield (1987) would famously call 'land managers' – in terms of the *social relations* within which they lived. This marked a significant departure, for it immediately called into question cultural ecology's depoliticizing language of 'adaptation' (which reduced culture to nature), and its tendency to locate agency in abstract entities like 'cultures' and 'ecosystems.' Instead, the turn to social relations focused attention on the social, ecological, and political contexts – at local, regional, and global scales – within which individual actors lived, and sought to investigate how *these* relations shaped environmental practices.

Political ecology and the turn to the social

We have now moved some distance toward our second 'moment,' political ecology. How did political ecology reconfigure how geographers approached the problem of the *relation* between culture and nature? In brief: by turning to the social. We will see shortly that this turn remained fully within the terms of Latour's 'modern Con-stitution,' despite its promise to do otherwise and despite its recourse to dialectics as a way of overcoming modern dualisms.

In geography, political ecology took root in the 1980s, but its sources are far too diffuse to allow it to be read solely as a reaction to the pitfalls of cultural ecology. Indeed the notion that political ecology merely 'advanced' or 'transcended' cultural ecology is belied by two observations: first, although its popularity has diminished, cultural ecology is far from dead, and continues to have influence in the discipline (see Butzer 1989; Turner 1989; Sluyter 1996, 1999), and, second, even during the heyday of cultural ecology in the 1970s, other scholars were approaching questions of culture and nature through terms that were similar to what would travel under the banner of political ecology in the 1980s and 1990s. The earliest uses of the phrase political ecology, for instance, date to the early 1970s and the work of the anthropologist Eric Wolf (1972), writer Hans Magnus Enzensberger (1974) and journalist Alexander Cockburn (Cockburn & Ridgeway 1979),whose writings made explicit a set of political questions around natural resources and the environment, including rights of access and control (see Watts 2001, Zimmerer 1996).

A complete genealogy of political ecology is beyond the scope of this essay, but a number of important threads can be identified. The 1970s were a decade of increased concern over environmental conditions, both in the developed economies of the West and in less developed regions in Asia, Africa, and Latin America. One influential response was neo-Malthusian, which placed the blame for environmental degradation on population growth, and thus firmly at the feet of those most affected by environmental change in the Third World (see Ehrlich 1968). Critics of neo-Malthusian ideas argued that it was not population growth, but poverty and its structural causes that were to blame. With this came far greater emphasis on structural relations, and increased attention to the affects of political and economic change (especially the transition from subsistence to market economies) as well as the role of economic and political actors such as the state, corporations and nongovernmental organizations. The 1980s also saw the resurgence of political economy – and social theory more generally – across the social sciences and humanities. This provided geographers with a very different toolkit through which to interrogate questions of 'culture' and 'nature' (now frequently discussed as 'society' and 'environment'). In place of cybernetics and general systems theory, researchers turned to Marxist political economy, structuration theory, Weberian sociology, and world systems theory, in order to understand the economic logics and social relations that shaped the decisions of environmental actors. Political ecology found an additional source in studies of 'natural hazards,' a field which was going through a similar transition, moving from seeing such hazards as floods, drought, and famine as caused entirely by nonhuman forces, to investigating their social, political, and economic causes and their radically uneven social effects (Sen 1981; Watts 1983; Smith & O'Keefe 1980; Hewitt 1983; Susman, O'Keefe, & Wisner 1983). As attention shifted to the social causes of environmental change, skepticism increased over the organic analogies, Darwinian terminologies, and systems theories that prevailed in cultural ecology. Increasingly, cultural ecology came to be viewed as apolitical and asocial, even if, like Bernard Neitschmann, its practitioners were deeply concerned with the peoples and environments they studied.

Today, what travels under the name 'political ecology' is remarkably diverse. This is in part because there is no single theoretical 'core' that anchors it, in contrast to the more unified project of cultural ecology. Nevertheless, for my purposes 'political ecology' usefully designates a number of key shifts that occurred in how the relation between culture and nature was conceptualized during the 1980s. Perhaps the most important was the transition – already noted – from a focus on culture and adaptation, to a focus on the actions of individual actors and their enabling and constraining social conditions. This approach demanded attention to *scale*, a point raised early by Eric Wolf (1972), and taken up more extensively by political ecologists in the years following. Exemplary in this regard was the work of Piers Blaikie (1985), whose study of soil degradation in South Asia focused on the resource manager (usually a peasant) and sought to understand the wider economic and political forces shaping their land-management decisions. A later edited collection with Harold Brookfield (Blaikie & Brookfield 1987) extended these insights in order to tackle the Malthusian assumptions prevalent during the period head-on, with its editors and contributors arguing that there was a causal – and cumulative – relation between poverty and environmental degradation. Conditions of poverty, they argued, led to poor environmental management strategies, often out of necessity. This in turn led to environmental degradation, which could exacerbate the poverty of the land manager. For Blaikie and Brookfield, the poverty of the land manager could not simply be blamed on overpopulation, but instead had to be understood through 'chains of explanation' which linked local decisions with wider social, economic and political structures (property rights, state power, market relations, ideas and ideologies).[5]

While the work of Blaikie and Brookfield was exemplary, it was far from unique. Increasingly, others working at diverse 'Third World' sites – Michael Watts, Suzanna Hecht, and Alex Cockburn, for instance – brought political economy to bear on environmental problems. Over time what constituted the 'social' factors linked to environmental change (through their impact on access and control over resources) would expand to include not only market capitalism, the state and property, but also international or multilateral organizations such as the World Bank and the IMF, the actions and strategies of transnational corporations, the practices of myriad non-governmental organizations (both local and international), and the tactics of local communities and individuals (for a survey, see Bryant & Bailey 1997). Likewise, analysis in terms of class difference was increasingly widened to include the connections between political struggles over resources and environment and questions of ethnicity (Watts 1998), gender (Rocheleau et al. 1996; Schroeder 1999) and nation. Richard Schroeder's *Shady Practices* (1999), a study of gender, nature, and politics in Gambia, exemplified this broadened political ecology. In this work he tracked the relation between gender politics and struggles over land tenure, while at the same time linking these struggles to the intersection of economic change, drought and famine, and placing these struggles – and their outcomes – in the context of shifting funding agendas and development paradigms of NGOs, large donor agencies, and organizations such as the World Bank. In one of the book's most innovative elements, Schroeder analyzed the changing terms of a *discourse* that linked 'women' and 'development,' and explored how this discourse was taken up within development programs and influenced the types of projects funded by international agencies during the 1980s and 1990s. By so doing Schroeder not only made important connections with the work of feminist critics of development (see Shiva 1988, Agarwal 1992, Jackson 1993), he also drew attention to the significance and politics of *language* and the role of struggles over *meaning*, for how 'development' and 'environmental change' proceeded in particular sites. This was evident within development agencies and state institutions, but also within the local communities affected by development and environmental change, in which individual actors struggled with and over 'words' at the same time as they struggled over land and access to resources. As we will see shortly, this attention to language and meaning would become increasingly important not only in political ecology, but more broadly in the study of the 'culture of nature' as the 1990s progressed.

Taken together, these diverse strands of political ecology represented a significant change in the terms that were now seen to govern the 'relation' between culture and nature. Where cultural ecology had imagined individual bounded culture groups adapting to environmental conditions, political ecologists sought to understand the environmental and resource-use practices of peasants in much wider political-economic, institutional, and discursive contexts. Where the scale of analysis of the former was decidedly – and usually unquestionedly – 'local,' questions of scale themselves became key for political ecologists, who insisted that 'local' events and practices be understood in terms of actors and institutions that operated at regional, national and international scales. This was not simply a matter of locating the correct scale of analysis, but of recognizing that scale was *relational* – that the 'local' was constituted in relation to events and actors at other scales, and vice versa. Further, whereas in cultural ecology, culture was seen as singular and monolithic – "a culture" – political ecologists placed increasing emphasis on politics and power, and moved the 'environment' from a neutral object that provided a template for culture, to a 'politicized' domain that was the object of intense political struggle. Finally, whereas for cultural ecologists nature and culture were understood to exist in a unity as a result of complex interactions and feedback loops that led to homeostasis (the thermostat metaphor), in political ecology, nature and culture were understood in a unity that was decidedly *dialectical* rather than *homeostatic*. Here the concerns of political ecologists intersected with those of historical materialists who understood human actions as part of nature's 'metabolism': people were understood as one of nature's constituent parts, but also as a *productive force* that continuously transformed nature and was transformed in the process (see Schmidt 1971, Smith 1984, Castree 1995). In this sense, nature was not something external to which people had to adapt – it was thoroughly 'social,' its future form to be determined by history and politics (Smith 1984, Braun & Castree 1998).

This final distinction is important. If cultural ecology resolved the culture/ nature dualism through collapsing culture into nature (accomplished through the generalization of the metaphor of 'ecosystem'), political ecology sought to resolve the dualism through a double move. Like cultural ecology it asserted a unity, but unlike cultural ecology, the arrow of determination was reversed: people were still considered a constituent part of nature, but the agency of nature was now replaced with an emphasis on *humans* as productive and transformative agents. Further, in contrast to cultural ecology, political ecology made no attempt to provide a single epistemology. Karl Zimmerer (1996) astutely notes that while cultural ecology imagined that it could study nature and culture as a single entity and through a single method (measuring flows of energy and matter), political ecology *divided* the study of ecology (and the ecological impacts of human actions) from the study of society and its structures, each of which was assumed to have its own 'autonomous' existence and laws or imperatives. To the physical sciences it gave nature and natural processes; to the social sciences it gave politics and social relations. This was encapsulated in the turn to dialectics, which understood 'nature' and 'society' in terms of a progressive *interaction* between different elements – a "constantly shifting dialectic between society and land-based resources, and also within classes and groups within society itself" (Blaikie & Brookfield 1987).

While political ecology's turn to the social appeared to resolve the problem of history and politics – that which cultural ecology lacked – it brought back history and politics at a price. On the one hand, it accepted without question the terms of the modern Constitution. It began by dividing the world into two separate domains – nature and society – and then sought to understand their relation. Dialectics provided a way of imagining this process, but while dialectics allowed for the 'interaction' of the two domains, it merely made the divide more permeable (Castree 2002). Worse, as critics quickly noted, political ecology granted agency, history, and politics to only one side of this dualism – 'society' – which was now conceptualized as a realm of struggle and contestation, the outcomes of which would be *imprinted* on the environment. To be sure, the old notion of 'feedbacks' was occasionally retained, such that human transformations of nature were seen to have subsequent effects, but for the most part the second domain – 'nature' – was merely imagined as a static entity – the 'ground' over which politics occurred, but most certainly not a dynamic actor in its own right. Ironically, and perhaps unwittingly, in its reaction to the depoliticizing language of cultural ecology, political ecology merely reversed its position, and thus reinstalled the very same dichotomy. Whereas cultural ecology collapsed culture into nature, political ecology did the opposite, turning the arrow of causation around but keeping the dualism in place.

This apparent erasure of nature's 'agency' would become an issue of considerable anxiety in the late 1990s (see below). But, significantly, this was *not* the source of the first criticisms of political ecology. Far from expressing concern that political ecology had lost sight of ecology, critics of political ecology focused on a different matter: that in their scramble to locate the *wider structures* that shaped human practices, political ecologists had managed to get the 'social' side of the equation wrong.

The cultural studies of the environment: challenging essentialisms, deepening dichotomies?

What had been political ecology's error? In the minds of its critics, it had fallen into two traps. On the one hand, its turn to social *structures* left it open to the accusation of replacing environmental determinism with social determinism. If, for cultural ecologists, individuals and communities were merely bearers of 'culture,' and culture was itself an adaptation to environmental conditions, then under political ecology, individuals and communities fared no better, for their actions were now determined by economic logics, state rationalities, and ideologies both beyond their control and beyond everyday consciousness. Indeed, it is notable that despite its claim to study a 'politicized environment,' political ecology often had as little to say about politics as had cultural ecology, for while cultural ecology had overemphasized the role of 'culture' as an overarching and unified set of beliefs and practices, political ecologists often did the same for the 'economy,' the 'state,' 'modernity,' and 'ideology,' such that the way that local communities and individuals negotiated, resisted, or helped constitute specific economic and political processes was vastly under theorized. Political ecology had a great deal to say about 'large' structures, but far less to say about how local actors came to passively accept the roles that these larger forces apparently had in store for them. In response to these problems, questions of resistance, and the ways that local communities and individuals appropriated or contested state projects, market relations, or even the plans of NGOs, increasingly found their way into the work of a second generation of political ecologists who were much more attuned to 'micropolitics' and to the performative aspects of cultural, political and spatial practices (Moore 1998, Moore 2000, Escobar 1996, Schroeder 1999).

A second charge – economism – was related to the first, but was directed specifically at the privileging of *political economy* in accounts of struggles over resources and environment. Here the concern was that too much emphasis was placed on economic forces, with many early accounts relying on a base–superstructure model that tended to see all other dimensions of social life as secondary, or as determined by the economic. Second-generation political ecologists would respond to this too, integrating into their analysis much greater attention to the cultural practices, scientific knowledges, and discursive relations that were equally important constitutive elements in political struggles over the environment and development. To conceptualize this, many turned to the work of the Italian Marxist, Antonio Gramsci, and the French historian and philosopher, Michel Foucault (see Moore 1998, Escobar 1996). From Gramsci was borrowed the notion that the rule of governing classes was enabled not only through force, but through the consent of the subaltern classes, brought about through the church, schools, and cultural institutions. This challenged the narrow economism of Marxist political economy, and rejected deterministic arguments about social structures. In a move that echoed Vayda and Rappaport's call to cultural ecologists to widen their scope beyond those cultural practices most obviously linked to the environment, political ecologists that followed Gramsci's lead took a much wider view of the *sites* at which struggles over access and control over resources occurred, no longer content to study state institutions and market reforms, but also schools, religion, historical narratives, and science.

Others turned to Foucault, whose reworking of conceptions of power, investigation of the relation between power and knowledge, and careful attention to processes of subjectification, proved immensely productive for rethinking how political ecologists conceived of 'social relations' and 'politics.' For Foucault, power was not something possessed by sovereign entities (institutions, individuals, dominant classes or the state) as if it were a thing, but rather was *immanent* to the world, present in, and working through, orders of knowledge, the organization of space, and the training of bodies. It was at once relational and capillary, diffused and everywhere, best understood as a 'field' or 'grid' of knowledges, practices, and spaces within which people and things were made visible and available to administrative or disciplinary mechanisms. In this sense power was *positive* or *productive* rather than *repressive*: it constituted subjects and enabled actions, including actions that undermined particular social orders. Often combined with Gramscian critiques of 'hegemony,' the influence of Foucault could be found in notions such as 'countermapping' (Peluso 1995), or in the 'micropractices' studied by Donald Moore (1998), who understood cultural practices around conservation in Zimbabwe as key sites of struggle over the fate of landscapes and communities.

Foucault's influence was also evident in the turn to the study of *environmental discourses* – those bodies of ideas, concepts and knowledges through which actors understand and engage with their ecological surrounds (see Darier 1999; Luke 1997). Studies of environmental discourse relied heavily on an interpretation of Foucault that took understandings of the world to be *effects of power*, and which simultaneously understood power to operate *in and through* forms of knowledge that infused everyday life. Often this was combined with other strains of poststructuralist thought (semiotics, deconstruction) which emphasized the arbitrary and unstable nature of 'reference,' and which understood the *legibility* of the world to be an effect of signification rather than something discovered and reflected in nature (see below). In short, poststructuralisms of various sorts were taken to have displaced the image of language (or thought) as the 'mirror of nature' (Rorty 1980) and replaced it with a notion of language as constitutive of what *counts* as nature. Over the past decade these arguments have been taken up by a number of scholars working on questions of nature, politics, and environment. Within political ecology, for instance, Arturo Escobar (1996), argued that representations were social facts – that language did not 'reflect' nature, it 'constituted' what counted as nature – and deployed this insight to interrogate the discourse of 'sustainable development' as it was employed in Columbia. This discourse, in which "nature is resignified as environment," Escobar argued, was thoroughly infused with relations of power. It was at once consistent with the emergence of a scientific gaze which Foucault had previously claimed "enabl[ed] one *to see* and *to say*" (quoted in Escobar 1996), and also crucial for the sustainability of capital today through intensive forms of environmental *management*, what Escobar called a new 'postmodern' form of capitalizing nature. For Escobar, the significance of interrogating discourses such as "sustainable development" lay in making visible the power relations that operated in its terms, attending to the relation between knowledge and administration (or *governmentality* – see Darier 1999; Luke 1997; Braun 2000), and calling attention to the increased significance of 'expert' knowledges at the expense of other knowledges, which came to be displaced or subjugated.

While poststructuralist theory had considerable influence on political ecology in the 1990s, its impact extended far beyond political ecology, and increasingly gave rise to novel approaches to the study of culture and nature. I will refer to this third 'moment' as the *cultural studies of the environment*. Again, a sharp distinction between more poststructuralist approaches to political ecology and cultural studies of the environment is somewhat arbitrary. Some, like the anthropologists Donald Moore and Arturo Escobar, fit well in both. However, to the extent that certain common themes can be identified, such a distinction may be warranted. These themes included the following: the study of 'nature' as a cultural construction; close attention to the relation between power and knowledge in struggles over resources and environment; greater emphasis on representational practices – science, art, literature – as sites where nature was called forth as an object of knowledge and contemplation; and an awareness that constructions of nature were never innocent, but instead intricately entangled with, and enabling of, governmental rationalities, racial and colonial discourses, and the construction of gendered, racial and ethnic/national identities.

If, like political ecology, cultural studies of the environment can be said to have a theoretical 'toolkit,' the tools of the latter are considerably different than those of the former, to such an extent that many scholars working in this area do not claim any direct affiliation with, or descent from, cultural or political ecology (see Sluyter 1997; Braun 1997b). Indeed, most have come to investigate the cultural politics of nature from other research agendas and very different theoretical and political concerns – studies of race and ethnicity, feminist and queer theory, explorations of colonialism and its technologies of rule, eco-politics and governmentality, critical race theory and post-Marxism. A complete genealogy would be daunting, but would most certainly take in semiotics (Barthes), the study of power/knowledge (Foucault), deconstruction (Derrida), poststructuralist feminisms (Haraway, Butler), and even, on occasion, psychoanalytic theory (Lacan), along with the cultural Marxisms of Gramsci and the English literary critic Raymond Williams.

This work is not limited to geography, and in many ways established itself elsewhere first. Alexander Wilson's (1992) immensely popular book, *The Culture of*

Nature, was one of the first to demonstrate the analytical power and political urgency of arguments that nature was 'culturally mediated' – known and understood through a vast array of images and ideas that circulated in film, literature, popular culture, advertisements and popular scientific narratives – and that this had consequences for the use and conservation of the environment. In a sense this updated and popularized the arguments of Raymond Williams (1980), who had earlier traced the changing fortunes of 'nature' within English literature and culture, drawing on Gramsci's notion of hegemony to link ideologies of nature with the power of ruling classes.[6] William Cronon's (1995) eloquent study of the concept of 'wilderness' also extended Williams' insight, revealing nature in the United States to be full of human history, both conceptually and materially. Like Wilson, Cronon's intervention was closely tied to an environmental politics, albeit one that conflicted with those American environmentalisms indebted to concepts and 'structures of feeling' bequeathed by Romanticism. His conclusion – that 'wilderness' took us to the wrong nature, since it presupposed a nature–culture dualism whereby that which was 'truly' natural was that which most fully excluded the human – vexed many. But it sought to raise awareness of how our tendency to dichotomize the world into these 'pure' domains made it tremendously difficult to develop an *ethical* and *political* relation to the world, since 'saving' nature – defined as the absence of the human – required eliminating people altogether, while spaces that could not easily be assigned to the category 'pristine' were inherently devalued (as 'modified' or 'degraded' landscapes) and not seen as worthy of ecological interest.

As noted above, others brought a decidedly semiotic approach, treating 'nature' as a signifier whose meaning was given by a system of signs. For the semiotician, 'nature' attained its meanings through the differential logic of a chain of signifiers rather than from the world itself. For structuralists like Ferdinand de Saussure, this differential logic of signification was both arbitrary, and in many respects, *fixed*. For poststructuralists, on the other hand, there was both nothing 'outside' language which could finally fix meaning once and for all and no necessary structure *to* language that governed meaning. Thus, it followed that the meaning(s) of 'nature' were always subject to the *play* of signification (Derrida 1976) and that how nature's meanings came to be provisionally established could be understood as a matter of both urgent scholarly investigation and ongoing political struggle (see Braun & Wainwright 2001).

Perhaps the most influential figure in this realm was the science studies scholar Donna Haraway (1992), who drew not only on semiotics, but was also influenced by Michel Foucault and his insistence that the world could be known only through the terms of specific (contested) discursive formations. Haraway drew a simple, but controversial, conclusion from her readings of poststructuralists: that what *counts* as nature could not exist separately from the practices through which it was rendered as a legible or knowable domain. Haraway's actual phrase – "nature cannot preexist its construction" – has been widely debated and often misunderstood. Some have suggested that this was an idealism of the worst sort, akin to claiming that the materiality of the world was merely 'in our heads.' Others claimed that arguments of this sort seriously damaged environmentalism, since it undermined the status of the very 'object' that environmentalists sought to save (see Soulé & Lease 1995).

The more common reading, and the one taken up by many cultural geographers, was actually far more consistent with the materialism that some thought Haraway was denying: that what counts as nature is necessarily the outcome of specific *practices* through which nature is given meaning. To say that nature was a 'trope,' not a thing, was therefore not a denial of materiality, it was an affirmation that language – and knowledge more generally – did not have an existence independent from the material practices by which statements about the world were produced. Here we might follow the geographer David Demeritt (1998), who has persuasively argued that Haraway should be read as advocating an 'artifactual constructivism' rather than a 'radical constructivism,' the difference being that while the latter takes the *world* to be our 'invention,' the former takes *knowledge* about the world to be a 'product' or 'artifact' (see also Latour 1987).

But it has been the connection between knowledge and power that has perhaps most defined the cultural studies of the environment. The phrase 'cultural' in this sense has largely referred to questions of representation (science, media, film), and struggles over, and debates concerning, the consequences of how 'nature,' 'organisms,' and the 'environment,' have been constituted as *objects of knowledge* and made *visible to power*. Often work in this vein has had explicit political intentions. Wolch and Emel (1998), for instance, have interrogated the way that 'animals' are set apart from 'humans,' a distinction which Kay Anderson (2001) has recently argued provides a basis for various racisms. Anderson (1998) has argued elsewhere that racialized knowledges have been produced not solely by the sciences of 'man,' but also, and perhaps more insidiously, by those sciences – like Linnaean botany – which take 'nature' as their primary object and field of investigation. Likewise, Jake Kosek (2002) has traced constructions of 'whiteness' and national identity in one of the most beloved icons in the United States: Smokey Bear. Indeed, the relation between constructions of nature and nationalism has become an important theme, from the Japanese context (Nakashima 1999) to German and Italian fascisms (Binde 1999) and English cultural nationalism (Bartram 1999). Likewise, the relation between nature and colonialism has recently seen considerable attention. In her work on ecopolitics and indigenous peoples in Australia, for instance, Jane Jacobs (1996) has explored the boundary stories that positioned aborigines in the domain of nature, and how these stories were produced, reinforced and contested in various Australian sites, including a proposed ecology center in Brisbane. Focusing on Western Canada, Bruce Braun (1997a, 2002) has traced the persistence of colonial relations in constructions of the 'temperate rainforest' by ecologists, foresters and environmentalists, and explored the significance of these images for recent political struggles over forestry and decolonization by First Nations. Derek Gregory (2001) in turn, has traced not only the workings of colonial power in how physical environments were described and known, but also how these representations invariably failed, with no little anxiety for colonial officials and agents for whom non-European natures were often sites of disorientation and terror (see also Taussig 1986). The argument in many of these texts – following on the work of postcolonial scholars such as Edward Said and Gayatri Spivak – is that constructions of nature (as *pristine*, *primeval*, *exotic*, *degraded*, or *unruly*) often provided justification for colonial projects which could then present themselves in the guise of civilizing missions, or as ordering a previously unmanageable landscape.

While many have applauded this cultural turn in studies of society and environment, it has also had its critics. Some have accused this work of trading in a 'discursive determinism,' merely replacing the structuralism of early political ecology with a new kind of determinism that views subjects, and their constitutive desires and knowledges, as effects of discourse rather than structures. Indeed, questions of agency have long been posed by critics of poststructuralisms, who have responded by pointing out that while they may have discarded the fixity of social, linguistic and economic structures, they have decidedly *not* done so in order to recuperate the sovereign subject of liberalism, with its sense of individual consciousness and agency. Other critics argue that the cultural studies of the environment has been little more than a diversion – that it gives its attention to 'texts' rather than 'material relations,' and to 'symbolic' rather than 'real' politics (see Harvey 1996). Such criticisms have been routinely dismissed as either misreadings of what is meant by 'textuality' (which is not just about 'texts,' but rather about how there is no transcendental location, no 'other' level, outside language and practice, from which to finally 'fix' meaning), or as complicit in a largely-discredited economism that dismisses cultural practices as merely 'superstructural.'

Far more serious objections have come from elsewhere, for if the 'cultural politics' of nature has become a prevalent theme in cultural geography in the past decade, so also has a countercurrent that has begun to question the ontological presuppositions that underwrite its claims, as well as those of cultural and political ecology. Informed by the philosophical writings of Gilles Deleuze and Félix Guattari, the work of sociologists of science Bruno Latour and Michel Calon, and the various interventions of Michel Serres, Isabelle Stengers and Manuel deLanda, among others, these critics have seized on the apparent *asymmetry* of many constructivist positions, in order to argue that by locating agency solely in the 'social' or 'cultural' domains, cultural studies is no longer able to say anything about what *nonhumans* contribute to the world, including to the social worlds of humans. To resolve this, some have suggested, it is necessary to abandon the 'nature–culture' problematic altogether, and substitute in its place a series of different concepts: hybrid networks, assemblages, abstract machines.

Beyond 'Culture' and 'Nature'? Nonmodern Ontologies

I will call this fourth moment 'nonmodern ontologies' for reasons that will soon become apparent. From this perspective the problem with political ecology and cultural studies of the environment is not that they propose nature as a social or cultural construction, and thus deny its autonomy, or that they reject language as a transparent medium for nature's representation. Rather, it is that their accounts presuppose a world divided into distinct ontological domains, and thus their accounts leave us with an impoverished understanding of the 'integrated networks' in which humans and nonhumans are entangled, in which entities (people, machines, words) continuously swap properties, and in which 'agency' is diffuse and relational, extending beyond humans to include all manner of other things. Each was guilty of accepting the terms of what Bruno Latour (1993) has called the 'modern Constitution.'

Latour coined the phrase 'modern Constitution' in order to call attention to the ontological presuppositions that underwrite modern society's self-understanding.

The word 'constitution' here has a double meaning. Much like a political constitution (i.e. the American Constitution), it refers to a set of governing principles and separations of power. It also functions as a foundational statement; that is, it calls a *political order* into being (or, in this case, a political ontology). This constitution is, quite literally, *constitutive* of our world, in the sense that it shapes how we understand the world, underwrites our actions, and informs the responsibilities we accept or deny.

Latour argues that modern societies constitute themselves *as* modern through enacting a series of dichotomies: the separation of humans from nonhumans; the separation of science from politics, and the retreat of God from the world. This allows us 'moderns' to accept three related assumptions: that society (or culture) is made by humans alone; that science (knowledge, and thus nature) is free of politics and power; and that God (morality) is either distant or something that dwells in our souls. Latour suggests that these modern mythologies – which separate people from things, divide knowledge from their constitutive practices, and relegate morality to the 'internal' space of our hearts – are immensely effective ('positive' in Foucault's terms, since they are constitutive), while at the same time they sanction an immense ignorance. Effective, because we go about our lives imagining that we make society ourselves (without the mediation of things), that science provides unambiguous truths (without being 'biased' by politics), and that morality is something we bring *to* the world (rather than something immanent in its organization). Each exists in its own domain. Precisely for this reason, we are unable to consider the way that people and things, science and politics, the world and morality, are all the while mixed together. On the one hand the modern Constitution gives us a belief in a world of distinct domains, while at the same time it leaves us blind to all the hybrid networks of people, things and politics that are being created, extended or ruptured.

Latour argues that 'we have never been modern.' Despite our belief in a world of distinct domains, these have always been tangled together. It is only we moderns who imagine that it is possible to assign things unambiguously to 'culture,' 'nature,' 'science,' and 'politics.' It is only we moderns who engage in these acts of 'purification' even as we continuously mix things together into hybrid networks through countless acts of 'translation' that go unacknowledged. It is only we moderns who imagine that ethics and politics is something that occurs solely in the realm of deliberation, rather than in the *organization* of the world. The recent professionalization of 'ethics' is merely a symptom of this, since questions of ethics are usually raised at the 'downstream' end of these acts of translation (Haraway 1997; Demeritt 2001). If there is anything that makes us truly 'modern,' Latour suggests, is our proclivity, first, to simultaneously purify the world into essences all the while furiously producing ever new heterogeneous associations, and, second, to only *subsequently* become anxious about the results. The proliferation of networks of 'quasi-objects/quasi-subjects' that result, Latour (1993) argues, have no place in the modern Constitution, and thus *cannot be represented*. At one level, Latour's argument represents a simple call to 'bring networks out of hiding,' and thus to begin to attend to how nature, culture, machines and politics are always already tangled together.

Our fourth 'moment' is in many respects a response to this call. Before exploring it further, however, let me pause to consider how this moment throws the claims of the previous three into crisis, since each can now be seen to accept the terms of this Constitution. Of the three, cultural ecology presents the most intriguing case, for its practitioners assumed that they had indeed managed to overcome the modern dualism that assigned 'nature' and 'culture' to separate domains. Recall, for instance, Clifford Geertz's (1963) assertion that cultural ecology did not separate the works of man from the processes of nature, but instead understood them as an *integrated whole*, since "material interdependencies . . . form a [single] community." Understood in this manner, "the sharpness of the division between analyses from the side of 'man' and analyses from the side of 'nature' . . . disappears" (p. 8). Is this not a statement that thoroughly *rejects* the modern Constitution? On the surface it would appear so. But we need to remember how this apparent unity was achieved. Again, drawing from Geertz, we learn that cultural ecology subsumes all processes "within a single analytical system, an ecosystem" (p. 2). And, moreover, we learn that cultural practices are 'adaptations' to ecological conditions, and thus essentially 'natural' in their own right. Far from providing us with a nonmodern ontology, cultural ecology fully accepts the terms of the modern Constitution. It divides the world into domains – 'culture' and 'nature' – and then collapses the former into the latter. Nothing could be more modern.

What then of political ecology? It too claims to locate a unity. Recall Blaikie and Brookfield's assertion that the world was constituted through a "constantly shifting dialectic between society and land-based resources, and also within classes and groups within society itself." Certainly this must avoid the trap that the moderns had set for themselves. Yet dialectics can be seen to simply deepen the error, imagining the world in terms of two separate domains – nature and culture – that continuously 'interact.' Worse, in practice it was only the second half of Blaikie and Brookfield's statement – the dialectical movement of "classes and groups within society itself" – that would be taken up at any length by political ecologists. Society and politics to the sociologist; ecology to the ecologist. What could be a more clear statement of the modern Constitution? On the one hand society making itself, and on the other, society 'interacting' with a nature posited as a separate, opposed, domain.

What might we say of cultural studies of the environment? For adherents of 'nonmodern ontologies' these studies would merely intensify the error, placing all the action on the side of the cultural, and leaving 'things' entirely mute and passive. For all its insights into how the world is 'made legible,' people – or language and discourse – are the only actors in these poststructuralist worlds and postcolonial dramas. As noted by Sarah Whatmore (1999, 2002), the so-called 'cultural turn' in geography resulted in the question of nature being reformulated as an exclusively epistemological one.

Against the terms of the modern Constitution and its great divides, Latour proposes a nonfoundational, or 'nonmodern,' ontology. This merits some discussion, since it speaks directly to the problematic of the relation between culture and nature with which we began, and since it also contrasts significantly with recent calls to 'bring nature back in' to cultural geography. In Western philosophy, ontology is conventionally taken to refer to the realm of Being, or the 'what is' of the world. It is commonly understood to name the immutable (which is why the turn to 'ontology' is often considered a turn away from politics). Epistemology, on the other hand, is the question of *how* we come to know the world. Politics is commonly taken to be located in the realm of the epistemological – how to provide an adequate account of the world that can guide human action. Where Latour departs from this is that for him ontology is not the realm of the given, but the realm of experimentation or practice – a realm of *becoming* in which the final result is not known in advance, but is instead the outcome of innumerable acts of mediation, communication and translation, or, to use Latour's phrase, the "exchange of properties" (Serres uses the sports metaphor of 'passing'). Nonmodern ontologies allow for the production of ever new and novel forms, the continuous deterritorialization and reterritorialization of the world through the proliferation of connections or sudden bifurcations (see also Deleuze & Guattari 1987; Thrift 1996; Doel 1999). Here Latour is drawing on an 'orphaned' philosophical tradition that includes such figures as Henri Bergson, Baruch Spinoza, Gilles Deleuze, Michel Serres, and a common source for many, the Greek physicist Lucretius. For these philosophers the world does not consist of discrete 'things' that are brought into relation through some sort of external determination (such as found in versions of dialectics), resulting in hybrids that are mixtures of pre-given pure forms, but instead consists of flows and connections within which things are continuously (re)constituted. The difference between an ontology of form and essence (modern ontology) and an ontology of flows and connections (nonmodern ontology), is striking. Whereas the former brings us to the problem of understanding how distinct things 'interact,' the latter asks how it is that things come to attain provisional form and a certain durability. In other words, while the former takes divisions as a starting point, the latter tradition *politicizes* these divisions, asking how they came to be in the first place.

There are a number of significant implications that follow from this. First, to accept the nonfoundational ontology outlined by Latour is to reject the terms of the modern Constitution: rather than the *relation* between nature and culture presenting a puzzle to be solved, it is the division of the world into these ontological domains that needs explanation (see Whatmore 1999). Viewed from the position of nonmodern ontologies, the world does not consist of 'nature' and 'culture' and their combination, but only of heterogeneous associations that bring together diverse objects, effects and aims (Thrift 1996). Second, this presents a significant challenge for the entire field of study that has historically taken as its problematic the 'relation' between nature and culture, since its founding terms are now thrown into question. Indeed, the challenge extends beyond cultural geography, or geography as a whole, to include the very divisions of knowledge that are institutionalized in the intellectual cultures of the Western academy, which can now be seen as the one institution above all others that maintains – and is deeply *invested* in maintaining – modernity's 'great divides.' In passing, it is worth noting that to the extent that calls to 'bring nature back in' retain the notion of nature as a distinct domain they remain firmly implicated in these divides. And third, it suggests new avenues for 'interdisciplinary' research, not in terms of dividing the world into disciplinary domains and then struggling to bring them into relation, but oriented towards 'bringing networks out of hiding,' to the tracing of associations and translations.

Studies of this sort have recently appeared in the discipline of geography, and have begun to transform the study of culture and nature. Indeed, so thoroughly has this work displaced these terms that we might suggest that the nature–culture problematic – much like the figure of 'man' – is on the verge of being erased by the incoming tide of 'nonmodern ontology.' This work has taken several forms. A number of geographers influenced by science studies have begun to explore the exchange of properties that occurs within technoscientific practices. To the extent that this research is directed toward understanding how knowledge about the world is produced, it retains similarities with the cultural studies of the environment. Yet, it departs in crucial ways. By diffusing agency throughout technoscientific networks so as to include 'things' such as machines and organisms, it refuses to imagine humans as the only actors (see Latour 1999, Haraway 1997). And, by assuming that we know reality through our connections with it, rather than by our distance from it, it throws into question the assumption that knowledge can be understood solely in terms of *signification*, and insists instead on the materiality of knowledge practices (Ingold 1995, Hayles 1995).

More recent work has begun to produce 'nonmodern' accounts of the heterogeneous associations that constitute our physical, political and cultural environments. Prominent in this area has been the work of Sarah Whatmore (2002) on topologies and political orderings of wildlife, Sally Eden et al. (2000) on river restoration, Neil Bingham (1996) on technological objects, Steve Hinchliffe (2001) on BSE, Nigel Thrift (1996, 2000) on the performativity of embodied knowledge (or 'nonrepresentational theory'), Katharyne Hayles (1999) and Neil Badmington (2003) on the 'posthuman,' and Jonathan Murdoch (1997a, 1997b) on geographical theory. As Whatmore (2002: 3) explains, work in this vein has produced

an upheaval in the binary terms in which the question of nature has been posed and a recognition of the intimate, sensible and hectic bonds through which people and plants; devices and creatures; documents and elements take and hold their shape in relation to each other in the fabrications of everyday life.

This has profound consequences, not only for how geographers imagine research (for instance, beginning 'in the middle of things,' rather than presupposing a world of separate domains), but also for ethical-political considerations. Not only does it become difficult to imagine an ethics exclusively in terms of humans, since the 'human' is immediately displaced into its constitutive relations, it also undermines the notion of 'rights,' since these are assumed to belong – like physical qualities – to discrete and static entities. Attempts to rethink the basis for ethics and politics have focused on notions such as relationality (Whatmore 1997), drawn on Spinoza's understanding of the body in terms of affect, or sought to situate ethical thinking in terms of experimentation (Deleuze & Guattari 1990), 'eco-art' (Guattari 2000), or in terms of the 'explosive corporeal productivity' of the earth (Casarino 2002).

Like the other moments I've explored, nonmodern ontologies (and especially actor-network theory, or ANT) has its critics. A favorite target has been Latour's argument that one could not adequately explain networks through appeal to 'macro' structures whose nature is determined in advance (capitalism, reason, modernity), since these kinds of structures do not exist apart from, or prior to, the networks that constitute them. Latour argues that one must begin 'in the middle,' which is where, in the words of Deleuze and Guattari (1988) things 'pick up speed.' Many have found this inadequate, since it appears to provide no way of understanding how certain structures or relations become generalized (such as an 'expansionary logic' inherent in capitalism). While generally convinced by Latour ontological arguments, these critics argue that ANT provides few tools for *analyzing* the world (see Castree 2002). Advocates have responded that the appeal to such explanatory categories such as the State, Capitalism or Science are more problematic, since they "render messy fragile net-workings as slick consolidated totalities" (Whatmore 2002: 168).

Others argue that ANT flattens the world in such a manner that all actors are seen as equivalent, and that this does not allow for the massive differences between people, animals, and machines (Laurier & Philo 1999). While this objection initially appears significant, it may be less so once one places in question the usual way that people are distinguished from animals and machines (i.e. through the capacity to reason). Latour and others have argued that we reason *through* things. Hence, that quality to which we appeal as humanity's most unique quality – reason – is shot through with the agency of nonhuman others. For adherents to a nonmodern ontology there is no separating people from things, subjects from objects, technologies from words. As Latour explains, even our most distinctively human propensities such as "knowledge, morality, craft, force, sociability are not properties of humans but of humans *accompanied* by their retinue of delegated characters" (1988: 310, emphasis added). In contrast to the claims of critics, what distinguishes modern human subjects is neither their mastery of, nor their alienation from, 'things,' but their extraordinary success in mobilizing them and their stunning inability to see that they are doing so! This *is* a significant distinction, but not the one that ANT's critics had expected to find.

Yet other critics have worried over the lack of normative foundations in nonmodern ontologies, since it appears that there is no basis on which to distinguish networks, assemblages, or events, whose effects are 'good,' from those whose effects are 'bad.' What kinds of associations and translations should be permitted, and which should not? No doubt Latour would respond that this is a matter of politics, since in the terms of the nonfoundational ontology that he outlines, there is no *transcendental* basis from which to evaluate. The world consists only of assemblages of different size, extent, and duration, and networks that 'fold' and 'refold' time and space in new and novel ways (see Serres & Latour 1995). What might it mean to live ethically in such a world?

Conclusion: Toward an Ontological Politics

Are we witnessing the passing of a problematic? If so, what consequences and possibilities might this open for thought and politics? At the very least the dichotomy between thought and politics would have to be discarded, since another consequence of nonmodern ontologies is to throw into question the assumption that thought is the realm of contemplation and politics the realm of action. Like the distinction between 'nature' and 'culture,' this distinction takes recourse to a notion of separate domains, and fails to understand the performative rather than reflective nature of representation. To draw again upon Deleuze and Guattari (1988), theories of representation worry over the relation between texts and meaning (or the text and the world), whereas nonrepresentational theories inquire about the way a text comes to be *connected* to other things (see also Thrift 1996). Once representation is placed on the same plane as practice, problems of representation resolve into questions of pragmatics – a matter of practice, of making connection, of creative involvement in the world.

This is not to say that the turn to 'nonmodern ontologies' should be uncritically embraced. Serious reservations have been raised about the *basis* for such ontological claims, which are often justified through recourse to mathematics, geometry, and the physical sciences (cf. DeLanda 2002). For critics, this move evades responsibility for the initial act of positing involved in any ontological speculation (Derrida 1994). Its adherents, however, suggest that in this turn we find a hint of what comes after the 'end' of the old problematic of the 'relation' between nature and culture. Once these purified domains have been abandoned and replaced by a nonmodern ontology of heterogeneous associations, they argue, we find ourselves facing a new analytical task: no longer that of determining which direction the arrow of causation points – nature to culture, culture to nature, or some 'middle ground' that combines the two – but instead something more modest and more pragmatic: the interrogation of networks and their consequences, the careful reckoning of our intimate connections to and with other things, human and nonhuman, in what Whatmore (1999: 30) calls "the everyday business of *living* in the world." Likewise, once politics is no longer preoccupied with policing the boundaries between nature and culture, its focus shifts to the art and practice of *making* connections and taking responsibility for how they are made. It becomes performative rather than theoretical, pragmatic rather than contemplative. The categories of 'culture' and 'nature' provided little of any guidance for such a project, since by definition they were *conservative* categories – categories that retained their value only through the constant work of conserving their integrity and autonomy. That the preservation of their autonomy *required* a great deal of work is increasingly evident. That critical project is now, perhaps, finally exhausted. In its place we see the faint outlines of something different: not a politics of representation that seeks to 'get it right' and assumes a world of 'fixed forms,' but instead an *ontological politics* (Mol 1999) or a *cosmopolitics* (Stengers 1996–7) that takes as its task the active shaping of the world, rather than its proper representation.

What this means for cultural geography is less clear. Certainly the very possibility of positing a 'cultural' geography that has its own distinct 'object' is increasingly open to debate. Already we are told that distinctions between 'cultural,' 'political,' and 'economic' have been thoroughly blurred. But if we accept nonmodern ontologies, the language of 'blurred' boundaries no longer makes sense, since these categories were simply the outcome of our practices of dividing the world into domains in the first place. As much as did the original categories, the language of 'blurred boundaries' gets in the way of understanding the world as it is. A nonmodern ontology refuses these realms as distinct, either today or in the past. It is not postmodernism that 'mixes together' culture and nature, for it is only we moderns who thought they were separate in the first place! We are at a juncture when disciplinarity must again be rethought. Neither creating new disciplinary divisions nor seeking interdisciplinarity will suffice. As Sarah Whatmore (1999) notes, it no longer makes sense to 'bracket off' environmental geography as a subfield, nor does it make sense to attempt the 'reintegration' of physical and human geography. These common responses to the modern predicament merely reproduce the original errors, as does an interdisciplinarity that seeks to 'combine' social, ecological, and economic facts. Perhaps what is needed are new ways of imagining and creatively engaging in the world, a new postdisciplinary pragmatics that accepts our *participation* in the worlding of our world and our connection to the many other 'actants' who constitute our worlds and our humanity. What we face, then, is the task of thinking in terms of a 'geophilosophy' (Deleuze & Guattari 1990) that attends to, and places us within, the creative becoming of the earth.

NOTES

1. Such 'passings' are, of course, continuously deferred, as Derrida (1982: 135) explains in the context of Heidegger's 'destruction' of humanism: "one risks ceaselessly confirming, consolidating, *relifting* [*relever*], at an always more certain depth, that which one allegedly deconstructs."
2. Clarence Glacken (1967) provides the most comprehensive historical account of the career of the nature–culture problematic in earlier periods of Western thought.
3. In a curious twist that challenges our usual temporal notions of intellectual progress, Christopher Johnson (1993) argues that cybernetics was highly influential to some French poststructuralisms in the 1960s, in part through the reception of the work of Gregory Bateson. Traces of this influence can be found in the early work of Jacques Derrida (see the opening sections in *Of Grammatology*) and more consistently in the writings of Gilles Deleuze and Félix Guattari. The poststructural turn in Anglo-American geography in the late 1980s and 1990s, then, contains certain unacknowledged repetitions.
4. Arguably 'material culture' returned in the late 1980s (see Appadurai 1986), and with a vengeance in the 1990s (see Michael 2000).
5. This was similar to the argument in favor of 'progressive contextualization' made by the cultural ecologist Andrew Vayda in 1983. Vayda and Harold Brookfield were both cultural ecologists who increasingly integrated the insights of political economy during the 1980s.
6. Williams was not the first to examine 'ideas of nature.' R. G. Collingwood's *The Idea of Nature* (1945) prefigured Williams by three decades.

REFERENCES

Agarwal, B. 1992: The gender and environment debate: lessons from India. *Feminist Studies* 18, 119–58.

Anderson, K. 1998: Science and the savage: the Linnean Society of New South Wales, 1874–1900. *Ecumene* 5, 125–43.

Anderson, K. 2001: The nature of 'race.' In N. Castree and B. Braun, eds., *Social Nature: Theory, Practice, and Politics*. Oxford: Blackwell, 64–83.

Appadurai, A., ed. 1986: *The Social Life of Things: Commodities in Cultural Perspective*. Cambridge: Cambridge University Press.

Aschmann, H. 1959: *The Central Desert of Baja California: Demography and Ecology*. Berkeley: University of California Press.

Badmington, N. 2003: Theorizing posthumanism. *Cultural Critique* 53, 10–27.

Bartram, R. 1999: The enclosure of nature in Stanley Spencer's *Hoe Garden Nursery*. *Ecumene* 6(3), 341–59.

Binde, P. 1999: Nature versus city: landscapes of Italian fascism. *Environment and Planning D: Society and Space* 17, 761–75.

Bingham, N. 1996: Objections: from technological determinism towards geographies of relations. *Environment and Planning D: Society and Space* 14, 635–57.

Blaikie, P. 1985: *The Political Economy of Soil Erosion in Developing Countries.* Harlow: Longman.

Blaikie, P. and Brookfield, H. 1987: *Land Degradation and Society.* London: Methuen.

Braun, B. 1997a: Buried epistemologies: the politics of nature in (post)colonial British Columbia. *Annals of the Association of American Geographers* 87(1), 3–32.

Braun, B. 1997b: On cultural politics, Sauer, and the politics of citation. *Annals of the Association of American Georaphers* 87(4), 703–8.

Braun, B. 2000: Producing vertical territory: geology and governmentality in late-Victorian Canada. *Ecumene* 7, 7–46.

Braun, B. 2002: *The Intemperate Rainforest: Nature, Culture and Power on Canada's West Coast.* Minneapolis: University of Minnesota Press.

Braun, B. and Castree, N., eds. 1998: *Remaking Reality: Nature at the Millennium.* London: Routledge.

Braun, B. and Wainwright, J. 2001: Nature, postructuralism, politics. In N. Castree and B. Braun, eds., *Social Nature: Theory, Practice, Politics.* Oxford: Blackwell, 41–63.

Bryant, R. and Bailey, B. 1997: *Third World Political Ecology.* London: Routledge.

Butzer, K. 1989: Cultural ecology. In C. J. Willmott and G. Gaile, eds., *Geography in America.* Washington, DC: Association of American Geographers and National Geographic Society.

Casarino, C. 2002: *Modernity at Sea: Marx, Melville, Conrad in Crisis.* Minneapolis: University of Minnesota Press.

Castree, N. 1995: The nature of produced nature: materiality and knowledge construction in Marxism. *Antipode* 27(1), 12–48.

Castree, N. 2002: False antithesis? Marxism, nature and actor-networks *Antipode* 34(1), 111–46.

Cockburn, A. and Ridgeway, J., eds. 1979: *Political Ecology.* New York: Times Books.

Collingwood, R. G. 1945. *The Idea of Nature.* Oxford: Clarendon Press.

Cosgrove, D. and Jackson, P. 1987: New directions in cultural geography. *Area* 19, 95–101.

Cronon, W. 1995: The trouble with wilderness: or, getting back to the wrong nature. In W. Cronon, ed., *Uncommon Ground: Toward Reinventing Nature.* New York: W.W. Norton & Co.

Darier, E. 1999: *Discourses of the Environment.* Oxford: Blackwell.

DeLanda, M. 2002. *Intensive Science and Virtual Philosophy.* London: Continuum Books.

Deleuze, G. 1991: *Bergsonism,* tr. H. Tomlinson and B. Habberjam. New York: Zone Books.

Deleuze, G. and Guattari, F. 1988: *A Thousand Plateaus: Capitalism and Schizophrenia,* tr. Brian Massumi. London: Athlone Press.

Deleuze, G. and Guattari, F. 1990: *What is Philosophy?,* tr. Hugh Tomlinson and Graham Burchell. New York: Columbia University Press.

Demeritt, D. 1994: Ecology, objectivity and critique in writings on nature and human societies. *Journal of Historical Geography* 20(1), 22–37.

Demeritt, D. 1998: Science, social constructivism and nature. In B. Braun and N. Castree, eds., *Remaking Reality: Nature at the Millennium.* London: Routledge, 173–93.

Demeritt, D. 2001: The construction of global warming and the politics of science. *Annals of the Association of American Geographers* 91(2), 307–37. Derrida, J. 1976: *Of Grammatology,* tr. Gayatri Chakravorty Spivak. Baltimore: Johns Hopkins University Press.

Derrida, J. 1982: *Margins of Philosophy,* tr. Alan Bass. Chicago: University of Chicago Press.

Derrida, J. 1994: *Specters of Marx: The State of Debt, the Work of Mourning, and the New International,* tr. Peggy Kamuf. New York: Routledge.

Doel, M. 1999: *Poststructuralist Geographies: The Diabolical Art of Spatial Science.* Edinburgh: Edinburgh University Press.

Duncan, J. 1980: The superorganic in American cultural geography. *Annals of the American Association of Geographers* 70, 181–98.

Eden, S. , Turnstall, S. M., and Tapsell, S. M. 2000: Translating nature: river restoration as nature culture. *Environment and Planning D: Society and Space* 18(2), 257–73.

Ehrlich, P. 1968: *The Population Bomb.* New York: Ballantine Books.

Enzensberger, H. M. 1974: A critique of political ecology. *New Left Review* 84.

Escobar, A. 1996: Constructing nature: elements for a poststructural political ecology. In R. Peet and M. Watts, eds., *Liberation Ecologies: Environment, Development, Social Movements.* London: Routledge, 46–68.

Foucault, Michel.1970: *The Order of Things: An Archaeology of the Human Sciences.* London: Tavistock.

Geertz, C. 1963: *Agricultural Involution: The Process of Ecological Change in Indonesia.* Berkeley: University of California Press.

Glacken, C. 1967: *Traces on the Rhodian Shore.* Berkeley: University of California Press.

Gregory, Derek. 2001: (Post)colonialism and the production of nature. In N. Castree and B. Braun, eds., *Social Nature: Theory, Practice, and Politics.* Oxford: Blackwell.

Guattari, F. 2000: *The Three Ecologies.* London: Athlone Press.

Gupta, A. and Ferguson, J., eds. 1997: *Culture, Power and Place: Explorations in Critical Anthropology.* Durham, NC: Duke University Press.

Haraway, D. 1992: The promises of monsters: a regenerative politics for inappropriate/d others. In L. Grossberg, C. Nelson, and P. Treichler, eds., *Cultural Studies.* New York: Routledge, 275–332.

Haraway, D. 1997: *Modest Witness@Second Millenium.Female Man© Meets OncoMouse*[TM]. New York: Routledge.

Harris, M. 1974: *Cows, Pigs, Wars & Witches: The Riddles of Culture.* New York: Random House.

Harvey, D. 1996: *Nature, Justice and the Geography of Difference.* Oxford: Blackwell.

Hayles, K. 1995: Searching for common ground. In M. Soulé and G. Lease, eds., *Reinventing Nature?* Washington, DC: Island Press, 47–64.

Hayles, K 1999: *How We Became Posthuman: Virtual Bodies in Cybernetics, Literature, and Informatics.* Chicago: University of Chicago Press.

Hewitt, K., ed. 1983: *Interpretations of Calamity.* London: Allen and Unwin.

Hinchliffe, S. 2001: Indeterminacy indecisions – science, policy and politics in the BSE crisis. *Transactions of the Institute of British Geographers* 26(2), 283–304.

Ingold, T. 1995: Building, dwelling, living: how animals and people make themselves at home in the world. In M. Strathern, ed., *Shifting Contexts: Transformations in Anthropological Knowledge.* London: Routledge, 57–80.

Jackson, C. 1993: "Women/Nature or Gender/History? A critique of ecofeminist 'development.' *Journal of Peasant Studies* 20(3), 389–418.

Jacobs, J. 1996: *Edge of Empire: Postcolonialism and the City.* London: Routledge.

Johnson, C. 1993: *System and Writing in the Philosophy of Jacques Derrida.* Cambridge: Cambridge University Press.

Kosek, J. 2002: *The Political Life of Forests in Northern New Mexico.* Ph.D. dissertation, Department of Geography, University of California, Berkeley.

Latour, B. 1987: *Science in Action: How to Follow Scientists and Engineers Through Society.* Cambridge: Harvard University Press.

Latour, B. 1988: Mixing humans and nonhumans together: the sociology of a door-closer. *Social Problems* 35(3), 298–310.

Latour, B. 1993: *We Have Never Been Modern*. Cambridge, MA: Harvard University Press.

Latour, B. 1999: *Pandora's Hope: Essays in the Reality of Science Studies*. Cambridge, MA: Harvard University Press.

Laurier, E. and Philo, C. 1999: X-morphising: review essay of Bruno Latour's *Aramis, Or the Love of Technology*. *Environment and Planning A* 31, 1047–71.

Luke, T. 1997: *Ecocritique: Contesting the Politics of Nature, Economy and Culture*. Minneapolis: University of Minnesota Press.

Michael, M. 2000: These books are made for walking . . . : mundane technology, the body and human–environment relations. *Body & Society* 6(3–4), 107–26.

Mol, A. 1999: Ontological politics. In J. Law and J. Hassard, eds., *Actor-Network Theory and After*. Oxford: Blackwell.

Moore, D. 1998: Subaltern struggles and the politics of place: remapping resistance in Zimbabwe's eastern highlands. *Cultural Anthropology* 13(3), 344–81.

Moore, D. 2000. The crucible of cultural politics: reworking 'development' in Zimbabwe's eastern highlands. *American Ethnologist* 26(3), 654–89.

Moore, O. K. 1957: Divination – a new perspective. *American Anthropologist* 59, 64–74.

Murdoch, J. 1997a: Towards a geography of heterogenous associations. *Progress in Human Geography* 21(3), 321–37.

Murdoch, J. 1997b: Inhuman/nonhuman/human: actor-network theory and the potential for a non-dualistic and symmetrical perspective on nature and society. *Environment and Planning D: Society and Space* 15, 731–56.

Nakashima, K. 1999: Representing nature and nation: national-land afforestation campaign and the production of the forest in 1960–1970s Japan. In T. Mizuuchi, ed., *Nation, Region and the Politics of Geography in East Asia*. Osaka: Osaka City University, 13–29.

Nietschmann, B. 1973: *Between Land and Water: The Subsistence Ecology of the Miskito Indians, Eastern Nicaragua*. New York: Seminar Press.

Odum, E. 1959: *Fundamentals of Ecology*, 2nd ed. Philadelphia: W. B. Saunders.

Peet, R. and Watts, M. 1996: Liberation ecology: development, sustainability, and environment in an age of market triumphalism. In Peet and Watts, eds., *Liberation Ecologies: Environment, Development, Social Movements*. London: Routledge, 1–45.

Peluso, N. 1995: Whose woods are these? Counter-mapping forest territories in Kalimantan, Indonesia. *Antipode* 27(4), 383–406.

Rappaport, R. 1967: *Pigs for the Ancestors: Ritual in the Ecology of a New Guinea People*. New Haven: Yale University Press.

Rocheleau, D., Thomoas-Slayter, B., and Wangani, E., eds. 1996: *Feminist Political Ecology: Global Issues and Local Experiences*. London: Routledge.

Rorty, R. 1980: *Philosophy and the Mirror of Nature*. Oxford: Blackwell.

Schmidt, A. 1971: *The Concept of Nature in Marx*. London: New Left Books.

Schroeder, R. 1999: *Shady Practices: Agroforestry and Gender Politics in the Gambia*. Berkeley: University of California Press.

Sen, A. 1981: *Poverty and Famine*. Oxford: Oxford University Press.

Serres, M. and Latour, B. 1995: *Conversations on Science, Culture and Time*, trans. R. Lapidus. Ann Arbor: University of Michigan Press.

Shiva, V. 1988: *Staying Alive: Women, Ecology and Development*. London: Zed Books.

Sluyter, A. 1996: The ecological origins and consequences of cattle ranching in sixteenth-century New Spain. *The Geographical Review* 8, 161–77.

Sluyter, A. 1997: On excavating and burying epistemologies. *Annals of the Association of American Geographers* 87(4), 700–3.

Sluyter, A. 1999: The making of the myth in postcolonial development: material-conceptual landscape transformation in sixteenth-century Veracruz. *Annals of the Association of American Geographers* 89(3), 377–401.

Smith, N. 1984: *Uneven Development: Nature, Capital and the Production of Space*. Oxford: Blackwell.

Smith, N. and O'Keefe, P. 1980: Geography, Marx and the concept of nature. *Antipode* 12(2), 30–9.

Soulé, M. and Lease, G., eds. 1995: *Reinventing Nature? Responses to Postmodern Deconstructionism*. Washington: Island Press.

Stengers, I. 1996–7: *Cosmopolitiques*, 7 vols. Paris: La Découverte.

Steward, J. 1955: *Theory of Culture Change: The Methodology of Multilinear Evolution*. Urbana: University of Illinois Press.

Susman, P., O'Keefe, P., and Wisner, B. 1983: Global disasters: a radical interpretation. In K. Hewitt, ed., *Interpretations of Calamity*. London: Allen and Unwin, 263–97.

Taussig, M. 1986: *Shamanism, Colonialism and the Wild Man: A Study in Terror and Healing*. Chicago: University of Chicago Press.

Thrift, N. 1996: *Spatial Formations*. London: Sage.

Thrift, N. 2000: Still life in nearly present time: the object of nature. *Body and Society* 6(3–4), 34–57.

Turner, B. L. 1989: The specialist-synthesis approach to the revival of geography: the case of cultural ecology. *Annals of the Association of American Geographers* 79(1), 88–100.

Vayda, A. 1967: Foreword. In R. Rappaport, *Pigs for the Ancestors: Ritual in the Ecology of a New Guinea People*. New Haven: Yale University Press.

Vayda, A. 1983: Progressive contextualization: methods for research in human ecology. *Human Ecology* 11, 265–81.

Vayda, A. and Rappaport, R. 1968: Ecology, cultural and non-cultural. In J. Clifton, ed., *Introduction to Cultural Anthropology: Essays in the Scope and Methods of the Science of Man*. New York: McGraw Hill.

Watts, M. 1983: *Silent Violence: Food, Famine and Peasantry in Northern Nigeria*. Berkeley: University of California Press.

Watts, M. 1998: Nature as artifice and artifact. In B. Braun and N. Castree, eds., *Remaking Reality: Nature at the Millennium*. London: Routledge, 243–68.

Watts, M. 2001: Political ecology. In E. Sheppard and T. Barnes, eds., *The Companion of Economic Geography*. Oxford: Blackwell, 257–74.

Whatmore, S. 1999: Human geographies: rethinking the 'human' in human geography. In D. Massey, J. Allen, and P. Sarre, eds., *Human Geography Today*. Cambridge: Polity Press, 22–39.

Whatmore, S. 2002: *Hybrid Geographies: Natures, Cultures, Spaces*. London: Sage.

Williams, R. 1980: *Problems in Materialism and Culture: Selected Essays*. London: Verso.

Wilson, A. 1992: *The Culture of Nature: North American Landscape from Disney to the Exxon Valdez*. Oxford: Blackwell.

Wolch, J. and Emel, J., eds. 1998: *Animal Geographies: Place, Politics, and Identity in the Nature–culture Borderlands*. London: Verso.

Wolf, E. 1972: Ownership and political ecology. *Anthropological Quarterly* 45, 201–5.

Zimmerer, K. 1996: Ecology as cornerstone and chimera in human geography. In C. Earle, K. Mathewson, and M. Kenzer, eds., *Concepts in Human Geography*. Lanham, MD: Rowman and Littlefield, 161–88.

Chapter 12

Cultural Ecology

Paul Robbins

A well-dressed extension agent, trained in a US land grant university somewhere in the Midwest, enters a dusty Indian village as part of a state service to introduce high-yielding varieties of wheat and maize, which together with industrial fertilizers and pesticides might increase local crop yields by more than 50 percent. After many group meetings with community members and groups, he becomes frustrated. While a handful of local farmers are interested in fertilizers, they are less enthusiastic about the seeds. Others are interested in maize but not in wheat. Many are reticent to implement any of the proposed changes, and they shake their heads at the fellow and return to their millets and legumes, thinking only of the backbreaking work of the day still ahead of them. The agent, employed by the state only to improve the lot of the local poor, is dumbfounded. He departs the village convinced that it is the *culture* of peasants like these, inherently conservative, frightened of change, and distrustful of progress, that keeps India poor, underdeveloped, and primitive in the face of rapid modernization throughout the developed world.

Had the man greater inclination or time to stop and listen to these farmers, he might have learned a great many things about the logic of local culture. The stalks of the high yielding wheat plants, designed to be short and therefore less wasteful of inputs into biotic production, provide far too little field stubble after harvesting to feed livestock, thus eliminating a key part of local subsistence. The water demands of the crop would require capital expenditures for well digging that would put most households in a precarious position of debt. The chemical fertilizer inputs that such crops require would create annual cash demands that are out of synchronization with household cash availability, which follows harvest. Moreover, the traditional fertilizer, goat and sheep dung, is known throughout the area to sustain yields over multiple cropping seasons far better than industrial urea. These stories of local production, however, go unattended by the agent.

Yet there is a long history of listening to such stories and asking the questions that inevitably follow. It is the project of Cultural Ecology – a field of Geographic and Anthropological research – to interpret and understand the logics, choices, and imperatives of daily environmental practice in a way that is sensible, practical, and universal. Cultural Ecology begins from the assumption that human ecological choices and practices are comprehensible and often optimal under the social and environmental conditions that prevail in place. As such, work in the field for the last century has consistently crossed the globe for explanations to the basic puzzles of life. Why would people choose lower risk over higher yields? Why do nomads move? Why do forest people cut forests? Why raise large families?

The answers to questions like these are more imperative than ever in a world searching for sustainable human systems and Cultural Ecology, despite shortcomings, thrives in many forms, quietly informing the work of local development organizations and even vast bureaucracies like the World Bank. Overshadowed in recent years by some other forms of cultural inquiry, Cultural Ecology can arguably said to have triumphed in many practical spheres, making the dismissive behaviors of the hypothetical extension agent described above increasingly unlikely in real life. For this reason alone, Cultural Ecology is worth exploring. So too, its highly empirical and synthetic efforts to analytically link environmental systems with the logics of the human world can inform geographical studies as few other approaches have yet proven to do (Netting 1986; Turner 1989). Finally, the field might yet provide a remedy for a range of pernicious, if persistent, ways of thinking about people and nature, including geographical determinism and apocalyptic Malthusianism, a pair of untenable arguments that seem never to go away.

Some Arguments Never Die

In the past, many crude arguments concerning the relationship between people and the landscapes in which they live often dominated accounts of human–environment interaction. Many of these arguments sought to explain cultural, political, and social systems by way of environmental limits. Others pointed to the ultimate limits the environment places on human society, especially constraints on growing populations. In the former case, the rise and success of European culture has been spuriously attributed to climate (Landes 1998), soils (Jones 1981), and a combination of landforms and rainfall (Hall 1985) (see Blaut 2000 for a full discussion). In the latter case, the limits of the earth's carrying capacity have consistently been used to predict demographic disaster and to justify the lifeboat ethics of denying aid to the poor and disenfranchised (Malthus 1992; Robbins 1998).

Curiously, these arguments have never fully disappeared, and reemerge from time to time. Despite the remarkable absence of any evidence in support of either geographical determinism or Malthusian apocalypse, the arguments endure. Parleying his training in evolutionary physiology to the study of global history in the recent book *Guns, Germs, and Steel* (Diamond 1997), Jared Diamond has argued for example that the rise of the "West" in world history resulted from the East–West orientation of the Eurasian continental axis, which allowed domestication, innovation, and diffusion. Echoing determinists of past eras, Diamond invokes "ultimate factors" in his explanation of history, insisting on the simple geographical determination of society by environment.

So too, authors like Paul Ehrlich (1968), who endlessly warn of overpopulation continue to sell copies of their prophecies in the millions. These arguments also survive constant revision as predicted disasters fail to arise (Ehrlich & Ehrlich 1991).

In light of these uncritically accepted views, rigorous investigation of human–environment interaction has never been more urgent. To truly evaluate and understand nature–society relations, however, requires exacting work on daily production, human adaptation, and the complex interworkings of resource use and production. Such work is too rarely performed because it is difficult, time consuming, and filled with complexity that makes simple reductionist arguments difficult to defend. Yet that is the very work of Cultural Ecology, the investigation into human production of, and adaptation to, environment.

In the following chapter, I will define the field of Cultural Ecology and trace some of the historic threads in its diverse research trajectory. In the process, I hope to introduce some of the *dramatis personae* that have inhabited this eclectic field over the last century with no pretense to the comprehensiveness of the account; the players, thinkers, and fieldworkers are too many and diverse. Even so, I intend to describe the field's diversity and highlight its most captivating areas of research, finally arguing that despite its flaws, Cultural Ecology is a crucial tool for exploring the combined questions of contemporary development, global poverty, and worldwide environmental change, issues as pertinent now as they were more than a century ago.

Auspicious Beginnings – In the Field with a Russian Anarchist

In 1865, in preparing for an expedition to a largely unmapped region of northern Siberia, Geographer Peter Kropotkin utilized for navigation a map prepared by a Tungus hunter, drawn with knifepoint on tree bark. The map, he said "so struck me by its seeming truth to nature that I fully trusted to it" (Woodcock & Avakumovic 1990: 72). That expedition, like several before it, demonstrated to the young Russian noble – who would later come to espouse a progressive policy of social anarchism – "the constructive work of the unknown masses, which so seldom finds any mention in books, and the importance of that constructive work in the growth of forms of society" (Woodcock & Avakumovic 1990: 59–60). Performed on horseback and foot, ongoing expeditions brought Kropotkin into contact with farmers, herders, plants, animals, and landscapes, that were to form the empirical basis for his best known argument, that evolution rests upon collective intraspecies mutual aid, cooperation, and collective organization (Kropotkin 1888).

More fundamentally, Kropotkin's fieldwork, his respect for local knowledge, his interest in the relationship between production and society, all reflect the auspicious beginnings of human/environment research and the hallmark traits of Cultural Ecology (Turner 1989). First, Kropotkin's work focused on *production* as a key site of social-environmental process. By investigating how people make a living from the land, he reasoned, we might better understand nature/society interactions. "The means of production being the collective work of humanity" (Kropotkin 1990: 14), he insisted, they provide the most direct window into the mechanisms of evolution.

Second, Kropotkin's work was marked by rigorous *archival and field-based* empirical research. His book *Mutual Aid* is filled with detailed observations of plant and animal life in Siberia and Manchuria, but also with careful accounts of the organization of society in places ranging from Rome to early Russia, all reconstructed from historical and archaeological accounts (Kropotkin 1888).

Third, Kropotkin held an explicit concern for *marginalized and disenfranchised* communities. In these communities, he saw the survival and innovation of "institutions, habits, and customs" that despite persistent exploitation by landlords and the state, locals preferred to maintain rather than adopt problematic solutions "offered to them under the title of science, but [that] are no science at all" (Kropotkin 1888: 260–1).

Fourth, Kropotkin had a strong interest in the position and power of *traditional environmental knowledges*. Though a strong supporter of innovation and modernization, he believed the elements of progress lay in the existing knowledge and ingenuity of local communities (Kropotkin 1985).

Finally, like many Cultural Ecologists to follow, Kropotkin held a keen interest in landscape as a central focus of explanation. Indeed, his earliest and most comprehensive contributions to theoretical Geography involved exploring for evidence of long-term desiccation and topographic change (Woodcock & Avakumovic 1990).

Though this picture of research comes from across a gulf of more than a century, it provides a sketch of the fundamental questions that remain on the minds of Cultural Ecologists. Why do people do things the way they do? What accounts for the vast diversity of economies and human ecologies around the globe? How does development work? Why does it fail? What are the links and feedbacks between vast civilizations and the soils, plants, and nutrient systems to which they are connected? Turning vast questions into an empirical project, Kropotkin was among the earliest geographers to explore the nature/society relationship in a grounded way. These efforts would soon be followed by others.

Theories of Culture and Change – Steward and Sauer

In 1955, the anthropologist Julian Steward offered a similarly comprehensive theory to account for the development and change of cultures, one that took seriously the environmental systems in which people are embedded without deterministic models of cause and effect. Coining the term "cultural ecology," he explained that the culture core – that "constellation of features which are most closely related to the subsistence activities and economic arrangements" – marked the starting point for investigations into human behavior and group practice (Steward 1972: 37). Why are certain hunting community groups arranged into bands? Is it related to the demands of subsistence? Where this is not the case, what other ecological and cultural factors impinge? Cultural Ecological research was therefore centered on human adaptation *to* the environment.

In a parallel but somewhat inverse fashion, Carl O. Sauer wrote in 1925, that "this contact of man with his changeful home, as expressed through the cultural landscape, is our field of work" (Sauer 1965: 349). Eschewing the various forms of environmental determinism that had swept through Geography in previous decades, he sought to create a field-based method to understand the way humans carve their histories into the land. How do the landscapes of cultivation function ecologically and how have they been formed to suit the demands of producers? How might that change with the advent of new cultivars or a change in markets? In complementary distinction to Steward, Sauer's Cultural Ecology was centered on adaptation *of* the environment. These two concerns and approaches would continue to define the field, both in philosophy as well as in terms of the mundane objects of study.

As later observers noted, this kind of work concerned culture at its most mundane and basic, and so perhaps its most universal (Murphy 1981). Explaining landscapes from human practice and human practice in an environmental context, it set the tone for much of what would follow. Cultural Ecologists would be interested in how people make a living in nature, how they adapt the landscape, and how their technology, labor, and knowledges link to complex environmental systems around them.

Adaptation – Exploring Human Capacity

The natural extension of this sort of thinking is to perform rigorous research into how people adapt to the environment, to spend time in communities undergoing change, and to explore the historical and archaeological records of past cultures searching for emerging adaptations. The resulting work on *adaptation* in Cultural Ecology seeks to explain how complex traditions and practices function ecologically. By explaining the ecological logic of a cultural event, like a festival, food system, or house type, adaptation research shows the endless variability and creativity of human life in nature.

In this way, otherwise mysterious or difficult to understand ways of doing things can be explained by virtue of their complex ecosystem functions, especially in cases where people are forced to make a living using simple tools in difficult environments. Agriculture on raised mounds can be shown to be an adaptation to soil moisture and temperature regimes in the tropics (Waddell 1972). Nomadic adaptations can be viewed as a highly functional way to spread risk and lower ecological impact, contrary to colonial and government efforts that sought to settle nomads (Johnson 1969; Sanford 1983). Large herd sizes and the culture of the "cattle complex," rather than being seen as irrational, can be viewed as effective adaptation to variability and herd mortality patters in semi-arid lands (Dahl & Hjort 1976).

The classic study in this area was Roy Rappaport's (1968) analysis of the livelihoods of the Maring people of New Guinea. Specifically, Rappaport sought to explain the complex, intermittently repeated, ritual behaviors of subsistence producers. He concluded that both periodic ritual warfare and pig sacrifice were the product of population cycles of both pigs and people, and that they interacted in complex metabolism to achieve equilibrium.

Another model study, Bennett's *Northern Plainsmen* (1969) is instructive both for its insights and its application to areas outside the traditional realm of underdeveloped contexts. Focusing his attention on farmers, ranchers, and indigenous people in Alberta, Canada, Bennett shows that each livelihood is an adaptation to a separate sphere or niche in a complex ecosystem – where ranchers adopt individuated practices, Hutterite farmers and land-poor Native Americans adapt cooperatively.

Moreover, such research suggests that adaptation is not simply a response to a single and isolated environment, since the spread and diffusion of adaptations is a hallmark of human practices. Diffusion research and variations in adaptation over space as well as time, became important strands of research showing the remarkable adaptively not only of people, but of the species they used, transported, and established far from the sites of their original domestication (Sauer 1952).

Excesses in Functionalist Thinking and the Teleology of Adaptation

For all of its strengths, this adaptation approach overextended itself seriously, and suffered from a fundamental teleological flaw: if people do it, it must be adaptive. Indeed, the logic of adaptation is arguably that those cultural features evident in populations, including and especially those "unusual" ones, that differ from more generic practices must be environmentally functional. This line of thinking was exhausted most thoroughly by anthropologist Marvin Harris, whose global examples and catchy titles (*Cows, Pigs, Wars, and Witches* in 1974 and *Cannibals and Kings* in 1977 most notably) made him an influential thinker in the area of environmental anthropology (Harris 1974). He argued, for example, that the cow became sacred in India since it made sense for the provision of milk proteins and traction power for agricultural production (Harris 1966). With little of the hallmark methodological practices of Cultural Ecology, especially long-term fieldwork and archival investigation, this field of "cultural materialism," as it became known, promulgated dozens of similar hypotheses, explaining the vast complexities of diet, conflict, and marriage with reference to simple adaptive principles.

Such functional adaptation usually did not survive empirical evaluation. Exacting fieldwork on India's sacred cattle, for example, revealed a far more complex picture of the adaptive and maladaptive features of animal keeping. Questions of cause and effect in cattle protection became prominent in careful investigation (Simoons 1979; Freed & Freed 1981): do adaptive uses lead to taboos creating surpluses or does the surplus of animals lead to adaptive uses?

Even where rich exploration of adaptation was the rule, however, fundamental and troubling problems remained. As Roy Ellen simply explained, "showing how things work is explaining neither why they came about nor why they persist. It does not provide a causal explanation" (Ellen 1982: 193). Adaptation researcher Alexander Alland (1975: 69) similarly warned that the role of adaptation "should not be exaggerated or we run the risk of substituting 'just so stories' for scientific explanations."

And the reductionism of this form of functional explanation did indeed lead to bizarre and untenable conclusions. Vastly complex Aztec human sacrifice traditions, for example, were explained to have resulted from protein deficiencies for which human flesh was a crucial supplement. Even ignoring the fact that the maize–legume combinations of domesticates in the region during this period could easily have met protein demands of people, the dismissive reduction of such a complex political, economic, and cultural system to a matter of protein needs, was concluded to be unsatisfying by even the most ardent supporters of the approach (Winkelman 1998).

More fundamentally, exploring adaptation of varying communities does little to illuminate why certain forms of human ecology prevail, especially when the broader forces acting within and between communities is ignored. In the obvious case of Bennett's *Northern Plainsmen*, a troubling silence prevails as to why native peoples in the region are land-poor and low on capital *in the first place*. Are they simply seeking out an "ecological niche" of poverty? Or are more profound historical power imbalances, land thefts, and conflicts part of the explanation? The obvious answer to these questions (yes), is made difficult in an approach centered on adaptation since even where people obviously respond to environmental signals, complex interactions at other scales (international, state, and community) condition and drive those responses (Trimbur & Watts 1976).

Even so, echoes of adaptation can be heard in strands of effective and illuminating research emerging in recent years. With increased concern on how people manage to thrive under ecologically and economically marginal and variable conditions in Africa (Mortimore 1989; Batterbury 2001), Latin America (Bebbington 2001; Rocheleau et al. 2001), and Asia (Robbins 1998), adaptation as a general line of inquiry continues to make sense (Batterbury & Forsyth 1999). While it remains short on explanatory power, by crediting the efficacy of environmental practices of local people, adaptation research helps to makes sense of the world.

Energetics and Systems Research – Putting a Number on Making a Living

Simultaneous to the emergence of interest in adaptive dynamics, more formalized and quantitative techniques of ecological assessment also began to thrive, and systems research in Cultural Ecology entered the computer age. Mirroring research in the science of Ecology, Cultural Ecologists sought a common metric through which they could track the metabolism of complex systems, which might include many species: humans, animals, and plants. A universal unit, they concluded, might include energy and nutrients. Using such common metrics, human social systems could therefore be compared in terms of productivity and efficiency.

In one prominent example, Bayliss-Smith compared the flow of energy between historical and contemporary farms in New Guinea, Polynesia, South India, England, and Soviet Russia in painstaking detail. He concluded that the highest output systems, the Soviet collective farm and contemporary English intensive practice, are far from the most efficient, a conclusion linked to the ecological price of fossil-fuel dependence.

The implications for this kind of work are especially evident for research into swidden (slash and burn) agricultural systems, where producers clear forest patches, burn the fallen biomass, and plant garden plots until the forest regrows into prohibitively thick secondary growth. Historically, colonial and development authorities described such systems as ineffective, destructive, and unsustainable.

Cultural Ecologists would reach rather different conclusions. As early as the 1950s, there was increasing recognition of the ecological similarities between swidden fields and the natural ecology of tropical forests (Conklin 1954). This work was followed by detailed and comparative case studies that showed that the biodiverse structure and physical canopy architecture of swidden cultivation sites made them miniaturized tropical forests (Geertz 1963). More formally, and working again among the Tsembaga of New Guinea, Rappaport documented the flow of solar and human energy in swidden cultivation. Measuring inputs in clearing, weeding, planting, and harvesting crops, as well as the biomass of crop yields, he concluded that swidden is far more efficient and ecologically stable than systems that depend upon high yielding varieties of cultivars and higher inputs (Rappaport 1975). Later research amended many of the misunderstandings found in this early work – the structure and sustainability of swidden systems is by no means identical to that of the standing forest it replaces – but continued to explore the practice in ecosystemic terms (Dove 1983). Research further demonstrated that swidden systems, though frequently maligned as practices of isolated peoples, are often well-integrated into market economies (Pelzer 1978).

Again, however, despite the power of systems approaches and quantitative energetics, questions arise about explanation. To have described the flow of energy in a system is by no means the same as explaining why the system looks the way it does or why it might change. As a result, much of the enthusiasm for this approach has waned in the last 20 years.

But even as Cultural Ecologists have abandoned energetics, engineers have begun to champion the approach, with specific attention to the thermodynamic cost efficiencies of many practices (Bakshi 2002). In so doing, they seek to perhaps allow a final answer to compelling practical mysteries like: "paper or plastic?" Systems approaches in Cultural Ecology have poor explanatory power ("why do people do things the way they do?") but continue to represent a powerful tool for exploring processes ("how do varying ways of doing things differ ecologically?").

Agrarian Landscapes – The Geography of Practical Reason

Beyond the internal characteristics of such human ecosystems, a central concern for Cultural Ecologists, and one that is truly geographic in emphasis and execution, is the study of agrarian landscapes. This interest has led to sustained research on the way internal logics and practical constraints of making a living on the land give rise to recognizable signatures and patterns. Whether exploring the distribution of agrarian systems across the hills and plains of New Guinea (Brookfield 1962), following Swiss peasants on the tasks of their daily work through their carefully produced patchwork landscapes of field, pasture, and garden (Netting 1981, 1986), or examining the vastly complex human-made ecosystems of sugarcane, silkworm, and mulberry in China (Zhong 1982), all this work emphasizes the remaking of the landscape to solve the practical problems of production. Landscapes are shown to be fitted to meeting household goals and making possible complex livelihoods that balance demands of both the environment and the market.

Because few variables for explaining such landscape change can easily be tracked or measured, however, especially over long histories, Cultural Ecologists tend to rely on population to explain much of this change. The theory and methods of this approach to landscape research, therefore, reflect "demand driven" concerns. When population rises, Cultural Ecologists suggest that there is pressure for innovation and increased yields resulting in landscape modification and land clearing. When populations fall, the reverse occurs and land is left for fallow and regrowth into native vegetation. This focus on population follows directly from revelations drawn from Esther Boserup's *Conditions of Agricultural Growth* (1965), a universally read and discussed volume in the field. This thesis, and its carefully assembled reasoning, shows the capacity of humans to expand the production of food by modifying the conditions under which it is produced, thus drawing into question long-held assumptions about absolute limits for populations.

However attractive and well-worn as such models may be, there are many forces and variables acting on farm households that remain unconsidered. Beyond population, commodity prices, political institutions, and a wide range of ideologies and traditions impinge on the way people make a living, few of which figure prominently in Cultural Ecological research. The reduction of explanation to demography therefore bedevils much otherwise excellent research into the production of landscape. But this approach nevertheless allows the formulation of many key questions and hypotheses for the study of agrarian change. Research has followed to explore the conditions under which intensification occurs, and the logic behind the acceptance and rejection of green revolutionary technologies including high yielding varieties of cultivars and important inputs like fertilizer and other agricultural chemicals (Turner & Brush 1987).

Exploration in this vein also continues to thrive in research on past environments, breaking new and important ground in both Geography and Archaeology. In particular, research shows the vast and complex alterations of the landscape made by pre-Columbian peoples (Butzer 1992; Doolittle 2000; Denevan 2001). Such research not only demonstrates the profound influence of Native American peoples on the landscape, underlining the adaptivity and creativity of these traditions, it further serves to dispel the myth of a "pristine" and Edenic pre-Columbian landscape, a misconception with no small ongoing influence in the popular, scientific, and political imagination of the Americas (Sluyter 1999).

Beyond Land and Water – The Limits of Cultural Ecology

But these many branches of research began to reach their limit in the last few decades of the century, as the landscapes of both research and subsistence began to change dramatically. In 1971, Barney Nietschmann set off for the Miskito coast of Nicaragua, a place where he had worked for several years prior, living with the Miskito Indians of Tasbapauni village to unlock the mysteries of adaptation using the techniques of energetics and ecosystem analysis. Paddling a dugout canoe back to his field base, however, he found a culture in flux, with scarcities of crucial foods, especially sea turtle, accompanied by an increasing pattern of commodification of land, labor, and crops.

Wishing to explain the changes he witnessed, Nietschmann was forced to transcend the traditional mode of explanation in Cultural Ecology. The explanation for change lay outside the Miskito village, and it was tied closely not only to increasing articulation with global markets, but also to the relative lack of power the Miskito held in regional and national Nicaraguan politics. Convincing explanation, as summarized in his classic account *Between Land and Water* (1973), would require a *political* as well as a cultural ecology. Moreover, the urgency of the problems facing the Miskito would lead Nietschmann in the following years to join the people of Tasbapauni in the struggle for rights to the land, water, plants, and animals that they had husbanded for centuries by establishing protected areas for productive use by the community.

Throughout Cultural Ecology, similar questions are being raised concerning the limits of the approach, and the larger questions that demand interrogation. Why, for example, should the household be the "natural" unit for analysis, when within the household, significant differences in knowledge and power between men and women directly cause and respond to social and environmental change (Rocheleau 1991)? Why should explanations of intensification remain fixed in local and regional patterns of demography when falling commodity prices and contractualization of peasant labor have driven intensification in agriculture for decades (Pred & Watts 1992)? Why should all cultural meanings and systems of knowledge serve ecological functions when disparate knowledges drive political schism both between and within subsistence groups (Robbins 2000)? Where the goals of local people exceed the opportunities of their locality, might explanations for ecological change lie in transnational processes of migration and remittance (Jokisch 1997)?

Perhaps more profoundly, however, Cultural Ecology faces the more general problems posed by postcolonial politics. What does it mean to have wealthy North Americans, Europeans, and Australians dwelling in villages of the Global South, seeking essential truths amongst "simple" people? Much has been said about this last problem, with accusations that the Cultural Ecological project is an extension of the grim, colonial, and racist projects of the previous century, which though usually benevolent in intent, were essential in the domination of what is now the underdeveloped world (Grove 1990; Bonneuil 2000). This charge has some resonance, especially in examining the most essentialist and reductionist work and its service to more global economic and political forces (Hyndman 2001).

Even so, few defenders of the rights, knowledge, and dignity of local peoples are more outspoken or knowledgeable than Cultural Ecologists. Indeed, many like Nietschmann, were so thoroughly transformed in their political consciousness by their time and work with local producers, that they apprenticed themselves to local political organizations, seeking to aid in the protection of local resources against the aggressive advances of "first world" economies and political forces.

As a result, a new and growing field of interrogation – Political Ecology – has emerged alongside Cultural Ecology, to more carefully examine the institutional, economic and power-laden contexts within which people make environmental decisions. The acorn, however, does not fall too far from the tree; political ecologists continue to be trained in Cultural Ecological theory and methodology and the efforts of researchers in both fields continue to shine light into shadowed questions that have been long neglected.

Forgetting the Lessons of Cultural Ecology: Diamond's Determinism and Ehrlich's Fatalism

The field of Cultural Ecology, despite its limits, therefore provides an empirical tapestry from which to evaluate a boundless range of important questions. By casting culture and nature together in an integrated way, Cultural Ecologists continue to direct attention both towards human adaptation *to* the environment and human adaptation *of* the environment.

First among the important sets of questions such an approach informs, are those raised by broad-brush ecohistorians and demographers like Jared Diamond and Paul Ehrlich, who have captured the public imagination by postulating that development is determined by the axis of continents and delimited by the growth of populations.

However compelling the simple logics of claims like these, rigorous work in Cultural Ecology demands their rejection.

Claims by Diamond, which rest on the limits produced by topography and climate, insisting for example that latitude and semi-aridity in the New World provided a barrier to the diffusion of agriculture northwards and therefore retarded Amerindian development, evaporate in the face of research. The diversity of pre-Columbian cropping systems across the Americas shows the staggering number of environments in which agriculture can emerge and thrive and across which it has diffused (Whitmore & Turner 1992).

So too, the dependency of "dominant" economies on the environmental knowledges and practices of other "failed cultures" undermines any such determinist argument. As evidence from research on rice cultivation by slaves in colonial America by Judith Carney (2001) shows, West African production knowledges and cultivars were brought to the New World by enslaved people. It is their ecological understandings of flooded and dryland rice production systems that was fundamental to the establishment of the rice economy, the major export crop of the antebellum Civil War period upon which future "cultural dominance" was leveraged. By showing the global scale of interactions prerequisite to domination, this kind of work undermines any hope of identifying a "western" agrarian history isolated from the incorporation of other knowledge systems around the world. Adaptation to the environment is a universal fact of global history, and the dominance of the west, to the degree that such a thing is true, is a product of global adaptations and coercions, not regional limits.

Claims of Ehrlich and others, on the other hand, that the natural limits of ecological systems fix and limit global populations, are rendered equally problematic by Cultural Ecological investigation. The vast boom and bust cycles of population expansion and contraction from prehistory to the present (Butzer 1990; Turner 1990), when investigated in careful detail, show complex relationships with the resource base, but continue to demonstrate the incredible capacity of humans to exist and thrive through adaptation of their environments. This is not to argue that Cultural Ecologists do not acknowledge varying carrying capacities under certain circumstances (Bernard et al. 1989), but the limits to growth are seen as the product of complex mutual adaptations between social and ecological systems, not simple – and easily known – limits. Again, determinism and fatalism are subverted by careful examination of adaptation, environmental knowledge, strategic behavior, and the inextricable linkages between social and ecological systems.

As a result, Cultural Ecology is poised to address the most far-reaching and important questions facing people today. How does articulation with globalizing markets influence environmental decision making and production of natural environments (Barham & Coomes 1996; Godoy et al. 2000; Godoy et al. 2000)? How are individual production decisions influenced and how do they, in turn, effect global land cover transformations (Klepis & Turner 2001; Turner et al. 2001)? These questions drive the next generation of Cultural Ecological research.

In the broadest sense then, Cultural Ecology teaches critical conceptual lessons that determinists and neo-Malthusians alike have failed to learn: Geography is a *process* not a preexisting, *a priori*, "natural" *condition*. Geography is *created* through the interaction of human and non-human agents, each mutually adapting and interacting over varying spatial and temporal scales. Geographies are *produced*, and are neither destinies nor prisons. In an era of underdevelopment and uneven distribution of basic needs, where many people face the daily prospect of misery even while resources are abundant and food is plentiful, such a lesson is all the more pressing. Thus Cultural Ecology is as timely as ever, providing a research platform for examining the myriad ways people produce and are produced by non-human actors in a complex world.

REFERENCES

Alland, A. 1975: Adaptation. *Annual Review of Anthropology* 4, 59–73.

Bakshi, B. R. 2002: A thermodynamic framework for ecologically conscious process systems engineering. *Computers and Chemical Engineering* 26(2), 269–82.

Barham, B. and Coomes, O. T. 1996: *Prosperity's Promise: The Amazon Rubber Boom and Distorted Economic Development*. Boulder, CO: Westview Press.

Batterbury, S. 2001: Landscapes of diversity: A local political ecology of livelihood diversification in south-western Niger: *Ecumene* 8(4), 437–64.

Batterbury, S. and Forsyth, T. 1999: Fighting back: human adaptations in marginal environments. *Environment* 41(6).

Bebbington, A. 2001: Globalized Andes? Livelihoods, landscapes, and development: *Ecumene* 8(4), 414–36.

Bennett, J. 1969: *Northern Plainsmen: Adaptive Strategy and Agrarian Life*. New York: Aldine.

Bernard, F. E., Campbell D. J., et al. 1989: Carrying capacity of the eastern ecological gradient of Kenya. *National Geographic Research* 5(4), 399–421.

Blaut, J. M. 2000: *Eight Eurocentric Historians*. New York: Guilford Press.

Bonneuil, C. 2000: Development as experiment: science and state building in late colonial and postcolonial Africa, 1930–1970. *Osiris* 15, 258–81.

Boserup, E. 1965: *Conditions of Agricultural Growth: The Economics of Agrarian Change under Population Pressure*. Chicago: Aldine.

Brookfield, H. 1962: Local study and comparative method: an example from central New Guinea. *Annals of the Association of American Geographers* 52(3), 242–54.

Butzer, K. 1990: The realm of cultural-human ecology: Adaptation and change in historical perspective. In B. L. Turner, ed., *The Earth Transformed by Human Action*. Cambridge: Cambridge University Press, 685–701.

Butzer, K. 1992: The Americas before and after 1492: current geographical research. *Annals of the Association of American Geographers* 82(3), 345–68.

Carney, J. 2001: *Black Rice: The African Origins of Rice Cultivation in the Americas*. Cambridge, MA: Harvard University Press.

Conklin, H. C. 1954: An ethnoecological approach to shifting agriculture. *New York Academy of Sciences, Transactions* 17(2), 133–42.

Dahl, G. and Hjort, A. 1976: *Having Herds: Pastoral Herd Growth and Household Economy*. Stockholm: Liber Tryck.

Denevan, W. M. 2001: *Cultivated Landscapes of Native Amazonia and the Andes: Triumph over the Soil*. Oxford: Oxford University Press.

Diamond, J. 1997: *Guns, Germs, and Steel: The Fates of Human Societies*. New York: W.W. Norton.

Doolittle, W. E. 2000: *Cultivated Landscapes of Native North America*. Oxford: Oxford University Press.

Dove, M. 1983: Theories of swidden agriculture and the political economy of ignorance. *Agroforestry Systems* 1, 85–99.

Ehrlich, P. R. 1968: *The Population Bomb*. New York: Ballantine Books.

Ehrlich, P. R. and Ehrlich, A. H. 1991: *The Population Explosion*. New York: Simon & Schuster.

Ellen, R. 1982: *Environment, Subsistence and System: The Ecology of Small Scale Social Formations*. Cambridge: Cambridge University Press.

Freed, S. A. and Freed, R. S. 1981: Sacred cows and water buffalo in India: the use of ethnography. *Current Anthropology* 225, 483–90.

Geertz, C. 1963: *Agricultural Involution: The Processes of Ecological Change in Indonesia*. Berkeley: University of California Press.

Godoy, R., Kirby, K., et al. 2000: Valuation of consumption and sale of forest goods from a Central American rain forest. *Nature* 406 (6 July), 62–3.

Godoy, R., O'Neill, K., et al. 2000: Human capital, wealth, property rights, and the adoption of new farm technologies: the Tawahka Indians of Honduras. *Human Organization* 59(2), 222–33.

Grove, R. H. 1990: Colonial conservation, ecological hegemony and popular resistance: towards a global synthesis. In J. M. MacKenzie, ed., *Imperialism and the Natural World*. Manchester, UK: Manchester University Press, 15–50.

Hall, J. A. 1985: *Powers and Liberties: The Causes and Consequences of the Rise of the West*. Oxford: Blackwell.

Harris, M. 1966: The cultural ecology of India's sacred cattle. *Current Anthropology* 7(1), 51–66.

Harris, M. 1974: *Cows, Pigs, Wars, and Witches: The Riddles of Culture*. New York: Random House.

Hyndman, D. 2001: Academic responsibilities and representation of the Ok Tedi crisis in postcolonial Papua New Guinea. *Contemporary Pacific* 13(1), 33–54.

Johnson, D. L. 1969: *The Nature of Nomadism: A Comparative Study of Pastoral Migrations in Southwestern Asia and Northern Africa*. Chicago: University of Chicago Press.

Jokisch, B. D. 1997: From labor circulation to international migration: the case of south-central Ecuador. *Yearbook Conference of Latin Americanist Geographers* 23, 63–75.

Jones, E. L. 1981: *The European Miracle: Environments, Economies, and Geopolitics in the History of Europe and Asia*. Cambridge: Cambridge University Press.

Klepis, P. and Turner, B. L. 2001: Integrated land history and global change science: the example of the southern Yucatan peninsular region project. *Land Use Policy* 18, 27–39.

Kropotkin, P. 1888: *Mutual Aid: A Factor in Evolution*. Boston: Porter Sargent Publishers.

Kropotkin, P. 1985: *Fields, Factories, and Workshops Tomorrow*. London: Freedom Press.

Kropotkin, P. 1990: *The Conquest of Bread*. Montreal: Black Rose Press.

Landes, D. 1998: *The Wealth and Poverty of Nations: Why Some are So Rich and Some So Poor*. New York: Norton.

Malthus, T. R. 1992: *An Essay on the Principle of Population* (selected and introduced by D. Winch). Cambridge: Cambridge University Press.

Mortimore, M. 1989: *Adapting to Drought: Farmers, Famines, and Desertification in West Africa*. Cambridge: Cambridge University Press.

Murphy, R. F. 1981: Julian Steward. In S. Silverman, ed., *Totems and Teachers: Perspectives on the History of Anthropology*. New York: Columbia University Press.

Netting, R. M. 1981: *Balancing on an Alp: Ecological Change and Continuity in a Swiss Mountain Community*. Cambridge: Cambridge University Press.

Netting, R. M. 1986: *Cultural Ecology*. Prospect Heights, IL: Waveland Press.

Nietschmann, B. 1973: *Between Land and Water*. New York: Seminar Press.

Pelzer, K. 1978: Swidden cultivation in south east Asia: Historical, ecological, and economic perspectives. In P. Kunstadter, ed., *Farmers in the Forest: Economic Development and Marginal Agriculture in Northern Thailand*. Honolulu: University of Hawaii Press.

Pred, A. and Watts, M. J. 1992: *Reworking Modernity: Capitalisms and Symbolic Discontent*. New Brunswick, NJ: Rutgers University Press.

Rappaport, R. 1975: The flow of energy in an agricultural society. In S. H. Katz, ed., *Biological Anthropology*. San Francisco: W.H. Freeman, 117–32.

Rappaport, R. A. 1968: *Pigs for the Ancestors: Ritual in the Ecology of a New Guinea People*. New Haven: Yale University Press.

Robbins, P. 1998: Nomadization in Rajasthan, India: migration, institutions, and economy. *Human Ecology* 26(1), 69–94.

Robbins, P. 1998: Population and pedagogy: the geography classroom after Malthus. *Journal of Geography* 97(6).

Robbins, P. 2000: The practical politics of knowing: state environmental knowledge and local political economy. *Economic Geography* 76(2), 126–44.

Rocheleau, D. 1991: Gender, ecology, and the science of survival: stories and lessons from Kenya. *Agriculture and Human Values* 8(1–2), 156–65.

Rocheleau, D., Ross, L., et al. 2001: Complex communities and emergent ecologies in the regional agroforest of Zambrana-Chacuey, Dominican Republic. *Ecumene* 8(4), 465–92.

Sanford, S. 1983: *Management of Pastoral Development in the Third World*. New York: John Wiley and Sons.

Sauer, C. O. 1952: *Agricultural Origins and Dispersals*. New York: American Geographical Society.

Sauer, C. O. 1965: The morphology of landscape. In J. Leighly, ed., *Land and Life*. Berkeley: University of California Press, 315–50.

Simoons, F. J. 1979: Questions in the sacred cow controversy. *Current Anthropology* 20(3), 467–76.

Sluyter, A. 1999: The making of the myth in postcolonial development: material-conceptual landscape transformation in sixteenth century Veracruz. *Annals of the Association of American Geographers* 89(3), 377–401.

Steward, J. H. 1972: *Theory of Culture Change: The Methodology of Multilinear Evolution*. Urbana: University of Illinois Press.

Trimbur, T. J. and Watts, M. 1976: Are cultural ecologists well adapted? A review of the concept of adaptation. *Proceedings of the Association of American Geographers* 8, 179–83.

Turner, B. L. 1989: The specialist-synthesis approach to the revival of geography: the case of cultural ecology. *Annals of the Association of American Geographers* 79(1), 88–100.

Turner, B. L. 1990: The rise and fall of population and agriculture in the central Maya lowlands: 300 BC to present. In L. Newman, ed., *Hunger & History: Food Shortage, Poverty, and Deprivation*. Malden, MA: Blackwell.

Turner, B. L. and Brush, S. B., eds. 1987: *Comparative Farming Systems*. New York: Guilford Press.

Turner, B. L., Villar, S. C., et al. 2001: Deforestation in the southern Yucatan peninsular region: an integrative approach. *Forest Ecology and Management* 154(3), 353–70.

Waddell, E. 1972: *The Mound Builders: Agricultural Practices, Environment, and Society in the Central Highlands of New Guinea*. Seattle, WA: University of Washington Press.

Whitmore, T. M. and Turner, B. L. 1992: Landscapes of cultivation in Mesoamerica on the eve of the conquest. *Annals of the Association of American Geographers* 82(3), 402–25.

Winkelman, M. 1998: Aztec human sacrifice: cross-cultural assessments of the ecological hypothesis. *Ethnology* 37(3), 285–98.

Woodcock, G. and Avakumovic, I. 1990: *From Prince to Rebel*. Montreal: Black Rose Press.

Zhong, G. 1982: The mullberry dike-fish pond complex: a Chinese ecosystem of land–water interaction on the Pearl river delta. *Human Ecology* 10, 191–202.

Chapter 13

Environmental History

Gerry Kearns

There was a time when almost all Western geography could be termed environmental history. In the late nineteenth century, physical geographers explained landscapes by describing how they had evolved. Likewise, human geographers saw society as shaped by the directing hands of the environment. By the 1960s this had very much changed. Process studies shortened the temporal framework in geographical explanation and cut the cord between nature and society. Now, physical and human landscapes were seen as responding to short-term fluctuations around a long-term steady state. Between the homeostatic systems of the geomorphologist and the isotropic surfaces of the economic geographer, there seemed to be no congress. For a number of reasons, environmental history now enjoys a renewed significance within human geography. I want to explore four sets of reasons why this is so. First, I will look at the continuing importance of an ecological tradition in geography that was always more than mere environmental determinism. In the second place, I will explore how geographical reasoning has continued to be of interest in what we might term big-picture histories. Thirdly, I want to consider how environmental history was treated within Marxist geography. Finally, I intend to consider how the New Cultural Geography has treated the subject. I will conclude by examining some studies that draw upon the best from these four approaches.

Ecological Reasoning in Geography

Environmental determinism was always a contested project within geography. There were those, such as Herbert John Fleure (1877–1969), who were worried by the biological determinism, even racism, of much contemporary geography. In Fleure's (1962) geography, social organization was a vital variable as was the interaction between peoples as they moved through and shared or contested the use of different regions. Population mixing, resource appraisals, and attention to the ways people got access to environmental resources complicate any simple determinism. The history of how societies change is, then, in part the history of how they have changed their ecological context. Ecological reasoning focuses on how the flows of natural matter and energy are garnered by different groups. Human life and economic development are impossible without this material basis. Without shelter, food, and tools, there is no society; and without nature there was no shelter, food, or tools. There are two aspects of Fleure's work that are still important: first, the emphasis upon racial impurity and, secondly, the emphasis upon the organization of work as a culturally variable and crucial factor in explaining how the environment is evaluated and used at various times and in particular places.

Impurity is significant because it makes it more difficult to use history for xenophobic purposes. Conservative thinkers such as Halford Mackinder (1861–1947) saw clear correlations between environment, race, and language and insisted that this explained and justified the division of the earth's surface into nations and empires. For Fleure any "simple linkage of race and language with the social group can, at most, have belonged only to very early times. Admixture came soon enough" (Peake & Fleure 1927: 121). It is striking to consider how far national histories see the past in terms of invasion, displacement and conquest. What if we see the past, instead, as characterized by miscegenation and by ongoing cultural and technological conversations between groups? Intermarriage has proved more fruitful for economies than has isolation: "[c]ulture contacts, except when involving complete destruction on one side or the other, have not only provided mutual enrichment by exchange, but have also stimulated fresh developments" (Peake & Fleure 1936: iii). Diffusion is about interaction not contamination. Fleure could never have agreed with Mackinder (1931: 326) that the English people were the inheritors of:

The English blood, one fluid, the same down through the centuries, on loan for the moment in the forty million bodies of the present generation. John Bull in his insularity is the exemplar of the myriad separate bloods and saps, each the fluid essence of a local variety or species of animal or plant.

Fleure (1951: 1), instead, maintained that: "[a]n outstanding feature of the story of man in Britain is that, in the course of the historic centuries, a considerable measure of unity has been achieved without a great deal of forcible repression of diversity. Unity in diversity . . . is a feature of Britain." The same was true of Europe and this made the pretensions of the sovereign nation-state dangerous. Writing to caution against the linguistic nationalism taken as the natural basis for political organization by the peacemakers planning Europe after the First World War, Fleure insisted that economic relations under industrialism must establish connections that transcend the localism of the agricultural societies that sustained earlier coherent nations. People were implicated in solidarities at multiple scales but Europe did not seem ready to think about this: "[t]he disastrous muddles made by the British Governments in Ireland have shown how little the idea of unity-in-diversity has been thought out by politicians, and we have to realise that in Europe we can have only unity-in-diversity" (Fleure 1921: 13).

Work is significant because it turns our attention to the way social groups set goals in seeking to secure a decent living from their environment. A common criticism of environmental determinism was that it treated society like a mobile plant. Once set in a particular place, it was the character of the local resources that determined if it would flourish. Work, however, is not like that. Work involves communication and is a cultural achievement. There are no Robinson Crusoes in human history. Furthermore, collective effort is almost always required for people to keep body and soul together. Land allocation is a social question, private property a cooperative achievement. The peasant agriculture of China, thought Fleure, required ways of sustaining families in their attempts to pass their enhancement of the soil down to their children. Things were very different for the commercial society of ancient Greece:

Whereas the Chinese agricultural system contrived to maintain the organization of society with the family emphasized as the most important unit around which almost everything was gathered, in the Greek lands with their specialization of crafts and their trade there was a tendency to make neighbourhood take the place of kinship to some extent in social organization. Thence there grew systems of law regulating intercourse between unrelated people . . . (Fleure 1921: 179)

Out of ways of making a living, then, a society develops its legal, philosophical and cosmological systems. The nomad, the peasant, and the merchant not only represent different ways that people can use their environment, where they dominate particular societies, they produce different systems of social organization and only through such institutions can society appropriate natural resources.

Another prominent critic of environmental determinism was Carl Ortwin Sauer (1889–1975). He rejected the notion that nature was the active, society the passive partner in ecology. Rather he emphasized the extent to which landscapes expressed the personality of a culture. He also paid close attention to people as geomorphic and biotic agents. In one of his last seminars, he told students that: "there are the simple and sturdy souls who identify vegetation with climate. And there are the people like myself who wonder every time there is something peculiar about a vegetation whether somebody didn't set fire to it" (Parsons 1987: 157). Landscapes, then, were cultural artifacts of very long gestation. This meant that Sauer was critical also of the process studies that narrowed geography's historical sweep. He saw this as produced by the euphoria of economic triumphalism when the United States stood lord of all the nature it surveyed, a "brief moment of fulfilment and ease" (Sauer 1941: 2). At that moment it seemed that nature was bent immediately and irrevocably to the short-term dictates of the economy. In a letter of 1948, Sauer expressed the belief that this hubris would soon receive its environmental check: "[i]t is quite possible that our whole western civilization in its modern form, based on ever increasing production and consumption, is a violation of natural order which will bring about its collapse. It is possible that the unparalleled malignancy of nationalism in our time is a sickness based on a pathologic industrialization, on increasing unbalance between population and resource with increasing failure of resource" (Martin 1987: xv).

Sauer provides further support for Fleure's emphasis on diffusion and upon work. However, I want to stress two further aspects of Sauer's work that distance his ecological reasoning from environmental determinism. The first is the idea that almost all environments are already what Hegel termed "second nature." In other words, the environment is a historical product of cycles of past human occupancy and use. The second, and related, lesson of his work is that the carrying capacity of a region depends upon how it is exploited and it is quite possible that current landscapes are degraded when viewed from the perspective of carrying capacity. For example, in his work on the transformation of the Caribbean under European colonialism, Sauer (1966) used archaeological as well as Spanish literary evidence to describe a form of farming that served local food needs rather than producing primary products for export. Sauer followed early Spanish observers in describing Hispaniola (now the Dominican Republic and Haiti) as a largely open landscape, cleared of its "natural" trees and mainly cultivated by mixed cropping on mounds of earth. Combined with fish and shellfish, this could support a very dense population. For the area under Spanish control, Bartholomew Columbus counted 1.1 million from the returns of the tax collectors he appointed in 1496. Sauer's estimate of about 3 million Indians on the whole island in 1491 was ten times higher than that accepted by Alfred Kroeber and Angel Rosenblat. This was the forerunner of a debate that soon produced similarly divergent population figures for many other parts of the Caribbean as well as both North and South America (Denevan 1992). Within a decade, the population of Hispaniola had been decimated and slaves were soon introduced from Africa. Without Indian labor, the arable areas retreated in some places before an expansion of pastoralism with its low intensity of labor and in others before scrub and then woodland. By 1518 the population decline had been exacerbated by the rounding up of Indians for slavery in the placer gold deposits and there their diet was under ignorant Spanish control. The fate of the Indians was sealed: "[a] well-structured and adjusted native society had become a formless proletariat in alien servitude, its customary habits and enjoyments lost. The will to live and to reproduce was thus weakened" (Sauer 1966: 204). Disease completed what malnutrition and despair had begun. By the 1530s there were hardly any Indians left. By the time anthropologists arrived to examine the few groups who survived beyond the activity space of the Europeans, their earlier way of life was not even a memory and it was all too easy to dismiss the earliest Spanish observers as romantics or even vainglorious conquerors exaggerating the military challenges they faced. By paying attention to the range of plants available and to the other food sources mentioned, Sauer was able to give ecological credibility to these earliest accounts of something akin to the "original affluent society" later described by Sahlins (1972).

Geographical Histories

Instead of building upon the ecological reasoning of such as Fleure and Sauer, human geographers, in the main, turned away from historical studies towards contemporary studies of economic space. Sauer himself saw American geography taken over by those he dismissed, in a letter of 1967, as "piddlers with forumulas of imaginary universals" (Martin 1987: xv). Nevertheless, the ecological perspective was repeatedly taken up by economic historians, many of whom offered explanations of Western development in which the environment played a key role. Environmental history was also taken up by scholars influenced by green politics and seeking to chart and explain the environmental degradation they saw advancing across the landscapes of both rich and poor countries. I want to show that the insights of Fleure and Sauer remain relevant to these modern studies.

Jared Diamond's (1997) explanation of why some peoples are rich and others poor paints a broadly Darwinian picture in which inter-continental contact produces conflicts which are ultimately settled by might backed up by technology and disease immunity. The argument rests upon an account of how agriculture develops in different environments. Eurasia had a great concentration of land in the mid-latitudes most conducive to the growing of the most nutritionally efficient grains. It also had a majority of the animals that have proved domesticable. Beyond that, western Europe has a varied topography producing small states rather than large empires and is thus prone to competition and innovation rather than to the technological conservatism of the autocratic empires of Asia. The Eurasian part of the argument is original to Diamond while the western European part derives from the work of Eric Jones (1981). I think Jim Blaut (2000) was broadly right in his criticisms of the antitropical bias in both Diamond and Jones. However, I think too that Diamond has an important argument to make about the relationship between populations and diseases. Many more people lived on the Eurasian than on the American land mass. Given the simplicity of the linguistic map of Eurasia, its peoples were probably in more intimate and frequent contact with each other than was the case in America. It is certainly the case that a greater number of large animals had been domesticated in Eurasia. Together these factors meant that the peoples of Eurasia were subject to epidemics of contagious diseases, such as smallpox, which had crossed over from animal reservoirs such as pigs, and which spread widely. What Diamond offers, then, is a way of relating agricultural development to patterns of disease and it is quite clear that the lack of any immunity to smallpox in particular was an important part of the decimation of Amerindian peoples upon contact. However, this cannot be the whole story, for at various points in its history Europe was subject to truly devastating plagues from which it took scores of years to recover. The crucial demographic feature in America is that virgin epidemics happened under the impress of colonialism and aboriginal populations got no opportunity to bounce back before their resources were simply taken away for use by Europeans. It is the social disorganization and the appropriation of their land by others that explains why Amerindian populations took so very long to achieve even modest recovery after epidemic or war. I think Sauer understood this better than does Diamond.

Jones's arguments have been heavily criticized by Blaut (1993) for their ethnocentrism. The environmental element of Jones's account of the rise of Europe is certainly deterministic. Jones says that Europe is tectonically stable and is subject to none of the uncertainties of the monsoon climates of Asia. The topography of Europe is varied, creating at the regional scale, a congeries of ecological niches with products that complement one another, and at a larger scale a series of drainage basins, separated by mountains, that cohere easily into states but are difficult to combine into empires. Europe and not Asia has been capable of sustained, long-term economic growth. Growth spurts in Asia are absorbed by population increases. Jones's argument is that the hostile climate and exploitative political system meant that Asian peasants simply faced greater insecurity than did Europeans. As such, they provided security in the form of children rather than running the risk of having fixed capital assets destroyed in war or taxed away by rapacious emperors. Given the different risk environments, Europeans and Asians made different but equally rational choices, the first to put goods before children, and the latter to value offspring over material wealth. It should be clear that this is not, although Blaut wants to suggest that it is, an argument about European rationality versus Asian super-stition. It is, however, an argument about how environments affect society and many of Blaut's criticisms of antitropical prejudice hold good here, as does his demon-stration of the tremendous diversity within Asia. I want to draw attention to a different problem. Jones's argument is not constructed on the basis of a properly comparative study of Asian and European societies before 1492. If you look at the evidence he relies upon, almost all the demographic material for places such as India come from a period after European interference with those economies and societies. To compare the famines in nineteenth-century India with the lack of extensive famines in Europe since the seventeenth century is not to bear witness to the fail-ures of climate but to the failings of colonial administration. As Sauer shows us, we cannot read back postcontact social, demographic, and agricultural systems into precontact times. Lack of evidence may drive us in that direction but the road to historical error is paved with such good intentions.

Big-picture histories often operate with spatial units that are chaotic rather than coherent (Lewis & Wigen 1997). They often make such units the bearers of a per-sonality in ways that emphasize the radical separation between societies and their deadly hostility towards each other. Culture replaces biology is the modern version of Mackinder's worldview and I feel that such as Samuel Huntington (1996) are susceptible to the very criticisms Fleure made of the environmental determinists; they pay too little attention to social organization and to the realities of economic and cultural interaction across borders. The lessons of Sauer and Fleure are also worth considering when looking at the second set of popular environmental histo-ries that I want to consider. Some historians have taken up the concerns of the green movement and tried to put them into a historical context by showing the unparal-leled damage done to the environment by capitalism or industrialism, as they vari-ously identify their enemy. Some of the most striking of these studies make up what has been called the New Western History (Kearns 1997).

In many ways, Donald Worster (1993) makes very much the case against indus-trialism that Sauer made. With industrialism, the homeostatic systems of Indian agri-culture are displaced and aquifers are squandered, soils reduced to dust and nature sacrificed to profits. In each case, I think their blanket dismissal of industrialism is unfeasible but in Worster's case I believe there is a further romantic denial of eco-logical realities. Worster, unlike Sauer, sees Indians as ecological primitives, barely marking the land. This, as Willems-Braun (1997) argued so well, is somewhat patronizing and leaves Indians no place in the modern world. There are only ver-sions of second nature available to us and purity cannot be an ecological virtue. There are only ever valuations placed on their environments by people. We may choose to celebrate color, or diversity, or biomass, or rare species, or unique eco-logical niches. Environmental history can remind us how certain of these valuations have come to be taken more seriously than others at various times. This, I think, is the great strength of Bill Cronon's (1991) work on Chicago and its hinterland. He describes the nineteenth-century conversion of pigs, and cows, and trees, and grasses into commodified pork, beef, pulp and grain. Production-line abattoirs change the social conception of life. There is a brutality and lack of respect in the meat packing plants and yet in the tins of corned beef a new vision of domestic life was also being projected. Environmental history can return us to a sense of responsibility for the ecological realities upon which our labor-saving cooking and cheap food rests. Commodities reside in ecological as well as economic chains and their forward and backward links equally bear consideration.

In engaging with the works of global economic historians and with "green" histories, human geographers have found ways to pick up again themes from scholars such as Fleure and Sauer, themes that had received but limited attention during the so-called quantitative revolution. These themes were also raised by developments within geography that explicitly confronted the ahistorical approaches swept into geography with that revolution.

Marxism

Marxists were vital in linking geography to a broad range of social and economic sciences. Marxism is inherently interdisciplinary. In some ways, it ignores academic disciplines altogether. For geography, the radical attacks on quantification for its political conservatism began a reengagement between geography and social theory that still continues. The philosophical and the political were inextricably linked. Marxism also aims at comprehensive explanation and thus a wide range of issues can be taken up and mapped back onto its core arguments. There are clearly dangers of reductionism in this but against that we have to recognize that before that point is reached the basic materialism of the Marxist approach sensitizes geographical inquiry to the exploration of a rich suite of interconnections, some of them environmental, many of them historical. Environmental history was never dominant in Marxist geography, which was focused in the main upon urban and economic geography. However, there were two ways that Marxism did engage with environmental history. The first is in its basic philosophical anthropology and the second is in its approach to natural hazards.

Neil Smith (1984), for example, engaged with the philosophical works of Alfred Schmidt (1962) and Sebastiano Timpanaro (1970), among others, to provide a reconsideration of the nature–society dialectic at the heart of geography. Smith explained that instead of seeing nature as an external force constraining social choices, we might consider how nature is transformed in the pursuit of social goals but also how the transformation of nature both socialized and empowered humans. Through work we make ourselves both human and social. Under capitalism, however, nature is privatized and people commit themselves to work, in the main, as to an external discipline necessary to get wages and thus to survive. Now, nature does appear before many as an alien power. It is a mistake, however, not to realize the historically contingent basis of this state of affairs. It is far from simply natural. Smith argues that the term "natural" serves to hide the way societies, economies and, yes, natures are the end points and not the starting points of production. There is very little historical detail in this philosophical work (there is, for example, greater historical detail in Harvey 1996) and there is even a dangerous tendency to treat capitalism alone as truly productive of nature due to its great technological capacity and to treat precapitalist societies as doing little more than scratching nature's surface. Smith (1984: 104) writes of "the natural economies of feudalism and other precapitalist modes of production" and tells us that "capitalism inherits a territorial division of labour rooted in natural differentiations." Second nature, the product of fire and of forest-clearing, has been general in almost all areas of human occupance for centuries before capitalism. The patchwork that Jones finds in Europe is the product of such selective transformations. Indeed, the grain of ecological differentiation has probably been made finer by human activity that it ever would be without. In medieval England, for example, the complementarity of pastoral and mixed-farming ecotones was established at the village level throughout lowland regions and many upland regions too. As Sauer and Fleure might remind us, the onset of capitalism is not the only historical transformation worthy of serious consideration in the study of the relations between society and nature.

Natural hazards research had remained an area within geography where human and physical approaches were at least neighbors as best exemplified in the work of Gilbert White (1973, 1974; Burton et al. 1978). The historical dimension was somewhat weakly developed within this research tradition for it amounted to little more than the investigation of the return-time of physical events of varying magnitudes. Marxist thought inspired two significant revisions of this work. Both underline the social nature of hazards. In the first place, geographers explored the significance of the fact that people now relate to nature as a form of property. Property relations structure access. These relations are historical products. They were different in the past and will no doubt be different in the future.

The pioneering work in this area was Michael Watts' (1983) study of food shortages in northern Nigeria. The famine of 1972–3 throughout much of sub-Saharan Africa fixed images of starving Black babies as a synecdoche for Africa. This imagery presented Africa as a place where nature was just too strong for a rather weak culture and technology, the dilemma of underdevelopment (Jarosz 1992). Watts (1983: xxiii) argued instead that "[a]ll climatic phenomena have social referents which are historically specific forms of society." When, during the nineteenth century, the area was the Muslim Caliphate of Sokoto, the climate was just as variable as under British colonial rule in the first half of the twentieth century. In the nineteenth century food shortages did not create mass starvation because the state mitigated its tax demands in times of difficulty for farmers. There were also forms of communal solidarity built into forms of labor tribute and gift reciprocity. In broad terms, this precapitalist economy, well used to the threat of food shortage, aimed at "the social provision of minimum income in the face of high risk" (Watts 1983: 89). In the first decade of the twentieth century, Britain took the area under colonial rule. It decided that no individual property rights had previously existed and thus it should nationalize all land and charge direct producers a tax for the annual use of their plots. Now the goal of property management was to maintain a constant tax-stream to sustain the colonial administration. This meant that producers were under great stress in times of shortage. Petty commodity production broke up collective solidarities. During the Second World War, for example, the consequences of a drought were magnified for the farmers by the state's demand for taxes and its control of food prices so that inflation would not affect the production costs of the tin produced for export. The result was that farmers fled to the towns or stayed put and ate their seed corn. The property relations were overlain by a political system that did not put rural living standards very high up its agenda. Food shortages are always refracted through such political and institutional prisms. They are never truly natural, and they never were.

There have been many further studies on the political economy of environmental change including Piers Blaikie's (1985) influential study of soil erosion and Judith Carney's (2001) study of technology transfer from Africa to Carolina in rice production. I want, however, to draw attention to a second way Marxist writings influenced the revision of the natural hazards tradition in geography. Property relations certainly affect how "natural" resources are transformed by work. They are also part of the power relations shaping how disasters reverberate through society. The Sahel drought of 1972–3 created widespread suffering, the English drought of 1976 prevented people legally watering their lawns for a while. There is no correlation between the scale of an environmental perturbation and the human consequences that follow upon it. Some people are more at risk than others and some people have a better chance of recovering their livelihoods than do others. Location, poverty, communal resources and insurance all go to form a social distribution of vulnerability that directs disasters towards their victims. This framework has been developed in a fantastic book, *At Risk* (Blaikie et al. 1994), and it has been applied to AIDS in Uganda (Barnett & Blaikie 1992). Barnett and Blaikie show that the upstream causes of vulnerability to HIV infection and the downstream impact of AIDS sickness and mortality follows social faultlines that can best be understood in terms of the political and economic history of Uganda. The transformation of the economy under the vicious rule of Idi Amin imposed price controls that simultaneously weakened the rural sector and placed a high premium upon the smuggling of products such as coffee out of the country. This had gendered consequences with men leaving villages to follow the contraband flows and women left behind with little access to markets in their own right. Under these circumstances, sex work at the truck stops along the smuggling routes became an all too understandable and dangerous survival strategy for many women. The transformation of the rural society under the impress of AIDS mortality also placed under great stress the coping mechanisms by which villagers had characteristically dealt with the occasional tragedy of the death of parents. Barnett and Blaikie show how under a new regime of labour, patterns of farming are transformed undermining the prospects of capital investment or food security. The perspectives of *At Risk* could usefully be applied to a wide range of hazards to produce a new kind of environmental history in geography (Kearns 2000).

The Cultural Turn

Marxism, then, has directed geographers' attention to the historical contingencies of property relations, which form the terms on which society achieves its material grounding. The historical relativity of this dialectic between nature and society had been occluded in much of the process-based studies that dominated geography in the 1960s and 1970s. The historical naivety of the way terms like nature were used in geography did not render them innocent of unexamined political and philosophical content. The normative content of the term "natural" has rarely been as carefully examined as it was in Clarence Glacken's (1967) great survey of the notion that nature might have a design benevolent to human purposes. Perhaps because his survey ended in the eighteenth century, it did not have the impact on contemporary geographical studies that it deserved to have. It was treated as a work on the history rather than the practice of geography yet its exploration of some of the central and contestable terms of the discipline anticipate much of what has since been taken up under the impress of the so-called "cultural turn." The cultural turn in the social sciences is a turn towards the explication of meaning as a sort of hermeneutics of suspicion. Social scientists have been directed towards a consideration of the untenable assumptions that hide behind the "big concepts" they use. Central to this interrogation has been a recognition that a model of the evolution of an "enlightened" West has been taken as normative in their theories. In asserting a single rationality, social scientists have more or less unwittingly elevated the world view of the heroic, bourgeois, white male to a position of unquestioned universality. Under the pressure of anticolonial, feminist, lesbian and gay criticisms, this universality has been revealed as partiality; its privileges reproduced where they are unexamined. Within geography these arguments have produced a new sort of environmental history, a history of the construction of environmental meanings. I want to examine two moments in this new history, the first contextualizes environmental knowings and the second questions their hidden violence.

The works of Raymond Williams (1973) and John Barrell (1980) have served as paradigms for geographical studies of the development of environmental ideas. Williams showed how a romantic view of a bucolic rural past served in nineteenth-century Britain as a way to point out the evils of unnatural industry. He also showed that the designing of some rural landscapes to replicate this imagined, Edenic vision was a way to hide the realities of production and exploitation upon which rural wealth was built. Landscapes screened work. Barrell showed that similar strategies lay behind contemporary landscape painting but that the pain of the derangement of village society under the modernizing and effacing drive of enclosure could yet be recovered from the works of such poets as John Clare. Art historians such as Timothy Clark (1985) and planning historians such as Donald Olsen (1986) took these arguments to town. We can see these approaches to landscape very clearly in the collection of geographical essays edited by Denis Cosgrove and Steve Daniels (1988). This is a thoroughly interdisciplinary field but I want to silence briefly that conversation and highlight a few of the contributions by geographers.

Daniels (1993), for example, has described the ways that representations of landscapes attempt to define the nation as a community with a certain set of values. Certain national realities were always evoked by English woodlands, which might, for example, be under royal ownership or earmarked for naval ships. Across the water in France, trees might recall quite different values, might recall indeed the trees of liberty planted throughout France after the Revolution. Cosgrove (1993) describes the way that the landscapes of Venice were redesigned in the sixteenth century so that they might serve as a setting for the inculcation of certain values in an attempt to consolidate and render natural a new political reality based on landed rather than purely maritime wealth. John Andrews (1975) has given an account of how the English effectively estranged the Irish from their own past by remapping and renaming the Irish landscape in the nineteenth century, replacing Irish names with English ones. In studies such as these, either landscapes are viewed as representations and their, often implicit, meanings decoded, or representations of landscapes are taken as expressive of certain sets of power relations.

Let me turn, now, to the second cultural strand that I want to draw out. I am concerned here with a more radical set of questionings. These scholars are not concerned to read landscapes or their representations as expressing social relations so much as questioning the positions from which landscapes were and are read. Instead of seeing the map as expressing a certain ideology, we might see it as suppressing other ideologies in the act of claiming any single authoritative viewpoint. By considering the direct othering of standpoints, we can explore the implicit constitution of an authoritative self who would feel comfortable looking in this way from this position. The topographical metaphor of surveying captures much of what is at stake here for it implies a single locus from which all meaning may be adequately gathered. But how might things appear to the sideways look? Brian Harley, for example, looked at maps as efforts to censor subaltern views of the world (Laxton 2001). Drawing upon Edward Said's (1978) use of the works of Michel Foucault, Harley went in search of the margins of maps. He tried to ask what interests were served by the silences imposed by the authoritative map.

Gillian Rose (1993) explicated the gendered dimensions of geographical knowledge in her wide-ranging *Feminism and Geography*. Environmental history is not only the story of the dispossession and separation of certain classes from the land through the assertion of property, it is also about the reproduction of patriarchy through gendered access to resources and the representation of gender through historically specific constructions of "nature." The two are related, of course. The allocation to women of tasks such as child rearing and the attendant devaluation of this work, sits alongside the exclusion of women from a full public life be that expressed in the market or the forum. Rose shows how these polarities run through geography with its devaluation of subjectivity in favor of a spurious objectivity, with the heroic explorer now seen in the hardy field scientist of physical geography, and the domestic entertainments of the butterfly collector now seen in the soft studies of the cultural geographer (Kearns 1997).

Rose also considers the pleasures of landscape and notes that the satisfaction of the imperial gaze depended firstly upon ownership but reminds us that this ownership was almost always male and, certainly in the nineteenth-century examples discussed by the cultural geographers above, extended from land to wife. If we examine, for example, the use of the pastoral aesthetic to embellish upper-middle-class suburbs in the cities of late nineteenth-century North America, we find a whole series of mappings of bodies onto places that inscribe contemporary patriarchy onto the land. Urban environments are expressive of gender and not only class. The curvaceous, lightly rolling aesthetic of places such as Riversdale (Chicago) was in marked contrast to the rectilinear landscape of the downtown Loop (Bluestone 1991). The soft lines of the suburb evoked "nature," in the comfort of whose bosom the male might recline at the end of a day in the public grip of Mammon. It was the place for families, for the safe reproduction of a social class. It was a domestic space. It was a place for women. Why, women might even walk about in public in the suburbs without inviting scandal. The aesthetic not only equated women with nature, but it also placed women. It placed them away from the public sphere. It left them where "their" men had put them while the men were free to disport themselves at will both home and away. These gendered activity spaces are clearly articulated in contemporary novels where women act through the disembodied emissary of the letter, whereas the men stroll around as they wish. The contrast between mobile Leopold and static Molly Bloom in James Joyce's *Ulysses* illustrates this perfectly.

A critical and effective environmental history might take up these concerns of the cultural geographers and explore how the making of environments, be they urban or rural, is always also the making of certain sorts of people through both expressing ideologies and by inviting us to read certain bodies in certain ways depending upon where we come across them (as in discourses of the "public" woman). This will mean imposing upon representations all the things they forget, the exclusions they find natural.

Conclusion

I have suggested that in various ways environmental history was devalued in geography after the demise of environmental determinism. I have also suggested that geographers in large part also turned their back upon the important lessons that contemporary critics of environmental determinism had developed in their own work. I have argued that environmental history has come to be of renewed importance in modern geography for three reasons. First, this form of geographical and ecological reasoning has proved of great interest to both global economic historians and to historians influenced by green politics. I have suggested that in each case, the lessons of earlier geographers might still have much to contribute to the development of these studies in environmental history. In the second place, interest in environmental history has been renewed in geography through human geographers' critical engagement with Marxist thought. I have proposed that paying attention to the property relations structuring the mutual constitution of societies and natures, and to the social distribution of vulnerability in the face of environmental risk create an agenda for a fruitful integration of geography and environmental history. Finally, I described some of the ways that geographers have engaged with certain of the issues raised by the so-called cultural turn in the social sciences and humanities. I have looked at landscapes as attempts to express and reinforce certain sets of power relations. I have also looked at them as attempts to silence various other readings and other voices.

I want to conclude by suggesting that these two ways of reinvigorating environmental history within human geography are inadequate without each other. This is argued quite magnificently in Don Mitchell's (1996) *The Lie of the Land*. Mitchell argues that landscape meanings relate to landscape use. He recalls Williams's (1973) argument about landscape as an aesthetic effacing the work upon which it is raised. To the victors, go the imperial gaze. They not only write the history, they also frame the vista that presents one contingent result as natural. The dominant view of California as a land of plenty, inhabited by sturdy yeomen, is one such vista. Mitchell describes the bloody battles that were won before the victors could survey the scene with such equanimity. By excavating the strikers, the Mexicans, the women- and child-laborers, and the communists who are buried beneath that defeat, he calls to our minds how it might have been, should have been, different. These alternative histories should also be part of our geographies. The relationship between aesthetics and property is often this violent.

This has more in common with Sauer on the dynamics of the Columbian encounter than Mitchell allows in his discussion of Sauer's organicism. It also returns us to the global economic histories I discussed above. If geography is in part about the study of how spatial differentiation is produced and reproduced, then, the violence of property relations must be brought within the remit of economic geography. Watts makes this clear. So, too, in a remarkable book, does Mike Davis (2001). *Late Victorian Holocausts* is precisely the sort of integration of environmental and historical-geographical perspectives that I am asking for. Like Sauer, Davis explores how landscapes become degraded under colonial rule. Here, however, we are dealing with the types of food shortages under the impress of commodification that Watts describes. Davis's argument pays attention to the murderous violence of the malignant neglect visited upon colonial subjects by their British rulers. Famines were exploited as opportunities to teach native people the discipline of the Malthusian realities they appeared to ignore. These realities were in fact shaped by the sort of property and tax regime that Watts describes for early twentieth-century Northern Nigeria. Davis proposes that the environmental perturbation of the failure of the rains was directed to do the work of breaking the subsistence economies of India, Brazil, and China so that all their production might pass through the market. So little came back from the market to the producers that they starved in their millions and were left helpless and desperate fodder for future rounds of capitalist exploitation, a docile because impoverished proletariat. This, he suggests, is the origin of the Third World. This work places environmental history at the heart of global economic history but it does so with a full recognition of the importance of the changing, and tragic, social organization of production.

REFERENCES

Andrews, J. H. 1975: *A Paper Landscape: The Ordnance Survey in Nineteenth-Century Ireland*. Oxford: Clarendon Press.

Barnett, A. and Blaikie, P. M. 1992: *AIDS in Africa: Its Present and Future Impact*. New York: Guilford Press.

Barrell, J. 1980: *The Dark Side of the Landscape: The Rural Poor in English Painting, 1730–1840*. Cambridge: Cambridge University Press.

Blaikie, P. M. 1985: *The Political Economy of Soil Erosion in Developing Countries*. London: Longman.

Blaikie, P. M., Cannon, T., Davis, I., and Wisner, B. 1994: *At Risk: Natural Hazards, People's Vulnerability, and Disasters*. London: Routledge.

Blaut, J. M. 1993: *The Colonizer's Model of the World, volume 1: Geographical Diffusionism and Eurocentric History*. London: Guilford Press.

Blaut, J. M. 2000: *The Colonizer's Model of the World, volume 2: Eight Eurocentric Historians*. London: Guilford Press.

Bluestone, D. M. 1991: *Constructing Chicago*. New Haven: Yale University Press.

Burton, I., Kates, R. W., and White, G. F. 1978: *The Environment as Hazard*. Oxford: Oxford University Press.

Carney, J. 2001: *Black Rice: The African Origins of Rice Cultivation in the Americas*. Cambridge MA: Harvard University Press.

Clark, T. J. 1985: *The Painting of Modern Life: Paris in the Art of Manet and his Followers*. London: Thames and Hudson.

Cosgrove, D. 1993: *The Palladian Landscape: Geographical Change and its Cultural Representations in Sixteenth-Century Italy*. Leicester: Leicester University Press.

Cosgrove, D. and Daniels, S., eds. 1988: *The Iconography of Landscape: Essays on the Symbolic Representation, Design and Use of Past Environments*. Cambridge: Cambridge University Press.

Cronon, W. 1991: *Nature's Metropolis: Chicago and the Great West*. New York: W. W. Norton.

Daniels, S. 1993: *Fields of Vision: Landscape Imagery and National Identity in England and the United States*. Cambridge: Polity.

Davis, M. 2001: *Late Victorian Holocausts: El Niño Famines and the Making of the Third World*. London: Verso.

Diamond, J. 1997: *Guns, Germs and Steel: The Fate of Human Societies*. London: Jonathan Cape.

Denevan, W., ed. 1992: *The Native Population of the Americas in 1492*, 2nd ed. Madison, WI: University of Wisconsin Press.

Fleure, H. J. 1921: *The Treaty Settlement of Europe: Some Geographic and Ethnographic Aspects*. Oxford: Oxford University Press.

Fleure, H. J. 1951: *A Natural History of Man in Britain; Conceived as a Study of Changing Relations Between Men and Environments*. London: Collins.

Fleure, H. J. 1962: Social organization and environment. In P. Wagner and M. Mikesell, eds., *Readings in Cultural Geography*. Chicago: University of Chicago Press, 491–505.

Glacken, C. J. 1967: *Traces on the Rhodian Shore: Nature and Culture in Western Thought from Ancient Times to the End of the Eighteenth Century*. Berkeley: University of California Press.

Harvey, D. 1996: *Justice, Nature and the Geography of Difference*. Oxford: Blackwell.

Huntington, S. P. 1996: *The Clash of Civilizations and the Remaking of World Order*. New York: Simon & Schuster.

Jarosz, L. 1992: Constructing the Dark Continent: metaphor as geographic representation of Africa. *Geografiska Annaler* B 74, 105–15.

Jones, E. L. 1981: *The European Miracle: Environments, Economies, and Geopolitics in the History of Europe and Asia*. Cambridge: Cambridge University Press.

Kearns, G. 1997: The imperial subject: geography and travel in the work of Mary Kingsley and Halford Mackinder. *Transactions of the Institute of British Geographers* NS 22, 450–72.

Kearns, G. 1998: The virtuous circle of facts and values in the New Western History. *Annals of the Association of American Geographers* 88, 377–409.

Kearns, G. 2000: Demography and industrialisation: a geographical overview. In A. Brändström and L.-G. Tedebrand, eds., *Population Dynamics During Industrialization*. Umeå: Demographic Data Base, 11–37.

Laxton, P., ed. 2001: *J. B. Harley: The New Nature of Maps*. Baltimore, MD: Johns Hopkins Press.

Lewis, M. W. and Wigen, K. 1997: *The Myth of Continents: A Critique of Metageography*. Berkeley: University of California Press.

Mackinder, H. J. 1931: The human habitat. *Scottish Geographical Magazine* 47, 321–35.

Martin, G. J. 1987: Introduction. In M. S. Kenzer, ed., *Carl O. Sauer: A Tribute*. Corvalis, OR: Oregon University Press, ix–xvi.

Mitchell, D. 1996: *The Lie of the Land: Migrant Workers and the California Landscape*. Minneapolis: University of Minnesota Press.

Olsen, D. J. 1986: *The City as Work of Art: London, Paris, Vienna*. New Haven: Yale University Press.

Parsons J. J., ed. 1987: "Now this matter of cultural geography": notes from Carl Sauer's last seminar at Berkeley [1964]. In M. S. Kenzer, ed., *Carl O. Sauer: A Tribute.* Corvalis, OR: Oregon University Press, 153–63.

Peake, H. and Fleure, H. J. 1927: *The Corridors of Time. III. Peasants and Potters.* Oxford: Clarendon Press.

Peake, H. and Fleure, H. J. 1936: *The Corridors of time. IX. The Law and the Prophets.* Oxford: Clarendon Press.

Rose, G. 1993: *Feminism and Geography: The Limits of Geographical Knowledge.* Minneapolis: University of Minnesota Press.

Sahlins, M. 1972: *Stone Age Economics.* London: Tavistock, 1974.

Said, E. 1978: *Orientalism.* London: Routledge and Kegan Paul.

Sauer, C. O. 1941: Foreword to historical geography. *Annals, Association of American Geographers* 31, 1–24.

Sauer, C. O. 1966: *The Early Spanish Main.* Berkeley: University of California Press.

Schmidt, A. 1962: *The Concept of Nature in Marx.* London: Verso.

Smith, N. 1984: *Uneven Development: Nature, Capital and the Production of Space.* Oxford: Blackwell.

Timpanaro, S. 1970: *On Materialism.* London: Verso.

Watts, M. 1983: *Silent Violence: Food, Famine and Peasantry in Northern Nigeria.* Berkeley: University of California Press.

White, G. F. 1973: Natural hazard research. In R. J. Chorley, ed., *Directions in Geography,* London: Methuen, 193–216.

White, G. F., ed. 1974: *Natural Hazards: Local, National, Global.* New York: Oxford University Press.

Willems-Braun, B. 1997: Buried epistemologies: the politics of nature in (post)colonial British Columbia. *Annals of the Association of American Geographers* 87, 3–31.

Williams, R. 1973: *The Country and the City.* London: Chatto and Windus.

Worster, D. J. 1993: *The Wealth of Nature: Environmental History and the Ecological Imagination.* Oxford: Oxford University Press.

Chapter 14

Ethics and the Human Environment

Jonathan M. Smith

The scope of this chapter is potentially very large, for ethics is far from simple and the human environment is made of many, many things. What is more, geographers have seldom studied the environment from the viewpoint of ethics, or ethics from the viewpoint of the environment, so there are few precedents for us to follow. The work that has been done, most notably by Tuan (1993), Sack (1997), and D. Smith (2000), identifies what we might call the spatiality of sympathy as a major problematic for those who would study moral geographies. They are, by my reading, interested in three general questions. First, to ask which sociospatial settings foster feelings of sympathy, affection, and responsibility for other humans, and what if any variety there is in these settings and feelings. Second, to ask why these feelings are very often partial, leading to ostracism and spatial exclusion of pariah groups and deviant behaviors (Sibley 1995). Third, to ask if, and if so how, we might enlarge feelings of sympathy and responsibility beyond the traditional spatial forms of the local community or nation state, and thereby create a flexible but universal ethic appropriate to the spatial form of the global economy.

Geographers interested in the spatiality of sympathy treat the physical environment as mere medium, a substance that social groups shape to inculcate ethical ideas, segregate moral communities, and increase the mutual sympathy or suspicion with which these communities view one another. This is only part of what we can or should ask about ethics and the environment. Before asking whether it is most ethical to shape the environment in this or that way, we surely must ask the more basic questions of whether, and if so to what extent, it is ethical to shape the environment in the first place. In this chapter I review general answers to this question, since every landscape, ethical or unethical, originates in a positive answer to it. Indeed, if geography is the study of earth-shaping processes and humans are moral agents, answers to this question are the foundation of human geography.

What follows will be in four stages. First I will discuss what I understand to be meant by the word ethical. This is not an exhaustive or deeply learned disquisition, but rather an attempt to outline some basic ideas in terms that I find helpful. I am most concerned to connect ethics with the concepts of ethical vision and moral community. Second, I will discuss premodern environmental ethics, connecting these to belief in a personalized environment of reasonable beings. In this and subsequent sections I will present something like Weberian ideal types to generalize about diverse beliefs. Third I will discuss modern environmental ethics as a consequence of disenchantment (Weber again) and the consequent belief that nature is dead matter not deserving moral consideration. In the fourth section I will discuss some postmodern environmental ethics, which is to say ethics proposed in conscious reaction against perceived environmental degradation caused by the modern environmental ethic of disenchanted nature.

Ethical Matters

The adjective ethical can be applied to a statement or an act. An ethical statement is an imperative that describes a person's duty, what he or she should or should not do. Ethical acts are described or directed by such imperatives. These imperatives and acts are further understood to be of a special sort, so that not all commands or commanded behavior is ethical. They are *categorical* imperatives, which means that they are absolute and unconditional duties incumbent on every person, or every person of a particular class in a particular situation. Children, obey your parents, is a categorical imperative.

Categorical imperatives are distinct from hypothetical imperatives, the former being absolute and the later conditional (Flew 1995). A hypothetical imperative normally takes the following form: if you desire or value X, then you should do Y. If you desire a slender body, for instance, then you should eat less. In a hypothetical imperative an individual human is the axiological ground or source of value, since, to continue with the example just given, he or she must decide whether a slender body is indeed valuable, as an end in itself or as a means to some further end. In a categorical imperative the axiological ground is something outside of or in addition to the self. This is evident if we state the general form of a categorical imperative is as follows: regardless of what *you* desire or value, do Y. Regardless of what *you* desire, for instance, you should telephone your mother once a week.

For a categorical imperative to have any sway over a person, that person must recognize the behavior denoted as Y as possessing a value other than or in addition to the value it has (or lacks) for himself. In other words, something capable of valuing, some other axiological ground, must value this act. Some examples are easy to grasp. All but the most impulsive among us recognize our future self as an axiological ground whenever we defer gratification and serve the interest of our future self. Unless you are an egoist, you almost certainly recognize and respect other humans as axiological grounds, and therefore recognize that their value as persons is primarily the value they have for themselves. This is why you see it as a moral obligation to treat other humans as ends and not means, to place the value they have for themselves ahead of the value they have for you. Additional axiological grounds can be posited. God, for instance. You may feel enjoined to do certain things, and to refrain from others, because you believe they are valued or discountenanced by God. Society or the cultural tradition may be taken as an axiological ground, so that the values of the group, including perhaps those of its deceased and future members, govern a person's behavior. As we will see, environmental ethics must always stipulate what sorts of beings are capable of having values that we humans should respect, values that legitimately constrain or compel behavior toward them or the things with which they are interested.

Ethics place more or less systematic limits on a person's behavior because they require him to recognize values other than his own, values that originate in an axiological ground other than his own, present self and its desires. This is no doubt why many think that ethics is a killjoy. But there is more to ethics than this. Any set of ethical rules purports to bring behavior into line with a transcendental reality that the authors and disciples of those rules believe lays beyond appearances (J. Smith 2000). Ethical rules are therefore the practical manifestation of a larger system of beliefs that, taken together, might be called the moral imagination or ethical vision, "a constant and self-renewing motive to action" (Scruton 2000: 12). Only in an ethical vision do humans perceive, or believe themselves to perceive, values that originate outside their present selves and their immediate aversions and desires. The ethical vision takes as its premise the assumption that the world apparent to the unaided eye is false, distorted by selfishness, ignorance, and impulse, but that this false appearance can be corrected by conscience, virtue, charity and piety. It seems to me that, regardless of specific substance, every ethical vision purports to be a sort of corrective lens. Indeed without an ethical vision, the world we experience would not be a human world, for it would be devoid of rights, duties, obligations, voluntary acts, and choices, as well as of virtues such as courage, temperance, justice, and charity (Scruton 1996). Taking ethical vision as a corrective lens that discloses the real nature of the world and our relations to it, we can understand why the limits ethics imposes on behavior are supposed to liberate, not limit. An ethical vision purports to free a person from the illusion of mere appearances, from the tyranny of passions aroused by these appearances, and from the evil consequences that follow upon taking these appearances for reality.

This is why ethical choices are often likened to a fork in the road, for the image of a traveler deliberating at a fork gives intuitive understanding of the concepts of freedom, duty, and moral choice. One *can* go either way, but only one of them is the right way. And it is a commonplace of such metaphors that to those without the proper ethical vision, the wrong path will appear most attractive. The most familiar trope is in Matthew, where Christ states that "wide is the gate and broad is the way that leadeth to destruction," but "strait is the gate, and narrow is the way which leadeth unto life" (Matthew 7:13–14). Virgil was also of the opinion that "the way down to Hell is easy" (*Aeneid*). Shakespeare suggested that it was also delightful, attractively bordered by the first – alas evanescent – flowers of spring, and therefore called the "primrose path."

An ethical choice at a metaphorical crossroads is therefore an affirmation of some transcendental reality behind the deceptive primroses of immediate appearance and egoistic desire, and as such it is an expression of identity. By choosing one path over another, and especially by abjuring what many see as the more attractive way, a person identifies himself as a member of a moral community. This social aspect of ethical behavior must be added to the prudential aspect, for in addition to the practical benefits that may accompany adoption of the corrective lens of an ethical vision, those who recognize a transcendental reality gain a feeling of membership and meaningfulness. The connection of morality and membership is evident in the close relation of the words ethics, ethos, and ethnic.

Humans have generally believed that their actions toward the environment are governed by categorical imperatives. Perhaps the most famous, and misunderstood, of these is the command given by God to Adam and Eve in the Garden of Eden. "Be fruitful and increase, fill the earth and subdue it, have dominion over the fish in the sea, the birds in the air, and every living thing that moves on the earth" (Genesis 1:28; see Callicott 1994: 14–24). Such an imperative discloses a super-natural reality beyond nature and natural impulse, for what primitive human could have supposed, simply on the evidence of his senses, that it was his place to subdue and have dominion over the natural world. This imperative served as a corrective lens, inspiring audacity in men who were weak, and it also served as a ground for meaning and membership in a moral community that was united in its ethical vision of a reality beyond nature.

Premodern Ethics and the Haunted Environment

It is difficult to discuss premodern environmental ethics in a short space, since they were always local products adapted to the contingencies of particular environments and cultures. The matter is further complicated by the fact that much of what we know about premodern environmental ethics is drawn from written documents, and there is good reason to doubt whether these speculations by the cultural elite closely resemble the beliefs and practices of ordinary folk. Nevertheless, some generaliza-tions are possible.

We should begin by observing that humans with a premodern view of the envi-ronment did not attempt to manipulate nature simply by *causing* it to behave in one way or another. They also gave the natural entities that were pertinent to their purposes *reasons* to behave in the desired fashion. To clarify this distinction, imagine that you are a cold camper with a single match endeavoring to light a fire in a damp forest. If you hold the lit match to dry tinder and ignite it, you *cause* it to burn. If you coax the waxing flame with words of encouragement, or threaten it with curses, you are giving the wood a *reason* to burn. To the extent that you think these words addressed to the wood increase the likelihood of it catching fire, your thinking is premodern.

This is because a premodern person assumed that objects had a nature in some respects like his own, that they were much more like people than like what we in the modern world call things (Barfield 1988: 42). Trees, springs, lakes, mountains, and stones were assumed to be quasi-persons, with something like a mind and a will of their own. They appeared as the mountain did to William Wordsworth, as beings animated "with voluntary power instinct" (*The Prelude*). Getting what one wanted from such an environment was, therefore, much like getting what one wanted from other people: it was a matter of giving natural entities good reasons to cooperate (MacCulloch 1961).

Because it took natural entities to be somewhat like humans, this view of the natural world is often described as anthropomorphic. It is also described as anama-tism or animism. Strictly speaking, animism describes a belief in spirits that are bound to particular bodies, much as an individual human spirit is tied to a particular human body, but it was often connected to belief in a more populous spirit-world. In addition to the animating spirits of things, this might include ghosts of dead humans, the dream-souls of metempsychosing witches and magicians, and those peripatetic spirits that Teutonic folklore represented as elves, dwarves, and giants. All such beings were presumed capable of affecting the material world to the boon or bane of human designs. Perception of an anthropomorphic, personal environment seems to have been universal among premodern peoples, and there is reason to suppose the human mind is congenitally disposed to perceive a spirit-haunted world.

In the West such thinking began to disappear in the sixteenth century. The personalities of the old folklore survive in children's literature, but with characters now so affable and benign that it is hard to remember that they were not always friendly beings. Most were indifferent to human happiness, bent on their own mysterious projects, unconcerned by human fortune and misfortune. Many were malevolent. Few could be counted as friends. Belief in beings bearing such dispositions toward humans served to make the ways of nature intelligible. It explained events in nature, and why these events were so often contrary to human interests.

The personalized human environment was thought to consist of *reasonable beings*, beings that act as they do because they believe they have reasons to act in these ways. The cause of a reasonable act does not work directly, but only through evaluation, judgment, and interpretation; its effect is not a necessary consequence, but rather a *deliberate* response. If you shoved me and caused me to fall, my body would not reflect on the impact and then determine that falling to the floor was the proper response. It would fall necessarily, like an upset tower of building blocks. Being a reasonable being, and assuming that you are analogous, I would, however, instantly question why you shoved me. What did the shove mean? In asking this question I change the shove, from an event that caused me to fall, to the act of a reasonable being that communicates a meaning and is itself reason for some response from me.

To be a reasonable being is, therefore, to engage in symbolic communication, and to demand that actions be justified. This is why we have, after Ludwig Wittgenstein, come increasingly to equate reason and personhood with language and other forms of symbolic activity (Scruton 1996). This is why a premodern person, living in what he took to be a personalized environment populated by reasonable beings, believed that the actions of these beings had a meaning he could understand, and that his own meaningful actions could be understood by these beings. Hence his efforts to influence the environment through symbolic behavior such as dances, charms, sacrifices, or disciplined conduct.

When entities in the natural environment are personalized, supposed to act for reasons, and supposed capable of symbolic communication, it is possible to describe the human environment in distinctly moral terms. This is, firstly, because natural objects could be held morally accountable. One could feel indignant over an undeserved catastrophe, call it an injustice, perhaps appeal to a higher authority. One might also feel a sense of obligation and pious gratitude toward beings that have been of use, or that have at least refrained from causing mischief. They might, after all, have withheld the favor or wreaked the havoc. Secondly, reasonable beings must be regarded as axiological centers, for reasons presuppose values and reasonable beings are necessarily intentional beings. In an environment so conceived, humans are not the sole source of value. Anthropomorphism precludes anthropocentrism. No particular environmental ethic follows from these assumptions, but it seems almost certain that *some* environmental ethic must have.

Modern Ethics and the Disenchanted Environment

Belief in a personalized, spirit-haunted world started to fade in the sixteenth century, when some educated Europeans began to view the environment as a collection of inanimate objects mindlessly moved by mechanical processes, rather like the works of a clock. This shift from an anthropomorphic to mechanistic ethical vision has continued down to the present. Indeed, disbelief in supernatural agents and embrace of materialism is a defining characteristic of the modern age. Anthropomorphism is now regarded as a superstitious solecism of the fanciful, delusional, and ignorant.

The sociologist Max Weber (1864–1920) described this shift as "the disen-chantment of the world" (*Die Entzauberung der Welt*), and regarded the exorcism as an event of great and lasting importance. For Weber, disenchantment was a pre-condition of modern control of nature because it opened up the possibility that "one can in principle master all things by calculation" (Weber 1946: 139). It was not a way of perceiving nature that arose as a result of technological mastery, as Marxists would claim, but a transcendental reality that had to be fully imagined before technological mastery could begin. As a commentator on Weber puts it, "*de facto* mastery is not a precondition for disenchantment. Rather the world is disen-chanted when it is perceived as a potential object of mastery" (Gilbert 1993: 28). This is because disenchantment depersonalized the environment, thereby removing the grounds on which premodern peoples had based their belief that there were limits to human mastery.

Mastery by calculation has four basic aspects. First, before one can master some-thing one must perceive that it has no other master. This was done by denying the existence of nonhuman persons and the values they had been thought to bestow. For instance, if there were such a thing as a wood nymph, it would presumably value the tree it inhabited much as a person values her own body. And it would have something like the same sort of moral claim on that tree. Therefore, to a person who believed in wood nymphs, felling a tree would be an act that, if not forbidden, would require some sort of compensation to the nymph, just as our justice requires compensation to persons whose property or bodies we damage or destroy. Disen-chantment removed from the environment all axiological grounds other than human beings, thereby eliminating the possibility that things in the environment might be valued by beings other than humans, might be in a moral sense *their* property. Thus was the way to anthropocentrism cleared.

In denying anthropomorphism, disenchantment also removed the grounds for attempting to give nature a reason to cooperate. Inanimate nature neither under-stands nor engages in symbolic communication, and so cannot be influenced by reasons. This put an end to the search for symbols with which to flatter, deprecate, or propitiate nature, and directed the whole of modern enquiry into a search for causes. This is the origin of modern technology. Abandonment of attempts to com-municate with nature followed the decision to disbelieve in personalized nature, but in turn changed the way humans understood nature. This is because attempts to influence nature with symbols seldom work, and frequent failure reinforced the idea that nature cannot be mastered, that it has a will of its own. Once causal techniques were discovered, however, attempts to influence nature with causes often did work, and this reinforced the idea that nature can be mastered.

The third way in which disenchantment opened up the possibility of mastery through calculation was by objectification. Beginning in the sixteenth century, intellectuals separated experience into those aspects that are the way they are because the object is what it is, and those aspects that are the way they are because the viewer is who he or she is: the objective and the subjective. René Descartes (1596–1650) proposed that qualities such as heat, sound, and color are not properties of objects, but rather effects that properties of certain objects have on the creature known as man. Terms like hot and cold, loud and muted, red and blue, were thus changed to descriptors of psychological events that are related to, but different from, the objective and quantifiable facts of temperature, amplitude, and spectral frequency. It is not objective to say that the coffee is hot, since it is decidedly cool when compared with, say, the core of the Sun; but is objective to say that the coffee is 110 degrees fahrenheit. Measurement and quantification thus became *the* way in which one understood objects in the environment.

This is why C. S. Lewis (1898–1963) described the shift to a materialist worldview as one in which "the object [was] stripped of its qualitative properties and reduced to mere quantity" (Lewis 1947: 82). Among the qualitative properties so removed, Lewis would certainly include color, sound, and heat, but his primary concern was with moral and aesthetic values that are visible only to those with an ethical vision, and this carries us to the fourth aspect of disenchantment. Just as humans are disposed to perceive some objects as hot, or big, or blue, so they are, when equipped with an ethical vision, disposed to perceive some objects as good and beautiful, and others as vile and foul. So long as such attributes are taken as the *property* of these things, and not something supplied by the viewer, certain ethical consequences will follow.

This point bears some elaboration. If I sit 12 inches from a roaring fire, there will in a definite number of seconds be certain quantifiable changes in my skin (known subjectively as damage) and certain quantifiable neurological impulses (known subjectively as pain). One can view this objectively if one is prepared to view me as an object. The heating of a human body is, after all, a physical event, different in detail but not perhaps in kind from the heating of a stone, a log, or the flesh of a butchered animal. Indeed this is just how it would appear to a cat. This calculation, in the sense of cold calculation, is accomplished by suppressing the ethical vision. Lewis described it as "repression of elements in what would otherwise be our total reaction." Such repression is "sometimes noticeable and even painful" to the person doing it, but is nevertheless necessary to those who would master their world because the ethical vision is "something that has to be overcome before we can cut up a dead man or a live animal in a dissecting room" (Lewis 1947: 81).

The human body remains the one thing that most stubbornly "resists" the "movement of mind" that "thrusts [things] into the mere world of [objectified] Nature" (Lewis 1947: 82). This is why, I trust, most of us feel, and do not attempt to repress the feeling, that there are things that should not be done to and with the human body. Torture and mutilation of the human body ought not to happen, and one properly feels horror when it does. This is why the crime of rape is, in Scruton's words, "a dragging of the subject [person] into the world of things" (Scruton 1996: 133). Torturers, murderers, and rapists who have, through suppression, lost the capacity for revulsion and horror, who have as we say hardened themselves, we quite rightly regard as nonhuman monsters.

It should be noted, however, that objectification of the human body *is* a precondition for mastery. In order to mend the body a surgeon must overcome squeamish aversion to blood. Soldiers must objectify the enemy in order to kill him, and think of civilian fatalities as collateral damage. It is instructive to think about the human body because it is, perhaps, the only thing that we today commonly regard as enchanted. We do this because our ethical vision discloses it as the embodiment of a person, a being who has intentions and values, who offers and responds to reasons, and who should not be objectified. It appears to us as something sacred, something that can be desecrated. This is why reflection on obscenity, which is objectification of the human body in pornography or violence, is perhaps the best way to begin to grasp the meaning of disenchantment, for obscenity is the human body disenchanted.

Disenchantment reduces nature to brute matter (quantification) that can be mastered (technology), and that there is no reason not to master (desanctification) if humans value this manipulation (anthropocentrism). At the very least, then, there is no ethical significance to environmental modifications that do not positively harm human values. Environmental manipulation by a person who views the world through this ethical lens is constrained and obliged only by consideration of the interests of other human beings.

Toward Postmodern Environmental Ethics

The modern environmental ethic of disenchanted nature places limits on the ways in which humans ought to think about the natural world. It is an ethical vision that discloses a transcendental reality, a vision of nature quite unlike that apparent to the unaided human eye. Like all ethical limits, these purport to liberate, and in a very real sense do liberate, for in adopting this ethical vision the modern person threw off the scruples that had trammeled his ancestors and, through science and technology, made himself veritable master of the natural world. The modern ethical vision imposed limits on what one might *think* about the environment even as it removed the moral limits on what one might *do* to the environment. Indeed, there were for it no *moral* limits. Human manipulation of the environment was constrained only by technical feasibility and the preferences of individual humans as these were expressed in politics or the market. It recognized and refrained from the impracticable, the unpopular, and the imprudent; everything else was fair game. As William James (1842–1910) put it, once belief in enchanted nature is discarded,

Visible nature is all plasticity and indifference, – a moral multiverse . . . and not a moral universe. To such a harlot we owe no allegiance; with her as a whole we can establish no communion; and we are free in our dealings with her several parts . . . to follow no law but prudence in coming to terms with such of her particular features as will help us to our private ends. (James 1923: 43–4)

James likens disenchanted nature to a harlot because it is treated as if it possessed only instrumental value; the prostitute, like the pornographic image, being a human body reduced to mere means or perfect instrumentality. To one outside the modern ethical vision however, this is obscene and desecrating, the mastery it permits is diabolical. As Oswald Spengler (1880–1936) put it, "he who was not himself possessed by this will to power over nature would necessarily feel all this as *devilish*" (Spengler 1932: 85).

Nineteenth-century Romantics were among the first to suspect that modern mastery was deviltry at heart, and through poetry, painting, fiction, and philosophy they attempted to reenchant nature. They failed. Rather than create a new ethical vision, Romantic art followed a course "of ever deeper mourning for the life of 'natural piety' which Enlightenment destroyed," and the characteristic Romantic attitude became languid longing for the world that was lost (Scruton 2000: 49). Individuals may find solace in Romantic reenchantment (most recently in new-age pantheism), but this does not arrest disenchantment.

In the twentieth century other skeptics began to suggest that the modern ethical vision of nature was a true primrose path, a deceptively attractive course by which the multitude might make their lazy way to hell. Some like Aldous Huxley (1894–1963) foresaw the disenchantment of the human body; others were alarmed by perceived environmental degradation. Much divided these skeptics, but they agreed on the need to fetter humans with something more permanent than temporary technological impossibility and fickle popular taste. It was in response to the fear that, in time, everything would be possible and every possibility would be desired, that the search for a postmodern environmental ethic first arose. This search generally consists of attempts to identify nonhuman axiological grounds within the nature that is known to natural science. It attempts to go beyond anthropocentrism without reverting, like Romanticism, to a spurious and untenable anthropomorphism. The argument has taken three general forms.

The first asks us to consider, more seriously than we presently do, our obligation to future generations. Humanity at some distant future date is thus an axiological ground outside present-day humanity, whose claims on resources deserves respect. Because humans have generally recognized some duty to posterity, this ethic is not odious to the general public, who rightly see in it little more than old-style conservation. Posterity ethics is not without problems, though. Foremost among these is that future generations do not yet exist and so cannot express preferences that we today are obliged to honor. Without knowing these preferences it is very hard to honor whatever rights future generations may have, since their right is not to any particular resources, but only to resources sufficient to permit them to live as well as we do. We might choose to conserve a resource that will in future have little or no value, due to technological change. What is more, denying ourselves such a resource must diminish output, and whatever we fail to make because the resource was left in the ground might be the very thing that future generations will need. The argument of duty to future generations is therefore tangled in paradox: for to save a resource may be in fact to waste it, and to use a resource by converting it into something else may be in fact to save it.

The second form is biocentric ethics, which holds that we should extend moral consideration to some set of nonhuman creatures, and regard these creatures as axiological grounds. This is often described in terms of rights such as animal rights. The various positions differ primarily in the suggested qualifications for admission into the moral community. More restrictive views limit the franchise to creatures that closely resemble humans, and thus may be thought to suffer in something like the way humans suffer. More expansive views extend moral consideration to all conscious, or even all living, beings.

Such ideas are already to some extent living in popular thought. It is, for instance, commonly believed that animals should be made to suffer and die only for good reasons. This is not anthropocentric because it recognizes that an animal may have a value to itself that is higher than at least some of the values that a human might assign to it (as a marksman's target, say, or medium of sadistic pleasure). This weak form of biocentric ethics maintains that human values do not always and everywhere trump other values, and therefore accepts the possibility that a human can treat an animal in ways that are morally wrong. Biocentric ethics takes a stronger form as it accepts fewer reasons why a human might justifiably impose his values on an animal, and thereby cause it to suffer.

The most basic problem with biocentric ethics is that it is impossible to extend the rights of the moral community without at the same time extending the ethical vision and its motivations. Imagine that we were to enlarge the moral community to include all mammals, and that we humans succeeded in treating all mammals with the moral consideration we presently give to other humans. Those who killed a mammal would, for instance, be charged with murder and forced to pay heavy retribution before readmittance to the moral community. Yet the lions would still kill and eat the gazelles, and there would be no way for a lion to repent and atone for the damage he did to the moral community. This would present us with one of three options: (1) redefine the community as one that tolerates killing within its ranks; (2) concede that some members of the community do not recognize community rules, and that the community does not, therefore, exist; (3) hold humans to a different standard, and thereby implicitly recognize the continued existence of a distinctly human community. All of these options strike me as intolerable.

The third approach is ecocentric ethics, which compel humans to act for the good of the ecosystem. It is thus a form of communitarianism, with the community here combining natural systems and human institutions. As a communitarian ethic it derives value from the whole, which it believes has intrinsic value. Individual parts possess instrumental value only insofar as they add to the stability of the community. The human individual is thus no longer an axiological ground, valuing and disvaluing according to his more or less unconstrained pleasure, but rather the object of an external source of value, valued or disvalued according to his more or less beneficial function.

At first glance such efforts to maintain the viability of the total community, or ecosystem, might appear no different than prudential maintenance of the environment on which human life depends, something that can be accomplished within the instrumental reason of the modern ethical vision. The essential difference, as I understand it, is that ecocentric ethics is animated by gratitude, not prudence. Prudence is a virtue, but it is a virtue of control, over one's self and one's affairs. Gratitude on the other hand is a warm sense of benefits received coupled with a desire to do something in return. To revert to language used earlier in this chapter, prudence speaks only in hypothetical imperatives. Gratitude entails categorical imperatives, for the grateful person recognizes and accepts that she lives under an indefeasible obligation to the social and natural systems that sustain her.

Although today associated in the minds of many with liberal or leftist politics, this manner of communitarian or ecocentric thinking is in spirit essentially conservative and antiliberal. It rejects as false the liberal view of the individual as essentially free and self-determining, as sovereign over himself and the relations he establishes with other persons and things. Instead it sees the individual as dependent on human society and the natural world, and due to this dependence, which begins in the womb, locked in obligations he has not chosen and cannot escape, but can only honor through a lifetime of gratitude and piety.

Such an attitude does not stipulate actual behavior, and must be taken as a mere foundation for a postmodern environmental ethic. Such an ethic will be postmodern not simply because it follows the modern vision, but because it incorporates and transcends that vision. Its sense of gratitude will be rooted in the knowledge of natural systems and organic interdependence that disenchanting science has revealed, but it will also understand that disenchantment is dangerous because it ultimately leads to disenchantment of ourselves. This may be avoidable if we do not again separate environmental from human ethics, but rather devise a fused ethic of the *human* environment as a foundation for future human geographies.

REFERENCES

Barfield, O. 1988: *Saving the Appearances: A Study in Idolatry*, 2nd ed. Middletown, CT: Wesleyan University Press.

Callicott, J. B. 1994: *Earth's Insights: A Survey of Ecological Ethics from the Mediterranean Basin to the Australian Outback*. Berkeley: University of California Press.

Flew, A. 1995: *Thinking About Social Thinking*, 2nd ed. Amherst, NY: Prometheus Books.

Gilbert, G. 1993: *A Discourse on Disenchantment*. Albany, NY: State University of New York Press.

James, W. 1923: *The Will to Believe and Other Essays in Popular Philosophy*. New York: Longmans.

Lewis, C. S. 1947: *The Abolition of Man*. New York: Macmillan.

MacCulloch, J. A. 1961: Nature, primitive and savage. In J. Hastings, ed., *The Encyclopedia of Religion and Ethics*, vol. 9. New York: Scribner's.

Sack, R. D. 1997: *Homo Geographicus: A Framework for Action, Awareness, and Moral Concern*. Baltimore: The Johns Hopkins University Press.

Scruton, R. 1996: *An Intelligent Person's Guide to Philosophy*. New York: Penguin.

Scruton, R. 2000: *An Intelligent Person's Guide to Modern Culture*. South Bend, IN: St. Augustin's.

Sibley, D. 1995: *Geographies of Exclusion*. London: Routledge.

Smith, D. M. 2000: *Moral Geographies: Ethics in a World of Difference*. Edinburgh: Edinburgh University Press.

Smith, J. M. 2000: When the landscape seems to break up, vacillate and quake. In J. Norwine
    and J. M. Smith, eds., *Worldview Flux: Perplexed Values among Postmodern Peoples*,
    Lanham, MD: Lexington Books, 1–20.
Spengler, O. 1932: *The Decline of the West*, tr. C. F. Atkinson. New York: A. A. Knopf.
Tuan, Yi-fu. 1993: *Passing Strange and Wonderful: Aesthetics, Nature, and Culture.*
    Washington, DC: Island Press.
Weber, Max. 1946. Science as a vocation. In H. H. Gerth and C. Wright Mills, eds., *From
    Max Weber: Essays in Sociology*. New York: Oxford University Press.

Part IV   Culture and Identity

Chapter 15

Nationalism

John Agnew

The best definition of nationalism I have been able to find comes from the historian Robert H. Wiebe (2002: 5), who wants to avoid demonizing nationalism (as is typical among many contemporary intellectuals) but nevertheless take it seriously as a powerful political sentiment and program in the modern world: "Nationalism is the desire among people who believe that they share a common ancestry and a common destiny to live under their own government on land sacred to their history." It is, therefore, the most territorial of political ideologies based on cultural beliefs about a shared space occupied by a kin-like, ethnic, or affinity group who face common dangers and bring to these a social bond forged through the trials and tribulations of a common history brought about by a common geography. The very space occupied by the group is seen as part and parcel of the group's identity in a way that is not the case with the major political ideologies with which nationalism has competed over the past 200 years or so: liberalism and socialism. When economic transactions are powerfully contained by state boundaries, nationalism gains a material basis that the other ideologies lack and which makes them ever vulnerable to collapsing into a nationalist form. It is no coincidence, therefore, that much socialism has been of the "national" or "in-one-country" varieties and that liberalism is usually hedged by claims about individual rights, property claims, and trade relationships that are enforced and defended by national states. Nationalism has benefited immeasurably from its alliance with states, but this has also led to its greatest excesses.

Writing about nationalism is fraught with intellectual and political dangers. On the one hand, there is a tendency to diminish nationalism because of the presumed intemperance it has generated in modern politics or the seemingly irrational challenge it poses to preferred brands of liberalism or socialism. On the other hand, there is a tendency to celebrate it as a means for groups subordinated by others to "liberate" themselves or to see it as reflecting deep-seated or primordial attachments to group and territory that provide "roots" in an otherwise chaotic and disturbing world. The political theorist John Dunn (1979: 55) captures this duality to nationalism eloquently when he writes:

Nationalism is the starkest political shame of the twentieth century, the deepest, most intractable and yet most unanticipated blot on the political history of the world since the year 1900. But it is also the very tissue of modern political sentiment, the most widespread, the most unthinking and the most immediate political disposition of all at least among the literate populations of the modern world.

Consequently, ignoring it is as dangerous as mindlessly celebrating it.

Defining it is one thing, but how is this explosive sentiment usually regarded? It is often thought of as a political ideology lauding a preference for and the superiority of one's nation and nationality in comparison to those of foreigners. One influential strand of thinking, associated above all with the early nineteenth-century philosopher Hegel and those following in his footsteps, views nationalism as an autonomous force or causal power that brings about the end of history with the emergence of the modern (national) state (Agnew 1989). Nationalism as the "spirit of the people" is a form of consciousness that will come to dominate all others. In fact, its history is intimately connected to the growth of popular sovereignty (the people should rule) in relation to state power and the challenge to state power from liberal and socialist ideologies (Yack 2001). But this history is also one in which nationalism has had to be *articulated* and *organized* as a form of political expression and has had to be *based* on popular support gained from populations with alternative political possibilities. In other words – and this is what a second strand of thinking emphasizes – nationalism is a practical politics and not an autonomous force. It is not just a popular sentiment but also a program of political action. In this light, nationalism's key claims are that (1) those who constitute a nation should have their own state; (2) the nation and the state should map onto one another by means of a common territory that is the historic "homeland" of the nation; and (3) a national identity (or sense of belonging) should win out over other possible political identities (Breuilly 1982; Conversi 1999; Yiftachel 2000).

The two strands of thinking – nationalism as an autonomous force in history and nationalism as practical politics – persist, even if the second is today somewhat ascendant. What is certain is that academic interest in nationalism has exploded since the 1980s after a long period, dating from the 1940s, when interest faded except among those focused on the independence movements in the colonies of Europe's declining empires. An undoubted revival of academic interest in nationalism since the 1980s after a long hiatus can be read as symptomatic of the revival of nationalism in the world at large following the end of the US–Soviet Cold War and the stability it imposed on the world's political map. But even this claim fails to engender consensus. Much of what is today often put down to "nationalism" is in fact either a revival of extreme religious beliefs (as in the usage of Islamic *jihad* by many groups such as *al-Qaeda* and *Hamas*) or an upsurge of local warlordism in the face of weak governments (as in Somalia and Afghanistan) rather than the expression of true national groups in search of or reviving states on their collective behalf (Wiebe 2002). Nevertheless, reports of nationalism's death or decline have proved premature before. Indeed, in contemporary Europe, Asia, and the United States nationalism seems anything but a spent force (e.g. Comaroff & Stern 1995). Perhaps seven specific aspects of nationalism define the main features of contemporary debate and dissent. In this chapter I take each of these in turn to illustrate the ways in which "nationalism" currently figures in cultural geography and closely allied fields.

Taking Nationalism More Seriously

With nationalism, as opposed to socialism and liberalism, many of those who study or make proclamations about it tend to see the people who subscribe to it as cultural dopes. "They should know better" is the implicit subtext, but they have been fooled or misled into it by self-serving state elites inventing traditions or by their own atavistic attachments to place and linguistic/religious groups. The implication is, obviously, that identifying by social class or pursuing individual interests are rational approaches to self-identification. In this way frequently undeclared and normative commitments to class and individual self as better sources of identification than nationality lead to a dismissal of nationalism as a legitimate type of political ideology.

Three ways of seeming to engage with nationalism but essentially dismissing it have achieved dominance in contemporary Western social and cultural studies. These must be challenged in order to take nationalism seriously as a powerful type of politics in the contemporary world. The first, associated most closely with the widely cited book by Benedict Anderson, *Imagined Communities: Reflections on the Origins and Spread of Nationalism* (1983), is that nationalism appeals simply to an "imagined community" that is created by and organized by the spread of books and reading in national vernacular languages. In fact, of course, "print capitalism," as Anderson terms it, is only one of a mass of technological and cultural innovations that have materially ordered the world into national-state spaces – from highways and railways radiating from capital cities, national currencies and economic regulation, and systems of weights and measures to school systems and educational credentials, national churches, government systems, and cultural production of books, films, and music. The appeal of nationalism rests initially and finally in the fact that in many parts of the world the political organization of territory into national states has created real, not simply imagined, *material* communities of interest and identity in which large numbers of residents see their fate tied to that of the national state or, if they do not have one of their own, obtaining one for themselves. The crucial alliance of putative nation (imagined as it certainly is) with state-organized territory, therefore, provides the breeding ground for nationalism (Mann 1992; Miller 1995; Smith 1999; Wiebe 2000).

Second, nationalism is often discussed independently of its ideological competitors, as if its development were separate from that of socialism and liberalism. With remarkably few exceptions, the study of nationalism has become separated from the study of the other great "isms" that took root in late nineteenth-century Europe and spread with it into the rest of the world with European colonialism. Yet, all three grew in the context of the disruption of local peasant societies by industrialization and urbanization, mass migration, and ideologies promising totalistic solutions to contemporary problems of exploitation (socialism), limited citizenship rights (liberalism), and increased economic and military competition (nationalism). Although they were often competitors, after 1914 they also became collaborators, with nationalism as the victor, as socialism and liberalism both came to define their goals in national-state terms. One important cause of nationalism's success was its ability to combine an appeal to fictive kinship with a clear identification of an "enemy" against whom the nation was embattled for this or that reason (economic, social, religious, etc.) Neither socialism nor liberalism had this mobilizing power: they could appeal to specific interests but not to the lethal combination of identity and interests fused with territory that nationalism encouraged (Dunn 1979; Brustein 1996; Hechter 2000).

Finally, nationalism undoubtedly developed in popular appeal alongside the growth of industrial capitalism and "modernization" in Europe in the late nineteenth and early twentieth centuries (Gellner 1983). It received a further boost during the process of decolonization in the years following the Second World War, both in former colonies as they embarked on "nation-building" and in the "home countries" as they adjusted to an unaccustomed smallness (Murray 1997). A good case can be made that in fact European colonialism provided a necessary circumstance for the development of nationalism in Europe in the first place, both with regard to competition between European states for overseas empires' stimulating national enmities and to empire-building's encouraging a sense of national-civilizational (and racial) superiority on the part of European nationalities over the colonized natives within "their" empires (Said 1993; Agnew & Corbridge 1995). But, the conventional wisdom suggests, following the view that nationalism is "caused" by, not just correlated with, modernization or industrial capitalism, that (1) nations are always the product of nationalism and (2) in the face of economic globalization and massive international migration nationalism can be expected to go into decline (e.g. Hobsbawm 1992).

With respect to the first of these points, it is not difficult to show, at least in many European cases, that some kind of proto-nation preexisted the arrival of nationalism (see, e.g., Smith 2002). Though nationalism is a modern phenomenon, therefore, there is no need to presume that nations or nationalities are likewise. This is a fallacy present in much of the contemporary literature. The second point, if anything, is made more insistently but is equally wrong-headed. To Nigel Harris (1990: 284), for example, "migration subverts the artificial cultural homogeneity which states have instilled in their citizens. . . . The greater the movement of peoples, the more that culture will come to be fashioned by people from many other sources." If anything, however, migration has often underwritten nationalism rather than written its epitaph. For example, the rise of Irish nationalism in the mid-nineteenth century is closely connected to emigration to the United States and the radical Irish nationalism of Irish Americans. Likewise, Jewish nationalism or Zionism grew out of large-scale international migration and the search for a Jewish homeland to bring the diaspora together in a single territory. Increased movement, therefore, can stimulate identity with a lost homeland rather than wipe it out. More generally, actually-existing nationalism is complexly related to religious, linguistic, and economic divisions all held in tension by a primary group commitment to occupation and domination of a common space or national territory. It is not and never has been simply a "functional" response to modernization, the rise of the state, or industrial capitalism. As a result, nationalism will not soon decline or disappear (Chatterjee 1986; Mortimer 1999; Peckham 2001; Wiebe 2002).

Nationalism and Territory

To geographers the most outstanding feature of nationalism is its unvarying claim to a territorial homeland (Anderson 1988; Murphy 2002; Yiftachel, 2000, 2002). This is the feature shared by all nationalisms regardless of how they came about or where they are. Many students of nationalism are confused about the relationship between nationalism and territory. Wiebe (2000: 54), for example, misses the point when he states that "nationalist loyalties are . . . geographically indeterminate. They move wherever people move; they do not bounce off boundary walls, as Anderson would have it." Here the fact that supporters of a nationalist movement may be widely scattered is used to deny that nationalism *always* involves claiming a physical national homeland or, in other words, that nationalism is inherently territorial in its central claim, as Wiebe (2002: 5) himself suggests elsewhere, to monopolize for their nation "land sacred to their history." The fusion of a piece of land with the symbolic and mythified history of the nation is what gives nationalism such symbolic power immediately related to the sites and circumstances of everyday life when compared to the often more abstract claims of liberalism and socialism. The Serb nationalist obsession with Kosovo as the "historic core" of Serbia and the competing claims of Zionists and Palestinian nationalists to the same patches of land are only two of the best known cases of this relentless focus by nationalists on "our" territory.

Two questions as to the precise character of the relationship between nationalism and territory have exercised considerable recent interest. One asks: when did the nation-in-its-territory become a subject of veneration? The purpose here is to ascertain how the map-image of the national territory and sense of "territorial destiny" figure in the genesis of nationalism. The other asks: how did nationalism reconfigure understandings of "home" such that the local (and familiar) became part of a nationalist "homeland?" The focus here is on the local production of the nation.

Responses to the first question tend to place the origins in either late medieval/early modern Europe or in Europe in the eighteenth century. Writers in the former camp tend to emphasize the experience of England and France as exemplary (see, e.g., Reynolds 1984; Hastings 1997; Schulze 1994). For example, Scattergood (2001) emphasizes how England was increasingly imagined as a separate space by poets and playwrights over the course of the fifteenth and sixteenth centuries in essentially modern terms – trade, merchants, money, networks of exchange. In accounts accepting this sort of genealogy, state elites elsewhere are then alleged to have later imitated the founding nations in pursuit of nationalist "modernity" (Greenfeld 1992). Those in the second group look to the eighteenth century, again largely also to England (now rewritten as "Britain") and France, as the period when popular political association with national territory crystallized (e.g. Colley 1992; Bell 2001). If in the British case wars served as the most important ingredient in promoting a popular British nationalism, in France it was the nationalist project that developed through the Revolution of 1789, notwithstanding the universalistic elements often seen in that moment of political upheaval. Yet, until the end of the century "the sense of a British nation was not geographically tied to

Britain itself" according to Stephen Conway (2001: 893), since it had a strong transatlantic element and was resisted by many in England who feared the rise of a culturally mixed "Britishness" (e.g. Ragussis 2000), and the nation-building project in France is probably better dated to the nineteenth rather than to the eighteenth century (e.g. Weber 1976). Nonetheless, the eighteenth century has a strong case as the founding period for what today would be the recognizably nationalist conception of territorial space. From this point of view, nationalism as a popular political project has its roots in the American and French Revolutions. They stimulated other nationalist projects as new states "invented" (Hobsbawm & Ranger 1983) or promoted (Wallerstein 1991) the nation as the "natural" territorial basis to statehood. With the decolonization of Europe's empires in the second half of the twentieth century nationalism became a worldwide phenomenon.

The second question has been more specifically addressed in contexts other than England and France. Germany and Italy figure particularly prominently. These are cases, perhaps not coincidentally, in which statehood dates only from the mid-nineteenth century but which have had much longer cultural-territorial histories as putative nations. The emphasis is on (1) what can be called the "local life of nationhood" (Applegate 1990; Confino & Skaria 2002); (2) the relation of local and regional to national identities (Agnew 1995; Agnew & Brusa 1999; Kaplan 1999; Núñez 2001); and (3) the "fluid" and "contested" identities of state borderlands (White 2000; Kulczycki 2001; Thaler 2001). The overall focus is on relating national identities to the geographical scales and contexts in which they are embedded rather than presupposing a nationalist "wave" that washes over a territory from either a center or the margins wiping out all other identities in its path. In this view the national is always forged in and through "the local." In Germany, for example, the idea of *Heimat* (homeland) has connected local and regional communities to the nation. In particular, and following the Second World War, "by talking about *Heimat*, Germans found a way to talk about that which was so problematic to talk about, namely the nation" (Confino & Skaria 2002: 11). The nation's territory is not a simple block of space but a complex set of relationships between local, regional, and national levels of social practice and geographical imagination. Nationalism relates to territory, therefore, in more complex ways than most students of nationalism have tended to believe.

Ethnic versus Civic Nationalism

According to the political theorist Bernard Yack (2001: 520), "A large part of the story of the emergence and spread of nationalism lies in the way that these two images of community, the nation and the people, have become entangled in our minds." Indeed, one of the major contemporary disputes about the nature of nationalism and whether there are "better" and "worse" kinds revolves around the interpretations given to the intersections between the two terms. On one side are those who distinguish between "ethnic" and "civic" nationalisms and on the other are those who fail to see the distinction or who see it as a false and misleading one. To the first group ethnic nationalism involves the exclusive identity of the people with the nation whereas civic nationalism involves the inclusive identity of the nation with the people. Thus, if ethnic nationalism is characterized by shared cultural loyalties, civic nationalism is all about shared political principles and institutions. Some writers, such as Greenfeld (1992, 1996), use the civic/ethnic dichotomy to distinguish more "democratic" (civic) from more "authoritarian" (ethnic) versions of nationalism. In this usage there is little if any ethical commitment to an idealized "civic nationalism." It is merely a taxonomic device to classify varieties of nationalism. Others, however, have attempted to reconcile nationalism with liberalism by arguing for a "civic" nationalism, like that said to exist in the United States, France, or Britain (e.g. Ignatieff 1993; Tamir 1993; Viroli 1995; and Miller 1995). In this understanding, the "main characteristic of the democratic national idea [is]: the effort to transcend the level of concrete identities and ethnic solidarities through citizenship" (Schnapper 1998: 234).

But, as the second group tends to maintain, both types of nationalism rest on claims to popular sovereignty on the part of nations that are necessarily exclusive and politicized. Even if they can be empirically distinguished, doubtful, they share a common historical trajectory: that of popular sovereignty. As Yack (2001: 529) makes the point:

You need to assume the existence of [territorial] boundaries between peoples before you can exercise the principle of popular sovereignty. Therefore, you cannot use popular sovereignty to determine where the boundaries between peoples should lie. Popular sovereignty can help guide us in determining our political arrangements. It cannot help us decide how to determine the shape of our collective selves.

Nicholas Xenos (1996) makes a somewhat different point in challenging the meaningfulness of the dichotomy. He contrasts the concrete "patriotism" of city-dwelling with the abstract imposition of both civic and ethnic nationalism. The affection displayed for place in classical republican patriotism is that of the city not of the modern nation-state. Thus, those who argue from classical and early-modern authors to justify a modern civic nationalism are guilty of misidentifying the object of patriotism (or belonging) articulated by such authors.

Long-distance Nationalism

Rather than simply a reflection of the association between a nation and its territory, the history of nationalism is also closely related to the experience of large-scale migration. With due regard to its peculiarities, Robert Wiebe (2002: 24) suggestively points to the linkage between migration and Irish nationalism, when following the Famine of the late 1840s:

While the Irish in Ireland buried the dead, nationalism survived by shifting its center of gravity across the Atlantic. In the years of O'Connell's ascendancy [over the Irish nationalist movement in the years before the Famine], the Irish in America had played only a minor role, cheering his cause and contributing money to it but otherwise simply watching from abroad. Now, as they took the initiative, they gave Irish nationalism its distinctive stamp: secular, public, and violent.

Typically, however, the influence of migration and more recent impacts of "space–time compression" due to the technological "shrinking" of the world are left out of both nationalist narratives and scholarly accounts of them (Mulligan 2002). In the stories of nationalists such external ties would undermine the seemingly natural connection between nation and territory; each begets the other. Scholarly accounts are similarly place-bound and often simply accept the claims of nationalist stories at face value. To the extent that the "long-distance nationalism" of "absent patriots" is taken seriously it is as a novel phenomenon tied to the nationalist proclivities of groups of recent immigrants from formerly colonial countries to the countries of Western Europe and North America. This is undoubtedly an important feature of contemporary world politics (see, e.g. Goulborne 1991 on Sikhs and Guyanese in Britain, or Schiller & Fouron 2001 on Haitians in the United States) but its novelty is exaggerated and the long-standing relationship between long-distance migration, romanticism about the land and people "left behind," and nationalism, is obscured. Long-distance nationalism did not arrive with the fax.

The erstwhile American radical, Tom Hayden (2002), is neither alone nor the first in adopting a romantic nativism in which his American "outside" disguises the fact that he is "Irish on the inside." All of the clichés of absent patriotism are present in his account, from the Irish sages who say that Irish culture is very ancient, older, of course, "than the English," and that the Irish soul is "like an ancient forest" to the "mystical courage" of the martyrs to the Irish cause. But this is not a joke. Rather, it is the essential core of the romanticism that inspires long-distance nationalism, even many generations and much intermarriage beyond the original migrants, many of whom often wanted to forget about where they came from. Of course, the "search for roots" in distant places need not always end up with the essentialized national identities that Hayden evokes. Catherine Nash (2002) shows nicely how investigations into personal genealogies can produce unsettling and complicated family pasts when the roots turn out to be less "purely" Irish than family lore might have suggested. Similarly, heritage tourism not only reproduces convenient national stories but also can offer local correctives that open to question dominant understandings of the national past particularly prevalent among absent patriots (Johnson 1999). If somewhat overstated, however, Ian Buruma's (2002: 14) commentary on Hayden's book captures what has often been at stake with the romantic nationalism of absent patriots: "Hayden is haunted by blood-thirsty ghosts. He is not alone. There are Sikhs in Toronto, Muslims in Britain and France, Jews in Brooklyn, and many others in far-flung places who seek to sooth ancestral voices by encouraging barbarism far from home. Some are prepared to die for their causes. Most are content to let others do the dying, while they work on their identities at home."

Religion and Nationalism

There are cases where religion and nationalism have been almost complete partners, as with the Greek and other Orthodox Christian churches, Iranian Shi'ite Islam, Orthodox Judaism, and the state churches of England and other northern European countries, on the one hand, and powerful nationalist movements and sentiments, on the other. In England, for example, the Protestant Reformation and the threat to it from the Catholic states served to unify the English into a national enterprise that was lacking in those states where church and state did not become mutually supportive. But there are others, as in many Moslem and predominantly Roman

Catholic countries where religious identities either compete with national ones or have complex relations to them. In Italy, for example, from 1870 until 1929 the Pope refused to recognize the Italian state because, in his view, it had usurped his temporal powers when it had annexed the papal territories of central Italy. Under threat of excommunication, active Catholics were required to abstain from active involvement in national politics and in the life of the nation.

At one time nationalism was seen as largely reflective of religious, linguistic and other cultural cleavages. Obviously this is problematic in an evident empirical sense. It is also problematic, however, because religion is frequently a banner for a wide range of differences and resentments that are only at most secondarily religious, in the sense of commitment to doctrines and beliefs: access to political power, availability of public offices, etc. (Harris 1990: 11). Indeed, and today, religious identities, particularly in the Moslem world, often cut across nationalist lines, except in the Iranian and Palestinian cases. The universalistic claims of Islam and Catholic Christianity have frequently coexisted uneasily with the particularistic claims of nationalist movements. Sometimes the character of religious belief, in the sense of popular as opposed to officially sanctioned belief, can also undermine national identities and nationalism in the interest of privileging local identities (see, e.g., on popular Catholicism in Italy, Carroll 1996).

Yet, there are two ways in which religion has intersected powerfully with nationalism down the years. The first is emphasized by Benedict Anderson (1983: 12) when he proposes that "nationalism has to be understood by aligning it, not with self-consciously held political ideologies [although I have challenged this assertion earlier], but with the large cultural systems that preceded it, out of which – as well as against which – it came into being." In this understanding, sacred languages such as Latin, Arabic, and Mandarin Chinese provided the core element to the civilizations that increasingly decomposed into "national" parts as vernacular languages replaced the sacred as the main media for popular literacy and public communication. Religion, by means of sacred languages, thus provided the common foundation (along with dynastic politics) upon which nationalism's "imagined communities" came to be imagined. The second has been religion's role in providing the material for the "tyranny of small differences" upon which most nationalist movements have relied to distinguish their nation from others. As Daniele Conversi (1994) has claimed, using even minor distinctions (in global terms) to define boundaries with the Other against whom you are defining yourself (e.g., the English for the Irish, the Germans for the French, the Pakistanis for Indians, etc.) is as if not more important to nationalist movements than is defining what makes you special without benefit of comparison and contrast. It is clear that religious differences have often played this role, for example in Irish, Welsh, and Scottish nationalism (Pope 2001).

Gender and Nationalism

Nationalism is frequently seen as the most masculinist or male-dominated type of politics. Not only did women's roles in politics seem to decline along with the rise of nationalism (e.g. Radhakrishnan 1992), nationalist ideologies seem to rest on a peculiarly gendered division of political labor with women allocated the role of nurturing the Motherland (or standing in for it symbolically as with the French national symbols of Joan of Arc [for the right] and Marianne [for the left]) by producing future generations, while men are given the directing role and charged with defending the homeland against or liberating it from its foreign enemies (Sharp 1996; Blom et al. 2000). In this understanding, and in the direst of circumstances, such as the bloody nationalist wars in the Balkans in the 1990s, women's bodies come to represent the very territory to be conquered or claimed and thus subject to rape and defilement (Skjelsbaek 2001). More mundanely, the metaphor of the nation as a "family" has carried much weight, sometimes to obscure the degree to which patriarchy is operative at multiple geographical scales but often, as in the late nineteenth century, to refocus the social life of the nation around an idealized household with men and women holding quite different social roles (Eley 2000).

In the light of recent research, however, this perspective on gender and nationalism seems not so much incorrect as overstated. Matters seem much more complicated than it suggests. First of all, women have not been simply passive bystanders to and symbols for nationalist movements even when seemingly marginalized within them. As Catherine Nash (1997) shows with respect to Ireland, it was not just exceptional and "famous" women, such as Maud Gonne and Countess Markievicz, but also a multitude of "ordinary" women who played a key part in the political protests of the nineteenth- and early twentieth-century nationalist movements. At the same time, questions of gender, sexual, and national identity are never simply linear and additive. Male–female and sexual identity differences do not line up on a single axis of nationalist politics with men and women and gays and heterosexuals on opposite sides and with competing roles (Dowler 2002; Marston 2002). As Nash (1997: 1234) concludes: "The history of Ireland and women's activism in contemporary Northern Ireland both point to the limitations of neat oppositions and single visions."

In the second place, sexual violence in the context of nationalist conflict, such as that directed at women in particular in the Balkans and elsewhere, seems related to the fear and advent of territorial partition rather than to nationalist politics per se. Mass rape as a weapon of war seems to occur almost entirely in specific settings in which partition of contested territory is under way, such as South Asia in 1947 and the Balkans in the 1990s. As the anthropologist Robert Hayden (2000: 33) plausibly claims:

Partition . . . is not only a liminal state but a time when the state itself is liminal, and the questions of whose state it is, and how the population will be defined are open. . . . After these issues are settled, mass rape will no longer be likely, because either coexistence will have been reconstituted or the newly consolidated groups will have separated.

Finally, women who have organized themselves in political organizations have sometimes been major independent proponents of nationalism. In the United States, for example, in the years between the Civil War and the First World War, women's organizations played a central part in generating American nationalism. Groups such as the Women's Relief Corps emerged in the aftermath of the US Civil War to insist adamantly that "patriotism knows no sex" (quoted in O'Leary 1999: 92; also see Rowbotham 1992). As O'Leary (1999) shows in detail, most members endorsed the idea of women's moral superiority to men and were opposed to limiting their work to serving veterans or staying within the bounds of domesticity. But just as they connected in the 1890s with the more partisan women's movement they also became major sponsors of patriotic events such as Memorial Day, the campaign to fly the flag at every school, petitioned for flag-desecration laws, and lobbied to include the pledge of allegiance in the public (state) schools (O'Leary 1999: 97). In sum, it turns out that nationalism has not consistently discriminated on the basis of sex after all.

Nationalism and Landscape

Tying the nation to territory has often involved identifying a prototypical landscape as representative of the collective identity. In this way the natural environment can be recruited for the national cause not only to naturalize the connection between nation and territory but also visually to communicate and reinforce identity with the nation. The physical images, buildings, monuments, and scenes encountered in everyday life come to provide a mundane or "banal" element to nationalism itself (Billig 1995; also see, e.g., Crameri 2000). The very familiarity of symbols seen on a daily basis makes the nation the "daily plebiscite" that Ernest Renan famously described it as being. Monumental spaces and other "places of memory" have been of particular significance in potentially bonding current residents to a common past (Till 2003). Through the landscape the memory of the nation is given concrete form as a reminder of what "we" have been through and why "we" need to remember.

More generally, however, a national landscape "imagery" is a visual technique that naturalizes particular images into a national narrative (Häyrynen 2000). Published and disseminated over long periods of time these images make the national territory concrete as a distinctive block of space and elicit shared values and meanings. If in some countries identification of a "national landscape" seems to have met with considerable success, in England, Finland, and Switzerland, for example, elsewhere this proved more elusive. In Switzerland after the founding of the modern federation in 1848, Alpine scenery not surprisingly provided both a geographical icon for the new state and, when combined with the image of virtuous peasants fruitfully tilling what soil there was, a "powerful symbol of republican will and cultural mediation" peculiar to Switzerland (Zimmer 2001). In Italy, however, attempts at using either Tuscan rural scenery or Roman ruins after unification to represent an idealized national landscape for the new nation-state came largely to naught (Agnew 2002: ch. 3). The combination of fragmented political identities in a physically divided peninsula, strong church–state tensions, the ambiguous legacy of ancient Rome, and the political incoherence of both liberal and Fascist regimes made crafting a national landscape ideal extremely difficult. Nationalism, therefore, is not invariably naturalized successfully through the creation of a national landscape imagery.

Conclusion

The self-sacrifice of the New York City firefighters who entered the twin towers of the World Trade Center as they were collapsing in the aftermath of the terrorist attacks of September 11, 2001 has come to symbolize the popular American reaction to the events of the day. The towers themselves have had somewhat less resonance in the American popular imagination. The memory of the firefighters as giving up their lives for others has gained a powerful hold, particularly in media re-creations. At the end of the day, it is sacrifice such as this, or interpreted as such, whatever any individual firefighter might have been thinking, that nationalism has to offer. It is also this focus on the sacrificial that other political ideologies find particularly offensive about nationalism. If its appeal still remains elusive, we nevertheless understand that nationalism is far from a spent force. If anything, nationalism has achieved even greater success recently than anyone would have pre-dicted 10 or 20 years ago. From India to Ireland, Israel, and Indonesia nationalism is a powerful element in everyday politics. Understanding the contemporary world, therefore, requires understanding nationalism as best we can. And we should remember that in many places it is still deeply rooted, wired into the routines and ephemera of everyday life. The poet and writer Patricia Storace (1996: 10) tells the story of Greek high school students who refused to read Virgil's *Aeneid*. "These particular students held it as dogma that the *Aeneid* was a cheap [Roman] imita-tion of the [ancient Greek] Homer, responding with a popular Platonism, present in both the ancient Greek preoccupation with sculpture and the modern Greek preoccupation with icons, that insisted there was one ideal original, and the rest of the genre was increasingly false and bloodless." The ideal original, of course had to be Greek. Whether that Greek would recognize himself in modern Greece is, for the nationalist, entirely beside the point.

REFERENCES

Agnew, J. A. 1989: Nationalism: autonomous force or practical politics? Place and nationalism in Scotland. In C. H. Williams and E. Kofman, eds., *Community Conflict, Partition and Nationalism*, London: Routledge.

Agnew, J. A. 1995: The rhetoric of regionalism: the Northern League in Italian politics. *Transactions of the Institute of British Geographers* 20, 156–72.

Agnew, J. A. 2002: *Place and Politics in Modern Italy*. Chicago: University of Chicago Press.

Agnew, J. A. and Brusa, C. 1999: New rules for national identity? The Northern League and political identity in contemporary northern Italy, *National Identities* 1, 117–33.

Agnew, J. A. and Corbridge, S. 1995: *Mastering Space: Hegemony, Territory and International Political Economy*. London: Routledge.

Anderson, B. 1983: *Imagined Communities: Reflections on the Origins and Spread of Nationalism*. London: Verso; rev. ed., 1991.

Anderson, J. 1988: Nationalist ideology and territory. In R. J. Johnston, D. B. Knight, and E. Kofman, eds., *Nationalism, Self-Determination and Political Geography*. London: Croom Helm.

Applegate, C. 1990: *A Nation of Provincials: The German Idea of Heimat*. Berkeley: University of California Press.

Bell, D. 2001 *The Cult of the Nation in France: Inventing Nationalism, 1680–1800*. Cambridge MA: Harvard University Press.

Billig, M. 1995: *Banal Nationalism*. London: Sage Publications.

Blom, I., K. Hagemann, and C. Hall, eds. 2000: *Gendered Nations: Nationalisms and the Gender Order in the Long Nineteenth Century*. Oxford: Berg.

Breuilly, J. 1982 *Nationalism and the State*, New York: St. Martin's Press.

Brustein, W. 1996 *The Logic of Evil: The Social Origins of the Nazi Party, 1925–1933*. New Haven: Yale University Press.

Buruma, I. 2002: The blood lust of identity. *New York Review of Books*, April 11, 12–14.

Carroll, M. P. 1996: *Veiled Threats: The Logic of Popular Catholicism in Italy*. Baltimore: Johns Hopkins University Press.

Chatterjee, P. 1986: *Nationalist Thought and the Colonial World: A Derivative Discourse*. Minneapolis: University of Minnesota Press.

Colley, L. 1992: *Britons: Forging the Nation, 1707–1837*. New Haven: Yale University Press.

Comaroff, J. L. and Stern, P. C. 1995: New perspectives on nationalism and war. In Comaroff and Stern, eds., *Perspectives on Nationalism and War*. London: Gordon and Breach.

Confino, A. and Skaria, A. 2002: The local life of nationhood. *National Identities* 4, 7–24.

Conversi, D. 1994: Reassessing current theories of nationalism: nationalism as boundary maintenance and creation. *Nationalism and Ethnic Politics* 1, 73–85.

Conversi, D. 1999: Nationalism, boundaries, and violence. *Millennium* 28, 553–84.

Conway, S. 2001: War and national identity in the mid-eighteenth-century British Isles. *English Historical Review* 116, 863–93.

Crameri, K. 2000: Banal Catalanism? *National Identities* 2, 145–57.

Dowler, L. 2002: Till death us do part: masculinity, friendship, and nationalism in Belfast, Northern Ireland. *Society and Space* 20, 53–71.

Dunn, J. 1979: *Western Political Theory in the Face of the Future*. Cambridge: Cambridge University Press.

Eley, G. 2000: Culture, nation and gender. In I. Blom et al., eds., *Gendered Nations: Nationalisms and Gender Order in the Long Nineteenth Century*. Oxford: Berg.

Gellner, E. 1983: *Nations and Nationalism*, Oxford: Blackwell.

Goulborne, H. 1991: *Ethnicity and Nationalism in Post-Imperial Britain*. Cambridge: Cambridge University Press.

Greenfeld, L. 1992: *Nationalism: Four Roads to Modernity*. Cambridge MA: Harvard University Press.

Greenfield, L. 1996: The modern religion? *Critical Review* 10, 169–91.

Harris, N. 1990: *National Liberation*. Reno: University of Nevada Press.

Hastings, A. 1997: *The Construction of Nationhood: Ethnicity, Religion and Nationalism*. Cambridge: Cambridge University Press.

Hayden, R. M. 2000: Rape and rape avoidance in ethno-national conflicts: sexual violence in liminalized states. *American Anthropologist* 102, 27–41.

Hayden, T. 2002 *Irish on the Inside: In Search of the Soul of Irish America*. London: Verso.

Häyrynen, M. 2000: The kaleidoscopic view: the Finnish national landscape imagery. *National Identities* 2, 5–19.

Hechter, M. 2000: *Containing Nationalism*. Oxford: Oxford University Press.

Hobsbawm, E. 1992: *Nations and Nationalism since 1780: Programme, Myth, Reality*. Cambridge: Cambridge University Press.

Hobsbawm, E. and Ranger, T., eds. 1983: *The Invention of Tradition*. Cambridge: Cambridge University Press.

Ignatieff, M. 1993: *Blood and Belonging: Journeys into the New Nationalism*. New York: Farrar, Straus and Giroux.

Johnson, N. C. 1999: Framing the past: time, space and the politics of heritage tourism in Ireland. *Political Geography* 18, 187–207.

Kaplan, D. H. 1999: Territorial identities and geographic scale. In D. H. Kaplan and G. H. Herb, eds., *Nested Identities: Nationalism, Territory, and Scale*. Lanham, MD: Rowman and Littlefield.

Kulczycki, J. J. 2001 The national identity of the "natives" of Poland's "Recovered Lands." *National Identities* 3, 205–19.

Mann, M. 1992: The emergence of modern European nationalism. In J. A. Hall and I. C. Jarvie, eds., *Transition to Modernity: Essays on Power, Wealth and Belief*. Cambridge: Cambridge University Press.

Marston, S. A. 2002: Making difference: conflict over Irish identity in the New York City St. Patrick's Day Parade. *Political Geography* 21, 373–92.

Miller, D. 1995: *On Nationality*. Oxford: Clarendon Press.

Mortimer, E., ed. 1999: *People, Nation and State: The Meaning of Ethnicity and Nationalism*. London: I. B. Tauris.

Mulligan, A. N. 2002: A forgotten "Greater Ireland" and the transatlantic development of Irish Nationalism. Paper presented at AAG Annual Meeting, Los Angeles, March.

Murphy, A. B. 2002: National claims to territory in the modern state system: geographical considerations. *Geopolitics* 7, 193–214.

Murray, S. 1997: *Not on Any Map: Essays on Postcoloniality and Cultural Nationalism*. Exeter: University of Exeter Press.

Nash, C. 1997: Embodied Irishness: gender, sexuality and Irish identities. In B. Graham, ed., *In Search of Ireland: A Cultural Geography*. London: Routledge.

Nash, C. 2002: Genealogical identities. *Society and Space* 20, 27–52.

Núñez, X.-M. 2001: The region as *essence* of the Fatherland: regionalist variants of Spanish nationalism (1840–1936). *European History Quarterly* 31, 483–518.

O'Leary, C. E. 1999: *To Die For: The Paradox of American Patriotism*. Princeton, NJ: Princeton University Press.

Peckham, R. S. 2001: *National Histories, Natural States: Nationalism and the Politics of Place in Greece*. London: I. B. Tauris.

Pope, R., ed. 2001: *Religion and National Identity: Wales and Scotland, c.1700–2000*. Cardiff: University of Wales Press.

Radhakrishnan, R. 1992: Nationalism, gender, and the narrative of identity. In A. Parker et al., eds., *Nationalisms and Sexualities*. London: Routledge.

Ragussis, M. 2000: Jews and other "outlandish Englishmen": ethnic performance and the invention of British identity under the Georges. *Critical Inquiry* 26, 773–97.

Reynolds, S. 1984: *Kingdoms and Communities in Western Europe, 900–1300*. Oxford: Clarendon Press.

Rowbotham, S. 1992: *Women in Movement: Feminism and Social Action*. London: Routledge.

Said, E. 1993: *Culture and Imperialism*. New York: Knopf.

Scattergood, J. 2001 "The Libelle of Englyshe Polyce": the nation and its place. In H. Cooney, ed., *Nation, Court and Culture: New Essays on Fifteenth-Century English Poetry*. Dublin: Four Courts Press.

Schiller, N. G. and Fouron, G. E. 2001: *Georges Woke Up Laughing: Long-Distance Nationalism and the Search for Home*. Durham, NC: Duke University Press.

Schnapper, D. 1998: Beyond the opposition: civic nation versus ethnic nation. In J. Couture, K. Nielsen, and M. Seymour, eds., *Rethinking Nationalism*, Calgary: University of Calgary Press.

Schulze, H. 1994: *States, Nations and Nationalism: From the Middle Ages to the Present*. Oxford: Blackwell.

Sharp, J. 1996: Gendering nationhood: a feminist engagement with national identity. In N. Duncan, ed., *Bodyspace: Destabilizing Geographies of Gender and Sexuality*. London: Routledge.

Skjelsbaek, I. 2001: Sexual violence and war: mapping out a complex relationship. *European Journal of International Relations* 7, 211–37.

Smith, A. D. 1999: *Myths and Memories of the Nation*. Oxford: Oxford University Press.

Smith, A. D. 2002: When is a nation? *Geopolitics* 7, 5–32.

Storace P. 1996: Marble girls of Athens. *New York Review of Books*, Oct. 3, 7–15.

Tamir, Y. 1993: *Liberal Nationalism*. Princeton, NJ: Princeton University Press.

Thaler, P. 2001: Fluid identities in central European borderlands. *European History Quarterly* 31, 519–48.

Till, K. E. 2003: Places of memory. In J. Agnew, K. Mitchell, and G. Ò Tuathail, eds., *A Companion to Political Geography*. Oxford: Blackwell.

Viroli, M. 1995: *For Love of Country: An Essay on Patriotism and Nationalism*. Oxford: Oxford University Press.

Wallerstein, I. 1991: The construction of peoplehood: racism, nationalism, ethnicity. In E. Balibar and I. Wallerstein, *Race, Nation, Class: Ambiguous Identities*. London: Verso.

Weber, E. 1976: *Peasants into Frenchmen*. Stanford, CA: Stanford University Press.

White, G. W. 2000: *Nationalism and Territory: Constructing Group Identity in Southeastern Europe*. Lanham, MD: Rowman and Littlefield.

Wiebe, R. 2000: Imagined communities: nationalist experiences. *Journal of the Historical Society* 1, 33–63.

Wiebe, R. 2002: *Who We Are: A History of Popular Nationalism*. Princeton, NJ: Princeton University Press.

Yack, B. 2001: Popular sovereignty and nationalism. *Political Theory* 29, 517–36.

Yiftachel, O. 2000: The homeland and nationalism, *Encyclopedia of Nationalism*. San Diego: Academic.

Yiftachel, O. 2002: Territory as the kernel of the nation: space, time and nationalism in Israel/Palestine. *Geopolitics* 7, 215–48.

Xenos, N. 1996: Civic nationalism: oxymoron? *Critical Review* 10, 213–31.

Zimmer, O. 2001: Forging the authentic nation: alpine landscape and Swiss national identity. In A. Dieckhoff and N. Gutiérrez, eds., *Modern Roots: Studies of National Identity*. Aldershot: Ashgate.

Chapter 16

Critical 'Race' Approaches to Cultural Geography

Audrey Kobayashi

For most of its history, human geography has tended to address the more positive aspects of human existence. Consider the founding legacy of the Berkeley School in establishing cultural geography, with its emphasis on the creative transformation of human landscapes, on the cohesive nature of human communities, and on the many fascinating ways in which cultural practices and artifacts differentiate one part of the world from another (see especially the collection by Wagner & Mikesell 1962). Indeed, when I was a student (some decades ago now), one of the things I found most exciting about my geography courses was the prospect of learning all the fascinating things I could about people in different parts of the world – and, about what made them different from one another.

More recently, although the tendency to study the world as an intriguing mosaic of difference remains very strong, 'critical' cultural geographers have placed a new emphasis on what makes human beings different from one another, replacing what many would view as a naive fascination with the exotic with a critical recognition that the exotic is a social production, both of the scholar and of the historical context in which the scholar works. In his recent text, Don Mitchell (2000) refers to "culture wars" as a more appropriate way of designating the struggles over identity, power, and territory that he – along with the majority of New Cultural Geographers – sees as inherent in the development of human culture. Arguably, the most unpleasant, and deeply troubling, product of the struggle for culture is 'race.'

I approach the concept of 'race' in two ways. First, it is a way of life, a fundamental product of Western cultures, deeply embedded in the European colonial past, lived out in the present as a taken-for-granted reality. Secondly, it is an analytical concept that has conditioned both academic and everyday ways of interpreting the world around us. For cultural geographers, it is important that 'race' was part of our earliest efforts, rooted in the geographical lore that accompanied the first European voyages of exploration that brought knowledge, riches, and power to the imperial/colonial dynasties. It was developed as a fully fledged theoretical system by Enlightenment thinkers whose treatises on such far-fetched theories as environmental determinism fit so neatly with the purposes of expanding European powers and with the by then highly developed sense of European cultural superiority and civilization. It was modified but by no means forgotten in the cultural theories of the twentieth century that eschewed environmental determinism in favor of culture as means of differentiating human systems, yet maintained an implicit belief in the fundamental differences that 'race' makes, and failed to apply a critical understanding to the human fallout of racialization: inequality; poverty; degradation; denial of human rights and dignity; erasure or exotification of the very cultures that we study with such enthusiasm. If cultural geographers are not directly culpable in the creation of inequality, they have certainly been complicit in erasure and exotification. (In the present volume, see especially Braun's chapter 11, as well as the chapters contained in part VI, on colonial and postcolonial geographies.)

In this short chapter, I am concerned with the latter definition of 'race.' I wish to show that geographies have geography; that our ideas are produced in context, and in turn contribute to the production of that context, as we express ourselves as members of cultural systems, and as our intellectual ideas and our actions as scholars influence the world around us. I wish both to chart some of the intellectual history of geographical ideas about 'race,' and to speculate on how the course of our history might be altered by critical assessment of our role in the process of racialization. The chapter begins with a review of the concept of 'race' as it is understood in contemporary antiracist geography, then moves to a brief analysis of how the production of antiracist geography has developed in three contemporary Western and Northern contexts.

The Geographical Concept of 'Race'

Recent cultural geography has seen a proliferation of studies of 'race,' embedded in a larger discourse on social construction. Although the concept of social construction is perhaps the intellectual hallmark of the paradigmatic shift that underlies all poststructuralist thinking, nowhere has the concept more salience than in understanding the construction of 'race,' or the process of racialization. Perhaps the most significant contribution of antiracist scholarship to the discipline of geography, then, is the development of this concept as part of its integration into virtually all areas of human geography.

What does the term 'social construction' mean? It suggests that the attributes that are historically associated with the human body – the qualities that are said to constitute gender or 'race' in particular – are socially constructed, or invented, rather than biologically determined. For example, traits associated with femininity, such as passivity, dependence or emotionality, or traits associated with 'race,' such as low intelligence or 'uncivilized' behavior, result from the ascription of such qualities to specific groups, not to some necessary or intrinsic aspect of their physical make-up. Similarly, opposite traits that are usually viewed positively, such as strength, rationality or the capacity for 'civilized' behavior, are ascribed historically to white males, again as socially constructed rather than physically necessary traits. It is through the practice of racism or sexism, therefore, that people are given attributes based on skin color or sex.

A theory of social construction also implies that *all* aspects of human being are socially constructed. There are not some areas that are socially constructed and others that are not – or that the 'invention' of some traits is somehow invalid, insignificant, arbitrary or 'not real' – but, rather, social construction constitutes the entire human experience. This point runs counter to any interpretation – for example, that of realism – that would suggest that some things are *only* socially constructed, as though there is some realm of human existence that is more basic. In other words, a social constructionist approach begins with social construction; it does not add it on to a 'natural' base. Indeed, in a social constructionist interpretation, the term 'natural' has no meaning, if that meaning concerns something that is prior to, determinate of, or independent of human discourse. Moreover, there is no need to resort to idealist interpretations that divide the world into that which is material and nonmaterial, since the world may be interpreted as material existence with meaning. Again, no part of the material world is without meaning. A social constructionist position is therefore simultaneously relativist, meaning that it is subject to change according to social context, and materialist, meaning that no social construction – including thought itself – occurs as anything except a material act.

A socially constructed world – filled with socially constructed human bodies – does not become less meaningful for having being invented. It is on the contrary *full* of meaning, replete with the tremendous range of discursive actions that constitute human life. There is no meaningless human life, no meaningless human act or gesture; nor is there any meaning that is not social. The term 'social' in this sense refers to all that is shared in being human, to common meaning based on shared history, filled with power and ideology, and systematically produced within social, cultural systems that are themselves socially constructed. Because social systems are systematically produced, however, it is also possible for some social constructions to be more meaningful, and more powerful, than others. Both concepts of 'race' and gender or sex are examples of extremely powerful constructions.

The socially constructed is also profoundly normative, as notions of good and bad, beautiful and ugly, civilized and uncivilized, strong and weak, are built into notions of the power, and the place, of human bodies within a social context. The strength of a social construction to regulate, or structure, human life depends very strongly upon its status as a normatizing concept, and therefore upon the ways in which human beings have invested it with power. The social constructions that are most powerful are those that display two main features: they are so deeply normatized that they seem to those who invoke or practice them to be natural ("well, *naturally*, black people have a tendency towards . . ."); and they are systematically embroiled within a wide spectrum of social life, including the family, the workplace, educational systems, expressions of national identity, and a range of cultural practices.

Recognition of the profound impossibility of accounting for any bodily trait as purely 'biological' has occurred largely through the collision of theoretical perspectives on the construction of sex, gender and 'race.' Second wave feminist theory underwent a series of disruptive shock waves when challenged to re-examine what had become a somewhat complacent view that gender is built upon biological sex. These waves became a major force when nonwhite feminists, arguing along the same lines, claimed that biological assumptions of difference and sameness underlay a pervasive whiteness within the feminist movement (for a review, see Lovell 1996). This recognition strengthened the understanding that we need to speak of feminisms and antiracisms – and by corollary of sexisms and racisms – because all are socially constructed and reflect specific historical circumstances. Nonetheless, the struggle to overcome whiteness in the feminist movement continues, as it does among those who would overcome racism. Theoretical understanding notwithstanding, both movements, and the relationship between them, have shown how hard it is to overcome our own normatized thinking, much less to marshal the social forces of change, fraught as these are with the results of historical constructions.

Building upon the historicity of the social construction of 'race,' it has become customary to refer to the process of 'racialization' as what Miles (following upon Fanon 1966; Banton 1977; and Guillaumin 1980) defines as:

a representational process whereby social significance is used to refer to certain biological (usually phenotypical) human features, on the basis of which those people possessing those characteristics are designated as a distinct collectivity. (Miles 1989: 74)

The concept of racialization implies that 'races' are constructed through historical processes, that they emerge in specific historical contexts without which they would have no meaning. By shifting from the *idea* of 'race' to its social production, we are also able to analyze racism – the belief in the concept of 'race' as a marker of human difference, as well as actions taken based on such a belief, whether implicit or explicit – as dynamic, discursive, and complex.

For the geographer, it is axiomatic to claim that all human processes *take place* in context. They occur within historically produced landscapes; they have spatial extent and distribution. It makes as much sense, therefore, to speak of 'spatialization' as it does racialization. Indeed, the two occur simultaneously. Racialization, therefore, is always a historical geography. In the context of western society, notwithstanding its considerable prehistory, most writers place the construction of 'races' within the so-called Enlightenment period of the latter half of the eighteenth century, simultaneous with the age of Imperialism, the spread of systems of capitalism, and the burgeoning and spread of modern scientific discourse.[1] During that period was established much of the geography of the world: the building of nation states based on ideas of inherent superiority and inferiority; the mapping of the world into 'civilized' and 'uncivilized' sections; the establishment of trade, production, and other economic factors that would profoundly influence human outcomes for centuries to come. During that period also the discipline of geography came into its own, as both a product and a producer of imperial, colonial systems. While cartographers mapped the world as a grid of political power, early human geographers speculated on whether climate was the dominant factor explaining the putative superiority of the white European man over the black African. In so doing, they legitimized and fed the notion of 'race' that would by the end of the nineteenth century become a thoroughly naturalized and normatized part of modern Western life. In retrospect, although perhaps they may have denied it at the time, they were entirely complicit in strengthening a racialized – and racist – society, while establishing the map as a significant statement not simply of location, but of moral values. As Livingstone's detailed account of the development of geography in the nineteenth century shows, the "interlacing of geographical knowledge and imperial drives" (Livingstone 1992: 219) in the expansion of imperial power represented not only an economic and political bid for power, but also an attempt to establish moral authority. The result was a racialized landscape that reflected the dominant values of the time.

Racialization, then, has a historical geography, in which we can understand the production of power, territory, and inequality in a systematic way, as systems through which the thread of 'race' runs deeply, justifying the actions of the white north against the black and brown south and east, as well as the production and justification of racial inequality in the creation of modern multicultural societies. The most important lesson of racialization, perhaps, is understanding not only that these large-scale historical processes have produced specific results, but also that such processes occur through the imposition of the human imagination upon specific landscapes. The human imagination is the collective – and usually also contested – discourse through which the normative, the taken-for-granted and the implicit is worked out, acted upon, coded and de-coded, as it is integrated into every aspect of living. I turn now to a brief discussion of the ways in which cultural geographies of 'race' have been thus produced, through the geographical imaginations of two social, cultural contexts.

Antiracist Geography in Context

It would be difficult, indeed hypocritical, to avoid the fact that the discipline of geography is dominated by Northern, Western, white scholars whose lives and careers have been constructed out of the very colonial systems that produced them. If the most important precept of critical thinking is continually to cast back our ideas upon themselves, examining not only their logical consistency but also the motives through which they are produced, then our ideas about 'race' are supremely susceptible to critical analysis. Part of that analysis, especially for the geographer, consists of recognizing that if racialization has a geography, so too does our attempt to understand it.

My purpose in this discussion, however, is not only to show that intellectual endeavors have a context. It is also to say something about the discourse of 'race' itself. One of the most important features of contemporary antiracist theory is the recognition that racisms are so highly variable and adaptable. This adaptability is based in what Foucault (see especially 1985) defines as a series of historical (and geographical) discourses mapping the "technologies of power" through which times and places gain their specific characteristics. As Laura Stoler (1995: 72) suggests:

race is a discourse of vacillations. It operates at different levels and moves not only between different political projects but seizes upon *different* elements of earlier discourses reworked for new political ends.

This observation rests on the assumption not only that racism – and by extension attempts to overcome racism – gain their power in specific contexts, but also that they are not "independently derived" (Stoler 1995: 72) but implicated in a series of overlapping and intersecting discourses that drive political and cultural goals. Is it not reasonable to expect, therefore, that a critical antiracist geography should be concerned with its own technologies of power and influence?

The British roots of racialized discourse

It is perhaps not too provocative to say that the very idea, 'British,' is historically synonymous with racial superiority. I shall not even attempt to do what others have done much more thoroughly in documenting the fundamental ways in which British society is built upon a racialized discourse rooted in colonial expansion (see, for example, Clayton 2003; Jacobs 1996; King 2003). We need only look to British imperial, social, scientific, and broadly intellectual history to see the forms of racialized discourse that have resulted both in the uneven development of colonialism, and in the construction of the racialized 'other' as inferior, uncivilized, and even inhuman. As Paul Gilroy (1987) put it, "*There Ain't No Black in the Union Jack.*"

During the 1980s and 1990s, British academics produced a series of powerful critiques of British colonialism. These works provided international leadership in understanding the fundamental relationship between 'race' and class, colonialism, and the downfall of Empire marked by racial tensions as Britons came to terms with social change during the 1970s. The editors of *The Empire Strikes Back* (CCCS 1982) depicted a national crisis in which the contradictions established during years of colonial domination were being worked out upon the postcolonial British landscape (Solomos et al. 1982).[2]

The crisis to which they refer began in Britain as a result of post-Second World War labor migration from former British colonies. This is not to say that British racialization began in the postwar period, especially if we consider the relative lack of nonwhite bodies in the British landscape prior to that time as itself a racialized expression. And, the fact that Britain was so dominantly white prior to the Second World War must also be seen as an expression of exclusion and of the notion of 'British' as an exclusively white race. Nonetheless, it was during the early 1950s that Britain underwent a transition from racialization at a distance, becoming the multicultural society that it is today through the movement of thousands of former colonial inhabitants to British cities, especially to London and the Midlands. Geographers such as Ceri Peach responded to the transformation of the British landscape with well-established methodologies to study changes in residential patterns (Peach 1975; Peach et al. 1981) that drew much from the rich dialogue between geographers and urban sociologists, in both Britain and the US, but particularly those of the Chicago School. The students of the next generation writing in the late 1980s, including such scholars as Anderson (1987, 1988), Jackson (1987, 1988), Keith (1987, 1988, 1989), and Smith (1989a, 1989b), built upon this perspective by applying the lessons of the new cultural studies approach, which Bonnett and Nayak (2003) have recently described as "representations of race and place."

Bonnett and Nayak describe more recent work, again occurring primarily but not exclusively in a British context, as moving generally from the study of representations to deeper critical cultural understanding of the symbolic meaning of such representations, that encompass "new theories of cultural identity: beyond 'race'" (Bonnett & Nayak 2003: 306–7). Strongly influenced by postcolonial theorists, such work begins with Jackson's (1995) *Maps of Meaning* and extends to Ruth Frankenberg's (1993) account of the meaning of landscape racialization in childhood, Heidi Nast's (2000) psychoanalytical account of the construction of family in racialized Chicago, Peter Jackson's recent work on the racialization of shopping patterns

(1998) or labor relations (Jackson 1992), Anderson's (1992) call to examine the nature of racialized discourse; and Kobayashi and Peake's (2000) discussion of whiteness as a basis for both local and national identity in the framing of the events at Littleton, Colorado, all of which share an emphasis on both the geographical and historical nature of racialized landscapes, and the very important perspective that we cannot understand the construction of 'race' as nonwhite without at least as much attention to the ways in which whiteness itself is constructed as a dominant metaphorical map for modern life. Bonnett's recent works (1993, 1997, 2000a, 2000b) draw out the theoretical implications of the turn to focus on whiteness as a geographical and historicized social product.

What stands out about Bonnett's and Nayak's account, however, notwithstanding its theoretical sophistication, is the fact that all of the works cited above (and others that, for reasons of brevity, are not fully cited here) occur at a methodological distance from the 'sites of struggle' in which racialized discourse occurs. Although a few of the works cited involve the collection of interview material, and all of them depend upon detailed archival research, none involves the immediate engagement of members of racialized communities, nor a political – much less activist – commitment to the places involved. The politics of difference and cultural identity are, therefore, constituted as analytical categories that – notwithstanding their obviously political roots – need to form the basis for scholarship:

We have argued in this chapter that it is only by understanding such normative terms as 'white' and 'western' – the ones against which others are defined as exotic – that wider systems of racial privilege can be brought into view. By making it clear that categories such as whiteness are also the products of racialization, that they too have a history and a geography and, hence, are changeable, we can help transform the critique of race and ethnicity from a 'subfield' into an essential theme running throughout a rigorous geographical education. (Bonnett & Nayak 2003: 309)

The American context

If British culture can be defined historically as racism at a distance, American society has by contrast been built upon the fundamental notion of a landscape shared, albeit unevenly and unequally, by white and nonwhite. Both the institution of slavery, and the practice of ridding the land of aboriginal cultures, are fundamental to what defines 'America,' and between the two account for most of the bloodshed that has occurred on American soil. The refinements associated with whiteness that are a trademark of British culture developed a much more blunted popular appeal as a result. While I would not wish to become too deterministic in this analysis, it is perhaps not insignificant that whereas British antiracist scholarship has been characterized as somewhat aloof and theory-driven, American scholarship has been on the whole more empirical, as well as more fraught and engaged with social struggle.

I have pointed out (Kobayashi 2003) that the roots of antiracist scholarship in the American context arose not through the direct application of social theory, but through a very raucous discourse over the moral obligations of geographers as citizens that began with an Association of American Geographers meeting in Ann Arbor Michigan in 1971, and led to the establishment of the journal *Antipode*. American antiracist scholarship has emerged from not only the deep social division of the legacy of slavery, but the post-Second World War social responses that include reactions to the Cold War, the civil rights movement in the context of the peace movement of the 1960s, and geographer's early attempts to combat racism on the ground through such pedagogic experiments as Bunge's 'Detroit Expedition' (Bunge 1971). For many American scholars, colonialism has meant not the construction of the other from a distance that spans all the pink on the globe, but colonialism represented by "the ghetto as neo-colony" (Blaut 1974). Others, while eschewing the rhetoric of radicalism as well as that of postcolonial theory, set their sights more immediately upon the lived conditions of African Americans, and upon a policy- as well as research-driven agenda for eradicating the results of a historical geography based on slavery (Rose 1970, 1972), while more recent work drawing upon that tradition but in addition applying an antiracist theoretical perspective calls for direct political action to intervene with and on behalf of racialized people (Gilmore 1998–9, 2002; Kobayashi 1994, 2001; Peake & Kobayashi 2002; Pulido 1996, 2000, 2002; Schein 2002; Wilson 2000a, 2000b; Woods 2002). These works discuss blood and guts, racialized killing, environmental degradation, the abuse of women and children, the burning of neighborhoods, and cultural genocide. They ask for an accounting not only of the cultural construction of whiteness, but of the power of whiteness to exclude in ways that are often violent (Dwyer & Jones 2000) or that invoke the potential violence of the state (Delaney 2002). The focus shifts in such works from the actions of the dominant majority to define and represent racialized subjects to the actual experiences of those subjects in everyday landscapes, with a reflexive agenda for the role of the geographer in his or her subjects' lives. In addition, the majority of the geographical scholars working in an American context are themselves members of racialized minority groups.

Having presented these two broadly-based approaches to the study of racism in geography, one dominated by British scholars and focused on postcolonial theories of cultural representation, the other dominated by American scholars and focused on on the-ground struggles that often involve participant activism on the part of the researcher, as well as coming-to-terms with the violence and human degradation that racism brings, I do not mean to present a clear-cut categorization of the two contexts. Indeed, there has been over the years, whether in the pages of *Antipode*, at both general and specialized academic conferences, as well as in joint publications, a great deal of interaction between the two contexts. Indeed, there is some overlap among the scholars whom I have named above, a number of them work in both broadly described fields and in a number of empirical sites. Not all can be categorized according to nationality.[3] Nor would I want to forget the contributions that have come from other parts of the world, notably southern Africa and the Caribbean. There are in addition a number of Canadians on the list – in addition to myself – whose work represents its own context, including that of recognizing the Aboriginal presence in Canada, but which often occurs in collaboration with both American and British colleagues. By all means, therefore, I wish to avoid lapsing into a new form of naive cultural reductionism.

In both countries, of course, the complexities of racialization cross-cut the landscape of racism in various ways. The two contexts are not unique, both because they have much cultural history in common, and because there is a wealth of collaboration among many countries. My distinction is therefore partly a heuristic one.

It illustrates, however, the important fact that the discernibly different manifestations of 'race' in the two national contexts need to be linked to the distinctive ways in which geographers have approached the study of racialization. The point is that the two countries illustrate the profound historical effects of such forces as colonialism, slavery and state policy, to the extent that these processes can become dominant, if by no means monolithic, forces in the development of racialized cultural conditions. The extent to which geographical scholarship reflects that dominance is both an expression of our reaction to a distinctive cultural milieu, and an expression of the extent to which our own work is normatized and reflects common experiences and conditioning discourses. I believe that the dominant historical fact in Britain of racism at a distance through the process of global colonialism (brought home most definitively in the postwar era), set against the historical fact of the legacy of slavery in the United States, with its legacy of deeply racialized and divided American cities and a particular history of social activism among American geographers, point to some significant contextual differences that, although I do not have the time nor space to develop them here, deserve serious further consideration. At least one major difference between the two contexts is that the British scene remains dominated by white geographers (hence an understandable focus on the significance of whiteness in geographical scholarship), while the American scene is much more diverse, but owes much of its legacy to both the scholarship and the dedication to social change of African American and other minority-group geographers. At the very least, my analysis points to a need to understand studies of racialization as themselves racialized.

Without also lapsing into yet another set of essentialized categories, therefore, I would simply make the point that there is a cultural geography of antiracist scholarship, that it matters not only where but *who* does the work (as well, no doubt, as who speaks to whom), that there can be no disengagement of the political and the academic without very serious consequences, and that in the end our discipline is thoroughly socially constructed, within a broader historico-intellectual context. My purpose here is to engage that process of construction, not only by pointing out discernible differences in intellectual contexts, but also by promoting dialogue between/among geographical cultures. For that project, too, is part of the political project of destabilizing the categories of 'race.'

NOTES

1. For accounts of the history of racialization see Malik 1996 or West 2002. While many writers see antecedents to racial thinking in certain Greek and Roman writings, the modern concept arises in the writings of eighteenth-century thinkers, whose power to normatize the concept was considerable (Kobayashi 2002; Livingstone 1992). I have confined my discussion here to racism in the western context, recognizing both that similar forms of creating difference exist in other contexts, and that there has been considerable historical overlap in various parts of the world, especially through the agency of colonialism. At the same time, however, I do not wish to reduce racialization to a single universal process.

2. I could also point to work done in France during the same era, especially that of Guillaumin (1980) or Fanon (1966), building upon the philosophies of Jean-Paul Sartre

and Hannah Arendt. But, while these works are of tremendous importance in geographical theories today, they did not play such a significant role in the production of geographical works in France at the time, and my purpose is to discuss the context of antiracist geography.

3. Indeed, I include my own work in reference to the context in which it has been published, not in reference to my own nationality, which is neither British nor American.

REFERENCES

Anderson K. 1987: Chinatown as an idea: the power of place and institutional practice in the making of a racial category. *Annals of the Association of American Geographers* 77: 580–98.

Anderson, K. 1988: Cultural hegemony and the race-definition process in Chinatown, Vancouver: 1880–1980. *Environment and Planning D: Society and Space* 6: 127–49.

Anderson, K. 2002: The racialization of difference: enlarging the story field. *Professional Geographer* 54(1), 25–30.

Banton, M. 1977: *The Idea of Race*. London: Tavistock.

Blaut, J. M. 1974: The ghetto as an internal neo-colony. *Antipode* 6(1), 37–41.

Bonnett, A. 1993: Forever 'white'? Challenges and alternatives to a 'racial' monolith. *New Community* 20(1), 173–80.

Bonnett, A. 1997: Geography, 'race' and whiteness: invisible traditions and current challenges. *Area* 29(3), 193–9.

Bonnett, A. 2000a: *White Identities: Historical and International Perspectives*. Harlow: Pearson.

Bonnett, A. 2000b: *Anti-Racism*. London and New York: Routledge

Bonnett, A. and Nayak, A. 2003: Cultural geographies of racialization – the territory of race. In K. Anderson, M. Domosh, S. Pile, and N. Thrift, eds., *The Handbook of Cultural Geography*. London: Sage, 300–12.

Bunge, W., Jr. 1971: *Fitzgerald: The Geography of an American Revolution*. Cambridge: Cambridge University Press.

Centre for Contemporary Cultural Studies, eds. 1982: *The Empire Strikes Back: Race and Racism in '70s Britain*. London: Hutchinson and the Centre for Contemporary Cultural Studies.

Clayton, D. 2003: Critical imperial and colonial geographies. In K. Anderson, M. Domosh, S. Pile, and N. Thrift, eds., *The Handbook of Cultural Geography*. London: Sage, 354–68.

Delaney, D. 2002: The space that race makes. *The Professional Geographer* 54(1), 6–14.

Dwyer, J. O. and Jones, J. P. III. 2000: White socio-spatial epistemology. *Social & Cultural Geography* 1(2), 209–22.

Fanon, F. 1966: *The Wretched of the Earth*. Harmondsworth: Penguin.

Foucault, M. 1985: *History of Sexuality*. New York: Vintage Books.

Frankenberg, R. 1993: Growing up white: feminism, racism and the social geography of childhood. *Feminist Review* 45, 51–84.

Gilmore, R. 1998/9: Globalisation and US prison growth: from military Keynesianism to post-Keynesian militarism. *Race and Class* 40(2–3), 177–88.

Gilmore, R. W. 2002: Fatal couplings of power and difference: notes on racism and geography. *The Professional Geographer* 54(1), 15–24.

Gilroy, P. 1987: *There Ain't No Black in the Union Jack*. London: Routledge.

Guillaumin, C. 1980: The idea of race and its elevation to autonomous scientific and legal status. In UNESCO, *Sociological Theories: Race and Colonialism*. Paris: UNESCO.

Jackson, P. J., ed. 1987: *Race and Racism: Essays in Social Geography.* London: Allen and Unwin.

Jackson, P. J. 1988: Street life: the politics of carnival. *Environment and Planning D: Society and Space* 6, 231–7.

Jackson, P. J. 1992: The racialization of labour in post-war Bradford. *Journal of Historical Geography* 18(2), 190–209.

Jackson, P. J. 1995: *Maps of Meaning: An Introduction to Cultural Geography.* London: Routledge.

Jackson, P. J. 1998: Constructions of 'whiteness' in the geographical imagination. *Area* 30(2), 99–106.

Jacobs, J. 1996: *Edge of Empire: Postcolonialism and the City.* London: Routledge.

Keith, M. 1987: "Something happened": the problems of explaining the 1980 and 1981 riots in British cities. In P. Jackson, ed., *Race and Racism: Essays in Social Geography.* London: Allan and Unwin, 275–303.

Keith, M. 1988: Racial conflict and the 'no-go areas' of London. In J. Eyles and D. M. Smith, eds., *Qualitative Methods in Human Geography.* Cambridge: Polity, 39–48.

Keith, M. 1989: Riots as 'social problem' in British cities. In D. T. Hiebert and D. M. Smith, eds., *Social Problems and the City.* Oxford: Oxford University Press, 289–306.

King, Anthony D. 2003: Cultures and spaces of postcolonial knowledges. In K. Anderson, M. Domosh, S. Pile, and N. Thrift, eds., *The Handbook of Cultural Geography.* London: Sage, 381–97.

Kobayashi, A. 1994: Coloring the field: gender, 'race,' and the politics of fieldwork. *The Professional Geographer* 45(1), 73–80.

Kobayashi, A. 2001: Negotiating the personal and the political in critical qualitative research. In M. Limb and C. Dwyer, eds., *Qualitative Methodologies for Geographers.* New York: Arnold and Oxford University Press.

Kobayashi, A. 2003: The construction of geographical knowledge – racialization, spatialization. In K. Anderson, M. Domosh, S. Pile, and N. Thrift, eds., *The Handbook of Cultural Geography.* London: Sage, 544–56.

Kobayashi, A. and Peake, L. 2000: Racism out of place: thoughts on whiteness and an antiracist geography in the new millennium. *Annals of the Association of American Geographers* 90(2), 392–403.

Livingstone, D. N. 1992: *The Geographical Tradition.* Oxford and Malden, MA: Blackwell.

Lovell, T. 2000 (1996): Feminisms of the second wave. In B. S. Turner, ed., *The Blackwell Companion to Social Theory.* Oxford and Malden, MA: Blackwell, 299–324.

Malik, K. 1996: *The Meaning of Race: Race, History and Culture in Western Society.* Houndmills: Macmillan.

Miles, R. 1989: *Racism.* London and New York: Routledge.

Mitchell, D. 2000: *Cultural Geography: A Critical Introduction.* Oxford and Malden, MA: Blackwell.

Nast, H. 2000: Mapping the 'unconscious': racism and the oedipal family. *Annals of the Association of American Geographers* 90(2), 215–55.

Peach, C., ed. 1975: *Urban Social Segregation.* London: Longmans.

Peach, C., Robinson, V., and Smith, S., eds. 1981: *Ethnic Segregation in Cities.* London: Croom Helm.

Pulido, L. 1996: *Environmentalism and Economic Justice.* Tucson: University of Arizona Press.

Pulido, L. 2000: Rethinking environmental racism: white privilege and urban development in southern California. *Annals of the Association of American Geographers* 90(1), 12–40.

Pulido, L. 2002: Reflections on a white discipline. *Professional Geographer* 54(1), 25–30.

Rose, H. M. 1970: The development of an urban subsystem: the case of the Negro ghetto. *Annals of the Association of American Geographers* 60, 1–17.

Rose, H. M. 1972: The spatial development of black residential subsystems. *Economic Geography* 48, 43–65.

Schein, R. 2002: Race, racism, and geography: introduction. *The Professional Geographer* 54(1), 1–5.

Smith, S. 1989a: *The Politics of 'Race' and Residence.* Cambridge: Polity.

Smith, S. 1989b: Race and racism. *Urban Geography* 10, 593–606.

Solomos, J., Findlay, B., Jones, S., and Gilroy, P. 1982: The organic crisis of British capitalism and race: the experience of the seventies. In Centre for Contemporary Cultural Studies, ed., *The Empire Strikes Back: Race and Racism in '70s Britain.* London: Hutchinson and the Centre for Contemporary Cultural Studies, 9–46.

Stoler, L. 1995: *Race and the Education of Desire: Foucault's History of Sexuality and the Colonial Order of Things.* Duke and London: Duke University Press.

Wagner, P. L. and Mikesell, M. W., eds. 1962: *Readings in Cultural Geography.* Chicago and London: University of Chicago Press.

West, C. 2002: A genealogy of modern racism. In P. Essed and D. T. Goldberg, eds., *Race Critical Theories.* Oxford and Malden, MA: Blackwell, 99–112.

Wilson, B. M. 2000a: *America's Johannesburg: Industrialization and Racial Transformation in Birmingham.* Totowa, NJ: Rowan & Littlefield.

Wilson, B. M. 2000b: *Race and Place in Birmingham: The Civil Rights and Neighborhood Movements.* Totowa, NJ: Rowan & Littlefield.

Wilson, B. M. 2002: Critically understanding race-connected practices: a reading of W. E. B. Du Bois and Richard Wright. *Professional Geographer* 54(1), 31–41.

Woods, C. 2002: Life after death. *Professional Geographer* 54(1), 62–6.

Chapter 17

Social Class

Nancy Duncan and Stephen Legg

Introduction

In this chapter we review the question of the relation between class and culture, first making brief reference to key texts in social and cultural theory. We then look at some of the more general statements on class in the geographical literature, with special attention to cultural geography. We end with some questions and remarks about how the issues of class and culture might be further explored by cultural geographers. Despite (some argue because of) the recent explosion of interest in subjectivity and identity formation in geography, class has remained the most neglected and problematic of those "agonizing etceteras": race, gender, sexuality, age, class, etc. (Butler 1990: 143). In cultural geography class is often used uncritically in the popular taxonomic and gradational sense of the term as a category with which to describe the social status or distinction of individuals, or as a variable based on education and income to be employed in statistical analyses. Class in various Marxian and Weberian dynamic and relational senses is too rarely brought under theoretical and empirical scrutiny or elaborated in specific cultural and historical contexts.

When Marxist definitions are invoked they are sometimes based on an overly simple, dichotomous, and essentialist model of capital and labor with little or no reference to self-identification processes, instabilities, hybridities, or multiplicities as these are seen to complicate the matter. When the model *is* refined, intermediate class fractions or contradictory class locations such as the propertyless middle class are often recognized (see Wright 1985, 2000). However, such complications as consciousness, especially its ambiguity, ambivalence, apathy, contingency, or other cultural, affective, experiential, or social-psychological aspects, are often thought to reduce the analytic power of the economic model. The fear, presumably, is that the analyst might come to see the world in all its baffling complexity rather than "cutting to the heart of the matter." We believe that it is possible to understand the nature of classes by using a dynamic and relational approach to the understanding of capitalist class processes which also acknowledges that popular understandings of class (both existential and articulated) refer to very real social differences (however fragmented and unstable) that enable recognition and subjectivity. These in turn are related in complex, if sometimes tangential, ways to class as political-economic processes. However, there are many problems with combining these different senses of class. Wright (1985: 79), for example, claims that status and class are unrelated and that questions of status have no place in class analysis. Crompton (1998: 118), however, points to the considerable empirical overlap between status (as prestige or lifestyle) and class (as defined in relation to production). Among the many problems is the fact that although class processes are being restructured globally, many of the studies of the social psychology of classes[1] are national or even regional in scope and usually based only on Western countries such as the US, Britain, or France.

Although there is clearly a perceived need to rethink class, recent introductions to cultural geography (Crang 1998[2]; Shurmer-Smith & Hannam 1994, and Shurmer-Smith 2002) still contain no significant consideration of the issue. As Norton (2000: 20) acknowledges, while political-economy remains important, "Class is not, however, central to much of the work in contemporary cultural geography." In fact Sadler (2003) speaks of a "limited engagement with class as an explanatory concept (*even*) within economic geography" (emphasis added). Various explanations have been offered to explain what Cooke (1996: 18) refers to as this "eclipse of class" in contemporary academic study and participatory politics. He states that economic and technological developments associated with a 'post-Fordist' or 'late capitalist' economy are thought to have fragmented traditional class formations while radical politics has given way to market-oriented and identity-based disputes. In the realm of theory, poststructuralist critiques of Marxist metanarratives and essentialism have led to an emphasis on studies that stress the relative autonomy of the cultural realm to the detriment of more materialist research. In this same vein Anderson and Gale (1999) believe that the currency of the concept of culture in geography reflects a "recent phase of economic and social restructuring in the West when old lines of class division are being fractured around new sources of identity and political mobilisation."

Neil Smith (2000) and David Harvey (2001) have been among the most vocal protestors against the decline of class as an object of geographical inquiry. As Smith (2000: 1012–14) points out, there has been unprecedented industrial expansion (especially in Asia) and new global class formations have arisen since the 1970s as globalization dramatically restructures class relations and "recalibrates" class, race, and gender divisions in society and the economy (2000: 1014). An ever-expanding global migration of labor has resulted in an intensified racialization of labor segmentation. Smith admits that while a renewed importance of class discourse is not, in fact, incompatible with an evolving politics of race, gender, and sexuality, it is difficult to "unpack the abstract theoretical categories of 'difference' in specific political context." He acknowledges that the "thuddingly inflexible" notions of class inherited from the seventies and eighties period of Marxist dominance in geography account, in part, for the turn to more nuanced understandings of identities as experienced. He admits that most Marxist work in geography failed to explore class subjectivity, class agency, and changing class structures. Nevertheless, he says, it would be distressingly ironic if at the beginning of the twenty-first century when there is a dramatic upsurge of class and class organizing globally (Sayer & Walker

1992), the concept of class continues to remain relatively undeveloped (Smith 2000: 1028; also see Harvey 2001). Another Marxist geographer, Richard Peet (1997: 46), calls for "a project linking economic with cultural analysis" which would be "supported by an embarrassingly rich array of intellectual resources, which only the blinkers of conventional economic thinking prevent us from fully using."

Thus, as cultural geography emerges from the limelight of the "cultural turn," there are growing calls for what Crang (1997: 9) describes as a renewed "political-economic return." Such a development should in theory turn the attention of cultural geographers to the concept of class. Jackson (2000: 13) has urged the "rematerialization of social and cultural geography," by which he means (in part) the need for culture to be "reconnected to a critical understanding of cultural materialism as practiced in the tradition of political economy, without simply 'reading off' symbolic meanings from the mode of production." At the same time Barnes and Hannah (2001) call for a more empirically grounded approach to geographical work through the use of quantitative methodologies. These, we agree, are appropriate (in conjunction with other methodologies) to the examination of class as a complex, large-scale political-economic phenomenon stretching well beyond the horizon of individuals' identities or quests for recognition. Statistical analyses of profound inequalities measured at various scales including the global also may be necessary to counter popular rhetoric about the disappearance of class as a structured political-economic phenomenon.

Ray and Sayer (1999) bemoan the fact that the so-called "cultural turn" in geography has not only neglected class as it relates to production, but that it has also resulted in a more general turning away from political economy as an important focus of research. They believe there "are many positive effects of the 'cultural turn' – both in taking culture, discourse, and subjectivity more seriously and in escaping from reductionist treatments of culture as a mere reflection of material situation" (Ray & Sayer 1999: 2). However, they see no good reason why the growing prominence of cultural geography should have resulted in (what they see as) a neglect of economic analyses rather than an enrichment of both. They make it clear, however, that theirs is not a call for the collapsing of culture and the economy or subsuming the economy under culture defined as a whole way of life. They see cultural and economic processes as internally related, but distinguishable and based in different logics. They argue further (1999: 13) that the emphasis in geography on cultural identity politics as a politics of recognition "endorses neo-liberal values and is convergent with the latter's defence of markets, especially where identity depends on consumption and images . . ." (On this see also Skeggs 2000; Brown 1995.)

Theorizing Class

Under the influence of various poststructural theories of subjectivity, cultural geographers have tended to reject the idea of a structurally defined, unified subject, let alone an idea of classes that are sufficiently homogenous and self-conscious to be politically effective. Gender, race, and sexuality are currently understood as fragmented, fluid, and ambiguous sets of relations, practices, and performances. But what about class? Is it an analogous concept? Class affiliations may be multiple, hybrid, or even contradictory; nevertheless people perform, embody, practice, and produce class as a project, albeit incomplete and never fully constituted. We have sophisticated analyses of the performance of class as lifestyle or consumption patterns that establish social distinction, but few that look at class structured through production or property relations in ways that are comparably nuanced.[3] Marx's famous distinction between "class in itself" and "class for itself" remains relatively undeveloped and unrefined compared to the sophisticated investigation and theoretical elaboration of similar relationships between structurings (albeit often fractured structurings) and group performances and self-understandings with respect to gender or sexuality, for example.

As we have suggested, in cultural geography and other cultural fields the term 'class' is most often used as a descriptive term referring to status, occupation group, or lifestyle and consumption patterns without sufficient critical attention to questions of ontology or to questions of class as exploitative, structured relationships, as lived and experienced, as an aspect of identity, or as regionally and historically variable. Should class be seen as a taxonomic, gradational category as it is often used in everyday speech? Or is it a (more or less) unified, reflexive social group that acts (or could potentially act) collectively? The latter is an empirical question. It depends, in part, on subjectivity or class consciousness.[4] It also depends on whether the concept of "act" is seen to include loosely structured, but largely uncoordinated, actions which have far-flung, unintended consequences and unacknowledged conditions. By using class in an unexamined, "commonsense," descriptive way geographers may be losing an opportunity to connect issues of class agency, subjectivity, and consciousness to political-economic structures.

If one conceives of class in a relational, interactional sense as a cluster of practices, is it potentially a force that can act in its own interest? Might classes be best understood as complex, heterogeneous networks of relations, institutions, and other resources structured, but unintended and undirected – possibly even having emergent and coherent properties? Must classes be classes for themselves in order to be classes in themselves? Taking a broad, non-individualistic notion of agency as found for example in Latour's (1999a, 1999b) actor-network theory, in Clegg's (1989) theorization of circuits of power, or Law's (1994) relational materialism, in which the social is seen as heterogeneously material, agency is not restricted to humans and need not be understood as intentional.

Resnick and Wolff (1987) see class as an adjective describing a set of processes. Gibson-Graham, Resnick, and Wolff (2000: 11) say that their "task is to open up new discursive spaces where a language of process rather than of social structure suggests the possibility of energetic and unconfined class identities." This perhaps suggests more fluidity and less structure than in fact exists: a triumph of hope over experience perhaps? But to oppose structure to process seems to undo some of the important theoretical developments over the last twenty or so years in overcoming such dualisms. We think that by acknowledging structured inequalities or structuration processes, one need not necessarily lose sight of changing, open, and multiple class positions; rather such acknowledgment serves to remind one also of the dangers of liberal individualism in assuming more choice, freedom, and mobility than in fact exists. However, we do wholeheartedly agree with Gibson-Graham, Resnick, and Wolff (2000: 9) when they say, "How class processes relate to individual and collective identities, the formation of social groups, and to other complexities such as power and property becomes an open question, something to be theorized rather than assumed."

Embourgeoisement theories are largely out of favor, as they are seen (like culture of poverty theories) to blame the victim (see Goldthorpe et al. 1969). But might it not be possible through in-depth, multifaceted study, including both social-psychological and political-economic approaches, to refine these types of explanation of class consciousness and alienation? Many theorists today refuse a distinction between objective and subjective bases of class, arguing that class includes practices, consciousness, and structures which are all mutually constitutive. The notion of false consciousness is widely thought to be too crude, unnuanced, and too wedded to a simplistic dichotomy between subjective and objective states of being. However, one might ask if there is a way to understand the complex and contingent structuration of inequalities, systematic disadvantaging, differential access to resources, and exploitation practices which exist (relatively) independently of class consciousness? If so what can be said about the relation of these structures to the understanding of class as experienced. Are there more accurate or subtle ways to understand the relation between common interests and class consciousness however defined?

As Wright (2000) points out, there are two distinct uses of the term 'class consciousness.' One sees it as a characteristic of classes as collective entities while the other sees it an attribute of individuals. He argues that imputing consciousness to a class is an "elliptic and rather awkward way of theorizing this emergent tendency" which runs the risk of teleology. Wright (2000: 193) argues that classes are not the kind of entity that can have minds or preferences. This is undoubtedly true, but what about class identification, class "feelings,"[5] romantic longings, or striving on the part of individuals who identify with a particular class and their understandings of its practices and cultural attributes? What is the relation between these "structures of feeling" and processes of production, exploitation, distribution, or domination? And does this relation not vary considerably cross-culturally? Awareness of class varies widely across cultures and through time. There are geographies of class processes which show how space "hides the consequences" (Soja 1989). For example, in the case of the most privileged and powerful, one might argue that residential separation and an aestheticization of lifestyles often obscures the social consequences of privilege, further reinforcing the status quo by naturalizing and supporting the bases of such privilege (see Duncan & Duncan 2003). Awareness of class clearly varies depending on how those in similar economic situations are fragmented ethnically and racially. Class processes are cross-cut by gender, ethnicity, race, language, citizenship, and immigration status within countries. Furthermore as class structures are increasingly globalized, then it is increasingly unlikely that the structures of class feeling will coincide with the geographical reality of class processes. If classes are in fact now global in scale, then do national boundaries and other separations obscure globally restructured class-based inequalities?

The inability to understand the links between class structure (class-in-itself) and consciousness (class-for-itself) have, in fact, stymied Marxist thought for well over a century now. One of the major theorists who have addressed this problem is Antonio Gramsci. Gramsci, and subsequent Gramscian cultural theorists, envisage class relations as maintained through a double helix of force and consent. Coercion and control are exerted through the institutions of 'political society' while consent is manufactured through cultural and moral norms in 'civil society' (Femia 1981; Guha 1997). As such, the sociocultural consent of the working classes is seen to explain the lack of a revolution in the face of exploitation in twentieth-century Europe. Raymond Williams's (1977) theory of cultural hegemony, similarly, sees class cultures as lived forms and cultural hegemony as articulated through "structures of feeling" that induce particular ways of acting which conform to an ideal of how society should operate. This hegemony then supports ruling class interests (Williams 1977: 131). In the US the classic work of Sennett and Cobb (1973) on the "hidden injuries of class" provides still useful insight into the workings of class hegemony at the level of "structures of feeling." They show through both intensive and extensive empirical research how the ideologies of individualism and class mobility supported class privilege and lead to the poor blaming themselves for their poverty rather than recognizing larger class processes. In Britain a classic cultural study of the development of class experience and consciousness and the "not so hidden" injuries of class is Willis's (1977) study of working-class boys. Both these studies point to the failure of individuals to recognize their own interests and to the ways their beliefs and actions reinforce the structures of inequality. They manage to perceptively explore these structures of class feeling and the failure of class militancy, without falling into the trap of cultural determinism. In fact, they manage to effectively counter "cultures of poverty" and underclass[6] type arguments which themselves blame the victim, failing to recognize the material force of the larger class structures of exploitation and failures of distribution at the root of poverty. The recent trend in social, cultural and geographical theory tends to emphasize instead resistance, knowingness, fragmentation, and incoherence in social relations and to downplay the coherence and power of dominant ideologies. This trend may unfortunately be more theoretically sophisticated than it is empirically substantiated.

The cultural work of Raymond Williams was also taken up by Stuart Hall and his colleagues at the Centre for Contemporary Cultural Studies at Birmingham University which throughout the 1980s developed its own brand of cultural studies and identity politics simultaneously considering race, gender, sexuality, and class. Although this work had its basis in Marxian critique (Hall 1996, 1997), it unfortunately tended to give the least attention to class. More recently, however, cultural studies has begun to recognize the need for a return to class as a decentered, relationally defined, aspect of identity. As Chen (1996a: 400) states, "[So] those terms that were excluded from cultural studies, in what I would call the middle period, when we were trying to get rid of the baggage of class reductionism, of class essentialism, now need to be reintegrated; not as dominant explanatory forms, but as very serious forms of social and cultural structural division, inequality, unevenness in the production of culture." Chen has further argued that revised forms of Marxisms (or 'post-Marxist' theories) emerging within poststructuralism and class-based analyses of cultural studies can be compatible. Both share, he claims, an emphasis on strategic alliances based on similar political concerns, framed within local studies of concrete struggles (Chen 1996b: 320).

Such theories maintain certain Marxist notions, such as "the perception that the organization of systems of ideas and the mode of their social operation can be satisfactorily understood only if primary consideration is given to their connections to the prevailing system of class relations" (Bennett 1990: 18). Other Marxian concepts including the mode of production and the dialectic are qualified. For example, any notion of 'being' prior to 'consciousness,' the 'real' prior to the 'ideology' that represents it, or 'society' prior to the 'discursive relations' which attribute meaning, are all called into question and seen as constitutive rather than separate.

Pierre Bourdieu has attempted to theorize class within a Marxist frame. He employs a notion of cultural "habitus" to articulate those spatially defined embodied rituals of everydayness by which a culture "reproduces and sustains the belief in its own 'obviousness'" (Butler 1999: 113). Although noncausal, habitus (or culture[7]) can inspire dispositions that incline people to act in certain ways. Habitus is, ultimately, thought to be determined by the social 'fields' from which it emerges, the most important of which is the market. Although Bourdieu devotes much of his attention to how class as status is expressed through taste, knowledge, and lifestyle and formed by cultural as well as economic capital, some sympathetic critics such as Judith Butler remain uneasy with the lingering primacy of the market in his work. Butler believes that where there should be opportunities for resistance within the improvisation and ambivalence that result from the imbrications of field and habitus, Bourdieu tends to see only conformity (Butler 1999: 118). On the other hand, we would argue that the question of whether to place emphasis on stability or instability, hegemony or strife should be resolved through empirical inquiry and should not be decided by theoretical debate. In fact there is evidence that Bourdieu shared this view and that he places more emphasis on contingency than many of his detractors suggest.

Post-Marxist theorists Laclau and Mouffe (1985: 70) question the assumption that the hegemony is necessarily based in class. Drawing upon Gramsci's work, they question the preexistence of fully constituted class identity, suggesting rather that people enter into political struggles in an attempt to shape their identities as well as their destinies. Just as biological sex does not preexist socially constructed gender, so the economy should not be seen to predate and determine politics or culture (Smith, 1998:151). Although class is identified as a subject position, it remains fragile and unfinished. Political discourses must promise to overcome the 'lack' (Laclau 1994: 2) between one's identity and one's subjectivity while forming links with residual, enduring and emerging institutions thus achieving a new, temporary, and partial hegemony (Smith 1998: 170).

However, while Laclau and Mouffe argue for an increased emphasis on class, what has occurred has been in fact is a radical devaluation. As Fraser (1995: 68) characterized contemporary debates:

In these 'post-socialist' conflicts, group identity supplants class interest as the chief medium of political mobilisation. Cultural domination supplants exploitation as the fundamental injustice. And cultural recognition displaces socio-economic redistribution as the remedy for injustice and the goal of political struggle.

While income inequality continues to rise (see Martin 2001), academics remain stuck in what Fraser (1995: 70) terms the "redistribution–recognition dilemma." Research tends to focus on cultural domination, nonrecognition and disrespect rather than exploitation, marginalization and deprivation. Important as the former cultural-symbolic issues are, they should not be considered without giving central consideration to socio-economic injustices.

Following Nancy Fraser's (1995, 1997, 1999) line of argument, Linda McDowell (2000) argues for a politics of social justice whose goal is recognition of cultural difference and economic redistribution. This as she explains raises many difficult issues concerning the relation between culture and the economy and the various competing definitions of class. McDowell (2000) argues that any combining of the politics of recognition with a politics of redistribution in which relations of production are radically restructured will necessarily "translate" binary distinctions into "networks of multiple intersecting differences that are demassified and shifting" (McDowell here quoting Fraser 1997: 31). Such translation (rearticulation, recontextualization) she says would require changes in the cultural definitions of various identities based on gender and ethnic as well as class. As economic inequalities are resolved there will be consequences in the realm of cultural differences that must be accommodated. Sayer (1999: 65) says cultural relations such as patriarchy and racism structure social relations within the economy and the "inequalities they generate are routinely taken advantage of by capitalist interests, whether in the super-exploitation of oppressed groups or the conversion of symbolic capital into economic capital." The interrelations between the cultural and the economic are highly complex; thus we can see that any truly significant change in economic relations will have cultural repercussions.

Class and Cultural Geography

As we have indicated above, within geography as a whole, analyses of class came to prominence in the late 1970s with the rise of a radical, generally Marxist approach. Yet, as with studies of class more generally, this prominence declined in the 1980s. Smith attributes this to causes both external and internal to geography. Externally, cultural studies focusing on feminism, racism, and sexuality tended to downplay class. Internally, the class categories used by geographers were often inadequate and inflexible (Smith 2000: 1020). Class structures were theorized abstractly and not always connected empirically to local class practices and formations. However, there have been some attempts over the past 20 years to rectify some of these problems and to revitalize the notion, as well as explore the distinctive contributions geographers may be in a position to make.

Thrift and Williams, for example, attempt to focus the analysis of class on the issue of space. They (Thrift & Williams 1987: xiii) state that "classes are organised (or disorganised) over space at a variety of scales and the degree and form of this spatial organisation will affect their integrity in myriad ways." They adopt an explicitly relational approach suggesting that class structure refers to the way in which people's capacity for action is limited by the institutionally mediated social relations of production. They supplement this politico-economic focus with attention to class formation, the process by which people are recruited to class politics. This formation is understood in relation to the three concepts of conflict, capacity, and consciousness. 'Capacity' refers to the ability of a class to reproduce itself and organize its members into a social force, which could lead to 'conflict' between class alliances. The result and source of these capacities and conflicts is 'consciousness,' the

awareness of class membership. However, they too have found that it is very difficult, if not impossible, to empirically determine when a class becomes "for-itself."

Many geographical analyses of class structure have been theoretical and abstract
in focus, such as those of Wallerstein or Harvey; capitalist structures are less often
studied empirically or located within place differentiated relations of production
and reproduction (but see Massey 1984). Thrift and Williams (1987: 15, 35),
however, argued that the regional scale should be used to look at class conflict and
capacity, while class-consciousness is best studied at the community scale. Some
geographical work began at that time to explore class practices and processes in
particular localities, localities being seen as the result of historically contingent
clusterings of heterogeneous processes and institutions (see Cooke 1989).

More recently geographical studies of urban form and processes have come to
examine class relationally and localities as networked into other spatial scales.
Kearns and Withers (1991) offer a critique of the sterility of urban ecological
approaches to class as a mappable variable. They (1991: 9) propose that studies of
class and community should be animated by explorations of the cultural, experiential aspects of the relations between classes. Relational studies of class should thus
emphasize the perceptions of class inequalities which they say are "invariably
framed by cultural factors" (1991: 10). They (p. 11) state that, "the study of how
society is structured by class relations leads us to explore a range of cultural phenomena that express the way individuals signified to people of similar standing and
to others the meanings they attributed to economic, political or demographic
processes."

The emergence of "new cultural geography" in the mid to late 1980s brought
mixed fortunes for studies of class. Earlier attacks on traditional cultural geography had criticized the reification of culture as an autonomous force and the consequent lack of attention to social process and social relations (Duncan 1980) as well
as the virtual non-existence of a "radical cultural geography" (Cosgrove 1983). It
promised an increased emphasis on social interaction especially power relations,
politics and contestation. However, a strong poststructural influence on much of the
later work, which was often based on an inherent critique of structural Marxism
as essentialist and totalizing, tended to lose the constitution of class as a primary
focus of research.

However, there is some work on landscape that does include significant contributions to class studies in cultural geography. Cosgrove and Daniels (1988) and
Cosgrove (1984) linked the emergence of capitalist class structures with the refor-
mulation of the landscape "way of seeing" as both a mode of representation and a
practical means for appropriating space. The bourgeois class sponsored the emergence of the linear perspective; it was used to represent their power and prestige
while erasing the laboring class whose exploitation created and maintained both
physical and representational landscapes (Cosgrove 1984: 27). Don Mitchell (2000:
99–100) shows how the landscape as a physical phenomena reproduces class relations. Like a commodity, the landscape embodies the labor and social struggle that
reproduces it. Likewise, Zukin (1991) views landscape as a product of social contestation. Duncan and Duncan (2003) analyze the aestheticization (mystification) of
the class and labor relations that are constitutive of suburban American landscapes
focusing attention on the tensions between Anglo elites whose identities are per-

formed through their landscape tastes and Latino workers whose labor maintains those landscapes. This and other cultural geographic work on consumption and cultural expressions of class,[8] much of it influenced by Bourdieu's (1984) in-depth study of social distinction, sees styles of life and cultural production as reinforcing and maintaining class structures.

Landscape is one of the principal themes in this recent work. Distinction and cultural capital in the form of taste are enacted in places; again the landscape is a principal medium along with housing and travel (Duncan & Duncan 2003; Philo & Kearns 1993). Some of these studies look at the production of new spaces in which capitalism operates and class identities and relations are formed as in studies of shopping malls (Crawford 1992; Shields 1992).

In cultural geography as elsewhere in the academy, poststructural conceptions of identity have had a significant impact. Identities are seen as fragmented, fluid, and relationally constituted, rather than essential. In response, Pred and Watts (1992) raise the question of how identities and identity politics that rest on internal fragmentation, difference and division can produce a common political ground with respect to class. The answer, they believe, requires "not a retreat from class, but a desperate need to re-theorize where class has gone and to rethink class in non-essentialist terms" (1992: 198). Non-essentialist conceptions of identity, however, have tended to focus on the performance of gender and sexuality, more than class. Among the few geographical works that truly take up the challenge of producing a non-essentialist definition of class as a heterogeneous social process is the highly innovative work of J. K. Gibson-Graham (1996, 1997). They argue that "a full or complex conception of class takes into account the ways in which groups are formed and subjective bases of group identification." Gibson-Graham quotes Massey (1984: 43), who states:

Production relations indicate the sites of class relations in the economic structure, but those sites do not designate whole classes as integral, empirical groups of men and women. The fact that people occupy similar places in the relations of production does not in itself imply any other empirical level of coherence, still less any kind of necessary political unity about pre-given common interests . . . All of which means that "whole classes" are rarely actual subjects.

Gibson-Graham's work on class addresses challenging questions concerning the successes and, especially, the failures and partial failures, of the cultural constitution of capitalist hegemony. In their work the complexity, fragility, and disarray of "actually existing" class processes and identities seems to have struck them more urgently than the fixity of traditional class structurings. They have attempted to re-generate a rich, historicized conception of class as fluid, fragmentary, and articulated with other equally important aspects of social existence and subject positions. As they put it elsewhere (Gibson-Graham et al. 2000: ix), "Its never *just* the economy, stupid!" The economy is not a rarified realm separated from culture. They call this mutual constitution of social positionings "overdetermination." Class according to Gibson-Graham is "overdetermined," by which they mean that it is constituted by every other aspect of social life. Cultural geography can potentially contribute to the understanding of these intersecting processes that constitute class relations.

Gibson-Graham (1996: 52) defines classes not as social groupings, but as processes and experiences of 'exploitation' – the producing, appropriating, and the distributing of surplus labor. In this they endorse a dynamic and relational approach defining classes in terms of ongoing, antagonistic, and mutually constitutive relations. They wish to simultaneously examine the large-scale political-economic structures of exploitation and intense feelings attached to the experience of exploitation. The emotional life of classes is clearly more than psychological in nature; there is a cultural dimension to be explored. There are cultural narratives of exploitation and appropriation that organize and stabilize emotional responses to class exploitation (Gibson-Graham et al. 2000: 1–22). Although they place perhaps undue emphasis on the power of these cultural discourses, they nevertheless present a beguiling thesis on the necessity of imagining beyond the hegemony of capitalism. They refuse to see capitalism as an all-powerful, all-encompassing totality; instead they seek out not only the contradictions of capitalism, but noncapitalist processes (including importantly unpaid domestic labor). They believe that such noncapitalist processes are far more prevalent and varied than those on either the right or the left tend to believe. They seek to examine various processes of exploitation through empirical investigation, rather than presuming the relations among exploitation, property ownership, domination and consciousness.

Analyses such as Gibson-Graham's productively question and complicate questions of consciousness, intentionality and complicity. We see cultural geographers as particularly well placed to continue the empirical research necessary to more fully understand the cultural and place-based dimensions of the lived and emotional experience of class – not to consider the cultural and discursive dimension as primary – but to see the investigation of these dimensions of class as important to the task of doing cultural geography. Although we assume that they are unstable, contradictory, fragmented, and porous, we nevertheless think that it makes sense to talk in terms of classes and perhaps most importantly to investigate how they are restructuring globally. A principal challenge then, is first to discover if we are correct in assuming that there is sufficient coherence to the notion of class for it to be a useful explanatory concept and second how the idea of culture may be of use in this pursuit.

Once various conceptual problems of defining class in empirically based, non-essentialist terms have been confronted and at least tentatively resolved, a revamped cultural geographic perspective on class and related processes could prove useful in the search for richer understandings of day-to-day practices and material conditions of power, exploitation, and oppression as they work out in particular places and as they participate in the production of particular places and relationships between places. Such class processes would include loosely structured, but largely uncoordinated actions which have unintended consequences and unacknowledged conditions. This perspective would entail a non-individualistic, relational perspective. Nevertheless it would have to connect to issues of agency, subjectivity, and consciousness to political-economic structurings. Understanding of the contingent, fluid, and complex, but nonetheless structured, relations among class, gender, nationality, and race can be broadened through studies of their interdependent constitution in (and through) particular places, types of spaces, and relations between places at a variety of spatial scales, including the global.

NOTES

1. An example of such studies is Argyle's (1994) *The Psychology of Social Class*, based on large-scale social surveys of attitudes such as attitudes toward work, lifestyles, neighboring, and child-rearing patterns, and psychological variables such as self-esteem, happiness, and mental health.
2. Crang 1998 includes an interesting chapter on "cultures of production," but class as a concept is barely addressed.
3. Exceptions include Charlesworth (2000), who attempts to convey "a phenomenology of the working class experience" – an in-depth sociological study of alienation in a deindustrializing town where unemployment is high and the sense of dignity and distinctive class culture is rapidly being lost.
4. Some theorists such as Giddens (1981) distinguish between class consciousness as antagonistic and class awareness as politically neutral. We use class consciousness here in the more general sense of class awareness.
5. An example of class feelings was recently reported in a Mori Social Values Survey (AOL Aug. 16, 2002). It showed that 68 percent of the British public claim to be "working class and proud of it," This is compared to 52 percent as recently as 1999. Furthermore of those who identified themselves as middle class 55 percent said they had "working class feelings". Richard Scase, a sociologist from Kent University, believes that job insecurity and disillusionment among professionals as well as a fashion he calls "working class chic" may explain these feelings. Whatever the reason it seems clear that people have class feelings which are very real and meaningful to them.
6. The term "underclass" was popularized by Myrdal (1962) and "culture of poverty" by Oscar Lewis (1969); these have been appropriated by the American right to blame the victims of poverty for their perpetuation of poverty through the generations and their dependence on welfare. These theoretical positions also tend to lay the blame on welfare programs. (For a critique see Philo 1995.)
7. Bourdieu (1968: 706) says that he would prefer to use the term culture if he were not afraid of being misunderstood because the term is "overdetermined."
8. See Jackson and Crang (2001).

REFERENCES

Anderson, K. and Gale, F. 1999: *Inventing Places: Studies in Cultural Geography*. Melbourne: Longman Cheshire.

Argyle, M. 1994: *The Psychology of Social Class*. London: Routledge.

Barnes, T. J. and Hannah, M. 2001: Guest editorial: The place of numbers: histories, geographies, and theories of quantification. *Environment and Planning D: Society and Space* A 19, 379–83.

Bennett, T. 1990: *Outside Literature*. London: Routledge.

Bourdieu, P. 1968: Structuralism and the theory of sociological knowledge. *Social Research*, 35, 681–706.

Bourdieu, P. 1984: *Distinction: A Social Critique of the Judgement of Taste*. Cambridge, MA: Harvard University Press.

Brown W. 1995: Wounded attachments: late modern oppositional political formations. In J. Rajchman, ed., *The Identity in Question*. New York: Routledge.

Butler, J. 1990: *Gender Trouble: Feminism and the Subversion of Identity*. London: Routledge.

Butler, J. 1999: Performativity's social magic. In E. Shusterman, ed., *Bourdieu: A Critical Review*. Oxford: Blackwell.

Charlesworth, S. 2000: *A Phenomenology of Working Class Experience*. Cambridge: Cambridge University Press.

Chen, K.-C. 1996a: Cultural studies and the politic of internationalisation: an interview with Stuart Hall by Kuan-Hsing Chen. In D. Morley and K.-C. Chen, eds., *Stuart Hall: Critical Dialogues in Cultural Studies*. London: Routledge.

Chen, K.-C. 1996b: Post-Marxism: between/beyond critical postmodernism and cultural studies. In D. Morley and K.-C. Chen, eds., *Stuart Hall: Critical Dialogues in Cultural Studies*. London: Routledge.

Clegg, S. 1989: *Frameworks of Power*. London: Sage.

Cooke, D. 1996: Is class a difference that makes a difference? *Radical Philosophy* 773, 17–26.

Cooke, P. 1989: *Localities: The Changing Face of Urban Britain*. London: Unwin Hyman.

Cosgrove, D. 1983: Towards a radical cultural geography. *Antipode* 15, 1–11.

Cosgrove, D. 1984: *Social Formation and Symbolic Landscape*. London: Croom Helm.

Cosgrove, D. and Daniels, S., eds. 1988: *The Iconography of Landscape: Essays on the Symbolic Representation, Design and Use of Past Environments*. Cambridge: Cambridge University Press.

Crang, M. 1997: Cultural turns and the (re)constitution of economic geography. In R. Lee and J. Wills, eds., *Geographies of Economies*. London: Arnold.

Crang, M. 1998: *Cultural Geography*. London: Routledge.

Crawford, M. 1992: The world is a shopping mall. In M. Sorkin, ed., *Variations on a Theme Park: The New American City and the End of the Public Sphere*. New York: Hill and Wang.

Crompton, R. 1998: *Class and Stratification: An Introduction to Current Debates*. Cambridge: Polity Press.

Duncan, J. 1980: The superorganic in American cultural geography. *Annals of the Association of American Geographers* 70, 181–98.

Duncan, J. S. and Duncan, N. G. 2003: *Landscapes of Privilege: The Politics of the Aesthetic in Suburban America*. New York: Routledge.

Femia, J. V. 1981: *Gramsci's Political Thought: Hegemony, Consciousness, and the Revolutionary Process*. Oxford: Clarendon.

Fraser, N. 1995: From redistribution to recognition? Dilemmas of justice in a post-Socialist age. *New Left Review* 212, 68–94.

Fraser, N. 1997: *Justice Interruptus: Critical Reflections on the Postsocialist Condition*. London: Routledge.

Fraser, N. 1999: Social justice in the age of identity politics: redistribution, recognition and participation. In L. Ray, and A. Sayer, eds., *Culture and the Economy After the Cultural Turn*. London: Sage, 25–52.

Gibson-Graham, J. K. 1996: *The End of Capitalism (As We Knew It): A Feminist Critique of Political Economy*. Oxford: Blackwell.

Gibson-Graham, J. K. 1997: Re-placing class in economic geographies: possibilities for a new class politics. In R. Lee and J. Wills, eds., *Geographies of Economies*. London: Arnold.

Gibson-Graham, J. K., Resnick, S. T., and Wolff, R. D. 2000: Introduction: class in a post-structuralist frame. In J. K. Gibson-Graham, S. T. Resnick, R. Wolff, and D. Class, eds., *Class and its Others*. Minneapolis: University of Minnesota Press.

Giddens, A. 1981: *A Contemporary Critique of Historical Materialism*. London: Macmillan.

Goldthorpe, J., et al. 1969: *The Affluent Worker in the Class Structure*. Cambridge: Cambridge University Press.

Guha, R. 1997: *Dominance without Hegemony: History and Power in Colonial India*. London: Harvard University Press.

Hall, S. 1996: Gramsci's relevance for the study of race and ethnicity. In D. Morley and K.-H. Chen, eds., *Stuart Hall: Critical Dialogues*. New York: Routledge.

Hall, S., ed. 1997: *Representation: Cultural Representations and Signifying Practices*. London: Sage.

Harvey, D. 2001: *Spaces of Capital: Toward a Critical Geography*. Edinburgh: Edinburgh University Press.

Jackson, P. 2000: Rematerializing social and cultural geography. *Social and Cultural Geography* 1, 9–14

Jackson, P. and Crang, P. 2001: Consuming geographies. In *British Cultural Studies*. Oxford: Oxford University Press, 327–42.

Kearns, G. and Withers, C. W. J. 1991: *Urbanising Britain: Essays on Class and Community in the Nineteenth Century*. Cambridge: Cambridge University Press.

Laclau, E. and Mouffe, C. 1985: *Hegemony and Socialist Strategy: Towards a Radical Democratic Politics*. London: Verso.

Laclau, E. 1994: Introduction. In E. Laclau, ed., *The Making of Political Identities*. London: Verso.

Latour, B. 1999a: *Pandora's Hope: Essays on the Reality of Science Studies*. Cambridge, MA: Harvard University Press.

Latour, B. 1999b: On recalling ANT. In J. Law and J. Hassard, eds., *Actor Network Theory and After*. Oxford: Blackwell, 15–25.

Law, J. 1994: *Organizing Modernity*. Oxford: Blackwell.

Lewis, O. 1969: The possessions of the poor. *Scientific American* 221, 114–24.

Martin, R. 2001: The geographer as a social critic: getting indignant about income inequality. *Transactions of the Institute of British Geographers* 26, 267–72

Massey, D. 1984: *Spatial Divisions of Labour: Social Structures and the Geography of Production*. London: Macmillan.

McDowell, L. 2000: Economy, culture, difference and justice. In I. Cook et al., eds., *Cultural Turns/Geographical Turns*. London: Longman, 166–81.

Mitchell, D. 1996: *The Lie of the Land: Migrant Workers and the California Landscape*. Minneapolis: University of Minnesota Press.

Mitchell, D. 2000: *Cultural Geography: A Critical Introduction*. Oxford: Blackwell.

Mori Social Values Survey, AOL, Aug. 16, 2002.

Myrdal, G. 1962: *Challenge to Affluence*. New York: Pantheon.

Norton, W. 2000: *Cultural Geography: Themes, Concepts, Analyses*. Oxford: Oxford University Press.

Peet, R. 1997: The cultural production of economic forms. In R. Lee and J. Wills, eds., *Geographies of Economies*. London: Arnold, 28–46.

Philo, C. 1995: Where is poverty? The hidden geography of poverty in the United Kingdom. In C. Philo, ed., *Off the Map: The Geography of Poverty in the UK*. London: Child Poverty Action Group.

Philo, C. and Kearns, G. 1993: *Selling Places: The City as Cultural Capital Past and Present*. Oxford: Pergamon.

Pred, A. and Watts, M. 1992: *Reworking Modernity: Capitalism and Symbolic Discontent*. New Brunswick, NJ: Rutgers University Press.

Ray, L. and Sayer, A., eds. 1999: *Culture and the Economy After the Cultural Turn*. London: Sage.

Resnick, S. and Wolff, R. 1987: *Knowledge and Class: A Marxian Critique of Political Economy*. Chicago: University of Chicago Press.

Sadler, D. 2003: Concepts of class in contemporary economic geography. In E. Shepard and T. Barnes, eds., *A Companion to Economic Geography*. Oxford: Blackwell, 325–40.

Sayer, A. 1999: Valuing culture and economy. In L. Ray and A. Sayer, eds., *Culture and the Economy After the Cultural Turn*. London: Sage, 53–75.

Sayer, A. and Walker, R. 1992: *The New Social Economy: Reworking the Division of Labour.* Oxford: Blackwell.

Sennett, R. and Cobb, J. 1973: *The Hidden Injuries of Class.* New York: Vintage.

Shields, R. 1992: *Lifestyle Shopping: The Subject of Consumption.* London: Routledge.

Shurmer-Smith, P. 2002: *Doing Cultural Geography.* London: Sage.

Shurmer-Smith P. and Hannam, K. 1994: *Worlds of Desire, Realms of Power: A Cultural Geography.* London: Edward Arnold.

Skeggs, B. 2000: The appearance of class: challenges in gay space. In S. Munt, ed., *Cultural Studies and the Working Class.* London: Cassell.

Smith, A.-M. 1998: *Laclau and Mouffe: The Radical Democratic Imaginary.* London: Routledge.

Smith, N. 2000: What happened to class? *Environment and Planning A* 32, 1011–32.

Soja, E. 1989: *Postmodern Geographies: The Reassertion of Space in Critical Social Theory.* London: Verso.

Thrift, N. and Williams, P. 1987: The geography of class formation. In N. Thrift and P. Williams, eds., *Class and Space: The Making of Urban Society.* London: Routledge.

Williams, R. 1977: *Marxism and Literature.* Oxford: Oxford University Press.

Willis, P. 1977: *Learning to Labour: How Working Class Kids Get Working Class Jobs.* New York: Columbia University Press.

Wright, E. O. 1979: *Class Structure and Income Determination.* London: Academic Press.

Wright, E. O. 1985: *Classes.* London: Verso.

Wright, E. O. 1989: *The Debate on Classes.* London: Verso.

Wright, E. O. 2000: *Class Counts: Student Edition.* Cambridge: Cambridge University Press.

Zukin, S. 1991: *Landscapes of Power: From Detroit to Disney World.* Berkeley: University of California Press.

Chapter 18

Sexuality

Richard Phillips

Introduction

By beginning to address questions of sexuality and sex, cultural and other geographers have not only drawn attention to some hitherto-uncharted human geographies, they have also thrown a new form of critical light upon some otherwise familiar places. To explain how they have done this and what it has achieved, I want to begin with a series of case studies, snapshots of real and imagined geographies: a scene from Gayfest, a gay and lesbian festival in Manchester, England; an illustrative map that appeared in a British colonial adventure story set in southern Africa; and a street scene in the United States suburb of Levittown (figures 18.1 to 18.3). These diverse images are associated with a variety of geography's overlapping subfields – including urban, historical, political, postcolonial, and cultural geographies. They do have something important in common, though, since each is shaped in some way by sexual identities and relationships. By sexual, I refer to both sexuality and gender. These are complex and interrelated. Put simply, a person's sex is defined by their anatomy as male or female, whereas their gender is defined with reference to the social roles they learn and perform as men or women. Sexuality has been defined differently in different historical and geographical contexts; today in western countries considerable attention is paid to the gender of a person's sexual partners, which define him or her as heterosexual, homosexual, or bisexual (though members of these groups sometimes use different terms to identify themselves). Rather than elaborating abstract definitions of sexuality and gender, though, I will suggest some of their tangible, geographical meanings and outcomes by introducing the images (which are examined in greater detail later on).

Gayfest presents an overtly compelling illustration of the way in which sexuality and gender can shape human geographies. The festival functions not only as a party but also, more seriously, a marginalized sexual group's assertion of their existence – and right to exist – in society and in a particular area, known locally as the 'gay village.' Gayfest reveals relationships between sexuality and space that are present, if less overtly or tangibly, elsewhere. The second image, an illustration that appeared in the opening pages of Rider Haggard's bestselling colonial adventure

Figure 18.1   Gayfest, Manchester, UK, 2001 (courtesy of Alexandra Hopps)

story, *King Solomon's Mines* (1885), shows a map that led the book's male heroes
to some treasure. It portrays the story's African setting as the body of a woman.
The map raises questions about how, why, and with what effect textual and other
intangible geographies have been sexualized. The final image appears to depict an
'innocently' asexual place: an area of 1950s suburban housing in the United States.
Yet this, perhaps more than anywhere, was constructed around expectations about
sexual behavior. It would be impossible to understand Levittown without understanding that the people who lived there were expected to form heterosexual relationships, the women to have babies and raise children.

The three snapshots raise questions about how geographies are shaped by sexual
relationships and identities. The remainder of the chapter examines these themes:
by charting the evolution of cultural geographies of sexuality and gender, with
emphasis upon the former (see chapter 6 for a fuller discussion of gender); by identifying present trends in these closely related subfields; and by pointing towards
some of the most exciting developments and research directions within this subfield.
These themes – evolution, trends, and directions – are examined with reference to
the two main forms of cultural sexual geographies, which correspond to a division
within cultural geography more generally, between the analysis of concrete and
representational spaces.

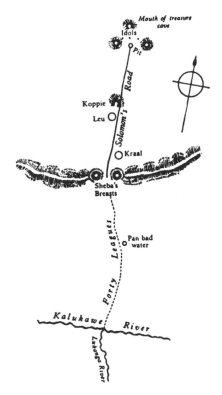

Figure 18.2 Map from *King Solomon's Mines*, by H. Rider Haggard (1885, frontispiece)

Figure 18.3 The US suburb of Levittown (Gans 1967, frontispiece)

(Sub)cultural Spaces

The image with which I began – that of a celebration, but also a policiticized assertion of identities, a territorial claim, and a critical transgression of dominantly heterosexual public space – invokes many of the issues that geographers began to
confront in the 1980s, when they first admitted questions of sexuality to the disciplinary agenda. These (mainly urban) geographers were interested in overtly sexualized spaces and groups, and paid particular attention to gay men and female
prostitutes (on the latter, see Symanski 1974; Hubbard 1998).

Manuel Castells' influential book, *The City and the Grassroots* (1983), mapped
the emergence and development of gay residential areas and "places where gays
gather" including bars and social clubs (Castells 1983: 148). Castells found that
maps of gay residential areas and gathering places correlated with those of gay
voting patterns. He argued that the emergence of San Francisco's Castro district as
a gay neighborhood contributed to the development of the city's gay community as
a politicized social movement. Researchers in geography, planning and related disciplines have further mapped and examined the significance of gay residential areas,
in works such as *Queers in Space: Communities/Public Places/Sites of Resistance*
(Ingram et al. 1997) and *Mapping Desire: Geographies of Sexualities* (Bell & Valentine 1995). Julie Podmore (2001) has extended Castells' project – originally limited
to gay men – to the analysis of lesbian spaces and community formations. Others
have begun to reflect more critically on the place of these communities within the
capitalist space economy. Quilley's (1997) analysis of the emergence of the gay
village in Manchester addresses the ambivalent mixture of displacement and urban
renewal that gay-identified gentrification has brought, not only to this district but
also to the surrounding areas that have absorbed and traded on its new-found chic.
Larry Knopp (1992) has positioned this form of gentrification within the context,
not of abstract liberation, but of the wider capitalist space economy and land
market. Peter Jackson has noted that only a small proportion – "the most politicized and vocal fraction" (Jackson 1989: 128) – of gay men and lesbians are represented in US gay- and/or lesbian-identified residential areas, and suggested that
some others have been economically excluded. A more critical geography of sexuality would recognize the large numbers of gay and lesbian Americans living in
poverty and/or homelessness, and address the limitations of a geography of sexuality dominated by patterns of consumption – of housing and services.

There are other reasons for the relative smallness of *urban* gay- and lesbian-
identified areas and communities. While many gays and lesbians continue to migrate
to large cities, others remain in or move back to smaller towns and rural areas,
where they tend to be less visible than their urban counterparts. In a study of rural
North Dakota, Jerry Lee Kramer (1995: 213) noted that while he used "the terms
homosexual, gay, lesbian and bisexual," he was "aware that many of the men and
women who do have homoerotic feelings, experiences and behaviors would not
identify as any of these." This finding has been interrogated in more detail by
Angelia Wilson (2000), with reference to the lives and identities of lesbians and gay
men in rural areas of the American South. She has suggested that lesbians and gay
men have found ways of coping and integrating socially and culturally in the wider
rural community. Their tendency not to identify with terms such as gay and lesbian

was not wholly the product of 'closeted' or unformed identities, but, in part, alternative strategies for organizing social and sexual lives. In other places and among other people, still other strategies have emerged. These range from identifying as 'queer' – a radical gesture that inverts a term of homophobic abuse – to eschewing all of these terms and refusing to be labeled. This range of sexual identities presents a partial explanation for the relative smallness of urban gay- and lesbian-identified communities, and it also underlines the complexity of relationships between geographies and sexualities.

Evidence for the geographical variability of gay and lesbian identities in the United States suggests that urban – and, in different ways, rural – spaces are significant for the formation of sexual identities. Sociologist Dick Hebdige helps to explain how and why, in *Subculture, the Meaning of Style* (1979), a book that has been particularly influential in social and cultural geography. Hebdige argues that the "expressive forms and rituals," the material culture and cultural spaces of "subordinate groups," enable members of these groups to recognize each other and also to be recognized by others (Hebdige 1979: 2). Symbolic objects and behaviors, which tend to be displayed and performed within identifiable subcultural spaces, "warn the 'straight' world in advance of a sinister presence – the presence of difference" (Hebdige 1979: 3). Though sometimes products of repression and exclusion, subcultural spaces may facilitate the formation of community and identity. For example, San Francisco's gay population was originally a product of the US Navy's discrimination against homosexuals. The city became a place of exile, but then of empowerment, to men and women who had been dishonorably discharged from their positions in the Pacific Fleet. Though not inevitably, concentrations of gay and lesbian residents and/or consumers may facilitate related processes of community and identity formation. Gill Valentine (1993) stresses that lesbian- and gay-identified areas do not cause communities or identities to form, but they do play an important part in the process, as individuals and groups pass through and draw upon these spaces in the course of their daily lives. With David Bell, she presents a site-specific and "performative" theory of sexuality and sexual identity:

To avoid a rupture of their 'identity' many lesbians use time-space strategies to segregate their audiences. These include establishing geographical boundaries between past and present identities, separating different activity spheres and hence identities in space, expressing a lesbian identity only in formal 'gay spaces,' confining their 'gay' socialising to homes or informal 'gay spaces,' expressing their lesbian identity only in public places at specific times, and altering the layout and decoration of private spaces to conceal clues about their sexual identity from specific people. (Bell & Valentine 1995: 147)

Material spaces become 'humanized' as spaces of community and identity in the course of individuals' and communities' encounters with and in them. More than simply material geographies, these places acquire meaning as they are reflected in the formation of personal and collective memories, bodily displays and performances, desires and fantasies.

Gay and lesbian subcultural spaces may also function as spaces of resistance. Defiant resistance to a homophobic police raid on the Stonewall Inn in New York is widely identified as marking the beginning of the modern struggle for gay and lesbian rights, in 1969. Gay Liberation flourished in the 1970s alongside other, more established civil rights movements including those of women and African Americans. This history of political engagement has continued, in new forms and in response to new challenges. Urban homosexuals have organized in response to AIDS, as Michael Brown has shown in his Vancouver-based study, *Replacing Citizenship: AIDS Activism and Radical Democracy* (Brown 1997). Gay and lesbian activists have also organized to assert their existence and sometimes their political objectives, notably in 'pride' marches and celebrations such as Gayfest and its more spectacular counterparts such as Sydney's Mardi Gras festival and parade.

The politicization of cultural processes by which sexualities are expressed and constituted extends not only to urban material geographies, the subject of this section and of the most important early works on sexual geographies, but also to a series of less tangible spaces. This is illustrated in an essay by Tracy Skelton, which examines resistance – and the spaces of resistance – to allegedly homophobic performances of Jamaican ragga music. Skelton concentrates on resistance to British and American gay organizations such as Outrage!, which led to certain tracks being banned in a number of places, and to action on the part of the record company, which then persuaded the performer to issue an apology. Skelton's analysis of "spaces of resistance" moves far from the concrete urban spaces examined above to consider representations of space and spaces of representation. She suggests, for example, that "in Britain the space of resistance has been predominantly the gay media" (Skelton 1995: 281). This points towards the significance of imaginative geographies of sexual identity and resistance.

Imaginative Geographies

Though traditional cultural geographers privileged material culture (see chapter 2), new cultural geographers have turned increasingly to expressive or imaginative forms including the textual geographies of film, literature, and art (see chapters 27 and 28). Indeed, it is in this area that cultural geographers have made some of their most distinctive contributions to the emerging exploration of geographies of sexualities.

Sexualized geographies have been portrayed in the media, for example, as cultural historian Judith Walkowitz has shown in her analysis of the press coverage of the 'Jack the Ripper' murders in London in 1888. Sensational media reports were accompanied by detailed accounts of their settings: illustrations of the streets where murders took place, maps of the murder sites including escape routes to the affluent and brightly-lit West End, and drawings of the victims. The stories moralized the places in which they were set, presenting the reading public with "an immoral landscape of light and darkness, a nether region of illicit sex and crime, both exciting and dangerous" (Walkowitz 1994: 193). They also promoted certain interrelated ideas about how 'respectable' women should behave and where they should be, particularly at night. The murder victims were portrayed as 'public women' – a euphemism for prostitutes – who held some of the blame for their own fate because of their presence on the streets at night, their defiance of the convention that unaccompanied women should remain within the home. The media-generated panic encouraged and legitimated the emergence of 'night patrols' by male vigilantes, who also called upon men to protect women and to repress brothels and street walkers

– and thereby sought greater control over the sexuality of women. In this manner, imaginative geographies were instrumental in shaping ideas about gender and sexuality, which in turn shaped peoples' sexual identities and lives.

The gendered and sexualized nature of imaginative geographies may also shape relationships between people and land or nature. In an early and influential contribution to feminist cultural history, Annette Kolodny argued that the European colonization and resettlement of North America revolved around gendered and sexualized ideas of nature and land. She identified within American culture an idealization of nature, which she termed pastoralism, and which constructed land as a metaphorical woman:

> Implicit in the metaphor of the land-as-woman was both the regressive pull of material containment and the seductive invitation to sexual assertion: if the Mother demands passivity, and threatens regression, the Virgin apparently invites sexual assertion and awaits impregnation. (Kolodny 1975: 67)

Kolodny argued that the relationship between 'patriarchal' (male-dominated) European-American society and its metaphorically, sexually feminine environment left tangible marks upon the landscape because it shaped the ways in which men regarded and treated the land, in the course of settlement and colonization.

The gendered and sexualized imaginative geographies of American settlement are echoed in other colonial contexts. An important colonial region – the vaguely defined 'East' or 'Orient' – was widely represented by geographers, as well as by painters and writers, as a "sexual *lieu*" (Kabbani 1986: 19). Colonial Africa and its inhabitants were portrayed in extremely sexual terms, as a footnote by Sir Richard Burton, a prominent Fellow of the Royal Geographical Society, illustrates:

> Debauched women prefer negroes on account of the size of their parts. I measured one man in Somali-land who, when quiescent, numbered nearly six inches. This is a characteristic of the negro race and of African animals; e.g. the horse. (Burton 1885: 6)

Europeans filled in the details of their colonial geographies largely according to their own tastes: some populated colonial regions with women in harems or on beaches (Kabbani 1986; Phillips 1999a), others with sexually available boys and men (Aldrich 1993; Phillips 1999b). The form and significance of the sexualization of colonial imaginative geography is illustrated in the map that appeared in the *King Solomon's Mines* (figure 18.2), which has been interpreted by Anne McClintock (1995: 1–3):

> On the one hand, it is a rough sketch of the ground the white men must cross in order to secure the riches of the diamond mines. On the other hand, if the map is inverted, it reveals at once the diagram of a female body. The body is spread-eagled and truncated – the only parts drawn are those that denote female sexuality. . . . At the center of the map lie two mountain peaks called Sheba's Breasts – from which mountain ranges stretch to either side as handless arms. The body's length is inscribed by the right royal way of Solomon's Road, leading from the threshold of the frozen breasts over the navel *koppie* straight as a die to the pubic mound. In the narrative, this mound is named the "Three Witches" and is figured

by a triangle of three hills covered in "dark heather." This dark triangle both points to and conceals the entrances to two forbidden passages: the "mouth of treasure cave" – the vaginal entrance into which the men are led by the black mother, Gagool – and, behind it, the anal pit from which the men will eventually crawl with the diamonds . . .

By portraying protagonists as heroic and virile, and the land as a sexual woman, Haggard was able to make the adventurous act of European conquest appear natural and legitimate – as 'natural' as a man's sexual conquest. Thus, in a general way, sexualized imaginative geographies have naturalized and legitimated colonial acts and power relations.

They have also naturalized certain ideas about sexuality and gender. It is now widely agreed that sexualities are not naturally or biologically determined, but are socially constructed. Michel Foucault's influential *History of Sexuality* (1978) traces the 'invention' of heterosexuality and homosexuality to sexologists in late-nineteenth-century Europe. Previously, sexualities were defined less by the gender of sexual partners than by the nature of sex acts, and the relevant laws reflected this (a man could be convicted of sodomy, for example, regardless of the gender of his sexual partner). New ideas about sexuality were expressed in a variety of contexts and by a variety of professional and amateur sexologists and professionals with interests in sexuality, including lawyers, legislators, doctors, religious leaders and academics – including geographers. For example, Burton, who signed many of his books simply as a Fellow of the Royal Geographical Society, described sexual customs and intervened in sexual politics. He mapped regions in which he claimed certain sexual practices were common – such as a 'Sotadic Zone' in which sex between men was commonly practiced and widely tolerated (Phillips 1999b). In his sexual geographies, Burton charted forms of sexuality and morality, which demonstrated the variety of sexual cultures and asserted the rights of individuals to live their sexual lives without interference. In an age when the government was increasingly regulating sexuality, his interventions were not entirely successful, but they do illustrate the part that geographers can play in shaping understandings of sexuality and sexual morality.

Sexualities are also represented and structured in a series of more abstract imaginative geographies, notably the 'closet.' Eve Sedgwick has called this "the fundamental architecture of gay oppression this century," which "evokes a sense of concealment and erasure typical of lesbian and gay desire" (quoted by Brown 1999: 185). Michael Brown poses the following rhetorical question: "If the closet represents the place where gay and lesbian desire remains hidden, what sort of space is it?" (Brown 1999: 185). His answer includes an analysis of the language of the closet, illustrated for example in a reading of travel writing by Neil Miller – *In Search of Gay America* (1989) and *Out in the World* (1992) – which concentrates on "travels into two of the most closeted places on his tours" (Brown 1999: 185). Figuratively moving between real and imaged closets, Miller's travel books demonstrate the interplay of these two spheres, which together act to structure sexual identities and lives. As a mechanism for the concealment of homosexuality, the closet may function as a vehicle of heterosexual power; this space is a marker and a maker of relationships between homosexual and heterosexual people and places. The next section critically examines heterosexual spaces.

Heterosexual Spaces

Sexuality is not just an attribute of sexual 'others' and their geographies, but of all people and all places – Levittowners and their suburban streets and homes, for instance. David Sibley has shown that it is impossible to understand the social and spatial margins without understanding the processes and imperatives that construct the social center; it is impossible to understand 'deviance' without understanding how certain powerful social groups invent their own 'normality' and use it to reproduce their social power (Sibley 1995: 25).

Overt expressions of sexuality may be particularly unwelcome in certain places, particularly those associated with the family such as homes and suburbs. Yet these places are sexualized in important ways – they are identified with normalized heterosexuality. Heterosexual spaces may reproduce the hegemonic (dominant) sexual order, both ideologically by making this construction of sexuality and the power relations inherent in it appear natural; and materially by physically accommodating and therefore encouraging or enforcing certain heterosexual lifestyles, which are historically constructed rather than 'natural' (Katz 1995). Thus, Julia Cream argues that it is important to make visible and problematize everyday sexual spaces:

We need to know how space is produced as uncontaminated, and shorn of its associations with sexuality. Sexuality is so often hidden away in the upstairs of homes, behind closed doors, or in the upper reaches of the disciplinary house. We need to expose the ways in which it has been excluded, obscured and rendered irrelevant . . . (Cream 1994: 122)

From a critical geographical perspective, this problematization of heterosexualities means seeking "to understand the straightness of our streets as an artifact; to interrogate the presumed *authentic* heterosexual nature of everyday spaces" (Bell et al. 1994: 32). This entails developing sensitivity to the taken-for-granted sexualization of everyday space, and an understanding of how this sexualization may be performatively constructed in places such as homes, streets, workplaces and (less tangibly) national and other symbolic landscapes.

Home, both a place and an idea, is closely linked to normative constructions of gender and sexuality. As a gendered space, it is fundamental to ideas about femininity and masculinity. These ideas were set out in unusually bold terms by the British Victorian moralist, John Ruskin, who labeled man "the doer, the creator, the discoverer" (Ruskin 1887: 135), woman the home-maker whose talents lay in "sweet ordering, arrangement, and decision" (Ruskin 1887: 136). Ruskin idealized the woman who stayed home and made it a "place of Peace; the shelter, not only from all injury, but from all terror, doubt, and division" (Ruskin 1887: 136). These ideas about the proper places of men and women, known as the ideology of the separate spheres, have changed over time but consistently identified the home as the sphere of women (see chapter 5). Society has continued to reward women who 'choose' to stay close to home and family, to spend their days in suburbs such as Levittown, by praising their femininity (Kelly 1993). This was particularly true in the United States in the postwar period, when the FHA (Federal Housing Authority) financed suburban homes for heterosexual nuclear families – while at the same time refusing mortgages to female-headed and other households, as Hayden (1984: 8) explains:

Levit's client was the returning veteran, the beribboned male war hero who wanted his wife to stay home. Women in Levittown were expected to be too busy tending their children to care about a paying job.

From the layout of its housing to the conditions of its mortgage provision, Levittown, like many other state-sponsored suburban housing projects, was a space of closely prescribed sexuality. Contemporary anthropologist Margaret Mead observed some of the sexual attitudes that fed into the design of postwar suburbs. She observed a dominant "belief that every family should have a home of its own" (Mead 1949: 325), and concluded that "all other forms of living are seen as having great disadvantages" (Mead 1949: 326). While people were expected to marry and have children, and while they were only considered worthy of housing if they did, their housing was also designed to ensure that only they were sexually active and reproductive. Their children were also to be segregated, partly in order to preserve their chastity, with boys and girls in different sleeping rooms. This provision, facilitated by the construction of housing with three or more bedrooms, further distinguished FHA housing from some of its predecessors, particularly urban tenements, in which crowded conditions meant multiple occupation of sleeping quarters (Kelly 1993; see Langford 2000).

Public spaces including streets and workplaces also function as heterosexual spaces. Mitchell (2000: 172) notes, for example, that:

heterosexual sex and sexuality have always been quite public. Take the very public marriage ceremony with its various ritual fertility rights, for example, or the simple acceptability of heterosexual couples kissing in public.

The voyeurism and hostility that generally greets equivalent public displays of affection by gays and lesbians underlines the dominance of public space by heterosexuals.

Similarly, many workplaces privilege and reward heterosexuality. In a study of merchant banks in the City of London, Linda McDowell found that the grooming and presentation of workers' bodies and the performance of heterosexuality, whether in the form of homosocial relationships between men or flirtatious heterosexual play between men and women, was central to their success in this potentially lucrative employment.

Being in control of your own presentation and image was vital not only in competition with fellow traders but also in managing relationships with clients – an importance reflected in the body culture of gyms and fitness clubs in the City. Men might adopt a clubby bonhomie with clients while women might deliberately play a mock game of 'seduction.' What this points to is the way that workers have to adopt a series of performances in the different spaces of their work. Gay workers would adopt a heterosexual role during the day to enable them to function in the dealing rooms; all men might have to adopt a stereotypical, thrusting, macho culture. (McDowell 1995: 75)

In this heterosexist environment, women and gay men were made to feel out of place, and/or to conform outwardly to the dominant heterosexual culture. Mc-Dowell concluded that "a hegemonic idealized notion of heterosexual masculinity is the dominant image in the world of merchant banking" (McDowell 1995: 86).

In addition to the home, street and work place, national landscapes are often heterosexual spaces. Sibley suggests that English symbolic landscapes – places and images that represent Englishness and are invoked in English nationalism – are particularly exclusionary, hostile to difference and deviance.

The countryside, as it is represented by those who have a privileged place within it, is the essence of Englishness, so those who are excluded from this purified space are also, in a sense, un-English. . . . I think we can recognize a number of building blocks or key sites of nationalist sentiment, including the family, the suburb and the countryside, all of which implicitly exclude black people, gays and nomadic minorities from the nation. (Sibley 1995: 108)

Sibley argues that in these symbolically important spaces there is a heightened sensitivity to the possibility of "pollution" by the presence of deviants or outsiders such as those mentioned above, whose presence may be seen as a threat to the purity and stability of the social order (Sibley 1995). Indeed, national landscape and nationalism have often been closely allied to reproductive heterosexuality (Mosse 1985). In national and nationalistic literature, for example, Lynne Pearce finds certain "contemporary Scottish and Welsh writers advocating, however indirectly, sexual endogamy – and preferably that which is heterosexual and reproductive" (Pearce 2000: 246). In Northern Ireland, Vincent Quinn notes a general adherence of both Nationalists and Unionists to heterosexual norms. But the heterosexual domination of nationalisms and national landscapes, like that of homes and streets, may be contested (Parker et al. 1992). Quinn suggests that 'coming out' as gay or lesbian in the province may destabilize sectarianism (the conflict between Irish Nationalism and United Kingdom Unionism) by promoting nonsectarian primary identifications (Quinn 2000). The heterosexuality of certain spaces may therefore be contested, and this may have far-reaching implications for the homes, workplaces, and nations that are affected.

Conclusions

Geographies of sexualities have drawn attention to the positions – often the plights – of sexual minorities. In so doing, they have addressed a broader set of academic questions and political issues, concerned with relationships between society and space. These questions and issues are concerned with social and spatial diversity; with spaces of inequality and exclusion; and with geographies and politics of identity. The mechanisms of exclusion and identity formation are complex. Most tangibly, for example, the United States has subsidized housing for nuclear families and excluded homosexuals from certain forms of employment (such as the military). Alongside these formal processes and material geographies, the identification and exclusion of certain groups has operated through a range of cultural representations and politics. Certain imaginative geographies and geographical discourses have been particularly significant for the construction of sexual identities and for resistance to exclusion and marginalization. It is here that cultural geographers have made some of their most important contributions to understandings of relationships between sexuality and space. Approaching this question at its broadest level, they have critically contextualized geographies of sexual minorities. Sibley in particular has shown how the marginality of some can only be understood as a product of the privilege and power of others, and how this has a spatial dimension. Thus, while geographies of sexuality may begin in urban enclaves, and with the important project of giving voice to and otherwise empowering sexual minorities, these critical geographies must ultimately reach out to other, less overtly sexualized people and places. By showing how these superficially 'normal' spaces actively normalize heterosexuality and thereby naturalize the power of heterosexuals at the expense of others, critical geographies of sexuality may help to disrupt compulsory heterosexuality and the particular form of patriarchy upon which it rests. This contributes not only to a gay and lesbian political agenda, but also to a much broader critical politics. Since sexuality is not a discrete area of social life, but one with close and complex relationships to others including gender and race, and one which structures a wide range of real and imagined geographies including homes, workplaces and nations, geographies of sexuality must leave no stones unturned. Geographies of sexuality may therefore work on a variety of levels to address a variety of issues, some long-standing, others more recent and urgent. At the local level, for example, they may address the family homes and classrooms in which discrimination on the basis of sexuality is often perpetuated. On the national and international level, geographies of sexualities may address such problems such as the spread and impact of HIV/AIDS and other sexually transmitted diseases in the context of a globalizing world (Altman 2001; Brown 1995). Critical geographies of sexuality may thereby play some part not only in explaining the world, but also in changing it.

REFERENCES

Aldrich, R. 1993: *The Seduction of the Mediterranean: Writing, Art and Homosexual Fantasy*. London: Routledge.

Altman, D. 2001: *Global Sex*. Chicago: University of Chicago Press.

Bell, D. and Valentine, G. 1995: *Mapping Desire: Geographies of Sexualities*. London: Routledge.

Bell, D., Binnie, J., Cream, J., and Valentine, G. 1994: All hyped up and no place to go. *Gender, Place and Culture* 1, 31–47.

Bell, D. and Valentine, G. 1995: The sexed self: strategies of performance, sites of resistance. In N. Thrift and S. Pile, eds., *Mapping the Subject*. London: Routledge, 143–57.

Brown, M. 1995: Ironies of distance: an ongoing critique of the geography of AIDS. *Environment and Planning D, Society and Space* 13, 159–83.

Brown, M. 1997: *Replacing Citizenship: AIDS Activism and Radical Democracy*. New York: Guilford.

Brown, M. 1999: Travelling through the closet. In J. Duncan and D. Gregory, eds., *Writes of Passage, Reading Travel Writing*. London: Routledge, 185–99.

Burton, R. F. 1885–6: *A Plain and Literal Translation of the Arabian Nights Entertainments, Now Entitled the Book of a Thousand Nights and a Night*. Benares: Kama Shastra Society.

Castells, M. 1983: *The City and the Grassroots*. London: Edward Arnold.

Cream, J. 1994: Review: sexuality and space. *Gender, Place and Culture* 1(1), 120–2.

Foucault, M. 1978: *The History of Sexuality, Volume 1*. London: Penguin.

Gans, H. 1967: *The Levittowners*. London: Allen Lane.

Haggard, R. 1885: *King Solomon's Mines*. London: Cassell.

Hayden, D. 1984: *Redesigning the American Dream*. New York: Norton.

Hebdige, D. 1979: *Subculture, the Meaning of Style*. London: Methuen.

Hubbard, P. 1998: Sexuality, immorality and the city: red-light districts and the marginalisation of female street prostitutes. *Gender Place and Culture* 5, 55–76.

Ingram, G. B., Bouthillette, A. M., and Retter, Y., eds. 1997: *Queers in Space: Communities/Public Places/Sites of Resistance*. Seattle: Bay Press.

Jackson, P. 1989: *Maps of Meaning*. London: Unwin Hyman.

Kabbani, R. 1986: *Imperial Fictions, Europe's Myths of Orient*. London, Pandora.

Katz, J. N. 1995: *The Invention of Heterosexuality*. New York: Plume.

Kelly, B. M. 1993: *Expanding the American Dream: Building and Rebuilding Levittown*. Albany: SUNY Press.

Knopp, L. 1992: Sexuality and the spatial dynamics of capitalism. *Environment and Planning D, Society and Space* 10, 651–69.

Kolodny, A. 1975: *The Lay of the Land*. Chapel Hill: University of North Carolina Press.

Kramer, J. L. 1995: Bachelor farmers and spinsters: gay and lesbian identities and communities in rural North Dakota. In D. Bell and G. Valentine, eds., *Mapping Desire: Geographies of Sexualities*. London: Routledge, 200–13.

Langford, B. 2000: *Margins of the City: Towards a Dialectic of Suburban Desire*. In R. Phillips, D. Watt, and D. Shuttleton, eds., *De-centring Sexualities: Politics and Representations Beyond the Metropolis*. London: Routledge, 64–80.

McClintock, A. 1995: *Imperial Leather: Race, Gender and Sexuality in the Colonial Contest*. London: Routledge.

McDowell, L. 1995: Bodywork: heterosexual performances in city workplaces. In D. Bell and G. Valentine, eds., *Mapping Desire: Geographies of Sexualities*. London: Routledge, 75–95.

Mead, M. 1949: *Male and Female, a Study of the Sexes in a Changing World*. London: Gollancz.

Mitchell, D. 2000: *Cultural Geography, A Critical Introduction*. Oxford: Blackwell.

Mosse, G. L. 1985: *Nationalism and Sexuality, Middle Class Morality and Sexual Norms in Modern Europe*. Madison: University of Wisconsin Press.

Parker, A., Russo, M., Sommer, D., and Yaeger, P., eds. 1992: *Nationalisms and Sexualities*. London: Routledge.

Pearce, L. 2000: Devolutionary desires. In R. Phillips, D. Watt, and D. Shuttleton, eds., *De-centring Sexualities: Politics and Representations Beyond the Metropolis*. London: Routledge. 241–57.

Phillips, R. 1999a: Sexual politics of authorship: reading the travels and translations of Richard and Isabel Burton. *Gender, Place and Culture* 6(3), 241–57.

Phillips, R. 1999b: Writing travel and mapping sexuality: Richard Burton's Sotadic zone. In J. Duncan and D. Gregory, eds., *Writes of Passage, Reading Travel Writing*. London: Routledge, 70–91.

Phillips, R. and Watt, D. 2000: Introduction. In R. Phillips, D. Watt, and D. Shuttleton, eds., *De-centring Sexualities: Politics and Representations Beyond the Metropolis*. London: Routledge, 1–18.

Podmore, J. 2001: Lesbians in the crowd: gender, sexuality and visibility along Montreal's Boulevard St. Laurent. *Gender, Place and Culture* 8(4), 333–56.

Quilley, S. 1997: Constructing Manchester's "New Urban Village": gay space in the entrepreneurial city. In G. B. Ingram, A. M. Bouthillette, and Y. Retter, eds., *Queers in Space: Communities/Public Places/Sites of Resistance*. Seattle: Bay Press, 275–93.

Quinn, V. 2000: On the borders of allegiance: identity politics in Ulster. In R. Phillips, D. Watt, and D. Shuttleton, eds., *De-centring Sexualities: Politics and Representations Beyond the Metropolis*. London: Routledge.

Ruskin, J. 1887: *Sesame and Lillies*. Orpington, Kent: George Allen.

Sibley, D. 1995: *Geographies of Exclusion: Society and Difference in the West*. London: Routledge.

Skelton, T. 1995: Jamaican Ragga and gay resistance. In D. Bell and G. Valentine, eds., *Mapping Desire: Geographies of Sexualities*. London: Routledge, 264–83.

Symanski, R. 1974: Prostitution in Nevada. *Annals of the Association of American Geographers* 64, 357–77.

Valentine, G. 1993: Negotiating and managing multiple sexual identities: lesbian time space strategies. *Transactions of the Institute of British Geographers* 18, 237–48.

Walkowitz, J. 1994: *City of Dreadful Delight: Narratives of Sexual Danger in Late Victorian London*. London: Virago.

Wilson, A. 2000: Getting your kicks on Route 66!: stories of gay and lesbian life in rural America, c. 1950–1970s. In R. Phillips, D. Watt, and D. Shuttleton, eds., *De-centring Sexualities: Politics and Representations Beyond the Metropolis*. London: Routledge, 199–216.

Chapter 19

The Body

Michael Landzelius

The Body Reembraced

In concluding his *The Production of Space*, Lefebvre asserted that "Western philosophy has *betrayed* the body; it has actively participated in the great process of metaphorization that has abandoned the body; and it has denied the body" (1991: 407). Despite roughly 2,000 years of betrayal, Lefebvre, writing in 1974, displayed optimism: "Today the body is establishing itself firmly, as base and foundation, beyond philosophy, beyond discourse, and beyond the theory of discourse. Theoretical thought, carrying reflection on the subject and the object beyond the old concepts, has reembraced the body along with space, in space, and as the generator (or producer) of space" (1991: 407). Lefebvre's account of the unfolding of the body–space nexus is situated in Marxism, yet also critically builds upon authors important in poststructuralism and deconstruction, such as Freud, Lacan, and Kristeva (see Blum & Nast 1996; Gregory 1997; Pile 1996), as well as Nietzsche and Heidegger (see Elden 2001; Merrifield 1995). Geographers such as Gregory (1994, 1997), Merrifield (1993), Pile (1996), Shields (1989, 1991, 1999), and Stewart (1995a), incorporate aspects of Lefebvre's theorization of the body. Yet his work continues to be controversial and has been variously characterized as romantic (Thrift 1997a), melancholic (Gregory 1997), teleological (Keith & Pile 1993), and masculinist (Blum & Nast 1996; Pile 1996).

The French edition of *The Production of Space* was published roughly 30 years ago, and the three decades since have seen the emergence of second and third wave feminism, poststructuralism, deconstruction, a renewed interest in psychoanalysis, the development of cultural studies, postcolonialism, queer, nonrepresentational, and actor-network theories – to name but a few important strands of thought which have dismantled Western metaphysics. Differences apart, a shared critique in this literature concerns the Cartesian subject's view from nowhere: the masculinist and simultaneously epistemological, moral, and political 'god-trick' (Haraway 1991: 189) through which "[t]he standpoint of the privileged, their particular experience and standards, is constructed as normal and neutral" (Young 1990b: 116). In emphasizing the production of knowledge, identity, ethics and politics as positioned practices embedded in particular social and cultural conditions, these strands of thought have turned to the body as a key site for understanding the workings and differentiation of society and thus also for the reworking of social theory as well as politics (for brief accounts, see Shilling 2001; Turner 2000).

The response in geography to this growing discourse on the body was slow. Through a number of theoretical avenues, geographers already engaged with issues that invoked the body. Behavioral research based upon environmental psychology as well as symbolic interactionism clearly implicated embodiment (see, for example, Cox & Golledge 1981; Moore & Golledge 1976). Yet, the constraints of behaviorism and mind/body dualism disallowed the articulation of the body as a particular site of inquiry. In critique of then fashionable spatial science approaches, humanistic geographers addressed the body–space nexus particularly from phenomenological perspectives (Buttimer 1976; Ley & Samuels 1978; Pickles 1985; Porteous 1990; Relph 1976; Seamon 1979; Tuan 1974, 1977). However, the influence of phenomenology decreased in a period when poststructuralist antihumanism highlighted diversity and questioned commonality and universalism. In addition, Hägerstrand's (1967, 1970) time-geography briefly surfaced among critical and feminist geographers in arguments that challenged universalist assumptions and anchored human behavior in the embodied time-spaces of everyday life (Dyck 1990; Miller 1983; Palm & Pred 1978; Pred 1981, 1984; Thrift 1983). Yet, it was soon claimed that "[t]he notation of the body in time-geography as a path which does not merge depends on this particular masculine repression of the bodily" (Rose 1993: 33; for other criticisms, see Gregory 1994; Harvey 1989).

The 1990s witnessed a radical increase in geographical research sensitive to positionality, particularity, and specificity. In this research, the body loses its definite article and becomes a plurality of differentiated bodies. Given this plurality, empirical work covers diverse social categories such as gender, sexuality, race, ethnicity, disability, illness, and age. Spatial contexts correspondingly vary from merchant banks of the present to colonies of the past. In terms of theory, geographers build upon approaches developed in other fields such as philosophy, psychoanalysis, general social theory and cultural studies. Foucault's theorizing of disciplined and different bodies as emerging out of different constellations of power and knowledge is immensely important. A vast number of citations in geographies of the body are also from works by Judith Butler, Moira Gatens, and Elisabeth Grosz. Frequently mentioned are also Susan Bordo, Rosi Braidotti, Gilles Deleuze and Félix Guattari, Donna Haraway, Sandra Harding, Julia Kristeva, and Iris Marion Young. In addition, many 'second hand' references to Jacques Lacan appear, whereas the psychoanalyst Paul Schilder and body theorists such as Pierre Bourdieu, Norbert Elias, and Maurice Merleau-Ponty are rarely cited. Without normative intent, one can make the observation that a geographical text on the body has yet to appear that could be called a 'paradigm' in terms of being not only cited but also applied by fellow geographers.

Geographical work on the body can to a large extent be characterized as a response and contribution to the discourse on identity politics, in which class politics as conventionally understood in terms of [male] labor versus [male] capital are displaced by interrogations of the nature and construction of subjectivity and selfhood. In this discourse, embodiment refers to how individuals literally incorporate social relations, psychological traits and cultural meanings, as well as to how bodily engagement in practices not only reiterates but potentially also transforms the world. This invocation of the body as a key site of personal experience, social distinction and political struggle results in a political edge different from class-based politics, as is clear in the employment of terms such as 'racism,' 'sexism,' 'heterosexism,' 'ableism,' 'ageism,' and so forth. A key issue in recent geographies of the body concerns how masculinist universalism in heteropatriarchal society produces normative spaces based upon the desires and characteristics of able-bodied and heterosexual men – distinctions understood to dominate over differentiation within this category in terms of, for example, class, education, race, and ethnicity. The resulting spaces are understood to exclude from recognition, in a both corporeal and discursive sense, 'deviant' groups and individuals and thus to both inhibit and devalue their particular embodied identities. In this fashion, much recent literature on body politics replaces analyses of class and structural economic conditions with analyses of subjectivation, oppression, and domination. While skeptical towards conventional modernist accounts of agency and intentionality, contemporary work explores spatial gaps in the conjunctions of power and conceives of the body as a potential force of political repositioning able to disrupt performative reiteration. In this context, Harvey approvingly observes that "a wide range of bodily practices and choices can be embedded in the circulation of capital" (1998: 412), yet further argues that to neglect the particular social relations of capitalism amounts to a foundational "body reductionism" that fails to identify "the direction as opposed to the locus of political action" (1998: 415). Such criticisms alongside Knopp's reasonable claim that "we construct sexuality and gender along with class, not independently of it" (1992: 652) show the importance of taking seriously the political as well as epistemological differences between positions.

The Body–Space Nexus

Different approaches to the body are indeed represented in geography, yet the majority of work is quite univocal in its reiterated references to the set of influential authors mentioned above. There is thus no clear articulation of a specifically geographical take on the body. In sociology, Turner critiques a "decorative sociology," which is "merely a description of the cultural representation of the body (2000: 481). Williams and Bendelow similarly argue that "sociology should itself be fundamentally embodied; theorising not so much about bodies . . . but from bodies as lived entities" (1998: 209). In geography, Thrift critiques a view, "pervasive . . . in current cultural geography" (1999: 318), "that human beings are engaged in building discursive worlds by actively constructing webs of significance which are laid out over a physical substrate" (1999: 300). Longhurst stresses that "[o]ne of the downsides of social constructionism . . . is that it can render the body incorporeal, fleshless, fluidless, little more than a linguistic territory" (2001: 23). In geography, such approaches are exemplified by analyses in which bodies are present only as particularized signifiers, and spaces are taken-for-granted as in themselves neutral, and as gendered, racialized or in other ways particularized and politicized only through the presence and discursive dominance of a certain individual or group.

Importantly, a number of themes in recent geographical research point towards a more clearly articulated geographical take on the body–space nexus that high-lights ways in which physical substrates and bodies are interdependently constituted as well as constitutive of social relations and cultural meanings. Before turning to these themes, it should be stressed that the body, as this companion clearly shows, is implicated in much recent work in cultural geography. Hence, as already noted, the body has been discussed in feminist, poststructuralist, and psychoanalytic approaches as well as cast in terms of the gendered and sexed body, the racialized body, the young body, and the performative body. These areas are all addressed in separate chapters in this volume.

Epistemology and the body

Feminist geographers in particular have identified masculinist, heterosexist, and universalist disciplinary foundations in geography. Grounded in asymmetrical active/passive binaries, the model researcher has been a disembodied male research-ing an object subjected to the male gaze and molded by incarnations of passive, woman, body, and nature. Such binaries are implicated not only in a general dis-avowal of the body and in the dominance of the conceptual over the corporeal, of culture over nature, but also in notions of core versus peripheral areas of the disci-pline, of active [male] exploration and mapping of a passive [female] landscape, and so forth (see Bondi 1997; Callard 1998; Chouinard & Grant 1995; Johnson 1994; Longhurst 1995, 1997, 2001; McDowell 1999; Nash 1996; Rose 1992, 1993, 1995; Stewart 1995a). Issues of disability, impairment, and illness have also encouraged reflection on established disciplinary assumptions. Chouinard (1997, 1999a) and Chouinard and Grant (1995) articulate academic responsibilities in face of the hege-mony of "ableist geographies," and Dorn and Laws critique bio-medical models of disease in arguing that geography needs a "politicized emancipatory phenomenol-ogy" (1994: 106) that incorporates social theory's rediscovery of the body. Simi-larly, Parr challenges medicalized notions of 'mental illness' in geography and suggests that the "mind/bodies of psychiatric patients are contested sites of control," and thereby part of "geographies of resistance" (1999: 197; see also Moss 1999).

Asymmetries between researcher and researched, and encounters with 'others' in fieldwork turn the question of how embodiment and positionality affects knowl-edge production into a particularly important issue. Thorny issues of relativism versus essentialism and objectivism thus unavoidably emerge out of the epistemo-logical incorporation of the body. Bondi identifies the risk that "geographical terms of reference do the work done by essences in other formulations" (1993: 98), and contends that "geographical metaphors of contemporary politics must be informed by conceptions of space that recognize place, position, location and so on as *created*, as *produced*" (1993: 99; see also Smith & Katz 1993). The body is indeed one such geographical term of reference, and a key site in discussions of essentialism. Rose explores how certain feminist alternatives to disembodied masculinism themselves serve to reproduce visualism and notions of control through "tactics [that] work by turning extraordinarily complex power relations into a visible and clearly ordered space that can be surveyed by the researcher" (1997: 310). In contrast to such 'trans-parent reflexivity,' Rose refers to the anti-essentialist concept of performativity in order to suggest that "research [is] a process of constitutive negotiation" (1997:

316) of positions, knowledges, and embodied identities. The quotations from Bondi and Rose illustrate how feminist reflection on positionality deeply implicates the embodiment of identities. Yet, opinions differ with regard to epistemological and methodological responses to this researcher's conundrum of being "captured and enmeshed" (Nast 1998: 110; see also Kobayashi 1994; McDowell 1992; Nelson 1999; Sparke 1998).

Essential here is whether geographers make a specifically spatial argument on embodiment and situatedness, and, accordingly, whether terms such as 'location' and 'position' mean something beyond discursive considerations of difference. Important is also whether the critique of the disembodied mind only concerns the limits of discursive knowledge and the biased constitution of the research object, or if it also invokes another conception of what should be counted as knowledge. Longhurst critiques binary thinking (1995, 1997) and builds an argument around how the fleshy and fluid messiness of bodies challenges established social and spatial boundaries concerning, for example, pregnancy, gender assumptions, workplace behavior, privacy, and exposure (1999, 2000, 2001). Her objective is to make space for politicized microlevel 'corpogeographies' that show how "specificity seeps into generality . . . lived messy materiality seeps into cerebral knowledge" (2001: 135). Yet, messiness in Longhurst's argument suggests specificity *of* discourse more than possibilities *beyond* discourse. Such possibilities, however, are suggested in Lefebvre's antihumanist claim that "long before the analysing, separating intellect, long before formal knowledge, there was an intelligence of the body" (1991: 174), as well as in present nonrepresentational theory and actor-network theory. Hence, Thrift proposes nonrepresentational forms of knowledge beyond discourse and stresses that "a practical or situated way of knowing is contextual, and rooted especially in embodiment" (1996: 33; see also Nash 2000). Similarly, Whatmore (1999) explores agency as a hybridized collective network capacity and then suggests a form of "sensible and relational knowledge of these hybrid worlds" which is dependent upon the human body as a corporeal organism and "the animal sensibilities of our diverse human being" (1999: 35). In terms of disciplinary consequences, questions here concern institutional academic constraints as well as what an epistemology of nondiscursive knowledge would entail in practice, with regard to methods, descriptive protocols, criteria, sharing of results, and so forth.

The body politic and the body

Explorations into relations between the body politic and the body of the individual from a geographical perspective have sought to move away from structural analyses of power towards an understanding of power as embedded in concrete spaces and bodily articulated. In this context, however, the body has been used "for contradictory theoretical agenda" (Longhurst 2001: 19) supporting accounts of disciplinary inscriptions of power as well as theories of empowerment and resistance. This state of affairs illustrates Lefebvre's remark on the body as a contested site that "cannot be destroyed without destroying the social body itself: the carnal, earthly Body is there, every day" (1976: 89). Lefebvre understands the body to be "the point of return, the redress – not the Logos, nor 'the human'" (1976: 89). His antihumanism turns the body into a differential space of hope in the midst of a growing diversity and dysfunctionality of abstract space: "Can the body in its quest for vindication use the resulting interstices as its way back?" (1991: 388). Similarly, much recent geographical work revolves around the body as simultaneously political battleground and site of resistance.

Cresswell (1997; 1999) as well as Sibley (1995; 1999) study how spatial processes of normalization and exclusion in the body politic are interdependent with the identification of individual bodies in terms of deviance through which denigrating meanings are mapped onto real or imagined embodied differences of, for example, female tramps and hobos, travelers, or immigrant communities. Addressing the politico-spatial effects of bodily metaphors of displacement, Cresswell suggests a focus on "geographical interpretation of metaphors as they are thought and acted out in the realms of politics and ideology" (1997: 343), while Sibley relies on object relations theory in his argument for the creation of "progressive, weakly bounded and heterogeneous places" (1999: 127) that are inclusive of difference. In an article on nineteenth-century San Francisco, Craddock studies "ways in which medical theory produced Chinese bodies" (1999: 352) and how this medical framing was underpinned by segregation, racialization, and pathologization of both spaces and bodies. Craddock and Dorn focus on the geography of "nationbuilding through the lens of medical discourse" (2001: 314) in a journal issue that explores how medical interpellations of bodies support exclusionary constructions of national values and identity through processes of othering in reference to health, hygiene, race, illness, and disability.

Addressing the public/private dichotomy, Duncan (1996) focuses on the public/private boundary as immediately related to a politics of the body, yet complexly articulated and spatialized in relation to contested terrains of gender and state intervention. Sharp (1996) explicates how the articulation of dichotomies such as public/private, male/female, and work/home in Eastern Europe under communism continues to have an impact on social struggles concerning symbolic as well as productive and reproductive linkages between women's bodies, the body politic, and nationalist politics. On racialized and heteronormative politics related to issues of public/private and state intervention, Elden argues that "sexual encoding of bodies was part of the larger racial landscape in South Africa during apartheid" (1998: 162), while Kesby, likewise, in a study of postindependence developments in Zimbabwe, shows that "the social construction of space and of gendered bodies is interlinked" (1999: 27). Sensitive to issues of scale, Yeoh (1999) studies ritual practices for dead bodies in Singapore, and how local communities' shifting perceptions of such practices affect how the living situate themselves in the body politic in relation to increasing secularization and nation-state policies and interventions.

The notion that resistance emerges out of embodied experiences just as much as from conscious considerations has been invoked particularly in studies of colonial and postcolonial contexts. In studying the gendering of bodies in rural Zimbabwe as entangled with knowledge and power as well as with spatial scales, Kesby seeks to "circumvent the material/textual binary" (1999: 31) in order to suggest new ways of destabilizing patriarchy. In a study on colonial India, Mills discusses how "architectural space affects social space" (1996: 126) with regard to how the spatial microarticulation of the public/private dichotomy allowed indigenous and colonizing women forms of spatial resistance through the body beyond "notions of confinement" (1996: 142). In her work on Latin America, Radcliffe asserts that "embodied subjectivities lie at a threshold of power, material resistance and representation" (1999a: 221) and concludes that the "constant ordering work of nation, race and gender nevertheless leaves interstices from which other orders, other geographies can be imagined and spoken" (1999b: 226). Similarly close to Lefebvre's notions, Pile, in his analysis of the spatialities of social struggle in colonial Algeria, suggests that resistance is a form of embodied creativity which employs and invents "discontinuous spaces . . . that lie beyond 'power'" (1997: 14, 5).

The economy and the body

The body is indeed a complex phenomenon, not least in relation to the capitalist space economy, which stakes out the body in a number of ways. First, the body is a commodity in its bare existence, as body parts and transplants on the organ market. Secondly, the body is a labor market commodity, as differentiated labor power in terms of manual, white collar, gendered, racialized, and so forth. Thirdly, the body is a site of survival needs and thus a site of consumption: of foods, clothes, housing, medical care, physical aids, and so forth. Fourthly, the body is a site of emotions, of desire and pleasure, with the effect of giving any kind of consumption symbolic signifying values while simultaneously enabling the emergence of a body-related economy of signs more or less disconnected from survival needs. In different ways, geographers have recently suggested that these four aspects are complexly entangled in one another. Harvey stresses that the body can never be free of capitalism's effects, which, however, will look "very different from the standpoints of production, exchange, and consumption" (1998: 414). Seager, in addressing sexuality and exploitation, points out that "[t]he world is lashed by networks of space, place, and economy that depend on the display, exchange, control, and use of women's bodies" (1997: 1522), and Knopp remarks that "the sociospatial construction of otherness, which has as much to do with representational and symbolic space as with physical space, has become key to the survival of capitalism" (1992: 664).

Some Marxist geographers have engaged with the notion of spatial scales (Brenner 1998; Smith 1993; Harvey 2000) in order to come to terms with the place of the body in the shifting landscape of capitalism. Hence, Smith outlines an incomplete and open-ended hierarchical typology that "stretches from the body to the global" (1993: 102), while Harvey sets out to elaborate a "foundational connexion" between the two based upon the fact that "globalization is about the sociospatial relations between billions of individuals" (2000: 16). Other geographical research exemplifies Lefebvre's general position that the body is "the generator (or producer) of space" (1991: 407), and suggests that the body, rather than being a discrete spatial scale, is nested with and constitutive of all spatial scales. Pred has posed the question: "Where are those social and economic practices, those routine and nonroutine daily practices, which do not involve embodied-corpo-real subjects?" (1995: 1066). In line with such reasoning, the economic deployment of bodies and interdependent construction of spatial scales are addressed in case studies such as Stewart's (1995b) study of slave codes as legal geographies that constituted the slave body, sovereign power and the plantation as a racialized spatial unit of exploitation, and in Pratt's work (1998) on how disciplinary subjectivation constrained domestic workers required to live in the middle-class Canadian homes of their employers. Yet, the issue of how spatial scales of capitalism are constructed through embodied practices concerns not only bodies enslaved. Bell and Valentine (1997) study how differentiated practices of shopping, preparing, and consuming food contribute to the shaping of distinct kinds of bodies, as well as to the structuring of "interconnections and disjunctions between scales" (1997: 207). Studying merchant banks, McDowell and Court (1994) and McDowell (1995) demonstrate how banking practices in the City of London are embodied gendered performances based upon power asymmetries and scripts firmly rooted in heteronormativity (see also Pile & Thrift 1995), while Hinchcliffe (2000) and Thrift (2000) engage in discussions of how business management has turned to issues of embodiment and non-representational learning processes in order to produce managers able to speed-up an already fast-moving global economy.

These examples illustrate that economic processes unavoidably pass through and make use of bodies that are concretely situated and complexly enmeshed in networks of social and cultural practices (see also Binnie 1995; Gibson-Graham 1998; Longhurst 2001; Massey 1994; Pratt 1998; Thrift 1996; Valentine 1999a, 1999b). In this vein, geographers convincingly argue that what some would call "the prevailing structures of political-economic power" (Harvey 1998: 420) cannot be reified as something global in contradistinction to a separate scale of the body, but that they are in themselves local embodied practices of decision-making particularly concentrated in white, upper-class males embedded in particular ways of being in a few select locations of power and privilege.

Impairment, illness, and the body

Some of the most integrative work on body and space has been written by scholars engaged in geographies of health and healthcare especially concerned with impairment and disability issues. Dorn's contention that "some poststructural feminists ignore institutional sedimentations in the built environment" (1998: 183) points to the fact that disability cannot be framed as a purely social relation in terms of how 'normal' bodies and 'disabled' bodies are discursively constructed due to prejudices and so forth. Disability issues unavoidably invoke spatiality and questions concerning physical constraints that contribute to the construction of impaired bodies *as* disabled and disempowered (see, for overviews, Gleeson 1999a; Imrie 1996a; Park, Radford, and Vickers 1998; Parr 2002a; Parr & Butler 1999). However, Dorn, in focusing upon how medical theory has been applied to give spaces and "anomalous bodies meaning" (1999: 46), makes the point that geographers themselves too easily have adopted disabling positions and need to "acknowledge the spatio-temporal structuring of the definition(s) of disability that they work with" (1999: 63). Considering such issues, Moss and Dyck argue that "the social model of disability, that emphasizes the social construction of disability through physical and social barriers, . . . did not take into account the nuances of bodily being that feminism has been able to provide" (2002: 12–13). In a study on possible effects of the Internet on experiences of health and bodily being, Parr discusses the tensions between a spatiotechnological expansion of the medical gaze through self-diagnosed inscription, and "the potential for an emancipatory disruption of the traditional canons" (2002b: 86) facilitated by internet users' access to alternative accounts, networks of support, and other sources for increased control of their own bodies.

Imrie and Hall (2001) focus upon the needs of people with impairments in a critical discussion of the professions particularly involved in shaping built space. In this research, the exclusionary character of ableist spaces is discussed in terms of careless planning and design, which contribute to the "estrangement of disabled bodies in the built environment" (Imrie 1999: 38). While sensitive collaborative design practices (Gathorne-Hardy 1999) and technological innovations (Golledge 1993, 1997) are suggested as remedies, the exclusionary landscapes of ableism are also seen as integrated parts of a capitalist space-economy that has "progressively devalued the labour-power of physically impaired people" (Gleeson 1999b: 109; see also Gleeson 1996; Golledge 1996; Imrie 1996b). Critical of technological utopianism, Gleeson rather asks for "a lasting transformation of the political-economic, institutional and cultural forces that shape our cities and societies" (1999b: 115). In general agreement with such a position, Dyck (1999), Moss and Dyck (1996, 2002), and Dyck and Moss (1999) address how women with chronic illness and disability forge their identities as corporeal sites of inscription and resistance at both home and work in relation to the multiple forces and social scripts that structure embodiment, while Butler and Bowlby discuss how estrangement and resistance in public spaces are related to both negotiation of constraints in physical space and oppressive "social discourses concerning disability and public behaviour" (1997: 428; see also Parr 1997). Touching upon aspects of such discourses in their interpretation of attitude surveys, Dear et al. suggest that the spatial repercussions of public opinions about disabled bodies can be understood in terms of a "landscape of (in)tolerance" (1997: 471; see also Gleeson 1997). In relation to encounters with intolerance, Dorn discusses embodied ways of knowing and being of a self-designated 'cripple' as "part of a counter-hegemonic field" (1998: 198), while Chouinard (1999a, 1999b) approaches experiences of disabled women's political activism as a form of resistance to the ranking of "bodies marked by difference" in a "corporeal class system" governed by "powerful groups such as capitalists" (1999b: 292).

Yet, capitalists come in different shapes, colors, and sizes, and the notion of a ranking system implies that othering concerns processes of hierarchization beyond both capitalist relations, and relations between an able-bodied heterosexual majority and different minorities. Hence, Valentine touches upon relations of power cutting across diverse social categories in a study of an impaired ex-miner's contradictory experiences and "the complex relationships which exist between hegemonic masculinities and disabled masculinities" (1999c: 168). Pain, Mowl, and Talbot (2000) point to overlapping effects of ableism and ageism in a study of older people and leisure spaces. Butler explicitly reflects upon "how and at what cost disabled people remain marginalised in the gay 'community,'" in which "obsessions with the perfect body . . . run deep" (1999: 203). She thereby raises questions concerning the omnipresence of power-relations and how they are embodied by individuals belonging to groups normally thought of as oppressed rather than oppressors.

Senses, practices, and nonrepresentational bodies

The body is deeply implicated in geographers' rethinking of vision and visualism, as well as in nonrepresentational theory and research on practices and the senses.

In a humanistic quest to "explore the possibilities of otherscapes" (1990: 17), Por-teous stresses that "[w]e live in a multisensory world, an allscape" (1990: 196), and Sui (2000) explores visualism in relation to epistemological and political implica-tions of a recent shift towards aural metaphors, which in his view "represents a sig-nificant – if still nascent – reconfiguration of geographical discourse during the late twentieth century" (2000: 334). In essence, this reconfiguration concerns more than metaphors, and within the broad field of work under discussion here, approaches can be differentiated with regard to focus as well as theories employed.

Recent work on body–space formation through sound accompany the shift towards aural metaphors. The aural sensing of space is a key aspect of a study on warehouse parties, in which Ingham et al. (1999) discuss how a specific place is defined through practices centered on the particular music played and the proper-ties of sound. Explicitly suggesting an analysis "beyond geography's visible worlds," Smith (1997) turns to the role of music in delimiting and spatializing identities of places as well as people. Continuing this path, Smith (2000) explores practices of performance and listening in terms of sonic knowledges and as embodied media-tion of power relations and particular social and spatial protocols. Addressing the politics of auditory space, Revill points out that music is "almost uniquely poly-semic" (2000: 605), yet gains authority and contributes to the construction of national identity through the time and place specific embodiment of musical meaning. In an edited volume on the role of music in the construction of place and scale, Leyshon, Matless, and Revill (1998) collect essays that include analyses of multisensuous and particularly sonoric landscapes of politics and place identity.

In a synthetic account of geographies of subjectivity and spatial behavior, Pile builds upon Freud, Lacan, and Lefebvre in suggesting "a psychoanalysis of space which correlates sexuality, geographic space and power with the body, meaning and (real, imaginary, symbolic) spatialities" (1996: 217). Yet, his treatise ends where a case-based and grounded psychoanalysis involving real spaces and real bodies would have begun. Suggesting a feminist revision of Lacan, Rose invokes "the existence of other visualised spaces of self/knowledge" (1995: 761) than those of phallocentric masculinism, while Nast and Kobayashi (1996) argue that "recorporealizing vision" makes it possible to distinguish between different modalities of masculinities and thereby to refine forms of resistance against heteropatriarchy (see also Pile 1996: 217). Nash (1994, 1996) turns to feminist art in searching for nonpassive depic-tions of the female body, identity, and landscape, and "reclaims" vision for a geog-raphy of landscape seen from subject positions that are not inherently oppressive. Related concerns inform Latham's exploration of "tactile, bodily, [and] habitually grounded practices" (1999: 452) in a reading of Walter Benjamin that suggests a non-authoritarian auratic experience "that undermines any dominance of the self over the object" (1999: 467).

In his critique of phallocentric abstract visualist space, Gregory calls on Lefebvre's unfinished project "to connect the history of the body with the history of space" (1994: 416). Lefebvre asserts such a connection in stating that capitalist development includes a process "whereby the visual gains the upper hand over the other senses" that ultimately reaches a point where "space has no social existence independently of an intense, aggressive and repressive visualization" (1991: 286). In addressing multisensuous and nonlinguistic signifying practices, Landzelius

(2001) discusses the segmentation of the body as a historico-spatial phenomenon of reciprocal interdependence with specific features of the built environment. Law (2001) argues that the senses *are* a situated practice, which Filipino migrants creatively engage to reconstruct multisensuous embodied experiences of home as well as to position themselves in new spaces of power. Relating similar concerns to epistemology, Harrison (2000) argues that mind/body dualism and notions of the body as a social effect have to do with how practices and "the *configuring* roles of the body" (2000: 504) are neglected in established discourse.

Geographical work in nonrepresentational theory and actor-network theory conceives of the mind–body–space nexus in terms of heterogeneous hybrid associations of networked 'actants' that include humans and animals as well as material constructs. This entails fundamentally rethinking agency and suggests that there are fuzzy boundaries between aspects and parts of 'humans' and 'things' normally understood to be discrete ontological entities (see Murdoch 1997a, 1997b; Nash 2000; Thrift 1996, 1997b, 1999; Whatmore 1999). Although sympathetic, Pred (2004) claims that actor-network theory "inadequately deals with power relations" in its primary concern with how networks form and develop, when power relations actually come in "myriad forms." Based on the position that "because of our corpo-reality . . . there is always a thereness, a somewhereness, a here-and-nowness to practice" (2004), Pred himself has in a long series of theoretically informed case studies focused on "embodied engagement in situated practices and the power relations and meanings with which they are unboundedly interfused" (1995: 1068).

Body–Space Reciprocity

Geography is concerned with the triad of economy, society and culture as spatialized, and the themes discussed above suggest that this spatialized triad must be understood through the body. The question of the geographical specificity of the body thus concerns the ways in which spaces emerge and are shaped interdependently with bodies. Geographical work in epistemology suggests that a shift towards the body and notions of positionality must be accompanied by an exploration of other forms of embodied, multisensuous, knowledge of spaces. Research on the body in relation to politics and economics suggests that matters of domination and exploitation, and questions of 'overarching' 'global' scales and processes, must be understood in terms of situated practices, and thus in reach of various forms of embodied attempts to resist and rescale present relations of power. Inquiries into issues of impairment and disability produce knowledge of how physical as well as discursive social constructs constrain bodies that is of relevance not only for emancipating 'deviant' bodies, but also for imagining possibilities beyond the everyday confines of 'normality.' Research into senses other than vision and the related stress on nonrepresentational, embodied ways of knowing in and through practices make the insufficiency of discursive approaches to the body–space nexus particularly clear.

Yet, I suggest that an embodied geography needs mediating concepts in theorizing the interdependent formation of bodies and spaces. The shaping of a body takes place through the senses, it is through the faculties of sight, hearing, smell, taste and touch including motility, that 'performative interpellations' (see Butler 1990; Nash

2000; Nelson 1999; Rose 1997, 1999) of bodies take place, and without the senses, an individual can take part in neither space nor discourse. Rodaway (1994) maps sensuous geographies across the world with regard to how different spaces enable and constrain practices in distinct kinds of ways, and thus result in different sensuous orderings of the body. In consideration of social interaction and psychological factors, such sensuous orderings can be articulated as the formation through reiterative practices of an individual's specific 'postural model of the body' (Schilder 1935; Merleau-Ponty 1962), 'habitual body' (Merleau-Ponty 1962), 'bodily hexis' (Bourdieu 1990), or 'body idiom' (Goffman 1963). Feminists such as Butler (1990), Grosz (1994), and Young (1990a) critique these authors to the extent that women's experiences are subordinated to a male norm, yet tend to agree that their ideas represent "enormously useful rethinking of mind/body relations" and contribute "crucial insights about the forms and structure of human embodiment" (Grosz 1994: 82, 108, on Schilder and Merleau-Ponty).

However, such body-concepts need to be articulated in conjunction with the spatially embedded process of incorporation, including the actual sensuous interpellations and practices by which the malleability of bodies is turned into the relative firmness of posture and flesh. Lefebvre's account of social space as power-laden and historico-geographically specific revolves around a usually overlooked notion of "formants" (1991: 285–91) that deeply implicate the body and the senses (see also Landzelius 2001: 170–3). In recursive fashion, formants differ between sociohistorical constellations, are enacted in spatial practice, affect social relations, and are materialized as sensuous hierarchies in the postural models of bodies as well as in built space. In further elaborating the geographical specificity of the body, concepts such as 'postural models' and 'formants' are useful. Not only do they direct attention to how malleable bodies are worked upon by situated interaction with other bodies differentiated in terms of particular postural models of class, gender, sexuality, race, ethnicity, disability, age, illness, and so forth. They also offer ways to understand how malleable bodies both work upon *and* are worked upon by a built space of sensuous hierarchies which in itself is continually reconfigured in terms of how, which, and where functions are enabled and constrained through situated practices of architectural-material sedimentation.

REFERENCES

Bell, D. and Valentine, G. 1997: *Consuming Geographies: We Are Where We Eat*. London: Routledge.

Binnie, J. 1995: Trading places: consumption, sexuality and the production of queer space. In D. Bell and G. Valentine, eds., *Mapping Desire: Geographies of Sexualities*. London: Routledge, 182–99.

Blum, V. and Nast, H. 1996: Where's the difference: the heterosexualization of alterity in Henri Lefebvre and Jacques Lacan. *Environment and Planning D: Society and Space* 14, 559–80.

Bondi, L. 1993: Locating identity politics. In M. Keith and S. Pile, eds., *Place and the Politics of Identity*. London: Routledge, 84–101.

Bondi, L. 1997: In whose words? On gender identities, knowledge and writing practices. *Transactions of the Institute of British Geographers* 22, 245–58.

Bourdieu, P. 1990: *The Logic of Practice*. Stanford: Stanford University Press.

Brenner, N. 1998: Between fixity and motion: accumulation, territorial organization and the historical geography of spatial scales. *Environment and Planning D: Society and Space* 16, 459–81.

Butler, J. 1990: *Gender Trouble: Feminism and the Subversion of Identity*. London: Routledge.

Butler, R. 1999: Double the trouble or twice the fun? Disabled bodies in the gay community. In R. Butler and H. Parr, eds., *Mind and Body Spaces: Geographies of Illness, Impairment and Disability*. London: Routledge, 203–20.

Butler, R. and Bowlby, S. 1997: Bodies and spaces: an exploration of disabled people's experiences of public space. *Environment and Planning D: Society and Space* 15, 411–33.

Buttimer, A. 1976: Grasping the dynamism of lifeworld. *Annals of the Association of American Geographers* 66, 277–92.

Callard, F. J. 1998: The body in theory. *Environment and Planning D: Society and Space* 16, 387–400.

Chouinard, V. 1997: Making space for disabling differences: challenging ableist geographies. *Environment and Planning D: Society and Space* 15, 379–87.

Chouinard, V. 1999a: Life at the margins: disabled women's explorations of ableist spaces. In E. K. Teather, ed., *Embodied Geographies: Spaces, Bodies and Rites of Passage*. London: Routledge, 142–56.

Chouinard, V. 1999b: Body politics: disabled women's activism in Canada and beyond. In R. Butler and H. Parr, eds., *Mind and Body Spaces: Geographies of Illness, Impairment and Disability*. London: Routledge, 269–94.

Chouinard, V. and Grant, A. 1995: On being not even anywhere near 'The Project': ways of putting ourselves in the picture. *Antipode* 27, 137–66.

Cox, K. R. and Golledge, R. G., eds. 1981: *Behavioral Problems in Geography Revisited*. London: Methuen.

Craddock, S. 1999: Embodying place: pathologizing Chinese and Chinatown in nineteenth-century San Francisco. *Antipode* 31, 351–71.

Craddock, S. and Dorn, M. 2001: Guest editorial: nationbuilding, gender, race, and medical discourse. *Journal of Historical Geography* 27, 313–18.

Cresswell, T. 1997: Weeds, plagues, and bodily secretions: a geographical interpretation of metaphors of displacement. *Annals of the Association of American Geographers* 87, 330–45.

Cresswell, T. 1999: Embodiment, power and the politics of mobility: the case of female tramps and hobos. *Transactions of the Institute of British Geographers* 24, 175–92.

Dear, M., Wilton, R., Gaber, S. L., and Takahashi, L. 1997: Seeing people differently: the sociospatial construction of disability. *Environment and Planning D: Society and Space* 15, 455–80.

Domosh, M. and Seager, J. 2001: *Putting Women in Place: Feminist Geographers Make Sense of the World*. New York: Guilford Press.

Dorn, M. 1998: Beyond nomadism: the travel narratives of a cripple. In H. Nast and S. Pile, eds., *Places Through the Body*. London: Routledge, 183–206.

Dorn, M. 1999: The moral topography of intemperance. In R. Butler and H. Parr, eds., *Mind and Body Spaces: Geographies of Illness, Impairment and Disability*. London: Routledge, 46–69.

Dorn, M. and Laws, G. 1994: Social theory, body politics and medical geography. *Professional Geographer* 46, 106–10.

Duncan, N. 1996: Renegotiating gender and sexuality in public and private spaces. In N. Duncan, ed., *BodySpace: Destabilizing Geographies of Gender and Sexuality*. London: Routledge, 125–45.

Dyck, I. 1990: Space, time, and renegotiating motherhood: an exploration of the domestic workplace. *Environment and Planning D: Society and Space* 8, 459–83.

Dyck, I. 1999: Body troubles: women, the workplace and negotiations of a disabled identity. In R. Butler and H. Parr, eds., *Mind and Body Spaces: Geographies of Illness, Impairment and Disability*. London: Routledge, 119–37.

Dyck, I. and Moss, P. 1999: Body, corporeal space, and legitimating chronic illness: women diagnosed with ME. *Antipode* 31, 372–97.

Elden, S. 2001: Politics, philosophy, geography: Henri Lefebvre in recent Anglo-American scholarship. *Antipode* 33, 809–25.

Elder, G. S. 1998: The South African body politic: space, race and heterosexuality. In H. Nast and S. Pile, eds., *Places Through the Body*. London: Routledge, 153–64.

Gathorne-Hardy, F. 1999: Accommodating difference: social justice, disability and the design of affordable housing. In R. Butler and H. Parr, eds., *Mind and Body Spaces: Geographies of Illness, Impairment and Disability*. London: Routledge, 240–55.

Gibson-Graham, J. K. 1998: Queer(y)ing globalization. In H. Nast and S. Pile, eds., *Places Through the Body*. London: Routledge, 23–41.

Gleeson, B. 1996: A geography for disabled people. *Transactions of the Institute of British Geographers* 21, 387–96.

Gleeson, B. 1997: Community care and disability: the limits to justice. *Progress in Human Geography* 21, 199–224.

Gleeson, B. 1999a: *Geographies of Disability*. London: Routledge.

Gleeson, B. 1999b: Can technology overcome the disabling city? In R. Butler and H. Parr, eds., *Mind and Body Spaces: Geographies of Illness, Impairment and Disability*. London: Routledge, 98–118.

Goffman, I. 1963: *Behavior in Public Places: Notes on the Social Organization of Gatherings*. New York: The Free Press.

Golledge, R. G. 1993: Geography and the disabled: a survey with special reference to vision impaired and blind populations. *Transactions of the Institute of British Geographers* 18, 63–85.

Golledge, R. G. 1996: A response to Imrie and Gleeson. *Transactions of the Institute of British Geographers* 21, 404–11.

Golledge, R. G. 1997: On reassembling one's life: overcoming disability in the academic environment. *Environment and Planning D: Society and Space* 15, 391–409.

Gregory, D. 1994: *Geographical Imaginations*. Oxford: Blackwell.

Gregory, D. 1997: Lacan and geography: the production of space revisited. In G. Benko and U. Strohmayer, eds., *Space and Social Theory: Interpreting Modernity and Postmodernity*. Oxford: Blackwell, 203–31.

Gregson, N. and Rose, G. 2000: Taking Butler elsewhere: performativities, spatialities and subjectivities. *Environment and Planning D: Society and Space* 18, 433–52.

Grosz, E. 1994: *Volatile Bodies: Toward a Corporeal Feminism*. Bloomington: Indiana University Press.

Hägerstrand, T. 1967: *Innovation as a Spatial Process*. Chicago: Chicago University Press.

Hägerstrand, T. 1970: What about people in regional science? *Papers of the Regional Science Association* 24, 7–21.

Haraway, D. 1991: *Simians, Cyborgs and Women*. London: Free Association Books.

Harrison, P. 2000: Making sense: embodiment and the sensibilities of the everyday. *Environment and Planning D: Society and Space* 18, 497–517.

Harvey, D. 1989: *The Condition of Postmodernity*. Oxford: Blackwell.

Harvey, D. 1998: The body as an accumulation strategy. *Environment and Planning D: Society and Space* 16, 401–21.

Harvey, D. 2000: *Spaces of Hope*. Edinburgh: Edinburgh University Press.

Hinchliffe, S. 2000: Performance and experimental knowledge: outdoor management training and the end of epistemology. *Environment and Planning D: Society and Space* 18, 575–95.

Imrie, R. 1996a: *Disability and the City: International Perspectives*. London: Paul Chapman Publishing.

Imrie, R. 1996b: Ableist geographies, disableist spaces: towards a reconstruction of Golledge's 'Geography and the disabled.' *Transactions of the Institute of British Geographers* 21, 397–403.

Imrie, R. 1999: The body, disability and Le Corbusier's conception of the radiant environment. In R. Butler and H. Parr, eds., *Mind and Body Spaces: Geographies of Illness, Impairment and Disability*. London: Routledge, 25–45.

Imrie, R. 2000: Disability and discourses of mobility and movement. *Environment and Planning A* 32, 1641–56.

Imrie, R. and Hall, P. 2001: *Inclusive Design: Designing and Developing Accessible Environments*. London: Routledge.

Ingham, J., Purvis, M., and Clarke D. B. 1999: Hearing places, making spaces: sonorous geographies, ephemeral rhythms, and the Blackburn warehouse parties. *Environment and Planning D: Society and Space* 17, 283–305.

Johnson, L. C. 1994: What future for feminist geography? *Gender, Place and Culture* 1, 103–14.

Keith, M. and Pile, S. 1993: Introduction part 2: the place of politics. In M. Keith and S. Pile, eds., *Place and the Politics of Identity*. London: Routledge, 22–40.

Kesby, M. 1999: Locating and dislocating gender in rural Zimbabwe: the making of space and the texturing of bodies. *Gender, Place and Culture* 6, 27–47.

Knopp, L. 1992: Sexuality and the spatial dynamics of capitalism. *Environment and Planning D: Society and Space* 10, 651–69.

Kobayashi, A. 1994: Coloring the field: gender, 'race,' and the politics of fieldwork. *Professional Geographer* 46, 73–80.

Landzelius, M. 2001: Contested representations: signification in the built environment. *The American Journal of Semiotics* 17, 139–99.

Latham, A. 1999: The power of distraction: distraction, tactility, and habit in the work of Walter Benjamin. *Environment and Planning D: Society and Space* 17, 451–73.

Law, L. 2001: Home cooking: Filipino women and geographies of the senses in Hong Kong. *Ecumene* 8, 264–83.

Lefebvre, H. 1976: *The Survival of Capitalism*. London: Allison and Busby.

Lefebvre, H. 1991: *The Production of Space*. Oxford: Blackwell.

Ley, D. and Samuels, M., eds. 1978: *Humanistic Geography: Prospects and Problems*. Chicago: Maaroufa Press.

Leyshon, A., Matless, D., and Revill, G., eds. 1998: *The Place of Music*. New York: Guilford.

Longhurst, R. 1995: The body in geography. *Gender, Place and Culture* 2, 97–106.

Longhurst, R. 1997: (Dis)embodied geographies. *Progress in Human Geography* 21, 486–501.

Longhurst, R. 1999: Pregnant bodies, public scrutiny: 'giving' advice to pregnant women. In E. K. Teather, ed., *Embodied Geographies: Spaces, Bodies and Rites of Passage*. London: Routledge, 78–90.

Longhurst, R. 2000: 'Corpogeographies' of pregnancy: 'bikini babes.' *Environment and Planning D: Society and Space* 18, 453–72.

Longhurst, R. 2001: *Bodies: Exploring Fluid Boundaries*. London: Routledge.

Massey, D. 1994: *Space, Place and Gender*. Cambridge: Polity Press.

McDowell, L. 1992: Doing gender: feminism, feminists and research methods in human geography. *Transactions of the Institute of British Geographers* 17, 399–416.

McDowell, L. 1995: Body work: heterosexual gender performances in city workplaces. In. D. Bell and G. Valentine, eds., *Mapping Desire: Geographies of Sexualities*. London: Routledge, 75–95.

McDowell, L. 1999: *Gender, Identity and Place: Understanding Feminist Geographies*. Cambridge: Polity Press.

McDowell, L. and Court, G. 1994: Performing work: bodily representations in merchant banks. *Environment and Planning D: Society and Space* 12, 727–50.

Merleau-Ponty, M. 1962: *Phenomenology of Perception*. London: Routledge and Kegan Paul.

Merrifield, A. 1993: Place and space: a Lefebvrian reconciliation. *Transactions of the Institute of British Geographers* 18, 516–31.

Merrifield, A. 1995: Lefebvre, Anti-Logos and Nietzsche: an alternative reading of *The Production of Space*. *Antipode* 27, 294–303.

Miller, R. 1983: The Hoover in the garden: middle-class women and suburbanization, 1850–1920. *Environment and Planning D: Society and Space* 1, 73–87.

Mills, S. 1996: Gender and colonial space. *Gender, Place and Culture* 3, 125–47.

Moore, G. T. and Golledge, R. G., eds. 1976: *Environmental Knowing: Theories, Research, and Methods*. Stroudsburg: Dowden, Hutchinson & Ross.

Moss, P. 1999: Autobiographical notes on chronic illness. In R. Butler and H. Parr, eds., *Mind and Body Spaces: Geographies of Illness, Impairment and Disability*. London: Routledge, 155–66.

Moss, P. and Dyck, I. 1996: Inquiry into environment and body: women, work, and chronic illness. *Environment and Planning D: Society and Space* 14, 737–53.

Moss, P. and Dyck, I. 2002: *Women, Body, Illness: Space and Identity in the Everyday Lives of Women with Chronic Illness*. Lanham, MD: Rowman and Littlefield.

Murdoch, J. 1997a: Inhuman/nonhuman/human: actor-network theory and the prospects for a nondualistic and symmetrical perspective on nature and society. *Environment and Planning D: Society and Space* 15, 731–56.

Murdoch, J. 1997b: Towards a geography of heterogeneous associations. *Progress in Human Geography* 21, 321–37.

Nash, C. 1994: Remapping the body/land: new geographies of identity, gender and landscape in Ireland. In A. Blunt and G. Rose, eds., *Writing Women and Space: Colonial and Postcolonial Geographies*. New York: Guilford Press, 227–50.

Nash, C. 1996: Reclaiming vision: looking at landscape and the body. *Gender, Place and Culture* 3, 149–69.

Nash, C. 2000: Performativity in practice: some recent work in cultural geography. *Progress in Human Geography* 24, 653–64.

Nast, H. 1998: The body as place: reflexivity and fieldwork in Kano, Nigeria. In H. Nast and S. Pile, eds., *Places Through the Body*. London: Routledge, 93–116.

Nast, H. and Kobayashi, A. 1996: Re-corporealizing vision. In N. Duncan, ed., *BodySpace: Destabilizing Geographies of Gender and Sexuality*. London: Routledge, 75–93.

Nast, H. and Pile, S. 1998: Everydayplacesbodies. In H. Nast and S. Pile, eds., *Places Through the Body*. London: Routledge, 405–16.

Nelson, L. 1999: Bodies (and spaces) do matter: the limits of performativity. *Gender, Place and Culture* 6, 331–353.

Pain, R., Mowl, G., and Talbot, C. 2000: Difference and the negotiation of 'old age.' *Environment and Planning D: Society and Space* 18, 377–93.

Palm, R. and Pred, A. 1978: The status of American women: a time-geographic view. In D. A. Lanegran and R. Palm, eds., *An Invitation to Geography*. New York: McGraw-Hill, 99–109.

Park, D. C., Radford, J. P., and Vickers, M. H. 1998: Disability studies in human geography. *Progress in Human Geography* 22, 208–33.

Parr, H. 1997: Mental health, public space, and the city: questions of individual and collective access. *Environment and Planning D: Society and Space* 15, 435–54.

Parr, H. 1999: Bodies and psychiatric medicine: interpreting different geographies of mental health. In R. Butler and H. Parr, eds., *Mind and Body Spaces: Geographies of Illness, Impairment and Disability*. London: Routledge, 181–202.

Parr, H. 2002a: Medical geography: diagnosing the body in medical and health geography, 1999–2000. *Progress in Human Geography* 26, 240–51.

Parr, H. 2002b: New body-geographies: the embodied spaces of health and medical information on the Internet. *Environment and Planning D: Society and Space* 20, 73–95.

Parr, H. and Butler, R. 1999: New geographies of illness, impairment and disability. In R. Butler and H. Parr, eds., *Mind and Body Spaces: Geographies of Illness, Impairment and Disability*. London: Routledge, 1–24.

Pickles, J. 1985: *Phenomenology, Science and Geography: Spatiality and the Human Sciences*. Cambridge: Cambridge University Press.

Pile, S. 1996: *The Body and the City: Psychoanalysis, Space and Subjectivity*. London: Routledge.

Pile, S. 1997: Introduction: opposition, political identities and spaces of resistance. In S. Pile and M. Keith, eds., *Geographies of Resistance*. London: Routledge, 1–32.

Pile, S. and Thrift, N. 1995: Conclusions: spacing and the subject. In S. Pile and N. Thrift, eds., *Mapping the Subject: Geographies of Cultural Transformation*. London: Routledge, 371–80.

Porteous, J. D. 1990: *Landscapes of the Mind: Worlds of Sense and Metaphor*. Toronto: University of Toronto Press.

Pratt, G. 1998: Inscribing domestic work on Filipina bodies. In H. Nast and S. Pile, eds., *Places Through the Body*. London: Routledge, 283–304.

Pred, A. 1981: Social reproduction and the time-geography of everyday life. *Geografiska Annaler* 63B, 5–22.

Pred, A. 1984: Place as historically contingent process: structuration and the time-geography of becoming places. *Annals of the Association of American Geographers* 74, 279–87.

Pred, A. 1995: Out of bounds and undisciplined: social inquiry and the current moment of danger. *Social Inquiry* 64, 1065–91.

Pred, A. 2004: Scientists without borders, or moments of insight, spaces of re cognition: situated practice, science, and the navigation of urban everyday life. In O. Kramsch, H. van Houtom, and W. Zierhofer, eds., *Bordering Space*. London: Ashgate.

Radcliffe, S. 1999a: Embodying national identities: *mestizo* men and white women in Ecuadorian racial-national imaginaries. *Transactions of the Institute of British Geographer* 24, 213–25.

Radcliffe, S. 1999b: Popular and state discourses of power. In D. Massey, J. Allen, and P. Sarre, eds., *Human Geography Today*. Cambridge: Polity Press, 219–42.

Relph, E. 1976: *Place and Placelessness*. London: Pion.

Revill, G. 2000: Music and the politics of sound: nationalism, citizenship, and auditory space. *Environment and Planning D: Society and Space* 18, 597–613.

Rodaway, P. 1994: *Sensuous Geographies: Body, Sense and Place*. London: Routledge.

Rose, G. 1992: Geography as a science of observation: the landscape, the gaze and masculinity. In F. Driver and G. Rose, eds., *Nature and Science*. London: IBG, Historical Geography Research Services, 8–18.

Rose, G. 1993: *Feminism and Geography: The Limits of Geographical Knowledge*. Cambridge: Polity Press.

Rose, G. 1995: Distance, surface, elsewhere: a feminist critique of the space of phallocentric self/knowledge. *Environment and Planning D: Society and Space* 13, 761–81.

Rose, G. 1997: Situating knowledges: positionality, reflexivities and other tactics. *Progress in Human Geography* 21, 305–20.

Rose, G. 1999: Performing space. In D. Massey, J. Allen, and P. Sarre, eds., *Human Geography Today*. Cambridge: Polity Press, 247–59.

Schilder, P. 1935: *The Image and Appearance of the Human Body: Studies in the Constructive Energies of the Psyche*. London: Kegan Paul & Co.

Seager, J. 1997: Reading the morning paper, and on throwing out the body with the bathwater. *Environment and Planning A* 29, 1521–3.

Seamon, D. 1979: *A Geography of the Lifeworld*. New York: St. Martin's Press.

Sharp, J. 1996: Gendering nationhood: a feminist engagement with national identity. In N. Duncan, ed., *BodySpace: Destabilizing Geographies of Gender and Sexuality*. London: Routledge, 97–108.

Shields, R. 1989: Social spatialization and the built environment: the West Edmonton Mall. *Environment and Planning D: Society and Space* 7, 147–64.

Shields, R. 1991: *Places on the Margin: Alternative Geographies of Modernity*. London: Routledge.

Shields, R. 1999: *Lefebvre, Love and Struggle: Spatial Dialectics*. London: Routledge.

Shilling, C. 2001: The embodied foundations of social theory. In G. Ritzer and B. Smart, eds., *Handbook of Social Theory*. London: Sage, 439–57.

Sibley, D. 1995: *Geographies of Exclusion: Society and Difference in the West*. London: Routledge.

Sibley, D. 1999: Creating geographies of difference. In D. Massey, J. Allen, and P. Sarre, eds., *Human Geography Today*. Cambridge: Polity Press, 115–28.

Smith, N. 1993: Homeless/global: scaling places. In J. Bird, B. Curtis, T. Putnam, and L. Tickner, eds., *Mapping the Futures: Local Cultures, Global Changes*. London: Routledge, 87–119.

Smith, N. and Katz, C. 1993: Grounding metaphor: towards a spatialized politics. In M. Keith and S. Pile, eds., *Place and the Politics of Identity*. London: Routledge, 67–83.

Smith, S. J. 1997: Beyond geography's visible worlds: a cultural politics of music. *Progress in Human Geography* 21, 502–29.

Smith, S. J. 2000: Performing the (sound)world. *Environment and Planning D: Society and Space* 18, 615–37.

Sparke, M. 1998: Mapped bodies and disembodied maps: (dis)placing cartographic struggle in colonial Canada. In H. Nast and S. Pile, eds., *Places Through the Body*. London: Routledge, 305–36.

Stewart, L. 1995a: Bodies, visions, and spatial politics: a review essay on Henri Lefebvre's *The Production of Space*. *Environment and Planning D: Society and Space* 13, 609–18.

Stewart, L. 1995b: Louisiana subjects: power, space and the slave body. *Ecumene: A Journal of Environment, Culture and Meaning* 2, 227–46.

Sui, D. Z. 2000: Visuality, aurality, and shifting metaphors of geographical thought in the late twentieth century. *Annals of the Association of American Geographers* 90, 322–43.

Thrift, N. 1983: On the determination of social action in space and time. *Environment and Planning D: Society and Space* 1, 23–57.

Thrift, N. 1996: *Spatial Formations*. London: Sage.

Thrift, N. 1997a: Cities without modernity, cities with magic. *Scottish Geographical Magazine* 113, 138–49.

Thrift, N. 1997b: The still point: resistance, expressive embodiment and dance. In S. Pile and M. Keith, eds., *Geographies of Resistance*. London: Routledge, 124–51.

Thrift, N. 1999: Steps to an ecology of space. In D. Massey, J. Allen, and P. Sarre, eds., *Human Geography Today*. Cambridge: Polity Press, 295–322.

Thrift, N. 2000: Performing cultures in the new economy. *Annals of the Association of American Geographers* 90, 674–92.

Tuan, Y.-F. 1974: *Topophilia: A Study of Environmental Perception, Attitudes and Values.* Englewood Cliffs, NJ: Prentice-Hall.

Tuan, Y.-F. 1977: *Space and Place: The Perspective of Experience.* Minneapolis: University of Minnesota Press.

Turner, B. S. 2000: An outline of a general sociology of the body. In B. S. Turner, ed., *The Blackwell Companion to Social Theory.* Oxford: Blackwell, 481–501.

Valentine, G. 1999a: Imagined geographies: geographical knowledges of self and other in everyday life. In D. Massey, J. Allen, and P. Sarre, eds., *Human Geography Today.* Cambridge: Polity Press, 47–61.

Valentine, G. 1999b: A corporeal geography of consumption. *Environment and Planning D: Society and Space* 17, 329–51.

Valentine, G. 1999c: What it means to be a man: the body, masculinities, disability. In R. Butler and H. Parr, eds., *Mind and Body Spaces: Geographies of Illness, Impairment and Disability.* London: Routledge, 167–80.

Whatmore, S. 1999: Hybrid geographies: rethinking the 'human' in human geography. In D. Massey, J. Allen, and P. Sarre, eds., *Human Geography Today.* Cambridge: Polity Press, 22–39.

Williams, S. J. and Bendelow, G. 1998: *The Lived Body: Sociological Themes, Embodied Issues.* London: Routledge.

Yeoh, B. S. A. 1999: The body after death: place, tradition, and the nation-state in Singapore. In E. K. Teather, ed., *Embodied Geographies: Spaces, Bodies and Rites of Passage.* London: Routledge, 240–55.

Young, I. M. 1990a: *Throwing Like a Girl and Other Essays in Feminist Philosophy and Social Theory.* Bloomington: Indiana University Press.

Young, I. M. 1990b: *Justice and the Politics of Difference.* Princeton: Princeton University Press.

Chapter 20

Consumption

James Kneale and Claire Dwyer

Cultural Geography and Consumption

Despite the fact that this is a relatively new concern in the social sciences and humanities, a bewildering range of theoretical and empirical studies of consumption have appeared in the last 10 or 15 years. Even more than other topics, it seems that academics studying the topic are not talking to one another or that they are unable to agree on how to approach the subject. This is partly because of the unusually wide range of disciplinary perspectives applied to consumption – economics, sociology, anthropology, cultural and media studies, history, human geography, and more – and partly because everyone already 'knows' what consumption means. Even so, it's hard to think of another 'hot' topic which has received as much attention and as little thought. Even in the 1990s a number of commentators were warning that too much work was based upon unexamined assumptions about consumption (Glennie & Thrift 1992; Miller 1995a). Daniel Miller is especially scathing about these 'myths of consumption,' arguing that these often add up to two all-pervasive assertions: 'consumption is good' or 'consumption is bad.' However, the fact that writers continue to rely upon and reproduce these myths is a testament to their power, and to the fact that we're still not thinking hard enough about what consumption means.

The steady growth of interest in consumption in human geography was largely due to the widening of the scope of the discipline following the 'cultural turn,' though the topic had already been addressed by geographers before this in discussions of housing (Hamnett 1989) and retail (Wrigley 1988). However, it seems likely that if geographers are confused about consumption this is a reflection of our indiscriminate borrowing from a long list of disciplines, often compounding existing problems and avoiding the challenge of integrating ideas from very different backgrounds. The dominance of ideas about the symbolic power of consumption suggests that of all the disciplines we have borrowed from, cultural studies has been the most influential. In this chapter we aim to clarify some of this confusion by taking an overview of different understandings of consumption. We also suggest that what is needed is a more sophisticated grasp of the *social* nature of consumption and more attention to its *materiality*, the physical presence of objects and living things that possess different abilities and attributes and occupy specific spaces and times. It has been argued that these twin concerns of sociality and materiality are also underemphasized within cultural geography as a whole (Philo 2000).

Thus we begin our chapter with an account of three different approaches to, and definitions of, consumption, which we would argue get increasingly more convincing. The approaches are not intended to be neatly exclusive, or to reflect the way ideas have developed: it's simply a useful framework. We then provide a review of some of the work done by cultural geographers and others, structuring our discussion around different spatialities of consumption. Because a full review would be impossible in the space available, this chapter could usefully be read in conjunction with other recent reviews of geography and consumption (see, for example, Jackson & Thrift 1995; Crang & Jackson 2001; Crewe 2000, 2001).

Defining Consumption, I: Uses and Needs

The *OED* defines consumption as "using up; destruction; waste . . ." Economists have typically contrasted consumption to *production*, and economic geographers, at least until very recently, used the term to refer to the purchase of manufactured goods or services by individuals or collectives (firms, nations, etc.). From this perspective the particular use to which the object or service is put is relatively unimportant – consumption is merely the necessary corollary of production just as leisure is secondary to work. Where economists did stop to consider the nature of this demand, they tended to attribute it to 'needs,' needs which are universally felt (for food, clothing, shelter, etc.) and easily satisfied.

While this viewpoint still dominates neoliberal economics, left-leaning academics are more likely to subscribe to a perspective which draws, in more or less faithful ways, on the writings of Karl Marx. Sometimes known as 'the production of consumption' argument and closely associated with the critical theorists of the Frankfurt School, it suggests that the nature of contemporary consumption is entirely due to the logic of capitalism and the expansion of mass production. Modern advertising and marketing have replaced standardized consumption with a more effective organization of consumption into many profitable niche markets. The notion of consumption has also been expanded so that, for example, the 'culture industry' which orchestrates the production of consumption also turns cultural forms – paintings, trips to the theater, and so on – into commodities (Adorno & Horkheimer 1979; Adorno 1991). From this perspective modern consumer society *manufactures* – rather than simply fulfilling – our needs and the 'real' values of objects are obscured by their market values (Rojek 1985).

In some accounts this view of consumption is closely linked with postmodernity. The widespread influence of Jean Baudrillard's explorations of signs (symbolic meanings) as commodities (1970) and the work of Fredric Jameson (1987) has led to a pervasive association between consumer society and postmodernity. For David Harvey (1989) the production of consumption is driven by a shift towards post-Fordist social organisation, producing a consumer society marked by plurality, difference, and novelty, which are all read as ways of manufacturing desire. Whether they accept this periodization or not, these arguments have been strengthened by analyses of the role of consumption in everyday life, such as studies of department stores in the nineteenth century (Williams 1982) and malls in the twentieth century (Chaney 1990; Hopkins 1990). Much of this work has taken a particular interpretation of Walter Benjamin's studies of the 'dreamworlds of consumption' of Second Empire Paris (1978), emphasizing hedonism, desire, and fantasy.

Miller (1995a, 1995b) points out that many of these accounts of consumption assume a set trajectory for this sort of social change: a fall from a premodern Eden into modern (or postmodern) materialism, commodification, and market exchanges and values. Anthropologists have used this trajectory to differentiate between advanced and 'primitive' cultures, even though systems of exchange, forms of 'money' and so on existed before (and beyond) Western capitalism.[1] The historical trajectory identified by Miller has its counterpart in geography, as this kind of consumer society is taken to be something which spreads from particular centers (the West, the USA) through globalization, displacing 'authentic' forms of consumption (Classen 1996). Again, as we suggest below, this is a model of consumption which has been subject to critique as studies have revealed the extent to which even the most seemingly 'global' of products, such as Coca Cola, are incorporated into highly localized cultures of consumption (Miller 1998b).

This first set of understandings of consumption all revolve around questions of need and use, and the key debate concerns whether these needs are 'real' ones or not. But what if consumption is not about the instrumental uses of objects but about their *socially-determined values*?

Defining Consumption, II: Making and Displaying Identities

From this second perspective consumption is a meaningful activity which helps us create social identities and relationships with others; as we do this the things we consume are given human values. Marx and Adorno recognized this but felt that these meanings were distortions of the true 'use-value' of objects because in a capitalist society commodities acquire 'fetishized' meanings through exchange (see Watts 1999; Castree 2001). The fetish, a term originally applied to ritual objects, refers to the attribution of human values to nonhuman objects. Think about a pair of trainers (or sneakers), for example. They could be described as 'sporty,' 'casual,' or 'sexy,' but literally speaking they are none of these things; to describe them in this way is to attach human values to them. Their use-value is a function of warmth, comfort, and other aspects of utility, while their exchange or fetish values are acquired through design, marketing, advertising, and so on. Both Marx and Freud were concerned that fetish objects stand in for (or replace) 'natural' human relations like those produced through labour or sexual desire (Dant 1999). Of course, ideas of the 'usefulness' of objects are themselves arbitrary (Doel & Clarke 2000), so that some trainers are better for running in, others for idle loafing. However, the power of these ideas lives on in our everyday condemnations of the 'materialism' of others.

In recent years this view has been largely replaced by a more positive conception of consumption, suggesting that it plays a key role in the production of identity and the communication of this identity to others. Consumers are held to be active and creative rather than passive 'satisficers' or dupes, and this is sometimes linked to a postmodern consumer culture where the line between high and low culture has been eroded and identities are put together in a 'pick-and-mix' style (Fiske 1989).

The work of Thorstein Veblen and Pierre Bourdieu on consumption and social hierarchy is commonly cited to justify this argument. Veblen's *Theory of the Leisure Class* (1994) argued that the late nineteenth-century *nouveau riche* displayed their wealth through leisure and 'conspicuous consumption' in order to differentiate themselves from their inferiors. Less convincingly, Veblen also suggested that tastes percolate downwards through society because those below *emulate* the tastes of those above, providing an ongoing logic for fashion as the leisure class looks for 'the next big thing' to stay one step ahead. This is a highly influential notion, but one which rests on all kinds of unlikely assumptions (Campbell 1987); this is especially obvious in the historical literature, where emulation is seen to drive the eighteenth-century 'consumer revolution' despite the fact that working-class tastes appear to run alongside, rather than behind, middle-class tastes (Glennie & Thrift 1992; Breward 1999). Bourdieu's much more convincing *Distinction* (1986) considers the nature of taste and argues that it is intimately tied up with class and (to a lesser extent) gender. 'Cultural capital,' the status acquired through tasteful and knowledgeable consumption, is passed on through education and socialization, and is consequently unevenly distributed throughout society. Despite his suggestion that class and gender are to some extent performed, for Bourdieu consumption largely reflects and reproduces preexisting identities (de Certeau 1984).

These writers are often used to support arguments which suggest that identities are defined by consumption rather than production, and consequently take the form of a fragmented set of lifestyles rather than the firm class identities associated with work. The consumer uses material and symbolic goods – clothes, food, musical tastes – to tell themselves and others who they are. While this has been a highly influential argument, we want to argue that there are two problems with this work. Firstly, the idea of communication through consumption, and secondly the assumption that it is done for the benefit of the self as a separate entity. The first point has been well made by Colin Campbell (1995, 1996). Campbell points out that the meanings of displayed objects are highly unstable, varying from person to person and from one context to another. While consumption is clearly meaningful, it is not a *language*:

One can indeed 'say it with flowers' (and with other things); that is to say, convey love, affection, gratitude, or the like . . . to one or more other people. However, in these circumstances not only is it the case that actual objects are transferred to specific targeted others, but such acts are themselves usually clearly situated in time and space, something which helps to determine their 'meaning.' (Campbell 1995: 115)

Campbell is arguing that consumption only makes sense as communication when the possibilities of misunderstanding are very much reduced. Giving your mum flowers will probably get your message across (though it could be thanks, sorry, or something else); handing them out to strangers on the street could mean anything. Similarly clothing can communicate something but it is only likely to be the simplest kind of information; even uniforms can be ambiguous.

As for the second criticism, anthropologists tend to study objects from the point of view of their place within social networks of exchange, so that their meaning is tied to the relationships that exist between giver and receiver. In this sense, consumption is as much about others as it is about ourselves. Daniel Miller's (1998c) ethnography of shopping in north London found that most of it was done by women buying food and essentials for their families rather than 'treats' for themselves. In fact Miller suggests that although many academics assume that shopping is mainly about buying 'treats,' it is in fact the exception that proves the rule. For Miller, shopping is all about love – the love family members bear for one another and the obligations that go with this. Consumption, then, builds familial and other relationships rather than purely individual identities. Of all the people Miller interviewed and observed, only teenagers could be said to consume in a self-indulgent way – and this is because at this stage in their lives their identities *are* being carefully constructed.[2]

Work influenced by these arguments has therefore sought to investigate the place of objects in everyday life without assuming that their symbolic meaning is merely a matter of individual interpretation.

Defining Consumption, III: Material cultures

In their critique of the economist's obsession with the uses of objects, the anthropologists Mary Douglas and Baron Isherwood suggested that we should

Forget that commodities are good for eating, clothing and shelter; forget their usefulness and try instead the idea that commodities are good for thinking; treat them as a nonverbal medium for the human creative faculty. (1996: 62)

For Douglas and Isherwood consumption actively organizes the world, "making visible and stable the categories of culture" (1996: 38). The allocation of objects to families and guests, prescribed ways in which they may or may not be used and other aspects of consumption *create* gender relations, distinctions between 'us' and 'them' and so on. As a result "consumption is the very arena in which culture is fought over, licked into shape" (p. 37). In this respect there are many similarities between contemporary consumption in the West and supposedly 'primitive' systems of exchange like the North American *potlatch* or the Melanesian *kula* (Mauss 2002). Ethnographies of consumption in the West should therefore avoid making presumptions about what commodities mean because consumption is an active and creative process at the heart of social life.[3] Marianne Gullestad's research on home-making in Norway, for example, argues that do-it-yourself home-making activities were not simply about the expression of individual identities, it is one way in which people go about 'constructing homes, genders and classes' (Gullestad 1993).

Arjun Appadurai notes that to study objects "we have to follow the things themselves, for their meanings are inscribed in their forms, their uses, their trajectories" (1988: 5). These 'cultural biographies' show us that commoditization is a *process*: objects become commodities when they pass into the sphere of market exchange, and pass out again when they are bought; they may be subsequently resold, and so on (Kopytoff 1986). At each stage they acquire different meanings. Douglas and Isherwood note that "It is all right to send flowers to your aunt in the hospital, but never right to send the cash they are worth with a message to 'get yourself some flowers'" (1996: 38). This is because commodities are more anonymous than gifts. Money marks the boundary between family and market since it can be used to convert commodities into gifts. The importance of this can also be seen in Peter Corrigan's ethnography of household clothing practices in Dublin (1989). Corrigan found that the daughters of the families refused to let their mothers buy clothes for them after they reached the age of about fourteen, receiving money instead. After this age, market relations are preferable to family ones. Corrigan explains this as a desire to loosen family ties, since a gift of money gives the daughter autonomy over her clothing decisions. This both reflects and produces the power relationship between mothers and daughters; daughters are resisting the power symbolized by previous gifts.

This kind of analysis shows how consumption plays an important role in making and changing social relationships (or social spaces). It refuses to make assumptions about what objects mean or to read them simply as symbolic meaning or individual identity. Instead both the social nature of consumption and the materiality of consumption practices and processes are acknowledged. It is this more contextual approach to consumption which has become increasingly influential within geography as the examples we now discuss suggest.

Geographies of Consumption

In this second part of the chapter we focus on the approaches taken to the study of consumption geographies. Like other reviews of consumption (see Jackson & Thrift 1995), we frame this discussion through an exploration of some of the different spatialities or geographies within which consumption might be analyzed. We begin by looking at sites or spaces of consumption suggesting that attention has shifted from spectacular sites of consumption like the mall to more informal spaces of consumption including domestic spaces. We then discuss the spatial structures of 'systems of provision' by focusing on the geographies of commodity chains as well as the idea of circuits or networks of 'commodity culture' (Jackson 2002). This approach to commodity circuits recognizes the complexity of the networks within which processes of commodification are entangled including the role of consumers themselves. We conclude our discussion, and our chapter, both by emphasizing this more social and materialist approach to the study of consumption and by highlighting some of the areas within which new work on the geographies of consumption might usefully be developed.

Sites and Spaces of Consumption

A focus on the geographies of sites of consumption, emerges particularly from economic geographies of retailing. This subdiscipline of economic geography has been transformed from a narrow focus on retail locations to a more complex study focusing in particular on retail restructuring and regulation but also on the experiences of both retail workers and shoppers (Wrigley & Lowe 1996). This transformation has provoked new attention on how key consumption sites might be understood. While attention had been focused on the mall as the iconic site of consumption

(Goss 1993; Shields 1992) or other spectacular sites of consumption such as world fairs and expositions (Ley & Olds 1988; Pred 1991), there has been a shift from interpreting such spaces as definitive sites of postmodern architecture and experience. Historical research has challenged the 'novelty' of contemporary consumer experiences (Domosh 1996; Blomley 1996) while others have argued for attention to the more mundane, everyday experiences of shopping centers. A good example of this is the detailed ethnographic study of Brent Cross and Wood Green shopping centers in north London (see Miller et al. 1998; Jackson & Holbrook 1995). Through their observations and discussions with groups of shoppers, Miller et al. argue that shopping malls should be seen as retail spaces which are actively socially and culturally constructed and contested. For example, ideas about ethnicity and national identity are actively constituted and reworked within the spaces of the shopping center – manifest for example both in the attitudes of some Wood Green shoppers towards 'foreign' products and in the construction of Brent Cross as a space for the (re)production of ethnic identities by others. Work on shopping centers also highlights questions about public space, surveillance and control (Jackson 1998) issues also emphasized in more critical studies of American shopping malls (Mitchell 2000). Miller et al. (1998) also emphasize the role of consumers not as passive 'dupes' but as complex actors involved in a process which involves social relationships and detailed consumer knowledge. As we suggested in our example of this relationship between social relationships and consumption drawn from Miller's work earlier, this ethnographic work revealed an understanding of shopping not as a site of fantasy or as the pursuit of hedonistic pleasure through the purchase of 'treats.' Focusing instead on 'shopping as provisioning' (1998c) reveals how shoppers were embedded in networks of care towards family members. Purchases were understood either directly as representing their love for their family, or more indirectly, for example in the valuing of thrift, as being evidence of their identities as 'good mothers'.

If some attention has been focused on understanding the complexity of what goes on within the shopping mall, other geographers have sought to expand our attentions to alternative sites of consumption. For example, Nicky Gregson, Louise Crewe, and Kate Brooks offer a detailed ethnography of the practices of consumption in the spaces of 'second hand' retailing including charity shops/thrift stores, vintage clothing stores, and car boot sales to emphasize that such places are significant for understanding how consumption practices and identities are produced (Gregson & Crewe 1994, 1997, 1998; Crewe & Gregson 1998; Gregson, Crewe, & Brooks 2001a). In particular, they emphasize how goods acquire meaning and distinction as they are recirculated within the commodity circuit. This parallels interesting work on the global circuits of second-hand clothing which also illustrates the transformations in the meanings of garments which occur during their passage through the commodity circuit (Hansen 1999). Another important finding of the work is the significance of the materiality of the purchase, particularly in relation to embodied purchases such as second-hand clothes. Work on these more informal spaces of consumption also help to challenge the distinctions between 'public' and 'private,' with their associated gender connotations, and indeed a number of theorists have turned their attention to domestic spaces of consumption including catalogue shopping and secondhand children's clothes sales (Clarke 1997, 2000).

Such studies again require attention to questions of consumer knowledge, but they also allow a much more nuanced understanding of how consumer goods are actively utilized and appropriated within the everyday spaces and social relationships of the home. Thus Clarke (2000) illustrates, through the medium of the sale of children's second hand clothes, how values such as what constitutes 'being a good mother' are also part of the transaction process.

It is not surprising that the home should be such an important focus; as Tim Dant reminds us, "As well as being a material entity in itself, a house is a locus for material culture, a meeting point for people and things, in which social relationships and material relationships are almost indistinguishable because both are bound together in the routine practices of everyday life" (1999: 61). Along with the home-oriented aspects of shopping, and the do-it-yourself literature mentioned earlier, the material culture of the garden has attracted some attention (Chevalier 1998; Bhatti & Church 2000, 2001). Geographers have also begun to consider the consumption of media (Burgess 1990), and its importance within domestic space (Kneale 1999). This work owes a great debt to research conducted within media studies, and to David Morley's research on television in particular (1986, 1995a). The vast amount of work which has followed (see Morley 1995b and Mackay 1997 for useful reviews) includes examinations of the close relationships that exist between the organization of domestic life and television (Silverstone 1994), radio (Moores 1988; Tacchi 1998), video recorders (Gray 1992), and domestic media technologies in general (Silverstone & Hirsch 1992; Silverstone 1999). While generalizations are risky, most of these authors agree that the practices of media consumption and domesticity are mutually constitutive. In this they differ from the much more private experience of reading (Radway 1994). Similarly, Sarah McNamee's study of children's use of domestic game consoles shows how arguments about access to these machines produced gendered identities and spaces (1997), an argument which is reinforced by the work of Sarah Holloway, Gill Valentine, and Nick Bingham on adolescents' use of information technologies in schools (Holloway et al. 2000; Valentine & Holloway 2002).

Thus work on the consumption of media within domestic spaces once again provides evidence for the value of understanding consumption practices within the context of social relations. An interesting example of this is Marie Gillespie's (1995) study of television and video use among young Punjabi Londoners in Southall. Gillespie's in-depth ethnographic study highlights the specificity of local, contextualized consumption practices. Thus British or Australian soap operas become vehicles for discussing and negotiating kinship, courtship, and marriage reflecting particular concerns of these transnational teenagers. In contrast, discussions about adverts for globalized brands such as Coca-Cola reveal a highly specific enthusiasm for a brand which symbolized for these respondents a concept of Americanization and 'cool' which was an alternative to both a parental Asian culture and an exclusionary Britishness. Gillespie's study reveals then both the importance of local and contextualized studies of consumption practices but also how consumption is embedded within social relations.

Obviously another important consumption practice which is particularly associated with domestic space is the consumption of food. Food has attracted considerable attention from geographers as consumption practice (Bell & Valentine 1997;

Valentine 1999). And again this research has been sensitive to understanding how the provisioning and preparation of food is centrally embedded within, and may also reveal, the complexity of social relations. The consumption of food has also been studied at a rather different scale linking the domestic consumption of food to the commodity chains associated with food provisioning (Whatmore 1995; Goodman & Redclift 1991). This alternative spatiality of consumption – the notion of commodity chains or what have been defined as 'systems of provisioning' (Fine & Leopold 1993) – is the focus of our next section as we move from the sites or spaces of consumption, to a consideration of commodity circuits.

Geographies of Commodity Chains and Circuits

Geographers have had a long-standing interest in researching the chains and networks associated with the production of goods (Dicken 1998). Such work has been important in illustrating at levels which can be both relatively simple and highly complex how systems of production are organized to produce goods for consumption. An example of a relatively simple commodity chain can be seen in the article 'Game, Set and Match: The Making of a Wimbledon Ball' from *The Guardian* newspaper (Abrams 2002). This traces the origins of a Wimbledon tennis ball, emphasizing the links across four continents. It also discusses the repetitive and sometimes dangerous tasks involved in its production by workers in factories and rubber processing plants in the Philippines, rubber plantations in Malaysia, and factories in Barnsley in the UK, not to mention those connected to the ball's production through the provision of raw materials from USA, Thailand, South Korea, Japan, New Zealand, and Greece. The story of the Slazenger Wimbledon tennis ball could be read alongside other often-cited examples of commodity chains such as Nike (Goldman & Papson 1998; Donaghu & Barff 1990) or indeed more popular accounts such as Naomi Klein's (2000) *No Logo*.

A strong theme within many such analyses of commodity chains is an argument about distanciation – both socially and spatially – between the consumer and the product. Geographer David Harvey takes the starting point of his own breakfast to reflect on his dislocation from the complex chains which have been required to assemble the food in front of him: "we can in practice consume our meal without the slightest knowledge of the intricate geography of production and the myriad of social relations embedded in the system that puts it on the table." Or, he continues, we can visit a supermarket and buy a bunch of grapes but "we cannot see the fingerprints of exploitation upon them or tell immediately what part of the world they come from" (Harvey 1990: 442–3). For Harvey this theme of distanciation is inherent in the process of commodity fetishism – consumers are distanced from the social relations underlying the product that they buy and the product itself is sold through processes of marketing which ensures that a shoe with the Nike label comes to signify a lifestyle and aspiration – it is not simply a shoe which is good for running in. Harvey thus argues that the role of academics is to 'unveil' the fetish, tracing back the social relations of contemporary consumption.

While 'unveiling' the fetish may actually be more difficult than it seems, as we discuss below, geographers have become increasingly interested in linking geographies of consumption with materialist commodity chain analysis (Hartwick 1998).

Work has focused particularly on the supply chains associated with food illustrating for example the internationalization of food provision (Goodman & Redclift 1991) and the complexity of these chains such as the links between major multinational corporations and subcontracted groups of suppliers (Arce & Marsden 1993). Yet alongside work on the globalizing tendencies of food producers is work which has considered how global processes are mediated through local specificities (Goodman & Watts 1997; Whatmore 1994). This more nuanced understanding of food commodity chains is reflected in a discussion of the complex networks underlying fair trade coffee (Whatmore & Thorne 1997; see also Smith 1996) or the symbolism underlying the production and consumption of exotic fruit (Cook 1994). Geographers have also used commodity-chain analysis to examine systems of supplier organization in the fashion industry (Crewe & Davenport 1992; Crewe 1996; Crewe & Lowe 1996), the cut flower trade (Hughes 2000), and soft furnishing industry (Leslie & Reimer 1999; Hughes & Reimer 2002).

As some of these studies suggest the idea of uncovering a straightforward 'commodity chain' is far from easy, and indeed the notion of a complex network involving many different actors (as well as nonhuman actants) which may reflect overlapping and sometimes contradictory interests rather than one single logic may be a more realistic way to explore consumption geographies. At the same time, some geographers have expressed dissatisfaction with an overly simplistic metaphor of 'unveiling' or 'unmasking' the fetish. Drawing on an ethnographic project about the consumption of food in north London, Phil Crang and Ian Cook (Crang 1996; Cook & Crang 1996; Cook et al. 2000) draw upon a set of different metaphors of 'entanglement' or 'displacement' to understand the networks within which both consumers and suppliers are involved. They argue that an understanding of food consumption networks requires an analysis of the geographical knowledges held by consumers about the meaning and significance of different foods. In turn these geographical knowledges – about food settings, food biographies and food origins – are themselves utilized in the commodification of new foods within the crowded food retail markets. Thus a process of 'double commodity fetishism' occurs as foods are repositioned within the consumption circuit. This argument might be read as another example of consumer disempowerment in the face of complex global circuits of culinary culture – and there is certainly a need for more work to be done about consumer mobilization and ethical consumption possibilities (Kaplan 1995; Hartwick 1998; Mitchell 1993). However, the thrust of Cook and Crang's argument is rather different as they seek a resistance which comes not from uncovering or unveiling the *fetish* to discover the *real* but rather to a relational or juxtapositional politics which provokes questions through unexpected conjunction or disruption.[4]

A similar argument is made by Jackson (2002) in a paper which draws on recent research about the transnational commodity circuits associated with the consumption of Asian food and fashion in Britain (see Crang et al. 2003; Dwyer forthcoming). This research seeks to understand the transnational spaces of British Asian commodity culture which are understood as multidimensional and occupied by many differently positioned actors including producers, suppliers, buyers, consumers and other cultural intermediaries such as journalists, advertisers and consultants. Drawing on the differences between two companies both selling pickles and sauces in the UK, Sharwoods and Pataks, Jackson illustrates the ways in which both companies must draw upon, although differently, discourses of authenticity and passion to sell their products. The issue is not which of these is most accurate but how and why such tropes are used. Similarly examples of the rise of so-called 'ethnic chic' in relation to Asian clothing are used to demonstrate the ways in which ideas about 'authenticity' or 'cultural integrity' may be challenged and subverted by both producers and consumers. A nice example of this is the British Asian fashion designer label Ghulam Sakina whose clothes emphasize both the heritage of 'traditional' Indian embroidery and textile skills alongside a 'multicultural' aesethetic of juxtaposition (Dwyer & Crang 2002). Jackson argues that although these approaches to commodity circuits may raise the risk of being too complex for their own good, the multiple connections which they emphasize may open up new spaces for intervention and resistance.

These approaches to consumption geographies incorporate the active role of consumers (although recognizing that these are a highly differentiated group) into the commodity circuit. Geographers have long been interested in the ways in which people are involved in 'consuming geographies' whether it is through the imagination of places and peoples through the consumption of 'exotic' food (May 1996; Cook & Crang 1996) or through the more direct experience of travel and tourism (Urry 1995; Desforges 1998). Such work has been important in forging new understandings of place – for example, considering how (and why) representations of 'otherness' are 'staged' (MacCannell 1989; Crain 1996) and recognizing that oppositions between 'here' and 'there,' 'global' and 'local' are not fixed but fluid and interrelated (Massey 1995; Crang & Jackson 2001).

Conclusion

We began this chapter by providing an overview of different understandings of the concept of consumption. This was followed by an illustration of some work on different spaces and spatialities of consumption. Our argument throughout the chapter is for an understanding of consumption which moves beyond the merely symbolic and seeks to understand the extent to which consumption must be studied as integral to, and constitutive of, social relations. Seeking to transcend the tension which often exists within geography between 'cultural' and 'economic' approaches (Jackson 2002) we have also argued for a materialist and materialized approach to the study of consumption which recognizes that 'things matter' (Miller 1998a). In making this argument through different ways of thinking about the spaces of consumption we want to emphasize again the ways in which these are related. As Crang and Jackson (2001: 2) argue: "consumption is profoundly contextual, embedded in particular spaces, times and social relations . . . but this contextuality is itself constituted from the materials and imaginations of far-flung commodity systems."

While, as we have suggested, we share some of the misgivings raised by other reviewers (Gregson 1995) about the dangers of ignoring the social and the material in consumption studies, our argument here has been to emphasize that studies of consumption geographies and commodity cultures can prove an important means by which broader social, economic or political geographical questions may be explored. Indeed in conclusion we want to emphasize the many areas which still require much further attention from geographers. Consumption geographies still remain highly concentrated on western contexts and there is a need to direct attention to a more worldwide focus. Notable here is the work being done about new sites of commodification – for example of water (Laurie & Marvin 1999; Page forthcoming) in developing countries. Such work might be particularly helpful in focusing our attention on developing new political interventions in relation to consumer power and consumer ethics. These interventions are tremendously important, and we should not be disheartened if contemporary critiques of the fetish leave us with complex questions, because "answering [them] involves the messy, contingent, context-specific work of politics: of naming the sites and subjects of social, cultural, economic, and environmental exploitation without somehow doing symbolic injustice to them" (Castree 2001: 1524). In that respect, the fact that geographers may now be less certain what consumption 'means' might, after all, be a good thing.

ACKNOWLEDGMENTS

We would like to thank Russell Hitchings for his comments on an earlier draft of this chapter.

NOTES

1. Even if this were not the case, careful attention to the development of modern consumer societies (e.g. Glennie & Thrift 1992; Glennie 1995) shows that there are a number of problems with the idea that capitalism and industrialization created a 'consumer revolution' (McKendrick, Brewer, & Plumb 1983).
2. This may be part of the reason that this idea of hedonistic consumption is so influential – a great deal of work in cultural studies was inspired by work on youth subcultures and their appropriations of objects like the motor scooter and the safety pin (Hall & Jefferson 1978; Hebdige 1979)
3. It is also worth noting Miller's and Campbell's suggestions that the two problems we've highlighted are related to methodological issues. Work in cultural and media studies which stresses hedonism is often based upon casual observation rather than rigorous ethnography. Miller points out that the idea of hedonistic consumption is so strongly embedded in everyday understandings of shopping that it always surfaced in his interviews with shoppers – yet his observations of their actual shopping practice produced very different results. Only ethnographic work would have got beyond this simplistic 'discourse of shopping.'
4. See Cook 2001 for an exploration about how this might be done in relation to pedagogy.

REFERENCES

Abrams, F. 2002: New balls, please. *The Guardian*, June 24.
 [http://www.guardian.co.uk/Archive/Article/0,4273,4446984,00.html]
Adorno, T. 1991: *The Culture Industry: Selected Essays on Mass Culture*. London and New York: Routledge.

Adorno, T. and Horkheimer, M. 1979 [1947]: *Dialectic of Enlightenment*, tr. John Cumming. London: Verso.

Appadurai, A. 1988: Introduction: commodities and the politics of value. In A. Appadurai, ed., *The Social Life of Things: Commodities in Cultural Perspective*. Cambridge: Cambridge University Press, 3–63.

Arce, A. and Marsden, T. 1993: The social construction of international food: a new research agenda. *Economic Geography* 69, 293–312.

Barthes, R. 1967: *The Fashion System*. Berkeley: University of California Press.

Baudrillard, J. 1970: *The Consumer Society*. London: Sage.

Benjamin, W. 1978: Paris, capital of the nineteenth century. In *Reflections: Essays, Aphorisms, Autobiographical Writing*, ed. P. Demetz, tr. E. Jephcott. New York: Schocken, 146–62.

Bell, D. and Valentine, G. 1997: *Consuming Geographies: You Are Where You Eat*. London: Routledge.

Bhatti, M. and Church, A. 2000: 'I never promised you a rose garden': gender, leisure and home-making. *Leisure Studies* 19, 183–97.

Bhatti, M. and Church, A. 2001: Cultivating natures: homes and gardens in late modernity. *Sociology* 35, 365–83.

Blomley, N. 1996: I'd like to dress her all over: masculinity, power and retail space. In N. Wrigley and M. Lowe, eds., *Retailing, Consumption and Capital*. Harlow: Longman, 238–56.

Bourdieu, P. 1986: *Distinction: A Social Critique of the Judgement of Taste*, tr. Richard Nice. London and New York: Routledge.

Breward, C. 1999: *The Hidden Consumer: Masculinities, Fashion and City Life 1860–1914*. Manchester and New York: Manchester University Press.

Burgess, J. 1990: The production and consumption of environmental meanings in the mass media: a research agenda for the 1990s. *Transaction of the Institute of British Geographers* 15, 139–61.

Campbell, C. 1987: *The Romantic Ethic and the Spirit of Modern Consumerism*. Oxford: Blackwell.

Campbell, C. 1995: The sociology of consumption. In D. Miller, ed., *Acknowledging Consumption: A Review of New Studies*. London and New York: Routledge, 96–126.

Campbell, C. 1996: The desire for objects and the meaning of actions: a critical note on the sociology of consumption and theories of clothing. *Journal of Material Culture* 1, 93–105.

Castree, N. 2001: Commodity fetishism, geographical imaginations and imaginative geographies. *Environment and Planning A* 33, 1519–25.

Chaney, D. 1990: Subtopia in Gateshead: the Metrocentre as cultural form. *Theory, Culture and Society* 7, 49–62.

Chevalier, S. 1998: From woollen carpet to grass carpet: bridging house and garden in an English suburb. In D. Miller, ed., *Material Cultures*. London: UCL Press, 47–71.

Clarke, A. 1997: Window shopping at home: classified, catalogues and new consumer skills. In D. Miller, ed. *Material Cultures*. London: UCL Press, 73–99.

Clarke, A. 2000: Mother swapping: trafficking in nearly new childrenswear. In P. Jackson, M. Lowe, D. Miller, and F. Mort, eds., *Commercial Cultures*. Oxford: Berg, 85–100.

Classen, C. 1996: Sugar cane, Coca-Cola and hypermarkets: consumption and surrealism in the Argentine NorthWest. In D. Howes, ed., *Cross-cultural Consumption*. London: Routledge, 39–54.

Cook, I. 1994: New fruits and vanity: symbolic production in the global food economy. In A. Bonanno, L. Busch, W. Friedland, L. Gouveia, and E. Mingione, eds., *From Columbus to ConAgra: The Globalisation of Agriculture and Food*. Lawrence: University of Kansas Press, 232–48.

Cook, I. 2001: Material culture and cyborg pedagogy. Paper presented at the Annual conference of American Geographers, New York, Feb.

Cook, I. and Crang, P. 1996: The world on a plate: culinary culture, displacement and geographical knowledges. *Journal of Material Culture* 1(2), 131–53.

Cook, I., Crang, P., and Thorpe, M. 2000: Eating into Britishness: multicultural imaginaries and the identity politics of food. In S. Roseneil and J. Seymour, eds., *Practising Identities: Power and Resistance*. Basingstoke: Macmillan.

Corrigan, P. 1989: Gender and the gift: the case of the family clothing economy. *Sociology* 23, 513–34.

Crain, M. M. 1996: Negotiating identities in Quito's cultural borderlands: native women's peformances for the Ecuadorean tourist market. In D. Howes, ed., *Cross-cultural Consumption*. London: Routledge, 125–37.

Crang, P. 1996: Displacement, consumption and identity. *Environment and Planning A* 28, 47–67.

Crang, P. and Jackson, P. 2001: Consuming geographics. In I. D. Morley and K. Robin, eds., *British Cultural Studies*. Buckingham: Oxford University Press, 327–42.

Crang, P., Dwyer, C., and Jackson, P. 2003: Transnationalism and the spaces of commodity culture. *Progress in Human Geography* 27, 438–56.

Crewe, L. 1996: Material culture: embedded firms, organisational networks and the local economic development of a fashion quarter. *Regional Studies* 30, 257–72.

Crewe, L. 2000: The besieged body: geographies of retailing and consumption. *Progress in Human Geography* 25(4), 629–40.

Crewe, L. 2001: Geographies of retailing and consumption. *Progress in Human Geography* 24(2), 275–90.

Crewe, L. and Davenport, E. 1992: The puppet show: changing buyer–supplier relations with clothing retailing. *Transactions, Institute of British Geographers* 17, 183–97.

Crewe, L. and Gregson, N. 1998: Tales of the unexpected: exploring car boot sales as marginal spaces of contemporary consumption. *Transactions of the Institute of British Geographers* 23, 39–53.

Crewe, L. and Lowe, M. 1996: United colours? Globalisation and localisation tendencies in fashion retailing. In N. Wrigley and M. Lowe, eds., *Retailing, Consumption and Capital*. Harlow: Longman, 271–83.

Dant, T. 1999: *Material Culture in the Social World: Values, Activities, Lifestyles*. Buckingham and Philadelphia: Open University Press.

De Certeau, M. 1984: *The Practice of Everyday Life*, vol. 1, tr. Steven Rendall. Berkeley, Los Angeles, and London: University of California Press.

Desforges, L. 1998: 'Checking out the planet': global representations/local identities and youth travel. In T. Skelton and G. Valentine, eds., *Cool Places*. London and New York: Routledge, 75–192.

Dicken, P. 1998: *Global Shift: Transforming the World Economy*, 3rd ed. London: Paul Chapman.

Doel, M. and Clarke, D. 2000: Cultivating ambivalence. In I. Cook, D. Crouch, S. Naylor, and J. Ryan, eds., *Cultural Turns/Geographical Turns: Perspectives on Cultural Geography*. Harlow: Pearson, 214–33.

Domosh, M. 1996: The feminised retail landscape: gender, ideology and consumer culture in nineteenth century New York City. In N. Wrigley and M. Lowe, eds., *Retailing, Consumption and Capital*. Harlow: Longman, 257–70.

Donaghu, M. T. and Barff, R. 1990: Nike just did it: international sub-contracting and flexibility in athletic footwear production. *Regional Studies* 24, 537–52.

Douglas, M. and Isherwood, B. 1996 [1979]: *The World of Goods: Towards an Anthropology of Consumption*. London and New York: Routledge.

Dwyer, C. (forthcoming) Tracing transnationalities through commodity culture: a case study of British-South Asian fashion. In P. Jackson, P. Crang, and C. Dwyer, *Transnational Spaces*. London: Routledge.

Dwyer, C. and Crang, P. 2002: Fashioning ethnicities: the commercial spaces of multiculture. *Ethnicities* 2, 410–30.

Featherstone, M. 1991: *Consumer Culture and Postmodernism*. London: Sage.

Fine, B. and Leopold, E. 1993: *The World of Consumption*. London: Routledge.

Fiske, J. 1989: *Understanding Popular Culture*. London: Unwin Hyman.

Gillespie, M. 1995: *Television, Ethnicity and Cultural Change*. London: Routledge.

Glennie, P. 1995: Consumption within historical studies. In D. Miller, ed., *Acknowledging Consumption: A Review of New Studies*. London and New York: Routledge, 164–203.

Glennie, P. and Thrift, N. 1992: Modernity, urbanism, and modern consumption. *Environment and Planning D: Society and Space* 10, 423–43.

Goldman, R. and Papson, S. 1998: *Nike Culture: The Sign of the Swoosh*. London: Sage.

Goodman, D. and Redclift, M. 1991: *Refashioning Nature: Food, Ecology and Culture*. London: Routledge.

Goodman, D. and Watts, M. 1997: *Globalising Food: Agrarian Questions and Rural Restructuring*. London: Routledge.

Goss, J. 1993: The "magic of the mall": an analysis of form, function and meaning in the contemporary retail built environment. *Annals of the Association of American Geographers* 83, 18–47.

Gray, A. 1992: *Video Playtime: The Gendering of a Leisure Technology*. London and New York: Routledge.

Gregson, N. 1995: And now it's all consumption? *Progress in Human Geography* 19, 135–41.

Gregson, N., Brooks, K., and Crewe, L. 2001: Narratives of consumption and the body in the space of the charity/shop. In P. Jackson, M. Lowe, D. Miller, and F. Mort, *Commercial Cultures: Economies, Practices, Spaces*. Oxford and New York: Berg, 101–21.

Gregson, N. and Crewe, L. 1994: Beyond the high street and the mall – car boot fairs and the new geographies of consumption in the 1990s. *Area* 26, 261–7.

Gregson, N. and Crewe, L. 1997: The bargain, the knowledge, and the spectacle: making sense of consumption in the space of the car-boot sale. *Environment And Planning D: Society and Space* 15, 87–112.

Gregson, N. and Crewe, L. 1998: Dusting down second hand rose: gendered identities and the world of second hand goods in the space of the car boot sale. *Gender, Place and Culture* 5, 77–100.

Gregson, N., Crewe, L., and Brooks, K. 2001: *Second Hand Worlds*. London: Routledge.

Gullestad, M. 1993: Home decoration as popular culture: constructing homes, genders and classes in Norway. In T. Del Valle, ed., *Gendered Anthropology*. London: Routledge, 128–61.

Hall, S. and Jefferson, T., eds. 1978: *Resistance Through Rituals: Youth Subcultures in Post-war Britain*. London: Hutchinson.

Hamnett, C. 1989: Consumption and class in contemporary Britain. In C. Hamnett, L. McDowell, and P. Sarre, eds., *The Changing Social Structure*. London: Sage.

Hansen, K. T. 1999: Second-hand clothing encounters in Zambia: global discourses, western commodities, and local histories. *Africa* 69, 343–65.

Hartwick, E. 1998: Geographies of consumption: a commodity chain approach. *Environment and Planning D: Society and Space* 16, 423–37.

Harvey, D. 1989: *The Condition of Postmodernity: An Inquiry into the Origins of Cultural Change*. Oxford: Blackwell.

Harvey, D. 1990: Between space and time: reflections on the geographical imagination. *Annals, Association of American Geographers* 80, 418–34.

Hebdige, D. 1979: *Subculture: The Meaning of Style*. London and New York: Routledge.

Holloway, S. L., Valentine, G., and Bingham, N. 2000: Institutionalising technologies: masculinities, femininities, and the heterosexual economy of the IT classroom. *Environment and Planning A* 32: 617–33.

Hopkins, J. 1990: West Edmonton Mall: landscape of myths and elsewhereness. *The Canadian Geographer* 34, 2–17.

Hughes, A. 2000: Retailers, knowledges and changing commodity networks: the case of the cut flower trade. *Geoforum* 31, 175–90.

Hughes, A. and Reimer, S. forthcoming: *Geographies of Commodity Chains*. Harlow: Prentice-Hall.

Jackson, P. 1998: Domesticating the street: the contested spaces of the high street and the mall. In N. Fyfe, ed., *Images of the Street*. London: Routledge.

Jackson, P. 2002: Commercial Cultures: transcending the cultural and the economic. *Progress in Human Geography* 26, 3–18.

Jackson, P. and Holbrook, B. 1995: Multiple meanings: shopping and the cultural politics of identity. *Environment and Planning A* 27, 1913–30.

Jackson, P., Lowe, M., Miller, D., and Mort, F., eds. 2000: *Commercial Cultures*. Oxford: Berg.

Jameson, F. 1987: Postmodernism and consumer society. In H. Foster, ed., *Postmodern Culture*. London: Pluto Press.

Jackson, P. and Thrift, N. 1995: Geographies of consumption. In D. Miller, ed., *Acknowledging Consumption*. London: Routledge, 204–37.

Kaplan, C. 1995: A world without boundaries: the Body Shop's trans/national geographies. *Social Text* 43, 45–66.

Klein, N. 2000: *No Logo*. London: Harper Collins.

Kneale, J. 1999: The media. In P. Cloke, P. Crang, and M. Goodwin, eds., *Introducing Human Geographies*. London: Arnold, 316–23.

Kopytoff, I. 1986: The cultural biography of things: commodification as a process. In A. Appadurai, ed., *The Social Life of Things: Commodities in Cultural Perspective*. Cambridge: Cambridge University Press, 64–94.

Laurie, N. and Marvin, S. 1999: Globalisation, neoliberalism, and negotiated development in the Andes: water projects and regional identity in Cochabamba, Bolivia. *Environment and Planning A* 31, 1401–15.

Leslie, D. and Reimer, S. 1999: Spatializing commodity chains. *Progress in Human Geography* 23, 401–420.

Ley, D. and Olds, K. 1988: Landscape as spectacle: world fairs and the culture of heroic consumption. *Environment and Planning D: Society and Space* 6, 191–212.

MacCannell, D. 1989: *The Tourist*. London: Macmillan.

Mackay, H. 1997: Consuming communication technologies at home. In H. Mackay, ed., *Consumption and Everyday Life*. London: Sage, 261–97.

Massey, D. 1995: The conceptualisation of place. In D. Massey and P. Jess, eds., *A Place in the World? Places, Cultures and Globalisation*. Oxford: Oxford University Press, 45–85.

Mauss, M. 2002 [1950]: *The Gift: The Form and Reason for Exchange in Archaic Societies*. London and New York: Routledge.

May, J. 1996: A little taste of something more exotic: the imaginative geographies of everyday life. *Geography* 81, 57–64.

McKendrick, N., Brewer, J., and Plumb, J. 1983: *The Birth of a Consumer Society: The Commercialization of Eighteenth-century England*. London: Hutchinson.

McNamee, S. 1997: *The Home*: youth, gender and video games: power and control in the Home. In T. Skelton and G. Valentine, eds., *Cool Places: Geographies of Youth Cultures*. London: Routledge, 195–206.

Miller, D. 1988: Appropriating the state on the council estate. *Man* 23, 353–72.

Miller, D. 1995a: Consumption as the vanguard of history: a polemic by way of an introduction. In D. Miller, ed. *Acknowledging Consumption: A Review of New Studies*. London and New York: Routledge, 1–57.

Miller, D. 1995b: Consumption studies as the transformation of anthropology. In D. Miller, ed., *Acknowledging Consumption: A Review of New Studies*. London and New York: Routledge, 264–95.

Miller, D. 1998a: Why some things matter. In D. Miller, ed., *Material Cultures*. London: UCL Press, 3–21.

Miller, D. 1998b: Coca-Cola: a black sweet drink from Trinidad. In D. Miller, ed., *Material Cultures*. London: UCL Press, 169–87.

Miller, D. 1998c: *A Theory of Shopping*. Cambridge: Polity Press.

Miller, D., Jackson, P., Thrift, N., Holbrook, B., and Rowlands, M. 1998: *Shopping, Place and Identity*. London: Routledge.

Mitchell, D. 2000: *Cultural Geography: A Critical Introduction*. Oxford: Blackwell, ch. 5.

Mitchell, K. 1993: Multiculturalism, or the united colors of capitalism? *Antipode* 25, 263–94.

Moores, S. 1988: "The box on the dresser": memories of early radio and everyday life. *Media, Culture and Society* 10, 23–40.

Morley, D. 1986: *Family Television: Cultural Power and Domestic Leisure*. London: Routledge.

Morley, D. 1995a: Television: more a visible object. In C. Jencks, ed., *Visual Culture*. London: Routledge.

Morley, D. 1995b: Theories of consumption in media studies. In D. Miller, ed., *Acknowledging Consumption: A Review of New Studies*. London and New York: Routledge, 296–328.

Mort, F. 1989: The politics of consumption. In S. Hall and M. Jacques, eds., *New Times: The Changing Face of Politics in the 1990s*. London: Lawrence and Wishart, 160–72.

Page, B. (forthcoming) Women and the social production of water in Anglophone Cameroon. In A. Coles and J. Davies, eds., *Cross-cultural Research on Women and Water*. Oxford: Berg.

Philo, C. 2000: More words, more worlds: reflections on the 'cultural turn' and human geography. In I. Cook, D. Crouch, S. Naylor, and J. Ryan, eds., *Cultural Turns/Geographical Turns: Perspectives on Cultural Geography*. Harlow: Pearson, 27–53.

Pred, A. 1991: Spectacular articulations of modernity: the Stockholm Exhibition of 1897. *Geografiska Annaler* 73B, 45–84.

Radway, J. 1994: *Reading the Romance: Women, Patriarchy, and Popular Literature*. Chapel Hill: University of North Carolina Press.

Rojek, C. 1985: *Capitalism and Leisure Theory*. London: Tavistock.

Shields, R., ed. 1992: *Lifestyle Shopping: The Subject of Consumption*. London: Routledge.

Silverstone, R. 1994: *Television and Everyday Life*. London and New York: Routledge, 24–51.

Silverstone, R. 1999: *Why Study the Media*. London: Sage.

Silverstone, R. and Hirsch, E. eds., 1992: *Consuming Technologies: Media and Information in Domestic Spaces*. London and New York: Routledge.

Smith, M. 1996: The empire filters back: consumption, production and the politics of Starbucks Coffee. *Urban Geography* 17, 502–25.

Tacchi, J. 1998: Radio texture: between self and others. In D. Miller, ed., *Material Cultures*. London: UCL Press, 25–45.

Urry, J. 1995: *Consuming Places*. London and New York: Routledge.

Valentine, G. 1999: Eating in: home, consumption and identity. *Sociological Review* 47, 491–524.

Valentine, G. and Holloway, S. L. 2002: Cyberkids? Exploring children's identities and social networks in on-line and off-line worlds. *Annals of the Association of American Geographers* 92: 302–19.

Veblen, T. 1994 [1899]: *The Theory of the Leisure Class: An Economic Study of Institutions.* New York: Penguin.

Watts, M. 1999: Commodities. In P. Cloke, P. Crang, and M. Goodwin, eds., *Introducing Human Geographies.* London: Arnold, 305–15.

Whatmore, S. 1994: Global agro-food complexes and the refashioning of rural Europe. In A. Amin and N. Thrift, eds., *Globalization, Institutions and Regional Development in Europe.* Oxford: Oxford University Press, 46–67.

Whatmore, S. 1995: From farming to agribusiness: the global agro-food system. In R. Johnston, P. Taylor, and M. Watts, eds., *Geographies of Global Change.* Oxford: Blackwell, 36–49.

Whatmore, S. and Thorne, L. 1997: Nourishing networks: alternative geographies of food. In D. Goodman and M. Watts, eds., *Globalising Food: Agrarian Questions and Global Restructuring.* London: Routledge, 287–304.

Williams, R. H. 1982: *Dreamworlds: Mass Consumption in Late Nineteenth-century France.* Berkeley: University of California Press.

Wrigley, N., ed. 1988: *Store Choice, Store Location and Market Analysis.* London: Routledge.

Wrigley, N. and Lowe, M., eds. 1996: *Retailing, Consumption and Capital.* Harlow: Longman.

Chapter 21

Public Memory

Nuala C. Johnson

Introduction

Roland Barthes observed in relation to the Eiffel Tower that it "is the only blind point of the total optical system of which it is the center and Paris the circumference" (Barthes 1964: 237). When speaking of the power of this public icon to capture the popular imagination both as a viewing spot for structuring the panorama that is Paris itself, and as symbolizing the city in a single sign, Barthes draws our attention to the significance of public monuments in the constitution of individual and collective meaning. Not all monuments have the iconic status of Paris's chief visual symbol, but the role of public sculpture and monumental architecture in framing the geographies of everyday life and in anchoring our collective social memory cannot be underestimated. While statues and the attendant grand architecture are found in cities of the ancient world, the massive proliferation of statuary and spectacular ritual that accompanied the nation-building projects of the past 200 years has become, in recent decades, a principal focus of scholarly attention.

These spaces of public display and ritual are what Boyer refers to as "rhetorical *topoi* . . . those civic compositions that teach us about our national heritage and our public responsibilities and assume that the urban landscape itself is the emblematic embodiment of power and memory" (Boyer 1994: 321). Rather than treating monuments as innocent, aesthetic embellishments of the public sphere alone, recent scholarship has emphasized the political and cultural meaning attached to them in the making of social memories. Indeed there is increased attention paid by cultural geographers to the *spatiality* of public monuments and ritual, where the sites are not merely the material backdrop from which a story is told, but the spaces themselves constitute the meaning by becoming both a physical location and a sightline of interpretation (Johnson 1994, 1995, 2003; Till 1999; Leib 2002).

Maurice Halbwachs (1992) observed that in the earliest religious rituals the most successful ones had a 'double focus' – a physical object of veneration and a shared group symbol superimposed on this object. Barthes also claims a 'double movement' where "architecture is always dream and function, expression of a utopia and instrument of convenience" (Barthes 1964: 239). Similarly when speaking of landscapes geographers have noted their duplicitous character materially experienced through the visual and other senses while simultaneously functioning as social symbols (Duncan 1990). Cultural geographers have been concerned centrally with the symbolic dimension of public monuments and their connections with social memory and identity politics. In this chapter I wish first to identify the relationship between time, representation and social memory. This will be followed by a discussion of the spatiality of memory and the role of geography in the construction of collective cultural identities. The final section of this chapter will examine how social memory is mediated by taking a selection of different examples of landscapes of mourning.

Time, Memory and Representation

The transmission and translation of meaning across time and space is central both to the rituals of everyday life and to the exceptional moments of remembrance associated with birth, death and other key events in personal and collective histories. Memory as re-collection, re-membering, and re-representation is crucial in the mapping of significant historical moments and in the articulation of personal identity. Consequently there are active practices of agency at work. As Jonathan Boyarin (1994: 22) has put it "memory is neither something pre-existent and dormant in the past nor a projection from the present, but a potential for creative collaboration between present consciousness and the experience or expression of the past."

Maurice Halbwachs' work *On Collective Memory* was the first critical attempt to give some sort of definition to the idea of social memory. For Halbwachs, collective or social memory was rooted in his belief that common memories of the past among a social group, tied by kinship, class, or religion, links individuals in the group with a common shared identity when the memories are invoked. Social memory is a way in which a social group can maintain its communal identity over time and it is through the social group that individuals recall these memories. But as Withers (1996: 382) has commented, this analysis itself is "rooted in that concern for continuities evident in the *longue durée* tradition of French *Annaliste* historiography and in acceptance of a rather uncritical, 'superorganic' notion of culture." While Halbwachs is right to socialize the concept of memory his analysis fails to historicize memory and embrace the notion that the very concept of the 'social' itself has a history and indeed a geography.

Conventionally the 'art of memory' since Romanticism has been ideologically separated from history in Western historiographical traditions where memory is subjective, selective and uncritical while history is objective, scientific and subject to empirical scrutiny (Yates 1978). With the demise of peasant societies, the social historian Nora (1989: 13) suggests that true memory "which has taken refuge in gestures and habits, in skills passed down by unspoken traditions, in the body's inherent self-knowledge, in unstudied reflexes and ingrained memories" has been replaced by modern memory which is self-conscious, historical and archival. More recent work on social memory has emphasized its discursive role in the articulation of an identity politics and in particular the role of elite and dominant memory, mobilized by the powerful, to pursue specific political objectives. The distinction between 'authentic' and modern memory is particularly persuasive when connected with a style of politics associated with nation-building programs. The development of extralocal memories have been intrinsic to the mobilization of an 'imagined community' of nationhood (Anderson 1983), and new memories necessitate the collective amnesia or forgetting of older ones. In particular where elites are concerned Connerton (1989: 51) suggests that "it is now abundantly clear that in the modern period national elites have invented rituals that claim continuity with an appropriate historic past, organizing ceremonies/parades and mass gatherings, and constructing new ritual spaces."

The democratization of political power in the nineteenth century shifted the focus from sculptural icons alone to a whole suite of associated collective rituals, with actors and spectators actively becoming involved in the re-presentation of the past. The erection of a monument to the French-Canadian politician Sir George Etienne Cartier (1814–73) is indicative of this process. Osborne (1998) has demonstrated how the memorialization of Cartier was used to embody the idea of a French-Canadian who combined loyalty to empire, nation, and race. The siting of this memorial in Montreal's Fletcher's Field–Jeanne Mance Park, near the interface of the city's English-speaking and French-speaking populations, was emblematic of the larger symbolic message encoded in the statue. In an elaborate unveiling ceremony in September 1919, representatives of the Canadian government, the Governor General, consuls from Canada's wartime allies, religious and industrial leaders, in addition to thousands of spectators and performers attended. As Osborne (1998: 439) has claimed, Cartier was "a figure who triangulated the values of a loyal French Canada, an expansionist Canada and an ever present Empire." In the second decade of the twentieth century this was an important unifying symbol for the Canadian state. A large-scale monument, accompanied by an elaborate unveiling spectacle transformed a popular recreational space in the city of Montreal into a site for narrating an official, elite view of Canada's history.

The role of re-membering the past – the putting together of its constituent parts into a single, coherent narrative – has been profoundly significant for the emergence of a popular nationalist identity. The deployment of the body as an analogy of the nation-state – a genealogy of people with common origins – coexists with a claim that the state acts as a guarantor of individual rights and freedoms that transcend historical time and the constraints of the past. Paradoxically, then, in the context of national identity, social memory as mediated through political elites both legitimates and simultaneously denies the significance of remembrance of things past.

While at its most basic level, memory can be said to operate at the scale of the individual brain and thus we avoid a concept of memory that suggests it has a super-organic quality, it is also necessarily the case that memories are shared, exchanged and transformed among groups of individuals. In this sense there are collective memories which arise from the inter-subjective practices of signification that are not fixed but are re-created through a set of rules of discourse which are periodically contestable. Till's (1999) analysis of the changing past that the Neue Wache memorial in Berlin represented is a compelling example. Originally built in 1816–18 under King Frederich Wilhelm III as a palace guard, the Neue Wache, located in Berlin's historic district has undergone a series of transformations. During the Weimar Republic it became a memorial to German soldiers killed in the First World War. The interior was redesigned to accommodate this new function by placing a large silver and gold plated oak wreath on top of a block of black marble and illuminating it by a beam of light emerging from a circular skylight. Under the Third Reich the building was redefined again as a memorial to represent a thousand years of German identity rather than a single historical moment. The historic meaning of the building was further transformed with the partition of Berlin and its location in East Berlin. Renovations in the postwar period under the German Democratic Republic (GDR) led the space to be rededicated to the victims of fascism. The interior room was remodeled to represent it as a site of antifascism. It contained the coat of arms of the GDR, an eternal flame and buried urns containing relics of soil from the concentration camps. For the 150 years or so of its existence, then, the past to which the Neue Wache made reference was reformulated several times over.

The real controversy over whose past the site would represent came with the redesigned building unveiled in 1993 as a new national memorial in a reunified Germany. Till (1999) disentangles the deep fissures that the debate about the new role of the building provoked. The interior was once again remodeled with an enlarged reproduction of Käthe Kollwitz's original 1937 statue *Mourning Mother With Dead Son* occupying the central space. While there was much public discussion about this rededicated building Till points out that West German interest groups' opinions were privileged overall. Three issues anchored the discussion. The first rotated around the tension of creating a 'national' memorial in a state with an uneasy relationship with the notion of the 'nation' and its underlying associations with extreme nationalism. The second concern was with the iconography of the statue itself. The implied Christian representation of suffering embodied in a Pieta style figurative monument and the construction of the past implied by that caused offence to the non-Christian population. The gendered depiction of suffering expressed through a representation of the 'universal' mother, although receiving less press coverage than other issues, also indicated a particular reading of the historical record. Thirdly, and perhaps most importantly, opponents of the redesigned Neue Wache questioned the manner in which the place remembered the dead. By dedicating it to *all* war dead it blurred the distinctions between victims and perpetrators. This suggested a leveling effect of death, which transcended the individual and collective identities of different social and religious groups. Critics feared that this mode of representation was in danger of collapsing difference, and relativizing historical and moral responsibility. In a compromise move, the Kohl administration added a plaque that listed separately different groupings killed in war. Through this fascinating case study Till has emphasized how the past at this site got reinscripted several times over. The debate in the 1990s brought into sharp focus the contested arenas of historical interpretation that undergirded the Neue Wache site. And even though she observes that "these discussions are still largely informed by a West German cultural hegemony" (Till 1999: 276), even within that context issues of historiography, gender and religion repeatedly surfaced.

Thus although there is a considerable literature emphasizing the politics of memory especially where dominant groups in society are concerned *vis-à-vis* their shaping of interpretations of the past, it is increasingly clear that the social process involved in memorialization is hotly contested with respect not only to form and structure but also to the meaning attached to a representation. Popular memory can be a vehicle through which dominant, official renditions of the past are resisted by mobilizing groups towards social action and also through the maintenance of an oppositional group identity embedded in subaltern memories. The deployment of local and oral histories in the formation of group identities can be a powerful antidote to both state and academic narratives of the past; especially where marginalized groups are concerned (Samuel 1994). The controversies surrounding the remembering of the Holocaust through the conversion of death camps into "memorial" camps to the genocide of the Second World War is a case in point. In Auschwitz, for instance, the competing aspirations of Polish nationalists, communists, Catholics and Jews to control the representation of the Holocaust there has influenced the physical structure of the site and the meaning attached to it by these various groups (Charlesworth 1994). In this sense rather than treating memory as the manipulative action of the powerful to narrate the past to suit their particular interests, a fuller account might follow Samuel (1994: 17) who suggests that one "might think of the invention of tradition as a process rather than an event, and memory, even in its silences, as something which people made for themselves." If memory is conceived as a recollection and representation of times past, it is equally a recollection of spaces past where the imaginative geography of previous events is in constant dialogue with the current metaphorical and literal spatial setting of the memory-makers.

Space, Memory, and Representation

The role of space in the art and the act of memory has a long genealogy in European thought. In the ancient and medieval worlds memory was treated primarily as a visual activity, one that focused on images more than written texts. The immense dialectical variation amongst linguistic groups and low levels of literacy perhaps account for the primacy of the visual image over other types of representation. Visual images, like the stained glass window and other religious icons, came to embed a sacred narrative in the minds of their viewers. They became mnemonic devices in religious teaching where sacred places became symbolically connected to particular ideal qualities.

Networks of shrines, pilgrimage routes and grottoes, sited for commemorative worship, formed a sacred geography where the revelations of a Christian God could be remembered and spatially situated (Carruthers 1990). Mappamundi too played a role in positioning the human within a sacred cosmology. The mapping of the narrative of Christianity through a predominantly visual landscape formed the basis of memory work through the Middle Ages.

While during the Renaissance and Enlightenment the conception of memory work changed scale (to the astral) and focus (towards the scientific rather than the religious), and was expressed, at times, architecturally by viewing the world from a height, it was during the period of Romanticism that a more introspective, personal, and localized view of memory came into focus. Memory in this guise came to be seen as the recovery of things lost to the past, the innocence of childhood and childhood spaces for instance, and it divorced memory work from any scientific endeavor to make sense of the world or the past. It transformed the role of memory to the scale of the individual and perhaps created the pre-conditions for divorcing history from memory and separating intellectually the objective spatial narratives of history from the subjective experience of memory-places. But Samuel (1994: X) persuasively argues that "far from being merely a passive receptacle or storage system, an image bank of the past, [memory] is rather an active, shaping force; that it is dynamic – what it contrives symptomatically to forget is as important as what it remembers – and that it is dialectically related to historical thought, rather than being some kind of negative other to it."

By treating memory as having a dialectical relationship with history, in constant dialogue with the past, we begin to see how the dualistic thinking underwriting the division of history and memory becomes more problematic. This is particularly the case in relation to the spatiality of history and memory. The gradual transformation of a sacred geography of religious devotion to a secularized geography connected with identity in the modern period destabilizes the rigid lines of demarcation drawn between objective/subjective narration; emotional/abstract sources of evidence; local/universal ways of knowing. Treating memory as a legitimate form of historical understanding has opened new avenues of research where subjective renderings of the past become embedded in the processes of interpretation and not as a counterpoint to objective facts. Nation-building exercises; colonial expansion of the non-European world; regional, ethnic and class identity formation; all embrace an imaginative and material geography made sacred in the spaces of remembrance and continuously remade, contested, revised and transmuted as fresh layers of meaning attend to them. Geographers, historians, anthropologists and cultural theorists are increasingly paying attention to the processes involved in the constitution and rooting of memory spaces, and especially to the symbolic resonances of such spaces to the formation, adaptation and contestation of popular belief systems. We come to understand their role through what Halbwachs (1992: 172) refers to as the "semiotics of space," that is, through treating space itself as a signifying system rather than just a material backdrop to interpretation.

In particular, studies have focused on the role of commemorative spaces and memory making in the articulation of national identity. In the context of the United States, the intersections between vernacular and official cultural expressions have been demonstrated to create a series of commemorative sites and rituals which attempt to combine some of the divergent sources of memory (e.g. local, ethnic, gender) with nationalizing ones. The vocabulary of patriotism is particularly important "because it has the capacity to mediate both vernacular loyalties to local and familiar places and official loyalties to national and imagined structures" (Bodnar 1992: 14–15). Similarly, because of the divergent allegiances generated by specific sites of memory, they operate multivocally and are read in divergent and at times contradictory ways. The commemoration of the American Civil War points to the underlying fissures evoked by remembrance of a divisive episode in a state's history. The spatiality of memory is not only mirrored in the physical distribution of commemorative sites but also in the interpretative apparatus embedded in them. For instance, the commemorative statue to General Lee in Richmond, Virginia focuses on his role as an American hero who fought out of loyalty to his home state and obscures the larger political and racial politics, which undergirded the war (Foster 1987). The equestrian statue on Monument Avenue was part of a larger speculative real-estate venture where an expensive residential subdivision of property was laid out along the long avenue. Linking business, art and memory-work the "legit-imation of Lee in national memory helped erase his status as traitor, as 'other,' leaving otherness to reside in the emancipated slaves and their descendants, who could not possibly accept Lee as their hero" (Savage 1994: 134).

Discussions of nation-building projects and the memory spaces associated with them have been analyzed as a form of mythology – a system of story-telling in which that which is historical, cultural and situated appears natural, innocent and outside of the contingencies of politics and intentionality. Drawing from semiology and lin-guistics such work claims that "the apparent innocence of landscapes is shown to have profound ideological implications . . . and surreptitiously justify the dominant values of an historical period" (Duncan & Duncan 1992: 18). Cultural geographers have extensively explored the promotion of specific landscape images as embodi-ments of national identity and historians have paid attention to the evolution of particular festivals, rituals, and public holidays (sometimes religious) in the evolu-tion of the 'myth' of nationhood. The materiality of a particular site of memory sometimes masks the social relations undergirding its production by focusing the eye on its aesthetic representation independent of the sometimes less visible ideas (social, economic, cultural power relations) underlying the representation. It is often then in the realm of the ideas, however contested and contradictory, that the meaning of memory spaces are embedded. What idea or set of ideas are stimulated by memories made material in the landscape?

The emphasis on visual interpretations of the memory landscapes that under-girded medieval sacred geographies continues to animate discussions of landscape interpretation today. The treatment of a landscape as a text which is read and actively reconstituted in the act of reading reinscribes the visual as the central action of interpretation (Barnes & Duncan 1992). While offering a more nuanced under-standing of landscape and the possibility of decoding the messages within any space, the text metaphor may overemphasize the power to subvert the meaning of land-scape through its reading without necessarily providing a space in which to change the landscape itself. Hegemonic and subaltern readings may in other words take precedence over hegemonic and subaltern productions (Mitchell 2000). The focus on the metaphor of the text also tends to underestimate the aural dimension of texts where, in the past, reading was a spoken activity. Reading texts aloud where the sounds, rhythms and syntax of the words are collectively absorbed directs attention to the social nature of interpretation which embraces senses other than the purely visual. Treating the landscape as a theater or stage broadens the imaginative scope of interpretation by suggesting that life gets played out as social action and social practice as much as it does by the reading implied by the text metaphor. As Cosgrove (1993: 1) argues "landscapes provide a stage for human action, and, like a theater set, their own part in the drama varies from that of an entirely discreet unobserved presence to playing a highly visible role in the performance." This notion of landscape as theater could be further extended not solely as the backdrop in which the action takes place but as actively constituting the action. The stage acts more than as the context for the performance; it is the performance itself.

The concept of public memory has been linked to the development of emotional and ideological ties with particular geographies. Memory is not simply a recollec-tion of times past, it is also anchored in places past and visualized in masonry and bronze, as well as in song and sound. The ordering of memory around sites of collective remembrance provides a focus for the performance of rituals of communal remembrance and sometimes forgetfulness. The continuous dimension of time is collapsed into a set of key symbolic dates and events and their public ritualization is expressed through what Nora (1989) refers to as "lieux de mémoire" or sites of memory. These sites become the landmarks of a remembered geography and history and they form the intersection between official and vernacular cultures. Public, collective memory then is "the dynamic process by which groups map myths (in an anthropological sense) about themselves and their world onto a specific time and place" (Till 1999: 254). This mapping process becomes part and parcel of the ongoing project of establishing individual and group identities, symbolically coded in public monuments.

The capacity which people have to formulate and represent their own memories, however, is regularly constrained by the discursive field in which they operate and literally the space in which their pronouncements both figurative and literal are made. As Sherman (1999: 7) reminds us, "commemoration is also cultural: it inscribes or reinscribes a set of symbolic codes, ordering discourses, and master narratives that recent events, perhaps the very ones commemorated, have disrupted, newly established, or challenged." If memory is conceived as a recollection and representation of times past, it is equally a recollection of spaces past where the imaginative geography of previous events is in constant dialogue with the current metaphorical and literal spatial setting of the memory-makers. This is clear in the recent debate concerning the placing of a memorial to Arthur Ashe in Richmond, Virginia. In a fascinating analysis Leib (2002) traces how the politics of race informed this debate. In a desire to remember the Richmond-born tennis star, philanthropist, and social activist "both African American supporters and much of the traditional white Southern population in Richmond tried to define and redefine their separate heroic eras (civil rights versus Civil War) within the same public space" (Leib 2002: 287). The proposal to locate the statue in Monument Avenue, the South's grandest Confederate memorial site, brought to the surface the deep tensions that the space represented to black and white occupants of the city. Both groups objected to the location. For African Americans the site in a white, prestigious neighborhood remote from many black children's everyday experiences and representing white Confederate ideology, seemed inappropriate for, what they regarded as, a hero of civil rights. By contrast, whites opposed the location on seeming aesthetic grounds, claiming that a statue of a casually-dressed Ashe would be incompatible with the statues to Confederate soldiers in full military dress. Ashe's statue would detract from the coherent symbolism of the avenue. This white aestheticized argument was supplemented with the suggestion that Ashe had not achieved enough in his life to be located adjacent to Confederate soldiers. While they acknowledged him to have been an excellent tennis player who should be commemorated in the city, a sports' star's achievements could not really be compared with the acts of heroism of a soldier. This argument sought to diminish Ashe's humanitarian actions, educational philanthropy and general political activism. While the city council eventually did decide to erect the Ashe memorial on Monument Avenue Leib (2002: 307) observes "that the meanings of monuments and the landscapes in which they are situated are never settled and are always open to contestation." And space was absolutely central to the conflict over Ashe. Moreover the geographies of remembrance are perhaps no more potently expressed than in war memorials and the landscapes of remembrance that societies create. I now wish to turn to some of these landscapes and to examine the contradictory memories that they evoke.

Landscapes of Mourning

In the aftermath of the First World War each combatant state attempted to inaugurate a landscape of national remembrance. In France, the issue of public commemoration converged around two areas of dispute. One related to the use of religious or secular iconography in monument design, the other focused on "the negotiation of local and national claims to memory of the dead" (Sherman 1994: 188). The French government agreed, where possible, to pay for the return home of soldiers' bodies, and memorials erected in towns and villages named individual soldiers killed in the community, localizing the act of remembrance.

The symbolic keystone of remembrance of the First World War in the United Kingdom was the building of the cenotaph (empty tomb), designed by Edwin Lutyens, and placed in Whitehall. This was accompanied by the burial of the unknown soldier in Westminster Abbey: "the unknown warrior becomes in his universality the cipher that can mean anything, the bones that represent any or all bones equally well or badly" (Lacqueur 1994: 158). Not all interests however were satisfied with the cenotaph. The *Catholic Herald* attacked the monument as "nothing more or less than a pagan memorial [which was] a disgrace in a so called Christian land" (quoted in Gregory 1994: 199). In an attempt to take the theological wind out of the sails of the Anglican Church the Catholic Church sought to reinforce their position as the true homeland of Christian morality, tradition and iconography. Nevertheless the cenotaph attracted huge crowds on the first anniversary of the Armistice and it continues to be the national centerpiece of commemorative activity each November. In towns across the United Kingdom smaller scale memorial spaces matched those in the capital. In Belfast, for instance, a catafalque was erected in the grounds of City Hall. The 1919 Peace Day celebrations were held in August rather than July to avoid clashing with the commemorative calendar of Orange Order parades, and the ceremonial centerpiece of the commemoration was the salute from the Irish Lord Lieutenant at the cenotaph.

The loaded role that space plays in the constitution of social memory can be seen in the Gallipoli peninsula. Site of the Allied Forces ambitious attempt to seize the Dardanelles and advance into Turkey, the peninsula became a site strewn with memorials, battlefield museums and cemeteries. While the early commemorative work of the 1920s was orchestrated by the Imperial War Graves Commission, by the 1950s the Turkish authorities had constructed a number of modernist structures at Cape Helles. By the 1990s these had been supplemented by a number of more traditional Islamic memorials and "a battle for monumental supremacy [had] been waged" (Gough 2000: 223). Located close together the Turkish and Commonwealth memorial spaces vied with each other for attention. In 1997 the Turkish government announced a competition for a park dedicated to peace at Gallipoli. Design teams were asked to address the larger issues of global peace while at the same time trying to resolve the antipathy between those national and patriotic interest groups that claimed moral ownership of the space. While none of the submissions fully reconciled the design remit, the winning entry by Norway proposed a network of footpaths that would be created and customized by individual visitors, and complemented by a website. Here an attempt was made to shift the responsibility on to individual visitors rather than imposing an interpretive superstructure. Consequently the design offered "a minimally invasive critique of existing memorial and preserved sites, raising through its website fundamental questions about reconciliation and commemoration" (Gough 2000: 224). While the battles of the First World War provided the impetus for creating a memorial landscape, more recent developments have been animated by the contemporary concerns surrounding global peace rather than national commemorative rivalries.

Although many of the spaces of memory dedicated to the First World War were reinscribed and recoded to accommodate the casualties of the Second World War, the specific circumstances of that conflict produced some different cultural practices. In Japan, for instance, the government designated Hiroshima a 'Peace City.' On August 6, 1945, the city had been almost obliterated by a nuclear bomb and over 80,000 people lost their lives. In subsequent decades the remaining physical and social fabric became the locus for the iconography of the antinuclear movement. The city was reconstructed and a 'Peace Hall' project comprising of a 12-hectare site at the epicenter of the bomb was redesigned to include a Peace Square, Peace Arch, and the preserved remnants of the Industrial Promotion Dome building. In addition, an 87-hectare plot, the 'Peace Park' project, was designed to include children's playgrounds and an International Culture Center. Although the city was promoted as a 'Mecca of Peace,' the uneasy relationship between local and global practices of memory surfaced. Many Japanese were troubled that the influx of tourists and the commercial revenue gained from this mass pilgrimage would profane the memorial space and undermine the sacred memories of the city's citizenry. The tensions between personal memories and public spaces became evident. Nonetheless the city has become the model for other peace projects and it acts "simultaneously as a reliquary, a funerary site, a civilian battlefield, and as a locus of political and social debate" (Gough 2000: 218).

Conclusion

In the past two decades scholars from a variety of disciplines have focused attention on the representation and articulation of social memories through the analysis of a variety of sites of memory. Connecting these public sites to gender, class, religious, national, and ethnic identities has proved a fruitful avenue of research. In particular, cultural geographers have sought to add to this work by underlining the significance of space in investigating and interpreting the sculpted icons and memorial landscapes that surround us. Rather less attention has been paid to the aural and oral dimensions of memory work. The role of music, song and story telling in evoking social memories could be a fruitful avenue for future research. While the monumental architecture and heroic statues of the good and the great may be less fashionable today than in the early decades of the twentieth century, it is evident nonetheless that the drive to construct and represent social memories in the public sphere continues. While writing this chapter the six-month anniversary of the assault on the Twin Towers in Manhattan passed. In New York City two moments of silence were observed and a ceremony of remembrance was held in Battery Park. Fritz Keonig's 1971 sculpture *The Sphere*, which had formerly stood in the fountain at the World Trade Center, and had survived, was rededicated at that ceremony. On the evening of March 11, 2002, two parallel beams of light, evoking the Twin Towers, were switched on as a temporary memorial radiating across the Manhattan skyline. While these are early acts of remembrance, there is no doubt that further public acts of commemoration will take place and these will provoke discussions about the appropriate ways and means of collectively and individually making sense of the past.

REFERENCES

Anderson, B. 1983: *Imagined Communities: Reflections on the Origins and Spread of Nationalism*. London: Verso.

Barnes, T. and Duncan, J. S., eds. 1992: *Writing Worlds: Discourse, Text and Metaphor in the Representation of Landscape*. London: Routledge.

Barthes, R. 1964: The Eiffel Tower. In R. Barthes, *Mythologies*, tr. Annette Lavers. New York: Hill and Wang, 236–50.

Bodnar, J. 1992: *Remaking America: Public Memory, Commemoration and Patriotism in the Twentieth Century*. Princeton: Princeton University Press.

Boyarin, J. 1994: *Remapping Memory: The Politics of TimeSpace*. London: University of Minnesota Press.

Boyer, M. C. 1994: *The City of Collective Memory: Its Historical Imagery and Architectural Entertainments*. Cambridge, MA: MIT Press.

Carruthers, M. 1990: *The Book of Memory: A Study of Memory in Medieval Culture*. Cambridge: Cambridge University Press.

Charlesworth, A. 1994: Contesting places of memory: the case of Auschwitz. *Environment and Planning D: Society and Space* 12, 579–93.

Connerton, P. 1989: *How Societies Remember*. Cambridge: Cambridge University Press.

Cosgrove, D. 1993: *The Palladian Landscape: Geographical Change and its Cultural Representations in Sixteenth Century Italy*. University Park, PA: Pennsylvania State University Press.

Davis, S. 1982: Empty eyes, marble hand: the Confederate monument and the South. *Journal of Popular Culture* 16, 2–21.

Duncan, J. S. 1990: *The City as Text: The Politics of Landscape Interpretation in the Kandyan Kingdom*. Cambridge: Cambridge University Press.

Duncan, J. S. and Duncan, N. G. 1992: Ideology and bliss: Roland Barthes and the secret histories of landscape. In T. Barnes and J. S. Duncan, eds., *Writing Worlds: Discourse, Text and Metaphor in the Representation of Landscape*. London: Routledge, 18–37.

Foster, G. M. 1987: *Ghosts of the Confederacy: Defeat, the Lost Cause, and the Emergence of the New South*. Oxford: Oxford University Press.

Gregory, A. 1994: *The Silence of Memory*. Oxford: Berg.

Gough. P. 2000: From Heroes' Groves to Parks of Peace: landscapes of remembrance, protest and peace. *Landscape Research* 25, 213–28.

Halbwachs, M. 1992 [1950]: *On Collective Memory*, ed. and tr. L. Coser. Chicago: University of Chicago Press.

Johnson, N. C. 1994: Sculpting heroic histories: celebrating the centenary of the 1798 rebellion in Ireland. *Transactions of the Institute of British Geographers* 19, 78–93.

Johnson, N. 1995: Cast in stone: monuments, geography and nationalism. *Environment and Planning D: Society and Space* 13, 51–65.

Johnson, N. C. 2003: *Ireland, the Great War and the Geography of Remembrance*. Cambridge: Cambridge University Press.

Lacqueur, T. W. 1994: Memory and naming in the Great War. In R. Gillis, ed., *Commemorations: The Politics of National Identity*. Princeton: Princeton University Press, 150–67.

Leib, J. I. 2002: Separate times, shared spaces: Arthur Ashe, Monument Avenue and the politics of Richmond, Virginia's symbolic landscape. *Cultural Geographies* 9, 286–312.

Lowenthal, D. 1996: *The Heritage Crusade and the Spoils of History*. London: Viking.

Mitchell, D. 2000: *Cultural Geography: A Critical Introduction*. Oxford: Blackwell.

Nora, P. 1989: Between memory and history: les lieux de mémoire. *Representations* 26, 7–25.

Osborne, A. 1998: Constructing landscapes of power: the George Etienne Cartier Monument, Montreal. *Journal of Historical Geography* 24, 431–58.

Samuel, R. 1994: *Theatres of Memory*, vol. 1. London: Verso.

Savage, K. 1994: The politics of memory: black emancipation and the Civil War monument. In R. Gillis, ed., *Commemorations: the Politics of National Identity*. Princeton: Princeton University Press, 130–45.

Sherman, D. J. 1994: Art, commerce and the production of memory in France after World War I. In J. R. Gillis, ed., *Commemorations: The Politics of National Identity*. Princeton: Princeton University Press, 170–98.

Sherman, D. 1999: *The Construction of Memory in Interwar France*. London: University of Chicago Press.

Sturken, M. 1991: The wall, the screen, and the image: the Vietnam Veterans' Memorial. *Representations* 35, 118–42.

Till, K. 1999: Staging the past: landscape designs, cultural identity and Erinnerungspolitik at Berlins's Neue Wache. *Ecumene* 6, 251–83.

Yates, F. 1978: *The Art of Memory*. London: Routledge.

Withers, C. 1996: Place, memory, monument: memorializing the past in contemporary Highland Scotland. *Ecumene* 3, 325–44.

Part V   Landscapes

Chapter 22

Economic Landscapes

Susan Roberts

Introduction

Just as cultural geography has its own sociohistorical geography – its own spatialized genealogy – so too does economic geography and so too do relations between economic and cultural geography. Although there is considerable intellectual traffic between geographers working in the English-speaking world (at least), and thus it is problematic to write of entities such as "British cultural geography," there are some real differences in the way subfields operate and change in different national contexts. In Britain, economic geography has been unevenly caught up in the so-called cultural turn in human geography. The face of British economic geography – as seen in textbooks, articles by well-known practitioners, and so on – has taken on a decidedly culturalist appearance (e.g., Lee & Wills 1997; Bryson et al. 1999; Bryson et al. 2000). This has not been without some argument and dissent (see e.g. Thrift & Olds 1996; Amin & Thrift 2000; Barnes 2001; Rodríguez-Pose 2001; Samers 2001). In North America, while the subdiscipline as a whole seems to have been less affected by such intellectual shifts, which in any case have been differently constituted and experienced, some of the most innovative and important work in economic geography has been marked by sustained attention to cultural matters (e.g., Gibson-Graham 1996; Pred & Watts 1992; Barnes 1996). Indeed, the story of a cultural turn (singular), with its implication of a recent, rapid, and coherent history, is simplified and exaggerated. It is easy to point to work in economic geography that has diligently and critically worked that boundary between culture and economy. This is especially true if we take a broad view of economic geography and include political economy and development geography (see e.g. Sidaway & Pryke 2000a, 2000b). It is perhaps not ironic that the cultural turn (as far as I can tell) began in part when cultural geographers worked to situate and analyze landscapes and their meanings within material historical political economies (especially Cosgrove & Daniels 1988; but see also Mitchell 1995, 1996; Roberts & Schein 1993; Schein's chapter 2 in this volume).

Expanding our considerations to a wider frame than geography and its subdisciplines, we can see that the worth of treating domains such as culture and economy as separate in any meaningful way, has increasingly been questioned (although cf. Sayer 1997). The rise of "culture" as a thing and as an object of study has been well documented (Williams 1976). Likewise, the epistemological establishment of a separate sphere or domain labeled as "the economy" has been charted by a variety of scholars (including Meiksins Wood 1981; Buck-Morss 1995). The economy, perhaps more so than culture, grew into a sphere that was (and still is, in mainstream/neoliberal frames) understood to be subject to its own processes and laws. It has become a taken-for-granted commonplace to refer to laws of the "market," of supply and demand, for example. Such a conceptualization of the economy made it (more than culture) available for scientific analysis (Visvanathan 1988). Hence, there are Nobel prizes for economics but not for anthropology. Moreover, the science of economics has been a practical one – aimed at once at analyzing and ensuring the "progress of opulence" (Smith 1976 [1776]). It has, contradictorily, been about the economy as an autonomous sphere, but also about its management and regulation, most notably by the modern capitalist territorial state. For the second half of the twentieth century at least, the economy meant the national economy. National economies, both so-called developed and developing (see Ferguson 1994 and Mitchell 1995) came, in the post-Second World War era, and until the rise of neoliberalism, to be seen as spatially bounded spheres to be managed and governed by the state with the aid of varieties of Keynesian economics (Berthoud 1992; Toye 1993). It is clear that the mainstream of economic thought has shifted to a more neoliberal logic that stresses the state-market binary and claims that the market is best left alone by the state – at least as a general principle (Watts 2000). Such arguments go hand in hand with descriptions and explanations of globalization that emphasize and celebrate a free-wheeling global market that encounters national regulatory structures only as undesirable causes of costly friction (e.g. Friedman 2000). While it is perhaps obvious that accounts of globalization such as Friedman's are cultural products, we can also see accounts of the economy (economics) and the economy itself then, as cultural products. Even concepts such as needs or poverty can be seen to be crystallizations of social and cultural practices (see Levine 1988 on needs, and Yapa 1996 [cf. Shresta 1997], on poverty, for example). Like all cultural products, knowledges of the economy and practices of its management possess or, better, are born out of particular times and spaces and are a mass of contingencies, even though they are not experienced this way by most. Likewise starting from culture, we can see that culture anywhere cannot be understood as outside of, or apart from, the ways people struggle to secure livelihoods. Relations of production and exchange, be they classically capitalist or not, are part and parcel of culture. Notice I did not say "are fundamental to" because I am keen not to replay the old base-superstructure (economy-culture [or ideology]) formulations (see also Mitchell's chapter 5 in this volume). Taking cues from much (western) social theory that has been devoted to exploring the many complex intersections and interrelations between the so-called cultural and the so-called economic, and the political, I wish to do so in ways that hold each in tension and do not accord a priori primacy to one or the other. It seems that this is in fact a central, if implicit, feature of much human geography, no matter the sub-discipline with which it is identified.

So, economic geographers and cultural geographers are themselves socially or sociologically categorized subjects, rather than being any kind of rationally ordered organizational reflections of an ontology ordered likewise. Of course, even though there is no essential "givenness" to the differences between cultural and economic geography, and even though we may be broadly invested in the same trajectory (as I argued above), there have been fierce antagonisms between cultural geographers and economic geographers in the past (see Hartshorne 1939; Butzer 1989). Further, there are still significant differences between cultural geography and economic geography as they are practiced today. These differences lie in theoretical inspirations and aspirations, key debates and animating concerns, research methods, and (to a degree) narrative styles (see Barnes 1996). The editors of this volume asked me to write as an economic geographer and discuss how I would approach the analysis of a landscape – a central activity of cultural geographers. How would an economic geographer approach, theorize, understand, explain this or that landscape? So, even though in this brief introduction I have argued against any assumed logic to the framing of such a task in terms of a culture-economy split, I shall proceed to carry out this exercise as a way of exploring how a place saturated with economic meaning – to the extent perhaps of making it appear only legible in economic terms, can be read as a nexus of all sorts of overdetermined relations (Gibson-Graham 1996: 26–9). Such relations refuse to completely settle in one or other realm, no matter that they are commonly exclusively ascribed to either economic, political, or cultural realms. In the study of aspects of the economy, and their associated places and landscapes, there is a substantial, even mainstream approach that is very much along such lines (see, as only a few examples of vast literatures, Corbridge, Martin, and Thrift 1994 on money and finance, or Herod 2001 or Kobayashi 1994 on work). Nonetheless there are some sorts of economic geography knowledges that remain more centered on the economy as their frame and as things taken to be 'economic' as their objects of analysis. Transport hubs, and particularly ports, have been treated this way. Here, I examine US maritime ports as places evincing a particularly interesting set of relations infused with economic, cultural, and (geo)political concerns.

Economic Geography and Transport Geography

In economic geography, there is an important tradition dealing with transportation. Transportation ought, in principle, to be a central concern of the subdiscipline, because it deals with distance. Distance is at the theoretical heart of space-time (Nystuen 1968; Massey 1993a, 1999) and of human geography. It has been at the center of capitalism's constant yet uneven restructuring – as David Harvey, above all others, has shown (e.g., 1989). Transportation geography has indeed emerged as an analysis of distance in capitalism – how it is calculated, meaningfully experienced (mostly by capital – the firm – rather than by labor), and articulated through material infrastructures or networks. Transportation geography has tended to include a large number of applied studies, and in general seems dedicated to the production of one sort or another of instrumental knowledge, most often via planning or policy (e.g., Tolley & Turton 1995). Methodologically, transportation geography has been closely associated with spatial science and with the application and development of quantitative analytical methods (see textbooks by Taaffe et al. 1996; Hoyle et al. 1998).

As transportation geographers recognize, the present globalization of policy prescriptions derived from neoliberalism is wreaking massive changes in the geographies of transportation at all scales and presenting them a tremendous opportunity. For example, the *Journal of Transport Geography*'s mission statement begins with this observation: "A major resurgence has occurred in transport geography in the wake of political and policy changes, huge transport infrastructure projects and responses to urban traffic congestion" (see *Journal of Transport Geography* 2003). The neoliberal insistence on liberalization cannot be realized without substantial material changes in the landscape. Specifically, it has resulted in considerable state sector and private capital investment in physical infrastructure designed to facilitate the opening of markets in material ways. Ports and airports, for example, are deemed in neoliberalism to be appropriate investments (and more appropriate than bread subsidies or social welfare measures) for the slimmed-down state. The World Bank and various bilateral aid agencies are heavily involved in such projects throughout the so-called developing world. Such civil engineering projects are just a part of the work entailed in making what is called globalization actually happen. Transportation geographers are seeking to map and understand such changes. Yet, for the most part, their analyses are not very critical of the general impulses of neoliberalism, even while they may be critical of various aspects of particular processes or policies.

Despite this overall state, transport geography has in the past been the site of some tremendously important critical work. For example, transport geography's methods were combined with elements from Hägerstrandian 'time geography' by feminist geographers Susan Hanson and Geraldine Pratt in their analysis of relations between journeys to work and the highly unevenly gendered urban spatialities of home and work (see Hanson 1995; Hanson & Pratt 1988a, 1998b, 1990, 1991). Hanson and Pratt's research in this area impacted transport geography, urban geography, and stands as a major contribution to feminist geography. Other areas in transportation geography seem less affected by concerns with social difference (e.g. gender), equity, or politics (more broadly conceived than in planning or policy terms) (although see Hine & Mitchell 2003 for an exception).

One part of transport geography that, it could be argued, has been only lightly touched by such concerns and that has had very little to do with cultural geography and vice versa, is port geography. Port geography has tended to be quite applied in orientation (see Hoyle 1996), although, because in many parts of the world old dock areas and waterfronts have become signal sites for urban redevelopment projects, some port geographers have moved closer to urban geography and more culturalist treatments of docklands developments (see e.g. Meyer 2003). On the other hand, it is interesting to note how few of the recent innovative cultural-urban geographies of Los Angeles pay any attention at all to the city's harbor/port (see Soja 2000, Scott & Soja 1996 as examples). This, despite the fact that the Port of Los Angeles is the biggest port in the US in terms of the volume of containerized traffic it handles. Together with the nearby Port of Long Beach the two southern Californian ports dwarf any other US port on any coast. Likewise, in terms of cargo value, Los Angeles and Long Beach if combined would rank first, even though separately they are only ranked below New York and Houston. For these rankings and one based upon cargo volume, see table 22.1 (see also figure 22.1).

Table 22.1 US Port Rankings, 2000

By cargo value (US$ millions)		By cargo volume (short ton 000s)		By container throughput (TEU 000s*)	
New York	19,732	S. Louisiana	217,757	Los Angeles	4,879
Houston	18,732	Houston	191,419	Long Beach	4,601
Long Beach	16,898	New York/NJ	138,670	New York/NJ	3,051
Los Angeles	16,732	New Orleans	90,768	San Juan PR	2,334
Hampton Rds	12,338	Corpus Christi	83,125	Oakland	1,777
Charleston	11,274	Beaumont	82,653	Charleston	1,629
Oakland	9,596	Huntington	76,868	Seattle	1,488
Miami	8,435	Long Beach	70,150	Tacoma	1,376
New Orleans	7,596	Baton Rouge	65,631	Hampton Rds	1,347
S. Louisiana	7,119	Texas City	61,589	Houston	1,074

Source: Compiled from data in AAPA 2002.

Note: A TEU is a maritime industry standard unit of measurement. It means 'Twenty Foot Equivalent Unit.' Containers typically come in 40-foot or 20-foot lengths. Using TEUs, various sizes of container can be counted in a standard unit.

Welcome to the Web site of the Port of Los Angeles, one of the world's largest, busiest, and most successful seaports. Located in San Pedro Bay, approximately 20 miles south of downtown Los Angeles, the port complex occupies 7500 acres of land and water along 43 miles of waterfront.

Your life is directly affected by what happens at the Port – from the clothes you wear, to the food you eat, to the well-being of the region you live in. The Port of Los Angeles could be "Your Best Liquid Asset." Thanks for taking the time to browse through our Web site to find out why.

Figure 22.1 Port of Los Angeles website welcome, 2003

The ports of Los Angeles and Long Beach are clearly significant in terms of the overall geography of US international trade. More than this, though, these ports are embedded in the regional economy and culture of southern California in a myriad of mundane ways, as the promotional greeting on the Port of Los Angeles website claims.

What would a more critical and more culturalist (and it should be clear by now that I do not equate these two attributes) economic geography of a port (landscape?) be like? In the remainder of this chapter I present a preliminary approach to the Port of New Orleans as a way to explore some of the challenges entailed in such a venture. In the process I should perhaps specify that my inspiration comes more from the political economy tradition in economic geography than from the spatial scientific tradition, for example. In addition, I have found it productive to bring in insights drawn from political geography, and particularly from critical geopolitics (see Herod, ÓTuathail, and Roberts 1998 for an earlier attempt to mesh these approaches).

Ports and Containers

If ever there was a place that, in a very material and quite obvious way, could be understood in terms of the intersections of myriad flows and overdetermined relations (see Massey 1993b, 1997) – a port would be a good candidate. Ports are scenes of comings and goings, of activity bundles (Pred 1977) bringing together the labor of greatly distanciated groups (of rubber tappers in Malaysia and stevedores in New Orleans, for instance) in the movement of commodities/products.

Ports are the hinges or valves articulating the national economy with the global economy. The US American Association of Port Authorities has 150 members. Public port authorities act in a variety of manager and landlord roles to oversee and coordinate the operation and development of the US's deep water ports. Through these 150 ports and others flow the bulk (in sheer volume, but also in value) of the national economy's tangible exports and imports. The US is trading as it never has, although the trade is unbalanced. At present the US has a truly enormous trade deficit with the rest of the world. According to official data, the trade deficit grew spectacularly through the 1990s. In 1991 it was valued at US$29.5 billion, but by 2002 it had reached over $435 billion (USTDRC 2000; USCB 2003).

Wal-Marts all across the US are filled to the brim with goods from China. From affordable clothing to toys to furniture, consumption by ordinary US shoppers nowadays is by importation. It is as if the commodity-hungry US economy sucks in sustenance every day, and much of that sustenance comes into the country through ports. Some high value commodities are imported via air freight, and a good deal of goods are transported via road or rail across the borders from Canada and Mexico, but the majority of imported "stuff" comes in through the country's ports. Bulk goods, like steel, lumber, and petroleum cannot be safely or efficiently containerized. However, most of the manufactured goods that fill the aisles of the country's over 3,000 Wal-Marts arrive in the US from Asia and elsewhere in standardized metal boxes known simply as containers. More than 50,000 containers arrive in the US each day (Bonner 2002: 14).

Containerization has had a revolutionary effect on the shipping and port industries, and has impacted a range of associated industries and labor, from rail and truck transportation to packaging and manufacturing of all sorts (Herod 1998, 2001; Winder 1999). In his historical study of this phenomenon as it impacted the Oakland port, Mark Rosenstein sums this all up:

Beginning in the 1950s, a revolution occurred in the technological foundations of the carriage of goods by ships. A labor intensive, piece-by-piece break-bulk method of loading and unloading cargo was replaced by a capital intensive, industrial process – containerization. This new technology, in which goods are packed into a metal box, transported as a unit, and unpacked only at the final destination, had far reaching impacts on stevedoring, ship operations and ports. The effects were even more widely felt, since containerization facilitated intermodal transport. Now, a container could be carried by ships, trains, and trucks, effortlessly moving between modes of transportation by a mechanized lift-off, lift-on transfer. Despite its advantages, previous attempts at containerization experienced only limited success. The efforts of Malcolm McLean and his firm Sea-Land Service, Inc. culminating with the departure of the vessel *Ideal X* carrying a deckload of containers from Port Newark en route to Houston in 1956 ushered in the modern era of containerization. (Rosenstein 2000: Abstract)

Containers themselves are fascinating commodities, technologies, and features of land- and seascapes. In the US, containers are showing up all over urban and rural landscapes. They are found at the back of shopping malls, as storage facilities for excess shop fittings or even inventory. They are seen all around construction sites where they function as tool sheds, cafeterias, offices, or latrines. Why are these 20 or 40 foot long metal boxes, originally manufactured for the ocean trade of commodities, showing up all over the US (and European) landscape? The answer partly lies in the seriously imbalanced global geography of trade. Every year, millions of standard steel shipping containers are manufactured – primarily in East Asia (China, South Korea). These are then filled with goods (and to a lesser extent commodities) for export. Giant ships (with displacements of over 70,000 gross tons), each loaded with thousands of containers then are unloaded in the ports of Europe and the US. The containers are typically put onto train or tuck chassis and off they go – intermodally – to the factories, warehouses, distribution centers, and stores. Some containers get re-used: they are filled with US made products for export and in turn get shipped to overseas ports, and so on.

The movement of containers around the globe is, at its most cost effective and neoliberal ideal, a perpetual motion of open circles. However because of two geographies of unevenness this does not happen. First, the simple developed-developing divide – where in the developing world there are barriers to entry in operation. Despite competitive pressures to up-grade, many ports cannot afford the sorts of investments necessary to support the handling of containerized cargo (see Airriess 1989; Hoyle & Charlier 1995; Wang 1998; and Song 2002 on interport competition). Such physical improvements require investments in dredging deep water channels, in reinforced wharves for storing containers stacked five high, and in large cranes that can lift heavy containers and that can reach across the largest classes of container ships (which can now be as much as 130 feet across the beam). These are major capital investments and, of course, displace much unskilled and skilled labor at the docks and in related industries (Herod 1998, 2001). So some parts of the world are not incorporated into these looping movements of containers. Most containerized traffic moves around (within and between) the three regional elements of the globalized economy – Europe, North America, Asia (east and southeast, primarily). The second geography of unevenness or asymmetry is the global pattern of trade surplus and deficit (Dicken 1998, 2002). Here, the US acts like a big sinkhole for goods and thus for containers. It is usually cheaper to buy a new container than to pay for the costs of shipping an empty one across the oceans. Thus, there is presently a huge oversupply of containers in the US. The industry of refurbishing, retrofitting and customizing containers has been an innovative sector and has produced a large range of adapted containers for sale, lease, or rent (see Seabox.com for example).

Containers appeared and still appear to assist the speeding-up and general efficiency of international trade. The doctrine (or dogma) of free trade or more generally of liberalization, would make the case for a geo-economy that is open, free of onerous regulatory controls, a sort of smoothed space of flows (Hardt & Negri 2000), wherein goods, services, financial instruments, and money can flow about according to the beating of the market's heart – of supply and demand. Even though the World Trade Organization essentially operates according to such logic, the global trading system, much less the geo-economy, is not an 'ideal' free market. As an aside, it is of course quite reasonable to point out that the whole idea of the free market is more of a mythic rationalizing end point than a sought after ideal state of affairs – it is not so much desired for itself as it is desired because of the things that can happen in its name. In the frame of liberalization the job of ports is to ensure the speediest, most efficient, cheapest, and smoothest transition as containers move from one "mode" to another (ship-rail or truck to ship for example). Certainly the shipping companies, the shippers, the brokers, the buyers and sellers of the commodities, all pressure ports and the myriad classes of port labor to reduce the "friction" at the port, so as to enable rather than impede the flows across the modes. However, in the present situation, there are very strong forces pulling in the direction of greater reinforcement of the US's national borders.

(In)security

On October 28, 2001, *The Seattle Times* ran a story with the headline "Big Hole in Nation's Defenses: Our Ports," by reporter Susan Kelleher. Since September 11, 2001, and the emphasis on 'Homeland Security,' a new set of geographies of fear have emerged. Built upon older mappings and practices aimed at securing the country's borders (such as 'Operation Gatekeeper' along the US–Mexico border), these post-9/11 mappings identify particular loci reasoned to be sites of danger. These included virtually all transportation networks, with particular anxiety focused upon nodes – places, such as airports, where complex logistical transfers seemed to present a landscape far too unruly to ever be easily surveilled, governed, and secured. It was not long before "our ports" came more sharply into focus as sites of anxiety over securing the homeland.

Within overall fears about "transportation networks and land and sea borders" (Flynn 2002: 60), the item upon which most anxiety is mapped is the container. The "black box" nature of the container with its unknown and, in these times, therefore suspect interiorized contents has come to be a potent symbol of fear. In Stephen E. Flynn's article on "America the Vulnerable," in the influential journal *Foreign Affairs*, the visual image is a large photograph of a container vessel in port (Flynn 2002: 65), although the article is about much more than containers. In addition, in a recent newsletter from the University of Pennsylvania's Wharton School of Business, an article appeared that was titled "How Far Should Business Go to Protect Itself against Terrorism?" (Wharton 2003). The five-page article is headed by one photograph and that depicts a container ship being loaded or unloaded by a crane with a single container suspended in mid-air. The article details the many possible arenas of concern for managers in the private sector – from the food industry to utilities, information technology, and financial service businesses. The issue of ports arises twice in the article and the potential dangers of containers were mentioned once, apart from their being signaled in the only visual image in the piece. Not that the focus on containers is wrong-headed. In October 2001 a container bound from

Italy to Canada was found to have been adapted to house a suspected terrorist who was locked inside (*The Times* 2001). Because ports are border sites, they have become loci of fear through which thousands of apparently unknowable containers arrive daily and enter the circulatory systems of the national territory. Ports, sitting on the edges of national territory, are sites where issues of geo-economics and geo-politics meet. Before September 11, 2001, it looked as though the globalizing economy was trumping the political geography of the world. Yet now, influential analysts such as Flynn and "front line" officials such as US Customs Commissioner Bonner, have pointed to lax border security as the "soft underbelly of globaliza-tion" (Flynn 2002: 61), a condition that makes the "hardening" of US borders an urgent task (Bonner 2002: 6).

In the contemporary US, doctrines of national/homeland security co-exist with a general tendency to accept liberalization (albeit with a *de facto* national interest ever present and at work). But at the same time, the national/homeland security doctrine demands that the borders of the US be secured against potential dangers (see Luke 1991; ÓTuathail 1996; Slater 1999). The borders are to be patrolled, policed, and guarded through action at or along the country's edges, and increasingly within and beyond these lines too (Bonner 2002). John Agnew has pointed out that in a world of states (in)security lies at the heart of geopolitical imaginings of the world and vice versa, For example, he states:

The focus on one's 'own' state and its security *vis-à-vis* the pre-emptive activities and poten-tial depredations of others reflects the profound ontological insecurity (loss of predictability and order) of people in the modern world. The geopolitical imagination has offered a reas-suring response. Our security was no longer vested in a transcendental religious order with earthly enforcers, such as the medieval Christian Church, a substitute had to be found. . . . The geopolitical simplification of the world into 'friendly' and 'dangerous ' spaces provided a practical means of giving order to this threatening and dangerous world. (1998: 70)

In the contemporary (post September 11, 2001) mappings of danger, security is seen as radically incomplete along every border and coast (Flynn 2002). Insecurity about terrorism has overlain extant fears of everything from child kidnappers to gun toting school children, and has been mapped onto the interior as well as exterior spaces of the nation-state. The current circumstances are not entirely brand new, but have resulted in a saturation of security regimes (most often referred to as 'measures') that have either been beefed up or newly installed in almost every space, from shop-ping malls in small towns, to ordinary workplaces, to student residence dorms (see Crang 2000 for a discussion of workplace surveillance for example). Along with this, security regimes have been even further embedded, enhanced, and extended at sites, such as airports and ports, identified as particular nexuses of vulnerability and hence fear. Security is in part a performative imperative – witness the recently man-dated rounds of screening at US airports. But the screening that passengers experi-ence is of themselves and their baggage. The movement of people has never been fully accommodated in the neoliberal view as it is found in the US. Liberalization is taken to justify the free movement of goods, services and finance as desirable, but this is not applied to people in general (see Sparke 1998). This uneven application of liberalization logics is, of course, one of the most often pointed-out contradic-tions of globalization more generally (see Sassen 1998, for example). While people do come in through ports, their primary traffic is in goods. Nonetheless, the ports of the United States are sites of intense regulatory and surveillant activity by the state – governing both the flows and the edges. Thus, for example, even a relatively small port – the Port of New Orleans – lists the following federal governmental agencies in its directory (PONO 2002):

Federal Bureau of Investigation
Federal Maritime Commission
US Border Patrol
US Coast Guard
US Customs
US Department of Commerce
US Food and Drug Administration
US Maritime Administration
US Postal Service
US Department of Agriculture, Animal and Plant Health Inspection Service
US Department of Agriculture Federal Grain Inspection Service

(In addition, at New Orleans, the federal government is present in the form of several agencies associated with the US Department of Defense such as the US Army Corps of Engineers and the Naval Reserve Force.) So while there is a general ascription to free trade doctrines, the US state continues its longstanding interests in monitoring and regulating the movement of goods through (but especially into) the national territory.

The regulatory and security imperatives present at the ports operate through the construction of physical barriers (fences, for example), and through visual inspections, but increasingly combined with and through information gathering and processing. US ports are intense activity bundles but they are also knowledge bundles, comprising massive amounts of information and information processing. While US ports are continually investing in their infrastructure, in the form of concrete and capital equipment (cranes and so on), they are also heavily investing in information technologies of many kinds. The Port of New Orleans, for example, as part of a large-scale investment in a new container facility (the Napoleon Container Terminal) is installing computerized portals through which every truck will pass. They will enable trucks equipped with in cab transponders to process "paperwork" before actually entering the port. Drivers of such trucks may not even handle paper manifests and transport instructions. Such technology is clearly dedicated to smoothing the transfer of container from ship to truck, but also fits easily into new security regimes. Thus, for example, the new Transportation Security Agency recently awarded the Port of New Orleans three and a half million dollars to install electronic access control gates at the entrances and exits of its road system (PONO 2002: 7). A container, no matter whether it is on a truck or rail chassis or a ship, has individual identification marks and usually a barcode. Such marks are used to track the container, and such tracking may be in the form of paper records and/or electronic data. An old freighter carrying say, bulk frozen chicken, needs an inventory specifying how much chicken it is carrying and who it belongs to, and where it is to go to. A container vessel of the new larger class, carrying over 6,000 TEUs brings along in its wake (so to speak) as many inventories as there are containers. A container full of antique furniture, say, is required by US Customs to be accompanied by a manifest listing every single item in it. Such a container may hold hundreds or thousands of individual itemized objects. In the aftermath of September 11, as one of a number of policies adopted to "harden our national borders" (Bonner 2002: 8), the US Customs proposed a "Container Security Initiative" (CSI) aimed at establishing a system of prescreening for container manifests to be done at their port of origin. The CSI is effectively extending the US border thus far (March 2003) to the ports of Rotterdam, Le Havre, Bremerhaven, Hamburg, Antwerp, Singapore, Yokohama, Vancouver, Montreal, and Halifax. CSI agreements have been signed with other ports and the system is supposed to include Hong Kong, Shanghai, Pusan (S. Korea), Kaohsiung (Taiwan), and other ports in Asia and Europe in due course. CSI operates similarly to the Advanced Passenger Information System that US Customs and airlines have been using for some years.

The collection and presentation of inventory data is driven by regulatory requirements, but has spawned its own mini-industry of tailored applications of information management and analysis, upon which shipping companies and others rely. In addition, with the rise of just-in-time (JIT) production methods (most famously in Japanese-owned auto plants in the US case), and more generally because of the time-sensitive nature of many transported goods (plastic eggs for Easter; lawn furniture for spring/summer seasons), keeping track of containers while en route has become of interest not just to the shipping companies themselves, but also to agents, brokers, and their customers. Very large shipping companies appear to compete in part on the basis of their information systems and how useful they can be to their customers. Which company offers the best real-time options for tracking your containers as they make their way from A to B? Figure 22.2 shows some of the information contained on a tracking record for a single 20-foot standard container shipped trans-Atlantic from a small town in the southeast of England, to a small town in central Kentucky, USA. Such a record is accessible to the party shipping the container, in real-time via the internet site of the shipping company. Additional tracking information showed the rail moves from Norfolk to Louisville and included 29 separate entries on the container's location (and time) along the route.

Although the discourses and practices of liberalization in the economic realm and homeland security in the political-cultural realm can seem to be opposed, the imperative to collect, order, and process information is common to both. It seems quite plausible to see these intersections of relations as working through one another, rather than in opposition to one another in the ports of the US (see also Dalby 1998: 309) In addition, the rapid expansion of apparently routine information processing and the way such practices are increasingly coming to be what places (such as ports) do, cannot be seen as unconnected to geopolitics or to the US's 'grand strategy' in the age of George W. Bush and his war-machine (Gowan 2002).

Conclusion

In *Ecology of Fear* Mike Davis catalogs the main elements in the "dialectic of ordinary disaster" haunting Los Angeles. The giant oil refineries next to the ports of Los Angeles and Long Beach are mentioned briefly as potential sources of major fires in the case of earthquake (1998: 42–3). Nowadays other geographies of fear and vulnerability are overlain on those detailed by Davis. The ports of southern

Container number TTNUXXXXXXX	Size 20-foot Dry Steel	
North American Customs Status		**North American Freight Status**
B/l number		
Place of receipt Little Chalfont, UK	**First activity date** 02-Nov-2002	
Place of delivery Midway, Kentucky, US		
CURRENT SHIPMENT		
Activity	Location	Date and time
Gate In Export Full	Felixstowe Trinity Terminal Felixstowe, UK	02-Nov-2002 13:40
Load Full	Felixstowe Trinity Terminal Felixstowe, UK	06-Nov-2002 04:17
Discharge Full	Norfolk Sea-Land, Norfolk Virginia, US	15-Nov-2002 08:37
Gate Out Import Full	Norfolk Sea-Land, Norfolk Virginia, US	16-Nov-2002 09:39
Gate In Import Full	Norfolk Sea-Land, Norfolk Virginia, US	16-Nov-2002 10:07
On Rail Full	Norfolk Sea-Land, Norfolk Virginia, US	16-Nov-2002 14.47
Off Rail Full	Norfolk Southern Railroad, Louisville, Kentucky, US	19-Nov-2002 04:50

Figure 22.2   Example of a container tracking record (excerpts)

California, like all ports, are no doubt doing their best to work with national and transnational capital and the US state to prevent disasters as part of the overall tightening of regulation and surveillance at ports, among the myriad practices going on in the name of 'securing the homeland.'

While obviously, a port is still basically a place "at which ships call to load and unload goods" (Moore 1975: 172), it can be seen a site through which all sorts of social relations, practices, and imaginings intersect. Ports, such as the Port of New Orleans, are places where the demand for cheap imported consumer goods, the uneven global geography of trade and current account "balances," the pervasive but differentiating mappings of fear, the technologically-mediated flows of information and goods, the interests of dock workers, shipping corporations, and the local state (port authorities) and the national state, are entangled in a dynamic and not at all settled mix. This mix, and the landscape it is part and parcel of, including the fences and electronic gateways, makes no sense only as something economic or something cultural. Rather, ports are just examples of places where what these terms mean, and what their material and discursive geographies may be, are being defined and re-defined in little (and some big) ways every day in and through the tangle of relations that intersect there.

REFERENCES

AAPA (American Association of Port Authorities). 2002: *Seaports of the Americas*. Alexandria, VA: AAPA.

Airriess, C. A. 1989: The spatial spread of container transport in a developing regional economy. *Transportation Research A* 23: 453–61.

Agnew, J. 1998: *Geopolitics: Re-visioning World Politics*. New York: Routledge.

Amin, A. and Thrift, N. 2000: What kind of economic theory for what kind of economic geography? *Antipode* 32,1, 4–10.

Barnes, T. J. 1996: *Logics of Dislocation: Models, Metaphors, and Meanings of Economic Space*. New York: Guilford.

Barnes, T. J. 2001: On theory, history, and anoraks. *Antipode* 33(2), 162–8.

Berthoud, G. 1992: Market. In W. Sachs, ed., *The Development Dictionary: A Guide to Knowledge as Power*. Atlantic Highlands, NJ: Zed Books, 70–87.

Bonner, R. C. 2002: Speech by US Customs Commissioner Robert C. Bonner before the Center for Strategic and International Studies, Jan. 17. Available at www.csis.org.

Bryson, J., Henry, N., Keeble, D., and Martin, R., eds. 1999: *The Economic Geography Reader*. New York: Wiley.

Bryson, J. R., Daniels, P. W., Henry, N., and Pollard, J., eds., 2000: *Knowledge, Space, Economy*. New York: Routledge.

Buck-Morss, S. 1995: Envisioning capital: political economy on display. *Critical Inquiry* 21(2), 434–67.

Butzer, K. W. 1989: Hartshorne, Hettner and 'The Nature of Geography.' In J. N. Entrikin and S. D. Brunn, eds., *Reflections on Richard Hartshorne's The Nature of Geography*. Washington, DC: Association of American Geographers, 35–52.

Corbridge, S., Martin, R., and Thrift, N., eds. 1994: *Money, Power, and Space*. Malden, MA: Blackwell.

Cosgrove, D. and Daniels, S., eds. 1988: *The Iconography of Landscape*. Cambridge: Cambridge University Press.

Crang, P. 2000: Organisational geographies: surveillance, display and the spaces of power in business organization. In J. P. Sharp, P. Routledge, C. Philo, and R. Paddison, eds., *Entanglements of Power: Geographies of Domination/Resistance*. New York Routledge, 204–18.

Dalby, S. 1998: Geopolitics, knowledge and power at the end of the century. In G. ÓTuathail, S. Dalby, and P. Routledge, eds., *The Geopolitics Reader*. New York; Routledge, 305–12.

Davis, M. 1998: *Ecology of Fear: Los Angeles and the Imagination of Disaster*. New York: Henry Holt/Metropolitan Books.

Dicken, P. 1998: *Global Shift: Transforming the World Economy*, 3rd ed. New York: Guilford.

Dicken, P. 2002: Trading worlds. In R. J. Johnston, P. J. Taylor, and M. J. Watts, eds., *Geographies of Global Change: Remapping the World*, 2nd ed. Malden, MA: Blackwell, 43–56.

Ferguson, J. 1994: *The Anti-Politics Machine: "Development," Depoliticization, and Bureaucratic Power in Lesotho*. Minneapolis: University of Minnesota Press.

Flynn, S. E. 2002: America the vulnerable. *Foreign Affairs* 81(1), 60–75.

Friedman, T. L. 2000: *The Lexus and the Olive Tree: Understanding Globalization*. New York: Anchor.

Gibson-Graham, J. K. 1996: *The End of Capitalism (As We Knew It): A Feminist Critique of Political Economy*. Malden, MA: Blackwell.

Gowan, P. 2002: The American campaign for global sovereignty. In L. Panitch and C. Leys, eds., *Socialist Register 2003: Fighting Identities: Race, Religion and Ethno-Nationalism*. New York: Monthly Review Press, 1–27.

Hanson, S., ed. 1995: *The Geography of Urban Transportation*, 2nd ed. New York: Guilford.

Hanson, S. and Pratt, G.1988a: Reconceptualizing the links between home and work in urban geography. *Economic Geography*, 64, 299–321.

Hanson, S. and Pratt, G. 1988b: Spatial dimensions of the gender division of labor in a local labor market. *Urban Geography* 9(2), 180–202.

Hanson, S. and Pratt, G. 1990: Geographic Perspectives on the Occupational Segregation of Women. *National Geographic Research* 6, 376–99.

Hanson, S. and Pratt, G. 1991: Job search and the occupational segregation of women. *Annals of the Association of American Geographers* 81, 229–53.

Hardt, M. and Negri, A. 2000: *Empire*. Cambridge, MA: Harvard University Press.

Hartshorne, R. 1939: The nature of geography: a critical survey of current thought in the light of the past. *Annals, Association of American Geographers* 24, 3 and 4.

Harvey, D. 1989: *The Condition of Postmodernity: An Enquiry into the Origins of Cultural Change*. Malden, MA: Blackwell.

Herod, A. 1998: Discourse on the docks: containerization and inter-union work disputes in US ports, 1955–1985. *Transactions, Institute of British Geographers* 23(2), 177–91.

Herod, A, 2001: *Labor Geographies: Workers and the Landscapes of Capitalism*. New York: Guilford.

Herod, A., Ó Tuathail, G., and Roberts, S. M. 1998: *An Unruly World? Geography, Globalization and Governance*. New York: Routledge.

Hine, J. and Mitchell, F. 2003: *Transport Disadvantage and Social Exclusion: Exclusion Mechanisms in Transport in Scotland*. Burlington, VT: Ashgate.

Hoyle, B. 1996: *Cityports, Coastal Zones and Regional Change: International Perspectives on Planning and Management*. New York: Wiley.

Hoyle, B. S. and Charlier J. 1995: Inter-port competition in developing countries: an East African case study. *Journal of Transport Geography* 5(2), 87–103.

Hoyle, B. S. and Knowles, R. D. 1998: *Modern Transport Geography*, 2nd ed. Chichester: Wiley.

Journal of Transport Geography 2003: Mission Statement. Available at http://www.transportconnect.net/jtrangeo/

Kobayashi, A., ed. 1994: *Women, Work, and Place*. Montreal and Kingston: McGill-Queen's University Press.

Lee, R. and Wills, J., eds. 1997: *Geographies of Economies*. London: Arnold.

Levine. D. 1988: *Needs, Rights, and the Market*. Boulder, CO: Lynne Rienner.

Luke, T. W. 1991: The discipline of security studies and the codes of containment: Learning from Kuwait. *Alternatives* 16(2).

Massey, D. 1993a: Politics and space/time. In M. Keith and S. Pile, eds., *Place and the Politics of Identity*. New York: Routledge, 141–61.

Massey, D. 1993b: Power geometry and a progressive sense of place. In J. Bird, B. Curtis, T. Putnam, G. Robertson, and L. Tickner, eds., *Mapping the Futures*. New York: Routledge, 59–69.

Massey, D. 1997: A global sense of place? In T. Barnes and D. Gregory, eds., *Reading Human Geography: The Poetics and Politics of Inquiry*. London: Arnold, 315–23.

Massey, D. 1999: Space-time, 'science' and the relationship between physical and human geography. *Transactions, Institute of British Geographers* 24, 261–76.

Meiksins Wood, E. 1981: The separation of the economic and the political in capitalism. *New Left Review* 127, 66–95.

Meyer, H. 2003: *City and Port: Urban Planning as a Cultural Venture in London, Barcelona, New York, and Rotterdam.* Utrecht: International Books.

Mitchell, D. 1995: There's no such thing as culture: towards a reconceptualisation of the idea of culture in geography. *Transactions of the Institute of British Geographers* 19, 102–16.

Mitchell, D. 1996: *The Lie of the Land: Migrant Workers and the California Landscape.* Minneapolis: University of Minnesota Press.

Mitchell, T. 1995: The object of development: America's Egypt. In J. Crush, ed., *Power of Development.* New York and London: Routledge, 129–57.

Moore, W. G. 1975: *A Dictionary of Geography.* Harmondsworth: Penguin.

Nystuen, J. D. 1968: Identification of some fundamental spatial concepts. In B. J. L. Berry and D. F. Marble, eds., *Spatial Analysis: A Reader in Statistical Geography.* Englewood Cliffs, NJ: Prentice-Hall, 35–41. (Originally published in *Papers of the Michigan Academy of Science, Arts, and Letters,* 1963, 48, 373–84.)

ÓTuathail, G. 1996: *Critical Geopolitics.* New York: Routledge.

Port of Los Angeles 2003. Website: www.portoflosangeles.com, accessed March.

Port of New Orleans. *Port Record* 2002. Sept./Oct. issue.

Pred, A. 1977: The choreography of existence: comments on Hägerstrand's time geography and its usefulness. *Economic Geography* 53, 207–21.

Pred, A. and Watts, M. 1992: *Reworking Modernity: Capitalisms and Symbolic Discontent.* New Brunswick, NJ: Rutgers University Press.

Roberts, S. M. and Schein, R. H. 1993: The entrepreneurial city: fabricating urban development in Syracuse, NY. *Professional Geographer* 45(1), 21–34.

Rodríguez-Pose, A. 2001: Killing economic geography with a "cultural turn" overdose. *Antipode* 33(2), 176–83.

Rosenstein, M. 2000: *The Rise of Maritime Containerization in the Port of Oakland 1950 to 1970.* MA Thesis, New York University. Available at www.apparent-wind.com/mbr/maritime-writings/

Samers, M. 2001: What is the point of economic geography? *Antipode* 33(2), 183–94.

Sassen, S. 1998: *Globalization and its Discontents: Essays on the New Mobility of People and Money.* New York: The New Press.

Sayer, A. 1997: The dialectic of culture and economy. In R. Lee and J. Wills, eds., *Geographies of Economies.* London: Arnold, 16–26.

Scott, A. J. and Soja, E. W., eds. 1996: *The City: Los Angeles and Urban Theory at the End of the Twentieth Century.* Berkeley: University of California Press.

Seabox.com 2003: website at www.seabox.com.

Shresta, N. 1997: A postmodern view or denial of historical integrity? The poverty of Yapa's view of poverty. *Annals, Association of American Geographers* 87(4), 709–17.

Sidaway, J. D. and Pryke, M. 2000a: The strange geographies of 'emerging markets.' *Transactions of the Institute of British Geographers* 25(2), 187–201.

Sidaway, J. D. and Pryke, M. 2000b: The free and the unfree: 'Emerging markets', the Heritage Foundation, and the 'Index of Freedom.' In J. Bryson, P. Daniels, N. Henry, and J. Pollard, eds., *Knowledge, Space, Economy.* New York: Routledge, 176–90.

Slater, D. 1999: Situating geopolitical representations: inside/outside and the power of imperial interventions. In D. Massey, J. Allen, and P. Sarre, eds., *Human Geography Today.* Cambridge: Polity Press, 62–84.

Smith, A. 1976 [1776]. *An Inquiry into the Nature and Causes of the Wealth of Nations, Volume One.* New York: Oxford University Press.

Soja, E. W. 2000: *Postmetropolis: Critical Studies of Cities and Regions*. Malden, MA: Blackwell.

Song, D.-W. 2002: Regional container port competition and co-operation: the case of Hong Kong and South China. *Journal of Transport Geography* 10, 99–110.

Sparke, M. 1998: From geopolitics to geoeconomics: transnational state effects in the borderlands. *Geopolitics* 3(2), 61–97.

Taaffe, E. J., Gauthier, H. L., and O'Kelly, M. E. 1996: *Geography of Transportation*, 2nd ed. Upper Saddle River, NJ: Prentice-Hall.

The Times. 2001: Business-class suspect caught in container. Oct. 25, p. 7.

Thrift, N. J. and Olds, K. 1996: Refiguring the economic in economic geography. *Progress in Human Geography* 20(3), 311–37.

Tolley, R. and Turton, B. 1995: *Transport Systems, Policy and Planning: A Geographical Approach*. Harlow: Longman.

Toye, J. 1993: *Dilemmas of Development*, 2nd ed. Malden, MA: Blackwell.

USCB United States Census Bureau 2003: *US International Trade in Goods and Services – Current, Prior and Compressed*. Washington, DC: US Census Bureau. www.census.gov/foreign-trade

USTDRC United States Trade Deficit Review Commission 2000: *Final Report. The US Trade Deficit: Causes, Consequences and Recommendations for Action*. Washington, DC: US Senate. (www.ustrdc.gov)

Visvanathan, S. 1988: On the annals of the laboratory state. In A. Nandy, ed., *Science, Hegemony and Violence: A Requiem for Modernity*. Tokyo: United Nations University/ Delhi: Oxford University Press, 257–88.

Wang, J. J. 1998: A container load center with a developing hinterland: a case study of Hong Kong. *Journal of Transport Geography* 6(3), 187–201.

Watts, M. 2000: Neo-liberalism. In R. J. Johnston, D. Gregory, G. Pratt, and M. Watts, eds., *The Dictionary of Human Geography*, 4th ed. Malden, MA: Blackwell, 547–8.

Wharton School of Business. 2003: How far should business go to protect itself against terrorism? *Knowledge@Wharton*, Feb. 26. Philadelphia: University of Pennsylvania, Wharton School.

Williams, R. 1976: *Keywords: A Vocabulary of Culture and Society*. London: Fontana.

Winder, G. 1999: Exploiting Technologies. In R. Le Heron, L. Murphy, P. Forer, and M. Goldstone, eds., *Explorations in Human Geography: Encountering Place*. Auckland: Oxford University Press.

Yapa, L. 1996: What causes poverty? A postmodern view. *Annals, Association of American Geographers* 86(4), 707–28.

Chapter 23

Political Landscapes

Karen E. Till

A graffitied "Wall" demarcates the boundary between the US and Mexico (figure 23.1). It is a political landscape defined by inclusions and exclusions. As a site of geopolitics and state power, this landscape expresses the sovereign right of one state to delimit political space through territorial spatial strategies, such as a material border, armed agents and soldiers, and a bureaucratic division, "Operation Gatekeeper," established in 1994 (Nevins 2001). This wall, established to keep undocumented immigrants from entering the US, *works* politically because it gives the appearance of a border under control. But the physical presence of this barrier conceals the unequal effects, economies, and consequences of its making. With the increase in Border Patrol officers, for example, there has been an increase in more sophisticated and expensive smugglers to evade those officers, a number of changes in worker-migrant mobilities (people stay longer once in the US and are less likely to migrate back to Mexico in off-season), and an increase in deaths of immigrants in the less policed mountain and desert areas of the border (Nevins 2000). This militarized border, in other words, is at once policing and peopled, and as such it is an embodied setting of *cultural practices* that may have political consequences despite of, or even because of, the strict controls of this place. People cross this border daily, they negotiate their and other people's movements, and they protest its presence, as evidenced by the graffiti stating "Stop Operation Gatekeeper!"

That this landscape expresses and creates so many meanings about political space should not be surprising. The various discursive and material meanings and functions of landscapes – as social environments, scenes, ways of viewing, representations of identity, nodes of capitalism, places of work, metaphors, and settings of everyday practice – are often used strategically by various actors to structure power relations and create understandings of 'the political.' Until recently, however, cultural geographers did not consider landscapes as a political concept nor did they view landscapes as outcomes and constitutive of political processes. Rather, scholars analyzed how cultures and human actions impacted the physical environment, resulting in "cultural landscapes" that could be read as an autobiography of a folk or as sedimented layers of social and cultural accretion (see Lewis 1979, 1983).

Figure 23.1 A Political Landscape: The US/Mexico Border/*La Frontera* (at San Diego, California and Tijuana, Baja California). The "Wall" extends out into the Pacific Ocean; political graffiti declares *Alto Guardian* ("Stop Operation Gatekeeper") (permission for use from Suzanne Michel; photo taken in Baja California, 2002).

Although some geographers paid attention to the role of processes and human activities in producing landscapes, those processes were often labeled 'cultural' and not considered political. Studies that treated 'landscape as everyday social space' (work often associated with J. B. Jackson's approach to studying 'ordinary' landscapes) also did not specify why certain landscapes should be privileged for study, such as why someone might want to research tenement districts as opposed to building types (Henderson 2002). These traditional approaches to cultural landscape tended to conflate vision with knowledge and legitimated a masculinist way of knowing about the world (Rose 1993). Geographers could seemingly take in a portion of the land 'at a glance' (as all-knowing and seeing observers of natural and human worlds) and write up "objective" descriptive inventories of those landscapes.

In recent years, geographers have called for studies that examine the processes, places, and people that went into the making of landscapes at multiple scales (Mitchell 2001; Schein 1997). Landscapes are theoretically understood as "arenas of political discourse and action in which cultures are continuously reproduced and contested" (after Duncan 1990, in Graham 1998: 21). Scholars analyze the ways that deliberate human action, discursive practices, economic relations, and everyday practices result in the establishment (and contestation) of particular material and symbolic landscapes that, in turn, structure social and political space. Moreover, by exploring the ways that landscapes are made, used, and circulated, geographers also analyze how landscapes reinforce and create meanings about the political realm and about social identities.

In this chapter I discuss three distinct approaches to the ways that landscapes constitute power relations and sociopolitical space: landscapes of state power, landscapes as work, and landscapes as everyday practice.[1] In the next section I describe how states, official institutions, and elites have constructed landscapes materially and discursively as political symbols. Geographers have drawn from various theories and methods to study the ways that officials and elites have imagined 'the nation' through paintings, representations, planning, and public monuments to gain or maintain access to political power and influence. In recent years, Marxist geographers have argued that scholars need to pay more attention to landscape as an expression of unequal social relations under capitalism, an approach to political landscapes I describe in section two. This perspective suggests that the production of landscape frames certain social relations and hides other relations, such as between labor and the making of landscape, and between labor and capital. Other recent research drawing from feminist and poststructuralist theories conceptualizes power in more diffuse ways than the first two approaches. In section three, I propose another approach, landscape as everyday practice, that draws from the strengths of the first two approaches yet is sensitive to the ways that social categories (gender, sexuality, race/ethnicity, class, and so on) interact and are created contextually. This approach would also examine the ways that multiple identity positions are performed in and through landscape. To explore the possibility of such an approach, I describe studies that may not explicitly theorize landscape but in some way examine how individuals and social groups self-consciously construct symbolic and material landscapes, or use the landscape in informal ways, to alter or question existing social and political relationships.

Landscapes of State Power: Imagining and Representing the Nation

As a form of geographical knowledge about how the world works, landscape is a central way of understanding social life and relations, including the relationships between a political community (an empire, regime, state, or even neighborhood) and its peoples. "Landscapes, whether focusing on single monuments or framing sketches of scenery, provide visible shape; they picture the nation," even though "there is seldom a secure or enduring consensus as to which, or rather, whose, legends and landscapes epitomize the nation" (Daniels 1993: 5). As symbols of national space (political territory) and time (social memory and heritage), national landscapes contribute to the everyday reproduction of a society (Gruffudd 1995; Johnson 1995). Cultural geographers have used different approaches to analyze how specific landscapes become dominant representations about how the world works that legitimate state and elite hegemony. Denis Cosgrove (1984) and Stephen Daniels (1993) describe the historical development of "landscape as a way of seeing" that accompanied the rise of linear perspective and was informed by the rational science of geometry. Further, this way of seeing material and social settings legitimated the emerging ideology of capitalism and the ruling, male-dominated, bourgeois class (see also Cosgrove & Daniels 1988; Rose 1993).[2] When understood as an epistemology, the all-seeing, knowing, and consuming masculine gaze, according to Gillian Rose (1993), constituted the landscape as a feminized object of desire to be conquered and possessed. Another approach, the poststructuralist "landscape as text" model developed by James and Nancy Duncan (1988), theorizes how landscapes function as one of many cultural texts through which political values are communicated and discourses enacted within particular societies. In addition, landscapes of state power have been analyzed as theater, a dramaturgical approach that captures the visual and routine nature of civic and state rituals (Cosgrove 1992;

Daniels & Cosgrove 1993). Common to all of these approaches is the view that the 'national' landscape is one of many competing articulations of powerful feelings and ideas that encapsulates a dominant image of how elites view 'a nation,' and perhaps even how 'a people' see themselves (see Duncan 1990; Olwig 2002).

Geographers have used these different approaches to landscape to examine how understandings of empire, state, and nation have been imagined, represented, and materially created through landscapes at particular moments in time. The common image of a bucolic landscape as being typically English, for example, emerged from eighteenth century landscape painting traditions in which scenes of flourishing estates depicted the virtues of progressive estate management (Daniels 1993). Such scenes were thought to reflect 'good taste,' being 'civilized,' and having a good social standing; being able to 'see' these landscapes properly also legitimated political authority (Nash 1999). Western, upper-class elite males claimed that only those who could objectively view the landscape had the rational detachment needed to properly see, rule, and govern. Those who worked the land lacked such visual objectivity because they were considered part of the landscape. Such ideas about and ways of seeing the landscape were connected to a historically specific model of freedom and individualism (differentiated by region, class, race, and gender) upon which commercial capitalism depended (Nash 1999). With the emergence of the nation-state, elites and others became nostalgic for bucolic landscapes that were supposedly lost with the early commercialization of agriculture, the rise of industrialization, and an increasingly internationalized England due to the expanding reach of the imperialist state (Agnew 1998a). Images of thatched cottages and pastoral countrysides during this moment in time became associated with *the* quintessential national landscape, that is, with what it meant to be English (Lowenthal 1991).

Scholars argue that the historical evolution of this romanticized English landscape ideal cannot be generalized to the experiences of other nations, even within Europe, nor should it be used as a general conceptual model for landscape (Agnew 1998a; Daniels 1993; Duncan 1995).[3] For example, Italy – a late-unifying state with a heterogeneous population – had a more difficult time in creating a representative national landscape (Agnew 1998a). Although the image of ancient Rome as the 'eternal city' came to represent Italian national identity after unification in 1865 (see below), other images were promoted, such as the Tuscan landscape as created by nineteenth century Macchiaioli painters in Florence.[4] As John Agnew (1998a: 230) points out, a long-lasting association between a particular landscape ideal and Italian national identity (as was the case for England) remained difficult because "the glories of ancient Rome and the Renaissance, [were] phenomena that the whole of Europe (or, even more expansively, the whole of Western civilization) claims as parts of its heritage."

While landscape images are historically specific forms of representing the nation in a given society, they have real political and material consequences, such as through land planning and in the projects of empire. Not only did wealthy British estate owners pay landscape architects to design properties to look like paintings and then had their properties painted (Duncan 1995), those very same images were used to legitimate and support colonial rule, and, in turn, to make and remake material landscapes abroad (see Pratt 1992). To make a place more familiar and more 'natural,' landscapes in overseas British colonies were changed to reflect Western homesteads and their related gendered and racialized roles (Nash 1999). Categories of people (men/women, settlers/natives, white/black) were assigned different locations within the material landscape as well as in landscape representations: white men worked, played, and conquered lands and mountain peaks, white women stayed at home, 'natives' were located elsewhere (Blunt & Rose 1994; Kearns 1997). After the phase of exploration was over, however, landscape stories and images indicated the contradictions between these landscape mappings and performed social identities. This may have been because such strict social divisions according to race, class, and gender, and between colonizer and colonized, were difficult to maintain in practice: colonial settler occupation depended upon hundreds of thousands of African workers who were legally classified as squatters or invaders, but without whom those farms would not have survived (Myers 2002). In addition, the very social categories themselves were inherently contradictory. Through a close reading of Eric Dutton's (1929) *Kenya Mountain*, Garth Myers (2002) examines a story of a failed climb and conquest to demonstrate how the dominant discourse of robust white Christian masculinity – defined by militaristic and athletic performances in the colonial landscape, and by refinement and tempering moral authority in (white) public and private spheres – was at odds with men's varied physical capacities and their lived experiences as clerks and shop-assistants in colonial society. Nonetheless, dominant colonial images of social relations continued to influence the ways that colonial and even postcolonial landscapes were planned. Jane Jacobs (1996) examines the ways that state-sponsored heritage projects in contemporary Australia represent 'authentic' Aboriginal cultures as belonging to the time-spaces of a more pristine (and imagined pre-contact) 'nature.' Through these projects, city planners and tourists continue to locate 'natives' in 'natural' landscapes, a way of viewing the social and natural environment that devalues contemporary urban and detribalized Aboriginal identities and cultures.

Elites have also created material landscapes as stages to display a distinctive national past and articulate an exclusive understanding of a cultural-political community. During the period of nation building in Europe, places of memory, like monuments, memorials, and museums, were established to maintain social stability, legitimate existing power relations, and provide institutional continuity (Johnson this volume; Till 2002b). Such places represented the nation in exclusive ways, according to gender, race, ethnicity, heteronormativity, class, religion, and/or region. According to Lorraine Dowler (1998), for example, war memorials and landscapes in contemporary Ireland exclude women (as well as other social groups) from being visible socially as leaders and active figures in the political realm. National landscapes also depict temporal continuity with past glories and the present state, evoking a sense of timelessness through material and symbolic means. The Vittorio-Emanuele II Monument in Rome, built in 1878–82 as a sacred altar honoring a dead king, was transformed in 1921 under Mussolini to celebrate the Cult of the Unknown Soldier (Atkinson & Cosgrove 1998). Symbolically located adjacent to the Imperial and Roman Fora, the stark white Brescian marble monument provided a new visual anchor for the city with its otherwise brown-tone buildings, an ordered vision of the world that materialized a mystical understanding of Italy as a transcendental classical empire, and linked a new political state to the mythical ancient acropolis of the 'eternal city' (Agnew 1998a; Atkinson & Cosgrove 1998).

Dramatic landscape inscriptions as these are typically built and rebuilt during times of political transition to maintain symbolic continuity and social stability (Foote, Tóth, & Árvay 2000; Till 1999). State officials and elites often invest much money and time through the establishment and remaking of symbolic national landscapes to accumulate 'symbolic capital' in the political realm and to project a particular worldview (Forest & Johnson 2002). Duncan (1990) describes how statues of British political figures – symbols of colonialism – were removed and replaced after independence by statuary commemorating Sri Lankan nationalist leaders in Kandy. This process, while reflecting a unified movement in the toppling of the British Empire, nonetheless reaffirmed the hegemonic political position of only one party (the United National Party) rather than a working alliance of parties opposed to colonial rule. In Taipei, Taiwan, after 1949, Chinese Nationalists renamed streets, schools, theaters, and other public buildings, squares, and spaces using names of Chinese national heroes, nationalistic slogans, and place names from the asserted living space of the Chinese nation-state (Leitner & Kang 1999). In contemporary Moscow, political elites co-opted, contested, ignored, or removed central Soviet-era public monuments after 1991 to engage in a symbolic dialogue with other politicians and the public and thereby gain prestige, legitimacy, and influence in cultural and political realms (Forest & Johnson 2002).

Recent research has indicated that material and symbolic landscapes of elite and state power – as ideology, way of seeing, stage, and text – cannot be necessarily used as "evidence" that those in power share similar ideas about the 'nation,' the 'state,' or the imposition of power. Nor does it imply that there is a one-directional flow of domination from ruler to ruled. Monumental landscapes may reflect the ideological incoherence, rather than popularity, of nationalistic agendas, as was the case in Mussolini's Rome (Agnew 1998b; see also Atkinson & Cosgrove 1998). In post-Soviet Moscow, Benjamin Forest and Juliet Johnson (2002) argue that the continuity between Soviet and Russian political elites constrained their ability to create Russian national symbols from Soviet ones, and so they chose to reinterpret, rather than erase, monumental landscapes (compare Bell 1999). Even then, these political elites, who controlled the resources to create national landscapes, must compete for symbolic capital, a process that means that these landscapes are not simply imposed on a passive 'public.' Their surveys of visitors indicated the limited appeal of these "new" (i.e. post-Soviet) monuments, suggesting that the past cultural functions of Soviet monuments may make it difficult to imagine a 'civic-democratic' Russian nation through such landscapes.

These approaches to political landscapes, while increasingly sensitive to the contradictions within state and national institutions and by elites with access to resources, still pay little attention to the histories and experiences of the individuals who actually make those landscapes. Further, as Don Mitchell (1996: 6) argues, "for all the importance of ideological, representational aspects of the idea of landscape, we need also to remember the geographical sense of landscape: the morphology of a place is in its own right a space that makes social relations. It is produced space." Marxist cultural geographers call for studies that examine the ways that landscape *works*, such as in the further economic development of a place, and is *a work* that is labored over. As I describe in the next section, this approach emphasizes how landscapes reproduce unequal power relations under global capitalism, and conceptualizes landscape as a scale or node that can function as a site of social struggle. In particular Marxist geographers theorize landscape struggle in terms of conflict over property (who owns what) and conflict over social divisions of labor (who does what).

'The Political Landscape' as a Work that Does Work

According to Don Mitchell (1996), the labor and economic relations that go into the material and symbolic production of landscape are hidden from the dominant 'ways of seeing' the landscape. He argues that the *work* of landscape in capitalist societies is to hide their function as symbolic systems that reproduce unequal social relations through their materiality. Marxist approaches like Mitchell's assume a conflict model of social theory in which power is defined by the oppression and domination of groups according to axes of difference (by class, race, gender, ethnicity, sexuality, and so on) (Henderson 2001). It further assumes that the world is in crisis due to the uneven structures of global capitalism. From this perspective, landscapes contribute to, even create, that crisis. They are products of labor and systems of meaning that naturalize uneven relations of capital.

As Mitchell (2000) describes, landscape is a place of recreation "where one basks in the leisure of a well-ordered scene" (Mitchell 2000: 136). It is a materially produced object and property within capitalist economic markets, as well as a system of signs that "advertise" meanings to their consumers and spectators. For example, the creation of a city or a part of the city *as* landscape in capitalist societies, according to Mitchell (2000: 137),

restores to the viewer (the tourist, the suburban visitor, or even the city residents) an essential sense of control within a built environment which is instead 'controlled' . . . through the creative, seemingly anarchic destruction of an economy over which they may in fact have very little control. Or more precisely, it provides an illusion of control in a space so highly designed, so carefully composed, so exquisitely 'set' by the owners and developers of that space that a visitor's control can only ever be an illusion.

Because landscapes conceal the inequalities and exploitation of their production under capitalism and the ways that people are controlled, Mitchell argues that landscapes can never be truly public spaces.[5]

Mitchell calls for studies that investigate the reasons why landscapes look the way they do (both in material form and through representation) by treating landscape as a social relation of labor.[6] Other geographers have also recently emphasized the relationships between landscape and property, such as Nick Blomley (1998) who understands both as forms of representation, sets of lived relationships, produced material forms, and sites of struggle (see also Blomley 1994). Andy Herod's (1999) edited volume interrogates how workers and capitalists mold and shape spatial relationships through landscape as a source of political power. George Henderson (1999) has eloquently analyzed – through literature and archival material – how landscape production in California was based upon and influenced changing geographies of capital circulation through the invention of branch banking, the labor of racially marked bodies, and complex systems of distributing and marketing crops. Gerry Kearns and Chris Philo's (1993) edited volume details the politics of using landscape as a cultural resource to promote places for capital gain. Jeff Crump (1999) also explores the processes of place-marketing through the case of Moline, Illinois. During a period of deindustrialization, Moline's landscape was reconstructed as a heritage site to attract tourism and investment. Town planners promoted a story of 'capitalist heroism' and selectively 'forgot' to include stories about working-class life and struggle. His case study demonstrates how "local" landscapes, including the built environment, memories, and representations, are framed and constituted by capitalist relations at scales beyond the local. These examples demonstrate the strengths of analyzing political landscapes as work, such as theorizing the complex relations and politics involved in the making of land-scapes at multiple scales or attempting to give voice to workers' stories.

As radical geographers have taught us, power relations are intricately related to (and created by) structured spaces, a "power geometry," to use Doreen Massey's (1994) words, that emplace and locate individuals and social groups differentially (including through landscape) according to the ways that people and places are interconnected to one another. Recent research has highlighted those scales and interconnections by detailing the complex ways that power relations are situated. Leila Harris (2002) describes landscape development and change in the Tigris-Euphrates basin, specifically through the Southeastern Anatolia water development project in Turkey, that resulted in a range of interrelated conflicts about landscape use that vary across scale. Conflicts have emerged about the meanings of sustain-ability, crop selection, livelihoods, household gender roles, village water practices, and the meanings of nationalist discourse related to Turkey's wars of independence, Middle Eastern regional wars (such as the Gulf War), and intrastate conflict (such as the Kurdish question). Although Harris does not explicitly treat landscape as a concept through which to examine these "conflict geographies," her work points to the ways that people are embodied with specific capacities in particular societies, bodies and practices that, in turn, result in differential access to, uses of, and trans-missions of power (see also Scott 1986). Recent research by feminist and environ-mental scholars similarly demonstrates how socio-political struggle cannot be understood without discussions of *everyday uses* of the landscape (Westwood & Radcliffe 1993). Because 'public' and 'private' political actions are intertwined and interdependent, Suzanne Michel (1998: 169) argues that "both individual courses of action and political-economic structures (such as the state) shape nature–society relations, landscapes, and identities."

According to Patricia Mann (1994) (cited in Domosh 1998), models of opposi-tional politics, including Marxism, do not recognize how class, race, sex, and other social categories interact in site-specific ways nor do they recognize the complexity of multiple identity positions. Moreover, because politics is defined as being located within the realm of the state and political economy, Marxist studies tend to focus on resistance, struggle, and action within the traditionally defined (masculinist) 'public realm,' ignoring other forms of politics, such as the politics of care (Domosh 1998; Michel 1998). Everyday practices, however, including using water, walking down a street, eating (or not), working (or not working fast enough), putting on clothes, or going shopping, may have a range of meanings that may be political depending upon who is carrying out those actions, how that person is performing an identity, and in what particular contexts these actions take place. When power is understood as not purely repressive and not simply about domination and oppression between coherent social groups, then the very meanings, categories, and settings of social relations need to be rethought. Power, as Michel Foucault (1977) reminds us, is never about a simple binary between those who dominate and those who are dominated; rather, power is internalized and transmitted through material and discursive acts that construct normative categories of belonging (like race and gender).

Power is also transmitted through embodied actors whose presence in particular settings may define social relations. From this perspective, people are not passive consumers, nor are they merely 'disciplined' transmitters of power. Moreover, landscapes are constitutive settings made and used by individuals performing a "recognizable" identity or even attempting to subvert that identity. As Dydia DeLyser (1999), Jon Goss (1999), and Stephen Hoelscher (1998) forcefully demonstrate, landscapes, including the dreaded shopping mall and tourist site, are more than objects to be consumed or defined only by relations of property (although they are that too).

Thinking about landscape and politics in these ways, as embodied everyday practices, suggests a different possible approach to political landscapes, one that combines the strengths of the first two approaches I have outlined above but allows for more sophisticated understandings of power relations, politics, and agency. In the next section I indicate a future direction for studies about political landscapes to move toward, what I call landscape as everyday practice.[7] While not all of the research below explicitly treats landscape as a conceptual category of analysis, they directly or indirectly examine how landscape use, change, and performance are significant cultural practices that stabilize and destabilize categories of social relations at multiple scales.

Political Landscapes as Everyday Practice[8]

Individuals and social groups create meanings about who should and should not belong to a particular social group, place, or political community through everyday practices, including landscape use and change. Through habits, cultural practices, and discourses, an individual's "identity" is created, often in opposition to other social categories. Although social identities are constituted through repetitive, day-to-day performances in particular settings (Butler 1990), because these everyday practices take place within the constraints of socially "acceptable" behavior (for a particular setting at a specific place and time), these actions are not freely chosen but are part of a choice within a system of schemes (Bourdieu 1977).

Individual actions within and upon a particular landscape, like a street, a church, or even a home in a suburb can be viewed as spatial "tactics" in the practice of everyday life (after de Certeau 1984 in Schein 1997 and Domosh 1998). Rich Schein (1997), for example, explores everyday practices that have created the suburban neighborhood of Ashland Park, Kentucky. There, landscape discourses, such as landscape architecture, insurance mapping, zoning, historic preservation, the neighborhood association, and consumption, are materialized and 'inhabited' through the tactics of individuals seeking to define normative understandings of what the suburban landscape *should be*. These dominant norms of home, neighborhood, and belonging, of course, can be challenged by non-political presence, such as the case of a homeless person who tries to find a place to sleep in the 'safe' landscape of Ashland Park or through racialized bodies in predominantly white cities, such as in Duisburg-Marxloh, Germany. Patricia Ehrkamp and Helga Leitner (2002) describe how conflicting ideas about what a 'typical' German city should look like, or who should be using a streetscape or particular building and in what ways, have shaped understandings of what it means to be a resident, and even citizen, of a place. Turkish immigrants feel tied to their (new) local places of residence through making and remaking the landscape, including the creation of neighborhood institutions or political demonstrations. These material and embodied expressions of belonging through more localized landscape practices, moreover, communicate a continued connection to transnational ties and identities. Some longer term residents of Marxloh, however, feel threatened and alienated by what they see as exclusive Turkish landscape practices, including veiling, predominantly male social spaces (teahouses), places of worship, or Turkish language signs (Ehrkamp 2002). Some ethnic German residents may even project their fears of potential economic loss, abandonment by the state, and even physical threat onto the bodies inhabiting 'Turkish' landscapes.

Individuals who are socially understood as being "out of place" may self-consciously assert their presence to challenge dominant discourses of "who belongs in the landscape." Tim Cresswell (1996) describes such acts and politics of transgression through graffiti, sit-ins, or political protest. Other recent research has documented landscape-based citizen activism that challenges taken-for-granted understandings of national belonging by making voices, scenes, and perspectives of marginalized social groups materially accessible and 'visible' in the landscape, including "The Power of Place" project in Los Angeles (Hayden 1995), the District Six Museum in central Cape Town, South Africa (http://www.districtsix.co.za/htm), or the Topography of Terror in Berlin, Germany (http://www.topographie.de/e/index.htm). The District Six Museum, for example, was established by ex-resident activists, in a Methodist Church shortly after the neighborhood was declared an area for whites only in 1996; at that time the area was bulldozed and its 60,000 residents displaced. Ex-residents decided to build a museum in this barren landscape to remember the individuals who fought against the forced removals; they also established a forum for the Land Restitution process that was successful after the fall of apartheid in 1998. Today museum visitors challenge the official national violence writ in the surrounding landscape by creating a socially vibrant memory of their home(land) through mappings, stories, a memory cloth, and neighborhood tours (Till 2002a). Another example of citizen activism that included protests, rallies, and landscape excavations is the Topography of Terror (Till forthcoming). In the late 1970s, this abandoned field next to the West Berlin Wall was 'rediscovered' by local historians who made public the National Socialist uses of the area as the former headquarters of the Gestapo, SS, and Security Service. Citizen groups understood this overgrown field as a metaphor for the German psyche and represented it as a symbol of national forgetfulness. Their demands to come to terms with the terrain resulted in the creation of a "documentation center" with an historical exhibition, outdoor mapping of the National Socialist terrain, educational programs, and a memorial. As these local activists have taught us, through the (re)making of landscape, critical understandings of national pasts and new political spaces may be imagined and made concrete.[9]

While such studies demonstrate the ways that transgressive actions confront existing social relations, recent research in sexuality studies and feminist geography explores the micropolitics of everyday action in streets, parks, or plazas that create or challenge new social relations *even as* they conform to socially dominant mores (Chauncey 1996; Domosh 1998; Kirkey & Forysth 2001; Thomas 2002). Mona Domosh (1998) explores these processes through the mid-nineteenth-century streets of New York City, landscapes that she treats as sites of complex social engagement as well as economic activity. She argues that because these streets were neither completely controlled public spaces nor totally open, they could be used as sites of micropolitical activity and tactical transgression. While promenades along Fifth Avenue were highly scripted rituals through which upper-class values were embodied on a daily basis, when African Americans engaged in those practices they simultaneously disrupted and supported (white) bourgeois standards. Such tactical gestures, argues Domosh, "are enacted and resisted through everyday spatial practices, but practices that are fragmentary, fleeting, and not in place" (1998: 212).

Everyday spatial practices such as wearing clothing, according to Anna Secor (2002), may not only produce particular urban landscapes but also enable and constrain a social group's experience of mobility through those landscapes. Secor describes women's choice to veil (or not) in the context of contemporary Istanbul, detailing the ways that women negotiate dominant social regimes of veiling through their individual subjective interpretations of femininity, religiosity, and urbanism. The presence of women's bodies may create exclusive gendered and sexed social landscapes through their veiling choices, but these choices also represent women's particular responses to their lived environments. As Secor's ethnographic research demonstrates, women in Istanbul do enact traditional narratives of nation, Islam, and modernity through veiling choices. Yet those daily practices may also traverse and remake gendered and classed urban environments: "The veil, whether read as a sign of religious belief, political protest or village heritage, comes to demarcate spatial and social arenas of inclusion and exclusion in the city" (Secor 2002: 19).

Concluding Notes: Landscape Projects in Geography

As I have suggested here, how we think about landscape and power as theoretical concepts and forms of geographical knowledge results in distinct ways to approach both political landscapes, and how those landscapes structure and create political spaces at various scales, from states, to global systems, to microgeographies of everyday space, to transnational ties. Cultural geographers examine the ways that landscapes are made and used to change social and power relations through studies of elite power, labor relations, daily practices, and acts of transgression. Their research demonstrates how landscapes "are part of complex processes through which individuals and groups define themselves, [and] claim and challenge political authority" (Nash 1999: 225). Furthermore, these studies indicate how political landscapes are open to interpretation and how their meanings change through time. Landscape practices, from monumental stagings of elite power to capitalist productions to veiling choices, are ways that individuals create meanings about who should be and should not be a member of what political community (and at what scales).

I have suggested that geographers should treat political landscapes as everyday practice, an approach that would pay attention to the particular contexts in which social relations are contextually situated and multiple positions of identity are performed, enacted, challenged, and negotiated. Such an approach would look critically at the ways that landscapes reinforce and have the potential to disrupt dominant categories of belonging, including categories of political community. It would also force us to interrogate such daily practices as "looking." Returning again to the image in figure 23.1, for example, think about the ways that looking locates a viewer in political and social space. Specifically, how are you connected to the other peoples and places assumed to be present (and absent) in this landscape? As a viewer, how are you related to the other viewers of this image (academics, students, a general reading public, undocumented migrants), to different discourses and ways of seeing the landscape (and in this instance to the interpretive spaces of this book), to those who made the image, and to those who made the material landscape depicted? What do you 'see' and what don't you see?

A reader of this edited volume may look at this image as defining a global North and South, each world characterized by unequal access to rights, resources, and citizenship – despite claims of increased integration and democratization under NAFTA. When placed in another context, for example, a regional or national newspaper, a US citizen may view this picture in indignant, nationalistic ways, arguing that the border is necessary to 'protect' an 'American way of life.' Another person may feel anger and personal feelings of loss. Still another might look at this image in fear, remembering that crossing may mean death, violent injury, or not being able to go back home. Such viewing positions and situated interpretations (and there are many other possible responses) remind us that political landscapes are always intensely humanized, embodied, and contextual settings – in terms of their construction, their situation, their symbolic use, their representation. Political landscapes render and express emotions, ideas, and cultural values at particular moments in time.

There are other, more obvious, ways that dominant discourses and material settings about "the border" are created through cultural practices. The day-to-day practice of traversing this border, for example, classify (and 'discipline') individuals according to the social categories of tourist, 'illegal immigrant,' worker, native, military agent, and so on. Yet as Schein (1997: 664) suggests, landscapes not only reconstitute a set of dominant discourses about social life, they also can be a "liberating medium for social change." The actions of immigration officers, *coyotes* (smugglers), personal relatives, human rights advocates, employers, government officials, and others, for example, result in "legal" and "illegal" openings and closings of this border as evidenced by the protest graffiti. As political graffiti, these skulls call attention to the very real human costs of the presence of US regulatory practices: tiny skulls form the letters *Alto Guardian*, each one representing a life lost at the border as a result of border enforcement practices.[10] But the graffiti does more 'work' than that. Because this message is quite literally painted onto the militarized

Figure 23.2 "Border Dynamics," created by Guadalupe Serrano and Alberto Morackis of Taller Yonke Public Art Workshop in Nogales, Mexico, commissioned by Beyond Borders Binational Art Foundation, 2002 (http://muralesfrontera.org/) (permission for use generously granted by Beyond Borders and Taller Yonke Workshop).

border, it demarcates the ghostly realities of this landscape as territorial border at the same time it points to the fluidity of that border.

The act of transgression depicted in the image also shows the potential of art to create landscapes as sites of contestation and as metaphors for progressive politics. This graffiti, like other proposed artwork along the border (figure 23.2), refocuses our attention away from the border as "the Wall" and toward the political potential of seeing this landscape as a "borderlands." As Joe Nevins (2000) writes, many of our dominant political imaginations do not allow us to see that "the US–Mexico boundary, as a line of control and division, is an illusion. Mexico and California are increasingly one." The image in figure 23.2 suggests a different political imagination, a "Border Dynamics" installation planned for both sides of the wall by the "Beyond Borders" binational, nonprofit artistic collaborative (http://muralesfrontera.org/). Four, 12-foot-tall metallic human figures lean into and press at and through the wall at the Nogales, Arizona, US/Nogales, Sonora, Mexico border. This 'public' art is intended to provoke questions about the state's authority to imagine political space, including the official (US) notion that this border separates two "peoples" (Kofler 2002). Indeed, these figures, "reflecting different levels of tenacity and spirit," create new political landscapes, border regions defined by "change, clash, and continuity"(Portillo Jr. 2002) rather than by boundaries, policing, and exclusions and inclusions.

ACKNOWLEDGMENTS

I would like to thank Dydia DeLyser, Patricia Ehrkamp, Ben Forest, Helga Leitner Andrea Kofler, Suzanne Michel, and Mary Thomas for their helpful ideas and suggestions on this chapter.

NOTES

1. For a discussion about the politics of producing "natural" landscapes see Braun (this volume); on national and postcolonial landscapes see Agnew, Johnson, and Ryan (this volume).
2. The etymology of the word 'landscape' dates back to medieval England when it referred to land controlled by a lord; in medieval German, it was a legal term defining the collective ownership of an area. By the early seventeenth century, landscape meant the representation of scenery in painting as well as the design of space (Cosgrove 1985; Olwig 2002; Rose 1993).
3. The information in this paragraph comes from Agnew (1998a).
4. Using Italian Renaissance traditions, and borrowing from English Romanticism and the French Barbizon School, the Macchiaioli painted landscape images that tied a noble past to the modern developing present. There was a deep relationship between their landscape impressions of native Tuscany and the development of the Risorgimento (revival through unification concerned with establishing Italy as a center of European civilization). The Macchiaioli were, however, to lose their cohesiveness after unification in 1865, and it was only under fascism (1922–43) that their work would be used again as supporting a fascist ultranationalist ideal. See Agnew 1998a.
5. Mitchell adopts a Habermasian definition of 'public' defined by open access and participation. Feminist political theorists have critiqued such a definition for various reasons, a topic that is beyond the scope of this essay. See, for example, Domosh 1998, Deutsche 1990, Fraser 1990, Ruddick 1996.
6. Mitchell (2001) cites the works in this paragraph as good examples of the direction landscape studies should move toward.
7. For a discussion of 'practice' as used in geography, see Crang 2000 and Painter 2000. For an overview of 'performativity' see Nash 2000.
8. The examples used in the next section are largely urban and from the 'first world,' a bias that reflects my own area of research and expertise. There is a large literature about everyday resistance in rural and developing countries; see for example, Scott 1986 and Westwood and Radcliffe 1993.
9. At the same time, both the District Six Museum and the Topography of Terror have become institutionalized and are now dealing with the difficulties and advantages of being more established tourist sites.
10. According to Joe Nevins (2000), the number of Border Patrol agents in the San Diego sector increased from 980 in 1994 to more than 2,200 as a result of Operation Gatekeeper. He argues that although Gatekeeper has made undocumented immigrants "less visible" at the US border, it has largely been unsuccessful even by its own terms: the numbers of people crossing have not gone down, more people have died (as of November 2000, 603 people have died), and people are not returning to Mexico once they cross successfully.

REFERENCES

Agnew, J. 1998a: European landscape and identity. In B. Graham, ed., *Modern Europe: Place, Culture and Identity*. London: Arnold, 213–35.

Agnew, J. 1998b: The impossible capital: monumental Rome under Liberal and Fascist regimes, 1870–1943. *Geografiska Annaler* 80 B, 229–40.

Atkinson, D. and Cosgrove, D. 1998: Urban rhetoric and embodied identities: city, nation and empire at the Vittorio-Emmanuele II monument in Rome 1870–1945. *Annals of the Association of American Geographers* 88, 28–40.

Bell, J. 1999: Redefining national identity in Uzbekistan: symbolic tensions in Tashkent's official public landscape. *Ecumene* 6, 183–213.

Blomley, N. 1994: *Law, Space and the Geographies of Power.* New York: Guilford Press.

Blomley, N. 1998: Landscapes of property. *Law and Society Review* 32, 567–612.

Blunt, Alison and Rose, G. 1994: *Writing Women and Space: Colonial and Postcolonial Geographies.* New York: Guilford Press.

Bourdieu, P. 1977: *Outline of a Theory of Practice.* Cambridge: Cambridge University Press.

Butler, J. 1990: *Gender Trouble: Feminism and the subversion of identity.* New York: Routledge.

Chauncey, G. 1996: 'Privacy could only be had in public': gay uses of the streets. In J. Sanders, ed., *Stud: Architectures of Masculinity.* Princeton: Princeton Architectural Press, 224–61.

Cosgrove, D. 1984: *Social Formation and Symbolic Landscape.* Totawa, NJ: Barnes and Noble.

Cosgrove, D. 1985: Prospect, perspective and the evolution of the landscape idea. *Transactions of the Institute of British Geographers* N.S. 10, 45–62.

Cosgrove, D. 1992: *The Palladian Landscape.* Leicester: Leicester University Press.

Cosgrove, D. and Daniels, S., eds. 1988: *The Iconography of Landscape.* Cambridge, New York: Cambridge University Press.

Crang, M. 2000: Relics, places and unwritten geographies in the work of Michel de Certeau (1925–86). In M. Crang and N. Thrift, eds., *Thinking Space.* London and New York: Routledge, 136–53.

Cresswell, T. 1996: *In Place/Out of Place: Geography, Ideology, and Transgression.* Minneapolis, MN: University of Minnesota Press.

Crump, J. 1999: What cannot be seen will not be heard: the production of landscape in Moline, Illinois. *Ecumene* 6, 295–317.

Daniels, S. 1993: *Fields of Vision: Landscape Imagery and National Identity in England and the United States.* Princeton, NJ: Princeton University Press.

Daniels, S. and Cosgrove, D. 1993: Spectacle and text: landscape metaphors in cultural geography. In J. Duncan and D. Ley, eds., *Place/Culture/Representation.* London: Routledge, 57–77.

De Certeau, M. 1984: *The Practice of Everyday Life.* Berkeley: University of California Press.

DeLyser, D. 1999: Authenticity on the ground: engaging the past in a California ghost town. *Annals of the Association of American Geographers* 89, 602–32.

Deutsche, R. 1990: Architecture of the evicted. *Strategies: A Journal of Theory, Culture and Politics* 3, 159–83.

Domosh, M. 1998: Those 'gorgeous incongruities': polite politics and public space on the streets of nineteenth-century New York City. *Annals of the Association of American Geographers* 88, 209–26.

Dowler, L. 1998: And they think I'm just a nice old lady: women and war in Belfast, Northern Ireland. *Gender, Place and Culture* 5, 159–76.

Duncan, J. 1990: *The City as Text: The Politics of Landscape Interpretation in the Kandyan Kingdom.* New York: Cambridge University Press.

Duncan, J. 1995: Landscape geography, 1993–94. *Progress in Human Geography* 19, 414–22.

Duncan, J. and Duncan, N. 1988: (Re)reading the landscape. *Environment and Planning D: Society and Space* 6, 117–26.

Ehrkamp, P. and Leitner, H. 2002: Beyond national citizenship: Turkish immigrants and the (re)construction of citizenship in Germany. *Urban Geography* 23.

Ehrkamp, P. 2002: *Becoming Turkish: Identity, Assimilation Discourse, and the Transformation of Urban Space in Duisburg-Marxloh, Germany.* Unpublished dissertation, Department of Geography, University of Minnesota, Minneapolis.

Foote, K., Tóth, A. and Árvay, A. 2002: Hungary after 1989: inscribing a new past on place. *Geographical Review* 90, 301–34.

Forest B. and Johnson, J. 2002: Unraveling the threads of History: Soviet-era monuments and post-Soviet national identity in Moscow. *Annals of the Association of American Geographers* 92, 524–47.

Foucault, M. 1977: *Discipline and Punish: The Birth of the Prison.* London: Allen Lane.

Fraser, N. 1990: Rethinking the public sphere. *Social Text* 25/6, 56–80.

Goss, J. 1999: Once-upon-a-time in the commodity world: an unofficial guide to Mall of America. *Annals of the Association of American Geographers* 89, 45–75.

Graham, B. 1998: The past in Europe's present: diversity, identity and the construction of place. In B. Graham, ed., *Modern Europe: Place, Culture and Identity.* London: Arnold, 19–49.

Gruffudd, P. 1995: Remaking Wales: nation-building and the geographical imagination, 1925–50. *Political Geography* 14, 219–39.

Harris, L. 2002: Water and conflict geographies of the southeastern Anatolia project. *Society and Natural Resources* 15, 743–59.

Hayden, D. 1995: *The Power of Place: Urban Landscapes as Public History.* Cambridge, MA: MIT Press.

Henderson, G. 1999: *California and the Fictions of Capital.* New York: Oxford University Press.

Henderson, G. 2002: What (else) we talk about when we talk about landscape: for a return to social imagination. In P. Groth and C. Wilson, eds., *Everyday America: Cultural Landscape Studies after J. B. Jackson.* Berkeley: University of California Press.

Herod, A., ed. 1999: *Organizing the Landscape: Geographical Perspectives on Labor Unionism.* Minneapolis, MN: University of Minnesota Press.

Hoelscher, S. 1998: *Heritage on Stage: The Invention of Ethnic Place in America's Little Switzerland.* Madison: University of Wisconsin Press.

Jacobs, J. 1996: *Edge of Empire: Postcolonialism and the City.* London: Routledge.

Johnson, N. 1995: Cast in stone: monuments, geography, and nationalism. *Environment and Planning D: Society and Space* 13, 51–65.

Kearns, G. 1997: The imperial subject: geography and travel in the work of Mary Kingsley and Halford Mackinder. *Transactions of the Institute of British Geographers* 22, 450–72.

Kearns G. and Philo, C., eds. 1993: *Selling Places: The City as Cultural Capital, Past and Present.* Oxford and New York: Pergamon Press.

Kirkey, K. and Forsyth, A. 2001: Men in the valley: gay male life on the suburban-rural fringe. *Journal of Rural Studies* 17, 421–41.

Kofler, A. 2002: Political realities in border cities: local forms of protest and their effects on life across borders. Paper presented at Rights to the City, International Geographical Union, Commissions on Political Geography and Public Policy, Rome, Italy.

Leitner, H. and Kang, P. 1999: Contested urban landscapes of nationalism: the case of Taipei. *Ecumene* 6, 214–33.

Lewis, P. 1979: Axioms for reading the landscape. In D. W. Meinig, ed., *The Interpretation of Ordinary Landscapes.* New York: Oxford University Press, 11–32.

Lewis, P. 1983: Learning from looking: geographic and other writing about the American cultural landscape. *American Quarterly* 35, 242–61.

Lowenthal, D. 1991: British national identity and the English landscape. *Rural History* 2, 205–30.

Mann, P. 1994: *Micro-Politics: Agency in a Postfeminist Era*. Minneapolis, MN: University of Minnesota Press.

Massey, D. 1994: A global sense of place. In *Space, Place and Gender*. Cambridge: Polity Press, 146–56.

Michel, S. 1998: Golden eagles and the environmental politics of care. In J. Wolch and J. Emel, eds., *Animal Geographies: Place, Politics, and Identity in the Nature–Culture Borderlands*. London and New York: Verso, 162–87.

Mitchell, D. 1996: *The Lie of the Land: Migrant Workers and the California Landscape*. Minneapolis, MN: University of Minnesota Press.

Mitchell, D. 2000: *Cultural Geography: A Critical Introduction*. Oxford and Malden, MA: Blackwell.

Mitchell, M. 2001: The Lure of the local: landscape studies at the end of a troubled century. *Progress in Human Geography* 25, 269–81.

Myers, G. 2002: Colonial geography and masculinity in Eric Dutton's Kenya Mountain. *Gender, Place and Culture* 9, 23–38.

Nash, C. 1999: Landscapes. In P. Cloke, P. Crang, and M. Goodwin, eds., *Introducing Human Geographies*. London and New York: Arnold, 217–25.

Nash, C. 2000: Performativity in practice: some recent work in cultural geography. *Progress in Human Geography* 24, 653–64.

Nevins, J. 2000: How high must operation gatekeeper's death count go? *Los Angeles Times*, Sunday, Nov. 19.

Nevins, J. 2001: *Operation Gatekeeper: The Rise of the "Illegal Alien" and the Remaking of the US–Mexico Boundary*. New York and London: Routledge.

Olwig, K. 2002: *Landscape, Nature, and the Body Politic: From Britain's Renaissance to America's New World*. Madison: University of Wisconsin Press.

Painter, J. 2000: Pierre Bourdieu. In M. Crang and N. Thrift, eds., *Thinking Space*. London and New York: Routledge, 239–59.

Portillo Jr., E. 2002: Art's meaning on the border is in the eye of the beholder. *Arizona Daily Star*, Wed. April 24 (available: http://muralesfrontera.homestead.com/files/arizonadailystar.jpg).

Pratt, M. L. 1992: *Imperial Eyes: Travel Writing and Transculturation*. London and New York: Routledge.

Pringle, R. 1999: Power. In L. McDowell and J. Sharp, eds., *A Feminist Glossary of Human Geography*. London and New York: Arnold, 216–18.

Rose, G. 1993: *Feminism and Geography*. Minneapolis, MN: University of Minnesota Press.

Ruddick, S. 1996: Constructing difference in public spaces: race, class, and gender as interlocking systems. *Urban Geography* 17, 132–51.

Schein, R. 1997. The place of landscape: a conceptual framework for interpreting an American scene. *Annals of the Association of American Geographers* 87, 660–80.

Scott, J. 1986: *Weapons of the Weak: Everyday Forms of Peasant Resistance*. New Haven: Yale University Press.

Secor, A. 2002: Women's dress, mobility, and Islamic knowledge. *Gender, Place and Culture* 9, 5–22.

Thomas, M. 2002: *The Social-Spatial Practices of 'Girl Power': Race, gender-sexuality, and teenage subjectivity in Charleston, South Carolina*. Unpublished dissertation, Department of Geography, University of Minnesota, Minneapolis.

Till, K. 1999: Staging the past: landscape designs, cultural identity and *Erinnerungspolitik* at Berlin's *Neue Wache*. *Ecumene* 6, 251–83.

Till, K. 2002a: Cosmopolitan places: historic site museums, national memory, and transnational networks. Paper presented at "Rights to the City," International Geographical Union, Commissions on Political Geography and Public Policy, Rome, Italy, May 29–June 1.

Till, K. 2002b: Places of Memory. In J. Agnew, K. Mitchell, and G. O'Tuathail, eds., *Companion to Political Geography*. Oxford and Malden, MA: Blackwell.

Till, K. forthcoming: *The New Berlin: Memory, Politics, Place*. Minneapolis, MN: University of Minnesota Press.

Westwood S. and Radcliffe, S. 1993: Gender, racism and the politics of identities in Latin America. In S. Radcliffe and S. Westwood, eds., *Viva: Women and Popular Protest in Latin America*. New York and London: Routledge.

Chapter 24

Religious Landscapes

Lily Kong

Inserting Religion in Geographical Analyses

Race, class, and gender generally are accepted as the primary axes of analyses across those disciplines concerned with understanding society.[1] So, too, within geography, they have constituted subjects, as both a priori and problematized categories of analysis. Religion has not received this same attention. This is not to say that it has been reduced to a residual category, or even that there is a paucity of research on geographies of religion. In fact, over the last two decades there has been a noticeable increase. Conceptual and theoretical attention to geographies of religion, however, has lagged behind, and only resurfaced in recent years (see Levine 1986; Kong 1990, 2001a).

Early Intersections of Geography and Religion

Several earlier reviews of geographical research on religion (Isaac 1959–60, 1961–2; Fickeler 1962; Sopher 1967, 1981; Levine 1986) illustrate a primary focus on religious landscapes, although research was not restricted to this focus only. For example, in the sixteenth and seventeenth centuries, ecclesiastical geography and biblical geography dominated. The former involved primarily mapping the spatial advance of Christianity and other religions in the world, often with an underlying aim of documenting which religions Christian missionaries found in what part of the world and how missions progressed among them (Isaac 1965: 10). The latter involved attempts to identify places and names in the Bible and to determine their locations, which illustrated the powerful influence of the Christian church during this period of geographic scholarship.

The focus on religious landscapes was to follow in the late seventeenth century and became particularly strong in the eighteenth and nineteenth centuries. In the physico-theological stance, scholars saw landscapes, and in particular, nature, to be divinely-created order for the well-being of all life (Glacken 1959, 1967; Buttner 1980: 94–5). Whether it was in the distribution of climates, the production of plants and animals in different zones, or the distribution of landforms, lakes and streams, it was argued that the earth and its geography was too advantageous to life and too well-reasoned to be accepted as fortuitous circumstances (Glacken 1959). Alongside this physicotheological school, environmental determinism was also developing in the eighteenth and nineteenth centuries under the influence of Montesquieu and Voltaire. Geographers sought to explain the essential nature of various religions in terms of their geographical environments (see, for example, Semple 1911; Huntington 1945; Hultkrantz 1966).

Weberian and Sauerian Influences

In the 1920s, Max Weber's ideas began to gain influence over environmental determinism. Research began to focus on how religion influenced and changed the environment, including physical landscapes. This approach spawned a body of empirical writings, so that by 1960 Isaac could define the 'geography of religion' as: "the study of the part played by the religious motive in man's [sic] transformation of the landscape." In his early conception of the subfield, the task of a geography of religion was "to separate the specifically religious from the social, economic and ethnic matrix in which it is embedded, and to determine its relative weight in relation to other forces in transforming the landscape" (Isaac 1961–2: 12).

The focus on religion's role in transforming landscapes reflects closely the work of Carl Sauer and the Berkeley school of cultural geography. These researchers have tended to treat religion as a superorganic construct influencing the cultural landscape. The processes through which these influences are effected were not very much studied while the focus remained chiefly on the form of the impacted landscape, such as their spatial extent. For example, studies have focused on spatial patterns arising from religious influences, including the spatial diffusion and expansion and the territorial demise of religious groups (for example, Crowley 1978; Heatwole 1986; and Landing 1982); the distribution of religious groups over space at particular points in time (for example, Shortridge 1978; Stump 1981; and Heatwole 1985); the delineation of culture regions based on religious characteristics (for example, Shortridge 1976 and 1977); and the impact of religion on the physical form of the landscape, with descriptions of sacred structures of particular groups, illustrating the unique imprint that each group leaves on the landscape. These have focused on the sacred structures of world religions, such as Buddhism (Tanaka 1984) and Hinduism (Biswas 1984), as well as folk religions (Curtis 1980; and Laatsch & Calkins 1986).

The interest in analyzing how religion influences landscapes is paralleled by a specific interest in how religion influences ecology, in direct opposition to an earlier environmental derterminism. This strand of research, variously termed 'religious ecology' and 'environmental theology' has progressed in two main areas. The first has focused on the role of religion in environmental degradation. Examples include Lynn White's (1967) "The Historical Roots of our Ecologic Crisis," which sparked a debate that involved the question of what caused the increasing environmental degradation that was evident on planet earth (see also Glacken 1967; Dubos 1969, 1972; Cobb 1972; Toynbee 1972; Passmore 1974; Hargrove 1986). The second has focused on the impact of religious thought on plant and animal ecology, and in turn developed along two main fronts. First, many have considered the influence of religion on attitudes towards animal life, for example, Hinduism and its approach to the sacred cow (see Harris 1966; Simoons 1979). Second, researchers have examined the question of religious influence on the domestication of plants and animals and their diffusion (Isaac 1962; Sopher 1964; Heiser 1973). The central tenet of such works is that domestication resulted not purely for economic reasons in many instances, but was closely associated with religious ceremonies and divinities instead.

Mapping 'New' Geographies of Religion: The Politics and Poetics of the Sacred

While the Sauerian approach emphasizing religious impacts on landscapes is still evident in some recent writings, the retheorization of cultural geography over the last decade and a half has also reframed the work of geographers interested in religion. In 1990, Kong highlighted various ways in which this was becoming evident. First, there has been increasing focus on societies with plural religious orientations, including secular ones, moving away from earlier tendencies to examine specific religions (and cultures) (as if they existed) in isolation. Second, and relatedly, there is growing acknowledgement of the intersections of the sacred and secular, of the political and cultural. This attention is often focused on religious landscapes and their relationship with other-religious and secular landscapes. Third, studies have begun to reflect increasingly a social geographical orientation in the focus on community studies, that is, in the study of religious groups as communities in a social and political context. Issues of identity constructions have therefore gained research attention. Fourth, there has been growing interest in the symbolic meanings of religious places, beyond more functional and descriptive efforts. Fifth, there have been greater attempts to understand the *processes* through which specific environmental objects, landscapes, and buildings become invested with meaning of a religious kind. Sixth, sacred experience at religious places has also been given attention.

While others have described the efforts as diffuse, incoherent and in disarray (Livingstone 1994: 373; Raivo 1997: 137), Kong (2001a) has argued that with some *a posteriori* conceptual thinking, there is in fact a certain theoretical coherence that may be cast around these emerging strands. She identifies these to be a politics and poetics of the sacred, in particular, a politics and poetics of religious landscapes and space, and a politics and poetics of religious identity and community. Such politics and poetics recognizes, as Durkheim and Lévi-Strauss did, that "nothing is inherently sacred," for the sacred is "a value of indeterminate signification, in itself empty of meaning and therefore susceptible to the reception of any meaning whatsoever" (Chidester & Linenthal 1995: 6). The sacred is tied up with, and draws meaning from, social and political relationships. This is the situational sacred, or the politics of the sacred. In contrast, the poetics of the sacred, or the "substantial" sacred is thought to have an "essential character" (Chidester & Linenthal 1995: 5), an essence and meaning in and of itself, inspiring and overwhelming, protecting but also frightening (Otto 1917; Kong 1992).

Politics of landscapes and space

Sacred space is contested space, just as the sacred is a "contested category" (Needham cited in Chidester & Linenthal 1995: 15). Sacred space reflects and reinforces "hierarchical power relations of domination and subordination, inclusion and exclusion, appropriation and dispossession" (ibid.: 17). Geographers (but also anthropologists, sociologists, and others) have therefore increasingly interrogated the "entrepreneurial, social, political and other 'profane' forces" that constitute the construction of sacred space (ibid.). Various politics and power relations have been explored in recent empirical work. These politics are focused on the production, management and maintenance of sacred place, the consumption of meaning, and insertion into everyday lived cultures.

In the production of sacred place, researchers have examined the politics of secular–religious relations and majority–minority relations, particularly in relation to the 'officially sacred' (Leiris 1938), such as churches, temples, synagogues, and mosques. In exploring secular-religious relations in the production of the 'officially sacred,' research has centered on illustrating the power of the secular in defining the location of the sacred, in the form of religious buildings. Such secular forces may be represented by "rational" urban planning principles, capitalistic principles of land values, and principles of multiculturalism (see Kong 1993a and Rath et al. 1991). On the other hand, as Kong (1993b) also illustrates, religious adherents may have other ideas about where to locate their religious buildings, following religious principles/guidance. When the power of the state transcends, religious adherents find ways of coming to terms with the primacy of the secular order, negotiating their conceptions of the sacred (Kong 1993b).

In exploring majority–minority relations and the connection with sacred space, there is sometimes a confluence of the religious majority with the state. For example, Philp and Mercer (1999) describe how the majority Buddhist government in Burma manipulates religion in its desire to represent Burma as a "harmonious Buddhist nation." For example, land is seized from a minority Kachin Baptist organization for the construction of a new pagoda. The majority position (a preferred construction of the "nation") is interpreted in religious terms, and sacred space is integral to the success of the majority's ideologically constructed assertions.

Also, a large multidisciplinary literature has emerged which examines the politics surrounding management and maintenance of religious places. The tensions and negotiations surrounding such management and maintenance are often between native people who revere sacred sites, and modern forces which want these sites for pragmatic, commercial, or even alternative religious purposes (Carmichael et al. 1994). Here, geographers have much to learn from other disciplines, such as archaeology and anthropology, and especially where specific work is done on cultural resource management. On the other hand, geographers have been much more active in exploring the nature of different meanings invested in the same sites. The politics surrounding meaning investment in religious places take various forms: tensions between secular and sacred meanings, interreligious contestations in multireligious communities, gender, class and race politics and politics between nations. I will elaborate below.

In conditions of modernity, sacred–secular tensions have formed a key focus of analysis. Various types of sacred sites have been studied in this regard, and Kong's (1999) review of work on cemeteries and crematoria illustrates the central arguments. For example, recent necrogeographical work has examined state discourse and practice surrounding burial and crematorial space, often hinged on secular utilitarian views of planning, adopting principles of efficient land use and taking on board concerns about sanitation, while local communities emphasized symbolic and religious meanings of graves as focal points of identity, expressions of relationships with the land and crucial to the practice of religious beliefs and rituals.

Yet, sacred spaces should not be conceptualized and understood only in terms of sites and locations, but in terms of religious routes as well. Graham and Murray (1997) illustrate this, focusing on the dichotomy between official and non-official appropriations of the pilgrimage route (not merely the site) to Santiago de Compostela, Spain.

Besides sacred–secular tensions, the acknowledgement of pluralities in societies has prompted analysis of interreligious contestations over meanings in multireligious societies. In Sydney, Australia, the refusal to allow mosques to be built represented religious prejudices designed to exclude the marginal 'other.' Councils and resident activist groups have frustrated the public practice of Islam and other non-Christian faiths so much so that they have been forced to worship secretly, in residential properties, or to use commercial premises. Where mosques are proposed, it is not uncommon for resident objectors to argue that members of Islamic groups proposing the developments are 'outsiders,' 'nonlocals,' 'they,' or 'them' (Dunn 2001), while opponents of mosques made very direct claims to local citizenship by describing and identifying themselves as 'concerned citizens,' 'concerned Christian,' 'legitimate resident,' 'locals,' and 'rate payer' in letters they write. Similarly, in London, UK, Naylor and Ryan (1998) have shown how local residents in a predominantly white Christian neighborhood perceive the mandir (Hindu temple) to be a threat to their homes, public areas and community, a "visual sign of intrusion and invasion of a predominantly white British space" (Naylor & Ryan 1998: 9).

The politics of religious spaces are also tied up with gender, race and class politics, and politics between nations. Patriarchy, classism and racism are often reflected in and reinforced by cemeteries, memorials and tombstones (see Kong 1999). For example, Morris's (1997) discussion of how the British War Graves Commission instituted a policy of uniformity for memorials so that wealthier families could not overshadow "what was seen to be the equal sacrifice of men from poorer social groups" (Morris 1997: 419; see also Heffernan 1995) opens up questions about how far death is a 'leveler' of class and social status. This may be extended to the issue of race, as Christopher (1995) illustrates in his study of racial segregation in cemeteries in Port Elizabeth, South Africa. He showed how, prior to 1948, this segregation was apparent within cemeteries, while after 1948, it became apparent through the establishment of completely separate cemeteries. Speck (1996), on the other hand, argues that women are not commemorated in war memorials, and when they are, are represented as the stoic woman to symbolize the community's sacrifice, or as mother figures (transformed from nurses), who are essentially passive, private and respectable citizens. This, she terms as representation of their maternal citizenship – they expressed their commitment as citizens in ways that were open to them primarily as wives and mothers. The marginalization of women is similarly evident in the principal rituals and ceremonies of commemoration, and in the memorial-making process (women sculptors, for example, have been awarded few major memorial commissions).

Deathscapes also illustrate the constructions of nations and the politics of internation relations. Whether it is about keeping a tangible colonial presence through the insistence on British war cemeteries in foreign soils (Morris 1997), or about the language used on headstones as an illustration of nationalistic allegiances (Mythum 1994), meanings are invested in deathscapes which speak about the power relations between nations. Such analyses of the politics between "nations" can be extended to other sites of religious significance, including technological "sites," from websites to audiovisual religious productions. As Kong (2001b) highlighted, various research questions deserve attention, for example, as technology and globalizing tendencies open up cultural borders, how are states dealing with the influence of international religious broadcasts in their countries? What kind of transnational religious developments might be facilitated via technology? If American involvement is strong in international Christian broadcasting, as Stump (1991) argues it is, what are the implications for a new cultural imperialism via religion, a kind of religious imperialism?

Politics and power relations are thus evident in the production and meaning of sacred landscapes. To take this a step further, other icons of religion may also be examined as "texts" produced in circuits of culture and transformed and taken up in everyday lives (Johnson 1986). For example, religious objects in temples, churches and synagogues may be laden with sacred meaning. Yet, they may be (re)produced and appear in museums, where different meanings become invested. As Grimes (1992) points out, religious objects do not exist in a void. The spaces that they inhabit can alter, even determine their meaning as well as viewers' comprehension of that meaning. In this regard, museums commoditize and singularize[2] religious objects; in the process, altering their meanings.

Poetics of place

A poetics of sacred place is often sought after, in people's search for the immanent and transcendent, though it is not always experienced. Geographers may still find inspiration in the work of Mircea Eliade (1959), who conceives of the sacred as erupting in certain places as revelations (hierophanies), causing them to become "powerful centers of meaningful worlds," set apart from ordinary, homogeneous space. Few geographers have examined empirically the poetics of place, though Lane (1988) has conceptually crystallized certain "axioms" of such sacred place: it chooses, it is not chosen; it is ordinary place, ritually made extraordinary; it is intimately linked to states of consciousness, such that it is possible to go by a place numerous times without recognizing it as sacred. When one does, however, one may experience it as the "numinous" (Otto 1917) or through a variety of emotions not unlike ordinary happiness, anger, fear and so forth, except as directed to the religious (James 1902; Kong 1992). Finally, sacred place is both local and universal and can drive one to a quest for a particular center of divine encounter but also drive one out from that center with an awareness that God is never confined to a single locale (Lane 1988: 15). This parallels two general spatial orientations in the study of religion, the locative and utopian: the former is fixed, bounded, and requires the maintenance of one's place and that of others in a larger scheme of things; the latter is unbounded and unfixed to any particular location, breaking out of a prevailing social order (Smith 1978).

In examining the poetics of religious place, scholars have been drawn to understanding the process of sacralization, that is, the manner in which place develops its sacred meaning. Anthropologists and geographers share a common interest in this. Hume's anthropological (1998) study notes how Wiccans[3] believe that sacred place can be set up anywhere. The processes of sacralization involve moments of quiet meditation prior to casting a circle, setting up the altar, laying out the witch's tools, ringing a bell to signal the commencement of the rite, and so forth. Mazumdar and Mazumdar (1993), focusing on the sacralization of the house in mainstream Hinduism, similarly emphasize the role of ritual in sacralization, purifying the outside (e.g. through consecration of the land and planting of ritually significant plants), and sacralizing the inside (e.g. through lighting the sacred fire, anointing participants with ashes from the fire, and walking a cow through the rooms).

These specific cases, of a new religious movement and mainstream religion respectively, illustrate the larger principle that Chidester and Linenthal (1995) identify as an integral part of sacralization: ritualization. Indeed, they argue that sacred place is ritual place, a location for "formalized, repeatable symbolic performances" (Chidester & Linenthal 1995: 9). Chidester and Linenthal (1995: 10) hold that the human body plays a crucial role in the ritual production of sacred place because ritual action "manipulates basic spatial distinctions between up and down, right and left, inside and outside, and so on, that necessarily revolve around the axis of the living body." With modernity and technology, however, questions must be asked about how conceptions of sacred place change, and the role of the living body-axis in that place. For example, as cyberspace invades myriad spheres of our lives, what happens to the maintenance of boundaries between inside and outside? What happens to the bodily axis? Are different rituals developed that perhaps emphasize the visual and kinetic less (such as ritual movement) and spotlight the aural/audio more (such as ritual songs and chants)? Might vicarious ritual action become important (performed elsewhere and watched on screen)? Will simultaneous living room rituals develop, or ritual in the form of songs/chants involving simultaneous others elsewhere become important (see Kong 2001b)?

In examining the poetics of sacred places, attention has refocused on some of the earlier contributions in humanistic geographies. Discussions about how religious places offer a sense of rootedness and identity find resonances with earlier ideas propounded by humanist geographers such as Tuan and Buttimer to nonreligious contexts. Kong (1992) has explored, for example, the personal and familial histories of religious adherents in Singapore and how they are tied up with churches and Hindu temples, contributing to the development of personal attachments and senses of place. Mazumdar and Mazumdar (1993) have focused on Hindu sacred place, arguing that the domestic *pooja* (prayer) area is viewed as a family heirloom and evokes a sense of rootedness. While representing continuities with the work of humanistic geographers, and illustrating the applicability of existing concepts, geographical research on religion has not contributed substantially to a reconceptualization of our understanding of place attachments. Attachment to religious place may be little different from attachment to secular place (see James 1902).

Poetics of community

Two major issues characterize writings about the poetics of religious communities. First, religious places are also social centers which facilitate community-building. Within the multidisciplinary literature on religion, attention has focused on religious places such as mosques and temples as social centers where adherents gather, not only to pray, but to engage in social activities as well. As long as people pray in the same place and "do things together," the assumption is often that they feel they "belong" together as a "community." Little attention has been paid to the fact that "belonging" to a parish or praying in the same place does not necessarily entail a feeling of integration and community with other worshippers. This somewhat uncritical treatment of religious places as social centers means that internal tensions have not been explored and attention has not been paid to the ways in which such tensions are mediated and resolved, and how these very mediations and negotiations are often part of the process of community-building. While it is important to understand the poetics of community, it is also crucial to interrogate the dialectics between the politics and poetics of community.

A second issue regards the role of place in the construction of a religious community. "Community" usually suggests some or all of the following: common needs and goals, a sense of the common good, shared lives, culture and views of the world, and collective action (Silk 1999: 8). These rely on interaction and communication between community members, which are much more likely when there is unmediated face-to-face contact between people, which, in turn, means locatedness in a place (see also Hillery 1955). However, communities may also be spatially dispersed ("place-free," "stretched-out") (Davies & Herbert 1993; Johnston et al. 1994: 80; Knox 1995: 214), and communicative media such as the telephone and the internet allow for the construction of communities without territorial base (Silk 1999: 9). Examples of such stretched-out communities might be nations (imagined communities) and ethnocultural diasporas.

Religious activities have also been influenced by technology through religious broadcasting and computer-mediated communication (email, discussion lists, websites). Such developments may have revitalized religion in some ways, rather than led to its demise, as some of the literature is wont to argue (see Kong 2001b). Few geographers have explored these media and their impacts on religious life, including the poetics of religious communities, and herein lies an additional area that deserves more research attention.

Politics of identity and community

"Traditional communities" as commonly conceived (as harmonious entities with shared needs, goals, values, activities, etc.) are a form of idealization. In fact, traditional communities are often characterized by various forms of oppression, "protecting the prevailing value system including its moral code" (Smith 1999: 25; see also Dwyer 1999), displaying an "intolerance of difference," since the "ideal of community" relies on a desire for "the same social wholeness and identification that underlies racism and ethnic chauvinism on the one hand and political sectarianism on the other" (Young 1990a: 303; Young 1990b).

Recent geographical work on religious 'communities' illustrates a willingness to engage with such reconceptualizations of community. Dwyer's (1999) work on young Muslim women in a small town near London examines the ways in which different constructions of community – both "local" and "globalized" – are used by young British Muslim women, which are simultaneously empowering and constraining. She reveals how 'community' is a source of security and strength but also of constraint and oppression. Participants in Dwyer's study spoke about a local 'Asian community,' evoked by the availability of specialized services such as halal meat shops, which signals for them a sense of security and acceptance (hence no racism) in the town. This is a construction of an 'Asian community' that corresponds to the ethnic community discourse of conventional multiculturalism in which the 'Asian community' is imagined in opposition to 'British society.' While this was positive, it came at a cost: living in an 'Asian community' meant all sorts of surveillance by other members of the 'community' about one's actions and behavior. This is the contradiction of community that confronts young British Muslim women.

Because the boundaries of 'community' are fluid, different imaginations of Muslim community can be evoked or denied. Dwyer (1999) explores contradictions within a 'community,' with those who construct and those who deny the existence of a 'Muslim community.' While some insist that divergences within the 'community' must be recognized, such consciousness of diversities are countered by those who seek to define an inclusive collectivity of Muslims, rejecting the salience of sectarian divisions such as Sunni, Shia, and Ishmaili Islam in their own 'community.' For them, banding together is important because Muslims the world over are deemed to be oppressed. Calling upon the global sense of a Muslim community (the *umma*) thus becomes a source of empowerment (see also Samad 1993; Eade 1993, 1994; Lewis 1994; Back 1996).

Religious places may play a role in constructing and maintaining the boundaries that sustain religious identities and communities. Control over religious places, be they schools, mosques, temples or other facilities can play an important role in community and family (see, for example, Saifullah-Khan 1977; Shaw 1988). Recent anthropological work points the way ahead for geographers.

Vertovec's (1992) study of different Hindu temples in London illustrates how members of the Caribbean Hindu Society's use the temple in a completely congregational manner, opening only for collective worship and remaining closed to individual and family-based worship on weekdays; organizing communal activities where food of the Caribbean-Indian variant is served; and reciting prayers congregationally, with the equivalent of church prayer books. The temple therefore becomes a significant means of consolidating and reproducing the Caribbean-Indian-Hindu community. Vertovec argues that this use of the temple has emerged because in Trinidad and Guyana, Hindus were at the bottom of the social structure and congregational worship provided a sense of mutual support and the maintenance of self-esteem, demonstrating and reinforcing their ethnic identity. When they migrated to Britain, they were still in an ethnic quandary, with the white British population thinking of them derogatorily as 'Paki' (subcontinental Indian); their official 'West Indian' status; and their harsh treatment by South Asians who saw them as a pariah group. For them, community has nothing to do with territory, coming from different parts of London, but everything to do with "cultural habits and mutual experiences of exclusion" (Vertovec 1992: 262). By contrast, where the need to consolidate and reinforce identity is not as marked, the temple does not play the important role of a "community center."

The desire to be recognized as a 'community' is also evident among the Hindu population in Edinburgh, as Nye (1993: 201) illustrates:

Nearly all Hindu temples in Britain make use of some type of congregational worship, but only certain temples are equating these congregations with actual communal groups, and in doing so are using the temple to create a sense of Hindu 'community.'

She argues that the notion that Hindus share a common identity and can therefore be considered a 'community' is a discursive construct, because the presence of Hindus in Edinburgh does not necessarily imply the presence of a Hindu community. Neither does the fact that people worship together (a congregation) make them a 'community.' Yet, there is 'common talk' among many sections of the population that they form a 'Hindu community,' with a common identity and purpose. This is primarily aided by the fact that the community has a physical manifestation, the Hindu temple.

In short, the notion of a 'religious community' is a contested one, at once liberating and constraining, contributing to the construction of place and relying on it at the same time.

'New' Geographies of Religion

Geographical interest in religion has a long history. As Glacken (1967: 35) pointed out:

In ancient and modern times alike, theology and geography have often been closely related studies because they meet at crucial points of human curiosity. If we seek after the nature of God, we must consider the nature of man [sic] and the earth, and if we look at the earth, questions of divine purpose in its creation and of the role of mankind [sic] on it inevitably arise.

A review of the existing literatures reveals how geographical research on religion reflects the key concepts and approaches in geography: the spatial, the environmental, the landscape, and the place-centered. The spatial is manifest in mapping exercises, in the exploration of diffusion patterns, and more recently, in spatial politics. Human–environmental relationships are mediated by religion, such as in environmental determinism and religious ecology. The landscape approach embraces explorations of religious landscape politics, but also religious landscape imprints in descriptive and symbolic terms. The focus on place recognizes the meaningful personal relationships between people and place, after the style of humanistic geographers, but also interrogates the significance of place in community-building. The role of physical place in a world increasingly mediated by technology also constitutes a subject of inquiry.

The literature on geographies of religion has thus been rich and varied. Yet, there are still other ways of expanding the agenda, and particular ways of framing this agenda conceptually. In what follows, I propose an agenda that is crafted in terms of various "differentiations," anchored in an interest to understand religion in/and modernity. This focus on differentiations draws from the understanding that modernity is characterized precisely by differentiations (Heelas 1998: 2), evident in the division of labor, the separation of home and work, public and private, the construction of 'national' and 'tribal' identities, the separation between God and nature, fractures between Protestant and Catholic, and differentiations between religion and politics (the secular), for example. It is rooted in a recognition that differentiations have emerged in multiple religious inclinations, from traditional, authoritative religions of the text to liberal teachings with a strong dose of humanism, to alternative spiritualities or New Age teachings emphasizing the expressive. Thus, I urge as a frame of reference for future work, differentiations of various complexions, in terms of (1) different sites of religious practice beyond the "officially sacred"; (2) different sensuous sacred geographies; (3) different religions in different historical and place-specific contexts; (4) different geographical scales of analysis; (5) different constitutions of population; (6) different dialectics; and (7) different moralities. Let me elaborate.

First, some of the emerging literature illustrates possibilities of extending the site of analysis, provoking research beyond the 'officially sacred.' Religious places such as indigenous sacred sites, religious schools, religious organizations and their premises (communal halls), pilgrimage routes (apart from the sites themselves), religious objects, memorials and roadside shrines, domestic shrines, and religious processions and festivals – the 'unofficially sacred' – fully deserve research attention. Further, with technological developments, new religious technological sites also require examination. Such new religiotechnological sites may shift the longstanding focus on visual and kinetic to aural/audio experiences and constructions of the sacred (see Kong 2001b). Arising therefrom, there is a second, and significant, need to foreground different sensuous sacred geographies, to understand how religious space may be carved out aurally, for example (Lee 1999).

Third, analytic categories must not be treated as substantive categories. Religion, like class, race and gender, must be a matter for historical and place-specific analysis rather than taken as *a priori* theory. The ways in which an Irish and a Filipino Catholic, or a rural and metropolitan Manila Catholic, experience and negotiate religious place, must be subject to specific contextual scrutiny (see Williams 1977: 80–1; Ling 1987: 11). Geography matters.

Fourth, the above discussion points to the need for analysis at various scales· global, national, regional, local and indeed, that of the body. The continuance of religious broadcasting and the emergence of the Internet suggest that certain religious groups have a more global reach than others, exercising influence that is nevertheless mediated by local contexts. Similarly, the reach of transnational religious groups set against the mediations of local forces demands attention, as does the question of how pan-religious identities and communities (e.g. the *umma*) conflict with local and national affiliations. Nagata (1999) argues that there is a trend towards religious globalization, characterized, *inter alia*, by a growing convergence and conformity between different religious traditions in which particular religious ideals are sought: regular congregational rituals, adoption of a sacred day a week, a centrality of scriptures and texts, an engagement with secular issues such as human rights, refugees, the environment, and so forth. These trends lend themselves to the development of a 'global' religious civil society. At the same time, with globalization and increasing migration of both highly skilled visible minorities and equally visible 'underbelly' illegal or low skilled ones, different religious diasporic communities have formed whose experiences deserve research attention. At the other end of the scale spectrum, the politics and poetics of the local – the school, the mandir, the communal hall, the pilgrimage site – have been examined more frequently, sometimes situated within larger national and even global contexts. More recent attempts at examining embodied geographies (Nast & Pile 1998) may also offer a fruitful scale for analysis. As Dwyer's (1998) analysis of Muslim women's dressing indicates, the body, and relatedly, dress, is both the expression of dominant ideologies and representations of 'Muslim women' as well as sites of contested cultural representation.

Mention of women directs attention to the fact that there are different geographies for different population constituents. A fifth way of differentiation that geographical analysis must consider is the way in which religious place holds different meanings and exerts different influences on such different constitutions as women, children, teenagers and the elderly. Their different geographies need to be theorized in different ways, for example, what do public and private spheres mean for and how are they experienced by men and women, children, adults and elderly, and how might these varied experiences and meanings alter conceptions of public and private?

At a theoretical level, there is a need to explore various dialectics, of public and private, politics and poetics, social and spatial. Research clearly needs to be advanced to interrogate public–private dialectics in the context of religious place and experience, as well as the sensitive integration of politics and poetics. In turn, the intersection of the social and spatial has quite frequently infused current work, a reflection of the firm hold of the society-and-space paradigm in geography in the last two decades.

Even while the above agenda for research calls for account to be taken of various differentiations, dedifferentiation is also evident from another perspective: in the ways in which multidisciplinary work creates crosscurrents to the extent that it is sometimes difficult to distinguish between contributions from different disciplines. In particular, a rapprochement with anthropology is growing. Perhaps this is a throwback to a long and early relationship between the two disciplines (see Wagner & Mikesell 1962). In addition, convergences are also sometimes evident with sociology, history, architecture and religious studies (Metcalf 1996). Indeed, Billinge (1986) has recognized the need to take on board the doctrinal content of religious traditions and not just the geographical impact. This emphasis on theology, not just geography, opens up avenues for collaboration with scholars of religion (see also Ley 2000).

Finally, moral geographies (landscapes and locations) have become more recent subjects for research (see Matless 1995: 396–7; Ó Tuathail 1996: 409–10) and the issue of social justice has attracted more research attention (Smith 1994; Harvey 1996). While morality and social justice may exist apart from religion, often, religion is the basis of morality and the impetus for social justice, as well as of intolerance and injustice. Yet, how different religions may inform the constructions of different moral geographies has not been explored, and how these constructed moral geographies contradict or are negotiated or reinforced by other secular agents of morality (for example, the state) requires examination (see Pacione 1999). In other words, how are competing constructions of good/bad, just/unjust played out in space, between different religious conceptions and between religious and secular conceptions? Such differentiations aside, the dedifferentiation between the secular–sacred boundary as the secular becomes "less obviously secular" (Heelas

1998: 3) is also evident in the moral geographies of social movements, some of which have religious undertones. Ecological movements, for example, take certain moral positions about what is good/bad and just/unjust, and while explicitly a secular movement, also approximates an "implicit religion" (Bartkowski & Swearingen 1997).

Geographers of religion have much to offer. On the one hand, through detailed empirical work, grounded in quotidian details from the field, they can contribute to refining theoretical understandings of the nature of the sacred (place, identity, and community). This reflects my belief that there is no "ascent" to theory without "descent" to case study. At the same time, those with more "applied" inclinations – whether proselytic (Cooper 1993), activist (Chouinard 1994: 5; Warf & Grimes 1997), or policy oriented (Dunn 1997) – will also find useful "real life" insights from further research in "new" geographies of religion that can inform praxis. In this way, the manners in which race, class, and gender have become primary axes of analyses in geography and other social science disciplines can begin to be true of religion as well.

NOTES

1. This chapter draws primarily from Kong (1990, 2001a). I am grateful to *Progress in Human Geography* for permission to reproduce certain paragraphs from Kong (2001a).
2. In economic theory, singularization is the opposite of commoditization. Singularizing something "takes it out of the market dynamics by treating it as precious, by attributing to it so much worth that it is beyond exchange" (Grimes 1992: 421). When museums purchase objects, they commoditize them momentarily but terminally, and in the museum, the object becomes "singular, unique, abstracted from its original context, protected from the market" (ibid.).
3. Wicca is a sub-branch of Paganism associated with witchcraft.

REFERENCES

Back, L. 1996: *New Ethnicities and Urban Culture: Racisms and Multiculture in Young Lives*. London: UCL Press.

Bartkowski, J. P. and Swearingen, W. S. 1997: God meets Gaia in Austin, Texas: a case study of environmentalism as implicit religion. *Review of Religious Research* 38(4), 308–24.

Billinge, M. 1986: Geography of religion. In R. J. Johnston, D. Gregory, and D. M. Smith, eds., *The Dictionary of Human Geography*, 2nd ed. Oxford: Blackwell, 403–6.

Biswas, L. 1984: Evolution of Hindu temples in Calcutta. *Journal of Cultural Geography* 4, 73–85.

Buttner, M. 1980: Survey article on the history and philosophy of the geography of religion in Germany. *Religion*, 86–119.

Carmichael, D. L., Hubert, J., Reeves, B., and Schanche, A., eds. 1994: *Sacred Sites, Sacred Places*. London and New York: Routledge.

Chidester, D. and Linenthal, E. T. 1995: Introduction. In D. Chidester and E. T. Linenthal, eds., *American Sacred Space*. Bloomington: Indiana University Press, 1–42.

Chouinard, V. 1994: Reinventing radical geography: is all that's Left Right? *Environment and Planning D: Society and Space* 12(1), 2–6.

Christopher, A. J. 1995: Segregation and cemeteries in Port Elizabeth, South Africa. *The Geographical Journal* 161, 38–46.

Cobb, J. B. 1972: *Is It Too Late? A Theology of Ecology*. Beverly Hills, CA: Bruce.

Cooper, A. 1993: Space and the geography of religion: a rejoinder. *Area* 25(1), 76–8.

Crang, M., Crang, P., and May, J., eds. 1999: *Virtual Geographies: Bodies, Space and Relations*. London and New York: Routledge.

Crowley, W. K. 1978: Old Order Amish settlement: diffusion and growth. *Annals of the Association of American Geographers* 68, 249–64.

Curtis, J. R. 1980: Miami's Little Havana: yard shrines, cult religion and landscape. *Journal of Cultural Geography* 1, 1–15.

Davies, W. K. D. and Herbert, D. 1993: *Communities within Cities: An Urban Social Geography*. London: Belhaven Press.

Dubos, R. 1969: *A Theology of the Earth*. Washington, DC: Smithsonian Institution.

Dubos, R. 1972: *A God Within*. New York: Scribner.

Dunn, K. M. 1997: Cultural geography and cultural policy. *Australian Geographical Studies* 35(1), 1–11.

Dunn, K. M. 2001: Representations of Islam in the politics of mosque development in Sydney. *Tijdschrift voor Economische en Sociale Geografie* 92(3), 291–308.

Dwyer, C. 1998: Contested identities: challenging dominant representations of young British Muslim women. In T. Skelton and G. Valentine, eds., *Cool Places: Geographies of Youth Cultures*. London and New York: Routledge, 50–65.

Dwyer, C. 1999: Contradictions of community: questions of identity for young British Muslim women. *Environment and Planning A* 31, 53–68.

Eade, J. 1993: The political articulation of community and the Islamisation of space in London. In R. Barot, ed., *Religion and Ethnicity: Minorities and Social Change in the Metropolis*. Kampen, the Netherlands: Kok, 27–42.

Eade, J. 1994: Identity, nation and religion: educated young Bangladeshi Muslims in London's 'East End.' *International Sociology* 9, 377–94.

Eliade, M. 1959: *The Sacred and the Profane: The Nature of Religion*, tr. W. R. Trask. San Diego: Harcourt Brace Jovanovich.

Fickeler, P. 1962: Fundamental questions in the geography of religions. In P. L. Wagner and M. W. Mikesell, eds., *Readings in Cultural Geography*. Chicago: University of Chicago Press.

Glacken, C. J. 1959: Changing ideas of the habitable world. In W. L. Thomas, Jr., ed., *Man's Role in Changing the Face of the Earth*. Chicago: University of Chicago Press, 70–92.

Glacken, C. J. 1967: *Traces on the Rhodian Shore*. Berkeley: University of California Press.

Graham, B. and Murray, M. 1997: The spiritual and the profane: the pilgrimage to Santiago de Compostela. *Ecumene* 4(4), 389–409.

Grimes, R. L. 1992: Sacred objects in museum spaces. *Studies in Religion* 21(4), 419–30.

Hardwick, W. G., Claus, R. J., and Rothwell, D. C. 1971: Cemeteries and urban land value. *Professional Geographer* 23, 19–21.

Hargrove, E. C., ed. 1986: *Religion and Environmental Ethics*: Athens, GA: University of Georgia Press.

Harris, M. 1966: The cultural ecology of India's sacred cattle. *Current Anthropology* 7, 51–66.

Harvey, D. 1996: Social justice, postmodernism and the city. In S. S. Fainstein and S. Campbell, eds., *Readings in Urban Theory*. Cambridge, MA: Blackwell, 436–43.

Heatwole, C. A. 1985: The unchurched in the Southeast. *Southeastern Geographer* 25, 1–15.

Heatwole, C. A. 1986: A geography of the African Methodist Episcopal Zion Church. *Southeastern Geographer* 26, 1–11.

Heelas, P. 1998: Introduction: on differentiation and dedifferentiation. In P. Heelas, ed., with the assistance of D. Martin and P. Morris, *Religion, Modernity and Postmodernity*. Oxford and Malden, MA: Blackwell, 1–18.

Heffernan M. 1995: For ever England: the Western Front and the politics of remembrance in Britain. *Ecumene* 2(3), 293–323.

Heiser, C. B., Jr. 1973: *Seed to Civilization: The Story of Man's Food*. San Francisco: W. H. Freeman.

Hillery G. 1955: Definitions of community: areas of agreement. *Rural Sociology* 20(1–4), 111–23.

Hultkrantz, A. 1966: An ecological approach to religion. *Ethnos* 31, 131–50.

Hume, L. 1998: Creating sacred space: outer expressions of inner worlds in modern Wicca. *Journal of Contemporary Religion* 13(3), 309–19.

Huntington, E. 1945: *Mainsprings of Civilization*. New York: John Wiley and Sons; London: Chapman and Hall.

Isaac, E. 1959–60: Religion, landscape and space. *Landscape* 9, 14–18.

Isaac, E. 1961–2: The act and the covenant: the impact of religion on the landscape. *Landscape* 11, 12–17.

Isaac, E. 1962: On the domestication of cattle. *Science* 137, 195–204.

Isaac, E. 1965: Religious geography and the geography of religion. *Man and the Earth*, University of Colorado Studies, Series in Earth Sciences no. 3. Boulder, CO: University of Colorado Press.

James, W. 1902: *The Varieties of Religious Experience: A Study in Human Nature*. New York: University Books.

Johnson, R. 1986: The story so far: and further transformations? In D. Punter, ed., *Introduction to Contemporary Cultural Studies*. London: Longman, 277–313.

Johnston, R. J., Gregory, D., and Smith, D. M., eds. 1994: *The Dictionary of Human Geography*, 3rd ed. Oxford: Blackwell.

Knox, P. 1995: *Urban Social Geography: An Introduction*, 3rd ed. Harlow, Essex: Longman.

Kong, L. 1990: Geography and religion: trends and prospects. *Progress in Human Geography* 14(3), 355–71.

Kong, L. 1992: The sacred and the secular: exploring contemporary meanings and values for religious buildings in Singapore. *Southeast Asian Journal of Social Science* 20(1), 18–42.

Kong, L. 1993a: Ideological hegemony and the political symbolism of religious buildings in Singapore. *Environment and Planning D: Society and Space* 11(1), 23–45.

Kong, L. 1993b: Negotiating conceptions of sacred space: a case study of religious buildings in Singapore. *Transactions, Institute of British Geographers* N.S. 18(3), 342–58.

Kong, L. 1999: Cemeteries and columbaria, memorials and mausoleums: narrative and interpretation in the study of deathscapes in geography. *Australian Geographical Studies* 37(1), 1–10.

Kong, L. 2001a: Mapping 'new' geographies of religion: politics and poetics in modernity. *Progress in Human Geography* 25(2), 211–33.

Kong, L. 2001b: Religion and technology: refiguring place, space, identity and community. *Area* 33(4), 404–13.

Laatsch, W. G. and Calkins, C. F. 1986: The Belgian Roadside chapels of Wisconsin's Door Peninsula. *Journal of Cultural Geography* 7, 117–28.

Landing, J. 1982: A case study in the geography of religion: the Jehovah's Witnesses in Spain, 1921–1946. *Bulletin, Association of North Dakota Geographers* 32, 42–7.

Lane, B. C. 1988: *Landscapes of the Sacred: Geography and Narrative in American Spirituality*. New York: Paulist Press.

Lee, T. S. 1999: Technology and the production of Islamic space: the call to prayer in Singapore. *Ethnomusicology* 43(1), 86–100.

Leiris, M. 1938: The sacred in everyday life. Reprinted in translation in D. Hollier, ed., *The College of Sociology 1937–39*. Minneapolis: University of Minnesota Press, 1988.

Levine, G. J. 1986: On the geography of religion. *Transactions of the Institute of British Geographers* NS 11, 428–40.

Lewis, P. 1994: *Islamic Britain*. London: I. B. Taurus.

Ley, D. 2000: Geography of religion. In R. J. Johnston, D. Gregory, G. Pratt, and M. Watts, eds., *The Dictionary of Human Geography*, 4th ed. Oxford and Malden, MA: Blackwell, 697–99.

Ling, T. O. 1987: *Buddhism, Confucianism and the secular state in Singapore*. Singapore: Department of Sociology, National University of Singapore, Working Paper no. 79.

Livingstone, D. N. 1994: Science and religion: foreword to the historical geography of an encounter. *Journal of Historical Geography* 20(4), 367–83.

Matless, D. 1995: Culture run riot? Work in social and cultural geography, 1994. *Progress in Human Geography* 19(3), 395–403.

Mazumdar, S. and Mazumdar, S. 1993: Sacred space and place attachment. *Journal of Environmental Psychology* 13, 231–42.

Metcalf, B., ed. 1996: *Making Muslim Spaces in North America and Europe*. Berkeley: University of California Press.

Morris, M. S. 1997: Gardens 'for ever England': landscape, identity and the First World War British cemeteries on the western front. *Ecumene* 4, 410–34.

Murray, M. and Graham, B. 1997: Exploring the dialectics of route-based tourism: the *Camino de Santiago*. *Tourism Management* 18(8), 513–24.

Mythum, H. 1994: Language as symbol in churchyard monuments: the use of Welsh in nineteenth- and twentieth-century Pembrokeshire. *World Archaeology*, 26(2), 252– 67.

Nagata, J. 1999: The globalisation of Buddhism and the emergence of religious civil society: the case of the Taiwanese Fo Kuang Shan movement in Asia and the West. *Communal/ Plural*, 7(2), 231–48.

Nast, H. and Pile, S., eds. 1998: *Places through the Body*. London and New York: Routledge.

Naylor, S. K. and Ryan, J. R. 1998: Ethnicity and cultural landscapes: mosques, gurdwaras and mandirs in England and Wales. Paper presented at the "Religion and Locality Conference," University of Leeds, Sept. 8–10.

Nye, M. 1993: Temple congregations and communities: Hindu constructions in Edinburgh. *New Community* 19(2), 201–15.

Otto, R. 1917: *The Idea of the Holy*, tr. J. W. Harvey, 2nd ed. Oxford: Oxford University Press.

Ó Tuathail, G. 1996: Political geography II: (counter) revolutionary times. *Progress in Human Geography* 20, 404–12.

Pacione, M. 1999: The relevance of religion for a relevant human geography. *Scottish Geographical Journal* 115(2), 117–31.

Passmore, J. 1974: *Man's Responsibility for Nature*. London: Duckworth.

Philp, J. and Mercer, D. 1999: Commodification of Buddhism in contemporary Burma. *Annals of Tourism Research* 26(1), 21–54.

Raivo, P. J. 1997: Comparative religion and geography: some remarks on the geography of religion and religious geography. *Temenos* 33, 137–49.

Rath, J., Groenendijk, K., and Penninx, R. 1991: The recognition and institutionalisation of Islam in Belgium, Great Britain and the Netherlands. *New Community* 18(1), 101–14.

Saifullah-Khan, V. 1977: The Pakistanis: Mirpuri villagers at home and in Bradford. In J. Watson, ed., *Between Two Cultures*. Oxford: Blackwell, 57–89.

Samad, Y. 1993: Imagining a British Muslim identification. Paper presented at *Muslims in Europe: Generation to Generation Conference*, St Catherine's College, Oxford, April 5–7.

Semple, E. 1911: *Influences of Geographic Environment: On the Basis of Ratzel's System of Anthropo-geography*. New York: Henry Holt; London: Constable.

Shaw, A. 1988: *A Pakistani Community in Britain*. Oxford: Blackwell.

Shortridge, J. R. 1976: Patterns of religion in the United States. *Geographical Review* 66, 420–34.

Shortridge, J. R. 1977: A new regionalization of American religion. *Journal for the Scientific Study of Religion* 16, 143–53.

Shortridge, J. R. 1978: The pattern of American Catholicism, 1971. *Journal of Geography* 77, 56–60.

Silk, J. 1999: The dynamics of community, place, and identity. *Environment and Planning A* 31, 5–17.

Simoons, F. J. 1979: Questions in the sacred-cow controversy. *Current Anthropology* 20, 467–93.

Smith, D. 1994: *Geography and Social Justice*. Oxford: Blackwell.

Smith, D. M. 1999: Geography, community, and morality. *Environment and Planning A* 31, 19–35.

Smith, J. Z. 1978: The wobbling pivot. In J. Z. Smith, ed., *Map is Not Territory: Studies in the History of Religions*. Leiden: E. J. Brill, 88–103.

Sopher, D. 1964: Indigenous uses of turmeric in Asia and Oceania. *Anthropos* 59, 93–127.

Sopher, D. 1967: *Geography of Religions*. Englewood Cliffs, NJ: Prentice-Hall.

Sopher, D. 1981: Geography and religion. *Progress in Human Geography* 5, 510–24.

Speck, C. 1996: Women's war memorials and citizenship. *Australian Feminist Studies* 11(23), 129–45.

Stump, R. W. 1981: *Changing Regional Patterns of White Protestantism in the United States, 1906–1971*. Unpublished Ph.D. thesis, University of Kansas.

Stump, R. W. 1991: Spatial implications of religious broadcasting: stability and change in patterns of belief. In S. Brunn and T. Leinbach, eds., *Collapsing Space and Time: Geographic Aspects of Communications and Information*. London: Harper Collins Academic, 354–75.

Tanaka, H. 1984: Landscape expression of the evolution of Buddhism in Japan. *The Canadian Geographer* 28, 240–57.

Toynbee, A. 1972: The religious background of the present environmental crisis – a viewpoint. *International Journal of Environmental Studies* 3, 141–46.

Vertovec, S. 1992: Community and congregation in London Hindu temples: divergent trends. *New Community* 18(2), 251–64.

Wagner, P. and Mikesell, M., eds. 1962: *Readings in Cultural Geography*. Chicago: University of Chicago Press.

Warf, B. and Grimes, J. 1997: Counterhegemonic discourses and the Internet. *Geographical Review* 87(2), 259–74.

White, L., Jr. 1967: The historical roots of our ecologic crisis. *Science* 155, 1203–7.

Williams, R. 1977: *Marxism and Literature*. Oxford: Oxford University Press.

Young, I. M. 1990a: The ideal of community and the politics of difference. In L. J. Nicholson, ed., *Feminism/Postmodernism*. London: Routledge, 300–23.

Young, I. M. 1990b: *Justice and the Politics of Difference*. Princeton: Princeton University Press.

Chapter 25

Landscapes of Home

James S. Duncan and David Lambert

Introduction

Home is a complex and ambiguous word. Because it bears such a weight of meaning in everyday life it can be considered one of the most emotive and powerful words in the English language. As Gathorne-Hardy (1999: 124) points out, "the word home can be seen as a vessel in which a tangle of abstract, cultural concepts are found." One would be hard pressed to think of a more important idea to people than that of home (Sopher 1979). One can read this importance in the notion of homelessness; a term which has come to stand for a condition of abjection, an indictment against affluent societies that are so uncaring as to allow so many of their citizens to go homeless (Somerville 1992). It is ironic, given the affective significance of the concept, that the home has until recently received only a modest amount of attention in the academy relative to that devoted to the public realm. There still appears to be a lingering sense that the home, as a site of reproduction or bourgeois pleasure, is trivial compared with the public worlds of business, politics, or even public pleasures. Staszak (2001b) argues that geographers have paid little attention to the home because they are uncomfortable working at such a small scale. Or perhaps academics shy away because of the very ambiguity of the term. For home, as Benjamin (1995: 2) points out, is "at once both concrete and abstract"; a place where one lives and a feeling of comfort – of feeling at home. Moreover, it is spoken of in ways that, without a sense of contradiction, range in scale from a mental state, to a house, to a continent (Bowlby, Gregory, & McKie 1997). A term that is made to do such work, which is stretched to such an extent, is probably going to be intellectually flabby (Rapoport 1995). And yet, it would be unproductive for academics to narrow its usage in the name of intellectual rigor, for in doing so they would lose much of its social meaning (Lawrence 1995).

Now with increased interest in the everyday, the production of space in a globalizing world (Massey 1994), with feminist destabilizing of the private–public dichotomy (Duncan 1996; Bondi 1998) and theorizing of unpaid domestic labor (Christie 1999), as well as renewed interest in the body (Nast & Pile 1998), emotions (Anderson & Smith 2001), and psychoanalysis (Sibley 1995; Bordo, Klein, &

Silverman 1998), the home as a topic of interest to geographers is beginning to come into its own. The concept of home has recently been explored in a number of edited collections. Benjamin (1995) draws together scholars working within an environmental design framework, Cieraad (1999) and Miller (2001) adopt more ethnographic perspectives, Staszak (2001a) brings together the work of Francophone anthropologists, architects, and geographers, and Mezei (2002) provides a forum for a wide variety of research on the home from within the humanities, social sciences, and design professions. McDowell (1999) and Bennett (2002) provide useful summaries of research on the notion of home. Classic work on changing conceptions of home by historians includes Davidoff and Hall (1987), Hareven (1982), and Hayden (1981). In this chapter we explore what we see as some of the more interesting cultural geographic questions concerning the idea of home. In doing so, we will range widely in scale, both temporally and spatially. We begin with a review of geographical approaches to the notion of home as the house or homeplace (such as one's neighborhood) and then attempt to broaden out the concept of homeland as composed by a "constitutive outside." Finally, with specific reference to the British Empire, we will address the issue of nostalgia for home and the "domestication" of nonmetropolitan spaces.

Geography of Emotions

One major focus of research on home has been the link between the home and the emotions. Structural anthropologists following Lévi-Strauss have tended to assume a connection between the house and the structure of mind. His (1967; 1972) classic work conducted among the Bororo and Sherente of Brazil and the work of others in the structuralist tradition (Bourdieu 1973; Tambiah 1969) are generally seen as ingenious but now mainly of historiographic interest due to the collapse of the Lévi-Straussian conception of mind. Within cultural geography, Lévi-Strauss's work has had little impact, a notable exception being Tuan's (1974) rather loose use of the perspective. An offshoot of structural analysis of the home survives (although one could hardly say that it flourishes) in the form of semiotics (Preziosi 1979). Like Lévi-Straussian structuralism, it is highly abstract and formalistic, but by remaining agnostic about the origins of the structures that it posits, it has survived where the former has foundered.

Another line of research, the phenomenological, has been inspired in part by the work of the philosopher Gaston Bachelard (1969: 72). For him, the house is a "psychic state," a site and bringer-into-being of deep feelings of value and caring. Within geography such a perspective has again been championed by Tuan (1974) whose notion of "topophilia," or love of place, has had wide appeal both within the field and within the cognate fields of architecture and landscape architecture. More recently Seamon and Mugerauer (1989) and Pallasmaa (1995: 143) have conducted more explicitly phenomenological research on home in which they argue for a "phenomenologically authentic" architecture that incorporates "the memories and dreams of the inhabitant."

Bell hooks (1990), like the phenomenologists, sees the home as a place of warmth, caring, and safety. For hooks the home is a powerful site of resistance where black women can fashion a space of solidarity and difference from a white racist society.

The phenomenologists, however, fail to recognize this politics of the domestic realm. Furthermore, unlike the phenomenologists, hooks is more careful not to overgeneralize and does not attempt to speak for a general black female experience. In fact, she points out that for black families there is often an ethic against public intervention and distrust of police scrutiny and control; hence black homes like white homes can sometimes be sites of domestic violence, a refuge perhaps for men, but oppressive for women who may be unable or unwilling to call on the often less than sympathetic public authorities. Much of this work, however, is based in philosophical and literary analysis, and tends to be empirically light.

There is also a small but significant literature on the loss of home, some of which is more empirically grounded. The classic statement in this area remains Fried's (1963) "Grieving for a Lost Home," a scathing indictment of the emotional damage wrought by urban renewal in the United States in the 1950s and 1960s. The theme of a sense of loss has been taken up more recently and extended cross culturally by Porteous (1989; 1995) and extended back in time within the context of British colonialism in India by Gowans (1999) and Thomas (2002). The latter two studies demonstrate how feelings of loss and memory intertwine in complex ways the notion of home as one's house with the notion of home as one's nation. Another fruitful line of research has been on the fear of needing to leave one's own home to live in an institution for the elderly or infirm. When such moves do occur, they tend to be characterized by an overwhelming sense of loss or even banishment (Wikstrom 1995; Hugman 1999; Valentine 2001). On the other hand, research by Mowl, Pain, and Talbot (2000) demonstrates that sometimes older men experience home less positively than women, associating it with the end of their productive lives in the public realm; consequently some retired men seek to avoid spending much time at home. Grieving for a particular home can be compounded by a move to a different style of dwelling. Collignon (2001), for example, documents poignant feelings of loss experienced by older Inuit women in the Canadian Arctic who were removed from traditional igloos into Anglo-Canadian style social housing. As Chapman (1999) demonstrates, one can even experience the loss of a home one does not actually leave. He argues that the experience of burglary for many people entails not simply the loss of household objects, but the "spoiling" of the identity of the home. Similarly home is often so closely associated with family. The loss of family members who either move away or die diminishes the fullness of a sense of home for many.

While most people associate it with caring and security, the home can also be a site of fear and danger as feminist and other researchers have pointed out (Gathorne-Hardy 1999; Massey 1992; Rushdie 1991; Duncan 1996; Goldsack 1999). Monk (1999: 160–1), for example, drawing on Klodawsky and Mackenzie (1987), argues that the contemporary notion of home as sanctuary (which draws on nineteenth-century romanticism) must be tempered by the knowledge that private homes are often sites of violence against women by their partners and are statistically more dangerous for women than public places. Dobash and Dobash (1992) claim that domestic violence against women, including marital rape, often stems from a man's perception that his partner has failed in her domestic duties. Klahr (1999a: 126) points out that domestic violence is in fact a primary cause of homelessness in women. One reason, of course, that the issue of the home as dangerous is not of greater concern to the general population is that the violence is privatized;

it may be much more common, but it is not as unpredictable as violence against women by strangers. Just as some women know they are in danger in their own homes, many other women know they are safe. If the violence were more randomly experienced, it would be a more highly publicized issue and would undoubtedly be more effectively controlled.

One of the largest-scale studies of the home and the emotions was conducted by Csikszentmihalyi and Rochberg-Halton (1981). They interviewed 315 Americans of various ages about their degree of emotional attachment to various objects in their homes. Bourdieu's (1984) similarly large-scale study of the French, although focused primarily on class as distinction and household objects as evidence of what he refers to as cultural capital, also explored emotional attachment to such objects. On a much smaller scale, Pennartz (1999) explores the emotional attachment to home as a site of "pleasantness" defined in opposition to the alienating realm of public space. The pleasantness of home may appear banal, but he concludes it is the central locus of emotional well-being.

Gender and Sexuality

During the nineteenth century in Britain and the United States, the spatial separation of men and women particularly in cities and suburbs increased significantly as men were seen to naturally occupy the public sphere and women an idealized domestic sphere (Hayden 1981). Although this is clearly the general pattern, recent work on the middle class in England by Tosh (1999), extending that of Davidoff and Hall (1987) and Hall (1992), shows that the relation of men to the home was fraught with tension and varied considerably during the course of the nineteenth century as gender relations evolved. The relations between gender and domesticity have continued to be complex, fluid, and contested. It is unrealistic to speak of such fluid and transforming gender relations abstractly, however. There is always a geography to social relations. Gender relations are very much embodied and thus "take place" in literal, material ways. As Butler (1990) and others have emphasized, gender is performed in places which are never merely backdrops, but which themselves help to constitute social relations. As a primary site of the transformation of gender relations, the home should be central to the study of the history of gender relations, work that must, of course, avoid reproducing the mind/body, public/private, and male/female sets of dualisms. Social relations are embodied everywhere not especially in the home, although it may be an especially important site to study the negotiation and transformation of gender relations.

By the mid-twentieth century, suburban housing developments in the United States had extended the scale of the privatized home from the house to the whole suburban landscape and thus suburbia came to be seen as a feminized, private realm of the family as distinct from the masculine, urban spaces of the public realm (Hareven 1993). The twentieth century also saw a continuation of the nineteenth-century endeavor to create the "ideal home" as a site of domestic reproduction organized by the "house wife." Silverstone (1997: 7) points out that as a result of middle-class women having experienced work outside the home during the Second World War, "post-war suburbanization was buttressed by a concerted effort by public policy and media images to re-socialize women into the home, and into the bosom of the nuclear bourgeois family." The idea of the "dream home," however, was criticized by feminist authors such as Friedan (1965) and Hayden (1981; 1984). More recent cross-cultural work continues this line of argument (Monk 1999) positing the nuclear family home as a site of patriarchal power, constraining as it is protective. The delegated organizational role of the woman in the home has tended to be circumscribed by the expectations of men of their home as a haven from the public world of work.

Housework, defined as "the work that ensures the smooth running of the domestic economy" (Christie 1999), has traditionally been defined as the realm of women. However the increasing move of women into paid employment outside the home has not necessarily brought about a radical shift in the gendered nature of housework (but see Lewis 2000). Many women feel that they hold two jobs, one paid and the other unpaid (McKee & Bell 1985; Morris 1993; Summerfield 1998; Christie 1999). Yet, some research suggests many women are untroubled by the disproportionate amount of domestic labor that they do (Valentine 2001; Baxter & Western 1998). And as Gregson and Lowe (1995) show, increasingly middle-class women who work outside of the home hire working-class women to clean their homes and serve as nannies for their children. There is an unfortunate irony in middle-class women, some of whom have adopted feminist perspectives, escaping housework by paying working-class women to stand in for them (on paid domestic workers and employers, see Pratt 1998). As McDowell (1999: 83) points out, "paid domestic work within the home not only challenges the socially accepted meaning of the home and its association with the private and the familial, but also makes plain the complex intersections of domesticity, class position and racial difference that distinguish women and create divisions between them."

Although in recent centuries in the West, the ideal middle-class patriarchal home has been defined as spatially separate from any labor other than female reproductive labor, economic restructuring has begun to produce an increase in piecework labor in the home (Klahr 1999b; Meulders et al. 1994). While homework has long been common among poor women especially in highly feminized industries such as garment manufacture (Phizacklea & Wolkowitz 1995) it is now more common among the middle class as well in the form of telemarketing (Oberhauser 1995) and various other forms of telecommuting.

It is interesting to see how gendered ideals of domesticity have been diffused, contested, and transformed in different contexts (Blunt 1999; Sinha 1995). For example, in the context of colonial India, Grewal (1996: 25) tells us that:

In India the English *memsahib* is seen as idle, useless, and too free in her associations with men; the Indian nationalists construct the Indian woman, a reconstruction of a middle-class Victorian woman, as the moral and spiritual opposite of the Englishwoman. Many Indians, especially those with an English education, used Victorian values to suggest Indian women as morally and spiritually superior and thus the proper symbol of "home."

In her studies of youth, gender and the family home, McNamee (1998: 204) believes that the notion of the house as a feminine space has been empowering in certain ways. She says that teenage girls resisted the boy's domination of the streets, by creating their own spaces to develop youth culture in their homes, especially their own bedrooms. Increasingly now, boys, especially middle-class boys with their own computers and video games, are reasserting their claims to homespace. She argues that the increased presence of boys in the home erodes the power of girls. She thus implies that the traditional gendered separation of the public and private spheres has in fact been empowering for girls. Gregson and Lowe (1995: 227) argue that with the increasing participation of women in the labor market and the increased participation of men in domestic work, "the home is no longer the primary space identified with women but rather one space amongst many, a situation which has contributed to the multiple, frequently contradictory nature of women's identifications."

The home is not only a site of gendered power struggle and intergenerational conflicts, it has also been traditionally been thought of as heterosexual space. Research by Valentine (1993), Johnson and Valentine (1995), and Elwood (2000) explains the difficulty of living a gay or lesbian life within the heterosexual family home. In this sense, as Valentine (2001) points out, the home fails to provide a basis for privacy or the development of one's own distinctive identity. While the creation of separate gay and lesbian households is a way of fashioning space for gay lifestyles and resistance to heterosexist norms, this solution is not unproblematic due to the not infrequent homophobia of neighbors who see homosexuality as "deviant" within a family residential area (Valentine 2001).

Housing and Identity

Homes and residential landscapes are primary sites in which identities are produced and performed in practical, material and repetitively reaffirming ways. Here we use the term perform as Austin (1975) defines it: productive, in contrast to denotative; and also as Butler (1990) uses it: to mean everyday self-constituting practices, embedded in a spatial context that is constituted by social practices while it is equally constitutive of them. Homes and residential landscapes evoke powerful sentiments, helping to constitute family and community values and playing a central role in the performance of place-based social identities and distinction (Bourdieu 1984; Duncan 1973; 1981; Duncan & Duncan 2003; Firey 1945; Hugill 1989; Miller 2001; Pratt 1981).

Moving to new homes can also mark changes, both positive and negative, in cultural identity. For example, Gelezeau (2001) shows how the shift in the 1990s in Korea for many families from the traditional hanok-style semidetached or detached house to western-style apartments is taken to be a way of acting "modern" and gaining social status. But she also shows how the adaptation to a new cultural type of spatial layout is tempered by a series of behavioral adaptations on the part of residents to make the space more Korean. Collignon (2001), on the other hand, shows that when cultural change is made under duress, although adaptations are made to new housing styles, identity can be severely undermined.

Valentine (2001: 63) reminds us that the home is a key site of contemporary consumption. Indeed, ever since the 1920s sociologists have explored the manner in which class identity is performed through objects in the home (Lynd & Lynd 1929; Chapin 1935; Warner 1953; 1963; Junker 1954; Davis 1955; Laumann & House 1970; Csikszentmihalyi & Rochberg-Halton 1981; Bourdieu 1984; Hummon

1989). Drawing inspiration from this work, anthropologists, geographers and historians have explored the role of home in the performance of class-identities in North America (Duncan 1973; Duncan & Duncan 1997; 2003; Hugill 1989; Pratt 1981), in Europe (McKibben 1998; Clarke 2001; Garvey 2001; Gullestad 1992; Dolan 1999; Cieraad 1999; Saarikangas 2002) and in South Asia (Duncan 1989; Duncan & Duncan 1976a; 1976b). People produce their identities in and through places, especially homeplaces: houses, gardens, neighborhoods, and towns. Such identities are defined not only in terms of attachment to one's home place, but also in large part in contrast to and *against* an outside world, real or imagined (Clarke 2001; Chapman & Hockey 1999), what some have termed "a constitutive outside." It is this quality of identity as produced both within the homeplace and in relation to other home places that can render place-centered identities insecure. Ironically, this can happen even among those with the resources (time, money and skills) to create what appear to outsiders to be ideal settings in which to substantiate desired social identities (Duncan & Duncan 2003).

Duany and Plater-Zyberk (1992) state that American suburbanites are "happy with the private realm they have won for themselves, but desperately anxious about the public realm around them . . . the late-20th century suburbanite's chief ideology is not conservatism or liberalism but NIMBYism: Not In My Back Yard." These residential landscapes of privilege serve as positional goods and in capitalist societies where identity is linked to possessions, the aesthetic plays a role in the depoliticization of class relations (Harvey 1989). Class relations have become aestheticized in the home realm redefined as lifestyle, taste, patterns of consumption and appreciation of the visual. As David Harvey (1989: 292) says, "the revival of basic institutions (such as the family and the community), are signs of a search for more secure moorings and longer lasting values in a shifting world." The retreat into the residential realm is often manifested in the celebration of the home and of a sense of homeplace that tends to be exclusionary, simultaneously a site of security and social injustice.

Transnational Homes and Communities

The word "home" clearly encompasses more than the house, neighborhood or home town. It includes homeland or nation, a country where one resides or perhaps more importantly where one "comes from." The notion of home can include a tension between these two meanings particularly for immigrants, exiles and expatriates of varying types. In his essay "The Migrant's Suitcase," Morley (2000) discusses objects which act as synecdoches for lost or unreachable homes. House keys (Seed 1999) and suitcases, full of mementoes and clothes, fulfill this function. Sometimes immigrants even buy and furnish houses in their countries of origin in hope of eventually returning. The notion of home as the place one comes from can extend over more than one generation and the country of origins can still be home, even among those who had never set foot there.

A recent chapter in the story of the production of transnational homes and communities has been elaborated in ways never before possible: e-mail and relatively less expensive telephone calls and airline tickets are allowing Latino immigrants to the US to maintain dual senses of home and of community. Politicians and other

influential decision-makers in both the communities of origin and destination sometimes participate jointly in community decision-making by holding conference
calls. Some countries are so anxious to maintain a close transnational community
that they even allow emigrants to vote in elections (dependence on *migradollars*, of
course, plays a role in this). Mike Davis (2000: 77) says, "To earn their living and
reproduce their traditional solidarities, hundreds of *ejidos*, *rancherias*, villages and
small towns in Mexico, Central America and the Caribbean have had to learn how
to live like quantum particles in two places at once." He says that unprecedented
amounts of investment in US homes and businesses should not be mistaken for
diminished commitment to immigrants' other homes and cultures. In fact, this is
seen as necessary to facilitate transnational ties. He writes (2000: 80):

The new logic of social reproduction under conditions of rapid and sometimes catastrophic
global restructuring compels traditional communities to strategically balance assets and population between two different, place-rooted existences.

Some villages in Latin America have half their population living in one neighborhood in the US. Suro (1998) offers the example of Randall's, a supermarket chain
in Houston, which hires more than 1,000 workers from a few neighboring villages
in Guatemala. He (1998: 45) tells of finding "out amid the freeways and strip malls
a thriving Mayan village improbably housed in a cluster of faux Georgian low rise
apartment houses." For some the hybridity of transnationalism has lead to fuller
cultural and economic opportunities, but for many others transnationalism is
equated with a type of homelessness. Many forced migrants often find little sense
of home or welcome in their adopted country and yet also feel estranged from the
home they came from. Differential attachment to the adopted homeplace between
generations also produces an unhappy ambivalence within families. Duncan and
Duncan (2003) describe the feeling of homelessness of many Guatemalan men who
say that can survive but not truly "live" in the New York State town where they
have come to work. Constituted as "other" by a large percentage of the local non-
Latino population they have difficulty achieving a sense of being "at home."

Home and Empire

The complex interplay between notions of home and the experience of transnationalism is not a new phenomena, nor it is associated only with contemporary
processes of globalization and postcolonial movements of people. It was also a
feature of the settlement and colonization that characterized Western imperialism
from the sixteenth to twentieth centuries. Much research in this area has tended
to emphasize the importance of "difference" in the experience and imagination of
imperial projects (Said 1979; Hulme 1986; Rabasa 1993). For instance, Arnold
(1996) argues that "torrid" or "tropical" environmental otherness was important
to the colonial vision of the non-European world. Nevertheless, Blunt (1999: 94)
reminds us that:

Imperial power and legitimisation relied not only on imaginative geographies of "other"
places (Said 1979) but also on imaginative geographies of "home," both between . . . [metro-
pole and colony] and within . . . [the colonial periphery] itself.

While early European contacts with other parts of the world may have been characterized by an initial "shock of difference," a persistent theme of European colonialism has been the domestication of the exotic, particularly before the emergence of Romanticism, through the translation of "New World" phenomena into "Old World" terminology (Greenblatt 1991; Pagden 1993). The empire was never simply a site of otherness, and the spaces of "home" and "away" did not exist in absolute separation. Indeed, one of the impulses of imperialism was the imaginative and material relocation of empire in the metropolitan core. This involved diverse activities ranging from the representation of colonial landscapes in exhibitions, pageants, adventure stories, travel writing and scientific studies (Ryan 1999) to the cultivation of exotic plant species in British gardens as a way of familiarizing unknown tropical lands (Preston 1999). Metropolitan cities were transformed into imperial cities, not only in ceremonial and monumental spaces, but also in the commodification of empire and the imperial labeling of suburban streets (Driver & Gilbert 1998). All these activities brought the empire "home" and represented one aspect of the impact of empire on metropolitan culture (cf. Schwarz 1996; Stoler & Cooper 1997; Burton 1994; Hall 2002).

Also of interest is the connected but somewhat reverse impulse: the transformation of colonial "terra incognito" into "landscapes of home," or what might be thought of as the domestication of empire. This involved the transference of a whole range of objects and ideas, from architectural styles and plant material, to legal systems and aesthetic visions. The emphasis here is not on an untroubled projection of homespace, however, and the recovery of the troubles of domestication exposes the imperial landscapes of home as a contested terrain rather than a confident imposition (cf. Colley, 2002).

Domesticating empire

A key form of the domestication of colonial spaces was their envisioning through the lens of metropolitan aesthetics. Places such as the Kandyan highlands of Ceylon and hill stations across British India were viewed and described in terms of metropolitan landscape models (Duncan 1998; Kenny 1995). Rural, pastoral and georgic idioms were particularly important in the familiarization of the exotic (Gilmore 2000; Sandiford 2000). In part, this had much to do with a nostalgia for the metropolitan home and pointed to feelings of loss amongst the settler populations. But this familiarization was also an act of imaginative colonialism and served specific political and cultural purposes by collapsing the difference between "home" and "away." For example, Seymour, Daniels, and Watkins (1998: 313) argue that the accommodation of the plantation landscape of the Caribbean through "conventional modes of representing and managing British landed estates," such as the pastoral, was important in the "assimilation of the islands as British colonies and in the integration of those with colonial interests into British elite society." Sandiford describes such strategies as "negotiation," whereby those who resided or had interests in the Caribbean sought to "win a tenuous and elusive legitimacy for an evolving Creole civilization, conflicted by its central relation to slavery and its marginal relation to metropolitan cultures" (Sandiford, 2000: 3). The imaginative domestication of empire extended into the postcolonial world; Dodds (1998), for example, argues that the reimagining of the Falkland Islands/Malvinas through rural aesthetics was an important part of the British government's attempt to mobilize popular support for the 1982 war to recapture them from Argentina. Dodds also notes that these imaginative geographies often collapsed under first-hand experience and there were clearly limits to how easily empire could be imaginatively domesticated. Within the "torrid zone," for instance, it tended to be sites of "ambivalent tropicality" (Duncan 2000), such as Barbados in the Caribbean or the more temperate highlands of India and Ceylon, that allowed such readings of colonial space as "home."

The (re)naming of colonial space after landscapes of home was another aspect of domestication. This arch-imperial gesture was part of an attempt to efface pre-colonial cultures (see Berg & Kearns 1996). Perhaps the ultimate manifestation of this kind of naming was the description of Barbados by visitors and settlers alike as "Little England" or "Bimshire," as though Barbados was a tiny fragment of England that had floated off into the Caribbean Sea (Greene 1987; Puckrein 1984; Lambert 2002b). This imagining of Barbados as "Little England" was greatly facilitated by the rapidity of colonial development, including land clearance and settlement (Watson 1979). This serves as a reminder that the domestication of empire was a material as well as imaginative process, which involved the introduction of European property laws, forms of planning, architectural styles, and agricultural practice. Kenny (1995) notes that the projection of British landscape models on to Indian hill stations influenced the actual development of these spaces in terms of the introduction of metropolitan varieties of trees, flowers and vegetables, as well as the architectural features of an elite pastoral landscape model based on a romanticized vision of pre-industrial England. The translation of such landscape models from their cultural and historical contexts lent them heightened ideological and political significance (Duncan 1989). Indeed, the construction of hill stations was just one of the strategies adopted by the British in India to strengthen imperial rule by countering the perceived threat to the colonizers posed by prolonged exposure to the tropical climate and native population. Such concerns were part of the "acclimatization" debate about the environmental limits to European expansion in tropical areas (Livingstone 1991; Kennedy 1990). Whereas sending children to be educated in Britain and periodic home leave for those serving and living in India involved returning to the landscapes of home, the construction and anglicization of hill stations involved cultivating aspects of home – 'English' aesthetics, more temperate conditions, white demographic dominance – in India.

The material transformation of empire was also part of the effort to utilize natural resources, and processes such as clearance, settlement, and planning both drew on and facilitated domesticating visions. Attempts to domesticate the tropical were often scripted in heroic masculinized discourses as part of a struggle to tame nature, a struggle in which women and children were seen as particularly vulnerable (Duncan 2000). Yet, this was not the only framework through which domestication was understood. The discourse of "improvement," which Gascoigne (1994) characterizes as the more efficient use of resources based on reason and the elimination of waste, transformed colonial space into a landscape of home by making it useful (Drayton 2000; Grove 1995). This was polite enlightenment rather than heroic taming and involved farming, breeding and cultivation. Blunt has also discussed the more feminized domestic discourses that framed the establishment of "homes" as part of the colonial project (Blunt 1999). Efforts to introduce white women to many colonies, especially from the mid-nineteenth century, were linked to a determination to emphasize racial divisions between colonizer and colonized, and also stemmed from fears about miscegenation and degeneracy – both fueled by the rise of scientific racism (Stoler 1992; 1996).

Material inscriptions of colonial space served ritual and symbolic purposes. Sites such as the grass lawn, the rose bed, and the hill station itself lay at the intersection of a series of environmental, aesthetic, political, and technological projects intimately bound up with colonialism. The cricket field is an illuminating example. First played across the empire by British soldiers during the Napoleonic Wars, the popularity of cricket was immense, particularly amongst white settlers, and pitches were laid across the Victorian empire. Participation in cricket was a way in which white settlers could "play at home" by reinforcing their links with metropolitan society and demonstrating that they had not succumbed to cultural or bodily degeneration (Beckles 1995; Stoddart & Sandiford 1998). The cricket field itself assumed a ritual purpose, being an example of what Baucom, after Nora, terms a *"lieu de mémoire"* – a place "where an identity-preserving, identity-enchanting (sic), and identity-transforming aura lingers, or is made to appear" (Baucom 1999: 19). Such sites were seen as sustaining the Englishness of settlers and colonial agents, *and* as a potential method for anglicizing colonial subjects. Certainly participation in cricket, particularly as spectators, was encouraged amongst black West Indians to legitimize the local and imperial social hierarchies. The cricket field was to serve as a metaphor and metonym for self-control, submission to rules and the acceptance of rank (Baucom 1999: 135–63; Beckles 1998a).

More generally, the domestication of empire was often accompanied by attempts to control the colonized both through the segregationist strategies that attended the creation of hill stations and European suburbs in colonial cities (Kenny 1997; Dossal 1991), and in the encouragement of assimilation through the promotion of metropolitan lifestyles (Duncan 1989). Urging colonial subjects to adopt European models of household organization and domesticity was key to this. Hall (1993), for example, discusses the attempts made by white missionaries to fashion a new society in the postslavery Caribbean through the establishment of "free villages" carrying the names of the pantheon of British abolitionism ("Sturge Town," "Clarkson Town"). These supposedly highly-ordered spaces were to be sites at which formerly enslaved black people could be anglicized – made Christian, hardworking, conforming to the gender roles of the English middle class and loyal to the "mother country" (Bhabha 1994; Blouet 1981; see also Scully 1997: 63–80).

The impact that the various attempts to domesticate empire had on colonized people is, of course, a moot point. It is perhaps significant that the West Indian poet, Edward Kamau Brathwaite, chooses the idiom of an idealized but misplaced landscape of home to characterize and criticize the persistence of colonial mimicry in the postcolonial Caribbean – this is the "snow was falling in the cane fields" way-of-thinking that he sees as typical of the educated West Indian imagination (Brathwaite 1974). Nevertheless, domesticating projects often failed or had unexpected effects, perhaps by sowing discontent within those sections of the colonized population excluded from the spaces and discourses of imperial domesticity (Duncan 1989). Moreover, as Baucom notes, "the pedagogical field can be made into a performative space" (Baucom 1999: 39), and a *lieu de mémoire* could also be a "contact zone" of transculturation, creolization, and hybridization (Pratt 1992). For example, the "free villages" fostered the development of an Afro-Caribbean political culture, which broke from the humanitarian networks that had helped to incubate it, and the cricket pitch became a place "to beat the master at his own game" (Beckles 1998b). This suggests that colonial "landscapes of home" were the sites of a complex interplay of inculcation, display, performance, and subversion.

Troubles of settlement

The reproduction and location of "home" in an imperial context was not untroubled. There were difficulties in attempting to separate "home" and "away," of defining a boundary between metropole and empire (Fletcher 1999). Nor was the imaginative and material transformation of colonial space into "landscapes of home" unproblematic. Rather it was attended by a whole series of anxieties, some of which stemmed from the very attempt to reproduce landscapes of home. Some arose from fears about the vulnerability of settler populations on the frontiers of empire (Colley 2002), others were predicated on environmental theories of white degeneracy and the concern that home could in fact never be reproduced in the tropics.

The transformation of colonial space often involved the use of colonized labor and this was frequently a source of anxiety. The presence of free or unfree nonwhite people in the empire belied the notion that the colonies were a copy of a racially homogenous "home" (itself a fiction, of course – see Fryer 1984; Lorimer 1978). Although their role in providing labor power or knowledge was marginalized in myths of settlement and colonization (Stewart 1995; Spurr 1993), this could never be fully achieved. Unfree labor was often seen as necessary because of doubts about the suitability of white labor in tropical climates and yet, at the same time, the presence of enslaved and coerced nonwhite labor was a striking manifestation of how the colonies were *not* home: slavery "symbolized the otherness of the tropics" (Arnold 1996: 160; see also Seymour, Daniels, & Watkin 1998). This would become a major issue from the late eighteenth century when plantation slavery came to be seen as a "problem" requiring metropolitan and humanitarian intervention (Davis 1996). Indeed, the participation of white settlers in slavery became a marker of their "un-Englishness" (Greene 1987) and of the "aberrant" status of the tropical "slave world," in contrast with a temperate "free world" and its developing wage-labor norms (Davis 1975; cf. Pope Melish 1998). The presence of unfree labor also undermined the claims of those who relied on it to share an identity with their metropolitan counterparts (Sandiford 2000; Lambert 2002a). On a different scale, Blunt (1999) and Stoler (1995) have discussed the imperial anxieties about the presence of nonwhite servants *within* colonial households, particularly those raised by practices of breastfeeding and childcare of white children by nonwhites. Various strategies were used to regulate the domestic other. For example, Kennedy (1987) notes that in the British settler colonies of Kenya and Rhodesia, where African men made up the majority of domestic servants, their infantilization and desexualization as "boys" was an expression of concerns about the safety of the domestic landscape of home and was symptomatic of the elaborate regulatory forms of behavior expected of both black men *and* white women.

Anxieties about the presence of native and colonized populations within the "landscapes of home" – be it the colony, the colonial city or the colonial household – centered on fears of racial mixing and hybridity (Young 1995), either the miscegenation that might transform the colonizing population into the "other" or the sexual danger that might accompany anticolonial resistance. Discourses of the home became a means of representing imperial fears of resistance. For example, in her discussion of accounts of the Indian "Mutiny" of 1857, Blunt demonstrates how "the severity of conflict came to be embodied by the fate of British women and the defilement of their bodies and their homes" (Blunt 2000: 403). She also shows how the violation of white femininity in imperial accounts of colonized insurgency was expressed through the theme of domestic defilement, perhaps because of the difficulties associated with representing rape and sexual assault (Sharpe 1991). Similarly, in the British Caribbean in the 1830s, concerns about whether the islands would remain "home" for the white settler population after the formal ending of slavery centered on anxieties about the safety and tenability of white domesticity (Lambert 2002a).

If the menacing presence of the colonized "other" was one source of anxiety about colonial landscapes of home, then concerns about the hybridity and degeneracy of white settler populations were another. Such anxieties often manifested themselves in unexpected ways. For example, Duncan has shown how hill stations became a draw for metropolitan British tourists, especially in the early twentieth century, as they were promoted for the desirable aesthetic mix of English and Indian landscape elements. Yet this was a source of concern for the inhabitants of such sites. As Duncan shows (1998: 152), the notion that their anglicized "home" could become a source of fascination and pleasure because of its hybridity was a real worry:

The British who were residents in, rather than visitors to, this picturesque place feared that they were part of the cultural decay of the place. They could not unambivalently maintain that distanced aestheticized view of the tourist, for they were not on the outside looking in – they were part of the landscape itself.

The different perceptions of visitors and residents point to a contested geography of "home." Moreover, the concerns of the British residents of Kandy in highland Ceylon point to a broader uncertainty about the place of white settlers in, rather than visitors to, colonial spaces. While the tendency of European settler populations to view the metropolitan country as "home" has been noted, settlement – particularly long-term – did produce a greater ambivalence about where home was. There was often a political dimension to this too, as, for example, in the humanitarian assertions that settler groups were not treating colonized populations in a manner consistent with their claims to be European (Lester 2001; 2002; Lambert 2002b). It is in the light of such concerns that the enthusiastic adoption of metropolitan cultural forms in the colonies can be understood – such as the phenomenal popularity of cricket in the West Indies – as these were means of demonstrating adherence to metropolitan values and of seeking to ensure continuing metropolitan support for settler interests. Nevertheless, this very enthusiasm often reinforced metropolitan notions that their colonial compatriots were "mimic men" and not "English English" (Anderson 1991: 93), or what Stoler terms "parvenus, cultural incompetents, morally suspect, and indeed 'fictive' Europeans, somehow distinct from the real thing" (Stoler 1992: 102). The effort to adhere to metropolitan cultural norms in building styles, the naming of streets after famous metropolitan originals and so on – indeed, the very description of a West Indian island such as Barbados as "Little England" by white inhabitants – added to the impression among metropolitan visitors that this was not a landscape of home, but a pale imitation, a landscape of mimicry.

The imaginative domestication of colonial space was an appropriating, colonising project – it made these places "already white, already home" (Spurr 1993: 31). Nevertheless, the attempt to create landscapes of home in the empire was attendant with concerns stemming from ideas of environmentally-induced degeneracy and the supposedly deleterious effects of proximity to nonwhite people, as well as from humanitarian claims about the brutality of settler populations. Such "tensions of empire" (Cooper & Stoler 1998) between core and periphery were often expressed through claims and counterclaims about landscapes of home. The key question was whether making home in the empire alienated one from the metropolitan home and it is in the light of the ambivalent place of white settler cultures within European empires that landscapes of home and away should be approached. Moreover, the role of the colonized, unfree, and enslaved in subverting the domestication of colonial space and defamiliarising the "landscapes of home" – perhaps through the very *lieux de mémoires* that were seen as sites for the ritual reproduction of "home" – remain relatively unexplored.

Conclusion

The romance and naturalization of the notion of home as "a haven from a heartless world," be it one's abode or one's homeland, highlights a poignancy to the ambivalence inherent in the notion. The idea of home has much cultural, ideological, and psychological work to do: from Thomas Wolfe's maxim that "you can't go home again"; increasing homelessness in the most affluent countries; the lesbian for whom "homophobia" refers to the fear of going home; widespread domestic violence across the socio-economic spectrum; Edward Said, the Palestinian writing from the United States who never feels at home anywhere; Hannah Arendt, the exile who, despite living for years in New York, never unpacked her bags; transnational Latinos living and working in the United States but voting in local elections in their "home" villages in the highlands of Nicaragua; the white West Indian planters for whom the cricket pitch was a link to the "mother country"; to the British residents of Ceylon who feared that their home was a source of voyeuristic pleasure for tourists. As perhaps the most emotive of geographical concepts, inextricable from that of self, family, nation, sense of place, and sense of responsibility towards those who share one's place in the world, home is a concept that demands thorough exploration by cultural geographers.

REFERENCES

Anderson, B. 1991: *Imagined Communities: Reflections on the Origin and Spread of Nationalism*. London: Verso.

Anderson, K. and Smith, S. 2001: Emotional geographies: editorial. *Transactions. Institute of British Geographers* 26, 7–10.

Arnold, D. 1996: *The Problem of Nature: Environment, Culture and European Expansion.* Oxford: Blackwell.

Austin, J. L. 1975: *How to Do Things with Words.* Cambridge, MA: Harvard University Press.

Bachelard, G. 1969: *The Poetics of Space.* Boston: Beacon Press.

Baucom, I. 1999: *Out of Place: Englishness, Empire, and the Locations of Identity.* Princeton, NJ: Princeton University Press.

Baxter, J. and Western, M. 1998: Satisfaction with housework: examining the paradox. *Sociology* 32, 101–20.

Beckles, H. 1995: The origins and development of West Indies cricket culture in the nineteenth century: Jamaica and Barbados. In H. Beckles and B. Stoddart, eds., *Liberation Cricket: West Indies Cricket Culture.* Manchester: Manchester University Press, 33–43.

Beckles, H. 1998a: *The Development of West Indies Cricket: Volume 1 – The Age of Nationalism.* London: Pluto Press.

Beckles, H. 1998b: *The Development of West Indies Cricket: Volume 2 – The Age of Globalization.* London: Pluto Press.

Benjamin, D. N. 1995: Introduction. In D. N. Benjamin, D. Stea, and D. Saile, eds., *The Home: Words, Interpretations, Meanings and Environments.* London: Avebury, 1–14.

Benjamin, D. N., Stea, D., and Saile, D., eds. 1995: *The Home: Words, Interpretations, Meanings and Environments.* London: Avebury.

Bennett, T. 2002: Home and everyday life. In T. Bennett and D. Watson, eds., *Understanding Everyday Life.* Oxford: Blackwell, 1–50.

Berg, L. D. and Kearns, R. A. 1996: Naming as norming: "race", gender, and the identity politics of naming places in Aoteroa/New Zealand. *Environment and Planning D: Society and Space* 14, 99–122.

Bhabha, H. K. 1994: Of mimicry and man. In *The Location of Culture.* London: Routledge, 85–92.

Blouet, O. M. 1981: Education and emancipation in Barbados, 1833–1846: a study of cultural transference. *Ethnic and Racial Studies* 4, 222–35.

Blunt A. 1999: Imperial geographies of home: British domesticity in India, 1886–1925. *Transactions of the Institute of British Geographers* 24, 421–40.

Blunt, A. 2000: Embodying war: British women and domestic defilement in the Indian "mutiny", 1857–8. *Journal of Historical Geography* 26, 403–28.

Bondi L. 1998: Gender, class and urban space: public and private space in contemporary urban landscapes. *Urban Geography* 19, 160–85.

Bordo, S., Klein, B., and Silverman, M. 1998: Missing kitchens. In H. Nast and S. Pile, eds., *Places Through the Body.* London: Routledge, 72–92.

Bourdieu, P. 1973: The Berber house. In M. Douglas, ed., *Rules and Meanings.* Harmondsworth: Penguin, 98–110.

Bourdieu, P. 1984: *Distinction: A Social Critique of the Judgement of Taste*, tr. R. Nice. Cambridge, MA: Harvard University Press.

Bowlby, S., Gregory, S., and McKie, L. 1997: Doing home: patriarchy, caring and space. *Women's Studies International Forum* 20, 343–50.

Brathwaite, E. K. 1974: *Contradictory Omens: Cultural Diversity and Integration in the Caribbean.* Mona: Savacou.

Burton, A. 1994: Rules of thumb: British history and "imperial culture" in nineteenth- and twentieth-century Britain. *Women's History Review* 3, 483–500.

Butler, J. 1990: *Gender Trouble: Feminism and the Subversion of Identity.* London: Routledge.

Chapin, F. S. 1935: *Contemporary American Institutions.* New York: Harper and Row.

Chapman, T. 1999: Spoiled home identities: the experience of burglary. In T. Chapman and J. Hockey, eds., *Ideal Homes? Social Change and Domestic Life*. London: Routledge, 133–46.

Chapman, T. and Hockey, J., eds. 1999: *Ideal Homes? Social Change and Domestic Life*. London: Routledge.

Christie, H. 1999: Housework. In L. McDowell and J. P. Sharp, eds., *A Feminist Glossary of Human Geography*. London: Arnold, 128.

Cieraad, I., ed. 1999: *At Home: An Anthropology of Domestic Space*. Syracuse: Syracuse University Press.

Clarke, A. J. 2001: The aesthetics of social aspiration. In D. Miller, ed., *Home Possessions: Material Culture Behind Closed Doors*. Oxford: Berg, 23–46.

Colley, L. 2002: *Captives: Britain, Empire and the World, 1600–1850*. London: Jonathan Cape.

Collignon, B. 2001: Esprit des lieux et modèles culturels. La mutation des espaces domestiques en arctique inuit. *Annales de Géographie* 620, 383–404.

Cooper, F. and Stoler, A. L., eds. 1998: *Tensions of Empire: Colonial Cultures in a Bourgeois World*. Berkeley: University of California.

Csikszentmihalyi, M. and Rochberg-Halton, E. 1981: *The Meaning of Things: Domestic Symbols and the Self*. Cambridge: Cambridge University Press.

Davidoff, L. and Hall, C. 1987: *Family Fortunes: Men and Women of the English Middle Classes, 1780–1850*. London: Routledge.

Davis, D. B. 1966: *The Problem of Slavery in Western Culture*. Ithaca: Cornell University Press.

Davis, D. B. 1975: *The Problem of Slavery in the Age of Revolution, 1770–1823*. London: Cornell University Press.

Davis, J. 1955: *Living Rooms as Symbols of Social Status: A Study in Social Judgement*. Unpublished Ph.D. dissertation, Harvard University.

Davis, M. 2000: *Magical Urbanism: Latinos Reinvent the US City*. London: Verso.

Dobash, R. E. and Dobash, R. R. 1992: *Women, Violence and Social Change*. London: Routledge.

Dodds, K. 1998: Enframing the Falklands: identity, landscape, and the 1982 South Atlantic War. *Environment and Planning D: Society and Space* 16, 733–56.

Dolan, J. A. 1999: "I've always fancied owning me own lion": Ideological motivations in external house decoration by recent homeowners. In I. Cieraad, ed., *At Home: An Anthropology of Domestic Space*. Syracuse: Syracuse University Press, 60–72.

Dossal, M. 1991: *Imperial Designs and Indian Realities: The Planning of Bombay City, 1845–1875*. Oxford: Oxford University Press.

Drayton, R. 2000: *Nature's Government: Science, Imperial Britain, and the "Improvement" of the World*. London: Yale University Press.

Driver, F. and Gilbert, D. 1998: Heart of empire? Landscape, space and performance in imperial London. *Environment and Planning D: Society and Space* 16, 11–28.

Duany, A. and Plater-Zyberk, E. 1992: The second coming of the American small town. *Wilson Quarterly* (winter).

Duncan, J. S. 1973: Landscape taste as a symbol of group identity: a Westchester County village. *Geographical Review* 63, 334–55.

Duncan, J. S., ed. 1981a: *Housing and Identity: Cross-Cultural Perspectives*. London: Croom Helm.

Duncan, J. S. 1981b: From container of women to status symbol: The impact of social structure on the meaning of the house. In J. S. Duncan, ed., *Housing and Identity: Cross-Cultural Perspectives*. London: Croom Helm, 36–59.

Duncan, J. S. 1989a: Getting respect in the Kandyan Highlands: the house, the community and the self in a Third World society. In S. M. Low and E. Chambers, eds., *Housing, Culture and Design*. Philadelphia: Pennsylvania University Press, 229–52.

Duncan, J. S. 1989b: The power of place in Kandy, Sri Lanka. In J. Agnew and J. S. Duncan, eds., *The Power of Place: Bringing Together Geographical and Sociological Imaginations*. London: Unwin Hyman, 185–201.

Duncan, J. S. 1998: Dis-orientation: On the shock of the familiar in a far-away place. In J. S. Duncan and D. Gregory, eds., *Writes of Passage*. London: Routledge, 151–63.

Duncan, J. S. 2000: The struggle to be temperate: climate and "moral masculinity" in mid-nineteenth century Ceylon. *Singapore Journal of Tropical Geography* 21, 34–47.

Duncan, J. S. and Duncan, N. G. 1976a: Housing as presentation of self and the structure of social networks. In G. T. Moore and R. G. Golledge, eds., *Environmental Knowing*. East Stroudsburg, PA: Dowden, Hutchinson and Ross, 247–53.

Duncan, J. S. and Duncan, N. G. 1976b: Social worlds, status passages and environmental perspectives. In G. T. Moore and R. G. Golledge, eds., *Environmental Knowing*. East Stroudsburg, PA: Dowden, Hutchinson and Ross, 206–13.

Duncan, J. S. and Duncan, N. G. 2003: *Landscapes of Privilege: The Politics of the Aesthetic in Suburban America*. New York: Routledge.

Duncan, N. G. 1996: Negotiating gender and sexuality in public and private spaces. In N. G. Duncan, ed., *Bodyspace: Destabilizing Geographies of Gender and Sexuality*. London: Routledge.

Duncan, N. G. and Duncan, J. S. 1997: Deep suburban irony: the perils of democracy in Westchester County, New York. In R. Silverstone, ed., *Visions of Suburbia*. London: Routledge, 161–79.

Elwood, S. 2000: Lesbian living spaces: multiple meanings of home. *Journal of Lesbian Studies* 4, 11–28.

Firey, Walter 1945: Sentiment and symbolism as ecological variables. *American Sociological Review* 20 (April), 140–8.

Fletcher, Y. S. 1999: "Capital of the colonies": Real and imagined boundaries between metropole and empire in 1920s Marseilles. In F. Driver and D. Gilbert, eds., *Imperial Cities: Landscape, Display and Identity*. Manchester: Manchester University Press, 136–54.

Fried, M. 1963: Grieving for a lost home. In L. J. Duhl, ed., *The Urban Condition*. New York: Simon and Schuster, 151–71.

Friedan, B. 1965: *The Feminine Mystique*. London: Pelican.

Fryer, P. 1984: *Staying Power: The History of Black People in Britain*. London, Pluto Press.

Garvey, P. 2001: Organized disorder: moving furniture in Norwegian homes. In D. Miller, ed., *Home Possessions: Material Culture Behind Closed Doors*. Oxford: Berg, 47–68.

Gascoigne, J. 1994: *Joseph Banks and the English Enlightenment: Useful Knowledge and Polite Culture*. Cambridge: Cambridge University Press.

Gathorne-Hardy, F. 1999: Home. In L. McDowell and J. P. Sharp, eds., *A Feminist Glossary of Human Geography*. London: Arnold, 124–5.

Gelezeau, V. 2001: La modernization de l'habitat en Corée du Sud. Usage et image des appartements de style occidental. *Annales de Géographie* 620, 405–24.

Gilmore, J. 2000: *The Poetics of Empire: A Study of James Grainger's The Sugar Cane (1764)*. London, Athlone Press.

Goldsack, L. 1999: A haven in a heartless world? Women and domestic violence. In T. Chapman and J. Hockey, eds., *Ideal Homes? Social Change and Domestic Life*. London: Routledge, 121–32.

Gowans, G. 1999: *A Passage from India: British Women Traveling Home, 1915–1947*. Unpublished Ph.D. dissertation, University of Southampton.

Greenblatt, S. 1991: *Marvellous Possessions: The Wonder of the New World*. Chicago: University of Chicago.

Greene, J. P. 1987: Changing identity in the British Caribbean: Barbados as a case study. In N. Canny and A. Pagden, eds., *Colonial Identity in the Atlantic World, 1500–1800.* Princeton, NJ: Princeton University Press, 213–66.

Gregson, N. and Lowe, M. 1995: "Home" making: on the spatiality of daily social reproduction in contemporary middle class Britain. *Transactions of the Institute of British Geographers* 20, 224–35.

Grewal, I. 1996: *Home and Harem: Nation, Gender, Empire and Cultures of Travel.* London: Leicester University Press.

Grove, R. H. 1995: *Green Imperialism: Colonial Expansion, Tropical Island Edens and the Origins of Environmentalism, 1600–1860.* Cambridge: Cambridge University Press.

Gullestad, M. 1992: *The Art of Social Relations: Essays on Culture, Social Action and Everyday Life in Modern Norway.* Oslo: Scandinavian University Press.

Hall, C. 1992. *White, Male and Middle Class: Explorations in Feminism and History.* Oxford: Polity.

Hall, C. 1993: White visions, black lives: the free villages of Jamaica. *History Workshop Journal* 36, 100–32.

Hall, C. 2002: *Civilising Subjects: Metropole and Colony in the English Imagination, 1830–1867.* Oxford: Polity.

Hareven, T. 1982: *Family Time and Industrial Time: The Relationship Between the Family and Work in a New England Industrial Community.* New York: Cambridge University Press.

Hareven, T. 1993: The home and the family in historical perspective. In A. Mack, ed., *Home: A Place in the World.* New York: New York University Press, 253–85.

Harvey, D. 1989: *The Condition of Postmodernity: An Enquiry into the Origins of Cultural Change.* Oxford: Blackwell.

Hayden, D. 1981: *The Grand Domestic Revolution: A History of Feminist Designs for American Homes, Neighborhoods and Cities.* Cambridge, MA: MIT Press.

Hayden, D. 1984: *Redesigning the American Dream: The Future of Housing, Work and Family Life.* New York: W. W. Norton.

Higley, S. R. 1995: *Privilege, Power and Place: The Geography of the American Upper Class.* Lanham, MD: Rowman and Littlefield.

hooks, b. 1990: Homeplace: a site of resistance. In *Yearning: Race, Gender and Cultural Politics.* Boston: South End Press, 41–50.

Hugill, P. J. 1989: Home and class among an American landed elite. In J. A. Agnew and J. S. Duncan, eds., *The Power of Place: Bringing Together Geographical and Sociological Imaginations.* Boston: Unwin-Hyman, 66–80.

Hugman, R. 1999: Embodying old age. In E. K. Teather, ed., *Embodied Geographies: Spaces, Bodies and Rites of Passage.* London: Routledge.

Hulme, P. 1986: *Colonial Encounters: Europe and the Native Caribbean, 1492–1797.* London: Methuen.

Hummon, D. M. 1989: House, home and identity in contemporary American culture. In S. M. Low and E. Chambers, eds., *Housing, Culture and Design.* Philadelphia: Pennsylvania University Press, 207–28.

Ingold, T. 1995: Building, dwelling, living: How animals and people make themselves at home in the world. In M. Strathern,, ed., *Shifting Contexts: Transformations of Anthropological Knowledge.* London: Routledge, 57–79.

Johnson, L. and Valentine, G. 1995: Wherever I lay my girlfriend that's my home: the performance and surveillance of lesbian identities in domestic environments. In D. Bell and G. Valentine, eds., *Mapping Desire: Geographies of Sexuality.* London: Routledge.

Junker, B. 1954: *Room Compositions and Lifestyles: A Sociological Study in Living Rooms and Other Rooms in Contemporary Dwellings.* Unpublished Ph.D. dissertation, University of Chicago.

Kennedy, D. 1987: *Islands of White: Settler Society and Culture in Kenya and Southern Rhodesia, 1890–1939*. Durham, NC: Duke University Press.

Kennedy, D. 1990: The perils of the midday sun: Climatic anxieties in the colonial tropics. In J. M. MacKenzie, eds., *Imperialism and the Natural World*. Manchester: Manchester University Press, 118–40.

Kenny, J. T. 1995: Climate, race, and imperial authority: the symbolic landscape of the British hill station in India. *Annals of the Association of American Geographers* 85, 694–714.

Kenny, J. T. 1997: Claiming the high ground: theories of imperial authority and the British hill stations in India. *Political Geography* 16, 665–73.

Klahr, R. 1999a: Homelessness. In L. McDowell and J. P. Sharp, eds., *A Feminist Glossary of Human Geography*. London: Arnold, 126.

Klahr, R. 1999b: Homework. In L. McDowell and J. P. Sharp, eds., *A Feminist Glossary of Human Geography*. London: Arnold, 126.

Klodawsky, F. and Mackenzie, S. 1987: Gender sensitive theory and the housing needs of mother-led families: some concepts and some buildings. *Feminist Perspectives/Feministes* 9, Canadian Research Institute for the Advancement of Women, Ottawa, 1–39.

Lambert, D. 2002a: *The Master Subject: White Identities and the Slavery Controversy in Barbados, 1780–1834*. Unpublished Ph.D. dissertation, University of Cambridge.

Lambert, D. 2002b: "True lovers of religion": Methodist persecution and white resistance to antislavery in Barbados, 1823–1825. *Journal of Historical Geography* 28, 216–36.

Laumann, E. O. and House, J. S. 1970: Living room styles and social attributes: the patterning of material artifacts in a modern urban community. *Sociology and Social Research* 54, 321–42.

Lawrence, R. J. 1995: Deciphering home: An integrative historical perspecive. In D. N. Benjamin, D. Stea, and D. Saile, eds., *The Home: Words, Interpretations, Meanings and Environments*. London: Avebury, 53–68.

Lester, A. 2001: *Imperial Networks: Creating Identities in Nineteenth Century South Africa and Britain*. London: Routledge.

Lester, A. 2002: Obtaining the "due observance of justice": the geographies of colonial humanitarianism. *Environment and Planning D: Society and Space* 20, 277–93.

Lévi-Strauss, C. 1967: *Structural Anthropology*. New York: Doubleday.

Lévi-Strauss, C. 1972: *Tristes Tropiques*. New York: Atheneum.

Lewis, C. 2000. *A Man's Place in the Home: Fathers and Families in the UK*. Findings Number 440. York: Joseph Rowntree Foundation.

Livingstone, D. N. 1991: The moral discourse of climate: historical considerations on race, place and virtue. *Journal of Historical Geography* 17, 413–34.

Lorimer, D. A. 1978: *Colour, Class and the Victorians*. Leicester: Leicester University Press.

Low, S. 2000: *On the Plaza: The Politics of Public Space and Culture*. Austin: University of Texas Press.

Lynd, R. and Lynd H. 1929: *Middletown*. New York: Harcourt, Brace and World.

Massey, D. 1992: A place called home? *New Formations* 17, 3–15.

Massey, D. 1994: A place called home. In *Space, Place and Gender*. Oxford: Blackwell, 157–74.

McDowell, L. 1999: *Gender, Identity and Place: Understanding Feminist Geographies*. Cambridge: Polity.

McKee, L. and Bell, C. 1985: Marital and family relations in times of male unemployment. In R. Roberts, R. Finnegan, and D. Gallie, eds., *New Approaches to Economic Life*. Manchester: Manchester University Press, 387–99.

McKenzie, E. 1994: *Privatopia: Homeowner Associations and the Rise of Residential Private Government*. New Haven: Yale University Press.

McKibben, R. 1998: *Classes and Cultures: England 1918–1951*. Oxford: Oxford University Press.

McNamee, S. 1998: Youth, gender and video games: power and control in the home. In T. Skelton and G. Valentine, eds., *Cool Places: Geographies of Youth Culture*. London: Routledge, 195–206.

Meulders D., Plasman, O., and Plasman, R. 1994: *Atypical Employment in the EC*. Hampshire, UK: Dartmouth Publishing.

Mezei, K., ed. 2002: Forum: Domestic Space. *Signs: Journal of Women in Culture and Society* 27, 813–900.

Miller, D. 2001: *Home Possessions: Material Culture Behind Closed Doors*. Oxford: Berg.

Mitchell, D. 2000: *Cultural Geography*. Oxford: Blackwell.

Monk, J. 1999: Gender in the landscape: expressions of power and meaning. In K. Anderson and F. Gale, eds., *Cultural Geographies*. Sidney: Longman, 153–72.

Morley, D. 2000: The migrant's suitcase. In *Home Territories: Media, Mobility and Identity*. London: Routledge.

Morris, L. 1993: Domestic labour and the employment status of married couples. *Capital and Class* 49, 37–52.

Mowl, G., Pain, R., and Talbot, C. 2000: The aging body and the homespace. *Area* 32, 189–97.

Nast, H. and Pile, S. 1998: *Places Through the Body*. New York and London: Routledge.

Oberhauser, A. 1995: Gender and household economic strategies in rural Appalachia. *Gender, Place and Culture* 2, 51–70.

Pagden, A. 1993: *European Encounters with the New World: From Renaissance to Romanticism*. London: Yale University Press.

Pallasmaa, J. 1995: Identity, intimacy, and domicile: a phenomenology of home. In D. N. Benjamin, D. Stea, and D. Saile, eds., *The Home: Words, Interpretations, Meanings and Environments*. London: Avebury, 33–40.

Pennartz, P. J. J. 1999: Home: The experience of atmosphere. In I. Cieraad, ed., *At Home: An Anthropology of Domestic Space*. Syracuse: Syracuse University Press, 95–106.

Phizacklea, A. and Wolkowitz, C. 1995: *Homeworking Women: Gender, Racism and Class at Work*. London: Sage.

Pope Melish, J. 1998: *Disowning Slavery: Gradual Emancipation and "Race" in New England, 1780–1860*. London: Cornell University Press.

Porteous, J. D. 1989: *Planned to Death*. Manchester: University of Manchester Press.

Porteous, J. D. 1995: Domicide: the destruction of home. In D. N. Benjamin, D. Stea, and D. Saile, eds., *The Home: Words, Interpretations, Meanings and Environments*. London: Avebury, 151–61.

Pratt, G. 1981: The house as expression of social worlds. In J. Duncan, ed., *Housing and Identity: Cross-Cultural Perspectives*. London: Croom Helm, 135–80.

Pratt, G. 1998: Inscribing domestic work on Filipina bodies. In H. Nast and S. Pile, eds., *Places Through the Body*. London: Routledge, 283–304.

Pratt, M. 1992: *Imperial Eyes: Travel Writing and Transculturation*. London: Routledge.

Preston, R. 1999: "The scenery of the torrid zone": imagined travels and the culture of exotics in nineteenth-century British gardens. In F. Driver and D. Gilbert, eds., *Imperial Cities: Landscape, Display and Identity*. Manchester: Manchester University Press, 194–211.

Preziosi, D. 1979: *The Semiotics of the Built Environment*. Bloomington: Indiana University Press.

Puckrein, G. A. 1984: *Little England: Plantation Society and Anglo-Barbadian Politics, 1627–1700*. New York: New York University Press.

Rabasa, J. 1993: *Inventing America: Spanish Historiography and the Foundation of Eurocentrism*. London: University of Oklahoma Press.

Rapoport, A. 1995: A critical look at the concept "home". In D. N. Benjamin, D. Stea, and D. Saile, eds., *The Home: Words, Interpretations, Meanings and Environments*. London: Avebury, 25–52 .

Rose, G. 1995: Place and identity: a sense of place. In D. Massey and P. Jess, eds., *A Place in the World? Place, Cultures and Globalization*. Oxford: Open University Press, 88–106.

Rushdie, S. 1991: *Imaginary Homelands: Essays and Criticism 1981–1991*. London: Granta Books.

Ryan, D. S. 1999: Staging the imperial city: the pageant of London, 1911. In F. Driver and D. Gilbert, eds., *Imperial Cities: Landscape, Display and Identity*. Manchester: Manchester University Press, 117–35.

Saarikangas, K. 2002: *Asunnon Muodonmuutoksia*. Helsinki: Suomalaisen Kirjallisuuden Seura.

Said, E. W. 1979: *Orientalism*. London: Routledge and Kegan Paul.

Samuel, R. 1995: *Theatres of Memory*, vol. 1. London: Verso.

Sandiford, K. A. 2000: *The Cultural Politics of Sugar: Caribbean Slavery and Narratives of Colonialism*. Cambridge: Cambridge University Press.

Saugeres, L. 2000: Of tidy gardens and clean houses: housing officers as agents of social control. *Geoforum* 31, 587–99.

Schwarz, B., ed. 1996: *The Expansion of England: Race, Ethnicity and Cultural History*. London: Routledge.

Scully, P. 1997: *Liberating the Family? Gender and British Slave Emancipation in the Rural Western Cape, South Africa, 1823–1853*. Oxford: James Currey.

Seamon, D. and Mugerauer, R. eds. 1989: *Dwelling, Place and Environment*. New York: Columbia University Press.

Seed, P. 1999: The key to the house. In H. Naficy, ed., *Home, Homeland and Exile*. London: Routledge.

Seymour, S., Daniels, S., and Watkin, C. 1998: Estate and empire: Sir George Cornewall's management of Moccas, Herefordshire and La Taste, Grenada, 1771–1819. *Journal of Historical Geography* 24, 313–51.

Sharpe, J. 1991: The unspeakable limits of rape: colonial violence and counter-insurgency. *Genders* 10, 25–46.

Sibley, D. 1995: Families and domestic routines: constructing the boundaries of childhood. In S. Pile and N. Thrift, eds., *Mapping the Subject: Geographies of Cultural Transformation*. London: Routledge, 123–37.

Silverstone, R., ed. 1997: *Visions of Suburbia*. London: Routledge.

Sinha, M. 1995: *Colonial Masculinity: The "Manly Englishman" and the "Effeminate Bengali" in the Late Nineteenth Century*. Manchester: Manchester University Press.

Somerville, P. 1992: Homelessness and the meaning of home: rooflessness or rootlessness? *International Journal of Urban and Regional Research* 16, 528–39.

Sopher, D. E. 1979: The landscape of home: myth, experience, social meaning. In D. W. Meinig, ed., *The Interpretation of Ordinary Landscapes*. New York: Oxford University Press, 129–52.

Spurr, D. 1993: *The Rhetoric of Empire: Colonial Discourse in Journalism, Travel Writing, and Imperial Administration*. Durham, NC: Duke University Press.

Staszak, J.-F., ed. 2001a: Espaces domestiques. *Annales de Géographie* 620.

Staszak, J.-F., 2001b: L'espace domestique: pour une géographie de l'intérieur. *Annales de Géographie* 620, 339–63.

Stewart, L. 1995: Louisiana subjects: Power, space and the slave body. *Ecumene* 2, 227–45.

Stoddart, B. and Sandiford K., eds. 1998: *The Imperial Game: Cricket, Culture and Society*. Manchester: Manchester University Press.

Stoler, A. L. 1992: Rethinking colonial categories: European communities and the boundaries of rule. In N. B. Dirks, ed., *Colonialism and Culture*. Ann Arbor: University of Michigan Press, 319–52.

Stoler, A. L. 1995: *Race and the Education of Desire: Foucault's "History of Sexuality" and the Colonial Order of Things*. London: Duke University Press.

Stoler, A. L. 1996: Carnal knowledge and imperial power: gender, race, and morality in colonial Asia. In J. W. Scott, ed., *Feminism and History*. Oxford: Oxford University Press, 209–66.

Stoler, A. L. and Cooper, F. 1997: Between metropole and colony: rethinking a research agenda. In F. Cooper and A. L. Stoler, eds., *Tensions of Empire: Colonial Cultures in a Bourgeois World*. Berkeley: University of California Press, 1–56.

Summerfield, C. 1998: *Social Focus on Men and Women*. London: HMSO.

Suro, R. 1998: *Strangers Among Us: How Latino Immigration is Transforming America*. New York: Alfred A. Knopf.

Tambiah, S. 1969: Animals are good to think and good to prohibit. *Ethnology* 8, 424–59.

Thomas, N. 2002: *Negotiating the Boundaries of Gender and Empire: Lady Curzon, Vicereine of India 1898–1905*. Unpublished Ph.D. dissertation, University of Oxford.

Tosh, J. 1999: *A Man's Place: Masculinity and the Middle Class Home in Victorian England*. London: Yale University Press.

Tuan, Y.-F. 1974: *Topophilia: A Study of Environmental Perception, Attitudes and Values*. Englewood Cliffs, NJ: Prentice Hall.

Valentine, G. 1993: (Hetero)sexing space: lesbian perceptions and experiences of everyday spaces. *Environment and Planning D: Society and Space* 11, 395–413.

Valentine, G. 2001: *Social Geographies: Space and Society*. Harlow: Pearson Educational.

Warner, W. L. 1953: *American Life: Dream and Reality*. Chicago: University of Chicago Press.

Warner, W. L. 1963: *Yankee City*. New Haven: Yale University Press.

Watson, K. 1979: *The Civilised Island, Barbados: A Social History, 1750–1816*. Barbados: Caribbean Graphic.

Wikstrom, T. 1995: The home and housing modernization. In D. N. Benjamin, D. Stea, and D. Saile, eds., *The Home: Words, Interpretations, Meanings and Environments*. London: Avebury, 267–82.

Young, R. 1995: *Colonial Desire: Hybridity in Theory, Culture and Race*. London: Routledge.

Chapter 26

Landscapes of Childhood and Youth

Elizabeth A. Gagen

Introduction

In March 2001 a poster campaign advertising Martin Amis's new autobiography *Experience* was banned by the London Underground. The poster displayed a photograph of Amis as a young boy scowling defiantly back at the camera, unlit cigarette balancing between his lips (see figure 26.1). The reason for withdrawing the campaign was said to be because it featured an illegal act – underage smoking – that might encourage other children to follow suit (*Guardian*, March 22, 2001: 1). The significance of this event, however, extends beyond these given reasons. Banning the advert was not an isolated incidence of moral or even legal judgment; rather, it has to be understood within what Gill Valentine (1996a: 581) calls the "moral landscape of childhood" – the evolving discourse through which the limits of childhood are established and negotiated. The photograph of young Amis was considered unacceptable because he was exhibited indulging in an adult act which challenges received notions of children as innocent, uncorrupted by adult vices, and marked by a lack of authority and agency. I suggest, therefore, that in addition to disapproving of the illegality of the action portrayed, the London Underground withdrew the advert because it breached the acceptable limits of childhood.

The nature of these limits – the discourses through which we know children – has become increasingly relevant in cultural geography; not simply because children as a social group have become a distinct focus of study but because there is an historical and cultural geography to discourses of childhood. The particular understanding of childhood innocence that mediated the debate between Amis's publisher and the London Underground is not constant; rather, in different contexts, the expectations, demands, and treatment of childhood are observably distinct. The initial assertion that childhood does not exist as a universal, timeless category was proposed by the historian Philippe Ariès (1962). In *Centuries of Childhood*, Ariès traces family life in Europe from the Middle Ages, arguing that childhood, as a conceptual category, emerged gradually from the sixteenth century. Prior to that, children, as we recognize them today, were simply considered to be miniature adults. At the age of 6 or 7 children were expected to assume adult responsibilities, but as

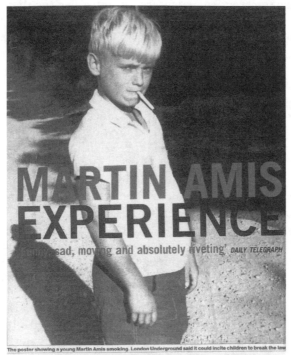

Figure 26.1 *Experience* by Martin Amis (reproduced by permission of The Random House Group Ltd and *The Guardian*)

young infants they were largely ignored. Aitken (2001a: 120) notes that this did not necessarily imply a lack of adult–child relations, but that "indifference rather than difference marked those relations." It was not until the Enlightenment philosophy of the eighteenth century, in particular the writings of Rousseau, that a modern conception of childhood becomes legible. Between the eighteenth and the nineteenth centuries, childhood developed as a culturally resonant, generationally defined concept. Children were gradually removed from adult spaces and provided with environments catering specifically for 'children's' needs. As many have observed, Ariès's substantive contribution to child studies is his conclusion that childhood cannot be thought of as an absolute age-based phenomenon; it exists contextually and indeed, at points in time, has not existed at all (Jenks 1996; James, Jenks, & Prout 1998; Aitken 2001a; 2001b; and Valentine 1996a; Valentine et al. 2000).

This observation has fueled a wealth of research on the progressive discourses through which childhood has been imagined, and forms a central component of new geographies of childhood, children, and youth.[1] Children have been a long-standing area of concern in geography since the 1970s and early 1980s. Early work by Jim Blaut and David Stea (Blaut & Stea 1971 and 1974) established a research agenda in children's geographical learning, including their capacity to learn mapping

skills and to cognate macrospatial concepts at an earlier age than was conventionally assumed by Piagetian models of development. From this work, a distinct
program of research on child development and spatial cognition established space
and place as fundamental aspects of children's knowledge acquisition (for example,
Matthews 1984; Downs 1985; Downs & Liben 1991; and Golledge et al. 1985).
While this work is no longer the dominant approach in children's geographies, and
has been criticized for applying instrumental ways of knowing to a phantom universal child (Aitken 2001b), it continues to produce new research and lively debate
(see for example Blaut 1997a; 1997b; and Liben & Downs 1997a, 1997b). A parallel strand of research also originating in the 1970s provides a more direct lineage
to current work. William Bunge's 'expeditions' in Detroit and Toronto began a more
ethnographic approach to the study of children (Bunge 1973; Bunge & Bordessa
1975). Their child-centered and politicized agenda can be linked to ensuing humanistic, ethnographic work such as Roger Hart's (1979) study of children's experience
of space and place in a small New England town (Aitken 2001b).

This latter strand of research – sociological and ethnographic in nature – has
been revived in the late 1990s to produce a flourishing area of research on children's
geographies. Influenced by similar developments in sociology, social anthropology,
and cultural studies (James, Jenks, & Prout 1998; Mayall 1994; Caputo 1995;
Qvortrup et al. 1994), geographers have engaged in a critical reorientation of child
studies. The determining feature of this work has been to urge researchers to "study
children as social actors, as beings in their own right rather than as pre-adult becom-
ings" (Holloway & Valentine 2000a: 5). This involves reimagining children as com-
petent decision-makers, self-aware individuals, and creative participants in social
life. The diverse and increasingly numerous contributions to this new field accept
this reformulation to varying degrees (see McKendrick 2000 for an inventory of
work to date). In this chapter, however, I focus primarily on that work which comes
from a cultural geographic perspective.[2] This is due in part to the nature of this
volume, but more importantly, because recent contributions to children's geographies are broadly sympathetic to cultural geographic themes. Before moving to the
main themes that organize this chapter, I briefly map out these theoretical affinities.

In the early 1990s a debate in *Area* highlighted the need for geography to engage
more directly with the geography of children (James 1990; Sibley 1991; Winchester
1991). With the exception of Sibley, however, the call demanded that children be
studied because they have unique characteristics, a distinctive geography, and are
demographically significant (James 1990). The following year, however, Philo (1992)
submitted a more specific proposal that the complex geographies of children, as
demonstrated by Colin Ward's work (1978; 1990), should galvanize specific attention from cultural geography. Philo identifies at least three themes in Ward's work
that resonate with cultural geography. First, children's social exclusion accords with
cultural geography's interest in "recovering the geographies of 'other' human groupings" (Philo 1992: 193). Second, Ward's observation that childhood is a social construction corresponds with cultural geography's focus on the instability of social
categories and its heightened attention to the representational qualities of social
life. And third, Ward's observance of both geographies of children and children's
geographies echoes the tension between structure and agency that pervades much
cultural geographic work.[3]

Over the last few years an increasing volume of work has theorized childhood and children's lives in ways that are compatible with the conceptual tools of cultural geography. The balance of this chapter presents a selection of current work on children's geographies that is loosely organized around the following themes: *Spaces of childhood* examines the changing nature of childhood and the various institutions and spaces through which childhood is negotiated; *Children's spaces* explores geographers' desire to understand the creative processes through which children live, including their appropriation and negotiation of adult spaces; *Methodological and ethical spaces* explores the dilemmas generated by researching children; and I conclude with a section on *Growing up?* in which I draw some brief conclusions about the future direction of children's geographies.

Spaces of Childhood

Despite the emphasis on children's viability as creative social actors, there remains considerable interest in the discourses and institutions through which childhood is reproduced. While this work retains a sense of children's competency, it prioritizes the discursive processes and institutional containment that constitutes children's lives. Referring to the current insistence on documenting children's autonomy, Mary Thomas (2000: 577) argues that we must also "acknowledge that childhood *is* a time of socialization, a phase of life when young individuals' times and spaces are structured, and institutionalized, by adults" (emphasis in original). The body of work I discuss in this section suggests that childhood is an ideological construct and that the norms and boundaries within which childhood *ought* to operate require careful attention. These are not simply abstract ideas, however. Discourses of childhood are invariably located in particular spaces: the home, school, playground, street, countryside, city, nation (Holloway & Valentine 2000a). Furthermore, these spaces are not discrete and bounded entities but operate in and through one another. Here matters of scale inflect the operation of discourses, in that the spatiality of nationhood is mediated through smaller scale institutional environments such as the school and the playground. Likewise, many authors illustrate how gender, sexuality, race and class operate within and through these spaces to constitute them in different ways. Through this relationship between discourse and space – what Holloway and Valentine (2000a: 15) call 'spatial discourses' – a geography of childhood emerges that attempts to fix a proper place for children. I end this section by examining the anxieties produced by children who exceed these limits.

Feminist geographers and historians have observed that during the nineteenth century there was a discursive reallocation of women and family to the private sphere and men and work to the public (Davidoff & Hall 1987; Nicholson 1986; Bondi & Domosh 1998). Of significance here is the fact that, along with women, the home emerged as *the* proper place for children. As James, Jenks, and Prout (1998: 53) write, during this period, home was constituted as a "space of childhood through its binding of the concepts of 'family' and 'home' into 'the modern domestic ideal.'" The importance of this condition is apparent throughout the twentieth century and into the twenty-first. In the morally charged discourse of parenting there remains pressure on working mothers to find child care facilities that "reproduce home-style environments for their children" (Holloway & Valentine 2000a: 16).

Similarly, the construction of the home as a site where women take care of children also impacts on the institution of fatherhood. Aitken (2000) finds this so pervasive that despite men's increased parenting responsibilities in the home, their role is still seen as 'helping out' rather than as the principal caregiver.

Since the early twentieth century, the allocation of children to the home has produced a tension between public youth culture and the private virtue of the family. Lisa Jacobson (1997) notes that the emergence of an autonomous youth culture in the United States in the early twentieth century alarmed the middle classes by threatening to reduce the moral influence of the family. An increasingly commercialized leisure industry available in the city, and in particular on the street, was seen as a morally inferior option to the safe play spaces of the home. In response, between 1920 and 1940, play rooms and nurseries were refashioned to combat the increasingly tempting commercial options. Moments like this provide precedence for late twentieth-century debates about the relative suitability of public versus private leisure: if home space is the 'proper' place for children, then public space – the street – is clearly 'improper.'

Gill Valentine (1996a, 1996b, 1997) has documented a particular rendition of this discourse that emerged in the 1980s and 1990s. During this period, North America and Western Europe witnessed rising panic over children's vulnerability in public space. The anxiety was connected to fear of sexual assault, abduction, and murder, so-called 'stranger danger,' and has been heightened yet further by the media frenzy surrounding the abduction and murder of 8-year-old Sarah Payne. This phenomenon is clearly not new, but feeds off and into well established discourses. Not only does it add a new dimension to the idea of home as sanctuary and street as dangerous, but, Valentine (1996a) observes, there is a simultaneous reinvigoration of the classic opposition between the innocence and wickedness of childhood. Jenks (1996) describes these identities as Dionysian and Apollonian, the former originating in the pre-Enlightenment belief that children are born with original sin that requires correction, the latter referring to Rousseau's judgment that children are born innocent and it is experience of the world that corrupts. Valentine (1996a) illustrates how both versions of childhood exist simultaneously in discourses about public safety. On the one hand, parents' desire to protect their children from the street draws on assumptions about children's innocence and vulnerability. These same parents, however, simultaneously demonize other children – those who *do* occupy the street – as necessarily corrupt and evil. It is clear that in a variety of contexts, the interpretation of child identity is constituted by their placing in space. Throughout the twentieth century, from the invention of the 'juvenile delinquent' in the early 1900s to the 'youth gangs' in the latter quarter, abnormality has been defined by children's occupation of the wrong space (Ruddick 1996).

In the process of constituting the nature of childhood spaces and children's identities, spatial discourses have significant effects on the way space is experienced. Numerous media-generated panics, including a warning issued by the National Society for the Prevention of Cruelty to Children urging parents not to let their children play unsupervised during the summer months (*Guardian*, Aug. 2, 1999), has produced an observable retreat of childhood back into the home. In 1999, statistics suggested only 2 in 10 mothers allowed their children to play unsupervised (BBC

Radio Four, July 22, 1999). Naturally, this retreat has effects on the dynamics of home space.[4] Sara McNamee (1998) finds that since boys traditionally enjoyed greater public freedom than girls, the effective curfew has resulted in boys recolonizing domestic space and eroding girls' sense of control within the home. On the other hand, children's increased use of domestic computers often subverts their supposed inferiority in the family hierarchy, since children are often more computer literate than their parents (Holloway & Valentine 2001).

Along with the home, the school is the single most important – in terms of time – institutional space in which childhood is experienced in Western societies. Much of the literature on childhood discusses the school in terms of discipline. The formal institutional space of the school is seen as a purposeful attempt to socialize children to conform to social norms, perform as individuals, accept authority, and interact sociably (Rivlin & Wolfe 1985). In other words, schools provide a space through which citizenly performances are reared. Aitken (2001b: 55) writes "[i]f the major purpose of school is to socialize children with regard to their roles in life and their places in society, then perhaps it also serves the larger stratified society by inculcating compliant citizens and productive workers who will be prepared to assume roles considered appropriate to the pretension of their race, class and gender identities." In illustrating precisely how school space is orchestrated around these intentions, many authors rely on Foucault's (1979) work on discipline (Walkerdine 1985; James, Jenks, & Prout 1998; Kirk 1998; Gagen 2000a). Such analyses examine school architecture, classroom seating, techniques of assessment, curriculum design, and physical exercise regimes as mechanisms and spaces through which disciplinary practices strive to ensure the correct development of children.

In doing so, however, authors observe that the school is not a bounded entity but is radically porous. Within the seemingly finite locations around the school – corridor, playground, or classroom – multiple discourses interpenetrate. While this applies to an infinite variety of networks, discourses of gender and sexuality have received particularly close scrutiny. For instance, Holloway, Valentine, and Bingham's (2000) work on the IT classroom in British secondary schools observes that through the use of computers, girls and boys police each others' gender and sexual identities, drawing from heterosexist understandings of normalcy. In particular, boys who are perceived as adept computer users are stigmatized as 'geeks' or 'nerds'; but crucially, this identity is further marginalized by being associated with femininity. Thus, they argue, computer competence is made legible through the operation of heterosexual norms of gender and sexuality. In addition, significant work has mapped the operation of gender and sexuality through girls' schooled bodies (Lesko 1988; Hyams 2000). In Melissa Hyams' (2000) work on adolescent Latinas in a Los Angeles high school she argues that girls' sexuality, understood through dress codes, bodily comportment, and expressive behavior, is regulated and self-regulated through its relationship to academic success. By allying success with propriety and failure with overt sexuality, the school encourages girls to dress and behave more conservatively. This confirms other authors' observation that since the advent of compulsory schooling in the late nineteenth century, education discourses have consistently rewarded boys for misbehavior, indeed it is taken as a marker of young masculinity, while girls are expected to be discreet and deferential (Walkerdine 1985; Brown 1990; Gagen 2001).

Gender and sexuality are just two dimensions through which children experience school space. As an open network of relationships, operating on a variety of spatial and temporal scales, the school represents a complex nerve center of social identities. Temporally, the school imagines itself as a preparatory ground for future identities. Similarly, the school connects a variety of other spaces laterally, from those that orbit its immediate surrounds, like the playground, playing field, or remote field site, to those that are more indirectly tethered, like the home, nation and empire. National spaces, for instance, are increasingly connected via the internet and email – often accessed from the classroom – and along with other global technologies, mediate the way children imagine other national identities (Hague 2001; Holloway & Valentine 2000b). Earlier in the century, nationhood played a more explicit role in the peripheral spaces of the school. In the United States, amidst fears that the nation was under siege from immigration and urban transformation, reformers instituted a regime of playground activities that sought to actively construct national consciousness through games and sport (Gagen 2000b). Similarly, Ploszajska (1998) uses the example of geography field trips to illustrate how the school symbolically recreated spaces of empire in order to instill colonial ideology in the fledgling nation. In these examples, the school literally and metaphorically reaches out to other spaces, drawing from, reconstituting and being reconstituted by a range of other, local, national, and global spaces.

Much of this section has been preoccupied with the spaces designated for childhood, examining, along the way, the enactment of discourses that mediate experience of these spaces. I want to end this section by turning briefly to examples of what happens when there is a mismatch: when children do not comply with the expected norms of childhood. If we cast back for a moment to the image at the opening of this chapter of the young Martin Amis flaunting his cigarette like a trophy of defiance, it doesn't stretch the imagination far to understand this as an 'unchildlike' act (Aitken 2001b). By this term, Aitken (2001b: 147) refers to those acts which "seem to ascribe to young people an independence, autonomy and self-interest that is irreconcilable with the nature of childhood as prescribed through most of the nineteenth and twentieth century." Child labor in the developing world is constructed along just such lines (Roberts 1998). The image of the child worker fails to conform to Western understandings of childhood which prescribe education, play, care, and protection rather than labor, responsibility, and hardship. The notion of unchildlike acts can also be usefully spatialized to recall Tim Cresswell's (1996) theory of transgression. For Cresswell, transgression does not simply imply improper acts, but rather, their performance in the wrong place. Throughout the work on spaces of childhood it is clear that there are proper and improper places for children to live, work, and play, as well as appropriate intervals in the lifecycle in which to assume those roles.

Children's Spaces

The child still scrawls and daubs on his [sic] schoolbooks; even if he is punished for this crime, he has made a space for himself and signs his existence as an author on it. (de Certeau 1984: 31)

The impulse to reinvent children as independent social actors has produced a body of work that explores children's spatial independence. Here, children are theorized as creative individuals, shaping and subverting the social world around them. Much of this work references – in spirit if not by citation – the early work of Roger Hart (1979) and Colin Ward (1978, 1990) whose research with children strove to document the different ways children make sense of the world through play, exploration and everyday being. "All children have an urge to explore the landscape around them, to learn about it, to give order to it, and to invest it with meaning – both shared and private" (Hart 1979: 3). While more recent contributions modify the universalizing tendency to speak of *all* children, they retain many of the methods and assumptions first established here.

Like those original pieces by Hart and Ward, recent work acknowledges the bequeathed nature of the social world in which children create spaces. Despite emphasizing the creative qualities of children's lives this work still regards children's actions as operating within or in response to an adult or 'adultist' structure of space (Valentine 1996b). There is an echo here of Michel de Certeau's (1984) notion of spatial practice. In everyday life, de Certeau identifies a set of practices which graft themselves onto the existing structures of life. He names these the *tactics* of the weak, in opposition to the *strategies* set in place by the powerful. De Certeau is more concerned with tactics than with strategies. He is interested in what he calls the poetry of everyday life: styles of action, modalities of operation that can only make use of "prefabricated space" (ibid.: 34). Similarly, the literature on children's geographies theorizes their actions as creative and cunning, but their worlds always exist within an 'official' space that is adult, permanent and more powerful.

To narrate children's worlds in this way relies on a fundamental assumption: that is, the belief that children are profoundly different from adults. This also has implications for children's methodologies, and I will return to this later in the chapter, but it is important here as it structures the way geographers understand children's spaces. Owain Jones (2000: 29), for instance, describes childhood as radically other: "The otherness of childhood is profound, as many of the symbolic orders which routinely but deeply structure adult life, such as time, money, property, sex, mortality and Euclidean space melt away." Thought of like this, children's spatial worlds become alien too. Children's blindness to adult mappings of space, their necessary ignorance of property boundaries, symbolic divisions, street patterns and pavements, and public/private allocations, results in an entirely different set of possibilities for spatial behavior. Children are more likely to contrive short cuts, to redefine spatial boundaries, or ignore them altogether, to rename places according to their own creative imaginaries, or reverse commonplace assumptions about fear and safety. For Jones (2000) these opportunities are magnified in a rural setting. Here, fears about children's safety are tempered by narratives of the rural idyll as parents appear more willing to permit their children the freedom to explore (although see Smith & Barker 2001, for evidence that rural childhoods are becoming more restrictive, and Tucker & Matthew 2001, for evidence that rural childhoods are becoming particularly restrictive for girls).

Similarly, Chris Philo (2000) explores the uniqueness of children's worlds, but does so using an adult's recollections of their own 'intimate geographies' of childhood. Philo's recounting of Hunter Diack's memories, reconstructed in the form of a novel, offers an experience of child space based on a remembered world. While this method is not unprecedented, either in its use of adult memories of childhood (see Sibley 1995b; and the coda to Hart 1979) or in its use of fiction to understand geographies of childhood (for example Phillips 1997), others question the ease with which these memories can readily access childhood. With such an insistence on the insurmountable gulf between the adult and child worlds, Jones (2001) suggests that adult memories are a problematic source of children's spatial experience. "Once childhood is superseded by adult stocks of knowledge, those filters can never be removed to get back to earlier states. Adult constructions and memories of what it is/was to be a child are invariably processed through *adultness*" (Jones 2001: 177).

Much of the literature on this theme concerns children's imaginative space making. An additional strand of work examines the practical rather than an imaginative reappropriation of space. This work is carried out in the context of debates about the increasing exclusion of young people from public space (as discussed earlier), and considers, instead, how young people make use of public space for their own needs. Despite the frequently observed retreat of children from public space, Matthews, Limb, and Taylor (2000: 64) argue that "[f]or a substantial residual of young people, the street remains an important part of their everyday lives, a place where they retain some autonomy over space." This is particularly notable in the case of girls, who are traditionally thought to have been excluded from street culture (Griffin 1985). Recent research finds, instead, that girls are able to use the street as a positive space, to chat, hang around, and exploit to their advantage (Skelton 2000). This work tends to look at young people's presence on the street as a marker of social relations rather than simply as a meaningful phenomenon in its own right.

A considerable volume of work on children's spaces focuses on play and leisure outside or on the street, perhaps because this is where the most creative opportunities lie. But with the expanding literature on children's geographies, many authors have explored children's spatial agency in other settings: in the classroom (Holloway, Valentine, & Bingham 2000), in cyberspace (Valentine, Holloway, & Bingham 2000), in the developing world (Punch 2000; Katz 1993, 1994), in nightclubs (Malbon 1998). Like other work, this focuses on the different ways children and young people experience, transform, and manipulate the everyday spaces of their lives.

Methodological and Ethical Spaces

Until quite recently, children's geographies had devoted limited space to ethical questions. While methodological issues have traditionally been more apparent, these too are now receiving more attention. There are a variety of reasons for this new awareness – legal, intellectual, and political – but almost invariably, researchers operate with two assumptions. The first, mentioned above, presupposes that child and adult identities are fractured by differences, which require unique methodologies to yield understanding. The second, following from the first, is that adult–child difference is characterized by an imbalance of power that places the onus on adults to negotiate research safely and ethically. The issues are both practical and philosophical: those that are preoccupied with techniques and strategies; and those that are concerned with underlying assumptions and problematics that inflect research with children. Of course, these can rarely be neatly separated.

The most obvious change in the way researchers approach children's geographies is in the terminology used to describe the relationship between researcher and researched. Whereas previously it was common to refer to research 'on' children, most now describe working 'with' children. This linguistic shift responds to the broader effort to see children as complete individuals to be engaged with rather than seen simply as inert objects to be studied. Consequently, many researchers consider qualitative, and specifically ethnographic, methods more appropriate for research 'with' children as it allows sustained interaction which treats children as individuals.

Throughout the research process, methodologies encourage children's full participation. As Valentine (1999: 142) reasons, "valid accounts of children's lives can only be obtained by engaging directly with children and treating them as independent actors." To begin with, children need to *consent*, rather than merely *assent*, to the research (Valentine 1999). As minors, their legal status as independent decision makers is ambiguous. But rather than rely on consent by proxy from parents or guardians, researchers should supplement that with permission from children themselves (Valentine 1999). Other strategies can also maximize children's control over their involvement in research. Valentine (1999) suggests allowing children to opt in rather than opt out of participation, while others advocate children's involvement in the actual design of the research, arguing that if children are responsible for the terms of their participation the research will elicit the most valuable responses (Skelton 2001). Alternatively, some methodologies inherently prioritize children's involvement such as autophotography, whereby children are given disposable cameras to document their individual visual experience of places (Aitken & Wingate 1993). These strategies are all designed to empower children throughout the research and minimize the power imbalance that structures adult–child relations (Matthews 2001).

An issue researchers have found particularly thorny relates to the geography of the research process itself; specifically, the selection of an appropriate location to conduct interviews. Since most research with young people involves school-age children, and access is often obtained via the school, it is an obvious location for interviews. Schools can offer safe environments, there are always plenty of people around, and it is a familiar space to children. Conversely, schools pose a number of problems. First, it is often extremely hard to guarantee privacy and therefore confidentiality (Valentine 1999; McDowell 2001), a particularly acute problem for research with vulnerable groups such as self-identified lesbian and gay young people (Valentine, Butler, & Skelton 2001). Equally, the home can be problematic for the same reasons. While a young person's bedroom can offer private sanctuary and therefore provide a safe interview space (Valentine 1999), McDowell questions the ethics of this choice. Citing guidelines drawn up by the Social Research Association, she suggests that researchers should "take scrupulous care to avoid situations that are open to the possibilities of abusive behaviour" (McDowell 2001: 92). This is doubly crucial for male researchers in the increasingly paranoiac climate surrounding pedophilia (Horton 2001). Both McDowell (2001) and Valentine, Butler, and Skelton (2001) agree that public or community spaces (youth centers, shopping malls) offer the safety and privacy to conduct sensitive conversations and provide a neutral space in which the hierarchies of educational institutions are temporarily set aside.

The issue of confidentiality raises important questions about intervention during the research. Interviews can often reveal compromising facts about children, and while most agree that information regarding young people's legal transgressions ought to be protected, if an individual is in danger, intervention is more justifiable (Valentine 1999). In other situations, particularly during participant-observation work, a researcher might witness abusive or oppressive behavior between children and have to contemplate intervening in the situation (Morris-Roberts 2001). Aitken (2001c: 125) argues that these kinds of questions arise in the 'immediacy of field-work' and cannot be resolved by "theoretical and philosophical pretensions." Rather, they need to be dealt with and judged in the urgency of that moment.

Like all social and cultural research, children's geographies has been obliged to reflect on the politics of representation. Again, the perceived gulf generated by adult–child difference is seen to produce an obstacle to understanding that requires negotiation. For Owain Jones (2001) this difference has to be transcended ethically to engage with children's lives. He writes, "[f]rom adult perspectives children's geographies may well appear bizarre and irrational, and the challenge is to translate these into the rational language of academic research and writing without, in the process, losing those very characteristics which may be at the center of understanding children's geographies" (Jones 2001: 177). For Jones this means giving up any aspiration to represent childhood completely. And while he applauds the various standards being established to make research with children more ethically responsible, he worries that this is "closing in on the otherness of childhood" (Jones 2001: 177–8). Rather than attempt to produce more accurate accounts of children's lives, representations of children should always acknowledge the ultimate unknowability of childhood.

The issue of representation is central to historical geographies of childhood; however, the imperatives described above are only relevant within current social contexts. Children's history provides no opportunities to seek consent, design participatory research, and intervene directly in children's lives. The dilemmas rest instead on the relationship between the historical text, the context, and the researcher. While representing experience is always a more problematic enterprise than many children's geographies of the present acknowledge, historical research is perhaps even more challenged. Here, the practice of writing child-centered histories has to rely on representations of children, produced by adults, for a particular purpose. Children's 'experience,' as such, is irreducible to a knowable account since their lives are always contained by the narrative of the archive. While this establishes a set of limits to the representation of childhood, it does not signal an interpretive impasse. Rather, it is often the case that archives record children's actions, and those actions, rather than some intangible notion of experience, reveal their participation in the world (Gagen 2001).

Conclusions: Growing Up?

In this chapter I have focused on those aspects of children's geographies that have thematic synergies with cultural geography. I began by looking at the construction of childhood in relation to particular spaces. This not only highlights the way children's identities are co-constituted spatially, but also illustrates the unease generated by unchildlike acts, particularly when those are defined by a breach of the spatial limits of childhood. The next section examined the various ways children creatively manipulate adult constructions of space to create their own imaginative geographies, or simply the ways they subvert commonplace uses of space, particularly public space. The final section on ethics and methodologies suggests some of the ways children's geographers have endeavored to ensure a safe and just research process that takes into account children's rights and independence.

The chapter is far from an exhaustive account of children's geographies to date, but outlines some of the principal themes that are allied with cultural geography. These are not, however, the only intradisciplinary connections; there are links to other geographical subfields – economic, environmental, behavioral, development – to name a few. As children's geographies reaches a critical mass, many of its advocates caution against partitioning the work in a discrete subfield, urging instead that it continues to reach across human geography's diverse interests. That said, there are other concerns, integral to the work itself, that need to be addressed. So far, children's geographies has been preoccupied with adult–child relations. This division forms the bedrock of analysis across the spectrum of research. While Valentine and Holloway (2001) argue that this is a necessary strategy to do justice to children as coherent social group, it is perhaps time to interrogate the many and varied lines of power *between* children that disrupt this coherence. Power saturates child–child relations too, and until the field engages with these, we risk neglecting the many ways children inflict harm and hurt on each other, and indeed on adults.

NOTES

1. Aitken (2001b) observes that there is a politics to the terminology employed in writing about children. He notes that it is significant to speak "of childhood and adolescence rather than simply children and young people. The former are placeless and abstract . . . They suggest a certain formal and sophisticated understanding of what and when it is to be a child or teenager, one that abstracts from the particularities of day-to-day lived experiences" (p. 21). I argue that it is vital to attend to both permutations of what it means to be a child, as neither, alone, can account for the meaning and experience of childhood. I should also clarify a point about age distinctions here. There is some ambiguity about the boundaries of 'childhood' and 'youth.' Adolescence is a notoriously 'fuzzy' zone which falls between adult and child worlds (Sibley 1995b). Much of the literature approaches each case individually, using the term youth, adolescence, children, childhood or simply young people as befits the context of the work. My review mirrors this ambiguity, drawing from literature on the very young to late teens.
2. Other work on children within geography drawing from environmental psychology, design and planning, transportation, policy, and development studies, is not covered here, but comprehensive statements and bibliographies can be found elsewhere (Matthews 1992; McKendrick 2000).
3. Matthew and Limb (1999) make similar demands for children to be studied by cultural geographers.
4. Other effects of parental fear over children's safety are the rise of commercial play-spaces and out of school clubs that aim to provide a safe alternative to unsupervised outdoor play (Smith & Barker 1999, 2001; McKendrick, Fielder, & Bradford 1999, 2000).

REFERENCES

Aitken, S. C. 2000: Fathering and faltering: 'Sorry, but you don't have the necessary accoutrements.' *Environment and Planning A* 32, 581–98.

Aitken, S. C. 2001a: Global crises of childhood: rights, justice and the unchildlike child. *Area* 33, 119–27.

Aitken, S. C. 2001b: *Geographies of Young People: The Morally Contested Spaces of Identity.* London: Routledge.

Aitken, S. C. 2001c: Fielding diversity and moral integrity. *Ethics, Place and Environment* 4, 125–9.

Aitken, S. C. and Wingate, J. 1993: A preliminary study of the self-directed photography of middle-class, homeless and mobility impaired children. *The Professional Geographer* 45, 65–72.

Ariès, P. 1962: *Centuries of Childhood: A Social History of Family Life.* New York: Knopf.

BBC Radio Four. *You and Yours.* July 22, 1999.

Blaut, J. 1997a: Children can. *Annals of the Association of American Geographers* 87, 152–8.

Blaut, J. 1997b: Piagetian pessimism and the mapping abilities of young children: a rejoinder to Liben and Downs. *Annals of the Association of American Geographers* 87, 168–77.

Blaut, J. and Stea, D. 1971: Studies of geographic learning. *Annals of the Association of American Geographers* 61, 387–93.

Blaut, J. and Stea, D. 1974: Mapping at the age of three. *Journal of Geography* 73, 5–9.

Bondi, L. and Domosh, M. 1998: On the contours of public space: a tale of three women. *Antipode* 30, 270–89.

Brown, V. B. 1990: The fear of feminization: Los Angeles high schools in the progressive era. *Feminist Studies* 16, 493–518.

Bunge, W. W. 1973: The geography. *The Professional Geographer* 25, 331–7.

Bunge, W. W. and Bordessa, R. 1975: *The Canadian Alternative: Survival, Expeditions, and Urban Change.* Geographical Monographs no. 2. Toronto: York University.

Caputo, V. 1995: Anthropology's silent 'others': a consideration of some conceptual and methodological issues for the study of youth and children's culture. In V. Amit-Talai and H. Wulff, eds., *Youth Cultures: A Cross-cultural Perspective.* London: Routledge.

Cresswell, T. 1996: *In Place/Out of Place: Geography, Ideology and Transgression.* Minneapolis: University of Minnesota Press.

Davidoff, L. and Hall, C. 1987: *Family Fortunes.* London: Hutchinson.

De Certeau, M. 1984: *The Practice of Everyday Life.* Berkeley: University of California Press.

Downs, R. G. 1985: The representation of space: its development in children and in cartography. In R. Cohen, ed., *The Development of Spatial Cognition.* Hillsdale, NJ: Lawrence Erlbaum.

Downs, R. G. and Liben, L. S. 1991: The development of expertise in geography: a cognitive-development approach to geographic learning. *Annals of the Association of American Geographers* 81, 304–27.

Downs, R. G. and Liben, L. S. 1997a: Can-ism and can'tianism: a straw child. *Annals of the Association of American Geographers* 87, 159–67.

Downs, R. G. and Liben, L. S. 1997b: The final summation: the defense rests. *Annals of the Association of American Geographers* 87, 178–80.

Foucualt, M. 1979: *Discipline and Punish: The Birth of the Prison.* New York: Vintage Books.

Gagen, E. A. 2000a: An example to us all: child development and identity construction in early 20th-century playgrounds. *Environment and Planning A* 32, 599–616.

Gagen, E. A. 2000b: Playing the part: performing gender in America's playgrounds. In S. L. Holloway and G. Valentine, eds., *Children's Geographies: Playing, Living, Learning*. London: Routledge, 213–29.

Gagen, E. A. 2001: Too good to be true: representing children's agency in the archives of playground reform. *Historical Geography* 29, 53–64.

Golledge, R. G., Smith, T. R., Pellegrino, J. W., Doherty, S., and Marshall, S. P. 1985: A conceptual and empirical analysis of children's acquisition of spatial knowledge. *Journal of Environmental Psychology* 5, 125–52.

Griffin, C. 1985: *Typical Girls: Young Women from School to Job Market*. London: Routledge and Kegan Paul.

The Guardian. 1999: Anger at child safety drive. Aug. 2, p. 1.

The Guardian. 2001: Young Amis caught in illegal act. March 22, p. 1.

Hague, E. 2001: Nationality and children's drawing – pictures 'about Scotland' by primary school children in Edinburgh, Scotland and Syracuse, New York. *Scottish Geographical Journal* 117, 77–99.

Hart, R. 1979: *Children's Experience of Place*. New York: Irvington.

Holloway, S. L. and Valentine, V. 2000a: Children's geographies and the new social studies of childhood. In S. Holloway and G. Valentine, eds., *Children's Geographies: Playing, Living, Learning*. London: Routledge, 1–26.

Holloway, S. L. and Valentine, G. 2000b: Corked hats and *Coronation Street*: British and New Zealand children's imaginative geographies of other. *Childhood* 7, 335–57.

Holloway, S. L. and Valentine, G. 2001: 'It's only as stupid as you are': children's and adults' negotiation of ICT competence at home and at school. *Journal of Social and Cultural Geography* 2, 25–42.

Holloway, S. L., Valentine, G., and Bingham, N. 2000: Institutionalising technologies: masculinities, femininities, and the heterosexual economy of the IT classroom. *Environment and Planning A* 32, 617–33.

Horton, J. 2001: 'Do you get some funny looks when you tell people what you do?' Muddling through some angsts and ethics of (being a male) researching with children. *Ethics, Place and Environment* 4, 159–66.

Hyams, M. 2000: 'Pay attention in class . . . [and] don't get pregnant': a discourse of academic success among adolescent Latinas. *Environment and Planning A* 12, 635–54.

Jacobson, L. 1997: Revitalizing the American home: children's leisure and the revaluation of play, 1920–1940. *Journal of Social History* 30, 581–96.

James, A, Jenks, C., and Prout, A. 1998: *Theorizing Childhood*. New York: Teachers College Press.

James, S. 1990: Is there a 'place' for children in geography? *Area* 22, 278–83.

Jenks, C. 1996: *Childhood*. London: Routledge.

Jones, O. 2000: Melting geography: purity, disorder, childhood, and space. In S. L. Holloway and G. Valentine, eds., *Children's Geographies: Playing, Living, Learning*. London: Routledge, 29–47.

Jones, O. 2001: 'Before the dark of reason': some ethical and epistemological considerations on the otherness of children. *Ethics, Place and Environment* 4, 173–8.

Katz, C. 1993: Growing girls/closing circles: limits on the spacing of knowing in rural Sudan and US cities. In C. Katz and J. Monk, eds., *Full Circles: Geographies of Women Over the Life Course*. London: Routledge, 88–106.

Katz, C. 1994: Textures of global change: eroding ecologies of childhood in New York and Sudan. *Childhood* 2, 103–10.

Kirk, D. 1998: *Schooling Bodies: School Practice and Public Discourse, 1880–1950*. London: Leicester University Press.

Lesko, N. 1988: The curriculum of the body: lessons from a Catholic high school. In L. G.

Roman and L. K. Christian-Smith, with E. Ellswork, eds., *Becoming Feminine: The Politics of Popular Culture*. Lewes, UK: Falmer Press, 123–42.

Malbon, B. 1998: Clubbing: consumption, identity and the spatial practices of every-night life. In T. Skelton and G. Valentine, eds., *Cool Places: Geographies of Youth Cultures*. London: Routledge, 266–86.

Matthews, H. 1984: Environmental cognition of young children: images of school and home area. *Transactions of the Institute of British Geographers* 9, 89–105.

Matthews, H. 2001: Introduction: Power games and moral territories: ethical dilemmas when working with children and young people. Special issue of *Ethics, Place and Environment*, vol. 4, 117–18.

Matthews, H. and Limb, M. 1999: Defining an agenda for the geography of children: a review and prospect. *Progress in Human Geography* 23, 61–90.

Matthew, H., Limb, M., and Taylor, M. 2000: The 'street as third space.' In S. L. Holloway and G. Valentine, eds., *Children's Geographies: Playing, Living, Learning*. London: Routledge, 63–79.

Mayall, B. 1994: *Children's Childhoods: Observed and Experienced*. London: Falmer Press.

McDowell, L. 2001: 'It's that Linda again': ethical, practical and political issues involved in longitudinal research with young men. *Ethics, Place and Environment* 4, 87–100.

McKendrick, J. H. 2000: The geography of children: an annotated bibliography. *Childhood* 7, 359–87.

McKendrick, J. H., Fielder, A., and Bradford, M. G. 1999: Privatization of collective play spaces in the UK. *Built Environment* 25, 44–57.

McKendrick, J. H., Fielder, A., and Bradford, M. G. 2000: Time for a party! Making sense of the commercialisation of leisure space for children. In S. L. Holloway and G. Valentine, eds., *Children's Geographies: Playing, Living, Learning*. London: Routledge, 100–16.

McNamee, S. 1998: Youth, gender and video games: power and control in the home. In T. Skelton and G. Valentine, eds., *Cool Places: Geographies of Youth Culture*. London: Routledge, 195–206.

Morris-Roberts, K. 2001: Intervening in friendship exclusion? The politics of doing feminist research with teenage girls. *Ethics, Place and Environment* 4, 147–52.

Nicholson, L. 1986: *Gender and History: The Limits of Social Theory in the Age of the Family*. New York: Columbia University Press.

Phillips, R. 1997: *Mapping Men and Empire: A Geography of Adventure*. London: Routledge.

Philo, C. 1992: Neglected rural geographies: a review. *Journal of Rural Studies* 8, 193–207.

Philo, C. 2000: 'The cornerstones of my world.' Editorial introduction to special issue on spaces of childhood. *Childhood* 7, 243–56.

Ploszajska, T. 1998: Down to earth? Geography fieldwork in English schools, 1870–1944. *Environment and Planning D: Society and Space* 16, 757–74.

Punch, S. 2000: Children's strategies for creating playspaces: negotiating independence in rural Bolivia. In S. L. Holloway and G. Valentine, eds., *Children's Geographies: Playing, Living, Learning*. London: Routledge, 48–62.

Qvortrup, J. et al. 1994: *Childhood Matters: Social Theory, Practice and Politics*. Aldershot: Avebury.

Rivlin, L. G. and Wolfe, M. 1985: *Institutional Settings in Children's Lives*. New York: John Wiley and Sons.

Roberts, S. 1998: Commentary. What about the children? *Environment and Planning A* 30, 3–11.

Ruddick, S. M. 1996: *Young and Homeless in Hollywood: Mapping Social Identities*. New York: Routledge.

Sibley, D. 1991: Children's geographies: some problems of representation. *Area* 23, 269–71.

Sibley, D. 1995a: *Geographies of Exclusion*. London: Routledge.

Sibley, D. 1995b: Families and domestic routines: constructing the boundaries of childhood. In S. Pile and N. Thrift, eds., *Mapping the Subject: Geographies of Cultural Transformation*. London: Routledge, 123–38.

Skelton, T. 2000: 'Nothing to do, nowhere to go?' Teenage girls and 'public' space in the Rhondda Valleys, South Wales. In S. L. Holloway and G. Valentine, eds., *Children's Geographies: Playing, Living, Learning*. London: Routledge, 80–99.

Skelton, T. 2001: Girls in the club: researching working class girls' lives. *Ethics, Place and Environment* 4, 167–72.

Smith, F. and Barker, J. 1999: From Ninja Turtles to the Spice Girls: children's participation in the development of out of school play environments. *Built Environment* 25, 35–43.

Smith, F. and Barker, J. 2001: Commodifying the countryside: the impact of out-of-school care on rural landscapes of children's play. *Area* 33, 169–76.

Thomas, M. 2000: Guest editorial. From crib to campus: kids' sexual/gender identities and institutional space. *Environment and Planning A* 32, 577–80.

Tucker, F. and Matthew, H. 2001: 'They don't like girls hanging around there': conflicts over recreational space in rural Northhamptonshire. *Area* 33, 161–8.

Valentine, G. 1996a: Angels and devils: moral landscapes of childhood. *Environment and Planning D: Society and Space* 14, 581–99.

Valentine, G. 1996b: Children should be seen and not heard: the production and transgression of adults' public space. *Urban Geography* 17, 205–20.

Valentine, G. 1997: 'Oh yes I can.' 'Oh no you can't': children and parents' understanding of kids' competence to negotiate public space safely. *Antipode* 29, 65–89.

Valentine, G. 1999: Being seen and heard? The ethical complexities of working with children and young people at home and at school. *Ethics, Place and Environment* 2, 141–55.

Valentine, G., Butler, R., and Skelton, T. 2001: The ethical and methodological complexities of doing research with 'vulnerable' young people. *Ethics, Place and Environment* 4, 119–24.

Valentine, G., Holloway, S. L., and Bingham, N. 2000: Transforming cyberspace: children's interventions in the new public sphere. In S. L. Holloway and G. Valentine, eds., *Children's Geographies: Playing, Living, Learning*. London: Routledge, 156–73.

Walkerdine, V. 1985: On the regulation of speaking and silence. In C. Steedman, C. Urwin, and V. Walkerdine, eds., *Language, Gender and Childhood*. London: Routledge.

Ward, C. 1978: *The Child in the City*. London: Architectural Press.

Ward, C. 1990: *The Child in the Country*, 2nd ed. London: Bedford Square Press.

Winchester, H. 1991: The geography of children. *Area* 23, 357–60.

Chapter 27

Landscape in Film

Robert Shannan Peckham

Introduction: Geographies of Cinema

Although films have long performed a pedagogical function within geographical studies, anthropology, and area studies, it is only recently that the cinema has itself become the focus of systematic study within these fields. The reason for this neglect, as Jacqueline Burgess and John Gold observed some time ago, may well be that, as components of popular culture, films have been overlooked because of their "ordinariness" (Burgess & Gold 1985: 1). The burgeoning interest in films within cultural geography could thus be taken to reflect a more thorough engagement with popular culture and an acknowledgment of the cinema's role in shaping individual and societal perceptions of space and place (Aitken & Zonn 1994; Cresswell & Dixon 2002).

Notwithstanding the theoretical interest in films within geographical research, however, and despite the converging preoccupations of geography and film studies evinced in collaborative publications such as the recent special issue of *Screen* devoted to the theme of Space/Place/City and Film (Lury & Massey 1999), geographers have yet to develop theoretically consistent approaches to the geographical dimension of the cinema (Kennedy & Lukinbeal 1997).

Research on the geography of cinema (a term that encompasses the business of making films as well as films taken collectively) has tended to concentrate on the ways in which space and place are represented in individual films or within generic groups of films. The concept of *mise-en-scène* or 'staging in action,' which originated in the nineteenth-century theater, refers in film studies to the constituent elements that compose a shot and create a specific 'screen space.' Amongst other prerequisites, including lighting and movement, props and costumes, setting is a crucial aspect of *mise-en-scène*. The setting is sometimes privileged as the leading character in a film, functioning not merely as an incidental background for the main action, but as an expressive component of the narrative itself (Bordwell & Thompson 1997: 169–209). Analyses have been made, for example, of the functions performed in Australian cinema by a distinctive bush setting, which pits the corrosive influences of the city against the salutary wilderness of 'authentic' outback Australia. The Australian filmmaker, curator, and critic Ross Gibson has argued, within this context, that the prominence given to the landscape in Australian cinema signifies the urge by a white society to historicize and root the Australian nation in an aboriginal territory. Seen from this perspective, the *Mad Max* film trilogy (1979, 1981, 1985), which engages with the conventions of the Western, may be said to exemplify the frustrated attempts by colonial explorers to subjugate the 'wilderness' (Gibson 1992).

The world as it is evoked in a narrative film is known as the film's *diegesis*, after the Greek term for narrated story. Diegetic components of a film include both the activities and places that make up the fictional world of the film, even when these are not pictured on-screen (Bordwell & Thompson 1997: 92). In film studies, given films are considered both as textual constructs, the product of an *auteur* or director who 'authors' the work, and as cultural products or commodities caught up in a dynamic network of political, economic and industrial systems. Films are analyzed in relation to their contents, style, form, and aesthetics. But they are also considered within the terms of their production, distribution and exhibition; aesthetic preoccupations are linked to social and economic environments. Indeed, there is a growing interest in the material circumstances within which films are produced and consumed. More than simply reflecting the environment, cinema actively participates in its configuration: "The city has been shaped by the cinematic form, just as cinema owes much of its nature to the historical development of the city" (Clarke 1997: 2). The cinema, and particularly Hollywood, remains influential in marketing ideas about the natural world (Zukin 1991; Wilson 1992). As the French theorist Jean Baudrillard remarked in his book *America*: "Where is the cinema? It is all around you outside, all over the city, that marvellous, continuous performance of films and scenarios" (Baudrillard 1989: 56).

Ideology and the Reality Effect

The invention of cinematic film in the 1890s constituted part of a modernist technological revolution that dramatically altered existing "ways of seeing." The cultural critic Walter Benjamin, writing about the advent of film in his essay "The Work of Art in the Age of Mechanical Reproduction" (1936), likened filmmaking to a surgical operation. Surgeons, like cameramen, he argued, were able to probe below the surface of the world and penetrate reality's "web." Film, Benjamin observed, "offers, precisely because of the thoroughgoing permeation of reality with mechanical equipment, an aspect of reality which is free from all equipment" (Benjamin 1973: 227).

As a mode of vision, the moving picture marked a key development in the modernization of vision, which had begun in the eighteenth century with the camera obscura (a darkened chamber where images of objects outside were projected onto a screen by means of a convex lens) and continued in the 1830s with the spread of photography. Ophthalmologic research and scientific studies of light and optics furthered understanding of vision and led, ultimately, to technical interventions such as the X-ray in 1895 (Crary 1992).

To view the inception of the cinema, however, simply as the culmination of an evolutionary drive towards the fulfillment of objective, 'natural' vision is misleading (Crary 1992: 26–7). Cinema may be considered instead as a cultural phenomenon linked to the new "spectacular realities" of modern mass-consumer society, such as the department store (Charney & Schwartz 1995; Schwartz 1998). Moreover, the notion of the cinema as the natural outgrowth of photography and the apogee of nineteenth-century scientific progress belies the fact that the cinema has frequently been mobilized to bolster political power, performing explicit and implicit ideological functions. As Jean-Louis Comolli and Jean Narboni remarked in a seminal article published in the radical French journal *Cahiers du Cinéma* (1969): "every film is political, inasmuch as it is determined by the ideology which produces it" (Comolli & Narboni 1993: 45).

The cinema constructs and legitimates an idea of the real. Realism is not a form of mimetic transparency that spontaneously reproduces the external world, rather verisimilitude is an "effect" (Barthes 1989) produced by the artful arrangement of signifying elements within a text according to specific conventions (MacCabe 1993).

Film Studies has developed different theoretical models to elucidate setting, drawing on a range of disciplines from literary and visual theories to cultural studies. The concept of the "chronotope," developed by the Russian theorist Mikhail Bakhtin, for example, provides one useful way of investigating the relationship of setting and genre. The "chronotope" is employed by Bakhtin to describe the specific conflations of time and place, which are inscribed in particular locales. Thus, the "chronotope" might be usefully deployed as a tool for analyzing the significance invested in the cocktail lounge, the nightclub and the bar within the postwar genre of film noir. All of these locales function as places "where the knots of narrative are tied and untied;" they are places out of real-life that have, over time, become associated "with fixed expressions and metaphoric patterns of thinking" (Sobchack 1998: 149). Considering realistic setting in this way opens up the relationship between text and context and reconnects "the historicity of the lived world" with the world of cinema (Sobchack 1998: 150).

Cinema and Postmodern Geographies

The geographer David Harvey has argued that studying films may be valuable in shedding light on ongoing theoretic debates about postmodern culture. Cinema, perhaps more than any other comparable media, he suggests, encapsulates the multifaceted relationship between temporality and spatiality in the postmodern age. For critics such as Harvey the term postmodernism alludes to a postindustrial economic and social order, characterized by the rapidity with which new digital technologies disseminate information and images globally. One feature of the postmodern condition thus defined is the concomitant compression of time and space, and the 'deterritorialization' of culture. Accordingly, identity is no longer firmly rooted in a specific place but constantly renegotiated among the shifting semantic contents of images and signs.

In a comparative analysis of Ridley Scott's 1982 cult movie, *Blade Runner*, which is set in the derelict streets of a futuristic and deindustrialized Los Angeles, and of Wim Wenders' *Wings of Desire* (1987), which takes place in Berlin, Harvey demonstrates how the two works are symptomatic of a crisis of representation. Both films, he contends, offer the audience a mirror, which reflects "many of the essential features of the condition of postmodernity;" namely, the fragmentation of time, space, history, and place (Harvey 1990: 308, 308–23).

Harvey's work intimates ways in which the theoretical models and insights developed in film studies may be usefully redeployed within cultural geography. At the same time, the writing of cultural critics such as Fredric Jameson, who has drawn upon the work of the geographer Kevin Lynch in developing his notion of "cognitive mapping," suggests how, reciprocally, film studies has drawn upon theoretical developments in cultural geography (Jameson 1991: 51–4, 409–17; Jameson 1992: 188–9). For Jameson, "cognitive mapping" describes the process through which individuals are able to locate themselves in relation to society, conceived as a totality. In a postindustrial world, he argues, there is a need for a political culture that "seeks to endow the individual subject with some new heightened sense of its place in the global system" (Jameson 1991: 54).

The Power of Cinema: Classical Hollywood and Beyond

The notion that postmodern films can self-reflexively comment on the condition of postmodernity is to suggest that films are somehow able to interrogate the circumstances of their production. In the twentieth century, however, the development of film has been closely connected with attempts by political authorities to curtail meaning in order to reinforce a given view of the world. The cultural critic Paul Virilio has shown, for example, how the history of film technologies and war technologies are intertwined. In the twentieth century film has formed part of "a perceptual arsenal" that has been crucial in conflicts from the First World War to the Gulf War and beyond. Films have been instrumental in strategies of surveillance and espionage aimed at the military subjugation of populations (Virilio 1989).

As a pedagogical tool within anthropological research, the documentary film – a term reputedly coined by the pioneering British filmmaker John Grierson (1898–1972) – has long functioned as a vehicle for mediating 'exotic' places and its inhabitants (Griffiths 2002). With the availability of hand-held cameras in the 1950s and 1960s, documentary filmmaking, known as *cinéma vérité* (cinema truth), developed with the ostensible aim of spontaneously recording objective, factual information. Documentary techniques were employed in the making of feature films. The directors of the so-called *Nouvelle Vague* or New Wave in France, such as François Truffaut, Jean-Luc Godard, and Eric Rohmer were influenced both by the emphasis on contemporary life in the work of Italian Neorealists, as well as by ethnographic filmmakers such as Jean Rouch. In the main they eschewed the studio and shot their films in actual locations using lightweight cameras that enabled greater flexibility, often casting nonprofessional actors and employing faster film to take advantage of natural light.

Although France produced the most influential group of new wave filmmakers, many other countries around the world, such as Japan and Brazil, saw the emergence of similar progressive groups during this period. Often the move towards documentary-style realism corresponded with a radical political agenda. In Greece, for example, the early realist films of Alexis Damianos, Theo Angelopoulos, and

Pantelis Voulgaris, which blurred the line between factual reportage and fiction, constituted a challenge to the authority of the dictatorship that ruled the country between 1967 and 1974.

Documentaries are always partial and informed by social and political assumptions. They do not offer unmediated, purely factual views of the world, but draw on narrative techniques and rhetorical strategies that are common to feature films (Nichols 1991). The controversy surrounding the editing of factual material in Michael Moore's documentary *Roger and Me* (1989) highlights the ambiguity of the documentary as a 'neutral' genre. Moore's film was offered as a factual account of a series of layoffs at General Motors' plants in the town of Flint, Michigan, during the 1980s, even though it transpired that the documentary rearranged events to dramatize its story more effectively (Cohan & Crowdus 1990).

Institutionally, at least, cinema is still marketed and studied as the product of specific geopolitical conditions. Hierarchical categories such as Hollywood Cinema, National Cinemas, and World Cinema are still widely employed as classificatory frameworks for defining films. The political role of cinema has been explored most thoroughly in the context of Classical Hollywood Cinema, which lasted from the 1920s to the 1960s. During the 1920s the US film industry amalgamated into the hands of a few large mass-production studio corporations, such as MGM, Fox, Warner Brothers, Universal, and Paramount, which controlled the production and distribution of films. Hollywood's studio system was organized around what may be called an industrial mode of production, where films were produced as commodities in a highly centralized production process (Naficy 1999). With the decimation of Europe's film industries during the First World War, Hollywood acquired unparalleled dominance of global screen entertainment.

During the 1970s, however, the studio system was transformed in order to come to terms "with an increasingly fragmented entertainment industry – with its demographics and large audiences, it diversified 'multimedia' conglomerates, its global(ized) markets and new delivery systems" (Tom Schatz quoted in Naficy 1999: 126). The preeminence of this 'new' Hollywood was secured by the global consolidation of US television networks and the availability of innovative audiovisual technology (Wasko 1994). Other factors were important, such as the widespread deregulation and privatization of the media, the unification of Europe, and the liberalization of former Communist countries during the late 1980s and 1990s. The case of India, a country with the second largest film industry in the world and a highly developed internal distribution network, remains an exception to the supremacy of Hollywood.

One consequence of Hollywood's hegemony, it is often claimed, is the impoverishment, both culturally and economically, of other less powerful nations. Hollywood cinema has been descried as an exemplar of US economic and political imperialism. While Hollywood is aggressively marketed and clearly does exert enormous economic and cultural influence, anti-imperialist criticism tends to simplify the ways in which viewers, both individually and collectively, mediate Hollywood films. By the same token, cultural imperialism, as opposed to economic imperialism, is notoriously difficult to evaluate with any precision. Recent research has confirmed how imported US popular culture may be appropriated in complex ways into indigenous cultural forms, while different individuals and audience groups impose divergent interpretations upon the same films, according to their backgrounds, experiences, and values (Liebes & Katz 1990).

In large measure, then, the concept of a 'national cinema' has emerged as a bulwark against the influence wielded by Hollywood Cinema. In many countries, the role of the state has been crucial in the financing of 'national' films, making the concept of 'national' cinema, in effect, a form of cultural protectionism. National cinema is frequently viewed in symbolic terms, as a synecdoche standing for a whole culture. French costume dramas of the 1980s (*film de patrimoine*), notably Claude Berri's *Jean de Florette* (1985) and *Manon des Sources* (1986), promoted a vision of France's heritage as a timeless, immemorial rural landscape linked to the Third Republic (1870–1940) (Forbes & Kelly 1995: 260). Such films obliterated the contemporary urban and multicultural realities of France and its attendant social problems in favor of the nostalgic idea of a stable and quintessential landscape, protected from the "discontents of modernity" (Nowell-Smith 1996: 766).

Ironically, however, 'national' films are often marketed for foreign export and, consequently, project an outsider's perspective on a local culture, homogenizing the differences within. The acclaim with which the work of Chinese filmmakers of the so-called Fifth Generation was greeted in the West prompted heated debates among Chinese critics about what constituted a 'Chinese' cinema and the manner in which specific images of 'China' were manufactured for external, Western consumption. Chinese filmmakers were caught in a double-bind: between accusations of fetishizing local culture for 'outsiders' and promoting an ethnocentric approach that suggested Chinese culture was somehow exclusive and impossible to represent for non-native audiences (Reynaud 1998: 545–6). As Chris Berry has remarked, however, critiquing the notion of a singular, essential 'China' does not entail debunking China as a fiction. On the contrary, 'China,' he contends, needs to be seen as a discursively produced and historically contingent entity. In this sense, it is not so much China that makes movies, he argues, but the movies that help to make different versions of 'China' (Berry 1994, 2000).

In African Cinema similar questions are being addressed, too, about the validity of African Cinema as a generic category, as well as the usefulness of Third World Cinema as a designation for non-Western productions. The debate has increasingly focused around the constitutive differences between African Cinema, Hollywood, and Second World Cinema, and the dilemma of how its distinctiveness is to be understood, given that the technology of filmmaking itself forms part of a colonial heritage (Diawara 1992; Ukadike 1994, 1998).

The category 'national cinema' suggests a community of like-minded viewers who share a vision of the world. Increasingly, however, the nature of the nation-state and national identity are being reassessed, following the influential work of Ernest Gellner (1983), Benedict Anderson (1983), and Eric Hobsbawm (1990). Much work has been done on demonstrating the ways in which films naturalize nationalist ideologies and help engineer and sustain a sense of identity. Sumita Chakravarty has shown, for example, how Indian popular films, after the creation of an independent India in 1947, reinforced ideas about the Indian nation at the same time as they created new ones (Chakravarty 1993). In Japan the *jidaigeki*, or historical drama, was similarly influential in forging a national identity, especially during the 1930s within the context of Japan's fraught relationship with modernity and the West

(Davis 1996). Like the novels of the nineteenth century, films may provide narratives in which individual viewers are able to associate themselves imaginatively with a collective community.

Thus, over recent years, the idea that films are the expression of specific geopolitical circumstances has been more openly debated. Cinema's categorization and the mechanisms of its funding have been widely researched. Questions have been asked about the political dimension of cinema's classificatory frameworks and about the disparate criteria (cultural, geographic, or economic) that render a film national in the first place. In addressing these issues film critics have emphasized both the political and industrial pressures and the aesthetic conventions that inform cinema as a cultural and economic activity.

Some critics allege that even reputedly 'conservative' Hollywood films contain structures of resistance, so that watertight divisions between experimental and non-experimental, popular, and art films are impossible. They maintain that Hollywood often subverts dominant ideologies by employing adversarial strategies, such as irony or parody, which self-consciously play with the viewers' expectations (Hutcheon 1989: 114). Far from projecting an unambiguous vision of the world, Hollywood films may offer different visions of the social order and self-reflexively draw attention to their own limitations.

An Oscar-winning blockbuster such as Anthony Minghella's *The English Patient* (1996), a film adaptation of the novel by the Booker Prize winner Michael Ondaatje, suggests how big production films can interrogate assumptions about race and culture. The narrative of *The English Patient* shifts between Egypt and Italy, where a Canadian nurse, Hana (Juliette Binoche), cares for the dying English patient (Ralph Fiennes) in an abandoned Tuscan villa. An analogy is drawn in the film between the cave paintings in the Sahara, testament to the demise of a once flourishing civilization, and the wasted Tuscan landscape, once the 'epicenter' of European culture and the birthplace of the Renaissance. In a scene that recalls the English patient's discovery of the cave drawings, a young Sikh sapper, Kip (Naveen Andrews), takes Hana to visit the frescoes of a medieval church. On one level, *The English Patient* may be read as a postcolonial allegory: it is the once peripheral colonial subject who defuses the bombs and becomes the emissary of civilizing values at the heart of a deserted metropolitan culture.

On another level, *The English Patient* promotes a vision of transcendence, of humanity undivided by the borders of class and nationality. In a war-film set against the backdrop of contested political borders, the repeated aerial shots of the desert are juxtaposed against the grisly gashes underneath the English patient's bandaged body. Indeed, the film draws a visual analogy between the undulating dunes of the Sahara and the erogenous contours of a female body. The desert obliterates distinctions and hierarchies and as such it stands opposed to the imperial partition of Africa and the Indian subcontinent, as well as the aggressive contestation of borders that has ravaged Europe. It comes as no surprise, perhaps, that the English patient's mistress, Katharine Clifton (Kristin Scott Thomas), confides her dream of "a life without maps" and elsewhere geography is described as being "sad." In short, a cursory reading of *The English Patient* suggests how successful big-budget films can explore difficult cultural issues and that often they do so through a complex engagement with place.

Conclusion: Watching Films

Although an increasing interest is being taken in the specific social contexts in which films are watched and the meanings of the activities that accrue around grounded sites of spectatorship from the multiplex to the art-house theater (Jancovich et al. 2003), there are still relatively few studies devoted to the geographical dimension of film spectatorship.

When considering the social context of the cinema, as a locale where individuals come to watch films, it is important to remember the conditions in which the cinema was born. The motion picture developed at a moment when populations in industrialized societies were migrating to the city. Indeed, it has been argued that the cinema reflected an impetus to bring order to the visual chaos of the urban environment. "The cinema," observes Paul Virilio, " gratified the wish of the migrant workers for a lasting and even eternal homeland, giving them a new kind of freedom of the city" (1989: 39). The cinema auditorium became a cenotaph or temple and "the site of a new aboriginality in the midst of demographic anarchy" (Virilio 1989: 39).

Today the cinema auditorium is being redefined in new ways. On the one hand, multiplexes in shopping malls are promoting forms of sociability that embed the experience of watching films in a wider context of consumption. On the other hand, the availability of digital technology and computer-mediated communications is effectively privatizing spectatorship by bringing cinema into the privacy of the home. While these transformations have given rise to a reconsideration of place, the bulk of critical work on postmodernity continues to stress, generally in abstract terms, the compression of space and time effected by the new technology. The focus has tended to be on the ways in which individuals are uprooted from locality and experience geography as a virtual reality (Morley 1999: 156–9). An investigation into the diverse ways in which individuals and groups experience cinema, and the different physical contexts of their spectatorship, remain profitable areas for cultural geography to explore.

REFERENCES

Aitken, S. and Zonn, L., eds. 1994: *Place, Power, Situation and Spectacle: A Geography of Film.* Lanham, MD: Rowman and Littlefield.

Anderson, B. 1983: *Imagined Communities: Reflections on the Origin and Spread of Nationalism.* London: Verso.

Barthes, R. 1989: The reality effect. In *The Rustle of Language*, tr. Richard Howard. Berkeley: University of California Press, 141–8.

Baudrillard, J. 1989: *America*, tr. Chris Turner. London: Verso.

Benjamin, W. 1973: *Illuminations*, ed. Hannah Arendt. Glasgow: Fontana.

Berry, C. 1994: A nation t(w/o)o: Chinese cinema(s) and nationhood(s). In W. Dissanayake, ed., *Colonialism and Nationalism in Asian Cinema.* Bloomington: Indiana University Press, 42–64.

Berry, C. 2000: If China can say no, can China make movies? Or, do movies make China? Rethinking national Cinema and national agency. In R. Chow, ed., *Modern Chinese Literary and Cultural Studies in the Age of Theory: Reimagining a Field.* Durham, NC: Duke University Press, 159–80.

Bordwell, D. and Thompson, K. 1997: *Film Art: An Introduction*, 5th ed. New York: McGraw-Hill.

Burgess, J. and Gold, J., eds. 1985: *Geography, the Media and Popular Culture*. London: Croom Helm.

Chakravarty, S. 1993: *National Identity in Indian Popular Cinema 1947–1987*. Austin: University of Texas Press.

Charney, L. and Schwartz, V. R., eds. 1995: *Cinema and the Invention of Modern Life*. Berkeley: University of California Press.

Clarke, D., ed. 1997: *The Cinematic City*. London and New York: Routledge.

Cohan, C. and Crowdus, G. 1990: Reflections on *Roger and Me*, Michael Moore and his critics. *Cinéaste* 17, 25–30.

Comolli, J.-L. and Narboni, J. 1993: Cinema/ideology/criticism. Tr. Susan Bennett. In A. Easthope, ed., *Contemporary Film Theory*. London: Longman, 45–52.

Crary, J. 1992: *Techniques of the Observer: On Vision and Modernity in the Nineteenth Century*. Cambridge, MA: MIT Press.

Cresswell, T. and Dixon, D., eds. 2002: *Engaging Film: Geographies of Mobility and Identity*. Lanham, MD: Rowman and Littlefield.

Davis, D. W. 1996: *Picturing Japaneseness: Monumental Style, National Identity, Japanese Films*. New York: Columbia University Press.

Diawara, M. 1992: *African Cinema: Politics and Culture*. Bloomington: Indiana University Press.

Forbes, J. and Kelly, M. 1995: *French Cultural Studies: An Introduction*. Oxford: Oxford University Press.

Gellner, E. 1983: *Nations and Nationalism*. Oxford: Blackwell.

Gibson, R. 1992: *South of the West: Postcolonialism and the Narrative Construction of Australia*. Bloomington: Indiana University Press.

Griffiths, A. 2002: *Wondrous Difference: Cinema, Anthropology, and Turn-of-the-Century Visual Culture*. New York: Columbia University Press.

Harvey, D. 1990: *The Condition of Postmodernity: An Enquiry into the Origins of Cultural Change*. Malden, MA and Oxford: Blackwell.

Hill, J. and Gibson, P. C., eds. 1998: *The Oxford Guide to Film Studies*. Oxford: Oxford University Press.

Hobsbawm, E. 1990: *Nations and Nationalism since 1790: Programme, Myth, Reality*. Cambridge: Cambridge University Press.

Hutcheon, L. 1989: *The Politics of Postmodernism*. London: Routledge.

Jameson, F. 1991: *Postmodernism, or, The Cultural Logic of Late Capitalism*. London and New York: Verso.

Jameson, F. 1992: *The Geopolitical Aesthetic: Cinema and Space in the World System*. Bloomington and London: Indiana University Press and British Film Institute.

Jancovich, M., et al. 2003: *The Place of the Audience: Cultural Geographies of Film Consumption*. London: British Film Institute.

Kennedy, C. and Lukinbeal, C. 1997: Towards a holistic approach to geographic research on film. *Progress in Human Geography* 21, 33–50.

Liebes, T. and Katz, E. 1990: *The Export of Meaning: Cross-Cultural Readings of Dallas*. Oxford and New York: Oxford University Press.

Lury, K. and Massey, D. 1999: Making connections. *Screen* 40 (Autumn), 229–38.

MacCabe, C. 1993: Realism and the cinema: notes on some Brechtian theses. In A. Easthope, ed., *Contemporary Film Theory*. London: Longman, 53–67.

Morley, D. 1999: Bounded realms: households, family, community, and nation. In H. Naficy, ed., *Home, Exile, Homeland: Film, Media, and the Politics of Place*. New York and London: Routledge, 153–68.

Naficy, H. 1999: Between rocks and hard places: the interstitial mode of production in exilic cinema. In H. Naficy, ed., *Home, Exile, Homeland: Film, Media, and the Politics of Place*. New York and London: Routledge, 125–47.

Naficy, H., ed. 1999: *Home, Exile, Homeland: Film, Media, and the Politics of Place*. New York and London: Routledge.

Nichols, B. 1991: *Representing Reality: Issues and Concepts in Documentary*. Bloomington: Indiana University Press.

Nowell-Smith, G., ed. 1996: *The Oxford History of World Cinema*. Oxford: Oxford University Press.

Powrie, P. 1997: *Jean de Florette* and *Manon des Sources*: nostalgia and hysteria. In P. Powrie, ed., *French Cinema in the 1980s*. Oxford: Oxford University Press, 50–61.

Reynaud, B. 1998: Chinese cinema. In J. Hill and P. C. Gibson, eds., *The Oxford Guide to Film Studies*. Oxford and New York: Oxford University Press, 543–9.

Schwartz, V. R. 1998: *Spectacular Realities: Early Mass Culture in Fin-de-Siècle Paris*. Berkeley: University of California Press.

Sobchack, V. 1998: Lounge time: postwar crises and the chronotope of film noir. In N. Browne, ed., *Refiguring American Film Genres: Theory and History*. Berkeley: University of California Press, 129–70.

Ukadike, N. F. 1994: *Black African Cinema*. Berkeley: University of California Press.

Ukadike, N. F. 1998: African cinema. In J. Hill and P. C. Gibson, eds., *The Oxford Guide to Film Studies*. Oxford and New York: Oxford University Press, 569–75.

Virilio, P. 1989: *War and Cinema: The Logistics of Perception*, tr. Patrick Camiller. London: Verso.

Wasko, J. 1994: *Hollywood in the Information Age: Beyond the Silver Screen*. Cambridge: Polity Press.

Wilson, A. 1992: *The Culture of Nature: North American Landscape from Disney to the Exxon Valdez*. Oxford and Malden, MA: Blackwell.

Zukin, S. 1991: *Landscapes of Power: From Detroit to Disney World*. Berkeley: University of California Press.

Chapter 28

Landscape and Art

Stephen Daniels

The currency of landscape in cultural geography during the last 20 years has been closely, if sometimes contentiously, associated with an engagement with the visual arts. There have been increasing studies of landscape art in a variety of media, with landscape as a subject, as in landscape painting and photography, as a material, as in landscape gardens and earthworks, and as a locus, as in site-specific sculpture and mural art. These studies have identified different genres of landscape art, in the worlds it represents, both within and beyond the boundaries of works, including the places portrayed, vantage points and spatial projections, relations of figures and landscape, locations where works are produced and consumed. Landscape art, in its various forms, is now, along with a variety of cultural representations, an established source in studies of the geographies of broad formations such as modernity, national identity, imperialism, and industrialism, usually through studies of specific subject matter such as rivers, cities and clouds. Geographical interest in art is part of broader, interdisciplinary exploration of the culture and meaning of landscape in the humanities and creative engagement with landscape as a genre in contemporary art practice.

This broad field of concern with landscape and art has, perhaps inevitably, been one of differentiation and dispute as well as collaboration and integration. The framed rural view, the historically dominant and still most popular form of landscape art, has been put into question, provoking representations of land and life which claim to oppose or radically revise landscape as a genre, and ideas of landscape which resist its register as an artistic, or even visual, image. Such critiques are nothing new, dating back in the Anglophone world to eighteenth-century disputes about the power of the picturesque as a landscape aesthetic (Copley & Garside 1994). These disputes are arguably a source of landscape's vitality as a form of art, field of vision, and arena of critical enquiry (Daniels 1989).

In this essay I chart the main currents of work on geography and landscape art in the Anglophone world since the mid-twentieth century, focusing on the period since the 1980s. This will involve traversing various cultures of geography, mostly various practices of teaching and research in the subject as instituted as an academic discipline, but also geography as an extramural pursuit and as an intellectual perspective in art history. In the process I want to consider 'art' as well as 'landscape' as a cultural keyword, for its connotation as a practical skill, in such accomplishments as mapping and mountaineering, as well as imaginative creation, as in painting and sculpture; in so doing I want to plot the shifting place of *landscape art* within a wider *art of landscape*.

Art and Environment

Mid-twentieth-century writings on visual art in geographical texts developed from traditions of work on culture and environment, on the aesthetics of scenery and regional surveying. Many of these writings are concerned with geographical teaching and its place in the curriculum of popular education, and if they paralleled a broader culture of travel and landscape appreciation, they are often set against its more passive and superficial pleasures, to produce alert and active citizens (Matless 1998). The appreciation and practice of art was part of geography's intelligence as an observational discipline, part of a repertoire of techniques, including map reading, lantern slide viewing, landform modeling, and section drawing, to instruct people in picturing the world and participating in it (Ploszajska 1999).

An article in *Geography* on 'The Influence of Geographical Factors upon the Fine Arts' (Robinson 1949) cites surveys of painting, architecture, sculpture, and cultural development to identify those 'material factors of the environment' which shaped artistic style (materials, subjects, symbolism) from rock and soil (pigment, potter's clay, building stone) to relief and climate (Japanese mountain motifs, Van Gogh's palette in Provence, Constable's clouds). The point was to identify geographical character and personality, national, regional and local. This line of thought, especially on climatic influence, can be found in popular texts on both physical geography, for example Gordon Manley's *Climate and the British Scene* (1952), and on the visual arts, notably Nikolaus Pevsner's *The Englishness of English Art* (1956). Originally broadcast as the Reith Lectures on BBC Radio, Pevsner describes his book as an essay in the "geography of art" and the "cultural geography of nations." The émigré author identifies England's "moist climate" along with "restless enterprise" and monosyllabic language ("its prams and perms, its bikes and its mikes") as key influences on a range of cultural artifacts, from Turner's late canvases to textile mills and hammerbeam roofs, which might collectively be identified as 'English art' (Pevsner 1956: 15–25). This national tradition encompassed the products of polite and vernacular society, and if it did not conform to a high cultural canon of art, as seen in museums, palaces and churches, it was an integral part of the cultural environment, inside and out, and a sign of its visual order.

The most sustained and wide-ranging studies of the geography of art were published as a series of articles in *The Geographical Magazine* from 1935 to 1958 during the founding editorship of Michael Huxley. The magazine promoted geographical knowledge (including assigning half its profits to a fund administered by the Royal Geographical Society "for the advancement of exploration and research") within the broad and popular educational field shared by other illustrated magazines of the period. In its mix of cultural enquiry and current affairs *The*

Geographical Magazine was pitched somewhere between *The Studio* and *Picture Post* and, with those magazines, provided an outlet for the revival of interest in landscape art in Britain, which in new work took on a literary, illustrative form (Mellor 1987). The cultural trajectory of *The Geographical Magazine* contrasted with that of the US produced *National Geographic* whose postwar photojournalism was criticized at the time for being frivolous and shallow, in presenting a bedazzlingly colorful tourist world driven by the development of Kodachrome (Bryan 1987: 286–305). Huxley commissioned over 20 generously illustrated essays on the visual arts for *The Geographical Magazine*, mainly painting, and a comparable number on literature, mainly poetry, from both established and new art historians, literary critics, and travel writers, to show "the relationship between art and environment." Some essays explored connections between painters and places, for example Poussin and Normandy, Van Gogh and Provence, Paul Kane and Western Canada, Edward Lear and Albania; others were more generic, such as 'Chinese Painting and the Chinese Landscape,' 'Gardens in Persian Miniature Painting,' 'Animals in Art,' and 'Scandinavian Sculpture.' They were part of a broader commitment to cultural issues, such as this list from the volume for 1946–7: Javanese classical dances, old Swiss maps, English porcelain figures, Egyptians and snakes, Butlin's holiday camps, and the diffusion of Greek culture. There were also at this time a number of essays on postwar reconstruction, particularly nation-building and rebuilding, to which those on art and environment can be connected (for example the article on 'The Albania of Edward Lear' followed one on 'The New Albania'). A key article in this year is 'Art and Environment in Australia' by art historian Bernard Smith, abstracted from his book *Place, Taste and Tradition*, one of the first to address the colonial dimension of art and the diffusion of conventions of landscape painting across contrasting physical and social settings. Smith focuses on the contrasting climatic regimes of native English and native Australian art, maintaining that "a culture does not spring from an environment but from the subtle interaction of the environment upon [*sic*] the activities, needs and ambitions of the people of the country." This expressly ecological perspective is extended to aboriginal art, and to the influence of such art upon Australian painters in a western, modernist tradition. Neglected "both in its homeland and abroad," Australian art offered evidence of a "maturing culture" of a postcolonial nation (Smith 1946–7). Visual art in *The Geographical Magazine* is presented as a positive cultural force, a language of international understanding.

The practice as well as appreciation of landscape art was part of the tradition of geographical education promoted by the Field Studies Council. Formed in 1943 with the intention of promoting a variety of outdoor studies, the Council established centers in contrasting ecological regions of England and Wales, the first at Flatford Mill, the hub of both the painter John Constable's family business and much of his art (Matless 1998: 256–7). Flatford Mill specialized in art practice, including courses on botanical illustration by the painter John Nash in the 1950s, but it was Geoffrey E. Hutchings, the warden of Juniper Hall in the Weald, and one of the founders of the Council, who took the lead in promoting a distinctively geographical art of landscape drawing. Towards the end of his career, Hutchings summarized the method and philosophy in *Landscape Drawing* (Hutchings 1960). Published by Methuen in a portable sketch-book format, this was part of a resurgent market in

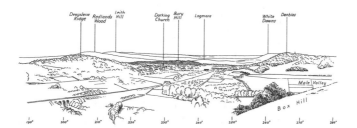

Figure 28.1 Geoffrey Hutchings, *Field Sketch of the Landscape Panorama. A Portion of the View from Precipice Walk, Dolgelly*, from *Landscape Drawing* (1960)

beginners' manuals for amateur artists, such as the books of Adrian Hill, a noted topographical artist of the 1920s, who made a new career on BBC television in the 1950s and 1960s with his *Sketch Club* programs.

In the face of the increasing popularity of photography in geography texts, and what he saw as its limitations as a medium of landscape *interpretation* (as opposed to *reproduction*), Hutchings set out a series of basic graphical guidelines, including advice on materials as well as techniques. Allied to the arts of drawing maps, sections, and profiles, landscape drawing could portray articulations of structure and scenery, land and life, and with annotations, specify details of land use, vegetation cover, and settlement pattern. Geographical drawing did not just reflect an informed knowledge of what is seen, it was itself an act of observation. The book is illustrated with Hutchings' annotated panoramic drawings (figure 28.1), a few by geography students, and also those in a century-old tradition, including examples by Archibald Geikie, A. E. Trueman, Alfred Wainwright, Edward Lear, David Linton, and, above all, John Ruskin. Ruskin's writings provide the rationale for the book's declaration that "learning to draw is, more than anything, a matter of learning how to look at things" (Hutchings 1960: 2). In his Foreword David Linton connected the "contemplative delight in landscape" expressed in landscape drawing more closely to that of "the angler, the farmer, the sailor, the field naturalist, or the geologist" than that of "the poet, painter and musician." Hutchings urged his readers to copy sketches, drawings, and engravings in books and periodicals published between 1880 and 1920. Hutchings acknowledges that the pictorial models he draws on are those "now designated 'traditional' or 'conservative' to distinguish them from what are supposed to be more 'advanced' forms of pictorial expression," but they were those which serve the purpose of popular geographical education (Hutchings 1960: 3). In a 1961 presidential address to the Geographical Association, Hutchings locates landscape drawing in a tradition of geographical field teaching which sought to challenge students who seemed "to accept the rural scene as something inevitable, immutable, earthy, picturesque," and "build up for themselves the geographical picture of the piece of country they were exploring," both in itself and to extend their visual experience. "Without such pictures they could not consider the operation of physical processes, organic relations and human activities" (Hutchings 1962: 3–4).

Disassociated from the pedagogy of field study, the empirical, explanatory register of geographical landscape drawing was displaced in the 1960s into the graphical repertoire of quantitative geography and spatial science. Landscape art reappeared, somewhat marginally, in the literature on human geography in the early 1970s in the study of environmental perception, landscape appraisal, and attitudes to the natural world. A number of works which explored environmental values and landscape tastes considered the visual arts as one source in a range of cultural evidence, including contemporary journalism and psychological experiments. The most specialized studies of landscape painting, by Heathcote (1972) and Rees (1973), are mainly surveys of secondary literature, using art as either a source of facts or expression of values. They drew on a burgeoning art-historical literature on landscape painting, notably Kenneth Clark's *Landscape into Art*, first published in 1949, with its retrospective view of the rise of landscape as an independent and civilized art form. Heathcote's sources, such as Bernard Smith's writings, and choice of examples, including aborginal art, atlases, explorer's sketches, and a multicultural vision of paradise from a 1967 Watchtower Bible, extended the culture of landscape art beyond the boundaries of Clark's book. The most systematic use of landscape art is in Jay Appleton's *The Experience of Landscape* (1975), in which the pictures are presented as evidence for the book's prospect/refuge thesis of landscape experience. If it overlooked, or looked through, the meanings of the paintings as works of art, significant in particular times and places, the book's scope appealed to some art and architectural historians searching for a conceptual framework beyond the confines of art historical connoisseurship (Appleton 1995: 235–55).

Iconographies of Landscape

Studies of the meanings of landscape art, of the way pictures and designs mediate cultural and material worlds through such conventions as perspective and symbolism, developed in the 1980s from an engagement between geography and the humanities. This was conducted both by consciously cultural human geographers, creating or recovering their own disciplinary heritage in the study of landscape aesthetics and the geographical imagination, and through explicitly interdisciplinary exchanges between geographers, art historians, painters, literary critics, archaeologists, and anthropologists. Moreover the field was increasingly presented as one of research, rather than pedagogy, in which artworks were studied in depth, using a range of primary sources, interpretative methodologies, and theoretical perspectives. This was in reaction to a style of writing about art and literature in geography which seemed casual and dilettante, and also to claim the explanatory power and precision conventionally reserved for human geography as a positivist or structuralist social science (Daniels 1985). The claim was strengthened by confidence in a broader warrant, for the currency of culture, space, and imagery in academic research and social life.

If human geography had a cultural turn, considering art among a range of artifacts and probing its representational power, including its material effects, the humanities had a complementary spatial turn, charting fields of visual culture and sites of knowledge and power. Landscape painting became a prime focus of research in art history and literature in Britain, concentrating on its currency in the political ideologies and material transformations of the eighteenth century (Barrell 1980; Bermingham 1986). Setting out the cultural force-field in which landscape was defined as a polite art, in its varied forms from engraving to gardening, involved charting connections between a variety of visual practices, from mapmaking to theater design, and written discourses, from poetry to political economy (Daniels 1999: 1–25). The practice of landscape art, looked down upon for much of the twentieth century as a conservative pursuit, the province of amateur painters and popular commercial artists, one peripheral to the trajectory of modern art, was revived as an art of creative, indeed avant-garde, engagement, and in the process ascribed a modernist pedigree (Wrede & Adams 1991; Alfrey 1993). Informed by contemporary cultural and environmental theory, artists sought to recover places, peoples and dimensions of nature and human nature screened out from traditional landscape painting and damaged by its social consequences (Gandy 1997; Nash 2000). Some did so by harnessing the power of mapping as a creative rather than coercive force (Curnow 1999). The spatial turn of art practice, in various forms from gallery installations to earthworks, and the inclusion of avant-garde art in the expanding domain of 'creative industries,' involved redrawing the boundaries between art and non-art, artistic and everyday space (Miles 1997). Art criticism too, especially in dissenting from the received historical canon, redefined itself geographically, charting sites and networks of creation, display, and consumption, and positions of identity (Pollock 1996; Rogoff 2000). Issues of landscape and imagery emerged in the world beyond the academy and the artist's studio, in the consumer culture of space and image, in the promotional refashioning of places as scenes of national heritage and multinational enterprise.

Denis Cosgrove's *Social Formation and Symbolic Landscape* situates discussions of European and American landscape painting and design within a wider thesis on the "idea of landscape" connecting the realms of art and design with broader currents in culture and society (Cosgrove 1984). The book's formulation of landscape draws on views of art in two widely influential books published in 1972, John Berger's *Ways of Seeing* and Michael Baxendall's *Painting and Experience in Renaissance Italy*. Landscape art is not a main subject of *Ways of Seeing*, indeed is something of an exception to its main thesis about the complicity of oil painting in the culture of western capitalism, but certain genres, such as the landed estate view (infamously exemplified by Gainsborough's conversation piece *Mr and Mrs Andrews*), offer scope for the standpoint of *Social Formation and Symbolic Landscape* that "landscape is a way of seeing the world," a visual ideology which mediated the structural transformations of land and society in western capitalist society. Neither is landscape art a subject of Baxendall's *Painting and Experience in Renaissance Italy*, but this book's approach offered another, more performative dimension to the thesis of *Social Formation and Symbolic Landscape*. Baxendall connects particular styles of Italian Renaissance art to accomplishments in the culture of patrons or buyers, social dancing, religious preaching, and mathematical gauging, and their attendant capacities to touch, hear and see. It is the practice of mathematical gauging, as both a commercial and philosophically speculative practice, which Cosgrove positions as central to the idea of landscape in Renaissance Italy, notably in its conventions of harmony, proportion, and perspective. Renaissance Italy is the main research focus of *Social Formation and Symbolic Landscape*, which is one reason why landscape then and there reaches high levels of cultural sophistication which it seldom regains in the subsequent history charted in the book; but another reason is the influence of two more traditional art-historical writings on the book's historical trajectory, Kenneth Clark's *Landscape into Art* and John Ruskin's *Modern Painters*. Enchanted with the Italian Renaissance, Clark, like Ruskin, regarded landscape, as an art form and mode of vision, as in terminal decline in the modern world, in response to developments in the landscape at large, such as industrial pollution and war, in pictorial media such as photography, in popular taste for tamely picturesque views and in the preoccupations of modern artists for exploring other worlds. The concluding chapter of *Social Formation and Symbolic Landscape* similarly announces the exhaustion of landscape as a creative concept in the twentieth century, a declaration belied by some of the author's own subsequent work in an expanding and differentiating field of study (Cosgrove 1998: xi–xxxvi).

A series of interdisciplinary collections examined the art and culture of landscape in various historical, geographical, and theoretical contexts. A conference on 'Landscape and Painting' hosted by Exeter College of Art and Design, and published in *Landscape Research*, enjoined geographers, art historians, and exhibiting art teachers to focus on work in the English landscape tradition (Howard 1984). Contributors drew attention to the various kinds of knowledge expressed in landscape art, of weather, agriculture, trade, and travel, although the practicing painters present tended to be more reticent about their art as an intellectual pursuit. The conference, published as *The Iconography of Landscape*, edited by Denis Cosgrove and myself, brought together a wider range of scholars and subject matter (Cosgrove & Daniels 1988). While the introduction frames the book from an explicitly art-historical perspective, as the study of symbolic imagery vested in particular cultural contexts, the following essays, including studies of maps, architecture, and ritual as well as painting, adopt a number of approaches to the social power of landscape meaning, including the dramaturgy of Victor Turner and semiotics of Roland Barthes.

What the various studies shared in these collections was an attention to the range of both visual and written material implicated in particular landscape images. I developed this intertextual approach in a series of studies of eighteenth-century landscape paintings (Daniels 1986, 1992, 1993). For example, by situating P. J. de Loutherbourg's *Coalbrookdale by Night* (figure 28.2) in a variety of overlapping discourses and practices, including stagecraft, technical drawing, tourism, apocalyptic Christianity, and rites of freemasonry, a painting which is usually presented as marginal, if not freakish, in accounts of landscape art, is revealed as a significant expression for the cultural moment of its first appearance at the height of the Napoleonic Wars. *Coalbrookdale by Night* reframes a range of polite and popular sensibilities, of knowledge, taste, and accomplishment, available to its audience at its first public exhibition, on the walls of Royal Academy, London, in 1801. In a highly competitive art world which sought to both to raise the cultural register of landscape painting to meet the academic standards of the institution and to make the kind of spectacle to be successful in a commercial market in which paintings competed with a variety of other commodities and entertainments, *Coalbrookdale by Night* redefined landscape art as a genre. The picture's significance has shifted, its meaning mutated. After disappearing from public view for a century and a half, *Coalbrookdale by Night* has been exhibited since 1952 on the walls of the Science

Figure 28.2   P. J. de Loutherbourg, *Coalbrookdale by Night* (1801). Courtesy the Science Museum, London

Museum, London, in a sequence of machines, models, and tableaux charting the history of Britain's 'industrial revolution,' an economic narrative unavailable to its original audience, which the picture is now conventionally seen to illustrate. Historical analysis of the kind undertaken in the essay on the painting can be seen as a form of restoration of the eloquence it once possessed (Daniels, 1993).

Collections published in the 1990s edited by literary historians, anthropologists, and archaeologists included studies of art in extending the scope of landscape beyond Eurocentric scenic definitions (Bender 1993; Mitchell 1994; Hirsch & O'Hanlon 1999). Some contributors sought to move analysis beyond art-historical notions of iconography to consider landscape as a form of representation more closely implicated in the reproduction of social life, as a medium of exchange within and between cultures as well with the natural world. Contributors to *The Anthropology of Landscape* (Hirsch & O'Hanlon 1995) identify an art and aesthetics of landscape in practices concerned with the loci of kinship in western Amazonia, shamanism and nomadic circuits in Mongolia, memory and embodiment in Melanesia, clear views and a primordial sense of place among the Zafimaniry of Madagascar, acoustic spaces in the forest habitats of New Guinea, and dreaming tracks along aboriginal ancestral grids in the western desert of Australia. These regions are sites of encounter with western views of landscape, held by colonizers, developers, missionaries, and, in these writings, by a largely Anglophone cast of scholars concerned to both extend landscape as an interpretative category and to identify cultural differences and conflicts as well as transcultural mixtures and transformations. Christopher Pinney considers the cultural geography of pictorial consumption in an industrial region of central India, in sites from the homes of Untouchables to the gates of a rayon factory, to chart an "inter-ocular field" taking in oleographs of deities in paradisial nature, prurient orientalist color postcards of a 'Bombay Olympia,' murals showing abstract spaces of industrial progress, and calendar prints in the "long-standing genre of women with bicycles" (Pinney 1999; see figure 28.3).

Figure 28.3   Calendar print with the actress Huma Malin (ca. 1985). Publisher unknown

The effect of this ethnographic turn in landscape research has been to estrange views of landscape art in the western landscape tradition. W. J. T. Mitchell identifies more than a projection of European pictorial conventions in *A Distant View of the Bay Islands, New Zealands* (1827), by the English born painter Augustus Earle; in the foreground is a carved Maori figure standing guard over tabooed territory, a recognition of another culture of landscape, a rival expansive culture with its own imperial ambitions (Mitchell 1994). Paintings of sites on the European mainland, internally colonized by metropolitan cultures, set out varied social and moral uses and valuations, including affiliations to cultures concerned with landscape as a physical shaping of land as well as its scenic consumption (Jensen Adams 1994). Even in the culture of urban tourist views, as projected in the topographical prints of nineteenth-century France, are "multiple moments, multiple activities and the intersection of multiple subjectivities." Such prints were, notes Nicholas Green, "commodities predominately produced and circulated through the economic and cultural circuits of the city . . . newspapers, luxury dealers, exhibitions, and boulevard entertainments," and looking at such pictures was part of a cultural ritual, no less than that which surrounds viewing a modern British TV soap opera like *Coronation Street*, "putting the tea on, getting the kids to bed, renegotiating domestic relations" (Green 1999). An exhibition and catalogue *At Home with Constable's Cornfield* (figure 28.4), considers the transformation of Constable's painting into a cultural icon through its reproduction on a variety of domestic goods, including wallpaper, firescreens, tea trays, thimbles, and decorative plates, and the meaning they have

Figure 28.4 From Colin Painter's exhibition, "At Home with Constable's Cornfield," National Gallery, London, 1996. Courtesy the artist

for the owners. Residents in south London tell their stories of the significance of the picture for individual and family life, through various remembered or imagined worlds, from an ancestry in English agricultural labor to a Creole childhood in Sierra Leone (Painter 1996).

Studies of landscape art since the 1980s have engaged with the identity politics of the period, around the cultural predicaments of nation, ethnicity, gender, and sexuality, and, if less assertively, social class. Issues of landscape and national identity emerged in a world in which accepted, state-defined forms of nationality were put into question by a series of developments: the globalization of institutions, the dissolution of the Soviet Union, the expansion of the European Union, the devolutionary pressures in the United Kingdom, the cultural confidence of formerly colonized peoples. Along with the work of writers, composers, architects, and planners, the works of landscape painters have been analyzed for their contribution to the making, remaking, and unmaking of national identity. Analyses focused on the way pictures and painters have been enlisted by various political interests, as well as the intentions surrounding their original production.

A theme issue of *Landscape Research* explored the anxieties, ambiguities, and cultural limits revealed in relations of landscape art and national identity, especially as the homelands of others were annexed in identity myths (Gruffudd et al. 1991). Paintings of north African deserts helped envision France's Second Empire: images of barrenness and ruins, histories of past fertility and prosperity under ancient empires. A modern empire might restore the landscape to its former glory, but, no less, the very wildness of the desert, its silences and vast horizons, might redeem the materialism of modern France, its spiritual decay. Such heroic visions could come aground – grandiose French schemes of settlement collapsed in the sands of the Sahara (Heffernan 1991). My book *Fields of Vision* concentrates on the work of painters and designers which had featured in exhibitions in the 1980s, and had been incorporated as part of its heritage industry; it explored the historicity of landscape conventions in England and the United States, both in their development and diffusion since the eighteenth century and their intersection with the narrative codes of national development (Daniels 1993). In *Landscape and Englishness* David Matless considers how the culture of landscape implicated a variety of material concerned with twentieth-century English identity; the art of landscape was a visceral as well as visual matter, conditioned by codes of physical conduct, by, in a phrase of the time, "an art of right living" (Matless 1998). In an issue of *Ecumene* on landscape art and Russian nationality, John McCannon explores the primeval landscapes of Nicholas Roerich, including the contribution of his stage designs, along with Stravinsky's music and Nijinsky's choreography to the 1913 premiere of the Ballet Russe's *The Rite of Spring*. After 1914, as Roerich migrated between India and the United States, so his mystic art was progressively detached from its Russian locus, loosened from its nationalist enclosure, even its topographical contour, and released into realms beyond the mundane world (McCannon 2000).

Geographical studies of contemporary art in Britain and Ireland have explored its critical engagement with landscape conventions, especially the pastoral nexus of body and land, using interviews with artists to extend the sources of interpretation. Phil Kinsman examines the place of race in the photographic works of the Guyanese-born artist Ingrid Pollard, notably the series *Pastoral Interludes* (1984), which, in image and text, project her own uneasy, sometimes fearful, experiences visiting idyllic English countryside through confronting the racist conjunctions of black figures and rural landscape and their location in a broader world of empire and diaspora. In its very making, Pollard's work is part of a broader project of critique and restitution, and informed by the contemporary cultural studies discourse of 'otherness,' 'difference,' and 'marginality'; the interpretative challenge, as with all theoretically conditioned artwork, is to both acknowledge this and interpret the work in terms of other frames of reference, in the case of Pollard's through broader historical and geographical issues of access to the iconography and actuality of landscape (Kinsman 1995). The interview with the artist underpinning David Matless and George Revill's field-based study of the Yorkshire-born land sculptor Andy Goldsworthy turns into a dialogue in which the glossary of physical geography is tentatively offered and accepted as part of the framework of meaning and making (figure 28.5). An art esteemed for its ecological integrity is analyzed for its incongruities, as emplaced art underpinned by property rites, reproduced as artwork through photography, and made on-site through a self-consciously solo

Figure 28.5   Andy Goldsworthy, circular drystone wall, Barfil Farm, Dumfriesshire, 1993. Photo courtesy George Revill

performance, characteristics it shares with a longer tradition of rural romantic landscape art (Matless & Revill 1995). Catherine Nash interprets the imagery of erotic landscape in works by Dianne Bayliss and Pauline Cummins in terms of debates on pornography and reproductive rights, and feminist approaches to issues of vision and space, gender and representation. Recuperating the pastoral tradition of libidinal landscape, of masculine viewer and feminine view, Bayliss and Cummins figure a male torso as a topographical site of sexual desire, Bayliss in *Abroad*, a photograph which elides the contours of body and land, Cummins in *Inis t'Oirr/ Aran Dance*, a slide and sound installation which shows an Aran sweater on a male body and describes a sexual encounter in the narrative language of knitting, "I'll spin you a yarn. / I'll weave you a tale" (Nash 1996). *Innis t'Oirr* is included in an exhibition Nash curated, *Irish Geographies*. A set of contemporary works by Irish artists which revision images of landscape and Irish nationality across a wide field of genres and media is interpreted in terms of a cosmopolitan human geography in which senses of place and identity are articulated through a consciousness of global movement and interconnection, a culture of both routes and roots (Nash 1997).

Landscape art has long been produced to commemorate and promote projects of commercial or social development, either as public commissions or private speculations. Two studies explore site-specific contemporary artworks in this tradition, both part of projects of 'postindustrialization.' George Revill examines a woodland sculpture trail commissioned to interpret transformations in the Forest of Dean, both commemorating the coal-mining and craft heritage of the region and promoting a new, mixed woodland economy of tourism and commercial forestry. The work is caught up in a wider web of complications, the legacy of forests as cultural landscapes as well as the conflicting demands of the present (Revill 1994). Tim Hall considers discourses of industrialism surrounding the site and symbolism of fiberglass sculptures installed outside the International Convention Centre, Birmingham, as

part of its urban regeneration program. Birmingham-born, Paris-based Raymond
Mason was commissioned by the City Council to produce *Forward*, a sculpture portraying sturdy artisans, representing the idea of industry as industrious individuals,
not an ensemble of mills and machinery, an iconography which draws on local narratives of industrial pride as well as national projections of industrial reorganization (Hall 1997). Perhaps it is a measure of the maturity of geographical studies of
art and material development that there are now no less than four successive analyses of one landscape painting and its place in urban redevelopment, moreover a
picture which has largely escaped the attention of art historians. Niels M. Lund's
The Heart of the Empire (1904), a panoramic view of the city of London from the
Royal Exchange, was originally purchased for the Lord Mayor and later donated
to the Corporation of London; it resurfaced in the 1980s as a rallying point for con-
servationists in disputes over the redevelopment of the site in its view, Bank Junc-
tion. Studies by Daniels (1994: 11–17), Jacobs (1996: 38–69), Driver and Gilbert
(1998), and Black (2000) variously interpret its vision of the city and empire in
terms of its phases of cultural significance and narratives of the city's rebuilding as
a financial center.

The Place of Art

Landscape art is now an established source for cultural geography, part of its repertoire of representations. The capacity and complexity of landscape's field of vision
has been recognized, and the way it encodes many forms and dimensions of geographical experience and imagination, many ways of perceiving, knowing, living in,
and moving through the world. There is more scope for connecting this world within
the frame of a work with the world beyond, with the geographies of creation,
display, reproduction, patronage, and exchange, say through the study of a particular region (Cosgrove 1993) or artistic career (Daniels 1999). There are opportunities for intensively researched case studies of places of landscape art, say artists'
colonies or quarters, and sites which are subject to sustained campaigns of portrayal
and design. Moreover these might be places off the cultural beaten track, *terra
incognita* which offer the opportunity for redrawing the art of landscape (Alfrey
2001).

Most geographical studies of visual art since the 1980s have operated with interpretative methodologies, largely iconographic and ethnographic analysis, applied to
finished works. New initiatives involving collaborations between academic geographers and practicing artists rework the art of landscape as a creative pursuit and
set in train exchanges between making and meaning. If techniques of field sketch-
ing and landscape drawing have disappeared from the geographical curriculum,
recent computer-based skills of spatial representation have opened a new meeting
ground for art and geography through the creation of objects, multimedia catalogues, and websites. A recent joint venture focuses on Margate, a declining English
seaside resort, "the other side of the coin of frantic urbanism valorized in much
twentieth century art." Pairings of five artists and five geographers address shared
themes of representation, Survey, Function, Networks, Landcover, and 3D Model
(figure 28.6), "multi-layered representations" which "begin a new process of understanding" (Hampson & Priestnall 2001).

Figure 28.6 Derek Hampson, *The Death of O* (oil on canvas); Gary Priestnall, *Brightness, Texture and Elevation* (digital print), from *Hawley Square* 2001

REFERENCES

Alfrey, N. 1993: Undiscovered country. In N. Alfrey et al., eds., *Towards a New Landscape*. London: Bernard Jacobson Ltd., 16–23.

Alfrey, N. 2001: *Trentside*. Nottingham: The Djangoly Gallery, University of Nottingham.

Appleton, J. 1975: *The Experience of Landscape*. Chichester: John Wiley.

Appleton, J. 1995: *The Experience of Landscape*, rev. ed. Chichester: John Wiley.

Barrell, J. 1980: *The Dark Side of the Landscape: The Rural Poor in English Painting 1730–1840*. Cambridge: Cambridge University Press.

Bender, B., ed. 1993: *Landscape: Politics and Perspectives*. Oxford: Berg.

Bermingham, A. 1986: *Landscape and Ideology: The English Rustic Tradition 1740–1860*. Berkeley: University of California Press.

Bishop, P. 1995: *An Archetypal Constable: National Identity and the Geography of Nostalgia*. London: Athlone.

Black, Ian S. 2000: 'The Heart of the Empire': bank headquarters in the City of London, 1919–1939. *Art History* 22, 153–66.

Bryan, C. D. B. 1987: *The National Geographic Society: 100 Years of Adventure and Discovery*. Oxford: Phaidon.

Copley, S. and Garside, P., eds. 1994: *The Politics of the Picturesque: Literature, Landscape and Aesthetics since 1770*. Cambridge: Cambridge University Press.

Cosgrove, D. E. 1984: *Social Formation and Symbolic Landscape*. London and Sydney: Croom Helm.

Cosgrove, D. 1993: *The Palladian Landscape: Geographical Change and its Cultural Representation in Sixteenth-Century Italy*. Leicester: Leicester University Press.

Cosgrove, D. E. 1998: *Social Formation and Symbolic Landscape*, 2nd ed. Madison: University of Wisconsin Press.

Cosgrove, D. E., ed. 1999: *Mappings*. London: Reaktion.

Cosgrove, D. E. and Daniels, S., eds. 1988: *The Iconography of Landscape: Essays on the Symbolic Representation, Design and Use of Past Environments*. Cambridge: Cambridge University Press.

Crouch, D. and Toogood, M. 1999: Everyday abstraction: geographical knowledge in the art of Peter Lanyon. *Ecumene* 6, 72–89.

Curnow, W. 1999: Mapping and the expanded field of contemporary art. In D. Cosgrove, ed., *Mappings*. London: Reaktion, 253–68.

Daniels, S. 1985: Arguments for a humanistic geography. In R. Johnston, ed., *The Future of Geography*. London: Methuen.

Daniels, S. 1986: The implications of industry: Turner and Leeds. *Turner Studies* 6, 10–18.

Daniels, S. 1989: Marxism, culture and the duplicity of landscape. In R. Peet and N. Thrift, eds., *New Models in Geography* 2, 196–220.

Daniels, S. 1992: Love and death across an English garden: Constable's paintings of his family's flower and kitchen gardens. *Huntington Library Quarterly* 55, 433–58.

Daniels, S. 1993: Loutherbourg's chemical theatre: 'Coalbrookdale by Night.' In J. Barrell, ed., *Painting and the Politics of Culture: New Essays on British Art 1700–1850*. Oxford: Oxford University Press, 195–230.

Daniels, S. 1994: *Fields of Vision: Landscape Imagery and National Identity in England and the United States*. Cambridge: Polity.

Daniels, S. 1996: The politics of landscape in European art. In S. West, ed., *Guide to Art*. London: Bloomsbury, 96–108.

Daniels, S. 1999: *Humphry Repton: Landscape Gardening and the Geography of Georgian England*. New Haven: Yale University Press.

Driver, F. and Gilbert, D. 1998: Heart of empire? Landscape, space and performance in imperial London. *Environment and Society D: Society and Space* 16, 11–28.

Gandy, M. 1997: Contradictory modernities: conceptions of nature in the art of Joseph Beuys
and Gerhard Richter. *Annals of the Association of American Geographers* 87, 636–59.

Gleason, J. 2000: 'Russkii inok': the spiritual landscape of Mikhail Nesterov. *Ecumene* 7,
299–312.

Green, N. 1999: Looking at the landscape: class formation and the visual. In E. Hirsch and
M. O'Hanlon, eds., *The Anthropology of Landscape*. Oxford: Clarendon Press, 31–42.

Gruffudd, P., Daniels, S., and Bishop, P., eds. 1991: 'Landscape and National Identity,' special
issue of *Landscape Research*, vol. 16.

Hall, T. 1997: Images of industry in the postindustrial city: Raymond Mason and Birmingham. *Ecumene* 4, 46–68.

Hampson, D. and Priestnall, G., eds. 2001: *Hawley Square*. Margate: Community Pharmacy
Gallery.

Heathcote, R. L. 1972: The artist as geographer: landscape painting as a source for geographical research. *Proceedings, Royal Geographical Society of Australasia, South
Australian Branch* 73, 1–21.

Heffernan, M. 1991: The desert in French Orientalist painting during the nineteenth century.
Landscape Research 16, 37–42.

Hirsch, E. and O'Hanlon, M., eds. 1995: *The Anthropology of Landscape: Perspectives on
Place and Space*. Oxford: Clarendon Press.

Howard, P., ed. 1984: 'Landscape and Painting,' theme issue of *Landscape Research*, vol. 9.

Hutchings, G. E. 1960: *Landscape Drawing*. London: Methuen.

Hutchings, G. E. 1962: Geographical field teaching. *Geography* 47, 1–14.

Jacobs, J. M. 1996: *Edge of Empire: Postcolonialism and the City*. London: Routledge.

Jensen Adams, A. 1994: Competing communities in the "Great Bog of Europe." In W. J. T.
Mitchell, ed., *Landscape and Power*. Chicago: University of Chicago Press, 35–76.

Kinsman, P. 1995: Landscape, race and national identity. *Area* 27, 300–10.

Matless, D. 1998: *Landscape and Englishness*. London: Reaktion.

Matless, D. and Revill, G. 1995: A solo ecology: the erratic art of Andy Goldsworthy.
Ecumene 2, 423–48.

McCannon, J. 2000: In search of primeval Russia: stylistic evolution in the landscapes of
Nicholas Roerich. *Ecumene* 7, 271–98.

Mellor, D., ed. 1987: *A Paradise Lost: The Neo-Romantic Imagination In Britain 1935–55*.
London: Lund Humphries.

Miles, M. 1997: *Art, Space and the City*. London: Routledge.

Mitchell, W. J. T., ed. 1994: *Landscape and Power*. Chicago: University of Chicago Press.

Nash, C. 1996: Reclaiming vision: looking at landscape and the body. *Gender, Place and
Culture* 3, 149–69.

Nash, C. 1997: *Irish Geographies: Six Contemporary Artists*. Nottingham: Djangoly Art
Gallery, University of Nottingham.

Nash, C. 2000: 'Breaking New Ground' (Tate Modern Special), *Tate* 21, 60–5.

Painter, C. 1996: *At Home with Constable's Cornfield*. London: National Gallery.

Pevsner, N. 1956: *The Englishness of English Art*. Harmondsworth: Penguin.

Pinney, C. 1999: Moral topophilia: the signification of landscape in Indian oleographs. In
E. Hirsch and M. O'Hanlon, eds., *The Anthropology of Landscape*. Oxford: Clarendon
Press.

Ploszajska, T. 1999: *Geographical Education, Empire and Citizenship: Geographical
Teaching and Learning in English Schools 1870–1944*. Historical Geography Research
Series 35. London: Historical Geography Research Group.

Pollock, G., ed. 1996: *Generations and Geographies in the Visual Arts*. London: Routledge.

Pugh, S., ed. 1990: *Reading Landscape: Country–City–Capital*. Manchester: Manchester University Press.

Rees, R. 1973: Geography and landscape painting: a neglected field. *Scottish Geographical Magazine* 89.

Revill, G. 1994: Promoting the Forest of Dean: art, ecology and the industrial landscape. In J. R. Gold and S. V. Ward, eds., *Place Promotion: the Use of Publicity and Marketing to Sell Towns and Regions*. Chichester: John Wiley, 233–45.

Robinson, H. 1949: The influence of geographical factors upon the fine arts. *Geography* 34, 33–4.

Rogoff, I. 2000: *Terra Infirma: Geography's Visual Culture*. London and New York: Routledge.

Smith, B. 1946–7: Art and environment in Australia. *The Geographical Magazine* 19, 398–409.

Wrede, S. and Adams, W. H., eds. 1991: *Denatured Visions: Landscape and Culture in the Twentieth Century*. New York: Museum of Modern Art.

Part VI   Colonial and Postcolonial Geographies

Chapter 29

Imperial Geographies

Daniel Clayton

Introduction

Wherever we look in the current annals of geography – in geography books, journals, postgraduate projects, and teaching curricula – we find palpable evidence of a postcolonial critical spirit. This spirit is perhaps most evident in a recent range of work on geography's historical ties with empire. But we find it more broadly in geographers' critical embrace of the postcolonial world in which they work – a world, Edward Said (2001: 65) has remarked, in which the white-male-Eurocentric intellectual establishment has been beset by "the non-European, genderized, decolonized, and decentered energies and currents of our times." These diverse 'postcolonial' energies and currents have made western scholars more sensitive to other voices and claims to difference, made work on the imperial/colonial past a highly marketable critical product, and made an academic home for themselves in the interdisciplinary field of postcolonial studies. This chapter sketches their impact on geography. It considers aspects of the recent 'postcolonial turn' in geographical inquiry. What happens when a discipline like geography starts to take its imperial heritage into account? And how have geographers wrestled with the postcolonial question of what it means to work 'after empire' and 'in the knowledge of' colonialism?

The following overview is inevitably partial and provisional. The geographical literature on questions of colonialism and postcolonialism is now enormous, and there is no consensus about the appropriate aims and methods of postcolonial analysis in geography or any other discipline. The chapter focuses on a body of geographical research that is ostensibly concerned with the imperial/colonial past, and on a limited set of postcolonial ideas (largely those that have had the most direct bearing on geographers' work).[1] I will start by situating geographers' work in an encompassing intellectual context and highlighting postcolonialism's trademark concern with the relations between culture and power, and then outline how work on the historical and cultural geographies of colonialism and empire has developed over the last 10 years.[2] I try to capture the eclecticism of research in this fast-growing area of geographical inquiry and guide the reader to a representative range of work. But I also tease out a number of distinctive themes, orientations, and debates in the geographical literature, and offer a partial evaluation at the end of the ways in which geographers' work can be called 'postcolonial.'

Postcolonialism and Culture

Postcolonialism can be characterized as an 'ameliorative' and 'therapeutic' project that is concerned with the impact of colonialism on colonizing and colonized peoples and places, and reexamines imperial/colonial history in the light of contemporary realities and especially the predicaments of decolonization (see Gandhi 1998: 1–15; Gregory 2000a). It is a hybrid and heterogeneous project – not least because it incorporates work from a wide range of disciplines and theoretical positions – giving us more differentiated and contested pictures of the making of modernity and the west. For some, the critical value of postcolonialism lies in its disclosure that colonization is a constitutive rather than tangential feature of western culture (see Hall 1996: 246). For others, its value lies in its attempt to question the postcolonial desire to forget the past and the west, to come to terms with the material legacies and psychological scars of colonialism, and to find new ways of talking about cultural difference (see Brennan 1997; Fanon 1963; Nandy 1983). Postcolonial thinkers and scholars have sought to debunk Eurocentric and historicist schemes of thought that configure the west as the self-contained fount of modernity and sovereign subject/center of world history. They point to the mutual (albeit asymmetrical and hierarchical) constitution of metropole and colony, and seek to critically revise understanding of the west (and historically Europe) in such a way that the Other can be treated as a subject rather than object of knowledge (see Blaut 1993; Hall 2000; Pratt 1992; Young 1991). But postcolonialism does not simply amount to an attack on western thought and the racism explicit in imperial/colonial projects and implicit in the current practices of western governments, corporations, and the media. It also extends a long history of anticolonial thought and activism, and is characterized by a new critical vigilance towards the successes and failures of anticolonialism before and after independence (see Young 2001). Postcolonial thinkers have been critical of the postindependence search for national and cultural origins and identities that are untainted by the experience of colonization. They insist that we will not find a critical position from outside of the historical configurations of colonialism and modernity from which a postcolonial society, discipline, or new global order will naturally arise (see Chatterjee 1999; Prakash 1999). As Gyan Prakash (1996: 189) insists, postcolonial projects can only work "*in medias res*" – from inside a story about colonialism that has not ended.

Postcolonialism imbues 'culture' with special significance. The momentum of western power is now deemed to lie as much in the 'cultures of imperialism and colonialism' – in language and knowledge, texts and discourses, images and representations, and the iconography of power – as in the political economy of imperial expansion and colonial incursion. There is no consensus about the conception of culture that shapes or best suits postcolonialism, largely, perhaps, because it is recognized that colonization set in train both a complex intertwining of communities, histories, places and geographies, and a long global history of conflictual cultural interaction. But one thing is clear: that we should resist totalizing and superorganic views of culture that cocoon 'the cultural' from other dimensions of human discourse. Rather, culture is taken to be an intrinsic and relational dimension of identity and difference, and a concept that focuses our critical attention on the uneven and unequal production and circulation of meaning. As Arjun Appadurai (1996: 13) suggests, culture is "a pervasive dimension of human discourse that exploits difference to generate diverse conceptions of group identity." Or as Derek Gregory (2001a: 130) notes, culture is seen "a series of representations, practices and performances that enter fully into the *constitution* of the world."

Postcolonialism's characteristic cultural emphases reflect its disciplinary origins in the fields of literary and cultural studies, and anthropology. More profoundly, however, this recourse to culture stems from the recognition that the break up of European colonial empires did not place decolonized nations on an equal cultural footing with the west. Western dominance and hegemony changed but continued. Political decolonization needed to be followed by a process of cultural and intellectual decolonization both inside and outside the west (see Pieterse & Parekh 1995). There needed to be a decolonization of thought and knowledge, and as Robert Young (2001: 65) notes, this necessarily involved western academic disciplines and "a decentring of the intellectual sovereignty and dominance of Europe, the critique of Eurocentrism." Postcolonialism seeks to undo what Ranajit Guha (1996: ix) has called the "government of colonialist knowledge" that has outlived empire and now infuses postcolonial politics. Postcolonialism is thus centrally concerned with the means by which the west arrogated to itself the authority to grant (and deny) cultural respect to others, and to decide on what counts as truth and knowledge (and what does not) (Seshadri-Crooks 1995). Or as one influential postcolonial thinker, Homi Bhabha (1994: 239) puts it, "the question of ethical and cultural judgement, central to the processes of subject formation and the objectification of social knowledge, is challenged at its 'cognitivist' core."

One crucial postcolonial tactic has been to recover and challenge the ways in which western dominance has revolved around binary (essentialist, dichotomous, and exclusionary) understandings of identity and difference. There has been a flood of postcolonial work on the binaries of center and periphery, civilization and savagery, colonizer and colonized, modernity and tradition, and so on, that drew material and imaginative lines of difference between colonizing and colonized cultures, and set peoples and places apart. Work in this direction received a decisive impetus from the writings of Frantz Fanon (1963: 37), who characterized colonialism as "a world divided into compartments," and latterly from Edward Said's *Orientalism* (1978), which examines how the Europe stereotyped the Orient as its 'inferior' and eternal Other, and emphasizes the west's propensity to demean and dominate the Other through language and knowledge. For many the power of Said's analysis lay in his representation of the Orient as a sort of 'distorting mirror' in which Europe defined and championed itself (Washbrook 1999: 597), and his account of the object- and reality-constituting power of discourse (a term he borrowed from Foucault). *Orientalism* inspired a new generation of scholars to examine how imperialism hinged on the production and codification of knowledge about different peoples and places, and on discursive strategies of cultural projection, incorporation, debasement and erasure (see Brennan 2000; Prakash 1994; Walia 2001). Indeed, the term postcolonialism is commonly associated with the critical analysis of colonial discourses – with the idea that imperialism works as a discourse of domination, and that colonialism works as a system of 'epistemic violence' (see Childs & Williams 1997). But Said's influence does not end here. Geographers have been particularly drawn to his acutely spatial sensibilities and the spatial turn he has nurtured in postcolonial inquiry – to his use of the term "imaginative geography" to capture the dichotomizing operations of colonial discourse, and his definition of imperialism as an incessant "struggle over geography" (Said 1993: 7; also see Gregory 1995; Jarosz 1992).

Critical energies have been focused on the universal–stable–immutable and diverse–precarious–contingent character of colonial discourses, and how post-colonial thinkers and scholars position themselves in relation to these poles of interpretation. Thinkers such as Homi Bhabha and Gayatri Spivak (1999) have heightened critical awareness of the ambivalences and contradictions inherent in the colonial psyche and the subject positions authored by colonialism. Nicholas Thomas's *Colonialism's Culture* (1994) is another important reference, in part because of the complaints that the book airs about postcolonialism. Thomas complains that postcolonial theory and scholarship fixates on the west, the agency (and anxieties) of the colonizer, and the analysis of texts; that it tends to over-generalize about colonial discourse and 'the' colonial condition; and that it is much too tightly focused on the colonial experience of particular parts of the world (India looms large in much postcolonial theory). This body of theory is ill-equipped to identify the specific sources of power in different colonial contexts because it is overcommitted to the configuration of colonialism as a transhistorical totality, and it tends to treat colonial discourse as "impervious to active marking and refor-mulation by the 'Other.'" Thomas sees colonialism as grounded, localized and partial yet encompassed by more widely held and enduring ideas and systems of representation (Thomas 1994: 2–4, 105–6). He captures a set of questions and con-cerns that have come to haunt the field of postcolonial studies (see e.g. Parry 1997; Bhabha 1994: 21–3; Spivak 1999). Postcolonialism runs a fine line between sub-verting and aggrandizing the grip of the colonial past on the present by placing colo-nialism too securely in the past or placing the colonial past too firmly in the present. As Prakash (1994: 1476) insists, we should acknowledge that postcolonialism's "critical apparatus does not enjoy a panoptic distance from colonial history but exists as an aftermath . . . [and] inhabits the structures of western domination that it seeks to undo."

The geographical literature to which we will now turn has developed in critical dialogue with these postcolonial agendas and concerns. We can find in geographers' work a similar engagement with questions of western intellectual sovereignty and colonial discourse, and a similar concern with the issues that Thomas raises. Yet different disciplines were not implicated in empire in the same way and do not have identical postcolonial motives and concerns. Geographers have tailored postcolo-nialism to their own interests and ends.

The Return of Empire to Geography

Geographers have a longstanding critical interest in questions of imperialism and colonialism (see e.g. Sauer 1938), but geographical research on such questions started to gain new intellectual momentum in the late 1980s through revisionist work on the history of geography and wider theoretical surveys of the discipline. On the one hand, there emerged a new historiographical literature that treated geography as a historically contingent, socially constructed, and power-laden set of concepts, knowledges, and practices rather than as an immutable, autonomous or impartial knowledge domain and field of study. On the other hand, postcolonial theory, and its complex articulation with Marxism, feminism, poststructuralism, postmodernism, and cultural studies, was used to raise important questions about what constituted a 'critical' human geography.

Some geographers sought to show that geography has long been a plural and contested discipline and discourse, and started to reroute the history of the subject through the power-laden context of empire. In his monumental study, *The Geographical Tradition* (1992: 352–8), David Livingstone argued that geography has meant "different things to different people at different times and in different places," and that it "has frequently cast itself as the aide-de-camp to militarism and imperialism." What Felix Driver (1992) dubbed "geography's empire" can be traced back to the fifteenth-century origins of European overseas expansion, and reached its climax at the end of the nineteenth century, when geography came into professional existence in tandem with the promulgation of imperialism as a 'civilizing mission.' This recourse to geography's imperial past did not just amount to a process of historical retrieval that would keep the discipline's imbroglio with empire at a comfortable distance from the present. From the start, geographers aimed to politicize as well as pluralize their understandings of 'the' geographical tradition. Driver (1992: 26), for instance, surmised that "the writings of our predecessors were so saturated with colonial and imperial themes that to problematize their role is to challenge the status of the modern discipline," and suggested that this was precisely what geographers needed to do if they were "to exploit present intellectual and political opportunities." He was referring to the critical opportunities opened up by Said's work, and that of other postcolonial scholars who paid attention to issues of geography and spatiality (e.g. Carter 1987; Mitchell 1988).

Other geographers became mindful of the contemporary theoretical implications of postcolonialism. There were pleas for geographers to see themselves as "situated actors engaged in the political work of representation and the production of knowledge" (Katz 1992: 496), to attend to their discipline's protocols of inclusion and exclusion (Rose 1995), and to "learn from other regions" (Slater 1992). Such pleas to rework – or decenter – geography's conventional 'maps of meaning' were wrapped up with the wider formation of the 'new cultural geography' within British and North American geography, and its concern with identity politics and place-based imaginations and practices. And postcolonialism can be seen as part of what Livingstone (2000a: 7) has described as a more general – postfoundationalist – "retaliation of the situated" against western protocols of science and objective knowledge that beset the western academy. But it was postcolonial theory that encouraged geographers to highlight the issue of geography's Eurocentric moorings. Gregory (1994: 165-203), for example, pointed to the incredible arrogance built into the idea that geography finds its *raison d'être* in the study of the variable character of the *earth's* surface, and insisted that geographers are the "creatures and creators of situated knowledges." Geographers, he noted, knew remarkably little about large parts of the earth, studied the world according to the mensural standards of the west, and blithely assumed that their models could be freely exported overseas with little modification (also see Gregory 1998). Postcolonial theory also helped geographers to see that some of their discipline's founding and characteristic practices – exploration, mapping, surveying, landscape reconnaissance, and spatial classification and planning – had been placed at the service of empire and honed in colonial contexts.

In these theoretical attempts to come to terms with the discipline's history, the imperial/colonial past was not simply construed as a revamped site of substantive investigation. A critical focus on geography's imperial habits of mind and colonizing gestures was also deemed to be a theoretical necessity. The recognition that colonialism casts a long shadow over geography's intellectual heritage – with some of the leading lights in the discipline's cognitive and institutional development (for example, Humboldt and Mackinder) holding the imperial torch – raised acutely epistemological questions about the nature and critical purpose of geographical inquiry. And as Jonathan Crush (1994) diagnosed, it was by no means clear what an alternative postcolonial geography might look like. If geography is a *quintessentially* Eurocentric and colonizing science, then would not the creation of a 'postcolonial' geography be an ironic – and perhaps even self-defeating – gesture? Would it needlessly refocus attention on the bumptious and aggressive aspects of geography's past – on geographical projects and practices that geographers no longer found acceptable, or on what many had simply forgotten about (see Barnett 1995)? Was work on geography's past that found its critical feet by dredging up onerous representations of foreign peoples and places meant to constitute some sort of enlightenment for the discipline? Were geographers documenting an injurious disciplinary past in order to demonstrate that 'we' now do things that are less harmful to others? Such questions have made 'the return of empire' of geography a complex and vexed affair.

Geographical research on the imperial/colonial past has proceeded apace from these kinds of critical coordinates, and we now have an expansive field of study. To list just 9 of the most prominent streams of research (though not in any order of importance), there have been surges of work on: (i) the 'imaginative geographies' and 'spaces of knowledge' that shaped colonialism and empire (e.g. Driver & Yeoh 2000; Livingstone 2002); (ii) the spatial construction of imperial/colonial subjectivities (e.g. Blunt 1994; Kearns 1997); (iii) imperial and colonial cities (Driver & Gilbert 1999; Yeoh 1996); (iv) how metropolitan and colonial spaces and landscapes were gendered, sexualized and racialized (e.g. Blunt & Rose 1994; Phillips 1997); (v) the links between cartography and empire (e.g. Edney 1997; Clayton 2000b); (vi) processes of environmental change in colonial settings, and the colonial production of nature (e.g. Head 2000; Gregory 2002); (vii) the articulation of global imperial networks and local colonial geographies (e.g. Lester 2001); (viii) questions of travel and transculturation (e.g. Duncan & Gregory 1999; McEwan 1998, 2000); and (ix) the making of regional colonial geographies and their relations with the present (e.g. Harris 1997; Morin & Berg 2001). This prodigious literature is not easily reviewed, and in some ways resists synthesis. Its substantive eclecticism mirrors the historical-geographical diversity of colonialism and empire, and its conceptual pluralism bears witness to postcolonialism's conceptual heterogeneity. However, it is possible to identify some distinct cleavages, and stock themes and problems, in the literature. In what follows, I will draw a distinction between a body of work that has a metropolitan and/or disciplinary focus and a more diffuse literature that deals with the colonial margins of empire – ultimately (though at the risk of great oversimplification) a distinction between work on imperialism and work on colonialism (see note 2). I will also remark on geographers' fraught attempts to decenter and decolonize their discipline, and attend to 'other' voices.

'Geography's Empire'

Over the last 10 years historical-cultural work on the links between geography and empire has grown and become one the chief manifestations of postcolonialism in the discipline. Landmark collections such as *Geography and Empire* (Godlewska & Smith 1994) and *Geography and Imperialism* (Bell, Butlin, & Heffernan 1995), and a gamut of articles and monographs, explore the imperial/colonial roles played by diverse producers and arbiters of geographical knowledge. The work of explorers, cartographers, surveyors, field scientists, geographical societies and professional geographers, which has long played a prominent role in narratives of the history of the discipline, have all been brought under the critical spotlight (see e.g. Bowd & Clayton 2003; Ryan 1995; Staum 2000; Withers 1995). So too have the geographical images, knowledges, and practices generated by a much wider range of agents, texts, and institutions of empire – artists, photographers, colonial administrators, merchant adventurers, geography school projects, adventure fiction, museums and exhibitions (see e.g. Braun 2002; Maddrell 1998; Myers 1998; Ogborn 2002; Ploszajska 1996; Phillips 1997; Ryan 1997).

Geographical discourses and practices that were once viewed as enlightened and disinterested are now seen as tools of material and intellectual dispossession, and stories of the west's triumphal and uncontested passage around the world are now told as halting and sometimes haunting tales of human struggle. Many geographers have used geographers' involvement in empire to remind us that 'geography' literally means 'earth-writing.' Special attention has been drawn to the images of 'backward' and 'pristine' space awaiting the arrival of modernity and the transformative hand of the west that pervade the intertwined 'earth-writing' projects of geography and imperialism. Great interest has also been shown in the 'spaces of knowledge' (e.g. the field and the study) in which imperial/colonial meanings were molded and disseminated. Geographers stress the practical and embodied nature of geography's empire. Their critical narratives point up the effort it took to draw geographical order out of chaos – to travel, collect, map, represent, govern, survive, and draw material and imaginative lines on the ground that both separated 'us' from 'them' and brought different peoples into anxious proximity (see Gregory 2000b). To resort to postcolonial lingo, this range of work seeks to expose and challenge the ways in which geography arrogated to itself the power to create and sustain some geographical knowledges and truths, and denigrate and block the emergence of other stories (see Withers 1999; Heffernan 2001).

Livingstone (1991, 1999, 2002), for example, discusses the formation of "moral geographies" of racial superiority that revolved around scientific observations and truth claims about the links between climate, virtue, and social development. Climate, particularly, he argues "became an exploitable hermeneutic resource to make sense of cultural difference and to project moral categories onto global space," with the temperate world being exalted over the tropical world (Livingstone 2000b: 93). In an allied vein, Matthew Edney (1997: 14–35) explores how 'The Great Trigonometrical Survey of India' (started in 1817) was central to the creation of "a conceptual image [of India and the British Empire] that consciously set the Europeans apart from the Indians they ruled." India was rendered as a bounded and unified cartographic entity that was cast in the image of western science, and that stood above 'fragmentary' and 'irrational' Indian knowledges of the land. And in an avowedly postcolonial reading of the "Africanist discourse" of the London-based Royal Geographical Society (RGS) during the mid-nineteenth century, Clive Barnett (1998: 244–5) argues that

The actual conditions of cross-cultural contact upon which the production of nineteenth-century geographical knowledge depended are retrospectively rewritten [for metropolitan audiences] to present ['racially unmarked'] European subjects as the singular sources of meaning . . . Without the use of local guides and interpreters, the exploits of men represented as untiringly perservering, independent and self-denying seekers of the truth [and nothing but] would have been impossible. But this routine *practical* dependence on local knowledges and information is not accorded any *epistemological* value. Local knowledge is refashioned as a hindrance, as a barrier to the arrival of the truth . . . Indigenous geographical meanings and knowledges are admitted into this discourse on the condition of being stripped of any validity independent of European definitions of scientific knowledge.

These and other studies read geography as a discourse in the sense that Said uses the term – as object- and reality-constituting – and trade on the 'epistemic violence' of geography's empire. Barnett and many others have underscored the importance of science as a duplicitous vector of geographical knowledge production, with non-European knowledge represented as "the confusion and noise against which European science takes shape and secures its authority" (Barnett 1998: 145; also see Anderson 1998).

As some of these snippets suggest, work on geography and empire takes on board postcolonialism's cultural concerns and bends them in more explicitly geographical directions. Driver (2000), for example, has argued that geographical exploration should be understood as "a set of cultural practices" that involved the mobilization of a wide variety of material and imaginative resources (equipment, guides, patronage, publicity, authority, texts, scholarship, myths, and so on). He charts the formation of a Victorian "culture of exploration" that centered on Africa, and revolved around a gentlemanly network of scholars, politicians and philanthropists who made the RGS an authoritative site for the promotion and dissemination of geographical knowledge. But he also shows that this culture was shaped by popular accounts of African exploration (such as those of Henry Morton Stanley) that were deemed sensational by the geographical authorities, and in public spaces of knowledge such as the museum and exhibition hall (Driver 2000: 7, 202, 216). Moreover, the motifs of manly adventure and exoticism that infuse the nineteenth-century configuration of Africa as 'the dark continent' are still at large in the advertising and tourism industries. In other words, students of geography's empire have to contend with contemporary forms of colonial nostalgia (see Gregory 2001b).

'Colonizing Geographies'

This plethora of work shows that geography's empire was far grander and more imposing than a narrow (if critical) disciplinary history could make it appear. Indeed, in recent years geographers have become increasingly interested in the broad implication of spatiality in the production of imperial/colonial power and identity. Gregory (2002) has coined the term "colonizing geographies" to convey the idea that geography and colonialism/empire work into one another in myriad ways, and can be approached from multiple positions. Let me briefly touch on two of these positions.

Geographical research on imperial travel, and feminist-geographical scholarship on empire, has been particularly effective at revealing the variegated and often paradoxical ways in which class, race, gender and sexuality were articulated in metropolitan and colonial locations, spaces and landscapes. Often based on the examination of sources that, until recently, were regarded as less than credible forms of geographical knowledge (e.g. guidebooks and women's diaries), this work gives us some important insights into the complex positionality of western men and women within the framework of empire (see McEwan 1998; Morin & Berg 1999). Jane Jacobs (2003: 349), for instance, observes that women were seen as

accessories to the masculinist project of empire building, often drawing on vectors of racial difference in order to assume a position of superiority denied to them within their own patriarchal social settings . . . [Yet their] very positioning . . . as peripheral to the privileged spheres of knowledge and action associated with empire building often placed them in relations with the colonized that unsettled those lines of difference and distinction.

Sara Mills (1999) and Judith Kenny (1995) explore how the complex gendering of imperial and colonial subject positions was tied to the creation of spaces of confinement and self-exclusion such as the urban cantonments and rural hill stations of British India. Alison Blunt (1994, 2000) and Cheryl McEwan (2000) have explored how the subject and viewing positions of women travelers and colonists changed as they moved between 'home' and 'away' and were presented in different ways before 'polite' and 'savage' audiences, and responded to alien environments (also see Gregory 2000b). Karen Morin and Lawrence Berg (2001) have started to open up important questions about how and why women became involved in indigenous practices of anticolonial resistance. And James Duncan (2000) has started to explore the fraught textual, physical, and psychical construction of colonial masculinity in natural environments – in his case, the tropical highlands of Ceylon – that were radically different than the ones from which the colonizers hailed.

The geographical literature on colonialism and empire arguably retains a much stronger concern with the materiality of discourse, the physicality of movement and interaction, and the geographical embodiment of power and identity than much postcolonial work that emanates, especially, from the fields of literary and cultural studies. It thus avoids one of the pitfalls of postcolonialism – its textualism – and augments the idea that geographical discourses are not free-floating constructions. Geographers routinely identify themselves as 'postcolonial' scholars and critics in this way. At the same time, it is important to point to the metropolitan and disciplinary biases in this work. Much of it takes the European-imperial arena as its prime historical context and Eurocentric knowledge as its chief critical referent. Mary Louise Pratt (2001: 280) has criticized recent geographical work on travel writing on this ground, observing that the experience of travel is "examined from within the self-privileging imaginary that framed the travels and travel books in the first place." European sensibilities remain of intrinsic interest, and while ideas of cultural negotiation and exchange are explored in methodological terms, they are rarely pursued in great substantive depth. Geographers working in metropolitan and disciplinary modes are teaching us a tremendous amount about what 'empire' meant to Europeans and how it was construed in geographical terms. But they often display a much shakier sense of the non-European and indigenous landscapes over which geography's empire ranged. Barnett's essay on the RGS illustrates these tendencies well. He is less interested in how and why Native people worked as guides and informants than in the denigration of Native knowledges and ways of knowing in European geographical science. Brenda Yeoh (2000) points out that work on the historical geography *of* colonialism overshadows the difficult but crucial task of uncovering "the historical geographies of the colonized world." In fact, we have a literature that is ultimately more concerned with the projection of empire and the west – with imperialism – than with the messy pragmatics of colonial contact (also see Lester 2000).

This is not a problem in itself. It only becomes a bone of critical contention when geographers who are working in this way claim that they are also bringing the world of the colonized more clearly into view. For in approaching the colonial world in this way, the colonized are only partially rendered as subjects rather than objects of knowledge. Jacobs (2001: 730) observes that it is a "vexed truth" that much post-colonial scholarship within and beyond geography tends to reinscribe the author-ity of the western events, agents and texts that it ostensibly seeks to expose and subvert. It often does so by focusing too exclusively on the white/Western histori-cal record and exaggerating the power of Western representations of foreign lands and peoples. A postcolonial politics of location that is premised on the courtesy of listening to the Other and working through the intersubjective nature of colonial encounters is frequently overridden by a metropolitan-intellectual politics of not speaking for the Other and using the colonial world to decenter/deconstruct the west (see Livingstone 1998). There has been a flurry of work by geographers on processes of othering, but much of it works at a great remove from its others – its objects of discourse. It is surely difficult to get at 'the native' side of the story from thoroughly lopsided archives that do not render knowledge about 'them' on 'their' terms. But geographers often exacerbate such problems by dealing with questions of native agency and otherness through the determining imprint of western dis-courses. Metropolitan-based geographical studies that conceptualize empire as situated, negotiated, contested, or anxiety-ridden often work much better in theory than in practice. Some geographers address this problem by recoiling from the analy-sis of native agency (by not attempting to speak for the Other), and sticking to the task of showing how dominant and demeaning knowledges were put together. This, to be sure, remains an important enough task in its own right, but this style of enquiry can come at a price. It can romanticize the Other, and make empire look too austere (and thus exaggerate the power of the west) or too precarious (and thus overinflate the agency of the critic who looks for this trait in the imperial/colonial archive).

Colonialism's Geographies

Such concerns are usually expressed most strongly by geographers who work on the contextually located nature of colonialism and what Jane Jacobs (1996: 1–3) has called "the politics of the 'edge' " (the subversive influence of the marginalized periphery on centrist practices of spatial demarcation). So let me now turn to another distinctive orientation in the geographical literature – a range of research on colonialism's geographies. Many geographical studies of the imperial/colonial past are regionally focused, treat colonialism as a situated (if unequal) process of cultural negotiation, and highlight the differences within and between specific colonial projects, regions, and formations. Geographers working at the colonial edges of empire stress the need to distinguish between Eurocentric and nation-centered imperial projects, and the different logics of power enshrined in settler- and dependent-colonial formations. They pursue the type of postcolonial project described by Dipesh Chakrabarty, who suggests (2000: 16) that if western thought is to be "renewed from and for the margins," we must acknowledge that both the margins and the centers are plural and diverse. Europe "appears different when seen from within the experiences of colonization or inferiorization in specific parts of the world." Scholarship on colonialism's geographies speaks of different – of specific and diverse – Europes (cf. Livingstone & Withers 1999; Scott 2002).

In fact, a good deal of postcolonial geographical work "from and for the margins" focuses on different parts of Britain's former settler empire – on Australia and New Zealand, North America, and southern Africa, which are not postcolonial in the same way as large parts of Africa and Asia. For geographers working on these parts of the world, disciplinary debates about "geography's empire" seem far off, and the type of globally ambitious (imperial?) postcolonial theory that emanates from India and other hot spots of postcolonial inspiration needs to be recontextualized. Postcolonial theory is used selectively, and regional historical literatures and conversations take on more importance (see Clayton 2002). Historical-geographical research on Australia and Canada is also set against the contemporary backdrop of aboriginal resistance to, and litigation over, the ongoing extension of colonial power, and is thus politicized in different ways than work on 'geography's empire' (see Sparke 1998; Stokes 1999; Howitt 2001). Geographers have to negotiate the discordant voices of natives and newcomers who have different and competing ties to the land, and some geographers have been actively engaged in indigenous struggles. Geographers working in such regions bring their geographical sensitivities to bear on a wide range of colonial spaces and geographies – colonial settlement systems, native reserves, Christian missions, the spaces created and exploited by capital, and the geographies of colonial governance (e.g. Christophers 1998; Hannah 1993).

This literature eschews any essentialized vision of either western power or native agency, and much of it extends Nicholas Thomas's arguments about the localized yet broadly transformative cast of colonialism. Cole Harris (2002: xvii), for example, has argued in relation to British Columbia that while "colonialism spoke with many voices and was often deeply troubled about its own contradictions," it tended to "override them with its own sheer power and momentum. Nor [he continues] is it clear that a culture is attenuated, or that the distinctions between it and another culture are destroyed, because the two have overlapped and exchanged some elements." Alan Lester (2001) has shown how British metropolitan discourses on southern Africa were heavily inflected by the competing visions of metropolitan politicians, colonial officials, humanitarians, and settlers, and the (often incongruous) colonial spaces they created. And one of the main themes in my work on the beginnings of native–western contact on Vancouver Island on Canada's west coast is that western agendas were not imposed on native territory in a uniform or mechanical fashion. The encounters, knowledges, and representations generated by western explorers, traders, cartographers, and politicians were influenced by native agendas, and local contacts and global imperial strategies became connected in complex ways (Clayton 2000a).

Work on these and many other colonial localities shows that imperial incursion kick-started diverse and often unpredictable interactions between 'Europe,' indigenous peoples, the environments in which they met, and the geographies of accommodation and resistance that they created (see Kenny 1999). So much so, Andrew Sluyter (2001) has suggested, that we urgently need to discuss whether it is possible (and indeed desirable) to generalize about colonialism in geographical terms, and how we might build geographical models of colonial landscape transformation that are robust enough to accommodate diversity, specificity, and contingency.

This literature also raises difficult questions about how native voices should be handled, especially if we hold the poststructuralist/postcolonial view that narratives and histories are social and cultural constructions. Do we apply one set of interpretative – or deconstructionist – techniques to the white historical record, and some other set to the native record? Is native testimony and evidence to be used to question the certainty of western knowledge (and reveal its hybridity), or to reconstruct an alternative narrative that points to incommensurable western and nonwestern worldviews? Either way, geographers realize how difficult it is to bring western and native evidence together in ways that bridge the intersubjective space of contact. They run the risk of subordinating 'other' voices to the secular codes of western academic discourse (to codes about the rational derivation and logical presentation of factual/archival evidence). Furthermore, in this age of globalized postcolonial study, in which ideas travel far and fast, scholarship has an interdisciplinary and international momentum, and we cannot know much about many of the places we read about, scholarly appreciation of local and regional studies of colonialism often assumes a methodological tone. We tend to focus on the approach taken by the scholar/critic rather than the locality/region in question. We think about the wider implications of a particular study and sometimes rather less about the facts and details that are being marshaled and how they are placed in local/regional debates. We often think in terms of how the part (the vignette, case study, locality) relates to the whole (to colonialism as such, or to the field of postcolonial studies).

Barnett (1997: 145) adds that attempts to restore hitherto excluded or suppressed voices to our accounts often conform to a western model of representation that "inscribe[s] colonial textuality within a quite conventional economy of sense which ascribes to voice and speech the values of expressivity, self-presence, and consciousness, and understands the absence of such signs as 'silence,' as an intolerable absence of voice, and therefore as a mark of disempowerment." This 'economy' belittles the idea that in some colonial situations and postcolonial projects, silence can be construed as a strategy of resistance and mark of subversion. The historical recovery of "the geographies of the colonized" raises questions of what Gayatri Spivak (1999) has termed "strategic essentialism" – of how we might contest some assertions of difference and not others, and articulate some archival findings but not others, for political (strategic) reasons. I have tried to show that the native groups of Vancouver Island felt anything but possessed or inferior to westerners during the early years of contact. Yet the story I tell of native tribal competition, warfare, and territorial change hardly squares with images of the 'ecological Indian' living in natural and social harmony that have played an important role in white-liberal sympathy for native causes, and the defense of native land claims in the courts.

Postcolonial Geographies?

This, in outline, is how geographical research on the imperial/colonial past has developed since the late 1980s. There is no simple way of summarizing or evaluating how this range of work is 'postcolonial,' but I will end with three general points.

First, Trevor Barnes and Derek Gregory (1997: 14) note that postcolonialism is centrally implicated in "the worlding of human geography"; it has made it "unacceptable to write geography in such a way that the West is always at the center of its imperial Geography." In part because of the advent of postcolonialism within geography, work in the expanding and increasingly fluid subfields of cultural and historical geography is now routinely framed around the notion that geography is a situated knowledge. Geographers have returned to, and in a way plundered, the imperial/colonial past to find out new things about themselves, and have found a new program of study in the postcolonial equation of power, knowledge and geography. Empire is now seen as a distorting mirror within which geography came to define and champion itself, and geographers are trying to come to terms with their discipline's imperial binds and conventions. They recognize that they are implicated in the power relations they study, and that they must therefore be concerned with the locations from which they apprehend the imperial/colonial past. They recognize that they work 'after empire' but in crucial respects not beyond colonialism.

Second, the geographical literature we have explored is animated by one of postcolonialism's most significant and obdurate analytical problems. Stuart Hall (1996: 249) puts the problem this way:

while holding fast to differentiation and specificity, we cannot afford to forget the over-determining effects of the colonial moment, the 'work' its binaries were constantly required to do to re-present the proliferation of cultural difference and forms of life . . . We have to keep these two ends of the chain in play at the same time – over-determination and difference, condensation and dissemination, if we are not to fall into a playful deconstructionism, the fantasy of a powerless utopia of difference.

Geographers have judiciously sought to recover the diversity, complexity, and contradictions of colonialism and empire, and in so doing, Livingstone (2000a: 8) reflects, have helped to relativize and pluralize understanding of "the historical geography of geography." They hold fast to multiplicity and dispersal, in part, no doubt, because geography is traditionally concerned with issues of diversity and areal differentiation. However, geographers have not lost sight of what Hall describes as the "over-determining effects of the colonial moment." One of main empirical insights to be gleaned from reading geographers' eclectic work on the imperial/colonial past is that heterogeneous geographical projects had more universal and uniform colonizing effects. Diverse colonial and colonizing geographies cohered in the bounding and classification of land and resources, the compartmentalization of peoples and places, the segregation of populations, the creation of center and peripheries of power, and in a logic of displacement and dispossession. As Harris (2002: xvii–xxi) puts it, "It may be important not to be too fancy with colonialism." Some basic – "primal" – lines of power were drawn on the colonial map (such as those between native reserves and the rest the land open to white settlement and exploitation). Harris insists that we cannot get away from colonialism's fundamental and changing geographies. However, we also need to remember that geographers' critical accounts of colonialism's logic of geographical violence are intellectual constructs, and that they are implicated in their constructions. Geographers write of colonizing geographies, normalizing discourses, and imperial imaginaries, and their critical attempts to decenter, decolonize, expose, and subvert to some degree depend on such standardized images of what colonialism and empire were about. They thus run the risk of presentism and of homogenizing understanding of colonialism's spatiality – of aggrandizing the grip of geography's imperial/colonial past on the present, and of accentuating difference by making assumptions about the sameness of imperial/colonial geographies (see Jacobs 2000). Driver's (1992) argument that geography has been "saturated" with imperial/colonial themes provides an instructive example of this first problem. To what extent is this a retrospective understanding that serves the needs of the postcolonial present? In the immediate aftermath of the Second World War, for instance, geographers complained about their discipline's shameful ignorance of colonial affairs (see e.g. Wooldridge 1947), and we might surmise from this that geography's imperial embrace was never as strong as many now want to think.

Third, this analytical problematic inevitably draws the positionality of the scholar into the critical frame, and geographers, like other postcolonial scholars, have a duty to work out the ways and extent to which their revisionist accounts get past the problem of Eurocentrism. What place do western disciplinary tools and concerns have in the analysis of colonialism? How and on whose terms are marginal voices and other ways of knowing incorporated into the center and the mainstream? Work on 'geography's empire' surely decenters geographical knowledge, may satiate geographers' thirst for multiplicity and dispersal, and may even be ameliorative for geography and therapeutic for geographers. But in what ways is it postcolonial? There is a danger that work on geography and empire can become a seductive but sanitized intellectual pastime that fixates on the power/knowledge equations that inhere in a discipline like geography and bypasses the practical problems faced by formerly and currently colonized peoples. I am not suggesting that historical work that is in touch with 'real' postcolonial places is more postcolonial or critically respectable than that which seeks to 'decenter' an academic center such as geography. Rather, I think there needs to be more dialogue between geographers working within the different orientations identified above, and that we need to remind ourselves that we are all creatures and creators of situated knowledge. Jacobs (2003: 534) suggests that while work on geography's empire is vexed, it does raise one viable question: "would it be possible for modern geography to effectively decolonize its practices without this kind of critical revisionist scholarship?" She suggests that we might only create alternate postcolonial geographies by looking back, for such geographies cannot emerge "outside of the histories . . . of the geographies that preceded them." This is surely one of the basic postcolonial messages that geographers should continue to heed, wherever they are working: that postcolonial geographies will only emerge *"in medias res."* It would be a mistake to think that we can find some great divide between a geography that was once complicit with colonialism and one that is now not. If geography forgets its place in the imperial/colonial past, and turns a blind eye to the place of that past in the present, it will narrow its critical compass and geo-graphic ambit.

NOTES

1. The focus of this chapter can be further qualified in three ways. First, I pass over a gamut of work on contemporary postcolonial issues, though it should be recognized that scholarship on the past works out of the present (and vice versa). Second, there are some biases and blinkers in the geographical literature that an overview like this can do little to rectify. Geographers who hail from Britain and its former colonial possessions seem more caught up with their countries' imperial/colonial past (and present) than geographers from other western countries (notably France and the US) seem to be with theirs, though there are obviously exceptions (see e.g. Bruneau & Dory 1994). Nor have geographers done as much as they might to assuage the false impression that imperialism and colonialism are exclusively modern western phenomena. There is a dearth of geographical research on nonwestern and premodern imperial/colonial dynamics. And third, the chapter says a great deal more about the impact of postcolonialism on geography than it does about the rich geographical tenor of postcolonialism. Suffice it to note that the terms place, space, location, and geography have become coveted critical commodities.
2. 'Imperialism' and 'colonialism' are complex and contested terms, but I will distinguish between them along the spatial lines suggested by Edward Said (1993: 9) and Ania Loomba (1998: 7): that imperialism is the metropolitan-based process that leads to domination, whereas colonialism is what happens in colonized areas as a consequence of imperial expansion, conquest, and rule.

REFERENCES

Anderson, K. 1998: Science and the savage: the Linnean Society of New South Wales, 1874–1900. *Ecumene* 5, 125–43.

Appadurai, A. 1996: *Modernity at Large: Cultural Dimensions of Globalization.* Minneapolis: University of Minnesota Press.

Barnes, T. and Gregory, D., eds. 1997: *Reading Human Geography: The Poetics and Politics of Geographical Inquiry.* London: Arnold.

Barnett, C. 1995: Awakening the dead: who needs the history of geography? *Transactions, Institute of British Geographers* NS 20, 417–19.

Barnett, C. 1997: 'Sing along with the common people': politics, postcolonialism, and other figures. *Environment and Planning D: Society and Space* 15, 137–54.

Barnett, C. 1998: Impure and worldly geography: the Africanist discourse of the Royal Geographical Society, 1831–73. *Transactions, Institute of British Geographers* NS 23, 239–52.

Bell, M., Butlin, R., and Heffernan, M., eds. 1995: *Geography and Imperialism, 1820–1940.* Manchester: Manchester University Press.

Bhabha, H. K. 1994: *The Location of Culture.* New York and London: Routledge.

Blaut, J. 1993: *The Coloniser's Model of the World: Geographical Diffusionism and Eurocentric History.* London and New York: Guilford Press.

Blunt, A. 1994: *Travel, Gender and Imperialism: Mary Kingsley and West Africa.* London and New York: Guilford Press.

Blunt, A. 2000: Spatial stories under siege: British women writing from Lucknow in 1857. *Gender, Place and Culture* 7, 229–46.

Blunt, A. and Rose, G., eds. 1994: *Writing Women and Space: Colonial and Postcolonial Geographies.* London and New York: Guilford Press.

Bowd, G. and Clayton, D. 2003: Tropicality, orientalism and French colonialism in Indo-China: the work of Pierre Gourou, 1926–1982. *French Historical Studies*, forthcoming.

Braun, B. 2002: Colonialism's afterlife: vision and visuality on the Northwest coast. *Cultural Geographies* 9, 202–47.

Brennan T. 1997: *At Home in the World: Cosmopolitanism Now.* Cambridge, MA: Harvard University Press.

Brennan, T. 2000: The illusion of a future: orientalism as travelling theory. *Critical Inquiry* 26, 558–83.

Bruneau, M. and Dory, M., eds. 1994: *Géographies des Colonisations XV–XX Siècles.* Paris: Hartmann.

Carter, P. 1987: *The Road to Botany Bay: An Essay in Spatial History.* London: Faber and Faber.

Chakrabarty, D. 2000: *Provincializing Europe: Postcolonial Thought and Historical Difference.* Princeton: Princeton University Press.

Chatterjee, P. 1999: *The Partha Chatterjee Omnibus.* New Delhi and Oxford: Oxford University Press.

Childs, P. and Williams, W. 1997: *An Introduction to Post-colonial Theory.* London and New York: Prentice-Hall.

Christophers, B. 1998: *Positioning the Missionary: John Booth Good and the Confluence of Cultures in Nineteenth-century British Columbia.* Vancouver: University of British Columbia Press.

Clayton, D. 2000a: *Islands of Truth: The Imperial Fashioning of Vancouver Island.* Vancouver: University of British Columbia Press.

Clayton, D. 2000b: On the colonial genealogy of George Vancouver's chart of the Northwest coast of North America. *Ecumene* 7, 371–401.

Clayton, D. 2002: Absence, memory and geography. *BC Studies* 132, 65–79.

Crush, J. 1994: Post-colonialism, de-colonization, and geography. In A. Godlewska and N. Smith, eds., *Geography and Empire.* Oxford: Blackwell, 333–50.

Driver, F. 1992: Geography's empire: histories of geographical knowledge. *Environment and Planning D: Society and Space* 10, 23–40.

Driver, F. 2000: *Geography Militant: Cultures of Exploration and Empire.* Oxford: Blackwell.

Driver, F. and Gilbert, D., eds. 1999: *Imperial Cities: Landscape, Display and Identity.* Manchester: Manchester University Press.

Driver, F. and Yeoh, B., eds. 2000: Theme issue on "tropicality." *Singapore Journal of Tropical Geography* 21.

Duncan, J. 2000: The struggle to be temperate: climate and 'moral masculinity' in mid-nineteenth century Ceylon. *Singapore Journal of Tropical Geography* 21, 34–47.

Duncan, J. and Gregory, D., eds. 1999: *Writes of Passage: Reading Travel Writing*. London and New York: Routledge.

Edney, M. 1997: *Mapping an Empire: The Geographical Construction of British India, 1765–1843*. Chicago: University of Chicago Press.

Fanon, F. 1963: *The Wretched of the Earth*. Paris: Présence Africaine.

Gandhi, L. 1998: *Postcolonial Theory: A Critical Introduction*. Edinburgh: Edinburgh University Press.

Godlewska, A. and Smith, N., eds. 1994: *Geography and Empire*. Oxford: Blackwell.

Graham, B. and Nash, C., eds. 2000: *Modern Historical Geographies*. London: Prentice-Hall.

Gregory, D. 1994: *Geographical Imaginations*. Oxford: Blackwell.

Gregory, D. 1995: Imaginative geographies. *Progress in Human Geography* 19, 447–85.

Gregory, D. 1998: *Explorations in Critical Human Geography*. Hettner Lectures, no. 1, University of Heidelberg.

Gregory, D. 2000a: Postcolonialism. In R. Johnston, D. Gregory, G. Pratt, and M. Watts, eds., *The Dictionary of Human Geography*, 4th ed. Oxford: Blackwell, 612–15.

Gregory, D. 2000b: Cultures of travel and spatial formations of knowledge. *Erdkunde* 54, 297–309.

Gregory, D. 2001a: (Post)colonialism and the production of nature. In B. Braun and N. Castree, eds., *Social Nature*. Oxford: Blackwell, 124–55.

Gregory, D. 2001b: Colonial nostalgia and cultures of travel: spaces of constructed visibility in Egypt. In N. AlSayyad, ed., *Consuming Tradition, Manufacturing Heritage: Global Norms and Urban Forms in the Age of Tourism*. London: Routledge.

Gregory, D. 2002: *The Colonial Present*. Oxford: Blackwell.

Guha, R. 1996: *A Rule of Property for Bengal: An Essay on the Idea of Permanent Settlement*, 2nd ed. Durham, NC: Duke University Press.

Hall, S. 1996: When was 'the post-colonial'?: thinking at the limit. In I. Chambers and L. Curti, eds., *The Post-colonial Question: Common Skies, Divided Horizons*. London: Routledge, 242–60.

Hall, C., ed. 2000: *Cultures of Empire: A Reader*. Manchester: Manchester University Press.

Hannah, M. 1993: Space and social control in the administration of the Oglala Lakota ('Sioux'), 1871–1879. *Journal of Historical Geography* 19, 412–32.

Harris, C. 1997: *The Resettlement of British Columbia: Essays on Colonialism and Geographical Change*. Vancouver–Toronto: University of British Columbia Press.

Harris, C. 2002: *Making Native Space: Colonialism, Resistance and Reserves in British Columbia*. Vancouver: University of British Columbia Press.

Head, L. 2000: *Second Nature: The History and Implications of Australia as Aboriginal Landscape*. Syracuse: Syracuse University Press.

Heffernan, M. 2001: 'A dream as frail as those of ancient time': the in-credible geographies of Timbuctoo. *Environment and Planning D: Society and Space* 19, 203–25.

Howitt, R. 2001: Frontiers, borders, edges: liminal challenges to the hegemony of exclusion. *Australian Geographical Studies* 39, 233–45.

Jacobs, J. 1996: *Edge of Empire: Postcolonialism and the City*. London: Routledge.

Jacobs, J. 2000: Difference and its other. *Transactions, Institute of British Geographers* NS 25, 403–8.

Jacobs, J. 2001: Touching pasts. *Antipode* 33, 730–4

Jacobs, J. 2003: After empire? In K. Anderson, M. Domosh, S. Pile, and N. Thrift, eds., *The Handbook of Cultural Geography*. London: Sage, 346–53.

Jarosz, L. 1992: Constructing the Dark Continent: metaphor as geographic representation of Africa. *Geografiska Annaler* 74B, 105–15.

Katz, C. 1992: All the world is staged: intellectuals and the projects of ethnography. *Environment and Planning D: Society and Space* 10, 495–510.

Kearns, G. 1997: The imperial subject: geography and travel in the work of Mary Kingsley and Halford Mackinder. *Transactions, Institute of British Geographers* NS 22, 450–72.

Kenny, J. 1995: Climate, race and imperial authority: the symbolic landscape of the British hill station in India. *Annals of the Association of American Geographers* 85, 694–714.

Kenny, J., ed. 1999: Colonial geographies: accommodation and resistance. Theme issue of *Historical Geography*, vol. 27.

Lester, A. 2000: Historical geographies of imperialism. In B. Graham and C. Nash, eds., *Modern Historical Geographies*. London: Prentice-Hall, 100–20.

Lester, A. 2001: *Imperial Networks: Creating Identities in Nineteenth-Century South Africa and Britain*. London: Routledge.

Livingstone, D. 1991: The Moral discourse of climate: historical considerations on race, place and virtue. *Journal of Historical Geography* 17, 413–34.

Livingstone, D. 1992: *The Geographical Tradition: Episodes in the History of a Contested Enterprise*. Oxford: Blackwell.

Livingstone, D. 1998: Reproduction, representation and authenticity: a rereading. *Transactions, Institute British Geographers* NS 23, 13–20.

Livingstone, D. 1999: Tropical climate and moral hygiene: the anatomy of a Victorian debate. *British Journal of the History of Science* 32, 93–110.

Livingstone, D. 2000a: Putting geography in its place. *Australian Geographical Studies* 38, 1–9.

Livingstone, D. 2000b: Tropical hermeneutics: fragments for a historical narrative. *Singapore Journal of Tropical Geography* 21, 92–8.

Livingstone, D. 2002: *Science, Space and Hermeneutics*. Hettner Lectures no. 5, University of Heidelberg.

Livingstone, D. and Withers, C., eds. 1999: *Geography and Enlightenment*. Chicago: University of Chicago Press.

Loomba, A. 1998: *Colonialism/Postcolonialism*. London: Routledge.

Maddrell, A. 1998: Discourses of race and gender and the comparative method in geography school texts, 1830–1918. *Environment and Planning D: Society and Space* 16, 81–103.

McEwan, C. 1998: Cutting power lines within the palace? Countering paternity and Eurocentrism in the 'geographical tradition.' *Transactions, Institute British Geographers* NS 23, 371–84.

McEwan, C. 2000: *Gender, Geography and Empire: Victorian Women Travellers in West Africa*. London: Ashgate.

Mills, S. 1999: Gender and colonial space. *Gender, Place and Culture* 3, 125–47.

Mitchell, T. 1988: *Colonising Egypt*. Cambridge: Cambridge University Press.

Morin, K. and Berg, L. 1999: Emplacing trends in feminist historical geography. *Gender, Place and Culture* 6, 311–30.

Morin, K. and Berg, L. 2001: Gendering resistance: British colonial narratives of wartime New Zealand. *Journal of Historical Geography* 27, 196–222.

Myers, G. A. 1998: Intellectual of empire: Eric Dutton and hegemony in British Africa. *Annals of the Association of American Geographers* 88, 1–27.

Nandy, A. 1983: *The Intimate Enemy: The Loss and Recovery of Self Under Colonialism*. Oxford: Oxford University Press.

Nash, C. 2002: Cultural geography: postcolonial cultural geographies. *Progress in Human Geography* 26, 219–30.

Ogborn, M. 2002: Writing travels: power, knowledge and ritual on the English East India Company's early voyages. *Transactions, Institute of British Geographers* NS 27, 155–71.

Parry, B. 1997: The postcolonial: conceptual category or chimera? *Yearbook of English Studies* 27, 3–21.

Phillips, R. 1997: *Mapping Men and Empire: A Geography of Adventure.* London: Routledge.

Pieterse, J. and Parekh, B. 1995: *The Decolonization of Imagination: Culture, Knowledge and Power.* London and New Jersey: Zed Books.

Ploszajska, T. 1996: Constructing the subject: geographical models in English schools, 1870–1944. *Journal of Historical Geography* 22, 388–98.

Ploszajska, T. 2000: Historiographies of geography and empire. In B. Graham and C. Nash, eds., *Modern Historical Geographies.* London: Longman, 121–45.

Prakash, G. 1994: Subaltern studies as postcolonial criticism. *American Historical Review* 99, 1475–90.

Prakash, G. 1996: Who's afraid of postcoloniality? *Social Text* 49, 187–203.

Prakash, G. 1999: *Another Reason: Science and the Imagination of Modern India.* Princeton: Princeton University Press.

Pratt, M. 1992: *Imperial Eyes: Travel Writing and Transculturation.* London: Routledge.

Pratt, M. 2001: Review of J. S. Duncan and D. Gregory, eds., *Writes of Passage. Journal of Historical Geography* 27, 279–81.

Rose, G. 1995: Tradition and paternity: same difference? *Transactions, Institute of British Geographers* NS 20, 414–16.

Ryan, J. 1995: Visualizing imperial geography: Halford Mackinder and the Colonial Office Visual Instruction Committee, 1902–11. *Ecumene* 1, 157–76.

Ryan, J. 1997: *Picturing Empire: Photography and the Visualisation of the British Empire.* London and Chicago: Reaktion Books.

Sauer, C. 1938: Destructive exploitation in modern colonial expansion. *Comptes Rendus du Congrès International de Géographie, Amsterdam*, vol. 2, sect. 3c, pp. 494–9.

Said, E. 1978: *Orientalism.* New York: Random House.

Said, E. 1993: *Culture and Imperialism.* New York: Alfred A. Knopf.

Said, E. 2001: Globalizing literary study. *Publications of the Modern Language Association of America* 116, 64–8.

Scott, H. 2002: Contested territories: arenas of geographical knowledge in early colonial Peru. *Journal of Historical Geography*, forthcoming.

Seshadri-Crooks, K. 1995: At the margins of postcolonial studies. *Ariel* 26, 47–71.

Slater, D. 1992: On the borders of social theory: learning from other regions. *Environment and Planning D: Society and Space* 10, 307–27.

Sluyter, A. 2001: Colonialism and landscape in the Americas: material/conceptual transformations and continuing consequences. *Annals of the Association of American Geographers* 91, 410–28.

Sparke, M. 1998: A map that roared and an original atlas: Canada, cartography, and the narration of nation. *Annals of the Association of American Geographers* 88, 463–95.

Spivak, G. 1999: *A Critique of Postcolonial Reason.* Cambridge, MA: Harvard University Press

Staum, M. S. 2000: The Paris Geographical Society constructs the other, 1821–1850. *Journal of Historical Geography* 26, 222–38.

Stokes, E. 1999: Tauponui a Tia: an interpretation of Maori landscape and land tenure. *Asia Pacific Viewpoint* 40, 137–58.

Thomas, N. 1994: *Colonialism's Culture.* Princeton: Princeton University Press.

Walia, S. 2001: *Edward Said and the Writing of History.* Cambridge: Icon Books.

Washbrook, D. 1999: Orients and Occidents: colonial discourse theory and the historiography of the British Empire. In R. Winks, ed., *The Oxford History of the British Empire, vol. V: Historiography*. Oxford: Oxford University Press, 596–611.

Withers, C. 1995: Geography, natural history and the Eighteenth-century enlightenment: putting the world in place. *History Workshop Journal* 39, 137–63.

Withers, C. 1999: Reporting, mapping, trusting: making geographical knowledge in the late seventeenth century. *Isis* 90, 497–521.

Wooldridge, S. 1956: Geographical science in education (1947). In *The Geographer as Scientist: Essays on the Scope and Nature of Geography*. London: Thomas Nelson.

Yeoh, B., 1996: *Contesting Space: Power Relations and the Built Environment in Colonial Singapore*. Oxford: Oxford University Press.

Yeoh, B. 2000: Historical geographies of the colonised world. In B. Graham and C. Nash, eds., *Modern Historical Geographies*. London: Longman, 146–66.

Young, R. 1991: *White Mythologies: Writing History and the West*. London: Routledge.

Young, R. 2001: *Postcolonialism: An Historical Introduction*. Oxford: Blackwell.

Chapter 30

Postcolonial Geographies

James R. Ryan

Introduction

... He sees that more children have raised their hands to ask questions.

"Yes, Joseph."

"You have told us about black history. You have been telling us about our heroes and our glorious victories. But most seem to end in defeat. Now I want to ask my question ... If what you say is true, why then was it possible for a handful of Europeans to conquer a continent and to lord it over us for four hundred years? How was it possible, unless it is because they have bigger brains, and that we are the children of Ham, as they say in the Christian Bible?"

He suddenly starts fuming with anger. He knows that a teacher should not erupt into anger but he feels his defeat in that question. Maybe the journey has been long and they have wandered over too many continents and over too large a canvas of time.

"Look, Joseph. You have been reading eeh, American children's encyclopedia and the Bible. They used the Bible to steal the souls and minds of ever-grinning Africans, caps folded at the back, saying prayers of gratitude for small crumbs labelled aid, loans, famine relief while big companies are busy collecting gold and silver and diamonds, and while we fight among ourselves saying I am a Kuke, I am a Luo, I am a Luhyia, I am a Somali ... and ... and ... There are times, Joseph, when victory is defeat and defeat is victory." (Ngũgĩ wa Thiong'o, *Petals of Blood*, 1977: 238)

This short passage is taken from Ngũgĩ wa Thiong'o's 1977 novel *Petals of Blood*. The story is set in Ilmorog, a new town on the edge of the Trans-Africa Highway in Kenya. In this scene Mr. Karega, a teacher and trade unionist, dreams about an incident in his classroom. Mr. Karega is one of four inhabitants of the town who become prime suspects following the murder of the local directors of the foreign-owned Theng'eta Brewery. The novel tells the story of these four characters, setting their uneasy relationships and personal histories within the setting of postindependence Kenya. In this postcolonial territory, as in the classroom scene dreamt by Karega, Kenya's history of colonial domination has evolved into new postindependence struggles against the combined forces of foreign capitalism and the interests of a new, propertied African elite. In *Petals of Blood*, as in many of his other novels, Ngũgĩ wa Thiong'o paints a vivid sense of Kenya's social and political landscape following its independence from British colonial rule in 1963. His novels are often powerful critiques both of British colonial mentalities as well as the ways in which colonial attitudes persist within economic, cultural, and social processes of post-colonial nationhood. His fifth novel, *Devil on the Cross* (1980), written while detained without trial by the Kenyan authorities, was dedicated "To all Kenyans struggling against the neocolonial stage of imperialism." This combination of literary imagination with a resolute political grounding in anticolonial struggle has ensured that Ngũgĩ's reputation extends well beyond his native Kenya. His work is widely read and admired in the West, where it is often categorized under the headings of "commonwealth" or "postcolonial" literature. I refer to Ngũgĩ here since he is one of a number of writers whose work deals with the territory of postcolonialism, not as some abstract theoretical concept but as the very landscape upon which the lives of individuals and societies are shaped. His work provides a useful starting point for an engagement with the theme of "postcolonial geographies" since it prompts the question: what does it mean to describe something as "postcolonial"?

Before I embark on an attempt to mark out some useful parameters of the "post-colonial" it is worth noting that the relationship between postcolonialism and cultural geography is a highly significant one. This may seem like an obvious point to make, given that this chapter is part of a section on "Colonial and Postcolonial Geographies" in a companion to cultural geography. However, the interest in post-colonialism marks one of the more striking ways in which cultural geographers (and indeed human geographers more generally) have been concerned to respond to major intellectual and theoretical currents within the social sciences and humanities in the last two or three decades. A curious parallel also exists in the nature of criticisms leveled at both cultural geography and postcolonialism. Each have had to withstand criticism that they promote studies that focus on the immaterial, the textual, and the symbolic, at the expense of the substantive, material processes of history and geography (Nash 2002: 220). Notwithstanding such charges, the terms "postcolonial" and "postcolonialism," as well as related concepts like "hybridity," now have a currency within human geography that they did not have 20 years ago.

Cultural geographers in particular have taken a profound interest in postcolonialism, both as a substantive research agenda and as a set of theoretical approaches, as is evidenced from recent guides to cultural geography (Crang 1998; Mitchell 2000; Shurmer-Smith & Hannam 1994; Shurmer-Smith 2002). Postcolonialism has prompted a huge variety of work in cultural geography, from explorations of different "imaginative geographies" to the accounts of the cultural dimensions of European colonialism; from the spatial strategies of colonial rule to the cultural spaces of anticolonial and postcolonial resistance, past and present. However, proliferation of postcolonial cultural geography has not always led to clarification. Indeed, the vast array of "postcolonialisms" being deployed within geographical texts has often resulted in little overall sense of what "postcolonial geographies" might actually be. It is only more recently that geographers, particularly those working within cultural, historical, political, and development geography, have begun to think more deeply about the aims and scope of "postcolonial geographies" (Blunt & Wills 2000; Graham & Nash 2000; Sidaway 2000; Yeoh 2000, 2001). In this way we might begin to reassess the kinds of distinctive contributions that geographers can make to this broad field.

What then are "postcolonial geographies"? Any attempt to answer this question is faced immediately with a whole range of complex questions concerning the scope and definition of the term "postcolonial." Try conducting a search under the subject headings "postcolonial" or "postcolonialism" in any major library catalogue, or – if you are feeling brave – on the internet, and you will be faced with a bewilderingly vast amount of material. This expanse of information, which seems to be increasing all the time, consists of a wide range of work in a number of different academic disciplines, including literature, anthropology, history, international relations, cultural studies, and geography. It also includes work – not all of it "textual" by any means – of artists, writers, and filmmakers. Given this range of users it is unsurprising to discover that what is meant by "postcolonialism" is both dynamic and diverse. Its appropriate meanings are often the subject of intense debate: is it a movement, an era, or a condition? Should there be a hyphen between "post" and "colonialism"? Or is it, like that other "post"-marked word postmodernism, too frequently and vaguely used to hold any effective meaning (Ashcroft et al. 1995: 2; see also Rattansi 1997)? Should we stop using the term altogether and seek an alternative? Robert Young, for example, favors using instead the term "tricontinentalism," a more precise geographical and cultural encapsulation of Latin America, Africa, and Asia that developed after the first conference of the Organization of Solidarity of the Peoples of Africa, Asia, and Latin America at Havana in 1966, which represented a key moment in anti-imperial struggle and the beginnings of postcolonial theory (Young 2001: 5).

Charting a course through this debate is not always easy. It is perhaps helpful to identify two main applications of the term postcolonialism, both of which circulate around the meanings of the prefix "post." In the first, and earlier, application postcolonialism describes the historical condition of people, states and societies *after* colonialism. In this context, "postcolonial" is applied to those states that experienced European decolonization, particularly in Africa and Asia, in the second half of the twentieth century (Alavi 1972).

A second way of thinking about postcolonialism is as a movement or set of theories, ideas, and practices committed to anticolonial struggle, to moving *beyond* colonialism. The foundations for such a movement of the term are to be found in the writings of novelists and critics engaged in anticolonial struggles, such as Franz Fanon and Ngũgĩ wa Thiong'o, and the varied articulations of "tricontinentalism" (Young 2001). The currency of this notion of postcolonialism was most firmly established through the development of postcolonial criticism and postcolonial theory. The varied work of Edward Said (1978, 1993), Homi Bhabha (1990, 1994), and Gayatri Spivak (1987), to take three well-known figures as examples, is thus part of broader development of a body of knowledge that takes as its object the language and practice of colonialism as well as the formation of colonial subjectivities. It is not my intention to review this literature here; there are now several useful guides to the varied field of postcolonial studies that accomplish this task (see, for example, Williams & Chrisman 1993; Ashcroft et al. 1989, 1995; Pieterse & Parekh 1995; Hall 2000; Young 2001). I merely wish to note that it is this second sense of postcolonialism that is most widely recognized within contemporary Anglo-American geography. Derek Gregory thus defines postcolonialism as:

A critical politico-intellectual formation that is centrally concerned with the impact of colonialism and its contestation on the cultures of both colonizing and colonized peoples in the past, and the reproduction and transformation of colonial relations, representations and practices in the present. (Gregory 2000: 612)

Such a notion of postcolonialism does not assume that colonialism has ended; rather it suggests that postcolonialism is an attitude of critical contestation of colonialism and its legacies (see also Blunt & Wills 2000: 167–8; Radcliffe 1997: 1331; Robinson 1999; Best 1999).

I have described two main applications of the term postcolonialism. Both sets of meanings have their limitations. A temporal meaning of "postcolonialism," as meaning "after" colonialism, for example, seems to suggest that colonialism simply ends with the independence of a former colony. However, as many have observed, forms of "neocolonial" or "neo-imperial" domination persist long after the flags of the Western colonial powers were lowered in their respective colonial territories. Indeed, the world today consists of "multiple colonialisms": "quasi-colonialism," "internal colonialism," and "neocolonialism" as well as the imperialisms of "breakaway colonial settler societies" (represented most dramatically in the twentieth century by the USA) and new ideologies of imperialism (Furedi cited in Sidaway 2000: 603). Given this geopolitical situation one might well ask if a complete end of colonialism and imperialism is ever possible in a world where economic, political, and cultural ties continue to sustain and structure global inequalities? As Sidaway (2000) notes, in a world of such complexity and rapid global political change, it is therefore essential that we reassess the political meanings of "postcolonialism" as it applies to the condition of different political entities. While there is debate about the relative importance of "old" and "new" applications of the term "postcolonial," those interested in "postcolonial geographies" would do well to maintain a critical perspective on different meanings, juxtaposing them with a view to debate and reconceptualization (Sidaway 2000; Lionnet 2000).

Many commentators have warned against the tendency to use the term postcolonial to describe a single or universal condition (McClintock 1995; Loomba 1998: 6). This warning also applies to the related terms colonialism and imperialism, which carry different, and specific, meanings. While colonialism refers generally to the establishment and formal colonization of territory by an alien, occupying force, imperialism is used to describe the broader exercise of political, economic, military, and/or cultural domination. For example, Argentina in the nineteenth century was clearly a recipient of British imperialism (largely through economic and cultural forces) but not British colonialism, since it was never formally colonized. Similarly, it is possible to distinguish different kinds of colonialism depending upon, for example, the type and degree of permanent settlement in the colonial territory. Such distinctions therefore also need to be made between postcolonialism in different spatial settings of, for example, settler and nonsettler colonies (see Mishra & Hodge 1994). In short, postcolonial geographies are as varied and specific as the forms of colonialism and imperialism that produced them.

At their most basic then, postcolonial geographies encompass studies that draw on postcolonial perspectives in order to challenge forms of colonial and imperial domination, in the past and in the present and across a diverse set of spatial locations. As a distinct dimension of contemporary academic geography, postcolonial geographies have been credited with an ambitious range of aims (Blunt & Wills 2000: 167–207). Jonathan Crush has identified the following varied agenda:

the unveiling of geographical complicity in colonial dominion over space; the character of geographical representation in colonial discourse; the de-linking of local geographical enterprise from metropolitan theory and its totalizing systems of representation; and the recovery of those hidden spaces occupied, and invested with their own meaning, by the colonial underclass. (Crush 1994: 336)

Building on and consolidating those aims identified by Crush, we might identify at least three broad themes within postcolonial geographies. Firstly, the different ways in which forms of geographical knowledge have shaped – and been shaped by – colonial power relations in different locations. Secondly, the spatiality of colonial power and its effects and expressions, past and present. Thirdly, the ways that colonial practices are encountered and resisted by different groups within the everyday worlds and spaces of colonized peoples. The remainder of this chapter takes a brief look at each of these three themes in turn in order to show the distinctive and diverse contributions geographers can make to this field.

Geography, Knowledge, and Colonialism

One major strand of postcolonial work in geography has focused on the relationship between geographical knowledge and colonial power (Driver 1992). The development of this theme has been strongly influenced by critical explorations of colonial discourse that have thrown into sharp relief the ways in which knowledge and power are together implicated in the operation of colonialism. Edward Said's 1978 book *Orientalism* marked a major initiative in this direction. In this book Said showed how the idea of the "Orient" was constructed in the Western imagination – as the "other" of the West. Said's critical analysis of texts, particularly those of the Western novel, exposed the ways in which Western cultural forms often accepted and legitimated the structures of colonialism. Said's work and the debates surrounding it across a range of disciplines have had a lasting impact within geography. Many geographers were particularly taken with his concept of "imaginative geography" and with his account of how categories such as "the East" and "the West," supposedly fixed blocks of geographical reality, are constructed through language and cultural imagery, and are shaped by grids of power (Gregory 1995a; Driver 1992).

Insights from postcolonial work on the relationship between forms of knowledge and the operations of colonial power have had a strong impact on work in the history of geography, fostering work that exposes the ways in which the discipline developed in the nineteenth and twentieth centuries went hand in hand with Western colonialism and imperialism (Bell et al. 1995; Driver 1992; Godlewska & Smith 1994). With its practices of exploration, cartography, and resource inventory, and its spatial languages of discovery and colonial conquest, geography was of considerable imperial significance. Indeed, one historian of the subject has described geography in the nineteenth century as the "discipline of imperialism *par excellence*"

(Livingstone 1992: 160). Further studies have been undertaken on how geographical institutions, ideas, and practices were bound up with nineteenth-century cultures of exploration and empire (Driver 2001; Barnett 1998). Others have charted how practices of cartography were instrumental in the fashioning of imperial space (Edney 1997; Clayton 2000b). Yet other studies have considered how geography teaching in British institutions in the nineteenth and twentieth centuries was used as vehicle for promoting imperial citizenship (Ploszajska 2000; Maddrell 1996).

While some of these accounts focus on the history of geography as a professional academic discipline, many are concerned with examining the relationship between empire and geographical knowledge more broadly defined. Here postcolonial geographical work considers the construction of "imaginative geographies" of empire through various cultural representations, from travel writing to photography (Gregory 1995b; Ryan 1997).

Of course, the boundaries between the academic discipline of geography and wider geographical discourse are neither fixed nor impermeable and there is a great deal of work to be done to chart the construction and movements of boundaries between different kinds of knowledge and their relations with colonial power. In particular, cultural geographers need to address how such categories are shaped in and through particular spaces of knowledge, from the colonial encounters on the margins of empire to the cultural arenas of knowledge production in the metropolitan centers of colonial calculation.

These questions of knowledge and power are also not exclusively historical issues. Indeed, they are an essential part of the project of decolonizing the discipline of geography, which is itself part of a larger postcolonial project of decolonization (Pieterse & Parekh 1995). Such a project is not simply a question of writing critical histories of the discipline of geography that expose its historical relationship to empire. It also involves rethinking the epistemological and institutional boundaries of the discipline, recasting what is encompassed by the Western geographical tradition as an "irredeemably hybrid product" that absorbed and appropriated many different forms of geographical knowledge from other times and places (Sidaway 1997: 76). Several commentators have noted how western geography continues to operate in an ethnocentric fashion where the interests and knowledge of the developed, privileged "West" are taken as the ultimate standard for geographical truth (Gregory 1994; Blaut 1993; McEwan 1998). Indeed, postcolonial perspectives challenge us not only to look beyond "the West," but to consider the ways in which geographical categories such as "the West" and "Western" are themselves formulated and constructed (Sidaway 2000).

Such categories are not easily put aside. Several critics have noted, for example, that the shift from "colonial" to "postcolonial" as a marker continues to label places solely in terms of their status as colony or ex-colony; in this way geography and history continue be seen from the perspective of Western colonial powers (McClintock 1995). Those engaged with "postcolonial geographies" certainly need to be sensitive to critiques of the eurocentric and totalizing tendencies of Western knowledge. As Sidaway (2000) puts it: "at their best and most radical, postcolonial geographies will not only be alert to the continued fact of imperialism, but also thoroughly uncontainable in terms of disturbing established assumptions, frames and methods" (pp. 606–7). While we need to be cautious of believing that it is possible to step entirely outside inherited categories of knowledge and language, one important task for those engaged in producing postcolonial geographies is to question the taken-for-granted narratives and frameworks of geographical knowledge.

Charting (Post)Colonial Spaces and Identities

A second major theme of postcolonial geographies, one that is closely allied to explorations of the relationship between geographical knowledge and colonial power, is a concern with the spatial operations of colonial power and with the expression of colonial and postcolonial identities. This theme includes, for example, expressions of colonial and postcolonial identities in the landscape, notably through practices of urban planning, architecture, and related cultural forms.

A number of studies within and beyond geography have considered how racial discourse and racial discrimination, so central to ideologies of colonialism, had distinctive spatial dimensions and effects in specific geographical and historical settings, from those of colonial Swaziland and the Eastern Cape Colony (Crush 1996; Lester 1998) to those of eighteenth- and nineteenth-century Ireland (Gibbons 2000). Racial discourses were invariably produced through a range of practices and related texts, including those of medicine, science, and acclimatization (Livingstone 1999). Contemporary theories of race and tropical disease were used in Sierra Leone, for example, to legitimate evolving colonial policies of racial segregation (Frenkel & Western 1988). Nineteenth-century colonial practices in "tropical" environments were similarly filtered through a range of discourses, including geography, medicine, and "race" (Driver & Yeoh 2000; Duncan 2001; Arnold 2000).

Many studies have emphasized the complex ways in which categories of "race," gender, sexuality, and class were interwoven and were forged across global colonial spaces (Blunt & Rose 1994; McClintock 1995; McClintock et al. 1997; Maddrell 1998). Ideas of domesticity in British India in the late nineteenth and early twentieth centuries, for example, were profoundly shaped by strongly gendered and spatially articulated meanings of "home" forged in both India and England (Blunt 1999).

Interest in the spatial networks of colonial power is evident in the growing interest in "imperial" and "postcolonial" cities (Driver & Gilbert 1999; Jacobs 1996; Yeoh 2001). Students of urban history and imperial historians have long been interested in the form of colonial cities. That is to say, how the evolution of colonial cities, from Delhi to Durban, was shaped by the forces of European colonialism. Anthony King, for example, has argued for the need to understand the evolution of such cities in the context of the global economy and the cultural dimensions of European imperialism (King 1990). More recently, a range of scholars have shown an interest in how the form, representation and use of European cities, notably capital cities such as London, Paris, and Brussels, have been shaped by colonial and postcolonial practices, politics, and performance. Just as we need to understand the cultural geography of a city such as Cairo by reference to the imperial networks that linked it to London and Paris, so we can only understand the changing geography of London with reference to its position at the hub of the British empire (Driver & Gilbert 1999).

Recent work has also sought to challenge the relative lack of attention given to suburbia as a site of modernity (Silverstone 1997) and to show how the evolution of suburbia is inextricably bound up with the cultural geography of empire (King 1990). Performances of imperial sentiment were often staged in suburban settings (Ryan 1999). The suburban vernacular architectural form of the bungalow has its origin in complex colonial cultures and networks (King 1984), and the physical development and ethnic make up of suburbs around major capital cities such as London have been shaped by large-scale global and imperial processes (see also Driver & Gilbert 1998).

Such work complements accounts of the cultural geography of modern (postcolonial) cities in its attention to the ways in which urban identities are imagined and performed. As Jacobs has observed: "In contemporary cities people connected by imperial histories are thrust together in assemblages barely predicted, and often guarded against, during the inaugural phases of colonialism. Often enough this is a meeting not simply augmented by imperialism but still regulated by its constructs of difference and privilege" (Jacobs 1996: 4). As Jacobs' accounts of postcolonial cultural geographies in Britain and Australia show, postcolonial perspectives are essential in understanding the intertwined geographies of "center" and "periphery," as well as how such constructs of difference and privilege continue to be applied and resisted within different spatial settings (Jackson & Jacobs 1996).

Postcolonial Geographies of Encounters and Resistance

A third major, but relatively underdeveloped, strand of work within postcolonial geography takes as its central concern those spaces of colonial encounter and resistance. As a movement, postcolonialism has long been concerned with the struggles of ordinary people against the forces of imperial and colonial power. Indeed, postcolonial theory and criticism emerged from anticolonial movements all over the world in which political practice and radical ideas were mobilized together against colonial domination (Young 2001). However, those least advantaged and most exploited groups in society – invariably the poor, women, children – have been often left out of studies of colonial history, anticolonial struggle, or political independence. One group of South Asian scholars – the Subaltern Studies collective – has pioneered work that sets out to recover the hidden voices and actions of "subaltern" groups through alternative readings of official or elite records, as well as oral history and songs (see, for example, Guha & Spivak 1988). Such work rejects the elitist models of both imperial history and nationalist history, focusing instead upon the experience of people whose lives and agency are ignored in such accounts. Some commentators have questioned the attempt to represent the lives of the marginalized, arguing that it is not possible to recover fully the hidden spaces and silenced voices of Indian subaltern women, because any act of dissent is also always entangled within the dominant discourses that it might be resisting (Spivak 1988). Instead, Spivak points to the necessity of exploring and decolonizing dominant discourses, notably of gender (Spivak 1987, 1988).

It has long been recognized that colonialism involves contact, conflict, and compromise between different groups within spatial settings; the "contact żone" where "disparate cultures meet, clash, and grapple with each other, often in highly asymmetrical relations of domination and subordination" (Pratt cited in Yeoh 2000: 162). However, many geographical accounts of colonialism and imperialism have concentrated on the processes and practices of domination, as understood and represented by the colonial powers, paying relatively little attention to perspectives of the colonized and processes of conflict, negotiation, and resistance. Brenda Yeoh has argued recently for "geographical accounts of the colonized world which move away from depicting it as a passive, flattened out world, stamped upon by more powerful others and fashioned solely in the image of colonialism" (Yeoh 2000: 162). Yeoh argues that geographers need to pay much closer attention to the everyday worlds of colonized people, to "re-filter colonial discourse through 'other' lenses" and to "reconceptualise the 'contact zone' in terms of contest and complicity, conflict and collusion, and to tackle the unwritten history of resistance" (Yeoh 2000: 149). One significant model for such an approach is Yeoh's own work on the colonial city of Singapore in which she explores the overlapping domains of the colonial project and the colonized world within the specific physical setting of a major colonial city (Yeoh 1996). Yeoh draws upon a range of historical sources to trace various kinds of resistance within late nineteenth- and early twentieth-century Singapore, from attempts by indigenous people to evade official strategies of disease control to the "Verandah Riots" of 1888, disturbances generated largely by Chinese reactions against restrictions on their use of urban space. In this way she charts the colonial city as a space of multiple conflict and negotiation; a space in which interconnected practices of resistance were entangled in complex patterns with discourses and practices of domination.

Recent accounts of the formation of imperial cities have also emphasized the heterogeneity of the imperial city and its role as a venue for alternative articulations of empire. Jonathan Schneer has shown, for example, how London provided the setting for the evolution of anti-imperial politics, particularly through the Pan-African conference of 1900, as well as through Indian and Irish nationalist movements (Schneer 1999). Moreover, urban spaces constructed to symbolize imperial power, such as Trafalgar Square in London, were appropriated as sites of protest and resistance (Mace 1976).

Another potentially fruitful avenue for cultural geographers is through the engagement with postcolonial countercultural praxis, notably in the work of community programs, artists, and filmmakers. Catherine Nash, for example, has explored the emergence of new cartographies of postcolonial and gender identities as represented in the landscape art of contemporary Irish women artists (Nash 1994). Jane Jacobs has also explored alternative postcolonial maps in her account of an Aboriginal art trail at J. C. Slaughter Falls near Brisbane in Australia. Both these studies show how specific projects of individual or community art can promote new kinds of cartographic renditions of space that creatively reappropriate colonial maps, subverting their conventional contours of power.

The innovative work of artists and filmmakers operating at the edges of the academy has often been underappreciated by academics. Paul Stotter has studied the films made in the 1940s, 1950s, and 1960s by the ethnographic filmmaker Jean Rouch, and shows how his work offered an incisive and sophisticated critique of the ethnographic encounter and French colonialism in Africa (Stoller 1994). One of Rouch's late films, *Petit à Petit* (1969), for example, portrays the experience of two

West African entrepreneurs, Damoré and Lam, visiting Paris, the heart of the French empire, to observe the habits of the French "tribe" in order to scrutinize them with a view to opening a luxury hotel in Niamey, Niger. With humor and dexterity, the characters turn the tables on Europeans – here it is Parisians, not Africans, who are being scrutinized and visualized. In one scene Damoré poses as a doctoral student and, wielding anthropometric callipers, sets about making bodily measurements of willing Parisians – in the Place Trocadero. In this and other work Rouch skillfully transformed the observers into the observed and exposed the complicity of the academy with colonial power and racism. By exploring such countercultural productions, from film to cartoons, cultural geographers can further broaden their critique of colonial knowledge as well as amplify the contested nature of colonial and postcolonial culture.

Conclusion: Locating Postcolonial Geographies

As I noted at the start of this essay, some commentators have been concerned that the term postcolonialism has been used so frequently, and often with little focus, that it might lose any effective meaning (Ashcroft et al. 1995: 2). Might "post-colonial geographies" be simply another variant on an already overextended theme, destined to produce more heat than light? Could "postcolonial geographies" be just marking an attempt by geographers to colonize academic territories of postcolonial studies and postcolonial theory (Barnett 1997)? These scenarios might materialize if geographers simply appropriate and rehearse existing or outdated ideas; if we apply "postcolonialism" in an uncritical, undifferentiated way, or if we fail to scrutinize and "decolonize" our own procedures and practices in producing knowledge. Geographers in general and cultural geographers in particular have a great deal to learn – and "unlearn" – from the interdisciplinary field of postcolonial studies as they strive to "decolonize" the geographical imagination (Pieterse & Parekh 1995; Ngugi 1986; Spivak 1988).

However, as I have tried to indicate in this chapter, the field of "postcolonial geographies" has much to contribute to the study of forms of colonial and imperial power. In particular, studies of the landscapes of postcolonialism often revolve around significant questions of space, place, and territory. As a number of commentators have observed, the work of postcolonial critics, from Said's explorations of "imaginative geography" to Bhabha's notion of a "third space" of hybrid identities, is often profoundly geographical in its theoretical emphasis (Blunt & Wills 2000). At the same time, many criticisms that have been leveled at theoretical analyses of "colonial discourse" argue that overgeneralized accounts have a limited relevance; what is needed, it is often claimed, is more studies that take account of the very specific conditions and circumstances in which colonial power operated (Thomas 1994). In an important way therefore, all postcolonial studies need to be concerned with geography; without the specifics of location in time and space "postcolonialism," like any other term, can only be applied in a very loose and general way. The conventional preoccupations of geographers with space and place make them well positioned to ground the often abstract debates of postcolonial studies within specific historical and geographical settings and, in so doing, to engage with the material as well as the discursive, the physical as well as the symbolic, dimensions of colonialism and its legacies (Driver 2001; Barnett 1997; Yeoh 2001).

I began this chapter by discussing how varied notions of postcolonialism have found an increasingly influential place within geography. It is now clear that this flow of ideas is not simply in one direction and that geographers in general, and cultural geographers in particular, have distinctive contributions to make to this expanding field. As Shurmer-Smith argues, cultural geographers are well placed to employ postcolonial theory in the "deconstruction" of a range of different post-colonial cultural artifacts, including films, novels, poems, music, and theater, in order to reveal and confront continuing forms of imperial and colonial prejudice and discrimination. However, she also urges cultural geographers to think more critically about "the very notion of postcolonial culture outside former colonies" as well as the process by which cultural products are legitimated through what Mitchell (1995) terms "postimperial criticism" emerging from metropolitan centers of authority (Shurmer-Smith 2002: 76). The production, legitimation and reception of (postcolonial) cultural products are intensely geographical processes. For example, in discussing the genre of what she calls "transnational novels" Shurmer-Smith notes that Arundhati Roy's 1997 Booker Prize winning novel *The God of Small Things* was translated from English into the major European languages before it appeared in any Indian language.

The making of postcolonial cultural geographies is not only a matter of deconstructing cultural representations for the marks of imperial and colonial power. As I have noted, it also involves exploring the everyday cultural worlds of colonial and postcolonial subjects and narrating the resistances and negotiations that shape the "contact zones" of colonial encounters and postcolonial landscapes, from London to Lagos. The fact that "postcolonial geographies," like postcolonial studies more generally, stem from Western and metropolitan institutions, notably universities, does not prohibit them from developing radically new perspectives or from fostering links with world wide political movements to highlight inequalities and promote social justice (see, for example, Blunt & Wills 2000: 198–203). The fact that some postcolonial critiques have shown how the language and techniques of geography placed it squarely as an imperial science should not stop us from attempting to explore as fully as possible the shape of postcolonial geographies.

As part of an evolving body of work, postcolonial geographies represent an important and diverse strand of work. As such, postcolonial geographies are set to occupy an increasingly important position within human geography in general and cultural geography in particular, as postcolonial perspectives continue to challenge geographers to think more deeply about the processes of colonialism and imperialism. The work of those who have pioneered postcolonial geographies in the last decade extends well beyond the usual confines of "cultural geography"; yet thinking more carefully about postcolonial geographies challenges cultural geographers in particular to employ new understandings of "culture" to understand better the operations of colonial power and to challenge dominant, eurocentric knowledges. The "culture" of colonialism is not to be located simply in the world of texts and representations, but in the material and performed realities of the everyday. Nor is "culture" to be treated as some separate domain, that can be isolated from, or explained by, the economic or political dimensions of colonialism; cultures of empire need to be considered in their full and complex articulations with other forms of colonial rule (Dirks 1992; Thomas 1994). Finally, postcolonial geographies need to be sensitive to the precise cultural and historical differences in the operation of – and resistance to – forms of colonial power. By undertaking work that locates colonial and postcolonial geographies more precisely in time and space, geographers are continuing to shape the development of this field and to probe the continuing effects of colonialism on the cultural landscapes of the present.

REFERENCES

Alavi, H. 1972: The state in postcolonial societies: Pakistan and Bangladesh. *New Left Review* 74, 59–82.

Anderson, K. 2000a: Thinking "postnationally": dialogue across multicultural, indigenous, and settler spaces. *Annals of the Association of American Geographers* 90, 381–91.

Arnold, D. 2000: "Illusory riches": representations of the tropical world, 1840–1950. *Singapore Journal of Tropical Geography* 21, 6–18.

Ashcroft, B., Griffiths, G., and Tiffin, H. 1989: *The Empire Writes Back: Theory and Practice in Post-colonial Literatures*. London: Methuen.

Ashcroft, B., Griffiths, G., and Tiffin, H., eds. 1995: *The Post-colonial Studies Reader*. London: Routledge.

Barnett, C. 1998: Impure and worldly geography: the Africanist discourse of the Royal Geographical Society, 1871–73. *Transactions of the Institute of British Geographers* NS 23, 239–52.

Barnett, C. 1997: "Sing along with the common people": politics, postcolonialism, and other figures. *Environment and Planning D: Society and Space* 15(2), 137–54.

Bell, M., Butlin, R. A., and Heffernan, M. J., eds. 1995: *Geography and Imperialism, 1820–1940*. Manchester: Manchester University Press.

Best, B. 1999: Postcolonialism and the deconstructive scenario: representing Gayatri Spivak. *Environment and Planning D: Society and Space* 17(4), 475.

Bhabha, H. K. 1990: *Nation and Narration*. London: Routledge.

Bhabha, H. K. 1994: *The Location of Culture*. London: Routledge.

Blaut, J. 1993: *The Colonizer's Model of the World: Geographical Diffusionism and Eurocentric History*. New York: Guilford Press.

Blunt, A. 1994: *Travel, Gender, and Imperialism: Mary Kingsley and West Africa*. New York: Guilford Press.

Blunt, A. 1999: Imperial geographies of home: British women in India, 1886–1925. *Transactions of the Institute of British Geographers* N.S. 24, 421–40.

Blunt, A. and McEwan, C., eds. 2002: *Postcolonial Geographies*. New York: Continuum.

Blunt, A. and Rose, G., eds. 1994: *Writing Women and Space: Colonial and Postcolonial Geographies*. New York: Guilford Press.

Blunt, A. and Wills, J. 2000: *Dissident Geographies: An Introduction to Radical Ideas and Practice*. New York: Prentice-Hall.

Clark, S. H. 1999: *Travel Writing and Empire: Postcolonial Theory in Transit*. London and New York: Zed Books.

Clayton, D. 2000a: The creation of imperial space in the Pacific Northwest. *Journal of Historical Geography* 26(3), 327–50.

Clayton, D. 2000b: *Islands of Truth*. Vancouver: University of British Columbia Press.

Clayton, D. 2001: Questions of postcolonial geography. *Antipode* 33(4), 3.

Cook, I., et al., eds. 2000: *Cultural Turns/Geographical Turns: Perspectives on Cultural Geography*. New York: Prentice-Hall.

Crang, M. 1998: *Cultural Geographies*. New York and London: Routledge.

Crush, J. 1994: Post-colonialism, de-colonization, and geography. In N. Smith and A. Godlewska, eds., *Geography and Empire*. Oxford: Blackwell, 333–50.

Crush, J. 1996: The culture of failure: racism, violence and white farming in colonial Swaziland, *Journal of Historical Geography* 22(2), 177–97.

Dirks, N., ed. 1992: *Colonialism and Culture*. Ann Arbor: University of Michigan Press.

Driver, F. 1992: Geography's empire: histories of geographical knowledge. *Environment and Planning D: Society and Space* 10, 23–40.

Driver, F. 2001: *Geography Militant: Cultures of Exploration and Empire*. Oxford: Blackwell.

Driver, F. and Gilbert, D. 1998: Heart of empire? Landscape, space and performance in imperial London. *Environment and Planning D: Society and Space*, 16, 11–28.

Driver, F. and Gilbert, D., eds. 1999: *Imperial Cities: Landscape, Display and Identity*. Manchester: Manchester University Press.

Driver, F. and Yeoh, B. S. A. 2000: Constructing the tropics: introduction. *Singapore Journal of Tropical Geography* 21, 1–5.

Duncan, J. S. 2000: The struggle to be temperate: climate and "moral masculinity" in mid-nineteenth century Ceylon. *Singapore Journal of Tropical Geography* 21, 34–47.

Duncan, J. S. and Gregory, D., eds. 1999: *Writes of Passage: Reading Travel Writing*. London: Routledge.

Edney, M. 1997: *Mapping an Empire: The Geographical Construction of British India, 1765–1843*. Chicago: University of Chicago Press.

Frenkel, S. and Western, J. 1988: Pretext or prophylaxis? Racial segregation and malarial mosquitos in a British tropical colony: Sierra Leone. *Annals of the Association of American Geographers* 78, 211–28.

Gelder, K. and Jacobs, J. M. 1995: "Talking out of place": authorizing the Aboriginal sacred in postcolonial Australia. *Cultural studies* 9(1), 150.

Gelder, K. and Jacobs, J. M. 1998: *Uncanny Australia: Sacredness and Identity in a Postcolonial Nation*. Carlton South, Aus.: Melbourne University Press.

Gibbons, L. 2000: Race against time: racial discourse and Irish history. In C. Hall, ed., *Cultures of Empire: A Reader*. Manchester: Manchester University Press, 207–23.

Godlewska, A. 2000: *Geography Unbound: French Geographic Science from Cassini to Humboldt*. Chicago: University of Chicago Press.

Godlewska, A. and Smith, N., eds. 1994: *Geography and Empire*. Oxford and Malden, MA: Blackwell.

Goldberg, D. T. and Quayson, A. 2002: *Relocating Postcolonialism*. Malden, MA: Blackwell.

Graham, B. and Nash, C., eds. 2000: *Modern Historical Geographies*. London: Prentice-Hall.

Gregory, D. 1994: *Geographical Imaginations*. Cambridge, MA: Blackwell.

Gregory, D. 1995a: Imaginative geographies. *Progress in Human Geography* 19, 447–85.

Gregory, D. 1995b: Between the book and the lamp: imaginative geographies of Egypt, 1849–50. *Transactions of the Institute of British Geographers* N.S. 20, 29–57.

Gregory, D. 1998: Power, knowledge and geography. *Geographische Zeitschrift* 86, 70–93.

Gregory, D. 2000: Postcolonialism. In R. J. Johnston et al., eds., *Dictionary of Human Geography*. Oxford: Blackwell, 612–15.

Guha, R. and Spivak, G. C., eds. 1988: *Selected Subaltern Studies*. Oxford: Oxford University Press.

Hall, C. 2000a: Introduction: thinking the postcolonial, thinking the empire. In C. Hall, ed., *Cultures of Empire: A Reader*. Manchester: Manchester University Press, 1–33.

Hall, C., ed. 2000b: *Cultures of Empire: A Reader*. Manchester: Manchester University Press.

Howell, P. 2000: Prostitution and racialised sexuality: the regulation of prostitution in Britain and the British Empire before the Contagious Diseases Acts. *Environment and Planning D: Society and Space* 18, 321–39.

Hudson, B. 1977: The new geography and the new imperialism: 1870–1918. *Antipode* 9, 12–19.

Jackson, P. and Jacobs, J. M. 1996: Postcolonialism and the politics of race. *Environment and Planning D: Society and Space* 14, 1–3.

Jacobs, J. M. 1996: *Edge of Empire: Postcolonialism and the City.* London: Routledge.

King, A. D. 1984: *The Bungalow: The Production of Global Culture.* London: Routledge.

King, A. D. 1990: *Urbanism, Colonialism and the World Economy: Cultural and Spatial Foundations of the World Urban System.* London: Routledge.

Kusno, A. 2000: *Behind the Postcolonial: Architecture, Urban Space, and Political Cultures in Indonesia.* London and New York: Routledge.

Landau, P. S. and Kaspin, D., eds. 2002: *Images and Empires: Visuality in Colonial and Post-colonial Africa.* Berkeley: University of California Press.

Lester, A. 2000: Historical geographies of imperialism. In B. Graham and C. Nash, eds., *Modern Historical Geographies.* Harlow, UK: Pearson Education, 100–20.

Lionnet, F. 2000: Transnationalism, postcolonialism or transcolonialism? Reflections on Los Angeles, geography, and the uses of theory. *Emergences: Journal for the Study of Media & Composite Cultures* 10(1), 25–35.

Livingstone, D. N. 1992: *The Geographical Tradition.* Oxford: Blackwell.

Livingstone, D. N. 1999: Tropical climate and moral hygiene: the anatomy of a Victorian debate. *British Journal for the History of Science* 32, 93–110.

Loomba, A. 1998: *Colonialism/Postcolonialism.* London: Routledge.

Mace, R. 1976: *Trafalgar Square: Emblem of Empire.* London: Lawrence & Wishart.

Maddrell, A. 1996: Empire, emigration and school geography: changing discourses of imperial citizenship. *Journal of Historical Geography* 22, 373–87.

Maddrell, A. 1998: Discourses of race and gender and the comparative method in geography school texts, 1830–1918. *Environment and Planning D: Society and Space* 16, 81–103.

McCarthy, C. and Dimitriadis, G. 2000: Art and the postcolonial imagination: rethinking the institutionalization of third world aesthetics and theory. *Ariel* 31(1/2), 231–54.

McClintock, A. 1995: *Imperial Leather: Race, Gender, and Sexuality in the Colonial Contest.* New York: Routledge.

McClintock, A., Mufti, A., Shohat, E., and Social Text Collective. 1997: *Dangerous Liaisons: Gender, Nation, and Postcolonial Perspectives.* Minneapolis: University of Minnesota Press.

McDowell, L. M. 1997: Colonial and postcolonial geographies. *Feminist Review* 57, 168.

McEwan, C. 1996: Paradise or pandemonium? West African landscapes in the travel accounts of Victorian Women. *Journal of Historical Geography* 22(1), 68–83.

McEwan, C. 1998: Cutting power lines within the palace? Countering paternity and eurocentrism in the "geographical tradition." *Transactions of the Institute of British Geographers* NS 23, 371–84.

McEwan, C. 2000: *Gender, Geography and Empire: Victorian Women Travellers in West Africa.* Aldershot: Ashgate.

Mishra, V. and Hodge, B. 1994: What is post-colonialism? In P. Williams and L. Chrisman, eds., *Colonial Discourse and Post-colonial Theory.* New York: Columbia University Press, 285–8.

Mitchell, D. 2000: *Cultural Geography.* Oxford: Blackwell.

Mitchell, W. 1995: Postcolonial culture, postimperial criticism. In B. Ashcroft et al., eds., *The Post-colonial Studies Reader.* London: Routledge, 475–9.

Moore-Gilbert, B. J. 1997: *Postcolonial Theory: Contexts, Practices, Politics.* London and New York: Verso.

Morton, S. 2002: *Gayatri Chakravorty Spivak*. New York: Routledge.

Nash, C. 1994: Remapping the body/land: new cartographies of identity, gender and landscape in Ireland. In A. Blunt and G. Rose, eds., *Writing Women and Space: Colonial and Postcolonial Geographies*. New York: Guilford, 227–50.

Nash, C. 2002: Cultural geography: postcolonial cultural geographies. *Progress in Human Geography* 26(2), 219–30.

Naylor, S. J. 2000a: "That very garden of South America": European surveyors in Paraguay. *Singapore Journal of Tropical Geography* 21, 48–62.

Naylor, S. J. 2000b: Spacing the can: empire, modernity, and the globalization of food. *Environment and Planning A* 32, 1625–39.

Ngũgĩ wa Thiong'o. 1977: *Petals of Blood*. London: Heinemann.

Ngũgĩ wa Thiong'o. 1981: *Detained: A Writer's Prison Diary*. Nairobi: Heinemann.

Ngũgĩ wa Thiong'o. 1982: *Devil on the Cross*. London: Heinemann.

Ngũgĩ wa Thiong'o. 1986: *Decolonising the Mind: The Politics of Language in African Literature*. London: Heinemann.

O'Brien, S. 1998: The place of America in an era of postcolonial imperialism. *Ariel* 29(2), 159.

Orlove, B. S. 1993: Putting race in its place: order in colonial and postcolonial Peruvian geography. *Social Research* 60(2), 301–36.

Pieterse, J. N. and Parekh, B. 1995: Shifting imaginaries: decolonization, internal decolonization and postcoloniality. In Pieterse and Parekh, eds., *The Decolonization of Imagination: Culture, Knowledge and Power*. London: Zed Books, 1–19.

Ploszajska, T. 2000: Historiographies of geography and empire. In B. Graham and C. Nash, eds., *Modern Historical Geographies*. Harlow, UK: Pearson Education, 121–45.

Radcliffe, S. A. 1997: Different heroes: genealogies of postcolonial geographies. *Environment & Planning A* 29(8), 1331.

Rattansi, A. 1997: Postcolonialism and its discontents. *Economy and Society* 26, 480–500.

Robinson, J. 1999: Postcoloniality/postcolonialism. In L. McDowell and J. P. Sharp, eds., *A Feminist Glossary of Human Geography*. London: Arnold, 208–10.

Ryan, J. 1997: *Picturing Empire: Photography and the Visualization of the British Empire*. London: Reaktion Books.

Ryan, D. 1999: Staging the imperial city: the Pageant of London 1911. In F. Driver and D. Gilbert, eds., *Imperial Cities: Landscape, Display and Identity*. Manchester: Manchester University Press.

Said, E. W. 1978: *Orientalism*. New York: Pantheon Books.

Said, E. W. 1993: *Culture and Imperialism*. New York: Knopf.

Sampat-Patel, N. 2001: *Postcolonial Masquerades: Culture and Politics in Literature, Film, Video, and Photography*. New York: Garland.

Schneer, J. 1999: *London 1900: The Imperial Metropolis*. New Haven and London: Yale University Press.

Shurmer-Smith, P. 2002: Postcolonial geographies. In P. Shurmer-Smith, ed., *Doing Cultural Geography*. London: Sage, 67–77.

Shurmer-Smith, P. and Hannam, K. 1994: *Worlds of Desire, Realms of Power: A Cultural Geography*. London: Arnold.

Sidaway, J. D. 1997: The (re)making of the western "geographical tradition": some missing links. *Area* 29, 72–80.

Sidaway, J. D. 2000: Postcolonial geographies: an exploratory essay. *Progress in Human Geography* 24(4), 591–612.

Simon, D. 1998: Rethinking (post)modernism, postcolonialism, and posttraditionalism: South–North perspectives. *Environment and Planning D: Society and Space* 16(2), 219.

Sluyter, A. 2002: *Colonialism and Landscape: Postcolonial Theory and Applications*. Lanham, MD: Rowman & Littlefield.

Somerville, M. and Hartley, L. 2000: Eating place: postcolonial explorations of embodiment and place. *Journal of Intercultural Studies* 21(3), 353–64.

Spivak, G. C. 1987: *In Other Worlds: Essays in Cultural Politics*. New York: Methuen.

Spivak, G. C. 1988: "Can the subaltern speak?" In C. Nelson and L. Grossberg, eds., *Marxism and the Interpretation of Culture*. London: Macmillan, 271–313.

Stoller, P. 1994: Artaud, Rouch, and the cinema of cruelty. In L. Taylor, ed., *Visualizing Theory: Selected Essays From V.A.R. 1990–1994*. New York: Routledge, 84–98.

Thomas, N. 1994: *Colonialism's Culture: Anthropology, Travel and Government*. Cambridge: Polity.

Thomas, P. 2002: The river, the road, and the rural–urban divide: a postcolonial moral geography from southeast Madagascar. *American Ethnologist* 29(2), 26.

Williams, P. and Chrisman, L., eds. 1993: *Colonial Discourse and Post-colonial Theory: A Reader*. New York: Columbia University Press.

Yeoh, B. S. A. 1996: *Contesting Space: Power Relations and the Urban Built Environment in Colonial Singapore*. Kuala Lumpur: Oxford University Press.

Yeoh, B. S. A. 2000: Historical geographies of the colonised world. In B. Graham and C. Nash, eds., *Modern Historical Geographies*. Harlow, UK: Pearson Education, 146–66.

Yeoh, B. S. A. 2001: Postcolonial cities. *Progress in Human Geography* 25(3), 456–68.

Young, R. 1990: *White Mythologies: Writing History and the West*. London: Routledge.

Young, R. 2001: *Postcolonialism: An Historical Introduction*. Oxford: Blackwell.

Chapter 31

Diaspora

Carl Dahlman

While the diaspora concept is not new, its contemporary usage within the western social sciences and humanities has moved well beyond any simple notion of a scattered population. Conventional treatments of the concept, which often focus on the Jewish diaspora and the culture of exile, have emerged in contemporary writings as a "special form" of transnational ethnic communities marked by a "persistent sense" of belonging among members "across borders and generations" (Clifford 1994; Castles & Miller 1998: 201; Safran 1991). As such, diaspora is increasingly part of the lexicon of the multicultural, transnational, and cosmopolitan moment in social inquiry, celebrating the disorientation and reorganization of global circuits of power (Hesse 2000; Tölölyan 1991; see also Cheah & Robbins 1998). Recent studies concerning migration and changing cultural landscapes of a globalizing world, have reworked the diaspora concept, denoting the cultural effects of shifts in capital and the extension and acceleration of transportation and communication networks (e.g. Nonini & Ong 1997). In this vein, authors have imagined diasporas as networks given over to new subject positions in which diasporic subjects are "enmeshed in circuits of social, economic, and cultural ties encompassing both the mother country and the country of settlement" (Lavie & Swedenburg 1996: 14; cf. Brah 1996: 196). Furthermore, diaspora has been held up as a site of progressive politics and antihegemonic subjecthood:

Diaspora formations currently define the post-colonial sense in the proliferation of and interaction between cultural differences that shape the transnational configurations of dispersed histories and identities within and against the cultural legislation of the western nation. (Hesse 2000: 20)

Despite the celebratory mood of its many advocates, the reality for would-be diasporic communities is more stark; an experience of exclusionary policies and intolerant attitudes held by host-societies, whose resident populations maintain tenacious biases in favor of racial, ethnic, and even civic national identity in which migrants are said to have no place (Geddes 2000; Harding 2000; Levy 1999; Sassen

1998: 31–53). The popular sentiment in industrialized countries, especially in western Europe, that they are awash with refugees, though dealing with but a fraction of the world's total, has contributed to a sense of siege; one in which anti-immigration platforms have well served right-wing political leaders in recent years. Such biases are most recently evident in the rise of nationalist and anti-immigration candidates across Europe (Cowell 2002; *Economist* 2002; Lyall 2002). For their part, migrants – both labor and refugee – are seeking to abandon the economic despair, political persecution or social instability endemic to an increasingly global-ized world and the convulsions accompanying the end of empires and the excesses of neoliberalism (Harding 2000).

Although much of the renewed interest in migration studies may be understood as a reasoned, even progressive, response to reactionary immigration policies, the cultural concepts emerging from this literature remain much debated. Criticism of these "new" theories of migration and culture – what some have termed "globaliz-ization from below" – focuses on both the conceptual duplicity between concept and reality and the narrowness of their explanatory vision. For example, Nagel argues that "concepts such as diaspora and transnationalism, while attempting to loosen conceptual boundaries, often revert to very rigid and traditional under-standings of culture, ethnicity, and locality" (2001: 247). Mitchell (1997) suggests that such decontextualized, celebratory declarations of the culturally ambivalent, new or cosmopolitan "may neglect the actual geographies of capital accumulation in which those spaces are produced" (p. 551). This essay follows from these criti-cal positions to more fully question the (geo)political significance of diasporas, specifically in the context of Kurdish emigration to Europe and North America.

Before considering diaspora as a geopolitical category, it is useful to recognize that diasporas denote quite specific sociospatial formations and cultural expressions distinct from many of the terms drawn in close association with migration. Three such terms are discussed here: transnationalism, multiculturalism, and hybridity. First, transnationalism, as typically understood in writings on diasporas, describes a condition in which somewhat regularized nongovernmental transborder relations persist among individuals who share a common culture and historical memory, a common experience of dispersal from and loss of a homeland, and a desire to symbolically maintain, or physically return to, that homeland (Cohen 1997: 26; see also e.g. Tatla 1999; Wahlbeck 1999). While broader interpretations of trans-nationalism include the emergence of culturally novel forms (Basch et al. 1994) or politically effective organizational relations (Risse-Kappen 1995), it is suffi-cient for our purposes to recognize that diaspora is often predicated on transna-tional social relations. However, transnationalism is not a sufficient condition for diasporas, which additionally imply a common sense of territorial identity among its members, nor are all transnational relations diasporic. Moreover, it is quite common to find an implied equivalence between transnationalism and diaspora, which threatens to evacuate any meaningful value from either term (see also Nagel 2001).

Second, authors often describe diasporic communities in terms of multicultural-ism, that is, thrusting into a host-society an "other" whose cultural difference cannot be wholly dissolved nor whose political loyalties can be fully won over. While mul-ticulturalism is typically understood to mean the inclusion of cultural difference within the formal institutions of representative government and civil society, it is best understood specifically to describe one possible political response by a host government to various forms of migrancy, which may or may not include diasporic projects. In any case, this concept implies an abandonment of strict ethnic or racial definitions of "nation" in favor of a more tolerant "civic national" enfranchisement of recently migrated or permanently resident noncitizens. In terms of diasporas, multicultural policies would appear to slacken apprehension over the "divided loyalties" of residents who seek a redemptive or reclaimant politics toward a homeland. In reality, multicultural projects generally disfavor the socially or politically extroverted communities that diasporas imply – focused as they are on the politics of a homeland.

Third, hybridity is frequently employed to describe the effects of migrancy on identity – the condition of being an in-between, out-of-place, or multiply-constituted subject (e.g. Bhabha 1994). Applied to the diaspora concept, it becomes apparent that hybridity opens the possibility of the diasporic subject to participate in two cultural registers or to be situated within two identity categories at once. Yet, this implies a degree of selective acculturation that many diasporic subjects, indeed many migrants, rarely achieve in light of the assimilative expectations or requirements they face, especially by participating in localized and nationalized political-economies. The imagination of a hybrid subject, one relatively accustomed or experienced in two or more distinct cultural registers confounds any attempt at precision – by what do we gauge it? – and fails to meaningfully explain the social significance of the concept, trapped as it is in psychological speculation. Instead, it refuses the moment of cultural synthesis, of the collapse of difference, in favor of a hyphenated and uncomfortable conjuncture of difference. The upshot of hybridity, when put in the context of migrancy, is that it replaces the homology of space and identity with two such homologies in tension, leaving relatively unexplored the social constitution of spatialized identities. Worse still, it appears from some treatments of hybridity that its application to social explanation depends on an unwarranted degree of voluntarism on matters of identity and political action.

Geopolitics, Diasporas, and Refugees

In reconsidering the diaspora concept from a more skeptical standpoint, and one that is concerned with the interaction of space, identity, and power, particularly at a geopolitical scale, it is useful to do so in the context of contemporary theories from international relations and the area of political geography termed critical geopolitics. Both literatures critique realist theories which describe international politics as a function of states operating in an anarchic, or unruly, environment. Within the international relations literature, authors such as Ashley (1987) have rejected the realist framework on the grounds that political interactions are not the actions of states *per se* but rather of a small network of specialist elites, such as foreign ministers and embassy officials, operating on behalf of states and who, when reconceived of as a social unit, may be recognized as sharing certain ideas and values that function as a form of power/knowledge. Once recognized as a socially constructed rather than naturally evolving condition, international politics is opened to social inquiry to explicate the practices that:

provide the framework, symbolic resources, and practical strategies for the coordination and legitimation of action, the disciplining of resistance, and, hence, the historical production and differentiation of the community, its boundaries, its objects, and its subjective agents. (Ashley 1987: 403–4)

Likewise, critical geopolitics seeks to identify and critique the practice of geopolitics from a position outside the received tradition of formal geopolitics. Committed to both heterogeneous and alternative practices of power and space, it also seeks to develop more fully an appreciation of nonstate geopolitics, including nonstate actors, shifting scales, unbound territorialities, and popular representational practices of the geopolitical (Ó Tuathail & Dalby 1998: 2–7). Agnew's argument that "the 'spatiality' or geographical organization of power is not necessarily tied for all time and all places to the territoriality of states" reminds us of the problems inherent in normalizing existing geopolitical space (1998: 49). To escape what Agnew terms the "territorial trap," we must recognize that a state's sovereignty, its exclusive spatiality, and its social "contents" are normative constructs that do not reflect the increasingly globalized and transnational character of contemporary social, economic, and even political interactions. In terms of the diaspora, as a political-cultural trope, one has to make a careful distinction between, on the one hand, an approach that reasserts the primacy and normality of territorially discrete nation-states favored by irredentist identity politics, and, on the other hand, an approach that recognizes diaspora as a socially constructed claim to territoriality. In consideration of these efforts, Dalby suggests "that 'alternative politics' is about more than resistance, social movements, and states. These arguments also show in a number of ways that critical geopolitics is about connections and community understood as other than place-bound political entities" (Dalby 1999: 181).

Though discussions of diaspora are steeped in the vocabulary of cultural studies, the concept is not without political and geopolitical import. Like nation, diaspora describes a relationship between space and identity though authors have tended to adopt one of two general schemes in specifying this relationship, each bearing quite different geopolitical implications. One approach to diaspora represents ethnic identity as organic and autochthonous; identity mapped onto specific territories or homelands. The loss of a homeland, usually through forced migration, heralds the emergence of a diasporic culture (that is a culture is displaced and also becomes a culture identifying itself with loss and the pain of exile). So while diaspora is much vaunted as "exemplary communities of the transnational moment" (Tölölyan 1991: 5), the concept has nevertheless, for some authors, become essentialized – it serves to reestablish the notion of territorially fixed and naturalized ethnic homeland as a norm from which a diasporic group was displaced: "the phenomenon of ethnic loyalty towards homeland is usually called a diaspora" (Tatla 1999: 2). The danger inherent in this use of the diaspora concept lies in its supposition of a natural order of places and peoples, which, *in extremis*, lends moral justification to nationalism, especially pernicious irredentist or revanchist policies. Malkki refers to this sensibility as the "national order of things": "the supposedly normal condition of being attached to a territorialized polity and an identifiable people" (1995: 516). The diaspora concept retains a sense of loss and longing for a cultural homeland that is attendant on loosely nationalist aspirations of the diasporic migrant: "The idea of 'homeland' can be seen as another criterion; the notion of diaspora thus indicates a nationalism in exile" (Wahlbeck 1999: 30). By extension, diasporic communities are defined by some authors according to a shared sense of common ancestral territory, an experience of dispersal or displacement from that homeland, and an implicit desire for its recovery or liberation (Cohen 1997: 26). The function of dispersal and loss as implied by the diaspora concept also serves to prefigure the refugee as a necessary diasporic subject. Taken further, diasporas are the site of political mobilization for homeland restoration and frequently imply a return migration (Tatla 1999). Ironically, nationalism's pernicious homology between space and identity, which endorses the diasporic subject's irredentist, romantic nostalgia for a homeland, also underpins the xenophobic and violent reactions of host-societies to those migrants.

A second approach to diaspora takes a very different tack from the first, insisting on the constructed and multiple nature of identity and refusing any necessary, or geographically normal, location. As such, diaspora represents less the loss of a cultural location than a reaffirmation of how culture, territoriality and identity are constructed in the first place. Donald Nonini and Aihwa Ong (1997), in a set of essays on Chinese transnationalism, argue "the necessity of reconceptualizing the relationship between the study of . . . identities and the place-bound theorizations of a preglobal social science, implied in such terms as *territory*, *region*, *nationality*, and *ethnicity*" (Nonini & Ong 1997: 5, emphasis in original). These authors view cultural forms, such as familial relations, identity and territorial attachments, as discursive tropes whose constructions have specific genealogies and intellectual antecedents that relate cultural epistemologies to the economic and geopolitical, not to mention academic, relations between China and the world. A "deterritorialized ethnography" that refuses any necessary equation between space and identity must, therefore, recognize the mobility and transience wrought by flexible accumulation, uneven geometries of power, and the emergence of global "third cultures," as described by David Harvey, Doreen Massey, and Mike Featherstone, respectively (Nonini & Ong 1997: 9–12). Their repeated refrain calling for a rethinking of how we understand the relationship between space and identity is highly appropriate, disinvesting as it does in the racist and ethnocentric tropes derived from European Enlightenment traditions and colonialism. As a result, Nonini and Ong reject the notion that diasporic persons are residual or inferior elements of some territorialized normal culture, but rather take "an affirmative view of diaspora as a pattern that marks a common condition of communities, persons, and groups separated by space, an arrangement, moreover, that these persons see themselves as sharing" (Nonini & Ong 1997: 18).

Finally, we turn to the specific issues surrounding the migrancy most closely associated with the diaspora concept, that of refugees or asylum-seekers. In as much as refugees are those forced to migrate or whose "well founded fear" of persecution precipitated flight, "the concept of diaspora seems to encompass the transnational and de-territorialized social relations of refugees as well as to outline the specific refugee experience" (Wahlbeck 1999: 30). Soguk (1999) argues that migrants, especially refugees, are disruptive of state territoriality while at the same time they are instrumental to the territorialization of the modern nation-state and citizenship complex (pp. 209–10). Put another way, the "state as container" analogy that Agnew warns against has as its corollary the demographic vision of the state and its citizens, a homology that migration brings to the surface by importing the foreign body into domestic space. This homology is underpinned by a sedentarist bias, which Foucault describes as necessary for the administrative control of territory and population (1991: 99–101), and which prefigures migrancy as a transgressive condition; of being out of place or a threat to the domestic order. This is readily apparent in the representation of refugee migration by the Trilateral Commission:

The most objectionable policy in the public mind is one where the nation appears unable to control a basic element of sovereignty, such as the choice of who resides in a country. This abdication of choice is what burgeoning asylum caseloads represent, and long-staying asylum populations symbolize national vulnerability. (Meissner et al. 1993: 48)

This realization, that migrants figure as threats to states but also provide states an unruly subject whose regulation reestablishes state power, highlights what Soguk refers to as the paradoxical and unequal relationship between sedentarized state projects and the reality of human mobility. Moreover, when those in motion are seeking exilic refuge from harm – mobility brought on by the failure of states – their transgressive acts of border crossings and domestic "disruptions" challenge the state system itself and by extension the sovereign principles through which "order" and "control" are recovered. This has led several authors to critically reconsider the refugee and the international refugee regime as a bundle of geopolitical practices, that is, processes enmeshed within international politics and concerned with the exercise of sovereign territorial power (Lippert 1999; Loescher 1990, 1996; Soguk 1999). Though the refugee is an almost inevitable outcome of the system of territorial nation-states, national governments present themselves as the necessary backstop and ultimate power broker in governing refugee migrations (Soguk 1999). That is, territorially sovereign states occupy the only base from which mastery of international space is possible. The deterritorialized refugee, on the other hand, is bereft of any position in the "national order of things" – the state-centric discourse that maps political rights to a sovereign territorial identity (Malkki 1995, 1997). Displaced from their country of origin, the refugee is reconfigured as the recipient of humanitarianism, bound to the limited participatory rights afforded by the host-state. As such, refugees become idealized as apolitical subjects, their access to the protections of refuge conditional on their docility and acquiescent social position. Indeed, the expectation that refugees should be apolitical is formalized by states in their immigration and asylum policy, yet we know that refugees are not only political subjects who seek consideration from their host-state but that their condition also bears witness to and is born of the geopolitical reality of the state system. As a result, we have little conceptual or empirical research to explain the intersection of refugee political identities and interests and the system of territorial nation-states that ensnares them. The following section takes up the question of how refugees and other migrants attempt to engage international politics by examining recent studies of Kurdish refugee migrations and the formation of Kurdish communities in exile.

Kurdish Diaspora

The Kurdish population is approximately 20 to 25 million people, and Kurds identify their homeland, Kurdistan, in a region transected by the boundaries of four states: Turkey, Iraq, Iran, and Syria. Linguistically distinct from both Arabic and Turkish, the Kurdish dialects are, like Farsi, part of the Indo-European family. Religiously, Kurdish society is roughly two-thirds Sunni Muslim with the other third comprising Alevi and Yezidi religious minorities with a small number of Christians and Jews. This means that Kurds are often religiously different from surrounding populations and are often held in suspicion by secularist regimes. Physically marginalized by their location in the mountainous terrain of Kurdistan, the Kurds have also been regularly conquered by regional empires. With the division of the Ottoman Empire after the First World War, the Kurdish population came under the rule of the four regional governments. The Kurdish experience in each country has been one of political disenfranchisement and cultural oppression, in which genocidal campaigns such as that in Iraq in 1988 have figured significantly. As a result, the last 80 years have witnessed steady Kurdish emigration from Kurdistan in search of either more stable conditions in larger cities like Istanbul or Damascus, or for more distant solutions in Europe and beyond. Kurdish refugee migrations have also numbered among the largest such movements of persons in recent years, much of it directed toward Europe. The Kurdish community in exile, what some Kurds refer to as the Kurdish diaspora, numbers approximately one million people living in Western Europe and North America.

Several authors have studied aspects of Kurdish refugee migration or Kurdish communities in exile as components of a Kurdish diaspora (Leggewie 1996; Van Bruinessen 1999, 2000; Wahlbeck 1998, 1999). While their approaches differ according to disciplinary interests, the research site, and the particular Kurdish sub-population under investigation, their conceptual conclusions direct our attention to issues at the heart of this chapter. Namely, these authors seek to understand better the relationship between Kurdish migration (both labor and refugee) and the obtaining geopolitical condition of Kurdistan, with particular emphasis on the struggle to gain full cultural and political rights and economic opportunities in the region. As such, the authors typically focus on the issue of Kurds from Turkey and the ensuing relations between European host-states and the Turkish government as it vies for accession to the European Union. What is most striking in these works is their shared view of Kurdish refugee mobilization as a form of globalization, a concept that attains a certain degree of geopolitical immediacy but which is more often left conceptually unexamined.

The political life of Kurdish exiles is often overlooked by social scientific studies that are more concerned with the sociology of community formation *vis-à-vis* resettlement policy. Extant contributions on this topic are rarely the result of fieldwork, but rather form analyses of current events and news stories. For example, Claus Leggewie discusses Germany as the "second front" of the Workers' Party of Kurdistan (PKK), the Kurdish movement in Turkey under Abdullah Öcalan (1996). It is true that many of the PKK's operations and brutal acts occur outside Kurdistan, thereby exporting the civil war to countries like Germany, where hundreds of thousands of Kurds migrated as *gastarbeiter* (guest workers) or as refugees. But Leggewie contends that many Kurds "did not discover their 'Kurdishness' until they came to Europe" where they could more freely participate in cultural and linguistic practices outlawed in Turkey (1996: 79). While this forms the basis for the Kurdish conflict with Turkey, along with the political and economic marginalization that propelled so many to Germany in the first place, it does not fully reflect the Kurdish dilemma in Germany. It is Germany's reluctance to grant full citizenship rights to refugees, guest workers, and even German-born Kurds – part of Germany's long-standing ethnic policy on citizenship – that further radicalizes Kurds in Germany.

In the face of these barriers, Kurdish nationalism has sprung up in Germany. In other words, Turks have become Kurds because the Turkish state denies them cultural recognition and the German state denies them political recognition. (Leggewie 1996: 79)

It is Leggewie's contention that Kurdish identity among Turkish *gastarbeiter* surfaced not through co-ethnic communal affinities in the urban quarters of Europe's working class but after Turkey's 1980 state of emergency in Kurdish southeast Anatolia and the ensuing criminalization of Kurdish culture that escalated to civil war. Their ensuing marginalization by German society as part of the "Turkish problem," seen as an inassimilable excess labor pool and the target of right-wing hate crimes, only hastened to radicalize Kurds toward a Kurdish nationalism that sought international and domestic political justice. What is most compelling in Leggewie's analysis is the equation of migration, whether "economic" or refugee, with the internationalization of political questions raised by separatist conflicts. The specific geopolitical map emerging from an internationalized conflict, begins to reconfigure Kurdish refugee communities as alternative, nonstate actors. Beyond the conflict between the PKK and the Turkish Armed Forces in southeast Anatolia, the 9,000 Kurdish activists and their 50,000 supporters in Germany point to a more complex reality: the Kurdish civil war is being funded by an extensive apparatus of the PKK that maintains cells in every Kurdish community in Germany and all around Europe (Leggewie 1996: 82–3). Further, a political movement of both PKK and pro-Kurdish activists in Europe has effectively used Turkey's application for membership in the European Union as a lever by which to alter the practices of the Turkish government.

The importance of Leggewie's study is that he successfully gives an empirical example linking the underconceptualized relationship between host-country resettlement policies and the geopolitical conditions in the sending region. He traces in both directions the otherwise unidirectional relationship between root causes and resettlement, tying what happens in exile to geopolitical developments back home – producing an ironic map that links the activities of the PKK in Germany to the amplification of conflict in Turkish Kurdistan, and a subsequent continued emigration of Kurdish refugees to Germany. These refugees often construct a typical chain-migration sequence, following kinship and communal relations in seeking asylum in Germany. Set against the backdrop of rising German and European resentment of immigration, this refugee migration puts into motion every scale of geopolitical interaction, including diplomatic conflict between Germany and Turkey, and Turkey and the European Union. Similarly, it puts additional strain on migrant–host relations, most noticeably through state-controlled channels, that is, migration policies, social benefits, economic participation, and political enfranchisement. Leggewie's study of Turko-German relations regarding the Kurdish question is not, however, easily generalizable to other Kurdish migrants living in Germany or elsewhere in Europe because his analysis hinges on the tactics of the PKK.

Noted Kurdologist Martin Van Bruinessen similarly recognizes the importance of exile communities as active sites of Kurdish politics (1999, 2000). Like Leggewie, Van Bruinessen focuses on Turkish Kurds in Germany and their political activism since 1980 when the migration of politicized Kurds from the southeast provided a "catalyst on the Kurds' ethnic awareness" in German cities (Van Bruinessen 1999: 11). Further, he stresses the inculcation of Kurdish identity in second-generation children of immigrants who most acutely face the failure of Germany's reluctant citizenship policies to more fully incorporate immigration communities into civic life. Two factors convinced the PKK that "Europe was the arena where the next phase in the Kurdish struggle was to be fought" (Van Bruinessen 1999: 17). First, Öcalan's expulsion from Syria and the catalytic effect his search for asylum had on both heightening European attention to the Kurdish situation and the consolidation of sometimes rival Kurdish organizations bore witness to the size and political effectivity of the Kurdish community in Europe. Second, the depopulation of the Turkish countryside in Kurdistan had led to an increasingly less effective campaign against the Turkish military, one that might be taken up more effectively outside Turkey. That is, there was greater strategic advantage in using Europe as both the grounds for the PKK campaign because it contained a reservoir of Kurdish political activism that could mobilize a diplomatic lever against the Turkish state. Van Bruinessen concludes, similar to Leggewie, that

Turkey's authorities apparently expect that the mass emigration from Kurdistan will ultimately lead to the assimilation of the Kurds and the gradual disappearance of the Kurdish question. The thrust of [this argument] has been to show that it was precisely because of this mass migration that Kurdish identity as well as the identities of smaller ethnic categories among the Kurds have been invigorated. (Van Bruinessen 1999: 20)

Van Bruinessen's study does not, however, clarify the extent to which the cultural and political activities of the Kurdish diaspora out of Turkey parallel that of or can be equally applied to Kurds from outside Turkey. To do so, we may examine three areas of transnational activity: linguistic and cultural maintenance; media technology; and transnational political organizations. For Van Bruinessen, the maintaining of mother tongue ability, or regaining this ability, is an important contribution to Kurdish culture made by Turkish Kurds living in exile. Because Turkey outlawed the Kurdish language and actively sought to replace it with a Turkish national language, it is in exile that an active scholarly community of Kurdish intellectuals and artists have reasserted the Kurmanci dialect of northern (Turkish) Kurdistan. The development of a Kurmanci literature is certainly important to Turkish Kurds who have lacked a significant and sophisticated literature in which to discuss their condition. It is similarly the case for Kurdish culture among those from Turkey – the recovery of community observances, such as *newroz* or new years, and customs long banned in Turkey are an important component of cultural revival. While the reemergence of Kurmanci and Kurdish culture among the Kurds from eastern Turkey suggests exile is an important site for their recovery of Kurdish identity, it does not necessarily hold true for Kurds from Iraq or the other countries. Although Iraqi Kurds have suffered regular conflict with Baghdad, their relatively autonomous status in northern Iraq has meant much less cultural and linguistic oppression, thus there is less of a linguistic and cultural renaissance among Iraqi Kurds in exile. Instead, the maintenance of Kurdish language ability and its instillation in the second generation is more easily recognized as a struggle against the assimilative forces of refuge and exile for Iraqi Kurds. The extent to which Iraqi Kurds maintain and instill Kurdish linguistic abilities and cultural identity in their community might indicate the extent to which these factors will contribute to their continued pressure and activism in recovering a homeland.

Media technology, especially satellite television and Internet resources, provide information and cultural programming that serve to bolster the expression of Kurdish identity and its attendant politics. In the case of Kurds from Turkey, satellite programming is provided by MED-TV, with production facilities located in the Netherlands. The programming concentrates on Turkey and the activities of the PKK and has had a wide appeal for Kurds throughout Europe, including Kurds from Iraq. More recently, satellite and Internet services directed at Iraqi Kurds have come online and in a form that is closely tied to transnational political organizations. The main Iraqi Kurdish political parties, the Kurdistan Democratic Party (KDP) and the Patriotic Union of Kurdistan (PUK), each have satellite television stations and Internet websites. These sites serve to maintain contact and relevancy with Iraqi Kurds living outside the region. Party officers interviews by the author noted the importance of keeping exile communities informed and aware, in preparation for the mobilization of either homeland defense or a return migration. The now-significant proportion of Iraqi Kurds living outside northern Iraq require that the political parties, as the only clear governing force on the ground, maintain their network of loyal members since, in the event of a return migration, the Kurds from exile will more likely have more money, skills, and new experiences to bring to bear on any new political situation.

To this end, the Iraqi Kurdish parties have reorganized their structures to more directly incorporate their membership living in exile. The Kurdish Parliament in Exile was convened in The Hague in 1995. Though it nominally seeks to represent all Kurds, its focus on the Kurdish question in Turkey, and Öcalan's case in particular, alienated some non-Turkish Kurdish parties and organizations, suggesting that it comes up short of being the "trans-state" organization that Van Bruinessen recognizes. Most certainly, because of its focus on the Kurdish question and its efforts to mobilize European governments on its behalf, the Kurdish Parliament in Exile is a transnational political organization. However, because it lacks significant organizational capacity in Turkey beyond the parties represented in it, it is transnational because of its efforts throughout Europe on behalf of issues in Kurdistan. The PKK does not enjoy official sanction to operate in Europe and is branded a terrorist organization by most governments. Nevertheless, their illicit activities in Europe effectively constitute a transnational political organization. It is important to recognize the multiple local competencies and on-the-ground capacities of an organization's activities in order to ascertain the geographical bearings of its particular brand of transnationalism.

Östen Wahlbeck's study (1998, 1999) examines the associational networks and activities of Kurdish refugee communities in London and Finland. Placed within the context of British and Finnish resettlement policy, he is able to more fully specify the effect of relocation on social relations within the communities than either Leggewie or Van Bruinessen. Focusing primarily on Kurds from Turkey, Wahlbeck notes the general split in refugee associational networks between Kurds from Turkey and those from Iraq, Iran, or Syria. Wahlbeck also observes that these associational networks and organizations, while focused primarily on assisting migrants, especially refugees, in their resettlement, were highly politicized and bore witness to "the same political allegiances and boundaries that can be found in Kurdistan [and] are thus recreated and modified in exile" (Wahlbeck 1998: 223). Kurdish political parties are frequently identified with different community centers or organizations, though management of these activities is never directly a function of party operations. While family structures are an important basis for social cohesion and organization, any explicitly "tribal" organization of Kurdish society has given way to a politically partisan organization, which serves to unite Kurdish ethnic identity, according to Wahlbeck, in place of religious or kinship-based solidarity (1998: 224). More importantly, his study suggests "social groups which are not politically organized, as well as nonpolitical or antipolitical individuals, will easily become marginalized in the Kurdish community" (1998: 225). Though Wahlbeck presumes that "Kurds from Iraq and Iran often were more alienated from Kurdish politics" (1999: 173), research conducted by the author suggests that these communities are each as well organized and cohesive as the Turkish Kurds. Explaining the difference is the outlaw status of the PKK as a terrorist organization and the politics of Turkey's accession to the European Union while Iraqi and Iranian political parties enjoy favor in most western capitals as opponents to "rogue regimes" in Baghdad and Teheran.

Deterritorialization and the Limits of Diaspora

The Kurdish community in exile is marked by a high degree of segmentation. Not only are Kurds divided in their homeland by state boundaries but their exile communities exhibit those same divisions, particularly in the separation of Turkish from Iraqi and other Kurdish groups. Likewise, within the Turkish and Iraqi exile communities, partisan differences obtain as the most salient social organizing principle, imputing nearly every event or organization with the subtle politics of internecine competition. These forms of imposed and self-inflicted segregation defy the very belief that most Kurds publicly express, namely, that "all Kurds dream of a united and independent Kurdistan." Such expressions of irredentist claims to Kurdistan as a homeland lost to the geopolitical depredations of Turkey, Iraq, Iran, and Syria and after the many years of their cultural, economic, and political repression of the Kurdish minority would appear to satisfy their condition as being one of diaspora. Yet the particularity of their political and cultural condition seems to confound any theoretical position that would characterize the present Kurdish communities in exile as comprising a diaspora. From the author's fieldwork in the Kurdish communities in Britain and North America, the very idea of diaspora is not common among refugees nor among most political leaders. While the Kurdish exile communities exhibit a high degree of transnationalism, particularly among its fragmented political organizations, there is no conceptual justification for understanding their condition to be particularly diasporic. There are, however, nascent in the vague and unmobilized common historical narratives of these exiles sufficient discursive potential for a future constructed diasporic identity that bridges the practical differences separating the Kurdish communities in exile and, perhaps, *in situ*.

If not a diaspora, then what describes the condition of Kurdish exile communities? Wahlbeck (1999) describes Kurdish communities in exile as deterritorialized, implying the maintenance of intensive social relations among actors who are not co-present but are connected by new communications technologies. That is, deterritorialized social relations are made possible through immediate and frequent uses of communication technology or social interaction. While Wahlbeck's use of the term is not unique, his generic rendering of "territory" as simple human co-presence departs from more geographical understandings of deterritorialization as a loosening of the connections between social practices and particular sociopolitical spaces. The distinction is important, for without a recognition that territorialization is the social process of mapping identity onto space we lose all value in understanding the social, cultural, and political changes wrought by migration of any kind. Deterritorialization, however, cannot be divorced from the political, or even geopolitical, context of displacement. The spatial metaphor of deterritorializing is not simply a challenge to the organicism of national identity theories. Instead, deterritorialization foregrounds the social construction of identity-in-place by recognizing the historiographic discourses that have mapped identity and space, and the modes of power and authority that maintain them. Further, there cannot be a deterritorialization without an ensuing reterritorialization, a renewal of the geographical specificity and unevenness of social life. In discussing these topics, Ó Tuathail suggests that geographers have a task

to theorize critically the polymorphous territorialities produced by the social, economic, political and technological machines of our postmodern condition rather than refuse this complexity and reduce it to singular dramas of resistant territorialization or unstoppable deterritorialization. (Ó Tuathail 1998: 90)

While Wahlbeck and van Bruinnessen recognize the role of deterritorialization in expanding the Kurdish geopolitical condition beyond the geographic bounds of the region, they fail to fully appreciate that the resettlement of Kurds outside the region portends significant and important changes in a reterritorialization of social and political (and even economic) geographies. Put another way, the geopolitical question of the Kurds has not been evacuated or diminished, *per se*, but rather its specific geographies realign the social interactions of identity and politics beyond the boundaries of the nation-state. This geographical expansion of social relations is typically thought of as a diminishing of ethnic intensity, a "watering-down" of identity-in-place and, therefore, a lessening of the meaning and attachment that historical and cultural practices map onto space. The study of migration often presumes that identity, in its "native" or ethnic varieties, is diminished by mobility *qua* deterritorialization; place-based social bonds or ecological practices that underwrite identity are exchanged, through assimilation, with those of the host-society. Empirically and conceptually, these presumptions fail to recognize that migration does not necessarily require an either/or outcome in terms of identity. What immigration theories have identified as unassimilated – or inassimilable – "ethnic enclaves" are frequently sites of complex social rearticulation. As such, it may be more useful to think of communities in exile, like those of the Kurds, less in terms of coherent and identifiable, if out-of-place, renditions of extant sociospatial identities, but rather as sites of cultural and political negotiation over the social and geopolitical terms of what it means to be Kurdish and what or where a Kurdish homeland ought to be. Furthermore, this negotiation is not constrained to "co-ethnics," but instead involves a series of interlocutors not limited to members of the host-society, those living in the "homeland," as well as state actors whose geopolitical interests may, at times, conflict with that of any presumed diasporic movement and its putative restorative claims to a homeland.

REFERENCES

Agnew, J. 1998: *Geopolitics: Re-visioning World Politics*. New York: Routledge.

Ashley, R. 1987: The geopolitics of geopolitical space: toward a critical social theory of international politics. *Alternatives* 12, 403–34.

Basch, L., Glick Schiller, N., and Szanton Blanc, C. 1994: *Nations Unbound: Transnational Projects, Postcolonial Predicaments, and Deterritorialized Nation-States*. Amsterdam: Overseas Publishers Association.

Bhabha, H. 1994: *The Location of Culture*. New York: Routledge.

Brah, A. 1996: *Cartographies of Diaspora: Contesting Identities*. New York: Routledge.

Castles, S. and Miller, M. 1998: *The Age of Migration: International Population Movements in the Modern World*. New York: The Guilford Press.

Cheah, P. and Robbins, B. 1998: *Cosmopolitics: Thinking and Feeling Beyond the Nation*. Minneapolis: University of Minnesota Press.

Clifford, J. 1994: Diasporas. In M. Guibernau and J. Rex, eds., *The Ethnicity Reader: Nationalism, Multiculturalism, and Migration*. Cambridge: Polity Press.

Cohen, R. 1997: *Global Diasporas: An Introduction*, Seattle: University of Washington Press.

Cowell, A. 2002: France's "hidden vote" helps underpin Le Pen. *The International Herald Tribune*. [online] May 4.

Dalby, S. 1999: Against "globalization from above": critical geopolitics and the world order models project. *Environment and Planning D: Society and Space* 17(2), 181–200.

The Economist. 2002: Anti-immigrant politicians: here we come – well, one of us. 16 Mar., p. 56.

Foucault, M. 1991: Governmentality. In G. Burchell, C. Gordon, and P. Miller, eds., *The Foucault Effect: Studies in Governmentality*. Chicago: University of Chicago Press.

Geddes, A. 2000: *Immigration and European Integration: Towards Fortress Europe?* European Policy Research Unit Series. Manchester, UK: Manchester University Press.

Harding, J. 2000: *The Uninvited: Refugees at the Rich Man's Gate*. London: Profile Books.

Hesse, B. 2000: *Un/Settled Multiculturalisms*. New York: Zed Books.

Lavie, S. and Swedenburg, T. 1996. *Displacement, Diaspora, and Geographies of Identity*. Durham, NC: Duke University Press.

Leggewie, C. 1996: How Turks became Kurds, not Germans. *Dissent* 43 (Summer), 79–83.

Levy, C. 1999: European asylum and refugee policy after the Treaty of Amsterdam: the birth of a new regime? In A. Bloch and C. Levy, eds., *Refugees, Citizenship, and Social Policy in Europe*. New York: St. Martin's Press, 12–50.

Lippert, R. 1999: Governing refugees: the relevance of governmentality to understanding the international refugee regime. *Alternatives* 24, 295–328.

Loescher, G. 1990: Introduction: refugee issues in international relations. In G. Loescher and L. Monahan, eds., *Refugees and International Relations*. Oxford: Oxford University Press.

Loescher, G. 1996: *Beyond Charity: International Cooperation and the Global Refugee Crisis*. New York: Oxford University Press.

Lyall, S. 2002: Far-rightists gain in UK. *International Herald Tribune* [online], May 4.

Malkki, L. 1995: Refugees and exile: from "refugee studies" to the national order of things. *Annual Review of Anthropology* 24, 495–523.

Malkki, L. 1997: Speechless emissaries: refugees, humanitarianism, dehistoricization. In K. F. Olwig and K. Hastrup, eds., *Siting Culture: The Shifting Anthropological Object*. New York: Routledge.

Meissner, D., Hormats, R., Walker, A., and Ogata, S. 1993: *International Migration Challenges in a New Era*. New York, Paris, and Tokyo: The Trilateral Commission.

Mitchell, K. 1997: Different diasporas and the hype of hybridity. *Environment and Planning D: Society and Space* 15, 533–53.

Nagel, C. 2001: Nations unbound? Migration culture, and the limits of the transnationalism diaspora narrative. *Political Geography* 20, 247–56.

Nonini, D. and Ong, A. 1997: *Ungrounded Empires: The Cultural Politics of Modern Chinese Transnationalism*. New York: Routledge.

Ó Tuathail, G. 1998: Political geography III: dealing with deterritorialization. *Progress in Human Geography* 22(1), 81–93.

Ó Tuathail, G. and Dalby, S. 1998: *Rethinking Geopolitics*. New York: Routledge.

Risse-Kappen, T. 1995: Bringing transnational relations back in: introduction. In Risse-Kappen, ed., *Bringing Transnational Relations Back In: Non-state Actors, Domestic Structures, and International Institutions*. Cambridge: Cambridge University Press.

Safran, W. 1991: Diaspora in modern societies: myths of homeland and return. *Diaspora* 1(1), 83–99.

Sassen, S. 1998: *Globalization and its Discontents: Essays on the New Mobility of People and Money*. New York: The New Press.

Soguk, N. 1999: *States and Strangers: Refugees and Displacements of Statecraft*. Minneapolis: University of Minnesota Press.

Tatla, D. 1999: *The Sikh Diaspora: Search for Statehood*. Seattle: University of Washington Press.

Tölölyan, K. 1991: The nation state and its other: in lieu of a preface. *Diaspora* 1(1), 3–7.

Van Bruinessen, M. 1999: The Kurds in movement: migrations, mobilisations, communications and the globalisation of the Kurdish question. Islamic Area Studies Working Paper Series no. 14. Tokyo: Islamic Area Studies Project, University of Tokyo.

Van Bruinessen, M. 2000: Transnational aspects of the Kurdish question. EUI Working Paper RSC no. 2000/22. Florence: Robert Schuman Center for Advanced Studies.

Wahlbeck, Ö. 1998: Community work and exile politics: Kurdish refugee associations in London. *Journal of Refugee Studies* 11(3), 215–30.

Wahlbeck, Ö. 1999: *Kurdish Diasporas: A Comparative Study of Kurdish Refugee Communities*. New York: St. Martin's Press.

Chapter 32

Transnationalism

Cheryl McEwan

Introduction

Transnationalism is not entirely new, but this phenomenon and its consequences reached a particular intensity at a global scale towards the end of the twentieth century. Within the social sciences, transnationalism has a multiplicity of meanings. It has been variously conceptualized as social morphology (diaspora and networks), a type of consciousness (diasporic and multiple identities), a mode of cultural reproduction (syncretism and hybridity), an avenue of capital (transnational corporations and global monetary flows), a site of political engagement (international NGOs and diasporic politics), and a reconstruction of place or locality (translocalities) (Vertovec 1999). Indeed, Vertovec (2001b: 576) argues that transnationalism as a concept has become "over-used to describe too wide a range of phenomena (from specific migrant communities to all migrants, to every ethnic diaspora, to all travelers and tourists)." Similarly, Guarnizo and Smith (1998: 4) caution against transnationalism "becoming an empty conceptual vessel." This chapter attempts to temper such skepticism by demonstrating that transnationalism is a useful concept in representing contemporary phenomena relating to mass migration and processes of political and cultural change across national spaces, and that geography can play a key role in understanding transnationalism and its consequences.

Recent literature has attempted to delineate and understand the growing phenomenon of "transnational communities" comprised of migrants who retain deep and extended attachments to people, traditions, and movements located outside the boundaries of the nation-state in which they reside (Vertovec 2001a). This interest is inspired by the fact that new forms of migration and travel are now occurring with different intensities of linkages with homelands, relating to the rapid development of travel and communication technologies and also to shifting political and economic circumstances in both sending and receiving countries. Evidence is growing for the considerable economic, social, and cultural impacts of these transnational communities (see, for example, Glick Schiller et al. 1992; Smith & Guarnizo 1998; Portes et al. 1999; Pries 1999; Vertovec & Cohen 1999). Mitchell (1997b) suggests that transnationalism is a "sexy topic" because of its transgressive qualities: it necessitates the crossing of borders, both literal and epistemological. Since borders are often associated with power (the power to keep in or out), movements across (national, disciplinary, theoretical) borders seem to be transgressive. Travel, and specifically migration, is thus an important means by which borders and boundaries are being contested and transgressed.

Scholarship on transnationalism in geography has tended to focus on economic globalization; however, less has been written about cultural globalization and the connections between cultural mobility and identities, citizenship, and transnational spaces. In what follows, therefore, I review the major debates that have been articulated in the social sciences and cultural studies relating to these issues. I suggest that geographers have much to contribute to understanding the implications of cultural globalization, including the paradox that the growth and intensification of global interconnection of people, processes, and ideas is accompanied by a resurgence in the politics of differentiation (Glick Schiller et al. 1992). I also suggest, following Mitchell (1997), that geographical scholarship opens possibilities for harnessing the progressive and transgressive potential of transnationalism that has perhaps not been apparent in some analyses of transnational processes and discourses.

Transnational Identities and Cultures

Theories of international migration tend to suggest that migrants cross borders, bringing their culture with them, and become relatively less or more assimilated to prevailing cultural norms of the new territory – they are either sojourners or settlers. Recently, however, theorists have attempted to link globalization to local transformations and struggles against modernity and marketization, instigating a reengagement with culture and transnationalism, often under the heading of "transnationalism from below" (Zhou & Tseng 2001; see also Henry et al. 2002). In contrast to seeing cultural identity as reflecting either the nation of origin or the host nation, it is more appropriate to see it as transnational.

The growing complexity of transnational communities is reflected in a rising concern with identity rather than with culture *per se*. Research on transnationalism generally reveals that large numbers of people now live in social worlds that are stretched between, or dually located in, physical places and communities in two or more nation-states. Hannerz (1996) describes the diverse "habitats of meaning" that are not territorially restricted and where multiple identities are constructed. As Vertovec (2001b: 578) argues, each habitat or locality represents:

a range of identity-conditioning factors: these include histories and stereotypes of local belonging and exclusion, geographies of cultural difference and class/ethnic segregation, racialised socio-economic hierarchies, degree and type of collective mobilisation, access to and nature of resources, and perceptions and regulations surrounding rights and duties.

Together, these create what have been variously termed "transnational social fields" (Glick Schiller et al. 1992), "transnational social spaces" (Pries 1999), or "translocalities" (Appadurai 1995). These concepts encapsulate a complex set of conditions that affect the construction, negotiation and contestation of cultural and social identities, and of individuals' places of attachment and sense of belonging. These new transnational social spaces are formed by combinations of dynamic "ties, positions in networks and organizations, and networks of organizations that reach across the borders of multiple states" (Faist 2000: 191).

Much recent scholarship has explored differing migration processes, collective and individual experiences, policy and institutional contexts, and cultural flows to suggest ways in which local identities are shaped by transnational factors (see for example Çağlar 2001; Riccio 2001; Al-Ali et al. 2001; Hansing 2001). As Çağlar (2001: 610) argues, people who live transnational lives "weave their collective identities out of multiple affiliations and positionings and link their cross-cutting belongingness with complex attachments and multiple allegiances to issues, peoples, places, and traditions beyond the boundaries of their resident nation-states." Vasile (1997: 177) suggests that globalization has constituted "the core of profound social and cultural transformations: new tastes, new forms of language, new deployment of symbols, new practices of worship." These global processes and forms are embedded in local social and spatial structures, so that both western and nonwestern localities give rise to as well as transform global practices as these pass through locally embedded histories and geographies (Mitchell 1995).

Social and cultural impacts of transnational migration are considerable and varied. As Vertovec (2001b) argues, intense linkages and exchanges between sending and receiving contexts are maintained by marriage alliances, religious activity, media, and commodity consumption; these transnational connections affect migrants as never before with regard to practices of constructing, maintaining, and negotiating collective identities. This has a significant bearing on the culture and identity of the "second generation," or children born to migrants. Vasile (1997), for example, demonstrates how, using a case study of Tunis, accelerated and increasingly dense transnational movements of capital, people, commodities and ideas have introduced new forms of architecture and dress, new gender relations and ethics of consumption and display, and new signifiers of power and position. Some of these innovations contradict or clash with existing social practices and values thought of as normatively Tunisian. However, working-class Tunisians, who might be thought of as marginal to these innovations, have actively reinterpreted and remade local cultural traditions and modern consumption practices, reworking and reviving Islamic religious practices. The transnational socio-political context of Islam, the collapse of state socialisms and the failures of free-market prescriptions for prosperity are woven through local geographies and into patterns of subsistence and sense of locality and home in Tunis.

Similarly, Faist (2000) explores transnational communities built around political or religious identities that last beyond the first generation of migrants. Here, there are usually strong ties of migrants and refugees to the country of origin and the country of immigration through social and symbolic ties. Faist argues that since the prerequisites for international migration include prior exchanges in economic (e.g. foreign investments), political (e.g. military cooperation or domination), or cultural (e.g. colonial education systems) dimensions, activities in transnational social spaces do not create transnational linkages *ex nihilo*, but usually evolve with preexisting linkages, building new ones and challenging existing arrangements, such as citizenship and notions of acculturation. In the country of immigration, obstacles to socio-economic integration and/or a denial of acculturation or cultural recognition are usually conducive to the transnationalization of political and cultural activities (e.g. Caribbean immigrants in the UK). In addition, if the countries of immigration are liberal democracies that do not assimilate immigrants by force, immigrant minorities have a good chance to uphold cultural distinctiveness and ties to the country of origin. The multicultural policies of the destination country are conducive to upholding the transnational ties of immigrants (again, Caribbean immigrants in the UK are a good example). Therefore, not only repressive policies and discrimination advance immigrant transnationalization, "opportunities to exercise multicultural rights and a liberal political environment can also further transnational activities and a border-crossing collective consciousness" (Faist 2000: 200).

Unlike assimilation and ethnic pluralism theories, immigrant cultures cannot be seen as baggage to be packed, uprooted and transplanted; they are instead structures of meaning engendered by and expressed in private and public spaces, images, institutions, and languages (Geertz 1973) and inherent in social and symbolic ties. The ongoing transnationalization of meanings and symbols through social and symbolic ties in transnational social spaces helps to sustain cultural border-crossing. This is enabled by modern technologies (satellite/cable TV, instant communications, mass affordable short-term long-distance travel), liberal state policies (polyethnic rights and antidiscrimination policies), changing emigration state policies, and immigrant capacities to mobilize resources (organizational, social, and human capital). The result is transnational syncretism of culture. The concept of border-crossing expansion of social space has, therefore, become more important in understanding issues of transnational cultures.

Transnational social spaces are also diasporic spaces. As Cwerner (2001: 28) argues,

Diaspora, as a transnational, multi-lateral socio-economic, political, and cultural formation, should be seen as a heterogeneous social space comprising communities, associations, networks of various kinds (family, friendship), cultural producers and ethnic businesses, as well as multilateral links established among host societies, and between these and the homeland.

Theorists are beginning to explore examples of transnational cultural activities in diasporic spaces. For example, Al-Ali et al. (2001) examine the activities of Bosnian and Eritrean refugees in Europe. These include musical, artistic and literary events where musicians, artists and writers from home countries are invited to perform in the host countries (e.g. the 1999 Eritrean Festival in Frankfurt); maintaining an active cultural calendar organized around national holidays and parties; promoting native language speaking and religious practice through special schools. Similarly, Çağlar (2001) explores Turkish youth cultures in Berlin and how they exhibit multiple and multilocal sources. She discusses, in particular, the importance of Turkish hybrid musical forms and Turkish café-bars, clubs and discos in the "non-ethnic" neighborhoods of the city. The references to Turkey in these new sites are different to those in the restaurants and cafés in the immigrant neighborhoods, since the references to Turkey are very selective and relate not to Turkey as a cultural space but to urban spaces in Turkey. As Çağlar (2001: 609) suggests,

By stressing the non-ethnic sources of the self, young people in [these] places . . . criticise the common binary opposition used in discourses on German Turks, and the belongingness and cultural formations that confine them either to German or to Turkish culture . . . This unmooring envisages new notions of community, membership and entitlement that cannot be conceptualised within a topos of *a priori* spatialised cultures and their spatial extensions through ethnic communities and ghettos.

Through these transterritorial sites, these young people are making claims to parts of the city from which they had been excluded.

In their study of Turkish Cypriots in Britain, Robins and Aksoy (2001) shift the focus of their analysis from cultural identities to cultural experiences. They connect Young's (1994: 146) notion of mental space (a place in and from which individuals symbolize and participate in cultures: an "intermediate area of *experiencing*, to which inner reality and external life contribute") to external geographies ("how we picture the world out there" (Robins & Aksoy 2001: 689). They suggest that the capacity to experience, and to learn from experience, is related to the ways in which transnational migrants conceive of and symbolize real-world geographies. Thus, despite the fact that "official" and ideological politics are still very much concerned with issues of identity, it is the responsibility of social scientists to move beyond cultural identity to consider particular cultural and experiential possibilities. In their interviews with Turkish-Cypriot women in Britain, they found that in some cases "it is no longer a question of cultural synthesis or syncretism, but of moving across both the British and Turkish cultural spaces" (2001: 704). All of the women refused to identify as British and were concerned about retaining their Turkish Cypriotism. But this was not about national sentiment, belonging and attachment; rather it was about "certain ethical and moral values, about how families and communities should function" and "about the way in which human beings should relate to each other." These things were more important to them than what is conventionally designated by the term "identity" (ibid.: 705); the different mental spaces of cultural experience and cultural thinking were most important. Thus the complexities of lived experiences, feelings, thoughts and narratives about being Turkish Cypriot cannot be captured through an imposed matrix of identity; experiences and thoughts were clearly more important to the women interviewed than identity (see also Dwyer 2002).

It is clear, therefore, that transnational processes and practices have put issues of cultural identity and cultural community into a new context. As Beck (2000) argues, questions of culture and identity have shifted from national contexts to postnational and cosmopolitan ones; in other words, identities have become unfixed. Robins and Aksoy (2001) ask whether new kinds of identities will, or will have to, emerge out of the processes of cultural transnationalization, or whether cultures will be organized around something other than identities. Crucial to this is mobility and boundary-crossing, the passage from one space to another, shifting between cultures, and the implications of this for transnational citizenship.

Transnational Citizenship

Changing global configurations of postcoloniality and late capitalism have resulted in the reinscription of space; this has profound implications for the imagining of national homelands and for discursive constructions of nationalism (Gupta 1999).

Transnationalism brings about the displacement of culture and identity from the nation, forcing (as discussed) a reevaluation of ideas about culture and identity but also enabling a denaturalization of nation as the hegemonic form of organizing space. As Kearney (1995) argues, transnational migrants move into and create transnational spaces that may have the potential to liberate nationals within them who are able to escape in part strong state hegemony. However, he also notes that deterritorialized nation-states may extend their hegemony beyond their national boundaries. President Aristide of Haiti, for example, has referred to Haitians living in the United States as the tenth Haitian province (Basch et al. 1994).

The political consequences of transnational phenomena are potentially far-reaching, since transmigration raises questions about the nature of citizenship and citizenship rights. Global flows and cross-border networks represented by transnational migrant communities challenge assumptions that the nation-state acts as a container of social, economic, cultural and political processes. A number of different theories have been formulated in recognition of these new processes, including "flexible" (Ong 1999), "postnational" (Soysal 1994), "diasporic" (Laguerre 1998), and "transnational" (Bauböck 1994) citizenship. As Faist (2000) argues, however, the implications of transnationalization for citizenship and culture have not been systematically explored.

Faist delineates three concepts for analysis of immigrant adaptation in the receiving countries. Where the latter seeks to assimilate immigrants on the basis of a unitary national and political culture, acculturation will normally take place, with adaptation of values and behavior to the nation-state's core. Where the receiving country supports ethnic pluralism on the basis of multicultural citizenship and recognition of cultural differences, cultural retention will occur, with practices maintained in a new context and collective identities transplanted from the emigration country. However, where the receiving country encourages border-crossing expansion of social space based on dual citizenship, transnational syncretism will occur, with a diffusion of culture and emergence of new types of cultural identities. This form of transnational citizenship does not deny the existence or relevance of borders and nation-states, but simply recognizes the increasing possibility of membership in two states. For example, the Mexican government uses immigrants as a support for conducting business at home and abroad (Smith 1999). In order to retain foreign revenue, some states (especially in Asia and Latin America) are attempting to capture migrants through rights to dual citizenship, health and welfare benefits, and property and voting rights. In January 2003, for example, the Indian government reversed its policy preventing Indians living overseas from attaining dual citizenship (BBC News 9/1/03). Other countries such as the UK, France, and Netherlands have tolerated dual citizenship and thus are replete with transnational social spaces.

Sexual politics is one arena where transnational phenomena have challenged national constructions of citizenship. Connections between travel, mobility, and sexuality have a long and complex history. As Binnie (1997: 242) argues, "contemporary transformations of the global economy have created new possibilities for the transformation of sexual cultures"; this is occurring in a range of cultural locations, shaped by transnationalism and its impacts on citizenship. In particular, the development of a European economic bloc could have consequences for the social and cultural politics around sexuality because the need for labor mobility has necessitated rights of free movement for workers between member states. Similarly, trans-migration is raising similar issues for citizenship globally. Major issues relate to rights of immigration for same-sex partners. The fact that same-sex partners now have rights to marriage in the Netherlands, for example, raises questions about whether these partnerships should be recognized in other EU member states.

The dilemmas raised by these issues emerged recently in South Africa, which has constitutional guarantees barring discrimination on the basis of sexuality. A test case was brought before the Constitutional Court in 2000 to challenge the constitutionality of the Aliens Control Act (1991), which allows preferential treatment to be given to a foreign national applying for an immigration permit who is the "spouse" of a South African resident (Stychin 2000). The national lesbian and gay rights lobbying group challenged this and the Court found the failure to recognize same-sex partnerships to be unconstitutional. Despite this, Stychin (2000: 606) argues that mobility should not necessarily be celebrated as the unproblematic basis for the constitution of lesbian or gay identities or rights to citizenship. Mobility is often constrained by relationships to class and consumption, which are often connected to gender and ethnicity, and might also be related more to forced migration, oppression and refugees than to voluntary travel. In addition, transnational migrants (especially when members of a minority ethnic group) are subject to intense state surveillance and surveillance within migrant communities, especially if they are women. This can create further layers of oppression for gay migrants. However, Stychin (2000: 623) also argues,

It is surely no coincidence that mobility has assumed such a central role in claims to sexual citizenship today. Both citizenship and mobility articulate to inclusion and exclusion. The hegemony of free movement in economic discourses of globalisation under late capitalism has proved a useful discourse upon which to graft sexual citizenship demands.

Globalization has facilitated the emergence of transnationalism in the politics of sexual citizenship, even though this tends to center on those already privileged within gay and lesbian communities. Changes in civil society resulting from transnational social, cultural, and economic processes are shaping citizenship claims and are having a material impact on people's lives.

Transnational migration, therefore, poses challenges to both the sovereignty of nation-states and to citizenship rules within nation-states. The former result in the decrease of the power of the state to control immigration flows due to international laws protecting the rights of immigrants and refugees, but also due to the increase in transnational flows of professional workers. Sassen (1998) refers to this as a *de facto* transnationalizing of immigration policy (see also Çağlar 2001 on recent changes to Germany's citizenship laws and the move away from *ius sanguinis* to *ius soli* principles of citizenship against the backdrop of the standardization of immigrant rights across western Europe). Exclusionist models of citizenship based on the nation-state are thus challenged by postnational or transnational models. In addition, actors embedded in transnational networks are having a significant impact on domestic policy and politics; the role of transnational feminist movements in the diffusion of gender-mainstreaming mechanisms is a clear example (Bickham Mendez & Wolf 2001; True & Mintrom 2001).

Critiquing Transnationalism

Analyses of transnationalism often celebrate new anti-essentializing concepts of subjectivity that emphasize plurality, mobility, hybridity, margins, and in-between spaces. As discussed, these concepts offer a powerful new way of thinking about the manifestations of culture such as ethnicity, gender, and sexuality, breaking down barriers and adhering to neither the "melting-pot" nor the "mosaic" idea of cultural mixing and identity formation. Authors such as Bourdieu (1984) and Bakhtin (1984) see popular hybridity as an exciting challenge to or subversion of dominant cultures and the exclusive lifestyles of dominant elites. By bringing together and mixing languages and practices from different and normally separated domains, they have the potential to disrupt dominant cultures by their "out-of-placeness." Clifford's (1992) notion of "traveling culture" perhaps best exemplifies this, where relations of movement and displacement are prioritized over locality and fixity. Culture, then, is located in a place of movement or a "site of travel" rather than in a fixed or controlled space. Similarly, Appadurai (1990) celebrates the deterritorialization created by new cultural mediascapes. Other critics have welcomed the reworking of multiple identities and syncretic cultural forms by cross-border movements. Bhabha (1994), for example, celebrates the spaces of the margins, of inbetweeness and hybridity, as privileged locations from which to challenge hegemonic notions of race and nation.

Similarly, Brah (1996: 208) refers to the many processes of cultural fissure and fusion that underwrite contemporary forms of transcultural identities, which seriously problematize the idea of a person being a "native" or an "insider." She argues that notions such as hybridity and diaspora allow for the recognition of new political and cultural formations that continually challenge the marginalizing impulses of dominant cultures.

Other critics have argued that the celebration of travel, hybridity, and multiculturalism is premature (see for example Spivak 1991; Shohat 1993; McClintock 1993). Those celebrating new transnational cultures and hybrid subject positions neglect the oppressive socio-economic forces underlying the changes and their material effects on individuals. Transculturation often takes place in profoundly asymmetrical ways in terms of relative power between different groups. The reality of transnational social spaces indicates that migration may not be definite and irrevocable and transnational lives in themselves may become a strategy of survival. For example, Morley (2001) cautions against the uncritical celebration of all notions of mobility, fluidity, and hybridity as intrinsically progressive. He argues that there is too much emphasis on people's abilities to remake and refashion identities rather than the inequality of distribution of forms of cultural capital through which people can refashion identities and the extent to which people are forced to live through identities ascribed for them by others. Mobility (rapid and over long distances) is celebrated as a condition of postmodernity, but actually only applies to 1.6 percent of the world's population (Morley 2001: 429). Transnational webs, therefore, also include large numbers of relatively immobile persons and collectives.

It is easily forgotten in celebratory accounts of transnationalism that, for many transnational travelers, mobility is involuntary or forced (Hannerz 1996). As hooks (1992) points out, the actual experience of crossing borders can be far from liberating; for people of color, it can often be terrifying. There is also a growing literature on sex tourism in transnational spaces where powerful images, fantasies, and desires (produced both locally and globally and inextricably bound up with race and gender) coincide with the economic vulnerability of young, poor, black women drawn into the sex trade to service white male tourists (see for example Brennan 2001). As Mitchell (1997a) argues, the heralding of positions at the margins too often neglects the actual marginalization of subjects; heralding the forces of deterritorialization inadequately addresses the powerful forces of oppression that accompany them (see also Visweswaran 1994). Nonini and Ong (1997: 13) are also critical of the dilution of research by a cultural studies approach "that treats transnationalism as a set of abstracted, dematerialized cultural flows, giving scant attention either to the concrete, everyday changes in people's lives or to the structural reconfiguration that accompany global capitalism." Furthermore, while marginal spaces might offer the potential for resistance, empirical studies suggest that they can also be used for less radical purposes. For example, Mitchell (1997c) has demonstrated that Chinese businessmen strategically use various diasporic, deterritorialized and hybrid subject positions for the purposes of capital accumulation. And she argues (1997a: 110):

Theorizing global processes with new conceptual tools enables alternatives to the "globalisation-from-above" model. But without "literal" empirical data related to the actual movements of things and people across space, theories of anti-essentialism, mobility, plurality and hybridity can quickly devolve into terms emptied of any potential political efficacy.

In the light of this, Mitchell argues that there is a need for analyses and understandings of lived experiences of travel and transnationalism before hybridity, third spaces, and drives towards cultural diversity can be celebrated. Tracing actual border crossings and the actual physical constraints encountered by refugees as they seek to cross borders, rather than theorizing transnational mobility in the abstract, acts as a material corrective to unimpeded "traveling cultures" and diasporic populations in some theories.

In the west, ideas of hybridity are currently popular with highly educated cultural elites, but ideas about culture, ethnicity and identity that develop in poverty-stricken underclass neighborhoods are likely to be of a different nature (Friedman 1997: 83–4). Evidence of racial tensions in many North American and European cities, the conflation in popular perceptions of asylum-seekers with illegal immigrants, and increasing xenophobia around the world point to the fact that class and local ghetto identities tend to prevail, with little room for the mixing pleaded for by cultural elites. The global, cultural hybrid, elite sphere is occupied by individuals who share a very different kind of experience of the world, connected to international politics, academia, the media, and the arts. In the meantime, the world becomes more polarized in terms of wealth, and heads towards increasing balkanization where regional, national and ethnic identities are perceived as bounded, threatened, and in need of protection. As Bhabha (1994) reminds us, hybridity seems an insufficient basis on which to consolidate new forms of collectivity that can overcome the embeddedness of prior antagonisms. Hybridity and transnational syncretism sound nice in theory, but do not necessarily exist outside of the realms of the privileged (McEwan, 2001). There is a need, therefore, for contextualized studies of how macro-forces (globalization, immigration, informal economies, and state regulation) affect the lives of individuals living in fragmented transnational spaces and how dispersed communities cope with the cultural alienation that often accompanies transnationalism (see for example Stoller & McConatha 2001).

Transnational migrations of wealthy individuals have provided an incentive for states to rework national ideologies around the concepts of race and nation. In addition, because wealthy migrants have economic and cultural power, they are able to challenge and in some cases transform notions that have served historically to exclude by race and class (see Mitchell 1993, 1997b on the Hong Kong diaspora). However, it must also be remembered that transmigration is deeply embedded in gender relations. As Salih (2001) argues, access to global mobility is gendered, yet in recent literature on transnationalism there is a tendency to ignore the ways in which nation-states and global economic restructuring are operating in gendered ways (see Willis & Yeoh 2000; Fouron & Schiller 2001; Robins & Aksoy 2001). Her focus on migrant Moroccan women in Italy illustrates a specifically gendered form of embeddedness within nation-state hegemony and, very often, a different experience of transnationalism between men and women. Conditions for moving transnationally are not always available to women, or are limited or framed within a set of normative and culturally gendered rules. Migrant women have qualitatively different experiences of citizenship in their country of origin and occupy different positions in their country of immigration (see for example Goldring 2001). Like Willis and Yeoh, Salih proposes a household approach to understand transnational women's culturally constructed reproductive roles in both countries. She also challenges celebratory stances towards transnationalism and highlights how transnational spheres are not only contingent upon the vulnerability of migrants within global economic systems, but are inscribed in specific cultural and normative constraints.

Conclusions

As Hall (1996: 233) argues, we should not view the current fashionability of hybridity and transnationalism in a wholly negative light. The celebration of both might be premature, but we should not forget the potential for the democratization of culture in this process, the increased recognition of difference and the diversification of the social worlds in which women and men now operate. This pluralization of social and cultural life expands the identities available to ordinary people (at least in the industrialized world) in their everyday working, social, familial, and sexual lives. As Hall (ibid.: 234) argues, "these opportunities need to be more, not less, widely available across the globe, and in ways not limited by private appropriation." For Bhabha (1994: 9), it is the interconnections of different cultural spaces and the overlapping of different cultural forms that create vitality and hold out the possibility of a progressive notion of culture and identity. A challenge for geographers, then, is to think about the place and meaning of transnationalism and cultural hybridity in the context of growing global uncertainty, xenophobia, and racism. We might consider why it is that both are still experienced as an empowering, dangerous or transformative force. Why is it that on the one hand cultural difference is celebrated through a consumer market that offers a seemingly endless choice of identities, subcultures, and styles, yet on the other hand transmigration continues to threaten and shock? Conversely, why do borders, boundaries and "pure" identities remain important, producing defensive and exclusionary actions and attitudes, and why are the latter so difficult to transcend?

Geographical understandings of transnational processes and discourses are particularly important. As Mitchell (1997a: 110) argues, geographers can contribute to contextualizing and grounding theoretical understandings of hybridity and margins, as well as deconstructing concepts such as capitalism and modernity, to enable transnationalism to serve a progressive politics of the future. Understanding geographical contexts on several different scales is essential to "force the literal and epistemological understandings of transnationalism to cohere" (ibid.). Significant strides in this direction have been made elsewhere. For example, Marcus (1995) provides a useful methodological outline of "multi-sited ethnography," which enables the tracing of cultural formations "across and within multiple sites of activity" (ibid.: 96) using methods "designed around chains, paths, threads, conjunctions, or juxtapositions of locations" (ibid.: 105). He advocates approaches that follow the people (especially migrants), the thing (commodities, money), the metaphor (signs, symbols, images), the plot (narratives of everyday experiences and memories), the life (biographies), or the conflict (issues contested in public space). The new work on transnational spatial ethnographies reviewed throughout this chapter also makes significant contributions in "bringing geography back in" (ibid.: 110) to studies of transnationalism.

Much of this work points to the fact that transnational processes rather than abstract cultural flows are located within the lived experiences of transnational migrants. Geographers might explore the literal movement across borders (of capital, people, cultures, information) that have dramatically increased recently, and interrogate the "epistemological celebrations of the spaces and positions astride borders, in-between nations and betwixt subjectivities" that have often been apparent in works on margins and hybridity (Mitchell 1997a: 101). In doing so, because of its different scales of analysis and its possibilities for forcing the contextualization of understandings of hybridity and margins, geographical analysis might help realize the transgressive potential of transnationalism.

REFERENCES

Al-Ali, N., Black, R., and Koser, K. 2001: Refugees and transnationalism: the experience of Bosnians and Eritreans in Europe. *Journal of Ethnic and Migration Studies* 27, 615–34.

Appadurai, A. 1990: Disjuncture and difference in the global cultural economy. *Public Culture* 2, 1–24.

Appadurai, A. 1995: The production of locality. In R. Farndon, ed., *Counterworks: Managing the Diversity of Knowledge*. London: Routledge, 204–25.

Bakhtin, M. 1984: *Rabelais and His World*, tr. Helen Iswolsky. Bloomington: Indiana University Press.

Basch, L., Glick Schiller, N., and Szanton Blanc, C. 1994: *Nations Unbound*. New York: Gordon & Breach.

Bauböck, R. 1994: *Transnational Citizenship: Membership and Rights in International Migration*. Aldershot: Elgar.

Beck, U. 2000: The cosmopolitan perspective: sociology of the second age of modernity. *British Journal of Sociology* 51(1), 79–105.

Bhabha, H. 1994: *The Location of Culture*. London: Routledge.

Bickham Mendez, J. and Wolf, D. 2001: Where feminist theory meets feminist practice: border-crossing in a transnational academic feminist organisation. *Organization* 8(4), 723–50.

Binnie, J. 1997: Invisible Europeans: sexual citizenship in the New Europe. *Environment and Planning A* 29(2), 237–48.

Bourdieu, P. 1984: *Distinction*. London: Routledge.

Brah, A. 1996: *Cartographies of Diaspora: Contesting Identities*. London: Routledge.

Brennan, D. 2001: Tourism in transnational places: Dominican sex workers and German sex tourists imagine one another. *Identities* 7(4), 621–63.

Çağlar, A. 2001: Constraining metaphors and the transnationalisation of spaces in Berlin. *Journal of Ethnic and Migration Studies* 27(4), 601–13.

Clifford, J. 1992: Travelling cultures. In L. Grossberg, C. Nelson, and P. Treichler, eds., *Cultural Studies*. London: Routledge, 96–112.

Cwerner, S. 2001: The times of migration. *Journal of Ethnic and Migration Studies* 27(1), 7–36.

Dwyer, C. 2002: "Where are you from?" Young British Muslim women and the making of "home." In A. Blunt and C. McEwan, eds., *Postcolonial Geographies*. London: Continuum, 184–99.

Faist, T. 2000: Transnationalization in international migration: implications for the study of citizenship and culture. *Ethnic and Racial Studies* 23(2), 189–222.

Fouron, G. and Schiller, N. G. 2001: All in the family: gender, transnational migration and the nation-state. *Identities* 7(4), 539–82.

Friedman, J. 1997: Global crises, the struggle for cultural identity and intellectual porkbarrelling: cosmopolitans versus locals, ethnics and nationals in an era of dehegemonisation. In P. Werbner and T. Modood, eds., *Debating Cultural Hybridity: Multi-cultural Identities and the Politics of Anti-Racism*. London: Zed, 70–89.

Geertz, C. 1973: *The Interpretation of Cultures*. New York: Basic Books.

Glick Schiller, N., Basch, L., and Szanton Blanc, C., eds. 1992: *Toward a Transnational Perspective on Migration*. New York: New York Academy of Sciences.

Goldring, L. 2001. The gender and geography of citizenship in Mexico–US transnational spaces. *Identities* 7(4), 501–37.

Guarnizo, L. and Smith, M. 1998: The locations of transnationalism. In M. Smith and L. Guarnizo, eds., *Transnationalism from Below*. New Brunswick, NJ: Transaction Publishers, 3–34.

Gupta, A. 1999: The song of the nonaligned world: transnational identities and the reinscription of space in late capitalism. In S. Vertovec and R. Cohen, eds., *Migration, Diasporas and Transnationalism*. Aldershot: Edward Elgar, 503–19.

Hall, S. 1996: The meaning of new times. In D. Morley and K.-H. Chen, eds., *Stuart Hall: Critical Dialogues in Cultural Studies*. London: Routledge, 223–37.

Hannerz, U. 1996: *Transnational Connections: Culture, People, Places*. London: Routledge.

Hansing, K. 2001: Rasta, race and revolution: transnational connections in socialist Cuba. *Journal of Ethnic and Migration Studies* 27(4), 733–47.

Henry, N., McEwan, C., and Pollard, J. 2002: Globalisation from below: Birmingham – postcolonial workshop of the world? *Area* 34(2), 117–27.

hooks, b. 1992: Representing whiteness in the black imagination. In L. Grossberg, C. Nelson, and P. Treichler, eds., *Cultural Studies*. London: Routledge, 338–46.

Kearney, M. 1995: The local and the global: the anthropology of globalisation and transnationalism. *Annual Review of Anthropology* 24, 547–65.

Laguerre, M. 1998: *Diasporic Citizenship: Haitian Americans in Transnational America*. London: Macmillan.

Marcus, G. 1995: Ethnography in/of the world system: the emergence of multi-sited ethnography. *Annual Review of Anthropology* 24, 95–117.

McClintock, A. 1993: The angel of progress: pitfalls of the term "postcolonialism." *Social Text* 10, 84–98.

McEwan, C. 2001: Geography, culture and global change. In M. J. Bradshaw et al., eds., *Human Geography: Issues for the 21st Century*. London: Pearson, 154–79.

Mitchell, K. 1993: Multiculturalism, or the United Colors of Capitalism? *Antipode* 25, 263–94.

Mitchell, K. 1995: Flexible circulation in the Pacific Rim: capitalisms in cultural context. *Economic Geography* 71, 364–82.

Mitchell, K. 1997a: Transnational discourse: bringing geography back in. *Antipode* 29(2), 101–14.

Mitchell, K. 1997b: Conflicting geographies of democracy and the public sphere in Vancouver, BC. *Transactions of the Institute of British Geographers* 22, 162–79.

Mitchell, K. 1997c: Different diasporas and the hype of hybridity. *Environment and Planning D: Society and Space* 15, 533–53.

Morley, D. 2001: Belongings: place, space and identity in a mediated world. *European Journal of Cultural Studies* 4(4), 425–48.

Nonini, D. and Ong, A. 1997: *Ungrounded Empires: The Cultural Politics of Modern Chinese Transnationalism*. London: Routledge.

Ong, A. 1999: *Flexible Citizenship: The Cultural Logic of Transnationalism*. Durham, NC: Duke University Press.

Portes, A. 1998: *Globalization from Below: The Rise of Transnational Communities*. Transnational Communities Programme Working Paper 98/01, School of Anthropology and Geography, University of Oxford. Available from www.transcomm.ox.ac.uk.

Portes, A., Guarnizo, L. E., and Landolt, P., eds. 1999: The study of transnationalism: pitfalls and promises of an emergent research field. *Ethnic and Racial Studies* 22(2), 217–37.

Pries, L., ed. 1999: *Social Spaces*. Aldershot: Ashgate.

Riccio, B. 2001: From "ethnic group" to "transnational community"? Senegalise migrants' ambivalent experiences and multiple trajectories. *Journal of Ethnic and Migration Studies* 27(4), 583–99.

Robins, K. and Aksoy, A. 2001: From spaces of identity to mental spaces: lessons from Turkish-Cypriot cultural experience in Britain. *Journal of Ethnic and Migration Studies* 27(4), 685–711.

Salih, R. 2001: Moroccan migrant women: transnationalism, nation-states and gender. *Journal of Ethnic and Migration Studies* 27(4), 655–71.

Sassen, S. 1998: The *de facto* transnationalising of immigration policy. In C. Joppke, ed., *Challenge to the Nation-State: Immigration in Western Europe and the United States*. Oxford: Oxford University Press, 49–87.

Shohat, E. 1993: Notes on the "post-colonial." *Social Text* 10, 99–113.

Smith, M. and Guarnizo, L., eds. 1998: *Transnationalism from Below*. New Brunswick, NJ: Transaction Publishers.

Smith, R. 1999: Reflections on migration, the state and the construction, durability and newness of transnational life. In L. Pries, ed., *Migration and Transnational Social Spaces*. Aldershot: Ashgate, 187–219.

Soysal, Y. 1994: *The Limits of Citizenship: Migrants and Postnational Membership in Europe*. Chicago: University of Chicago Press.

Spivak, G. 1991: Neocolonialism and the secret agent of knowledge: an interview. *Oxford Literary Review* 13, 220–51.

Stoller, P. and McConatha, J. T. 2001: City life: West African communities in New York. *Journal of Contemporary Ethnography* 30(6), 651–77.

Stychin, C. 2000: "A stranger to its laws": sovereign bodies, global sexualities and transnational citizens. *Journal of Law and Society* 27(4), 601–25.

True, J. and Mintrom, M. 2001: Transnational networks and policy diffusion: the case of gender mainstreaming. *International Studies Quarterly* 45, 27–57.

Vasile, E. 1997: Re-turning home: transnational movements and the transformation of landscape and culture in the marginal communities of Tunis. *Antipode* 29(2), 177–96.

Vertovec, S. 1999: Conceiving and researching transnationalism. *Ethnic and Racial Studies* 22(2), 447–62.

Vertovec, S. 2001a: Transnational challenges to the "new" multiculturalism. Paper presented at the ASA Conference, University of Sussex, Brighton, March 30 to April 2. Available at www.transcomm.ox.ac.uk.

Vertovec, S. 2001b: Transnationalism and identity. *Journal of Ethnic and Migration Studies* 27(4), 573–82.

Vertovec, S. and Cohen, R., eds. 1999: *Migration, Diasporas and Transnationalism.* Aldershot: Edward Elgar.

Visweswaran, K. 1994: *Fictions of Feminist Ethnography.* Minneapolis: University of Minnesota Press.

Willis, K. and Yeoh, B. 2000: Gender and transnational household strategies: Singaporean migration to China. *Regional Studies* 34(3), 253–64.

Young, R. 1994: *Mental Space.* London: Process Press.

Zhou, Y. and Tseng, Y. F. 2001: Regrounding the "ungrounded empires": localisation as the geographical catalyst for transnationalism. *Global Networks* 1(2), 131–54.

Index